The Bradford Studies of Strategic Decision Making

Classic Research in Management
General Editor: Derek S. Pugh

Titles in the Series

Managerial, Occupational and Organizational Stress Research
Cary L. Cooper

Managing Democratic Organizations, Volumes I and II
Frank Heller

The Bradford Studies of Strategic Decision Making
David J. Hickson, Richard J. Butler and David C. Wilson

The Tavistock Institute Contribution to Job and Organizational Design, Volumes I and II
Eric Miller

The Aston Programme, Volumes I, II and III
Derek S. Pugh

The Bradford Studies of Strategic Decision Making

Edited by

David J. Hickson
Richard J. Butler
David C. Wilson

Routledge
Taylor & Francis Group
LONDON AND NEW YORK

First published 2001 by Ashgate Publishing

2 Park Square, Milton Park, Abingdon, Oxon OX14 4RN
605 Third Avenue, New York, NY 10017

Routledge is an imprint of the Taylor & Francis Group, an informa business

First issued in paperback 2021

A Library of Congress record exists under LC control number: 00029953

ISBN 13: 978-1-138-72409-9 (hbk)
ISBN 13: 978-0-367-24937-3 (pbk)

Contents

PART III ORGANIZATIONAL FEATURES

PART IV NATIONAL FEATURES

PART V SUCCESSFULLY MANAGING IMPLEMENTATION

Acknowledgements

The editors and publishers wish to thank the following for permission to use copyright material.

Annual Reviews for the essay: David J. Hickson (1987), 'Decision-Making at the Top of Organizations', *Annual Review of Sociology*, **13**, 165–92. With permission from the Annual Review of Sociology, vol. 13. Copyright © 1987 Annual Reviews.

Blackwell Publishers Ltd for the essays: David C. Wilson, Richard J. Butler, David Cray, David J. Hickson and Geoffrey R. Mallory (1982), 'The Limits of Trade Union Power in Organisational Decision Making', *British Journal of Industrial Relations*, **20**, pp. 322–41; Runo Axelsson, David Cray, Geoffrey R. Mallory and David C. Wilson (1991), 'Decision Style in British and Swedish Organizations: A Comparative Examination of Strategic Decision Making', *British Journal of Management*, **2**, pp. 67–79; W. Graham Astley, Runo Axelsson, Richard J. Butler, David J. Hickson and David C. Wilson (1982), 'Complexity and Cleavage: Dual Explanations of Strategic Decision-Making', *Journal of Management Studies*, **19**, pp. 357–75; David Cray, Geoffrey R. Mallory, Richard J. Butler, David J. Hickson and David C. Wilson (1988), 'Sporadic, Fluid and Constricted Processes: Three Types of Strategic Decision Making in Organizations', *Journal of Management Studies*, **25**, pp. 13–39; David Cray, Geoffrey R. Mallory, Richard J. Butler, David J. Hickson and David C. Wilson (1991) 'Explaining Decision Processes', *Journal of Management Studies*, **28**, pp. 227–51; Graham K. Kenny and David C. Wilson (1984), 'The Interdepartmental Influence of Managers: Individual and Sub-unit Perspectives', *Journal of Management Studies*, **21**, pp. 409–27; Richard Butler, Les Davies, Richard Pike and John Sharp (1991), 'Strategic Investment Decision-Making: Complexities, Politics and Processes', *Journal of Management Studies*, **28**, pp. 395–415; David C. Wilson and Richard J. Butler (1986), 'Voluntary Organizations in Action: Strategy in the Voluntary Sector', *Journal of Management Studies*, **23**, pp. 519–42; Geoffrey R. Mallory, Richard J. Butler, David Cray, David J. Hickson and David C. Wilson (1983) 'Implanted Decision-Making: American Owned Firms in Britain', *Journal of Management Studies*, **20**, pp. 191–211; Suzana Braga Rodrigues and David J. Hickson (1995), 'Success in Decision Making: Different Organizations, Differing Reasons for Success', *Journal of Management Studies*, **32**, pp. 655–78. Copyright © 1995 Blackwell Publishers Ltd.

Elsevier Science for the essay: David J. Hickson, W. Graham Astley, Richard J. Butler and David C. Wilson (1981), 'Organization as Power', in L. Cummings and B. Staw (eds), *Research in Organizational Behavior*, Volume 3, Stanford, CT: JAI Press Inc., pp. 151–96. Copyright © 1981 JAI Press Inc.

Susan Miller (1997), 'Implementing Strategic Decisions: Four Key Success Factors', *Organization Studies*, **18**, pp. 577–602. Copyright © 1997 Susan Miller.

Henry Mintzberg and Jim Waters, A.M. Pettigrew, and R. Butler (1990) 'Studying Deciding: An Exchange of Views Between Mintzberg and Waters, Pettigrew, and Butler, *Organization Studies*, **11**, pp. 1–16. Copyright © 1990 EGOS.

Plenum Publishing Corp for the essays: David C. Wilson, Richard J. Butler, David Cray, David J. Hickson and Geoffrey R. Mallory (1986), 'Breaking the Bounds of Organization in Strategic Decision Making', *Human Relations*, **39**, pp. 309–31. Copyright © 1986 Tavistock Institute of Human Relations; Graham K. Kenny, Richard J. Butler and David J. Hickson, David Cray and Geoffrey R. Mallory and David C. Wilson (1987), 'Strategic Decision Making: Influence Patterns in Public and Private Sector Organizations', *Human Relations*, **40**, pp. 613–31. Copyright © 1987 Tavistock Institute of Human Relations.

Sage Publications, Inc. for the essay: David C. Wilson, David J. Hickson and Susan Miller (1996), 'How Organizations Can Overbalance: Decision Overreach as a Reason for Failure', *American Behavioral Scientist*, **39**, pp. 995–1010. Copyright © 1996 Sage Publications, Inc.

Taylor & Francis Ltd for the essay: David J. Hickson (1988), 'Ruminations on Munificence and Scarcity in Research', in A. Bryman (ed.), *Doing Research in Organizations*, London: Routledge, 136–50.

Walter de Gruyter and Co. for the essay: David J. Hickson, in association with Richard J. Butler, David Cray, Geoffrey R. Mallory and David C. Wilson (1986), 'Governmental Influence Upon Decision Making in Organizations in the Private and Public Sectors in Britain', in Rolf Wolff (ed.), *Organizing Industrial Development*, Berlin/New York: de Gruyter, pp. 107–16.

David C. Wilson (1982), 'Electricity and Resistance: A Case Study of Innovation and Politics', *Organization Studies*, **3**, pp. 119–40.

Every effort has been made to trace all the copyright holders, but if any have been inadvertently overlooked the publishers will be pleased to make the necessary arrangement at the first opportunity.

Series Preface

As the history of management and management thought continues to attract greater interest among scholars, the Ashgate/Dartmouth series of collections of articles on the *History of Management Thought* has been successful in making more readily available historically important academic papers in key areas of the subject. *Classic Research in Management* complements the *History of Management Thought* by presenting the contribution of outstanding research programmes whose sustained output of work has had a defining effect on the development of the field of business and management as a discipline.

Classic Research in Management presents, for each research programme, a comprehensive set of papers which have had a major impact on subsequent research and thinking. In many cases these research reports and articles have appeared in books which are now out of print, or are in early issues of journals which are not easily available to libraries. The present series provides a new opportunity for wider access to the research. Each volume has been collected and presented by a scholar who played a leading part in the original research programme. Each chosen article is reproduced in full. The volumes enable a detailed analysis of the distinctive contribution of each research programme in its historical context. The series offers an important resource for use by academics and advanced students in the field of increasing their knowledge and understanding of the historical development of the management discipline.

DEREK S. PUGH
General Editor
Classic Research in Management
Open University Business School, UK

Introduction: Aims, Means and Results

Filling the Gap

The Bradford team set out to plug a gap by widening the view, which was – to scramble the metaphors even more – a tall order. They did not know how long their work would continue nor how difficult it would be to sustain it. As those who look back often say, 'Had we known then what we know now, we might never have started', notwithstanding the achievements.

The gap was the absence of comparative empirical research on managerial decision making. There were, at the time, a small number of studies of single examples of decisions, but no systematic comparisons across a number of cases. Hence a wider view was needed to fill the gap because, although the description of one or two cases can yield insights, its usefulness is limited if no one knows whether the cases are typical or exceptions. If the case description generates ideas, do these apply elsewhere or not?

Comparing different decisions in differing organizations requires concepts that can show which cases have more and which have fewer of particular characteristics – that is, concepts capable of tracing variation and change. The Bradford studies therefore define concepts which can be applied empirically as variables, and which are appropriate to any kind of decision in any kind of organization. They are empirically flexible.

They could also be seen as relatively mundane. Yet apparently mundane variables, used comparatively, opened up entirely novel views of what happens at the managerial apex of organizations. Decision making at this level is seen to be either *sporadic* in character or *fluid* or *constricted.* These terms pick up the inherent nature of processes through time – a bumpy ride or a smooth one. Sporadic decision making is 'informally spasmodic and protracted' – a relatively bumpy ride – whereas fluid decision making is 'steady paced, formally channelled and speedy' – in a word, smoother. Constricted decision making includes something else. It may be somewhat sporadic, it may be somewhat fluid, but distinctively it is more tightly controlled or 'narrowly channelled' than either.

Further, when it comes to putting a decision into effect, there are two previously unnoticed ways in which management can go about it. Implementation can be managed either by the *know-how route* or by the *readiness route.* If management knows enough to see how implementation should be managed, then it can go ahead by the know-how route. If it knows less but all concerned are receptive to pushing ahead anyway, then it can follow the readiness route. Where possible, a combination of both will usually work best.

More will be said about these lead ideas later, as well as the many offshoots and derivative ideas that have arisen from the research programme.

The Research Programme

The Bradford studies are a programme more in retrospect than in intent. They were not designed as such, but grew and extended as more questions beckoned and ideas began to come. Yet they did, and do, have a guiding hope: namely, that empiricism can pay off theoretically; that a fertile source of ideas lies in the interaction between data and concepts; that puzzling over problems – such as 'How can processes which at first seem so indefinable and incomparable be compared?', or 'Can such an unlikely correlation mean anything?', or 'What can explain this?' – can bring inspiration.

Second, the studies also have a guiding focus. They concern the more strategic of the decisions taken in organizations. 'Strategicness' is a matter of degree. Fully strategic decisions which are wholly unprecedented and set an organization's direction for years to come, such as large-scale mergers or ventures into new markets, shade off into those where something similar was done before and are of less consequence, and so on into recurring decisions such as budgets, and then into everyday choices and operating decisions. Every instance in over 300 cases that have been studied in different ways is not fully strategic, but the vast majority of them are.

Third, the Bradford studies are prompted and guided by a core project. The other projects included in this volume have arisen from it. It was the first to begin, is the longest running, and its publications continue beyond this volume. This is the study of how 150 varied decisions were made in organizations in Britain, and how the implementations of 55 of them were managed, and why.

The longest involved in this core research have been the editors of this collection of published work, Richard Butler, David Wilson and myself. Others have been involved – some for many years, some not so long – although contributions are not measured by time alone. They are Graham Astley, Runo Axelsson, David Cray, Geoff Mallory and Sue Miller. Yet others have carried out projects stemming from that core research – namely, Carlos Arruda Oliveira, Runo Axelsson, Graham Kenny, Les Davies, Richard Pike, Suzana Rodrigues and John Sharp.

The conception of this core work could probably be traced back to a gleam in my eye when I came to Bradford Management Centre in 1970. I sought a colleague with whom I could share an interest in power and influence in organizations, and launch fresh research. Richard Butler joined me in 1973, returning from New Zealand and the United States with both industrial experience and research training. We set off to see what needed doing.

At that time, Stewart Clegg was the first PhD candidate with whom I worked, and although his research on embedded power was not directly about decision making, at this early stage his critical and profound views were thought-provoking.

Runo Axelsson had a particular defining influence on what was done. With a background of research in Sweden on decision making, he argued that the power and influence in which we were interested was manifest in decisions and that decisions should therefore be our empirical focus. The better part of three decades later they still are.

David Wilson had already joined us with degrees from Leeds University. He took the empirical lead with exploratory in-depth case studies. Another long-term stalwart, Geoff Mallory, joined after taking a Bradford undergraduate degree as a mature student following a spell in industry. Graham Astley, a second Englishman returned to England from an American training, clarified for us the difference between political and technical elements in decision making – a distinction that has shaped our explanations of what is done by managers ever since.

The work on decision making was dogged by failure to raise sufficient funding for long enough to enable the team to concentrate free of worries about jobs. The strains are described in the final essay in this volume which is about munificence and scarcity in research. When morale was at its lowest, it was largely David Cray who turned the team around, when he replaced Graham Astley. This time it was an American from Wisconsin who brought the American training, but most of all he brought a cheery disposition that revitalized everyone. Geoff Mallory and David Wilson had held on through the worst with Richard and me, and now, in the early 1980s, we moved forward again.

It became intuitively apparent that some decision making was more fluid and some less so, and gradually repeated analyses and discussions elaborated this into the threefold sporadic, fluid and constricted typology of processes. This typology was still getting into print, and the team had dispersed except for Richard and myself, when David Wilson, now at Warwick Business School, remarked with telling effect that it was time we followed up some at least of the decisions we had studied. We had spent time and energy in researching how they were made, but what happened during implementation? The lead in this further phase of the research through the 1990s was given by Sue Miller who, working with a separate set of cases, pioneered the systematic comparison of implementation management. Subsequent research by the three of us – Sue, David and me – has revealed the two 'routes' in implementation management mentioned earlier, and still continues.

Of the related projects which grew out of this core work, the most substantial was by Richard Butler and his colleagues on investment decisions. Otherwise, Graham Kenny and David Wilson analysed Australian data on manager influence, Runo Axelsson and our colleagues studied Swedish decision making, I worked with Carlos Arruda to compare Brazilian and English decision making, and Suzana Rodrigues studied decision success. There is more about these developments in the following section.

The driving interest behind the Bradford studies has not been a concern with management as such. It has not been a desire for immediate practical application, nor for the rewards of consultancy. It has been a longer-term interest in understanding and explaining organizational phenomena. This can be criticized as 'research for its own sake', but that epithet is misguided for the ultimate aim of the research – as of all research which takes the same approach – is teachable theory, accumulating via academic publications and thereon into teaching and training, so to influence practical capabilities. The difference between it and work aimed directly at managerial applications is in the freedom to choose the theoretical aim and the longer time-scale required.

The Essays in this Volume

'Does Decision Get in the Way?', ask Mintzberg and Waters (1990) in the title of their essay which spurs the 'Exchange of Views' at the outset of Part I, 'Issues and Ideas'. They fear that it is likely to. For what happens is not so much decisions as sequences of actions that may or may not have been decided upon. To isolate and study 'the decision' is to miss that process. Pettigrew is sympathetic to this challenging view, stressing, as he does, the interconnectedness of change. Butler replies by arguing that existing theory on decision making can accommodate these doubts. Not only deciding but implementing are also matters of degree in diffuse processes.

He maintains that a steady step-by-step accretion of theory has been possible. Hickson (Chapter 2) draws this theory and the underlying empirical research together.

The duality of thinking running through the Bradford studies, which see decision making being affected both by the subject of decision and the political involvement in it, is signalled by Astley *et al.* in Chapter 3 who discuss what they then called (in 1983) the complexity of the topic and the cleavage of interests. So as Hickson *et al.* (Chapter 4) put it: 'The balance of power in an organization becomes a matter of a dialectic between the technical and political perspectives worked out in a decision making arena.'

In Part II, 'Decision Making Processes', seven essays describe and explain the processes in that arena. The first two, both by Cray *et al.* (1988 and 1991), present the principal findings of the core research on the making of decisions. They show how a series of variables such as expertise and informal interaction and elapsed time, though earlier here downplayed as relatively mundane, were the vital means of comparing elusively differing processes and then inspired the sporadic, fluid and constricted typology. The 1991 essay (Chapter 6) goes on to explain why each of the three arises in a typical causal context of both task (or technical) and political ingredients.

More detailed findings and case illustrations are given in the greater page space of the book by Hickson *et al.*, *Top Decisions* (1986). There the particular features of decision making on various topics (new factories, changing financial services, municipal reorganizations, and so on) and in various organizations (manufacturers, health services, utilities, universities and so on), are examined, and it is concluded that 'the matter for decision matters most' in forming decision making processes – more than does the kind of organization. It is not possible to include extracts from the book here.

In Chapter 7 Wilson recounts the most vibrant single case among the 150 of the core research, a power*full* contest between two directors of a chemicals manufacturer. He joins Kenny (Kenny and Wilson, Chapter 8) to point out, from an analysis of data on Australian managers, how power bases remain latent until exploited by individuals in this way. Their scope is greatest in 'unbounded' decisions (Wilson *et al.*, Chapter 9).

That scope is, of course, for managers. It is they who hold the greater sway over what happens. Even at a time of trade union ascendance in Britain, union influence on the making of top decisions was minimal (see Wilson *et al.*, Chapter 10). The most that unions can do is to modify implementation.

With a different group of Bradford colleagues, Butler studied a different set of cases of decisions, all of which required capital investment (Butler *et al.*, Chapter 11). They, too, found politically imbued and uncertain processes which led to decisions that they later found were judged in two ways (see Butler *et al.*, 1993). Attaining objectives was the overriding consideration, as would be expected, but learning from the experience was also valued.

Comparisons between privately owned and public or state owned organizations figure in Part III, 'Organizational Features'. These organizations are more similar at the top than might be expected. There is a 'bureaucratic homogeneity' in the patterns of interest units (internal departments and external organizations) that are involved in decision making in both (see Kenny *et al.*, Chapter 12). But influence differs. Most obviously, the sales and marketing function has more say under private ownership. More surprisingly, governmental bodies can influence private sector decisions. Hickson *et al.* (Chapter 13) confirm this, showing in addition that governmental influence is most effective in both public and private sectors when its agencies intervene pointedly on particular occasions rather than through the usual run of subsidizing and regulating.

Decisions are integral to strategies, as Wilson and Butler (Chapter 14) find in an excursion into the third sector, voluntary organizations. Their study of the NSPCC (National Society for the Prevention of Cruelty to Children), the Metropolitan Community Transport Service (linking with the Council for Voluntary Services), the RNLI (Royal National Lifeboat Institution) and Oxfam, reveals that the strategies of these organizations primarily follow their resource dependencies, much as those of other kinds of organizations do, despite their very different purpose.

Part IV, 'National Features', shows clearly how societal differences – most interestingly, those of a cultural nature – colour how decisions are handled. It is regrettable that time, money and energy have not so far been available for the Bradford studies to do more in this respect, because what has been done is so promising.

Cultural influence can be marked even when its transmission is tenuous. Mallory *et al.* (Chapter 15) detected the influence of American management style on the British managers of faraway subsidiaries in Britain. The decision making of these British managers was relatively 'informal within a formalised frame' – American in manner – contrasting with the 'formal within a non-formalised customary pattern' that is the British way when there is no transatlantic influence. But although the Americans are reputed to make decisions most rapidly, the British get there faster than the Swedes (Axelsson *et al.*, Chapter 16). This equates with the Swedes' more consultative and egalitarian style.

Decision making in Latin lands is different again. In Brazilian cases, contrasted with English cases by Arruda and Hickson (Chapter 17), there was sharper chief executive influence over more urgent and quicker decisions, yet comparatively 'meandering' sociable meetings and personal interaction. However, this study also reveals the 'common managerialism' that may well pervade decision making everywhere, despite the culturally saturated idiosyncrasies.

The managing of implementation, ensuing from the making of decisions, is the unfinished business of the Bradford studies. Part V 'Successfully Managing Implementation' contains essays that, though complete in themselves, are a prelude to later work. Suzana Rodrigues, herself Brazilian but researching organizations in England, opens this section with a study of the conditions seen as conducive to success (Rodrigues and Hickson, Chapter 18). Whereas, in business firms, a sufficiency of information and resources is paramount, in universities and hospitals the process of deciding itself – a process in which 'the right people participate and the people at the very top do not interfere too much' – is more important to subsequent success. This organizational difference adds to those already mentioned in Part III.

It is Sue Miller's research (Chapter 19) that leads directly to the substantial current work on implementation success, as described earlier. Distinguishing those factors that *realize* success from those which *enable* that realization, she highlights support for what is to be done, clear aims and planning, and a conducive climate. That all do not succeed is vividly evident in the unfortunate cases of overreach and thence overbalance recounted by Wilson *et al.* (Chapter 20).

Doing the core research on decision making and then decision implementation was, and is, not easy, as Hickson recounts in Part VI, 'Doing the Research'. The sharp contrast between this experience in Britain and experience previous to that in Canada exposes the greater difficulties that can beset researchers in Britain.

The World of the Top Decision Maker

The portrayal of decision making in the work of top decision makers drawn by the research at Bradford gives an exceptionally wide and long view. It is a view derived from a very large number of cases of decisions of every kind in every form of organization, over many years of research into cases themselves covering many years. It is, of course, probabalistic, not deterministic.

To summarize some of its features, the consequential matters – the big ones that excite interest and interests – occupy the minds of decision makers for a long time. It may, indeed, be up to four years before a conclusion is reached. Some decisions do get made in a few months, but the mean is consistently around a year. To then put decisions into effect – to implement them once the go-ahead is legitimized – takes as long again and, in some cases, much longer.

With decisions as serious as these, there are no snap judgements – or, if there are, these judgements are then tested out, for there is always a process of scrutiny and discussion. Yet the scope of that process is often narrowed down. In as many as one decision in three, the outcome is more or less a foregone conclusion. This is quasi-decision making, going through the motions, although that can be a useful check.

Processes swirl and straggle in decision arenas full of interests through and around which decision makers wend their way. There are many who have something at stake. Some are involved rarely but influentially, some are involved frequently but with little influence. The heavyweights, continually involved and consistently influential, are the production, sales and finance functions, by whatever names they may be called in different kinds of organization. The lightweights include purchasing and personnel functions, competitors, trade unions and, usually, government agencies. The 'big three' of production, sales and finance are the main connectors of decision to implementation, carrying the organizational memory through from their active part in decision making to an active part in implementation.

Decision makers find themselves drawn into processes which, unbeknown to them, bear them along sporadically, fluidly or constrictedly. The probability of which is going to happen is set less by what the decision is nominally about – a product, a reorganization, or whatever – or by what organization it is in, than by its inherent complexity and politicality. An executive who moves from one organization to another will intuitively recognize what is going on because every organization will experience each kind of process. He or she will have known the feel of it before, even if purposes and problems differ.

The newcomer will also recognize how implementation is being managed, although no one may be explicitly aware of what prompts them to go about it in one way rather than another. Two conditions sway the managerial approach. If enough is known to enable the means to be planned, it will take the know-how route. If not enough is known, but there is a receptiveness for action, then it will take the readiness route, pushing ahead with the utmost priority. To take neither route is risky, one alone will be adequate, but it is when managers are in a position to take both routes together that the chances of success are highest.

Although learning from the decision making experience is useful, it is first and foremost the attaining of objectives that matters, and success in this is never certain. It is no surprise to find that deciding and implementing is a risky business, but just how risky it is can now be demonstrated. Only about a third of decisions turn out really well. As many as half show poor or declining performance. This means that, if an implementation is not well managed, by either route, it is highly likely to perform indifferently, having no more than a one in ten chance of a thoroughly satisfactory outcome.

Here, decision makers are caught up in the 'forwards and backwards' causal connectedness of the decision making and the implementation. If they are in contention during decision making, this carries forward into a reduced backing for, and understanding of, implementation. If they anticipate an intricate implementation, this recoils back into more interactive and prolonged decision making beforehand.

The faces in this densely drawn portrayal of strategic deciding at the top are British. This is an English picture. There is fascinating variation between this and other cultures – too much for a single picture to contain. Variation, however, does not mean unrecognizable difference. In managerial decision behaviour there is likely to be a recognizable cross-societal homogeneity around which the cultural variation takes place.

Within the frame of this small picture is just a part of the research results. There is more in this volume, and more beyond it, as has been indicated. Further, much of what is sketched on implementation is from ongoing work not yet published.

The picture shows that doubts at the outset about the practicability of validly comparing ephemeral processes which move through time were needless. This can be done, and has been done, by a predominantly cross-sectional-cum-historical method of analysis. It has yielded concepts which convey movement – for example, sporadicity in process or routes in managing. It has exposed the unusual cases, such as the electricity generation and overreach cases, with no risk that they are mistakenly generalized from because they are known to be exceptional. Likewise, it has revealed, and is still revealing, what the majority are like.

The picture shows, too, that a focus on cases of decisions is fruitful. It does not tell all, by any means. Much that surrounds decisions in the stream of action and events is missed. But only a celestial camcorder could record all that happens, and only a cosmological computer could analyse it. Researchers are forced, always, to make do with skimming and slicing time and, among such artificial cuts, a decision case is not a bad one.

DAVID J. HICKSON

References

Butler, Richard J., Davies, Les, Pike, Richard and Sharp, John (1993), *Strategic Investment Decisions*, London: Routledge.

Hickson, David J., Butler, Richard J., Cray, David, Mallory, Geoffrey R. and Wilson, David C. (1986), *Top Decisions*, London/New York: Blackwell/Jossey-Bass.

Part I
Issues and Ideas

[1]

Studying Deciding: An Exchange of Views Between Mintzberg and Waters, Pettigrew, and Butler

Preface

This exchange of views on the study of decisions and change in organizations was prompted by the question, 'Does decision get in the way?', which is asked in the opening piece by Henry Mintzberg and James Waters. They distrust the concept of decision itself; so does Richard Butler, but he tries to prevent any throwing out of the baby with the bathwater, arguing that existing theory can cope with this distrust. Andrew Pettigrew prefers to enlarge the scene so that the changing activity around the baby in the bath is not missed.

Sadly, Henry Mintzberg's colleague, Jim Waters, died suddenly before this exchange could be published. It has become a posthumous memorial to him and his work.

David Hickson
Editor-in-Chief

Does Decision Get in the Way?

Henry Mintzberg
Department of Management,
McGill University,
Montreal, Canada

Jim Waters
Graduate School of Management,
Boston College,
Chestnut Hill,
Mass., U.S.A.

Organization Studies
1990, 11/1: 001–016
© 1990 EGOS
0170–8406/90
0011–0001 $1.00

'Decision' is one of the most widely and firmly accepted concepts in the field of organization theory. With the ambiguities that surround so many of the field's other concepts — decentralization, participation, planning, etc. — there tends to be a sense of security about decision. Everyone knows that it exists and what it is. True there may be some overlap with concepts such as 'problem'; debates may have continued over the extent to which organizations really can make choices; and much ambiguity certainly remains about how organizations make decisions. But *that* they make decisions which determine their actions is universally accepted. Even so strident a group of critics of conventional views of decision-making as March and his colleagues nonetheless seem to accept as given the assumption that organizations do make 'choices' and 'decisions' (see, e.g., March and Olsen 1976: 10–13).

For years, we studied the process of strategy formation based on the definition of (realized) strategy as 'a pattern in a stream of decisions' (e.g., Mintzberg 1972, 1978; Mintzberg and Waters 1982). Eventually it occurred to us that we were in fact not studying streams of decisions at all, but of actions, because those are the traces actually left behind in organizations (e.g., stores opened in a supermarket chain, projects started in an architectural firm). Decisions simply proved much more difficult to track down. As Barnard noted many years ago:

'Not the least of the difficulties of appraising the executive functions or the relative merits of executives lies in the fact that there is little direct opportunity to observe the essential operations of decision. It is a perplexing fact that most executive decisions produce no direct evidence of themselves and that knowledge of them can only be derived from the cumulation of indirect evidence. They must largely be inferred from general results in which they are merely one factor, and from symptomatic indications of roundabout character.' (1970:192–193)

If a decision is really a *commitment* to action (see Mintzberg, Raisinghani, and Théorêt 1976), then the trace it leaves behind in an organization can range from a clear statement of intent — as in the recorded minute of a meeting — to nothing.

To proceed with our research, based on the definition we were using, we made the implicit assumption that decisions inevitably preceded actions, that if an organization *did* something, then it must have previously *decided* to do so. As Barnard suggested, it was just a matter of tracking the decision down, but, on reflection, another interpretation is possible: that decisions are difficult to uncover because sometimes they don't exist, in other words, that the relationship between decision and action can be far more tenuous than almost all the literature of organization theory suggests (Weick 1979, being one notable exception). To quote Nicolaides in his rarely cited dissertation on decision-making:

'It is evident on the basis of [my] analysis that an organizational decision is in reality a constellation or a galaxy of numerous individual decisions. Some of these decisions are "registered" in the book of the organizational activities, while others remain hidden in the inner sanctum of the human psyche. When and where a decision begins and ends is not always clear.' (1960:173)

Let us consider some of the ambiguities associated with the concept of decision.

For one thing, action can occur without commitment to act — as when a doctor strikes one's knee. Even the law recognizes such a phenomenon. Section 214 of the Canadian Criminal Code states that 'Murder is first degree when it is planned and deliberate,' otherwise it is second degree. In other words, a person can murder without deciding. In a collective context, Swanson (1971) has described 'commensal heteronomy,' as a 'set of legitimated procedures for collective action' in which problems are informally talked over and talked around 'until a kind of common view emerges [which becomes] the basis for action':

'In some societies, all small in population and localized in residence, the whole people, or the men, or all adults, will gather informally, once a day, to gossip, socialize, and debate . . . There is no agenda, no machinery for making decisions, and no apparatus for the people's acting jointly to carry out a collective task or to authorize some participants to represent or enforce the common view. There is an informal "leader" whose position depends upon the respect his abilities warrant.

He periodically summarizes the drift of the discussion and continues to do so over whatever period of hours, days, or weeks it continues; this until there is no substantial dissent from his report.' (pp. 613–614)

For those who think this is a far cry from the behaviour of formal organizations, consider the comment by an executive of the largest corporation in the world, remarkably similar to Swanson's words above:

'We use an iterative process to make a series of tentative decisions on the way we think the market will go. As we get more data we modify these continuously. It is often difficult to say who decided something and when — or even who originated a decision . . . I frequently don't know when a decision is made in General Motors. I don't remember being in a committee meeting when things came to a vote. Usually someone will simply summarize a developing position. Everyone else either nods or states his particular terms of consensus.' (Quoted in Quinn 1980:134)

But social systems can act even without censensus. The story circulated in Europe several years ago that the top management of another large automobile firm had hired consultants to find out who in their company had 'decided' to introduce a major new model. Perhaps someone really did decide, in a clandestine manner; the consultants would then track him or her down. But conceivably no one did. Perhaps someone merely sketched a new speculative design, someone else picked up on that to see what a mockup would look like, and, like a rolling snowball, these activities developed their own momentum: thousands of 'decisions' and actions later — concerning bumpers and assembly lines and advertising campaigns — a new model appeared. In effect, 'decisions', like strategies, can emerge inadvertently.

To further complicate matters, the environment can sometimes 'decide' too, as we noted in our study of an architectural firm (Mintzberg et al. 1988). It was prepared to do a variety of projects, taking whatever work came along that was up to its standards. As it happens, what came along in disproportionate numbers, for a time, were performing art centres. The firm had received considerable publicity for the first one it did, and so the world of such centres beat a path to its door. In effect, the firm ceded those decisions to its clients, who chose for it by asking it to do this particular kind of work. From the firm's point of view, its actions reflected its performance more than its decisions.

One fundamental problem with decision is the difficulty of identifying commitment in the collective context of organization. Must there always be a clear *point* as well as a clear *place* of commitment? What, in effect, is commitment? Associating it with some specific document may simplify the problem of identification, but sometimes at the price of distortion.

Consider the example of a company that announces the 'decision' to build a new factory. Tracing back, one might find the minute of a meeting in which the decision was 'made', which really means recorded. But perhaps the real commitment preceded that minute by six months, when the president visited the site and made up his mind. Here, then, commitment (i.e., decision) has to be traced back to someone's mind, indeed perhaps even to that person's subconscious, and that can become rather problematic.

Shift this into the more complex organizational setting where the commitment must be collective, and the problem of identifying decision magnifies enormously. Given that an action was taken, and that broad support preceded it, we must find out when and where consensus emerged — for that must be the real 'point' of decision. Unfortunately, it may not be a point at all, but a gradually unfolding and subtle process, as the comment of the General Motors executive suggested earlier, and as Snyder and Paige (1958) noted about the United States decision in 1950 'to resist aggression in Korea'. The stages they identified in their research 'do not reveal and cannot reveal when the individual decision-makers made up their minds. What is revealed is the time when group opinion coalesced and was made official . . .' (p. 369). In essence, commitment — and, by direct implication, decision — is an elusive concept, at the limit no more than some presumed psychological state, individual or collective.

Another associated problem with decision in an organizational context is that it reinforces an undifferentiated, mechanistic image of one or few central decison-makers, thereby diverting attention from the fact that organizational actions do not always correspond directly to leadership intentions. For example, in a study of a film-making agency (Mintzberg and McHugh 1985), the formal decision was made to fund a short documentary film. But the film inadvertently ran long, and so had to be marketed as a feature. The organization 'acted' though the management never 'decided'. There are other instances when a central decision is consciously subverted by others in the organization, so there is decision but no action. To explain this, conventional management theory falls back on the convenience of 'implementation'. The 'organization' (meaning its top management) decided, but failed to implement its choice, but might it not be equally correct — indeed descriptively more illuminating — to say that the 'organization' (meaning the true collectivity) never really did 'decide'?

A focus on decision can also mask the ways in which general commitments are reshaped, elaborated, and defined over time through complex processes within and without organizations. For example, a company may announce a decision to diversity its related businesses, but, over the years, based on the firms available for acquisition (and their prices) and the company's own successes and failures with those it does buy, the result comes to look like conglomerate diversification. In effect, the pattern (the many actions, forming the *realized* strategy) subverted the original commitment (the single decision at the outset), indeed, ironically in this instance, probably at the management's own hand. Thus, preoccupation with *the* decision runs the risk of imputing a direct relationship between the abstraction of mental intention at the individual or small group level and the concreteness of realized action at the organizational level. A great deal of real-world behaviour can get lost in between.

As a result of all this, in our research we were drawn into defining strategy as 'a pattern in a stream of actions,' instead of decisions (Mintzberg and Waters 1985). For us, realized strategy came to mean consistent behaviour, whether or not decisional. (Indeed, and fully in the spirit of our own research, which set out to study behaviour and work back to intention, our actions reflected this before we became aware of what was happening and then 'decided' to change our formal definition!) It made more sense for us to study streams of actions, and then go back and investigate the role of decision, *if any*, in determining these actions.

The implications of this go well beyond our research on strategy, however. The important general conclusion is that the concept of 'decision' may sometimes serve to confuse things. In essence, decision, like so many other concepts in organization theory, can sometimes turn out to be an artificial construct, one that in this case imputes commitment to action. We have seen that, for individuals as well as for organizations, commitment need not precede action, or, perhaps more commonly, the commitment that does precede action can be vague and confusing. This view does for decision what the thrust of our research does for strategy: just as the *pattern* in behaviour (strategy) may or may not have been intended, so too the *single* behaviour may or may not have involved prior commitment (decision).

Of course, it is in one context in particular, the traditional machine-like bureaucracy, that decision is assumed to precede action. Administrators are supposed to decide on all things, and then have those decisions formally authorized at a higher level before others implement them down below. Likewise, in a bureaucratic society, citizens are expected to decide formally and receive approval before acting, whether it be to enlarge a house (get a building permit), to engage in work (get put on the payroll), sometimes even to propagate the species ('Even the decision to bear a child is usually made by the [Chinese work] unit; the married women within the group decide whose turn it is to become pregnant' [Mathews and Mathews 1983:19]). A research community intent on operationalizing its concepts falls into the same trap, forcing itself, however inadvertently, to restrict its study to the context of machine bureaucracy, and likewise ends up bureaucratizing its own procedures, for the sake of 'scientific rigor'.

Not all organizations or all society, not even all research, is fully bureaucratic (yet), and so we must apply our concepts with care. 'Decision' can sometimes get in the way of understanding behaviour.

References

Barnard, C. I.
1938 *The functions of the executive*. Cambridge, Mass.: Harvard University Press.

March, J. G., and J. P. Olsen
1976 *Ambiguity and choice in organizations*. Bergen, Norway: Universitetsforlaget.

Mathews, J., and L. Mathews
1983 *One billion: a China chronicle*. New York: Ballantine Books.

Mintzberg, H.
1972 'Research on strategy making'. *Proceedings of the 32nd annual meeting of the Academy of Management*. Minneapolis.

Mintzberg, H.
1978 'Patterns in strategy formation'. *Management Science* 24: 934–948.

Mintzberg, H., and A. McHugh
1985 'Strategy formation in an adhocracy'. *Administrative Science Quarterly* 30: 180–197.

Mintzberg, H., S. Otis, J. Shamsie, and J. A. Waters
1988 'Strategy of design: a study of architects in co-partnership' in *Strategy management frontiers*. J. Grant (ed.). Greenwich, CT.: JAI Press.

Mintzberg, H., D. Raisinghani, and A. Théorêt
1976 'The structure of "Unstructured" decision process'. *Administrative Science Quarterly* 25: 465–499.

Mintzberg, H., and J. A. Waters
1982 'Tracking strategy in an entrepreneurial firm'. *Academy of Management Journal* 25: 465–499.

Mintzberg, H., and J. A. Waters
1985 'Of strategies, deliberate and emergent'. *Strategic Management Journal* 6: 257–272.

Quinn, J. P.
1980 *Strategies for change: logical incrementalism*. Homewood, Ill.: Irwin.

Snyder, R. C., and G. D. Paige
1958 'The United States decision to resist aggression in Korea: the application of an analytical scheme'. *Administrative Science Quarterly* 3: 341–378.

Swanson, G. E.
1971 'An organizational analysis of collectivities'. *American Sociological Review* 36: 607–624.

Weick, K. E.
1979 *The social psychology of organizing*, 2nd ed. Reading, Mass.: Addison-Wesley.

Studying Strategic Choice and Strategic Change. A Comment on Mintzberg and Waters: 'Does Decision Get in the Way?'

Andrew M. Pettigrew
Centre for Corporate Strategy and Change, University of Warwick, Coventry, U.K.

All academics are wordsmiths. Social Science academics are incorrigible wordsmiths. So does it matter beyond mere taste whether one describes choice behaviour in an organizational context as problem-solving, decision-making, or strategy formulation? No doubt the sociologist of knowledge would tell us that words rise and fall in potency depending on features of socio-political context. Thus in expressing his/her ideas the academic is not making free scholarly choices but is reflecting deeper contextual forces, some relating to broad societal consideration, and others to stages in the development of particular disciplines or fields of study.

In adding to the points raised by Mintzberg and Waters, and Butler, I will argue that words do matter. Beneath the words lie ontological and epistemological assumptions which open up and close down fields of inquiry. I agree with Richard Butler that a focus around organizational decision-making has been theoretically and empirically additive. I would also argue that recent advances in the field of business strategy and policy studies have benefited greatly from twenty years or more of scholarly activity on decision-making. But it is also clear that decision-making can close down wide areas of concern for organizational scholars and my current preference is to approach the study of strategy with a vocabulary that leans rather more heavily on change than choice.

I was first made aware of the strengths and limitations of the vocabularies of strategic choice and change at an international gathering of researchers interested in how strategic decisions are made and implemented. The proceedings of this 1983 conference were eventually published by Pennings (1985). Penning's introductory and concluding chapters to that volume still contain some of the most perceptive analytical comments about the literatures on strategic decision-making and change. Part of the difficulty of studying strategic decisions is the very nature of what is being studied. Thus Pennings accurately portrays such decisions as significant, unstructured, complex, collective and consequential. Strategic decisions can also be portrayed as a process, a structure, or an outcome. Furthermore, they can be analysed across a variety of levels of analysis, using concepts from a range of disciplines, and be discussed in a more or less prescriptive or descriptive mode. No wonder there is also multiplicity in the research strategies available to study strategic decisions. No surprise indeed that Mintzberg and Waters, and Butler should come to different conclusions about the analytical power of mobilizing empirical inquiry around 'decision making'.

An interesting re-labelling exercise took place as Pennings' conference moved from formulation to implementation. The focus in the pre-conference documentation moved from 'strategic decision-making in complex organizations' to a 1985 book of proceedings entitled *Organizational Strategy and Change*. Now the change of label could have been due to marketing consideration by the publishers, but an equally plausible explanation could be a noticeable move during the conference discussions towards change and away from choice as the prime mobilizing concept for the proceedings.

What are some of the limitations of 'decision' in organizational analysis and do they extend beyond the points made by Mintzberg and Waters?

Neither Mintzberg and Waters, nor Butler dwell on the levels of analysis problem, but this can be a critical analytical limitation for decision-making studies. Is the unit of analysis the decision episode? If the unit of analysis is the discrete decision event abstracted from the series of decisions and other actions of which it is a part, this can be a severe analytical and empirical limitation. Hardy (1985) in her work on the organizational closure of factories and hospitals was very clear to build antecedent conditions into her analysis. Thus she did not take the closure decision to mean the point when the management finally made the closure decision and announced it, but when initial moves were made to restrict investment and allow the factory to die on the vine. This decision not to invest preceded the final decision and announcement by around five years.

Equally well, a concern with the decision episode may also lead to a preoccupation with the front-end decision to-go-ahead stage and the consequent neglect of key implementation processes. Research on processes of choice and change in the NHS by Pettigrew, McKee and Ferlie (1988) reveals the clear gap that frequently exists between statements of strategic intent and operational implementation. A focus on front-end choice processes to the neglect of on-going choice and change processes would present a rather partial view of organizational life in the NHS. If the analytical choice is between the decision episode or event as the unit of analysis and decision-making as a continuous process in context, the latter must be the preferred option.

So the language of decision-making can be more powerful when decision-making is understood as a continuous process in context. Decision-making is also more attractive as a construct when it can include the front stage of visible decisions and the back stage of non-decision-making, Bachrach and Baratz (1962). Difficult as non-decision-making is to study, ideas such as the mobilization of bias do push the analyst of decision-making to features of the content and context of decisions which can crucially shape decision process.

Interestingly, although the Bradford studies of strategic decision-making (Hickson et al. 1986) can be criticized for treating the decision episode as the unit of analysis and for downplaying the significance of non-decision-making, the Bradford work more than most decision research does try to get to grips with how variability in the content and context of decisions shapes decision process. Hickson et al. (1986) prefer to call decision content, 'decision problem or decision topic,' but whatever the language, the message is clear. There are extensive differences in decision process, and why?; because 'the problem raised, and the interests implicated, by one decision are not the same as those encountered by the previous decision' (1986:240). 'To know the process, first know the complexity of the problems and the politicality of the interests' (1986:241).

What is the role and significance of context in shaping decision process? Does the nature of the decision problem and interests shape the process more than the organization context through which the process proceeds? Here again, Hickson et al. are clear 'it is the complexity and politicality of what is under decision which matters rather than the organization' (1986:247). Now this is an important empirical finding, and one entirely consistent with a preoccupation with the decision episode as the unit of analysis. Would the Bradford studies have produced this finding if they had taken a more dynamic view of decision-making (as a continuous process and not an episode) and placed the decision process in a context which includes not only the inner context, but also the outer context of the organization (Pettigrew 1985a, 1987)?

Penning's view in 1985 was that the more dynamic and contextual decision-making is seen to be, the less useful becomes the mobilizing construct of strategic decision-making. 'In fact, the Starbuck, Normann and others view of organisations . . . is so encompassing that they prefer to speak about strategic change and strategic development rather than specific socially and temporally bounded actions. They appear to hint at the futility of efforts to artificially lift a specific decision, however defined, out of its context because of the ubiquitous continuity of organizational behaviour', Pennings (1985:475).

This line of argument takes us back to some of the tensions evident in the

Mintzberg and Waters, and Butler exchange. Decision is the more exclusive and limiting concept. While decision can get in the way of understanding behaviour, it is also evident that scholars of decision-making have been the most active in developing alternative process theories of action and behaviour. I refer here to the well known and much used boundedly rational, incremental, political and garbage-can theories of choice. When the focus of explanation moves from a particular choice process to wider concerns with the strategy or strategic development of the organization, then the more inclusive vocabulary of continuity and change rapidly supersedes the language of the language of choice and strategic decision-making.

As I have argued in detail elsewhere (Pettigrew 1985b, 1989), research on strategic change should be context and process sensitive. Until recently, the change literature was blighted by the same ahistorical, aprocessual, and acontextual limitations evident from work on strategic decision-making. Thus there has been a tendency to treat the change episode as the unit of analysis and thus fall into the same methodological trap regarding the decision event or episode as the unit of analysis. Where the change project is treated as the unit of analysis, the focus is on a single event or a set of discrete episodes somehow separate from the immediate and more distant antecedents that give these events form, meaning, and substance. Such episodic views of change not only treat innovations as if they had a clear beginning and a clear end but also, where they limit themselves to snap-shot time-series data, fail to provide data on the mechanisms and processes through which changes are created. Studies of transformation are, therefore, often preoccupied with the intricacies of narrow changes rather than the holistic and dynamic analysis of changing.

The suggestion made here is that one way to respond to the above weaknesses in the literature on change is to encourage a form of research which is contextualist and processual in character (Pettigrew 1985b, 1989). A contextualist analysis of a process such as change draws on phenomena at vertical and horizontal levels of analysis and the inter-connections between those levels through time. The vertical level refers to the interdependencies between higher or lower levels of analysis upon phenomena to be explained at some further level; for example, the impact of a changing socioeconomic context on features of intraorganizational context and interest-group behaviour. The horizontal level refers to the sequential interconnectedness among phenomena in historical, present, and future time. An approach that offers both multilevel or vertical analysis and processual, or horizontal, analysis is said to be contextualist in character.

In summary, the key points to emphasize in analysing change in a contextualist mode are:

(i) The importance of interconnected levels of analysis

- target changes should be studied in the context of changes at other levels of analysis
- the search is for patterns of reciprocal connectivity between levels

- a source of change is the asymmetries between levels of context
- processes at different levels have their own momentum, rates, pace and trajectory
- some levels of context may impact more visibly and rapidly than others and thus, in the short term, sources of change may appear unidirectional rather than multidirectional.

(ii) The interconnectedness of the past, present and future

- antecedent conditions shape the present and the emerging future. History is not an event in the past but is alive in the present
- history is about events and structures, acts and underlying logics
- there are no predetermined timetables; trajectories of change are probabilistic and uncertain because of changing contexts

(iii) The importance of context and action

- it is not a question of nature *or* nurture, or context or action, but context *and* action
- context is not just a stimulus environment but a nested arrangement of structures and processes where the subjective interpretation of actors perceiving, comprehending, learning, and remembering helps shape process.

(iv) The nature of causation about change

- causation is neither linear nor singular. Changes have multiple causes and are to be explained more by loops than lines. 'The shifting interconnectedness of fused strands' as Mancuso and Ceely (1980) put it.
- the directions of change follow multiple paths; there is no necessary path to development, the trajectory could involve growth, decline, decay, death or regeneration.

Thus contextualism offers an analytical mode to study change that is not tied to a particular theory of change. It provides an approach capable of drawing on concepts from a variety of disciplines and several levels of analysis. Featherman and Lerner (1985) conclude their review of what they call developmental contextualism by drawing attention to its intellectual pluralism. 'Different modes of analysis and causal explanation do not need reduction or integration into one over-arching theoretical paradigm: evidence from distinct paradigmatic approaches can accrue or co-exist to account for a complex phenomena' such as change. Featherman and Lerner (1985:672). Furthermore, contextualism offers a meta level approach capable of exploring several content areas of change in multifareous contexts through time. Thus reality can be caught in flight while, at the same time, there is a commitment to embeddedness as a principle of analysis.

References

Bachrach, P., and M. S. Baratz
1962 'The two faces of power'. *American Political Science Review* 56: 947–952.

Featherman, D. L., and R. M. Lerner
1985 'Ontogenesis and Sociogenesis: problematics for theory and research about development and socialisation across the lifespan'. *American Sociological Review* 50/5: 659–676.

Hardy, C.
1985 *The management of organizational closure*. Aldershot: Gower.

Hickson, D. J., R. J. Butler, D. Cray, G. R. Mallory, and D. C. Wilson
1986 *Top decisions: strategic decision making in organizations*. Oxford: Basil Blackwell.

Mancuso, J. C., and S. G. Ceely
1980 'The self as memory processing'. *Cognitive Therapy and Research* 4/1: 1–25.

Pennings, J. M.
1985 *Organizational strategy and change*. San Francisco: Jossey Bass.

Pettigrew, A. M.
1985a *The awakening giant: continuity and change in ICI*. Oxford: Basil Blackwell.

Pettigrew, A. M.
1985b 'Contextualist research: a natural way to link theory and practice' in *Doing research that is useful in theory and practice*. E. E. Lawler (ed.), 222–249. San Francisco: Jossey Bass.

Pettigrew, A. M.
1987 'Context and action in the transformation of the firm'. *Journal of Management Studies* 24/6: 649–670.

Pettigrew, A. M.
1989 'Longitudinal field research on change: theory and practice' in *New frontiers in management*, R. M. Mansfield (ed.), 21–49. London: Routledge.

Pettigrew, A. M., L. McKee, and E. Ferlie
1988 'Understanding change in the NHS'. *Public Administration* 66 (Autumn): 297–317.

Decision-making Research: Its Uses and Misuses. A Comment on Mintzberg and Waters: 'Does Decision Get in the Way?'

Richard Butler
Management Centre, University of Bradford, Bradford U.K.

There is no problem in agreeing with the final sentence of Mintzberg and Water's short 'think piece,' namely that ' "decision" can sometimes get in the way of understanding behavior' if this is taken to mean that over-concentration upon one concept in social theory can produce a distortion in the kind of understanding that is arrived at, but then, this problem applies to any concept used in social theory; organization, group, role, strategy and the like are all concepts which we find useful, but all are capable of misuse.

It is now half a century since Barnard (1938) put decision-making at the core of organization theory and the study of managerial work. At that time, there was a good reason for this since the predominant model of industrial and commercial organization was a mechanistic–bureaucratic model against which Barnard's insights represented a break from the principles of Scientific Management. Decision-making, with the attendant processes of communication and cooperation, gave a model of executive work which involved discretion, choice, delegation and the development of trust. Through these ideas theory was able to progress, especially through the work of Simon (1947), and Cyert and March (1963) who, in different ways, developed the image of an organization as a kind of satisficing coalition. Underlying this image was a model of man as intendedly rational but the extent to which that rationality could be achieved was limited by the complexity of the actual situation of decision-makers.

Later works by authors such as Allison (1971) and Pettigrew (1973) revived a more Machiavellian image of organizational decision-making by deliberately introducing an overt political dimension, an image that matched a wider societal interest in the processes of power. Mintzberg, Raisinghani and Théorêt (1976) were also able to make a distinct contribution to organizational decision-making research by pointing out that the way in which decisions are made in organizations (i.e., the decision processes) varies between decisions, but that it is possible to draw up patterns of these variations, showing that some decisions can, for instance, be made very smoothly while others experience considerable interruptions and disruptions. Hickson, Butler, Cray, Mallory and Wilson (1986) in the Bradford studies also explored this theme empirically over a sample of 150 decisions. An addition to theory from the Bradford research is that it provided an explanatory framework for the three predominant patterns they observed using, in particular, a set of variables capturing the dual notions of the complexity and the politicality of the decision issue or topic under consideration as major explanatory dimensions. Up to this time explanation had tended to be subordinated to description.

In this way it is possible to trace a history of decision-making research, as applicable to the field of organizations, which demonstrates a steady step by step accretion of theory. By any account, this is not a bad record, which demonstrates well the way in which programmatic research can build up our understanding of a concept and of its place in the wider field of organization theory. If Mintzberg and Waters now suggest a discarding, or at least a revision of the framework underlying this research, we can only assume that dissatisfaction with the usefulness of existing theories has grown to the point where we can no longer make accommodations in this programmatic way. If they are on the threshold of a new conceptual framework this would indeed be significant for an author who has already greatly contributed to the area; we need to sit up and take note.

Before inventing a new framework and concepts (and the field of organization and management is not short of these) perhaps we should see whether the problems raised by the authors can be accommodated within existing theory. Although I cannot guarantee to have captured every aspect of their argument, I found it useful to develop a series of maxims which attempt to capture the gist of their argument. Six such maxims, given below, seem to give adequate coverage to their ideas.

1. The connection between decision and action is problematic. If we accept that a decision is an intention to act, the extent to which action follows becomes, as Mintzberg and Waters suggest, a matter of implementation since the problem they raise is that some intentions get translated more perfectly into action than others. In other words, degree of implementation becomes a variable of decision-making, an important one that remains to be investigated in more detail. An interesting question here, and one of potentially great practical significance, is why some decisions achieve a greater degree of implementation than others. Two types of low decision implementation could be posited. The first is that the original intention was only weakly implemented; quoting Mintzberg and

Water's example, perhaps the new store that opened was smaller than intended, or that no store was opened after all. The second type of weak implementation would be when the implementation was of a completely different substance than the original intention; taking the new store example, this might mean that no store was opened but that the land was sold at a great profit for development as a leisure park. In short, there can be unintended outcomes from a decision, either beneficial or not. This is not a new idea since the notion of the unintended consequences of action have been well established in sociology at least since Merton (1968).

2. *In an organization, the locus of decision-making can be diffuse.* Thompson (1967) points out that some decisions in an organization can be attributed to one person, an attribution that is more likely to hold under the condition of low or modest complexity. It is central to the research of Cyert and March (1963), March and Olsen (1976), Thompson (1967), Hickson et al. (1986), and others, that complexity, uncertainty or ambiguity (whichever term one wishes to use) concerning ends/means relations will tend to increase the diffuseness of decision-making as more specialists and interest units get involved as an organization attempts to resolve uncertainty. Concurrently, a large number of specialists also tends to increase the uncertainty over outcome preferences because there are more interests with a stake in the decision, and hence the chances of political behaviour increases. The precise terminology varies between the different authors but the direction of the argument does not. Under these conditions, the locus of the decision cannot be tied down to one point in the organization since it traces out a trajectory (Hage 1981) as the attention given by different interests shifts both horizontally and vertically in the organization.

It is by providing a mapping technique helping us to describe the nature of this trajectory as a decision goes through different phases that Mintzberg, Raisinghai and Théorêt (1976) made their particular contribution to organizational decision-making theory. The Bradford studies also produced decision profiles by subjecting the scores of their 150 decisions on a set of descriptive variables to cluster analysis; three dominant profiles emerged, the sporadic, the fluid and the constricted. The sporadic decision type comes nearest to describing the kind of process that Mintzberg and Waters are concerned with when they raise the problem of not being able to identify a single decision-making locus; a sporadic decision involves many interests, it tends to move both horizontally and vertically in the organization and exhibits stops and starts. Where is such a decision made? Not in any one place, but it is made, nevertheless, through a diffuse and complex organizational process.

Also related to this question is the distinction between ratification and the use of real power in the decision-making process. Sporadic decisions involve the highest levels in the organization, but the decision is not only made there. In some cases it is possible to see ratification more as a symbolic process, and indeed an interesting variable to investigate would be the extent to which ratification is symbolic and separated from the executive power. A constitutional monarchy is an example of almost complete separation between executive power and symbolic ratification, but one can sometimes see a similar symbolic role in some large complex organizations.

3. Action without a decision is possible. This maxim is the converse of number one above. Yes, quite true and in biological organisms this is known as reflex action. In social organization there is already a vocabulary to describe this, perhaps best known by March and Simon's (1958) notion of programmed decisions. Again, the question is containable within existing theory.

4. Action in an organization can occur without consensus. The coalition model of organization states quite clearly through the notion of quasi-resolution of conflict (see Cyert and March) that only sufficient consensus is needed for decisions to proceed. This point was further elaborated by Thompson through the notion domain consensus, a concept which never implied that everybody had to agree before anything could happen, but just that sufficient consensus had to be achieved. What is meant by 'sufficient' remains undefined; there is room for further research here but at present there is no reason to suppose that this question cannot be contained within the existing framework.

5. Exogenous events can trigger decisions. Mintzberg and Waters describe the case of client demand for designing performing arts centres pushing an architectural firm towards specializing in this kind of work. Sometimes decisions can be reactive, but in this particular example a decision still had to be made. From the description given, this would sound like what the Bradford group called a fluid decision: there were a number of new product or service decisions in their study that came into that category. Of course, the clients or customers get listened to in this type of decision but the essential point from a decision theory angle is how those preferences get taken into account in the decision-making process; it tends not to happen through direct involvement but through information gleaned from the environment. If, indeed, this was a fluid decision, it would tend to happen fairly quickly and be made upon the basis of summary, formalized information and to be decentralized. What we need to emphasize is that the nature of decision-making processes can vary according to the type of issue or topic under consideration.

6. Decisions are made within a context and help to influence the context for future decisions. Context is also set by a set of factors exogenous to a particular decision. The first part of this statement can be put into systems language if we say: the output from decision 1 forms part of the input for decision 2. This is an important point and one that needs further attention. The developing theory of institutionalization (Meyer and Scott 1983) is of some help here. Institutionalization theory attempts to explain the setting of the 'Rules of the game' under which decision-making takes place, how those rules get reinforced by successive decisions, and, more precariously, how a long-term performance gap between expected and actual performance might begin to force a change in these rules. Decision-making theory is just beginning to get to grips with this aspect but, again, to say that the existing theory is inadequate is not sufficient cause for abandoning the underlying framework; rather it should provide an impetus for further research until that framework has been demonstrated as inadequate.

Elaboration of the above points has been used to emphasize that the problems with regard to decision-making theory raised by Mintzberg and Waters can be attended to within the framework of theory, what I have in general terms called the satisficing coalitional model of organizational decision-making, that has evolved over the past 50 years or so. There is scope for development, but no overwhelming evidence of a need to invent a completely new vocabulary, if indeed this was what Mintzberg and Waters had in mind.

I should emphasize the doubt as to what they do have in mind, since we learn towards the end of their piece that it is not really decision-making that they wish to study, but strategy. Now the problem here might be that Mintzberg has allowed himself to be confounded by his own previous definition of strategy which he describes as 'a pattern in a stream of decisions'. This has never struck me as a particularly satisfactory view of strategy since, by definition, strategy must surely involve a degree of intention to act, a kind of plan which is to be put into effect. The word strategy belongs, after all, to a language borrowed from the study of military campaigns translated into the business arena. A military commander who, when asked to describe his strategy, had to say 'I can only tell you after the battle' could not really be said to have a strategy. Certainly, one can attempt to retrospectively reconstruct a strategy by looking at the kinds of decisions made and the actions taken by a general over time. If one did this, decision processes cease to be dependent variables and now become independent variables, that is, one might use a description of decision processes to attempt to work out whether there was a plan, or an intention, worked out beforehand; process would become an explanation of strategy.

In conclusion, I must say to Mintzberg and Waters that if they wish to go and study strategy, then go and study strategy; do not be constrained by feeling that they have to define all aspects of strategy in terms of decision-making processes. There are many factors that go to make up the strategy of an organization. Patterns in decision processes and of actions may be part of that explanation but to rely entirely on this would, indeed, be to allow decision to get in the way of understanding behaviour.

References

Allison, G. T.
1971 *The essence of decision: explaining the Cuban missile crisis*. Boston: Little-Brown.

Barnard, Chester I.
1938 *The functions of the executive*. Cambridge, Mass: Harvard University Press.

Cyert, R., and J. G. March
1963 *The behavioral theory of the firm*. Englewood-Cliffs, N.J.: Prentice-Hall.

Hage, J.
1981 *Theories of organizations: form, process and transformation*. New York: Wiley.

Hickson, D. R., R. J. Butler, D. Cray, G. R. Mallory, and D. C. Wilson
1986 *Top decisions: strategic decision making in organizations*. San Francisco: Jossey Bass. Also Oxford: Basil Blackwell.

March, James G., and Johan P. Olsen
1976 *Ambiguity and choice in organizations*. Bergen: Universitetsforlaget.

March, James G., and Herbert A. Simon
1958 *Organizations*. New York: Wiley.

Merton, Robert K.
1968 *Social theory and social structure*. New York: Free Press.

Meyer, John W., and W. Richard Scott
1983 *Organizational environments: ritual and rationality*. Beverly Hills: Sage.

Mintzberg, H., D. Raisinghani, and A. Théorêt
1976 'The structure of "unstructured" decision processes'. *Administrative Science Quarterly* 21/2 (June): 246–275.

Pettigrew, A.
1973 *The politics of organizational decision making*. London: Tavistock.

Simon, H. A.
1947 *Administrative behaviour*. New York: Free Press.

Thompson, James D.
1967 *Organizations in actions*. New York: McGraw-Hill.

[2]

Ann. Rev. Sociol. 1987. 13:165–92

DECISION-MAKING AT THE TOP OF ORGANIZATIONS

David J. Hickson

University of Bradford Management Centre, Bradford BD9 4JL England

Abstract

Strategic decision-making processes at the top of organizations are examined. Research is reviewed on types of process movement, on the matters under decision, the problems raised, the interests implicated, the rules of the game, and its outcomes and implementation. Methodology is found to have gone through a conventional sequence of development from the small-scale intensive study to the large-scale extensive study, the latter very recently. Methodology has been catching up with theory, which has long been well developed. There are three main theories, overlapping and complementary—the incrementalism theory, the garbage-can theory, and the dual rationality theory. Five areas for further research are indicated.

WHAT THEY LOOK LIKE: THE MAKING OF STRATEGIC DECISIONS

From the vantage point of some researchers, the making of big decisions by those at the top of organizations appears like a football game. But which kind of football? By some, it has been seen as an "unconventional soccer match" (Weick 1976). Instead of the usual oblong soccer pitch, the field is round. Instead of two teams each attacking a goal at the other end, goals are scattered around haphazardly, and people can come on and off as they please and aim at any goals they like. The field is sloping. And yet "the game is played as if it made sense" (Weick 1976, and also March & Romelaer 1976).

While some Americans have this view of decision-making as a kind of crazy European soccer, those on the other side of the Atlantic see it as a sort of riotous American football! It is seen as a game of powerful groups in which some teams are much bigger and have "thicker protective padding and harder helmets" (Hickson et al 1986). Boundaries are elastic, the field is bumpy, and the number of teams in play fluctuates. They disagree as to where the ends of the field are, but eventually "one team or coalition of teams pushes its way through holding the ball to where it says the end is" (Hickson et al 1986). This is a game in which the heavier or better protected players have a greater chance of shaping what is going on and where it is going to. The shape of the ball itself can be changed.

Whichever of these two fanciful analogies may be the more fitting, they have in common the view that what happens on the way to a decision is not always straightforward. The matter under decision may bounce around from hand to hand in a way that can be difficult to follow. So this essay is an attempt to discuss, in a more or less orderly way, processes that may not take place in an orderly way, and to discuss one by one things that may happen all together.

Admitting that, then it begins by examining the main features of strategic decision-making: The kinds of processes that occur, the strategic matters that come up for decision, the uncertainty encountered, and the influence of interests; the basic rules of the game, its outcomes, and their implementation. The doubts and divisions over research methodology are then commented upon, and its historical development is reviewed. Some of the principal concepts and theories are discussed, and a new maturity is discernable in both methods and ideas. Finally, some of the least known and least understood aspects are pointed out as possible areas for future research. However, this is an essay, and it does not pretend to be an encyclopedia of absolutely everything that has ever been done on decision-making.

The Process in Motion

Just as the ball moves across a football field toward a goal, so the matter under consideration moves toward a decision. The answer to the question "what is process" is that process is movement. The process of strategic decision-making moves a strategic matter from A to B through an organization through time.

The difficulty is in defining A and B. Where is the start and where is the finish? Ultimately this is asking where are the ends of time, for there are no finite beginnings and endings. Everything can be traced back further and further and further. As historians know, periods have to be chopped out of the human saga at junctures that help to make sense of it, and that is sufficient justification. Most students of decision-making at the top of organizations have chopped out periods of overt and acknowledged decision-related activity. Typically, "the decision process encompasses all those steps taken from the time a stimulus for an action is perceived until the time the commitment to the action is made" (Mintzberg 1979:58), that is from "first proposal" to "final decision outcome" (Hage 1980:117). Such periods do not include the whole story. There is much to tell both beforehand and afterwards (and this is referred to later in this essay), but these periods of deliberate managerial movement towards a decision are the focus of the tale.

How long are they? How long does it take to reach a major decision? Not very long as a rule. Most of the big choices are made in two years or less. The mean period is about a year, and such decisions are quite commonly made in a few months since there is a modal point around six months (Hickson et al 1986, Mallory 1986). On the other hand, a few are prolonged indeed. While a new dean was chosen in an American university in just nine months (March & Olsen 1976: Chapters 6 & 15), many matters are undecided for up to four years (Mintzberg et al 1976, Hickson et al 1986, Mallory 1986). Some persist even longer—as did the maneuverings over computer equipment in a British retail business, which went on for seven years (Pettigrew 1973).

As Hage (1980:110) visualizes it, this movement through time towards a decision follows a "trajectory" which bounces around like that of a molecule in a bubble chamber. Certainly the trajectories often do bounce to and fro in a lively, though not necessarily erratic, manner. Those concerned may well feel that they know what they are doing, at the time anyway, even if hindsight brings second thoughts. But what they do can twist and turn and repeat itself. This has been nowhere better revealed than by Mintzberg et al (1976) who studied 25 cases of decision-making, one each in a variety of Canadian organizations. They identified no less than seven kinds of processes: simple impasse, political design, basic search, modified search, basic design, blocked design, and dynamic design processes. Of the 25 processes, 15 were broken up by "interrupts" ("sudden events that interrupted them and caused changes in pace or direction"), and all showed cycling and recycling, that is the reassessing of information and alternatives again and again. Mintzberg and his coworkers (1976) faced quite a problem in trying to diagram these uneven and repetitive sequences of events! The same sort of thing is suggested by Nutt (1984) from the analysis of a decision process in each of 73 health-related service organizations in the United States. Burgelman (1983) noted that new product proposals were forced up through a business corporation until they reached the attention of those at the top. In the course of this they were the subject of repetitive entrepreneurial moves from below and administrative manipulations from above, with feed-forward and feed-backward loop effects.

So those at the pinnacle of the hierarchy often run into delays or doubts about the available information or opposition, many of which either give them the chance to go over the ground again or force them to do so. [Hickson et al (1986) enumerate nine kinds of impediments of this nature.] Even if they follow a textbook course that begins by identifying a problem, goes on to search for pertinent information, evaluates alternative solutions to find which is best, and finally makes a choice—they are not very likely to move step by step through these phases in a neat orderly way once and for all. They may do so, but more often they will repeat some phases or parts of phases more than once before they come to a conclusion.

"Muddling through" the process in this fashion is "disjointed" partly because it looks for solutions bit by bit, that is, as a succession of limited "incremental" comparisons (Lindblom 1959, Braybrooke & Lindblom 1963). Since to attempt to achieve the "rational deductive ideal" of amassing and evaluating all possible information on all possible alternatives would be mind blowing, decisionmakers content themselves with enough information to make limited comparisons between alternative decisions, most of which would be mere increments added on tentatively at the point where the last decision finished off. Disjointed processes move first one way, then another, feeling the way ahead in small steps. Most senior managers and administrators are likely to approach decisions this way. For even though Lindblom first saw these characteristics in public administration (Lindblom 1959), Quinn argues persuasively that a similar "logical incrementalism" pervades private industry (Quinn 1978, 1980).

Of course, these insights indicate broad tendencies, a matter of degree in many instances but not all. Some decisions can be all or nothing, too indivisible to be tackled incrementally (Schulman 1975, Lustick 1980).

Indeed, it has to be asked whether the whole image of a volatile molecule—or football—bouncing sideways and backwards as often as forwards, and making progress only little by little in fits and starts, is not too lurid. It is a brilliant and invaluable cartoon which describes what happens in a way that gives penetrating understanding, although while it may well hold much of the truth much of the time, there is strong evidence that it does not represent all of the truth all of the time.

The Bradford studies of decision-making by my colleagues and myself (Hickson et al 1985, 1986) derived a characterization of the movement of strategic decision-making processes from 150 cases, 5 each in 30 diverse organizations in Britain. The most distinctive summary features of these cases were their discontinuity and their dispersion. That is, they differed first in the extent to which they had proceeded steadily and continuously, and second in the extent to which they had proceeded throughout the organization or were relatively confined. While many were *dis*continuous or, in more colorful terms, did seem to bounce around, many were comparatively continuous; and they varied similarly in *dispersion*.

Three types of movement emerged from an analysis of 136 cases that had the necessary data. There were *sporadic processes*, "informally spasmodic and protracted", as when in a state-owned industry a decision to buy a one-third share in a large customer firm was taken over a period of a year and a half, in irregular bursts of activity and flurries of negotiation with other interested corporations. There were *fluid processes*, "steadily paced, formally channelled, speedy," as when in a city government, a decision to launch a lottery, an unprecedented and potentially controversial source of funds at the time, was rushed through the framework of municipal committees in a month or so. And there were *constricted processes*, "narrowly channelled", as when in an insurance company, a decision was taken to defend its autonomous existence via an updating and centralizing of its data handling, a decision-making process that revolved around the chief executive in a tried and recognized manner. Some matters for decision and kinds of organizations are prone to one type of process rather than another.

Although the sporadic processes showed symptoms of the discontinuous excitation that the general image of decision-making leads one to expect, the fluid processes showed far fewer symptoms of this. The constricted group were divided either way but, more significantly, were the opposite of dispersed, as the word constricted denotes. The process moved in well-worn channels under the control of a chief executive or similar figure and did not flow around the organization as sporadic and fluid processes tended to do. In short, the salient impression given by at least a half the cases (the fluids and many of the constricteds) was of smooth continuity or limited movement or both. We should avoid drawing an over-excited image of what goes on along the corridors of decision.

The Strategic Matter in Motion

Impressions of what strategic decisions are about can also be unbalanced. Media stories focus attention on the big product launch successes and failures, such as the well-known cases, in American industry, of IBM's computer, Du Pont's Corfam shoe, and Ford's Edsel car which Hage (1980) cites as examples of high risk decisions. Yet among decisions that have been studied, those chosen by executives as being strategic matters, new products in manufacturing are only one category (Quinn 1978). In published comparative research (Drenth et al 1979, Nutt 1984, Mintzberg et al 1976, March & Olsen 1976, Hickson et al 1986: see Table 2.2 in the last reference), new technology and investments in buildings and equipment, internal reorganizations, and electronic data processing and related planning, all bulk large among topics for decision (computers and the like have been a favorite among researchers ever since the early case histories published by Cyert et al (1956), Cyert & March (1963), Carter (1971), and Pettigrew (1973). Decisions to introduce new services in private commerce and in the public sector are quite common, even more so than new product designs in manufacturers. Then there are a range of less frequent topics such as market and price decisions, personnel grading schemes, takeovers and mergers, the raising of capital, and whether to move the main organization to a fresh location. In summary, the principal strategic preoccupations of those at the top appear from research coverage to be: how the organization is to be equipped (by investment in productive technology or in data processing equipment), what the best structure is for the organization, and what the organization is to do. This is reassuringly obvious. These are the sorts of topics that governing elites would be expected to be dealing with.

The matter in hand is labeled as the new plant decision or the merger question, or whatever it is, by those involved in the process. This topic label identifies it at the time and subsequently but does not necessarily convey all that is at stake. Any matter is liable to be the surface expression of long-standing underlying issues—such as how far to go in diversifying a firm, or what the balance should be between research and teaching in a university—issues not signified by the simple topic label that the matter acquires.

Even so, the ostensible topics do offer a first grasp on what is afoot. They frequently embody intentional managerial strategies that can be seen in the way in which one decision leads to another (Hickson et al 1986). However, it is questionable whether the decisions actually carried out are always the same as the intended strategy. "A pattern in a stream of decisions" (Mintzberg 1978) can expose the actual strategy that has emerged in practice. Mintzberg & Waters (1982) show this in the patterns of store openings and closings, of financing, and of related activities over many decades in a Canadian retail chain. After tracing in the same way the patterns of films that have been produced by the National Film Board of Canada, Mintzberg & McHugh (1985) go further and suggest that strategies emerge from all the "grass-roots" operating decisions in organizations as well as from deliberate strategic decisions higher up.

The Problems Raised

The handling of each matter for decision is partly shaped by the problems it raises; the uncertainty these problems bring is thought to be especially telling. All strategic matters are by definition largely beyond the routines evolved to deal with repetitive matters in a programmed way. They are comparatively nonprogrammed because of the uncertainty about how to deal with them and what conclusion to reach (Simon 1960). There may be no accepted assumptions about cause and effect, so that the consequences of choosing this alternative rather than that are unforeseeable (Thompson & Tuden 1964). The factors to be weighed may be numerous, varied, and changing, as they were in the Swedish schools and colleges investigated by Axelsson & Rosenberg (1979).

It is contended that organizations attempt to avoid uncertainty so that their central activities can continue undisturbed (Thompson 1967, Cyert & March 1963). The word "avoid" is misleading if it is taken to mean that executives always run away from anything uncertain; indeed, many major decisions, particularly reorganizations and relocations, are "an unprecedented step into the unknown" (Hickson et al 1986). The point is more accurately understood as meaning that executives take risks only so far as they must and at a time when they hope their organizations can hold down the uncertainty. Specialist departments gain influence from developing a capacity to cope with areas of uncertainty (March & Simon 1958, Hickson et al 1971, Hinings et al 1974), and they feed in information and recommendations during the making of strategic decisions.

"Problemistic search" spurred by the immediate problem is more important than is the steady routine accumulation of information on, say, sales or costs (Cyert & March 1963). By sorting through case material on decisions in 73 hospitals and governmental agencies, insurance companies, and consulting firms in the health field, Nutt (1984) discerned 5 ways in which ideas were sought (and 11 subvariations on these 5 ways). Most common (41%) was the "historical process" which used "concepts drawn from the practices of others." Almost as common (30%) was the "off-the-shelf" process in which "aggressive and overt search" attempted to find "the best available ideas." "Nova" processes (15%) deliberately aimed at innovation. In other words, if what appeared to happen in these health related organizations can be generalized, the thrust of the search for ideas is about evenly divided between looking backward at what has been done before and more energetically looking forward and outward to what might be done. Nutt (1984) found also a minority of more defensive "search" processes which "lacked a workable idea," and "appraisal" processes which assessed "an idea that has an unknown or contentious value."

Whether or not this typology is exactly transferable to other kinds of organization, there is no doubt of either the limited capacity of the human mind or its susceptibility to believing what it wants to believe. Cognitive limits set a "bounded rationality" within which things make reasoned sense, though looked at in a wider context they make no sense at all (March & Simon 1958, Simon 1960, Cyert & March 1963). Motivation limits bias the acquisition of information, so that those concerned go for the most easy to come by and least controversial information which they come to treat as more certain that it originally was (O'Reilly 1983). Thus, decisions ensue from narrow perspectives and distorted data!

Despite this, organizations survive, and these pages are written by an employee of one. Even though the makers of decisions grope around in a probabalistic world in a selective self-justifying way and there is always an element of chaos as a result, coherence persists in most organizations and most societies most of the time.

The Interests Implicated

Within each organization, as within a whole society, this coherence must somehow contain multiple interests. In the understanding of decision-making in organizations, the early brilliance of the ideas from the "Carnegie school," principally those of Cyert, and of March, and of Simon (for examples, March & Simon 1958; Simon 1945, 1960; Cyert & March 1963), outshone all else and led to an emphasis on the information processing aspect of decision-making rather than the political aspect. This was not an altogether fair reflection of the Carnegie school which comprehended both aspects, even if its writings did not make this sufficiently plain, but probably it was more a reflection of the selective perception of academics in business education at the time. Since then, through the 1970s and 1980s, greater attention has come to be paid to the political nature of strategic decisions. It is well recognized that the way each matter is handled is shaped by the interests it implicates as well as by the problems it raises.

Each interest exerts influence or "kinetic power," as it has been called (French & Raven 1959), in the "bureaucratic politics" (Allison 1969) of decision-making. "Politics refers to the active influence process, but power is latent, referring to the ability or capacity to influence" (Miles 1980). Departments submit reports, consultants make recommendations, suppliers indicate possible prices, and so on. The more influential the interest, the more likely it is that the information and/or views it offers will be acted upon (O'Reilly 1983). The timing of an intervention is crucial, since everyone cannot attend to everything at once, and so there are right moments and wrong moments: "Every entrance is an exit somewhere else" (March & Olsen 1976). Thus, timing when to come in and when to stay out demands political judgment. There is "fluid participation" (Cohen et al 1972). It has been suggested that while most of the action takes place during the middle phase of a decision-making process (DIO International Research Team 1983), it is vital to influence the start and the finish (Heller et al 1987).

Each decision-making process involves a subset, or "decision-set" (Hickson et al 1986) of the interests in the "organizational coalition" (Cyert & March 1963, Pfeffer & Salancik 1977) of the internal and external interests that sustain the organization in being. An average of about seven "interest units" per decision has been found, including both "heavyweights" and "lightweights" in terms of the influence they exert and the number of decisions they become involved with (Hickson et al 1986). Among the heavyweights are production departments (and the equivalent in service organizations), sales and marketing, and accounting; from outside the organization the customers or clients may be involved, although only now and again. Governmental departments and agencies, and trade unions, are relatively uninfluential lightweights. On rare occasions, however, when the moment and the circumstances are right, a governmental interest may bring pressure to bear for a particular decision and it then may manage to exert considerable influence.

Games of position are played in which interests are protected in a "concatenation of maneuver" (March 1981) across "bargaining zones" (Abell 1975). Indeed, an organization can be regarded as an "ensemble des jeux" (Crozier & Friedberg 1980). Two memorably vivid case histories come from British experience. One, mentioned earlier, describes the manipulation of information and of access to authority figures in the retail business (Pettigrew 1973). The other tells how an otherwise smooth process in a chemicals producer was inflamed by a career struggle between the two directors, both of whom used it in their endeavors to attain the managing directorship (Wilson 1982, Hickson et al 1986). In the American corporation studied by Burgelman (1983), if a product innovation were to become part of the corporation's strategy it had to be thrust upwards by its "champion" until it secured a positive top-level decision, a process in which "gatekeeping, idea generating and bootlegging activities" could all be found. Political success allowed initial "strategic forcing" of the product into the market by its supporters; this, if successful, won sustained corporate management support.

There is a sense in which the political game turns a decision-making process around back to front. Interests in its outcome are already there before the process begins, insofar as most of those whose interests may be implicated know their objectives, their preferences, and their *logiques d'action* (Karpik 1972, Weiss 1981) irrespective of which topic arises. Thus, solutions exist *before* problems arise, and the game is to find a problem to which you can attach your solution (Cohen et al 1972, March & Olsen 1976).

In a decision-making process, therefore, the search is not only for problem-solving information but for interest-accommodating alternatives. Cognitive limits are paralleled by acceptability limits. Since there are multiple interests, all of which cannot be met at once, there is "sequential attention to goals" (Cyert & March 1963) with first one and then the other claiming priority. Since differing interests are built into an organization—sales versus production, surgical versus medical, sociology versus biology, and so on—each decision is only a "quasi-resolution of conflict": The differences remain and will come out again next time (Cyert & March 1963). Grandori (1984) puts forward a rather simplistic classification of procedures that logically should fit different levels of conflict and uncertainty, running from "computation" of value maximizing choices when there is agreement and certainty, to random casting around when there is a great deal of disagreement and uncertainty.

A prime social mechanism for the management of potentially conflicting interests is the committee by whatever name (the council, board, senate, committee, subcommittee, working party, project team, etc). A committee makes political behavior less obtrusive and more legitimate, and it diffuses responsibility (Miles 1980). Universities probably have more of these creations than any other known form of organization but, strangely, they do not seem to slow decision-making in universities nor anywhere else despite the popular impression that they clog it up (Hickson et al 1986).

The contemporary view of the making of a strategic decision therefore sees it as an essentially political process (Pfeffer & Salancik 1974) in which problems are defined and information is used with the interests of a range of insiders and outsiders in mind implicitly, if not explicitly. Emphasizing this in American private industry, Donaldson & Lorsch (1983) make what is nevertheless a general point about "unlimited ambition, limited choice": "Top management's freedom to set strategic direction in the mature industrial corporation is significantly constrained."

Even so, "the managerial prerogative is in no danger of being usurped" (Heller et al 1986). Power and counter-power offset one another (Rus 1980), and by and large the multiple interests are contained within a "malleable constrained domination" by the general executives at the top (Hickson et al 1986).

The Rules of the Game

Most of the time, then, the elite keep a grip on what is going on, though no one would suggest that it is entirely within their control. Behind this grip lie the rules of the game as these are expressed in the constitution and structure of the organization itself. Whether the organization is in a relatively 'capitalist' or a relatively 'communist' state, (for what these terms are worth), those who have power to do so set it up on a legal basis with basic resources that frame their intentions on what should and should not be done.

Overtly, the management of an organization has a given autonomy to make decisions to the extent that its position in any owning group allows and within the laws of the state. Thus, in business firms with a divisional structure, the divisional and even departmental managements are able to play a part in initiating and pushing through proposals requiring major investments that is greater than would be feasible in more centralized structures (Ackerman 1970). Further, the more independent an organization is of external entanglements the wider the range of decisions open to its management. The more it is dependent upon others (e.g. suppliers or customers or, most obviously, owners such as another corporation or a government), the less autonomy it is likely to have in decision-making and, in addition, the more centralized it is likely to be within itself (Pugh et al 1969, Pugh & Hickson 1976). The ultimate in dependence is the small subsidiary unit that takes all its inputs from others within the same group and sends them all its outputs, and whose managers are that in name only, locked within either a private or a state-owned corporation or government administration.

Covertly, beneath this overt exclusion of some matters for decision from the legitimate authority of the management of the organization in question, there are several further levels of "nondecision" (Bachrach & Baratz 1962), if that expression may be stretched to cover them all. First there is what has been called "quasi-decision making", where the forms of decision-making must be proceeded with even though it is apparent to some or all of those involved that the decision has already been made (Hickson et al 1986). A good third of decision-making seems to be like this. Then there are the potential issues that are never allowed to break the surface to become labeled as matters for decision (Abell 1977, Lukes 1974): "I wouldn't bring that up if I were you." Higher levels control lower levels by "structuring an internal selection environment" (Burgelman 1983). Beneath this again lie the taken-for-granted values and managerial language that may divert or suppress the formulation by powerless interests of matters they would otherwise bring forward (Lukes 1974, Clegg 1975). Taken together, all these levels of "nondecision" mean that each decision-making process must wend its way between a series of unquestionable assumptions and unthinkable options. Power rests as much in "its ability to be the natural convention" as in any overt action (Clegg 1977).

Insightful though this comment is on the nature of what is happening, it rests more on supposition than on empirical research. For instance, if there are different rules of the game, should this not be apparent in differences in the decision-making in different organizations? There is very little to go on here, and what there is seems ambiguous. March & Olsen (1976) titillate us with colorful visions of "organized anarchy" in universities and colleges that "do not know what they are doing". Yet what they are doing in decision-making mostly goes through in comparatively smooth "fluid" or "constricted" processes, that are not conspicuously anarchical (Hickson et al 1986). Again, while, in general, public ownership is held to load the chances in favor of a greater proportion of comparatively agitated "sporadic" processes (Hickson et al 1986) and probably prolongs them (Mallory 1986), the aims of managers under public ownership look much the same as their aims under private ownership (Aharoni & Lachman 1982). That could be held to mean the opposite, that public sector processes should not differ much from those in the private sector.

Outcomes and Implementation

There is a similar lack of research on which kinds of processes lead to what outcomes. Indeed, it may be questioned whether processes lead to outcomes at all (*outcome* here meaning the choice made between alternatives, the formal decision)? If interested parties already know their preferred choices before the process begins, as suggested earlier, and if during the process all sorts of problems and choices intermingle, then how far can a decision-making process be thought logically to lead to a choice? It has been asked whether a process can be partly "decoupled" from its outcome (Cohen et al 1972, March & Olsen 1976)? If it can be, then there is no manifest rational link between the decision made and the ostensible moves that look as if they lead up to it?

Perhaps not, but even if the precise choice made is therefore something of a surprise, the alternative chosen is unlikely to be very novel. Some argue that a search for a solution seems rarely to look far away from the point reached by the last decision. It is a "simple-minded" (Cyert & March 1963) examination of the simpler alternatives about which a lot is known already and will not disturb the status quo very much. Each step in this "incrementalism" (Lindblom 1959, Braybrooke & Lindblom 1963) adds just an increment to the previous conclusion, thereby avoiding too much uncertainty and the need for overmuch information. The small step is more common than the big leap.

A small step can be in a new direction, of course, and it has been argued that a succession of small steps is easier to make than one big one because the risk is less. Thus, changes can be made as rapidly by a series of small steps as by drastic but infrequent steps (Lindblom 1959). Empirical research does suggest that in a substantial proportion of cases decisionmakers do search for novel ideas or at least for fresh ideas taken "off-the-shelf" (Nutt 1984), and they do reach "custom-made" solutions much more often than "ready-made" ones (Mintzberg et al 1976).

However, if the recorded discussions between President Kennedy's advisers in 1962, when Soviet missiles were discovered on Cuba, are anything to go by, reaching a decision is less a weighing up of the merits of possible alternatives than it is an acknowledging of objections to them. It is likely to be "decision making by objection" (Anderson 1983). In this, alternatives are sought that are least likely to make things worse, and they are objected to iteratively, one by one, until the sequence of binary yes/no choices is brought to an end by finding one that is more or less acceptable. "Acceptable level decision rules" (Cyert & March 1963) mean that the search stops when a solution is found which is just about compatible with other decisions and will do for the time being. Such an outcome is "satisficing," the term coined by Simon (1960) to describe decisions that are neither wholly satisfactory nor wholly sufficing but which will get by with a little of both. It is the reverse of optimizing, that almost mythical outcome which all managers and administrators are supposed to strive for but which the Carnegie school shrewdly suspect is hardly ever achieved. In their famous analogy, which never loses its impact, decision-making is not about searching for the sharpest needle in a haystack but about finding one that is sharp enough to sew with (March & Simon 1958).

It is easy to take from published research the mistaken impression that all strategic decisions are positive. They are not. Although the majority are positive, such as to extend buildings, to reequip, to raise capital, or to buy a subsidiary, a minority of decisions are negative. They either decide to do nothing and leave the situation as it is (not to make a takeover bid, not to enter a market), or they decide to undo something (to shut down shops, to close hospitals). Of the 150 cases covered by the Bradford studies, as many as 12 (8%) were negative (Hickson et al 1986).

Whether positive or negative, once a decision has been made it represents such an accumulated effort, and probably such a careful reconciliation of interests, that there is great reluctance to change it. Indeed, even if when it is implemented it turns out to have been a bad decision, there is a pronounced tendency to keep going and "pour good resources after bad," in the hope that all that is needed to pull things round is a little more money or time or effort, less than would be needed to start all over again in another direction. There is an "escalation of commitment" (Staw 1981).

After all, everything is not cut and dried once the decision is taken. Great uncertainty may exist about implementation (Mumford & Pettigrew 1975), and this can be frustrated not only by unforeseen difficulties but by unreconciled interests. Perhaps these interests failed to stop the decision during the decision-making process, or perhaps they were never in on the process because they were kept out or because they kept themselves out. For example, trade unions in Britain are both kept out and keep out; as a result their influence on the process of making a major decision is relatively negligible (Wilson et al 1982). They do not count. They make themselves felt, if at all, after the decision is taken, during its implementation. At this stage they can slow down and mollify what is done, in defence of what they see as their members' interests. But they cannot change the decision.

In fact, Heller et al (1987) conclude that the importance of the implementation stage has been underestimated. Even in terms of time it takes much longer than they had believed. Certainly executives do try and peer through the uncertainty a long way ahead when making strategic decisions. They do not anticipate the first effects of their decision to show up for a couple of years (Mallory 1987), and they expect the effects to last many years beyond that. They anticipate that the overall consequences will endure for around eight years on average, and even longer for reorganization and relocation decisions because they are especially tricky to change or to supersede until many years have passed (Hickson et al 1986).

METHODOLOGY

The Doubts and the Data

Humankind's study of itself has always been beset with doubts and divisions over how it should be done. Should such study be more an artistic distillation of impressions or a scientistic interpretation of data? The study of elite strategic decision-making processes poses this puzzle as acutely as anything does. The description of decision-making given here (perhaps a caricature of it in some respects) is wholly the result of the methods that produced it. So what methods have been and are feasible and acceptable?

The crux of the difficulty for researchers is the vaporous quality of a decision-making process. Its outcome, the decision itself, can usually be found in the deliberations of a board or council meeting, and the resulting new product or share issue or reorganization or whatever can be seen to have happened. But where is, or was, the *process* of reaching the decision? Workers or clerks can be studied, after a fashion, because where they are, or are supposed to be, is known and the researcher can go there and talk to them or watch them or even work with them. They can be got at. So can an individual manager, though not so readily since a manager moves about more. Still, spot checks and self-recorded diaries yield a fairly standard picture (for example, Mintzberg 1973, Stewart 1976). But the social process of moving toward a decision is located nowhere in particular. Put the other way around, it can be anywhere in general.

Does it then require its own special methods of study? Here there is great appeal in data for data's sake. The story of what happens is itself interesting—with luck sensational—in a way that a story of workers working or clerks clerking or lecturers lecturing is unlikely to be. Here is power with the lid off! What may be the best record ever made was produced in the early 1970s not by researchers but by television camera crews filming hundreds or maybe thousands of hours of meetings and conversations in the offices and corridors of the nationalized steel corporation in Britain. Cut down to a remarkable couple of hours, this was an inside view of a cliffhanger plant investment decision. It went out on the public television network and has been widely used for teaching ever since. It was and is absorbing data, showing as nothing else can do how the process does become manifest in a phone call, a few words around an executive desk, a conflict of views in the board, or a nod in the chairman's room. Yet even this is inevitably a small selection of all that occurred and, most significantly, in the television rendering there is nothing that an academic researcher would call analysis. It is data and only data.

Researchers have never equalled what the resources of a television company can do, but they have often tried to go as far as they can. An inclination to tell all is distinctive to this field of work. Cyert et al (1956) reported their

"Observation of a Business Decision," and this was followed by some more case histories in Cyert & March (1963). In the 1970s Pettigrew's (1973) well-known case story centered on the manager "Kenny" in a retail firm; some detailed Scandinavian descriptions were collected in March & Olsen (1976). Most recently, each stage of each of the 73 cases studied by Nutt (1984) is set out in a summary page after page. The Canadian National Film Board is exposed at great length by Mintzberg & McHugh (1985), and the book in which the bulk of the results of the Bradford studies are presented begins with the "tale of Toxicem" on its first page, an instant immersion in data (Hickson et al 1986). These few examples suggest that, in the study of decision making at this elevated level in organizations, not only do researchers like to tell their stories they also seem to feel that readers need to be convinced. Not many of them personally inhabit the more rarified layers of a hierarchy and unless given a mass of description, they may not understand what it is like there, nor will they credit the researcher with having found out. The case study method is not special to decision-making research, of course, but the urge to regale the reader with the data it produces is pronounced.

Researchers have tended not to venture outside the bounds of the case study method, but understandably so. Long ago, Bachrach & Baratz (1962) criticized political scientists for concentrating on what did happen rather than what did not (what they called the "non-decisions"); their point has been uncomfortably at the back of researchers' minds ever since. It was restated and reinforced (for instance by Lukes 1974 and Clegg & Dunkerley 1980) under the impulse in the 1970s of radical and ethnomethodological criticisms of the sociology of organizations and organization theory (for example, Silverman 1970; Zey-Ferrell & Aiken 1981). The feeling persists that if any method has a chance of getting underneath the decision-maker's carpet, it is the close personal familiarity of the intensive case history. An associated fear has been that to move so far out of the case narrative as to apply variables to cases would somehow "de-nature" the data itself.

But ideas and not data are the prize. In decision-making research, as elsewhere, data for data's sake is sterile. While descriptive data are absolutely indispensable to revealing the human experience as a basis for understanding it, ultimately data are the means to the end of devising concepts with which to interpret that data.

To this end researchers need not only the case study method and the narrative history but any and every other method of data collection and data analysis to use alongside it. Among others, Galtung (1967) wrote of the "data matrix" in which one axis was the number of dimensions or variables—or concepts—employed, from one to many, and the other axis was the number of units or cases studied, also from one to many. Research on decision-making should not pay undue attention to the advantages to be gained by working on one side of the matrix, the part with just a few cases, without making an equal effort to see what can be gained from the other side, many cases. And on both sides, the more ideas the better.

Coming of Age

Research on decision-making seems to be beginning to spread more evenly across the data matrix than hitherto. Indeed, research on decision-making may not be special at all and has probably been developing through a most conventional scientistic progression—not from bad to better but from the cautious use of some methods to the ability to work anywhere across Galtung's (1967) data matrix according to the needs of the research and the researcher.

Take three elements of empirical method—sample, data collection, and data analysis and presentation. There has been an extension from small samples with some form of intensive case study data collection (personal observation and conversation) and narrative presentation, through various middling approaches, to comparatively large samples with some form of structured interview or questionnaire and analysis by variables. At the smaller scale and narrative end, illustrative examples are the description by Cyert et al (1956) of an electronic data processing decision, accounts by Cyert & March (1963) of four cases including a similar electronic data processing decision, and the intricate story of a computer purchase decision, told by Pettigrew (1973), all of which have already been referred to. A number of case histories are included in March & Olsen (1976), such as decisions on departmental changes in a university, and one (never implemented) on racial desegregation and on a new open class structure in schools. Latterly, Wilson (1982) reviews the Toxicem case that has been mentioned here and Wilson et al (1986) compare it and another in the same company with cases in a university. Hence, the classic case study method is in no sense being supplanted. But researchers have been successfully trying out other possibilities as well, and these enable a wider coverage.

The collection of data on as many as 25 cases by Mintzberg and his students (Mintzberg et al 1976) was "historically a milestone" (Butler et al 1979–1980), opening the way to larger numbers and heartening others working in the same direction. Quinn (1980) tackled nine privately owned manufacturers of household-name repute and Nutt (1984) subsequently followed up with data from no less than 73 health-related service organizations as mentioned before. The characteristic of the middling approach taken by these studies is the collection of data by substantial interviews, moderately structured, and the analysis of the data by comparison of cases in words and diagrams, rather than by numbers.

Numerical analysis, and the definition of variables as explicit means of comparison, has become prominent in print during the 1980s, reflecting research launched in the 1970s. For instance, Heller and his colleagues (Drenth et al 1979, DIO International Research Team 1983, Heller et al 1987) have used unstructured and structured interviews to obtain data on 217 decisions in 7 companies, 102 of which were classed as strategic. They compared these by a combination of verbal case discussion and the numerical analysis of variables such as influence, satisfaction, and trust. Yet another example is the progression of the Bradford studies over ten years from intensive case studies, both concurrent and historically traced, to substantial structured interviews commencing with case histories and moving eventually to mailed questionnaires. With 6 early depth cases as a base (Wilson 1980, Wilson et al 1982), the research amassed a further 146 cases of strategic decisions in 30 organizations by interview alone (including covering the original six again, a total of 150), and then applied comparative analysis by variables to processual data (Hickson et al 1986). The variables included, for instance, disruption by delays, formality and informality of interaction, and the number of sources of information, as well as the seriousness of the matter and the contention of interests. Although a prior attempt by Stein (1981a, b) had not seemed at all encouraging, Mallory (1986) went on to "do the impossible" by producing process data on a further 56 cases not merely by questionnaire but by a *mail* questionnaire covering four sides of paper. The likely validity of this is attested by the results available which so far match those from the study of 150 cases in places where the two studies coincide. One extraordinarily precise example is the duration (as defined at the beginning of this essay) of the processes in the two studies which were (Mallory figures second): means 12.4 months and 12.4 months, standard deviations 10.6 months and 10.9 months, ranges 1–48 months and 2–48 months!

Clearly, therefore, it is possible to apply the customary range of social science methods of data collection and analysis to these kinds of decision-making processes, however vaporous such processes might seem to be. Equally clearly, the methods of data collection differ in what they rely upon. The depth case study relies on the personality and accuity of what is usually a lone researcher. This method is limited because the researcher, or even a small team of researchers, cannot be everywhere all at once; they often have to make do with being told what has happened rather than with being on the spot as it happens. The interview and the questionnaire rely even more on the executive as a recording device. That is, they are limited by reliance on the informant's longer term memory; in the depth case, the memory is usually more recent, of course. On the other hand, the interview or questionnaire does get an overview of the basic events and the character of a completed story.

Essentially the methodological pros and cons are those of any other area of study. In this sense, the field has come of age.

Common Difficulties

Coming of age does not remove the difficulties that affect sampling, data collection, and data analysis—e.g. difficulties in collaboration, costs, and classification, respectively.

Sampling is hampered by the difficulty of persuading top executives to collaborate by giving up their time and, especially, giving it up to talk of something about which they feel apprehensive, lest they betray some innermost managerial secret. It is difficult to gain permission to follow one case in detail, or to question many managers in many organizations briefly, in person or by questionnaire. Frequently researchers obtain collaboration by exploiting a teaching or a consulting type link (for example, Nutt 1984, Quinn 1980) but this carries the inevitable risk of compromising the research relationship. Otherwise, the form of words and the appropriate degree of confidence with which to present researcher and research in a way that is understandable and appealing has to be found by trial and error. Random sampling or any other deliberate selection has so far been out of the question: A third at least of those contacted are likely to say no (Hickson et al 1986).

Even when collaboration is achieved, costs hamper data collection. Following a process along as it happens is enormously expensive in researcher time, and there is always the risk that the researcher may have to finish—or be shown the door—before a decision is reached. Extensive interviewing is also expensive in time and travel; this tends to force expedients such as using students as interviewers (Mintzberg et al 1976) (when each different case may be perceived through the medium of different and relatively inexperienced individuals) or relying on comparatively few principal informants (for example, Nutt 1984; Hickson et al 1986) when more would be more readily and manifestly persuasive, even given the reassurance of various cross-checks (Hickson et al 1986).

Thirdly, the difficulty of classification is shared with every other field of study, social science and otherwise. How many categories make sense? Too few cases in too many categories makes classification complicated and unrevealing, adding little to leaving the cases separate and unclassified. Categories have utility when each contains a substantial number of cases. On the other hand, too few categories could result in over simplification. The classification of decision-making processes has sharp contrasts in this respect. For instance, Stein (1981b) construed as many as 16 categories from 63 questionnaires (only 4 cases per category, on average); Mintzberg et al (1976) proposed 7 process categories (and a range of possible "routines" within each) for 25 cases; Nutt (1984) suggested 5 types and 11 subvarieties to cover 73 cases, and Hickson et al (1986) arrived at 3 types covering 53, 42, and 41 cases in a total of 136 processes.

First and foremost, however, the value of a classification is in the insightfulness and generalizability of the concepts that define the categories. This essay now turns to concepts and theories.

CONCEPTS AND THEORIES

Concepts

The comprehension of strategic decision-making began with concepts of its problems and their solutions. The emphasis then gradually shifted to the politics and movement of the process. These two emphases are not mutually exclusive. The one grew to complement the other, and both are indispensable to any full comprehension.

The most penetrating and lively concepts of decision-making problems and solutions have come from March and Simon and their colleagues of the one-time "Carnegie school," and from those who think likewise. Among their illuminating concepts included in this essay are the notions of *sequential attention to goals* (that decisionmakers cannot balance everything at once but turn first one way and then the other); of *uncertainty avoidance* (whereby decisionmakers seek ways to protect and stabilize their organization); and of *simpleminded search* (whereby decisionmakers prefer alternatives that are not far away from what is being done already) (Cyert & March 1963). These lead to *satisficing* decisions, it has been said, rather than to optimizing ones, on the more consequential and more novel *non-programmed matters* (Simon 1960).

Those whose contribution has been rather more to concepts of the *politics and movement* of decisionmaking have not yet equalled this Marchian flair for evocative terminology! Had they done so we might have had a spectacular vocabulary with which to appreciate its political essence and action.

Nevertheless, we do have "*ensembles des jeux*" (Crozier & Friedberg 1980), a conception of an organization as a setting for political games and, in horseracing parlance, jockeying for position. These games are played across *bargaining zones* (Abell 1975) to protect or promote *interests*. Movement toward a decision is broken by *interrupts*, and it often *cycles* back upon itself (Mintzberg et al 1976). It has both *duration* in chronological time and *pace* in the eyes of those involved, and the two are not at all the same (Mallory 1987). Its character may be *sporadic, fluid,* or *constricted* (Hickson et al 1986).

These concepts and others (this does not pretend to be a complete list) are the basis for the main theories that have been put forward to explain what happens in decision-making.

Theories

The study of decision-making has been the playground of contestants who, with a little license, might be called either the "managerial systemetizers" or the "behavioral debunkers." The managerial systematizers are those whose necessary normative mission it must be to advocate to managers, and to students aspiring to be managers, the means to an orderly controllable world. Decision trees, planning charts, cost-benefit analyses, and the like are aimed at easing the manager's lot when confusing and worrisome decisions have to be taken. Against these, the behavioral debunkers have delighted in pointing out the mental and political limits that hinder their use. Just as psychologists have relished citing articles showing poor human reasoning and decision-making rather than good (Christensen-Szalanski & Beach 1984), so the debunkers of managerial decision making have bolstered their own position by puncturing managerial reasoning!

The contest has been productive, nonetheless. From it have emerged three ways of thinking about and explaining decision-making that have appeared again and again in this essay. These three theories are *incrementalism*, the *garbage-can model*, and *dual rationality*.

Incrementalism originates very obviously in the contest between systematizers and debunkers. Incrementalism contrasts the "synoptic" approach, that aims at the "rational deductive ideal," with the mundane practicabilities of "successive limited comparisons" of information and alternatives, and with compromises by "mutual partisan adjustment," (Lindblom 1959, Braybrooke & Lindblom 1963). This bit by bit approach, or "disjointed incrementalism," is explained by the limited information handling capacities of the decision-makers and by their need to pick a way through the "partisan" viewpoints. Doing a bit at a time in this way is said to be the most generally applicable and successful tactic.

The second theory, the *garbage-can model*, rests on the same assumptions about mental and political limits. Its evocative terminology conjures up the tangled innards of a garbage can as an alternative to the vision of rational orderliness (Cohen et al 1972, March & Olsen 1976, March & Olsen 1984). Inside the can, there are quite a few oddities, or so they appear. Individuals fight for the right to participate and then do not exercise it; information that is available is ignored, more is requested, and then that too is ignored; there is acrimonious contention over the adoption of policies, but relative indifference to whether policies are implemented; and so on. To account for what goes on, the model turns the conventional view back to front. Instead of assuming that one thing causally leads to another in a logical "consequential order," which is not the way things seem to happen, it postulates "*temporal order*" as being the more apposite.

Into the can tumble streams of problems, solutions, and participants. It is not their logical ordering but their temporal simultaneity that accounts for decision-making. When compatible problems and solutions coincide in time, then there is a choice opportunity that may enable a decision. Whether it does so or not depends upon who has time and attention to give to it, since no one can attend to everything all at once; in short, "the process is sensitive to load" (March & Olsen 1984).

The model is flexible and can be adjusted to different streams of problems, solutions, and participants, and to different conditions of time and attention. It shares with incrementalism the explanation that what happens is due to the possibilities being bounded both cognitively and politically, but it reverses the presumed order of things. Solutions come *before* problems, in the sense that participants know what they want and await a chance to get it, and the occurrence of a chance that catches their attention is the necessary circumstance. Among the handy inferences drawn are that participants should choose their time, should persist if they fail since another chance may come, should give due import to symbolic issues, and should "overload the system" with proposals since even if one proposal misses its moment another may succeed (March & Olsen 1984).

The model goes so far and no further, of course—as those who devised it frankly say. It does not encompass the powers that define what streams of problems, solutions, and participants may flow and that set the situation so that some are more likely to coincide than others. Empirically, the theory is grounded in the experience of educational organizations, but in other organizations decision-making may be less like this.

Thirdly, in a more prosaic manner, the *dual rationality theory* is an attempt to draw together the ingredients that appear commonly in one form or another in research in this field. These ingredients so permeate thought that it is tempting to indulge current fashion and refer to them as the dominant paradigm. Very simply, they are the assumptions—inherent in both the incrementalism and the garbage can explanations—that decision-making is a process of handling both problems and politics.

Beginning as a "dual explanation" (Hickson et al 1981, Astley et al 1982, Hickson et al 1986), this may better be termed a dual rationality theory. It argues that every matter that arises for decision must *both* raise problems and implicate interests. Because the problems raised and the interests implicated by one matter are not the same as those encountered by the previous one, nor will they be the same as those in the next, the process of arriving at each decision will differ. Greater complexity of problems and greater politicality of interests ginger up activity and involvement; lesser complexity and lesser politicality allow a more quiescent process.

Three prevalent combinations of complexity and politicality have been identified empirically. Most complex and political are the "weighty and controversial" *vortex* matters. Less complex and least political are the "unusual but non-controversial" *tractable* matters. Least complex, but rather more political than tractable matters, are the "normal and recurrent" *familiar* matters. Each combination tends to generate a typical kind of movement towards a decision. A vortex matter is likely to generate a sporadic process, a tractable matter a fluid process, and a familiar matter a constricted process.

Each matter is approached by the élite of the hierarchy in accordance with dual implicit managerial or administrative rationalities. On the one hand, they aspire to handle its complexities by the classic problem-solving rationality whose limitations the incrementalism and garbage-can theories expose so piercingly, yet which remains a guide to action. On the other hand, although there is no equivalent explicit model in the literature for handling politicality, there is an implicit interest-accommodating rationality that weighs up what is at stake for each interested party and what the range of acceptable alternatives may be. However, the product of two different rationalities is not necessarily "rational" in the original textbook sense of that word, since the solving of the problems is shaped by the accommodating of the interests.

In this formulation, both the definition of the matter on hand and the guiding rationalities derive from the rules of the game inherent in the organization itself. A framework of power prescribes what an organization is for and who in the last resort determines what it is for. That framework sets the rules for what can and cannot be decided and how it may be decided. Managerial focusing upon the matter in hand means that "the matter for decision matters most" for the character of overt decision-making processes, but for covert nondecision processes—if processes is the right word—it is the power that frames the organization which matters even more.

What do these three theories try to explain? In a uniquely stringent assessment of what passes for theory about decisions, Mohr (1982) argues that there is no theory adequate to the explanation of why one choice is made rather than another. No theory gives reasons for the decision or *outcome* in which the decision-making process culminates. Neither a variance explanation nor a processual explanation is offered. The former kind of explanation, "variance theory," would attempt to explain the variance in a dependent variable. Since variables of the decision or outcome are not specified, however, nor are independent variables, this is not accomplished. The latter kind of explanation, "process theory"—or is it processual theory?—would attempt to explain a phenomenon as the result of "a series of occurrences in a sequence over time," but decisions or outcomes have not been defined in a way that enables this to be done, except perhaps at too particular or too general a level.

Rather than attempting either of these kinds of explanation of the outcomes of decision-making, research has concentrated on *describing* decision-making processes. In the same way that "description is often called theory in science not because it is an explanatory generalization or set of interrelated laws but because it is both important and conjectural" (Mohr 1982: 160), this has produced valuable descriptive theory, full of inspired conjectures about what goes on as decisions are made.

However, although the three theories summed up here as incrementalism, garbage-can model, and dual rationality may not have yielded explanations of the outcomes of decision-making processes, they do explain the *processes*. Process is and should be the focus of research, says Mohr (1982).

All three theories are putative explanations of the managerial social processes in which decisions are formed. The first, incrementalism, suggests that the more complex and indefinable is the matter for decision, the more disjointedly incremental the process of deciding is likely to be. The second, the garbage-can model, suggests that the more "loosely coupled" an organization is, and the more "anarchic," the more the model will account for what occurs. In other words, in organizations that lack tight hierarchical control, where means and ends are not clear, garbage-can style processes are more likely to be characteristic—for example, in universities and colleges in the Western world.

Most recently, the dual rationality theory brings prior thinking together, doing so because of a fresh step, namely, the application to process data of what Mohr (1982) calls variance theory. Variable characteristics of organizations (e.g. ownerships and functions), and of the problems raised and the interests implicated by the matters on hand (e.g. their consequentiality and influence) are used to explain the probabilities that one type of decision-making process will occur rather than another. Dual rationality theory attempts explicit explanation, over and above description. Dual managerial problem-solving and interest-accommodating rationalities are inferred to account for the relationships between the variables that make up the explanation.

These three theories are not in competition. They are overlapping and complementary. Between them, the explanation of decision-making processes is well advanced. In this field, theory has been ahead of the methodology rather than lagging behind. It is the methodology that has to catch up, and it is doing so.

SOME GROUND TO BE COVERED

All research is bad research, inasmuch as it could always be done better and there is always more to do. The ground to be covered is infinite. And those who study decision-making have been accused of devoting too much intellectual energy to a priori modelling and too little to empirical enquiry (Smith & May 1980). From the infinity, five areas of empirical interest will be picked out here as possibilities for further research—namely nondecisions, organizational and decisional differences, the matter for decision, successful decision-making, and societal differences.

Nondecisions

The covert side to decision-making may be described as being at three levels of nondecision: (*a*) quasi–decision making, where it is tacitly accepted that the decision has already been made, (*b*) the suppression of issues that then do not become matters for decision, and (*c*) the establishing of taken-for-granted values and language that obscure some matters and promote others. The difficulty is that the scanty publications about this aspect of decision-making have an air of the dark thriller about them, the lights low and the language mysteriously multisyllabic. They are fascinating, they are suggestive, but they do not rip the curtain aside and reveal all. Where are the researchers who can find means to confirm empirically that nondecisions at any level are all they are said to be?

Since organizations constitute the rules of the game for strategic decision-making, the study of any form of nondecision almost certainly requires the investigation of more than one organization, otherwise the rules may not be noticed by the researcher. They are more likely to be detected in the contrasts.

Organizational Differences and Decisional Differences

While the study of nondecisions might be aided by comparison between organizations, the study of overt decisions requires also the comparison of different decisions within any one organization. There is a glaring empirical gap here. Most explanations of decision-making are weakened because they say nothing about what may be due to the nature of the organization as against the nature of the matter for decision. The overwhelming portion of empirical research is one-in-one, that is, one case of decision-making in one organization. This prevents any comparison of different decisions in the same organization or of the same kinds of decision in different organizations. It confounds organizational and decisional explanations. They should be disentangled.

What Is The Matter?

The question "What is the matter?" needs asking more bluntly and answering more clearly. This essay began lightheartedly by wondering whether decision-making is more like soccer football or American football, and in the terms of that analogy we need to know more about the shape of the ball. In other words, what is the shape of the matter under decision? How does the incipient matter for decision begin to form during what has been called the gestation period prior to its surfacing as the subject for overt decision making? Indeed, does this reveal the rules for nondecisions? Once surfaced, how does the matter get redefined along the way, and how likely is it to finish as it began? Much of this appears in many case narratives, but rarely is it brought to the forefront of interest in the analysis.

Asking about the matter for decision confronts us with the problem of comparing like with like. This essay purports to be about "strategic" decisions. Yet who knows whether one researcher's strategic decision is the same as another's? The word is appealing to researchers who by using it imply that the research is really up there in the big time, but there is hardly any discussion of how different grades of decision might be operationally defined, and no way of knowing how far different studies are about the same or somewhat different classes of decision. A thoughtful, laborious, but important task of definition has yet to be done.

What Works Best?

Which kind of process leads to the best decision is a question bound to arise in any discussion of decision-making, whether with students or faculty or managers and administrators. Everyone in their heart of hearts hopes to find a clue to how they could do it better or see that it was done better. So far the question has no straight answer.

In fact, it is not one question but several. If processes are partly uncoupled from decisions, then which are more uncoupled and which more logically connected, and is it best to be uncoupled or coupled? Further, does the kind of process affect how and how fully the decision is implemented? Is the process an end in itself? There is some evidence for this in universities and hospitals, at least, where participation in the process of making a decision can be as important, even more important, than whether there is any means to implement it (Rodrigues 1980)!

The definition of a good decision is relative, of course. Are the criteria the costs, or profits, or the greatest satisfaction of the greatest number, or what? And what are the evaluations of those who participated in the decision-making process, of those who had most influence and those who had least, of those who formally "made" the decision by authorizing implementation, and of those affected by implementation?

Whose Processes Are They Anyway?

It must be confessed that this essay has been written as if the people taking part in decision-making processes are everywhere the same, in the same economic and political circumstances. Obviously they are not! They are American or Chinese or Russian or Indian or Arabic or Germanic or Latin European, and so on. Yet it has not been possible to review research on the *processes* of making strategic decisions in such a way as to show differences between national or cultural settings. This is because the available published material on which this essay has had to rely is solidly "Anglo-Nordic," that is, it comes from empirical work in Canada, the United States, Britain, Scandinavia, and The Netherlands. Nothing has been used from African, Arabic, Asian, East European, or Latin lands.

Within the Anglo-Nordic sphere, nothing has stood out sharply as a feature that characterizes one nation or one culture (or is it subculture?) more than another, but then the published work pays no attention to this possibility. Yet it is impossible to believe that social processes, including those decision-making processes that take place at the apex of an organization's hierarchy, are not deeply affected by national wealth and economic structure and by culture. Even though person-to-person interaction, which might reveal cultural differences most vividly, has not been directly dealt with here, the process properties that have been discussed must surely be affected? After all, the incessant comparisons of American and Japanese management practice suggest more prolonged and consultative processes among Japanese executives. Decisions in Africa have to be made in particular national political contexts which must affect their making. Those in Latin countries cannot be unaffected by hierarchies where blockages to vertical communication are frequent. In the People's Republic of China, centralization of decisions recurs despite efforts to decentralize. Indeed "socialist" economies typically struggle with endemic centralist tendencies and with what the role of the ruling party should be in strategic decision-making.

So although research on processes of decision-making at this level has a history of vigorous theoretical development, and it is maturing methodologically, there is as always much to be done and nowhere more so than in cross-national and cross-cultural investigation and explanation.

Acknowledgments

Although all omissions and commissions herein are my own, I could never have attempted the task but for what I learned in the Bradford studies of decision-making from my colleagues, notably Richard Butler, David Cray, Geoffrey Mallory, David Wilson, Runo Axelsson, and Graham Astley.

Literature Cited

Abell, P. 1975. Organizations as bargaining and influence systems: Measuring intraorganizational power and influence. In *Organizations as Bargaining and Influence Systems*, ed. P. Abell, pp. 10–40. London: Heinemann

Abell, P. 1977. The many faces of power and liberty: Revealed preference, autonomy and teleological explanation. *Sociology* 11(1):3–24

Ackerman, R. W. 1970. Influence of integration and diversity on the investment process. *Admin. Sci. Q.* 15(3):341–53

Aharoni, Y., Lachman, R. 1982. Can the manager's mind be nationalized? *Organ. Stud.* 3(1):33–46

Allison, G. T. 1969. Conceptual models and the Cuban missile crisis. *Am. Polit. Sci. Rev.* 63(3):689–718

Anderson, P. A. 1983. Decision making by

objection and the Cuban missile crisis. *Admin. Sci. Q.* 28(2):201–22

Astley, W. G., Axelsson, R., Butler, R. J., Hickson, D. J., Wilson, D. C. 1982. Complexity and cleavage: Dual explanations of strategic decision making. *J. Manage. Stud.* 19(4):357–75

Axelsson, R., Rosenberg, L. 1979. Decision-making and organizational turbulence. *Acta Sociol.* 22(1):45–62

Bachrach, P., Baratz, M. S. 1962. The two faces of power. *Am. Polit. Sci. Rev.* 56: 947–52

Braybrooke, D., Lindblom, C. 1963. *A Strategy of Decision.* New York: Free Press

Burgelman, R. A. 1983. A process model of internal corporate venturing in the diversified major firm. *Admin. Sci. Q.* 28(2):223–44

Butler, R. J., Astley, W. G., Hickson, D. J., Mallory, G. R., Wilson, D. C. 1979–1980. Strategic decision making: Concepts of content and process. *Int. Stud. Manage. Organ.* 9(4):5–36

Carter, E. E. 1971. The behavioral theory of the firm and top-level corporate decisions. *Admin. Sci. Q.* 16(4):413–28

Christensen-Szalanski, J. J. J., Beech, L. R. 1984. The citation bias: Fad and fashion in the judgment and decision literature, *Am. Psychol.* 39(1):75–78

Clegg, S. 1975. *Power, Rule and Domination.* London: Routledge & Kegan Paul

Clegg, S. 1977. Power, organization theory, Marx, and Critique. In *Critical Issues in Organizations.* ed. S. Clegg, D. Dunkerley, pp. 21–40. London: Routledge & Kegan Paul

Clegg, S., Dunkerley, D. 1980. *Organization, Class. and Control.* London: Routledge & Kegan Paul

Cohen. M. D., March, J. G., Olsen, J. P. 1972. A garbage can model of organizational choice. *Admin. Sci. Q.* 17:1–25

Crozier, M., Friedberg, E. (1977) 1980. *Actors and Systems,* Chicago: Univ. Chicago Press

Cyert. R. M., Simon, H. A., Trow, D. B. 1956. Observation of a business decision. *J. Bus.* 29:237–48

Cyert, R. M., March, J. G. 1963. *A Behavioral Theory of the Firm.* Englewood Cliffs: Prentice Hall

DIO International Research Team. 1983. A contingency model of participative decision making: An analysis of 56 decisions in three Dutch organizations. *J. Occup. Psychol.* 56(1):1–18

Donaldson, G., Lorsch, J. G. 1983. *Decision Making at the Top.* New York: Basic Books

Drenth, P. J. D., Koopman, P. L., Rus, V., Odar, M., Heller, F., Brown, A. 1979. Participative decision making: A comparative study. *Ind. Relat.* 18(3):295–309

French, J. R. P., Raven, B. 1959. The bases of social power. In *Studies in Social Power,* ed. D. Cartwright, pp. 150–67. Ann Arbor: Univ. Mich. Press

Galtung, J. 1967. *Theory and Methods of Social Research.* Oslo: Universitetsforlaget

Grandori, A. 1984. A prescriptive contingency view of organizational decision making. *Admin. Sci. Q.* 29(2):192–209

Hage, J. 1980. *Theories of Organizations: Form, Process and Transformation.* New York: Wiley

Heller, F., Drenth, P., Koopman, P., Rus, V. 1986. *Decisions in Organizations: A Three Country Longitudinal Study.* New York: Wiley

Hickson, D. J., Astley, W. G., Butler, R. J., Wilson, D. C. 1981. Organization as power. In *Research in Organizational Behavior, Vol. 3,* ed. L. L. Cummings, B. Staw, pp. 151-96. Greenwich, Conn: JAI

Hickson, D. J., Butler, R. J., Cray, D., Mallory. G. R., Wilson, D. C. 1985. Comparing 150 Decision Processes. In *Organization Strategy and Change,* J. M. Pennings and associates, pp. 114–43. San Francisco: Jossey-Bass

Hickson, D. J., Butler, R. J., Cray, D., Mallory, G. R., Wilson, D. C. 1986. *Top Decisions: Strategic Decision Making in Organizations.* Oxford: Blackwell; San Francisco: Jossey-Bass

Hickson, D. J., Hinings, C. R., Lee, C. A., Schneck, R. E., Pennings, J. M. 1971. A strategic contingencies theory of intraorganizational power. *Admin. Sci. Q.* 16(2):216–29

Hinings, C. R., Hickson, D. J., Pennings, J. M., Schneck, R. E. 1974. Structural conditions of intraorganizational power. *Admin. Sci. Q.* 19(1):22–44

Karpik, L. 1972. Les politiques et les logiques d'action de la grande enterprise industrielle. *Sociol. Travail* 1:82–105

Lindblom, C. 1959. The science of muddling through. *Public Admin. Rev.* XIX(2):79–88

Lukes, S. 1974. *Power: A Radical View.* London: Macmillan

Lustick, I. 1980. Explaining the variable utility of disjointed incrementalism: Four propositions. *Am. Polit. Sci. Rev.* 74:342–53

Mallory, G. R. 1987. *The Speed of Strategic Decisions.* PhD thesis. University of Bradford, Yorkshire

March, J. G. 1981. Decisions in organizations and theories of choice. In *Perspectives on Organization Design and Behavior,* ed. A. H. Van de Ven, W. F. Joyce, pp. 205–44. New York: Wiley.

March, J. G., Olsen, J. P. 1984. *Garbage can models of decision making in organizations.* Presented to a workshop on Decision Making in Military Organizations. Montreal, Canada

March, J. G., Olsen, J. P. 1976. *Ambiguity and Choice in Organizations*. Bergen, Oslo, & Tromso: Universitetsforlaget

March, J. G., Romelaer, P. J. 1976. Position and presence in the drift of decisions. In *Ambiguity and Choice in Organizations*, ed. J. G. March, J. P. Olsen, pp. 251–76. Bergen, Oslo and Tromso: Universitetsforlaget

March, J. G., Simon, H. A. 1958. *Organizations*, New York: Wiley

Miles, R. H. 1980. *Macro organizational Behavior*, California: Goodyear

Mintzberg, H. 1973. *The Nature of Managerial Work*. New York: Harper & Row

Mintzberg, H. 1978. Patterns in strategy formation. *Manage. Sci.* 24(9):934–48

Mintzberg, H. 1979. *The Structuring of Organizations*. Englewood Cliffs, NJ: Prentice-Hall

Mintzberg, H., McHugh, A. 1985. Strategy formation in an Adhocracy. *Admin. Sci. Q.* 30(2):160–97

Mintzberg, H., Raisinghani, D., Theoret. A. 1976. The structure of "unstructured" decision processes. *Admin. Sci. Q.* 21:246–75

Mintzberg, H., Waters, J. A. 1982. Tracking strategy in an entrepreneurial firm. *Acad. Manage. J.* 25(3):465–99

Mohr, L. B. 1982. *Explaining Organizational Behavior*. San Francisco: Jossey-Bass

Mumford, E., Pettigrew, A. 1975. *Implementing Strategic Decisions*. London: Longman

Nutt, P. 1984. Types of organizational decision processes. *Admin. Sci. Q.* 29(3):414–50

O'Reilly, C. A. 1983. The use of information in organizational decision making: A model and some propositions. In *Research in Organizational Behavior, Vol. 5*, ed. L. L. Cummings, B. M. Staw, pp. 103–40. Greenwich, Conn: JAI

Pettigrew, A. 1973. *The Politics of Organizational Decision Making*. London: Tavistock

Pfeffer, J., Salancik, G. R. 1974. Organizational decision making as a political process: The case of a university budget. *Admin. Sci. Q.* 19:135–51

Pfeffer, J., Salancik, G. R. 1977. Organization design: The case of a coalitional model of organizations. *Organ. Dynam.* 6:15–29

Pugh, D. S., Hickson, D. J. 1976. *Organizational structure in its context: The Aston Programme I*. Farnborough: Gower (and formerly D. C. Heath)

Pugh, D. S., Hickson, D. J., Hinings, C. R., Turner, C. 1969. The context of organization structures. *Admin. Sci. Q.* 14:91–114

Quinn, J. B. 1978. Strategic change: Logical incrementalism. *Sloan Manage. Rev.* Fall 1978:7–21

Quinn, J. B. 1980. *Strategies for Change: Logical Incrementalism*. Homewood, Ill: Irwin

Rodrigues, S. B. 1980. *Processes of Successful Managerial Decision Making in Organizations*. PhD thesis. University of Bradford, Yorkshire

Rus, V. 1980. Positive and negative power: Thoughts on the Dialectics of Power. *Organ. Stud.* 1(1):3–20

Schulman, P. R. 1975. Nonincremental policy making: Notes towards an alternative paradigm. *Am. Polit. Sci. Rev.* 69:1354–70

Smith, G., May, D. 1980. The artificial debate between rationalist and incrementalist models of decision making. *Policy Polit.* 8(2):147–61

Silverman, D. 1970. *The Theory of Organizations*. London: Heinemann

Simon, H. A. 1945. *Administrative Behavior* New York: Free Press 2nd Ed.

Simon, H. A. 1960. *The New Science of Management Decision*. New York: Harper & Row

Staw, B. M. 1981. The escalation of commitment to a course of action. *Acad. Manage. Rev.* 6(4):577–87

Stein, J. 1981a. Contextual factors in the selection of strategic decision methods. *Hum. Relat.* 34(10):819–34

Stein, J. 1981b. Strategic decision methods. *Hum. Relat.* 34(11):917–33

Stewart, R. 1976. *Contrasts in Management: A Study of Different Types of Managers' Jobs*. New York: McGraw Hill

Thompson, J. D. 1967. *Organizations in Action*. New York: McGraw Hill

Thompson, J. D., Tuden, A. 1964. Strategies, structures and processes of organizational decision. In *Readings in Managerial Psychology*, ed. H. J. Leavitt, R. Pondy, pp. 195–216. Chicago: Univ. Chicago Press

Weick, K. E. 1976. Educational organizations as loosely coupled systems. *Admin. Sci. Q.* 21(1):1–19

Weiss, J. W. 1981. The historical and political perspective on organizations of Lucien Karpik. In *Complex Organizations: Critical Perspectives*, ed. M. Zey-Ferrell, M. Aiken, pp. 382–96. Glenview, Ill: Scott, Foresman

Wilson, D. C. 1980. *Organizational Strategy*. PhD thesis. University of Bradford, Yorkshire

Wilson, D. C. 1982. Electricity and resistance: A case study of innovation and politics. *Organ. Stud.* 3(2):119–40

Wilson, D. C., Butler, R. J., Cray, D., Hickson, D. J., Mallory, G. R. 1982. The limits of trade union power in organizational decision making. *Br. J. Ind. Relat.*, 20(3):322–41

Wilson, D. C., Butler, R. J., Cray, D., Hickson, D. J., Mallory, G. R. 1986. Breaking the bounds of organization in strategic decision making. *Hum. Relat.* 39(4):309–32

Zey-Ferrell, M., Aiken, M. 1981. *Complex Organizations: Critical Perspectives*. Glenview, Ill: Scott, Foresman

[3]

Journal of Management Studies, 19, 4, 1982

COMPLEXITY AND CLEAVAGE: DUAL EXPLANATIONS OF STRATEGIC DECISION-MAKING [1]

W. Graham Astley, Runo Axelsson, Richard J. Butler,
David J. Hickson and David C. Wilson
Organizational Analysis Research Unit, The Management Centre, University of Bradford

ABSTRACT

This paper presents a framework for the comparative analysis of strategic decision-making processes. It draws together and integrates predominant but previously disparate theories of decision-making. Examples are given of how decision-making processes may be characterized and, hence, facilitate comparison across all types of strategic decisions. Explanation of why decision processes may differ is from two perspectives. First, the complexity of the topic may lead to particular characteristics of the decision process. Secondly, the cleavage of interests which a topic arouses may also lead to particular aspects of decision processes. We argue that each decision topic has varying levels of both complexity and cleavage and four examples of strategic decisions are analyzed on these dimensions. We identify four profiles of decision-making processes associated with varying levels of complexity and cleavage and we finally suggest that our model may explain and empirically demonstrate variations across a large number of diverse strategic decisions.

INTRODUCTION

The study of strategic decision-making remains of paramount importance in the field of organization theory and management. By forming and implementing chosen strategies, organizations shape both themselves and the society in which we live (Cherns, 1980; Freeman, 1978). Decisions to launch radically new or different products, to expand into other areas of business or non-business, or decisions to invest in new technology, for example, all contribute substantially to fashion the characteristics of our organized society (Colignon and Cray, 1980). These decisions help to determine, for instance, which international markets are entered, which services are available to the public, or decree how coming generations are to be educated.

Yet conceptual development in the study of organizational decision-making remains fragmented, precluding the construction of a unified and empirically researchable theory. The volume of published works on decision-making is, however, immense. We know from this literature, for example, that decision-making may be seen as a process of 'muddling through' (Lindblom, 1959) toward a satisfactory and sufficient outcome (what March and Simon (1958) called satisficing). From these perspectives, later research has focused upon the question of which features of the decision-making process contribute to such satisficing and muddling through behaviour. Pettigrew (1973) and Abell (1975) have concentrated on the negotiable nature of decisions, positing that the division of labour creates and reinforces distinct and separate interests. Decisions, they argue, are the result of conflicts and compromises between competing interests each with a difference perspective on how decisions should proceed and what they should resolve. The roots of this perspective may be traced back to Cyert and March's (1963) work on coalition formation and behaviour and, more recently, Mintzberg *et al.* (1976) who have pin-pointed the repetitious and hesitant nature of some decision-making processes.

Tending to eschew the politics of decision-making, Simon (1947) and March and Simon (1958) emphasize the inherent cognitive limitations upon the outcomes of decision-making processes. Human cognition is severely limited when confronted with the complexities of reality. March and Simon argue that the rational utility assignments of Churchman's (1961) 'systems approach' are circumscribed in practice since decision-makers' cognitive shortcomings limit their search for alternatives, hinder their facility for ranking preferred utilities and curtail their ability to calculate costs and benefits. Rationality is bounded. Search is truncated before optimal alternatives can be identified, resulting in satisficing decisions which tend to select familiar and acceptable rather than novel solutions.

In the same vein, Cyert and March (1963) indicate how problem-spurred activity, mildly innovative learning processes and 'simple-minded search' detract from 'omniscient rationality', but nevertheless make 'adaptively rational' sense in the face of complex uncertainty. Lindblom (1959, 1968) proposes the method of 'successive limited comparisons' for dealing with that uncertainty. Decision-makers move cautiously in small incremental steps, edging forward from historically determined precedents.

Underlying this perspective is the presumption that decision-making activity is evoked by the occurrence of problems and so is orientated toward solutions. Thus it is an intendedly rational instrumental activity. Decision-making processes only have significance as reflecting the technical means to achieve an end. Their imperfections as information-processing exercises, therefore, are manifested as technical difficulties encountered in the pursuit of such solutions.

In contrast to this predominantly apolitical and problem-solving view of decision-making, March and Olsen (1976) lay their emphasis on the process of decision-making in its own right. Often, the process 'does not appear to be much concerned with making a decision' (p. 11). It 'erects a stage for many dramas' (p. 12) with the result that 'outcomes are not a direct consequence of process' (p. 21). Decision processes are portrayed as anarchic, wherein action has primacy and goals are discovered through it.

According to Cohen *et al.* (1972), decision-making outcomes are not always devised in response to problems because the nexus of problems and choices is partially uncoupled. A particular solution may exist before a specific problem arises, and may then be attached to it as it comes along, however oddly in a logical sense. 'From this point of view, an organization is a collection of choices looking for problems' (Cohen *et al.*, 1972, p. 2). The choices are, of course, somebody's choices, and the solutions are somebody's solutions. In a scenario where all is held to be veiled by mists of ambiguity, the 'ambiguity of self-interest' and of goals as they shift with fluctuating participation brings the sense of 'organized anarchy' which characterizes this perspective.

From another perspective, political theories of decision-making have evolved from an analysis of the power of the institutional framework of organizations. This perspective subjugates the negotiations and bargaining between separate interests to the meta-power exercised by institutions. When procedures exclude items from direct attention, they control the decision-making agenda (Bachrach and Baratz, 1962). Similarly, the programming of decision-making routines simultaneously removes uncertainty from the process and confers power on advantageously positional interests (Wilson *et al.*, 1982a). Mechanic (1962) and Karpik (1978) have both pointed to the selective endowment of power to those who can use routinized decision-making procedures to their own advantage. Knowledge of procedure confers power in the decision-making process. Wilson (1982) illustrates this phenomenon in a case study of innovation in a chemical firm where an individual was able to secure promotion to Chief Executive as a result of his accurate knowledge of the decision-making procedures of the organization. The entrenched and often unquestioned nature of these procedures is well documented by Lukes (1974) and Clegg (1979) and the political weight of institutions in decision-making is discussed, for example, in Heydebrand (1977), Salaman (1978), and Clawson (1980).

Despite this proliferation of literature, however, no integrated theory of decision-making exists, as yet. Many of the theoretical stand-points remain mutually exclusive. Either one examines the process of decision-making itself, or examines the outcomes which are the culmination of such processes. Or one examines the bounded rationality of individuals in processing information, or one examines the institutionalized rules by which those procedures are enacted.

This paper is an attempt to construct a more holistic model. In so doing, it represents an integration of many of the foregoing theoretical perspectives. Its value, therefore, lies not in producing a brand new theory of decision-making (by focusing on specific parts of the process for example) but in producing an integrated and empirically testable framework for the analysis of organizational decision-making, across a wide range of organizations.

THEORETICAL FRAMEWORK

Complexity and Cleavage

We have already seen that much of existing decision theory pays allegiance to either complexities in the nature of the problem to be solved, or to inherent political imbalance and subsequent conflicts in the decision-making process. In building our model we start by considering two key concepts which summarize these two main arguments offered as explanations of decision-making. The concepts cover the technical *complexity* of what is to be decided and the political *cleavage* of the interests involved. An integrated theory of decision-making must, therefore, be able to incorporate both explanations of decision behaviour. It must be able to assess both the independent and the relative contributions of each explanation in fashioning the characteristics of decision-making processes. Our model begins with an exposition of what constitutes complexity and cleavage and, later, develops a scheme for characterizing the variable nature of the decision-making process. The final section of the paper shows how complexity and cleavage may be used to account for variations in decision-making processes and gives four examples of strategic decisions to illustrate the model.

Complexity examines the extent to which the topic that engages the decision-making is intricate (2). The topic may involve multiple considerations each of which is difficult to evaluate. This may be due to equivocality (or ambiguity) over what is being done (Weick, 1969), or to the many-sided nature of prevailing issues, or to the uncertainty of the consequences involved in embarking upon a particular course of action (Axelsson and Rosenberg, 1979). Each topic will vary in the extent to which it is complex. For example, a rare or totally novel topic would arguably be more complex than one which comes up repeatedly. Organizations faced with decisions on topics which occur regularly, tend to set up fairly standard and routine decision-making procedures which effectively simplify the decision-making process by removing uncertainty from it. This distinction may be found in new product decisions where it is possible to distinguish totally new products (reorientations) from modifications to an existing range of products (variations). Normann (1971, p. 205) notes that variations can be accommodated within the existing system of organization, whilst reorientations often involve changes to the system itself.

Although it is not the purpose of this paper to cover all the possible variables of complexity and their operationalization, the extent to which a topic is novel to the organization would obviously be an important and empirically demonstrable variable of complexity (3). So, too, would be the extent to which a topic can be precisely assessed. Thompson (1967, p. 134) refers to 'inspirational' decision-making in those situations where precise predictions are impossible over what the topic should be, or what are the likely cause-effect relations of the choice process. He goes so far as to suggest that, often, decision-making is unlikely to occur at all in extreme cases. Clearly, the less precision of assessment there may be, the greater is the degree of complexity in the decision-making process.

Cleavage, on the other hand, denotes the political face of decision-making. Irrespective of the level of complexity, each topic is subject to the diverse and often conflicting views of the various interests which participate in the decision-making process. Interests are defined internally in an organization by the division of labour, which creates 'local' perspectives on each topic (Abell, 1975; Cyert and March, 1963). Interests may also be external to an organization. Examples would be suppliers, customers, organs of government, trades unions, and group headquarters in the case of subsidiary companies (Axelsson *et al.*, 1977; Hickson *et al.*, 1978; Wilson *et al.*, 1982b).

Taken together, external and internal interests form a *constellation* of interests around a topic (4). The number of interests, or the ratio of external to internal interests does not necessarily predict the amount of conflict there may be over a particular topic. Their views may be congruent in consensus rather than disparate in mutual antagonism. We must, therefore, identify the extent to which various interests disagree over what the topic should achieve or how the decision-making process should proceed. The notion of cleavage captures this variation by suggesting that the more disparate are interests and the more influential they are, the greater is the degree of cleavage (Rae and Taylor, 1970). Empirically, a full range of cleavage is possible ranging from none at all to a great deal in each decision-making process. Indicators of the level of cleavage would be, for example, the number of objectives expressed by participant interests and the level of disparity between them. Also of relevance would be the distribution of the influence exerted to advance such objectives as well as the density of contacts between interests, and the 'influence coalitions' (Bacharach and Lawler, 1980).

Theoretically, the two concepts of cleavage and complexity are interrelated and an adequate theory of decision-making must examine both factors. A more complex topic may draw in more interests and, simultaneously, more interests may make the matter more complex. Particular characteristics of organizational technology, the competitiveness of the market and the number of regulatory rules and laws both create and maintain dependencies and disparate perspectives between various interests in the constellation (Crozier, 1973; Perrow, 1967). Similarly, 'beliefs about causation' (Thompson, 1967, pp. 134–35), which underly much of the disparity between interests, are often rooted in the ambiguity surrounding possible outcomes of decision topics.

Although there is a vague understanding that complexity and cleavage will make decision-making more difficult, the precise consequences of various levels of cleavage and complexity over decision-making processes have so far not been systematically explored in decision-making theory. High levels of cleavage are reported to be instrumental in lengthening the time taken to make decisions (Pettigrew, 1973) or in creating hold-ups and delays in the process (Mintzberg *et al.*, 1976), but beyond these isolated studies (one of them on one case only) we have no adequate theoretical model against which empirical results can be compared across different decisions. Pettigrew's (1973) case study of the purchase of a new computer, for example, may equally be analyzed in terms of the complexity of the topic which was to be decided upon. It is arguable that this decision was protracted and delayed due to the lack of specific information about computers and their capabilities rather than solely due to Kenny's manoeuvres to curry favour with particular suppliers of computer equipment. We certainly are given no assessment of the *relative* contributions of complexity and cleavage to the duration and hesitancy of the decision-making process. In order to achieve this, we introduce the notion of a decision-making arena.

Decision Making Processes

In addressing this problem we now need to develop concepts of the decision-making process itself which can be applied across various decisions. These concepts must capture what goes on in a decision-making arena (Butler *et al.*, 1979), but this arena will be more than a 'bargaining zone' in which gladiatorial contests between competing interests take place (Abell, 1975) and more than the organized anarchy of March and Olsen's (1976) 'garbage can'. It will be an arena in which technical problems as well as political conflicts are resolved.

Within this arena, we can expect to find that some decisions are tossed to and fro from committee to committee for increased scrutiny of information and the voicing of disparate interests. Other decisions may be held up as more research on technical problems is conducted or because of blocking by powerful interests. Not all decisions will be like this, however. Some will go through 'on the nod' (Pahl and Winkler, 1974) and will display evidence of little interruption or discontinuity. Others, although of great import to the organization, can be precisely evaluated and, similarly, encounter little delay or hesitancy. In essence, we aim to characterize what Hage (1980) has called the difference 'trajectories' (or profiles) of decision-making processes.

In order to achieve this, we propose a number of concepts, each of which are capable of illustrating such variability, and the full schema is shown in figure 1.

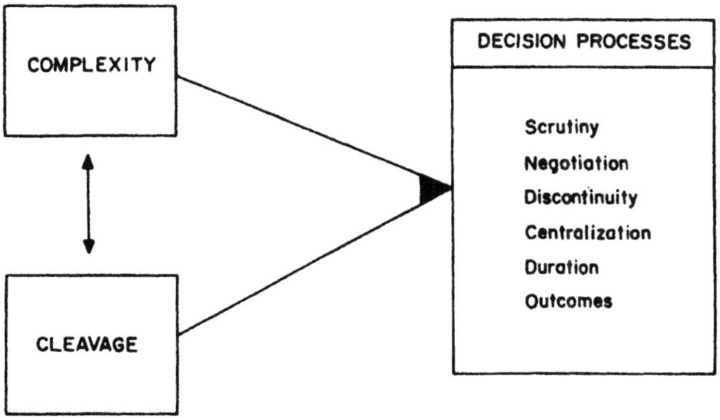

Figure 1. Dual explanations of strategic decision-making

Central to most accounts of decision-making processes is the *scrutiny* of information. This includes searching, collecting, evaluating and diagnosing activities. For example, do participants in decision-making rely upon limited amounts of information that are readily available and choose between options by the re-application of established organizational repertoires, or do they utilize project groups, strategic planning departments and brainstorming committees to generate multiple and novel alternatives and opportunities? These aspects of scrutiny are similar, but not the same as, Cyert and March's (1963) notions of search since it is not to be regarded simply as a tailored response designed to produce a solution to a pre-selected problem. It also refers to activity which generates entirely new goals and, indeed, activity which is conducted for its own sake. Generally speaking, the more that presented choices trigger scrutiny, the larger and more fluid will be the sphere of activity which is energized in the decision-making arena.

Another aspect of scrutiny that has received considerable attention is the extent to which it is programmed (March and Simon, 1958) or routinized. Routinization examines those aspects of decision-making that are peculiarly organizational. Decision-making processes may be more or less 'bounded' within parameters and socially predefined constraints (Wilson *et al.*, 1982a). Topics for decision are channelled into existing standard operating procedures which will not only apply problem-solving rules to the decision unit but also preclude and constrain the surfacing of conflicting interests. Scrutinizing activity may often be conjoined to high degrees of *negotiation* as negotiation interjects new items into existing agendas. Pettigrew (1973), Abell (1975) and Mintzberg *et al.* (1976) each have emphasized its role as a central dynamic of organizational life.

From these perspectives, negotiation is the result of cleavage and conflict among powerful interests but negotiation also has a coordinating function in the sense that Thompson (1967) refers to mutual adjustment—the two-way flow of information between individuals and groups as they try to adjust their activities to each other. As Thompson points out, the need for mutual adjustment increases in line with the complexity of the tasks being coordinated. Such activity, therefore, represents the intended rationality of coping with complex problems rather than the rationality of vested interests trying to push their items onto agendas. By intendedly rational we mean striving towards a common organizational goal rather than towards local, interest-specific goals.

Closely related to scrutinizing and negotiation are the stops and starts (or discontinuities) in the decision process. Sometimes decisions can be put on the shelf awaiting further developments, as Wilson *et al.* (1982a) report concerning a decision to introduce a new course in a university. This can sometimes occur in firms who develop products and await the appropriate market conditions to materialize before deciding to launch the product. Mintzberg *et al.* (1976) emphasize strongly the extent to which decision processes may be smooth or discontinuous. Discontinuities may cover delays due to awaiting further information; due to 'interrupts' (sudden unexpected events); due to recycling to aid comprehension and to gain commitment from participants. Again, we emphasize that discontinuities can result from intendedly rational problem-solving by participants seeking information and clarification, or can result from interests trying to time events to suit their purposes.

Centralization is also a well-known concept and is focused upon the function of hierarchy in decision-making. Simon (1962) and Thompson (1967) have both emphasized the utility of a hierarchy in coordinating activities. However, hierarchy also relies upon the ability to be able to measure activities and allocate them to subordinates (Butler, 1982). Consequently, when problems are complex centralization of decision-making is less likely than with simple problems. From the viewpoint of cleavage a higher authority with sufficient power may be brought in to resolve conflicts which occur at lower levels, resulting in more centralized decision-making. Lack of that higher authority, that is *de*-centralization, could therefore arguably be associated with unresolved cleavage.

A predominant characteristic of decision-making, popularized by writers such as Parkinson (1964) is the length of time decisions take, that is, their *duration*. Mintzberg *et al.* (1976) have also shown the widely varying temporal extent of decisions and the duration of decision-making constitutes one of our key concepts of processes. Both complex and highly politically cleaved decisions are expected to lengthen the time a decision process takes until final authorization. On the one hand, complexity may increase the need for and the scope of information inputs, all of which take time to achieve and, on the other hand, high cleavage of interest will lengthen decision process time as disagreements are sustained or whilst compromises are being reached.

Following March and Olsen (1976, p. 45), we argue that 'choice processes are important independent of the substantive outcomes that result from them'. Substantive outcomes can, of course, refer to the launch of a new product following an innovation decision-making process. The product is the outcome here. However, we also argue that outcomes also refer to non-substantive aspects of decision-making. Thus, we may refer to an outcome as *incremental* if it deviates only to a small extent from previous practice (Lindblom, 1959). A decision to launch a new product only marginally different to existing outputs is an incremental outcome to the decision-making process. A radically new and different product, launched after a process of careful consideration of alternative courses of action is, on the other hand, a 'synoptic' outcome (Braybrooke and Lindblom, 1963). In much the same way, outcomes can be *acceptable* or *optimal*. They may be sufficient for solving present problems in a satisfactory way to all concerned. Such an outcome would be the acceptable, 'satisficing' decision outcome proposed by March and Simon (1958). Indeed, the portmanteau word satisficing comprises both what is *satis*factory and suff*icient* for present problem-solving.

Finally, outcomes may be *anticipated* or *crescive*. A seemingly obscure term, crescive has, in fact, well-founded roots in Sumner's (1906) discussion of 'crescive systems' and in Gouldner's (1959) concept of 'natural systems'. We use the term to differentiate between goal-directed decision-making processes (where outcomes are anticipated) and those processes where the nexus of process and outcome is uncoupled and progress toward an outcome is without goal-orientation or premeditated plan (crescive outcomes).

Dual Explanations of Decision-Making Processes

Having outlined the main explanatory concepts of cleavage and complexity, we can anticipate particular profiles of decision processes that may result from various levels of complexity and cleavage. These profiles are characterized by our concepts of the decision-making process. Suppose we examine a particular decision profile of high levels of discontinuity, limited scrutiny and high levels of negotiation. We may explain such a profile by reference to complexity and cleavage. Both sustain tenable arguments.

From one perspective, a decision topic may be *complex* insofar as it encompasses multiple unclear goals, is unprecedented in its occurrence and lacks criteria by which it can be evaluated. Technical effectiveness in handling this task complexity demands that the decision-making arena includes many relevant interests (probably specialists) who are free to negotiate possible solution of discussions in existing committees or in specially set up working parties. Scrutiny would be limited to practicable alternatives and to those sources of information that are known to be reliable. Due to limitations on individual cognitive capacity, problems would be worked through with a high level of discontinuity in order to back-track and double check. Slow progress toward the final outcome would be the result, and acceptable rather than radically different outcomes would avoid leaping into the unknown. Satisficing and incrementalism thus ensue from the inherent complexity of the topic for decision.

On the other hand, a decision topic may display a high level of cleavage initiated by the intrusion of divergent interests. If the distribution of power between the interests is roughly equal and balanced against each other, each will wish to secure effective representation in the decision-making arena in order to voice their opinions. According to this political *cleavage* argument, each interest will limit search activities and scrutiny to its own localized perspectives and preferences, resulting in bouts of negotiation and consequent discontinuity. Again, the tendency would be toward acceptable outcomes rather than radical solutions since some degree of compromise must be sought between conflicting interests, and collective goals would be lost to sight amidst the competing pressures from the interests involved. From this perspective, satisficing and incrementalism ensue from the political cleavages of those who wield power.

Similarly, an organization may be faced with a decision topic of such rarity that existing procedures built up over the years to handle such questions cannot cope. Existing committees, for example, feel unable to deal with such a topic in an adequate manner. Routine is bypassed, and the decision is taken straight to the top. The same result would arguably ensue from a constellation of interests in stalemate, where financial or temporal pressure demand that the chief executive uses his hierarchical power to push the decision through. Both complexity and cleavage can push decision-making up the hierarchy and centralize authorization.

It is interesting to note that both Mintzberg *et al.* (1976) and Wilson (1982) show that where the complexity of the topic breaks existing institutional bounds, then the cleavage of interests also comes to the fore. Empirically, this implies that whilst complexity and cleavage will both independently predict decision process characteristics there will also be an interactive effect between them.

In order to illustrate the ability of our model to both characterize and explain the nature of strategic decisions, we now describe four examples of decision-making. These are taken from our sample of 150 cases of strategic decision-making (see note 3). The intention is to demonstrate the validity of our model and, whilst four cases do not provide such a rigorous test as more extensive results, they can serve as exemplars of comparison using our theoretical model.

INITIAL RESULTS

Four Strategic Decisions

These decisions have been intentionally selected in order to maximize the variations in complexity and cleavage and, hence, to maximize the test of our model. Figure 2, therefore, incorporates four combinations of low and high complexity coupled with low and high levels of cleavage.

COMPLEXITY	CLEAVAGE: Low	CLEAVAGE: High
Low	Case 1 Decision: to introduce a lottery Organization: a local authority	Case 2 Decision: to resist HQ's new product launch Organization: subsidiary chemical company
High	Case 3 Decision: new product launch Organization: independent chemical company	Case 4 Decision: to change the committee structure Organization: a university

Figure 2. Four strategic decisions: their complexity and cleavage

Case 1 is a decision to introduce a lottery in a Local Authority. The decision was focused upon a common concern in the organization to find ways of raising money independently of the local rates levied on commercial and domestic properties. The idea was not new. Lotteries are common in other countries and central government and some other Local Authorities were already operating such schemes. As a decision topic, it is hardly complex. Lotteries can be bought ready-made through agents and they have a predictable return. A chance meeting between a lottery agent and the Finance Committee Chairman of the Authority whilst both were on holiday initiated the idea of the lottery. On his return, the Chairman brought the issue before the Council. Within just over two months the scheme was authorized and, remarkable for a Local Authority, there was little cleavage apparent between the opposing political parties. It seemed that the ease with which the lottery could overcome a problem of common concern to all was sufficient to defuse political differences on that occasion.

The profile of case 1 (and the three subsequent decisions) is shown in table 1 where complexity and cleavage levels as well as the decision process concepts are rated high or low. The three characteristics of outcomes are also indicated in the table.

The lottery decision, low in complexity and cleavage, displays little evidence of the high levels of scrutiny for information postulated by Kickert (1979), and Hage (1980). There were no special committees, working parties or special reports. In addition, there was no evidence of negotiation between opposing interests to solve either political differences or to resolve any doubtful technical problems. Nonetheless, the lottery was a strategic decision for the Local Authority. Its process was, however, simple and non-controversial.

Table 1. Profiles of decision-making

DECISION CONCEPTS		CASES: 1. Introduce Lottery in Local Government	2. New Product in Chemical Company	3. Resist HQ's Product Launch in Subsidiary Company	4. New Committee in University
	Complexity	LOW	HIGH	LOW	HIGH
	Cleavage	LOW	LOW	HIGH	HIGH
Process	Scrutiny	LOW	HIGH	HIGH	HIGH
Process	Negotiation	LOW	LOW	HIGH	HIGH
Process	Discontinuity	LOW	LOW	HIGH	HIGH
Process	Centralization	LOW	LOW	LOW	HIGH
Process	Duration (years)	0·2	3	2	2
Outcomes	Synoptic/Incremental	× (Synoptic)	× (Synoptic)	× (Synoptic)	× (Incremental)
Outcomes	Anticipated/Crescive	× (Anticipated)	× (Anticipated)	× (Anticipated)	× (Crescive)
Outcomes	Optimal/Acceptable	× (Optimal)	× (Optimal)	× (Optimal)	× (Acceptable)

Above all, it was a quick decision with a duration of only 0·2 years (10 weeks). Considering the outcome dimensions of this decision, we would see it as synoptic, anticipated and optimal. It was a clear-sighted process, the only alternative being not to introduce the lottery, aimed at a specific and commonly shared goal of raising finance by means other than the rate levy. In addition, the outcome of the lottery decision was fairly easy to calculate (money raised *per annum*) unlike the following case described next.

Case 4 is a decision to change the committee structure in a University. We take this case next as it represents one of the most complex and politically cleaved decisions in our sample. It is, therefore, in direct contrast to case 1. A full account of this decision is in Wilson (1980). Dissatisfaction amongst the academic and non-academic staff plus a recommendation from the Association of University Teachers (A.U.T.) sparked off a decision-making process which was to consider a rearrangement of existing committees plus the introduction of a new committee designed solely to handle staffing procedures. The decision was highly complex primarily because of the size of the existing committee system. This intricate web of overarching committees and sub-committees needed unravelling before any progress could be made on designing a new committee. In addition, the assessment of university staff whether for appointments, promotions, or any other reason is difficult due to the lack of easily measured performance criteria which are commonly accepted across academic departments. From a political cleavage perspective, the redesigning of committee systems is a topic wracked with divergent and conflicting interests. The existing structure favoured some interests and not others resulting in staunch defenders of the *status quo* and equally adamant antagonists who demanded change. Fears of the erosion of existing powers coupled with changes in the legal charter of the university fuelled the cleavage of interests.

One Pro-Vice-Chancellor was given charge of the decision. He formed a working party, itself a difficult task since the working party had to have the appearance of representing the broad range of interests in the topic. Aware that they were dealing with large and complex issues, the working party members concerned themselves primarily with the feasibility of creating a new committee. Enormous scrutiny activity followed, evident in a barrage of reports, working papers, brainstorming sessions, visits to other universities and lengthy discussions. All were aware that such scrutiny not only served to examine the new committee problem but also allowed full voice to the cleavage amongst the interests. Consequently, negotiation was at a high level coupled with a number of delays and stoppages as powerful interests had their say and as complex problems were encountered (such as sources of finance or the overall pervasiveness of Senate's influence). This decision-making process was characterized by its high discontinuity.

Finally, a decision to install a new committee was reached and ratified by Senate. It had taken two years—ten times longer than case 1. Yet this university decision had only touched the surface of a much bigger issue and the final incremental solution was characterized by its slow and cresive build up. Reference to table 1 shows how cases 1 and 4 are diametrically opposed on all aspects of the decision-making process. Such a stark contrast lends support to our theoretical model using complexity and cleavage as predictors of decision-making characteristics. Nonetheless, we need to examine intermediate cases of complexity and cleavage in order to test the model more completely.

Case 2 is the decision of a chemical company to launch a radically new product in the face of stiff competition at home and abroad. The case is reported in detail in Wilson (1980). The product, a dyestuff pigment, was outside the company's manufacturing and marketing expertise. The technical problems with the product were considerable, both in terms of research and development, expertise required and the new manufacturing skills to be learned. In our model, it is a complex decision. Yet cleavage is low (see figure 2) since all senior managers (that is, the powerful interests) covering the production, research and development, finance, sales and purchasing functions were in full agreement over the necessity to launch the new product in order to capture a new segment of the market.

Nevertheless, scrutiny is at a high level (see table 1) in this case, not to resolve divergent interests as in case 4, but to gather information about the product, likely technical problems, costs and potential market domain. Although we see little negotiation between conflicting interests, we do see that the decision takes three years—longer than both of the previous cases. This result supports Normann's (1971) argument that radically new product decisions are characterized by their relatively lengthy duration. We also argue that this decision conforms to what Braybrooke and Lindblom (1963) have termed a 'synoptic' process, displaying orderly and continuous progression to a preconceived common goal. In addition, the decision tended toward the optimal rather than the acceptable as there were primarily only two options open (introduce or not introduce) and, once introduction had been decided upon, the best possible product was designed and launched. It is now one of the company's fundamental and most profitable products.

Case 3 is the decision of a subsidiary chemical company to resist their parent company's insistence upon them to launch a new product. The parent company wished to use the subsidiary to test out new products in the market six times *per* year. This was strongly resisted by the management of the subsidiary but the parent company had a stranglehold over them. We therefore count this as a case in which there is high cleavage (see figure 2) between subsidiary and parent. It was however hardly a complex decision since the subsidiary had a very clear idea, from their experience, on each occasion as to the likely outcome of such market testing. To them it was a waste of their time and resources and hence their resistance was strong.

This decision is characterized by high levels of scrutiny, negotiation and discontinuity. Reports and documents justifying the subsidiary's resistance to the product went back and forth to headquarters. Each report contained increasingly detailed information which supported the case for not launching the product. The parent company was, however, insistent and consequently negotiation levels were high and discontinuities evident as each side gathered information to support its arguments.

In this analysis, the decision is tending toward the pattern of the high complexity, high cleavage case 4, suggesting a possibly stronger reaction of these process variables to cleavage than to complexity. This view is reinforced by the relatively long duration of the decision (two years, see table 1). Unlike case 4, however, the resist product launch decision is de-centralized. The eventual decision to totally resist any product of this kind was taken amongst a group of functional and middle managers in the subsidiary organization. We regard the outcomes of this decision process as synoptic, anticipated and optimal (from the subsidiary's point of view), since the issues were quite clear to the participants and the eventual decision not to launch the product was exactly what they wanted.

The two intermediate cases, therefore, display a correspondingly intermediate pattern of decision-making. Where cleavage is high and complexity is low, there is a trend toward high levels of scrutiny, negotiation and discontinuity. On the other hand, low cleavage and high complexity lead to a different pattern of decision-making processes tending toward the continuous and non-negotiable (see table 1) but coupled with a high level of scrutiny for information. These variations in the patterning of decision processes lend further justification to our model, although more extensive empirical testing is required to examine whether such variation is consistent across a wide range of decision and organizational types. This work is forthcoming and is reported in Butler *et al.* (1982).

CONCLUSIONS

The purpose of the dual explanations model has been to integrate previously disparate strands in the literature of decision-making and to demonstrate how the decision-making process may be described and related to the inherent cleavage or complexity of the topic itself. Hence, using four cases we have shown how the model may be used to develop profiles of decision-making processes and, from the descriptions of each of the cases, we can claim general support for our model.

Although based on a small sample, the strength of the results described here lies in their comparability across the decision-making characteristics. This goes much further than the frequently found 'one-shot' case studies of decision-making which, as Campbell and Stanley (1966) point out, are virtually uninterpretable. The counterposing of a simple 2 × 2 matrix of decision cases paves the way for more sophisticated, multivariate analyzes and techniques which can examine a wide range of variables within the theoretical model. The discussion of the four cases has emphasized patterns of profiles of decision process characteristics. This has involved an examination of table 1 vertically column by column and comparing each of the four decisions. In addition, of course, we could compare decisions by examining table 1 horizontally and focus upon a specific aspect of decision-making.

For example, centralization of decision-making may be singled out for study. Three of our four cases are relatively decentralized. Centralization, however, seems to come into play when *both* complexity and cleavage are high as in case 4. This concurs with both Thompson (1967) and Hage (1980). Thompson's fundamental assumption is that managers and administrators will try to avoid complex and politically riven decisions wherever possible—he calls this the desire to reduce uncertainty—but that where such decisions are unavoidable, the tendency will be to centralize their authorization. Hage (1980) argues that centralization in these circumstances is a predictable manoeuvre by the power élite in order to protect any possible threats to their dominance (pp. 114–20).

Similarly, we could argue from our four cases that it is only when decisions are simple and without cleavage that the decision-making process is relatively fast (see case 1, figure 2). Mintzberg *et al.* (1976), show this to be the case in their analysis of 25 decision processes, although Hage (1980, p. 128) argues that simple, low cleavage decisions should take longer as they are decentralized and, hence, promote negotiation and prolonged discussion. Our further empirical work should reveal whether this assumption holds true.

Finally, it must here be restated that complexity and cleavage pertain to a particular decision topic. They describe the nature of each decision topic. This perspective may be criticized by pointing to the institutional setting of an organization within which decision-making takes place. For example, Salancik and Pfeffer (1974), March and Olsen (1976) and Butler *et al.* (1979) all point to the over-riding political nature of university decision-making. Axelsson and Rosenberg (1978) point out this consistent pattern of university decision-making in the face of environmental turbulence. Conversely, Rodrigues (1980), illustrates the prevailing institutionalized decision-making processes of business organizations as largely synoptic and apolitical, and Lindblom (1959) has pointed out that the over-riding characteristic of public administration decision-making is that of incrementalism.

These institutional stereotypes, however, have their exceptions and these may only be illustrated at the level of analysis of specific decision topics. Wilson (1980, 1982) and Rodrigues (1980) have both shown that business organizations are not always synoptic in their decision-making but that they are often faced with highly complex and highly cleaved topics which are consequently discontinuous, slow and incremental. Our model, therefore, also allows us to examine the extent to which decision-making processes correspond to or differ from postulated institutional characteristics and for what reason. The theoretical model thus provides us with a framework for describing decision-making across a wide range of topics and across organizations of all kinds. We believe this to be essential for the further development of decision-making theory.

NOTES

[1] We wish to thank our colleagues Geoff Mallory and David Cray for the support they have given us; and Terry Connolly of the Georgia Institute of Technology for his thorough criticisms. This research was supported by the British Social Science Research Council.

[2] In an attempt to clarify the vagueness of much decision-making terminology, the following definitions are evolved and used in this paper:
An ISSUE is a continuing problem or opportunity faced by an organization.
A TOPIC is a label attached to an issue when it becomes the subject of a decision-making process.
A DECISION is a choice arrived at through the processing of an issue.

[3] In the empirical study based on the theoretical framework presented here, a total of 26 variables were used to characterize complexity, cleavage and decision processes. One hundred and fifty decision topics were analyzed and the sample covered 30 organizations. Full operationalization of all the variables may be found in Butler *et al.* (1982).

[4] For the purposes of the theory, the term 'constellation' of interest is preferred to the term 'coalition' as used by Cyert and March (1963). The coalition of shareholders, suppliers, managers *etc.* is a constant for an organization, whereas the constellation or assembly of interests changes from topic to topic. In any case, the word coalition often brings confusion because it commonly means also a particular alliance such as might occur within a constallation of interests as a subset of it: as Bacharach and Lawler (1980) put it, coalitions occur within 'influence networks'. Further, the expression 'organization-set' as used by Evan (1971) covers only part of the meaning of constellation since it refers to external interests only and not to internal interests.

REFERENCES

Abell, P. (1975). *Organizations as Bargaining and Influence Systems.* London: Heinemann.

Axelsson, R. *et al.* (1977). 'Organization power in organizational decision-making'. In Warner, M. (Ed.), *Organizational Choice and Constraint.* Farnborough: Saxon House.

Axelsson, R. and Rosenberg, L. (1978). 'Decision-making and organizational turbulence'. *Acta Sociologica*, **22**, 45–62.

Bacharach, S. B. and Lawler, E. J. (1980). *Power and Politics in Organizations.* San Francisco: Jossey-Bass.

Bachrach, P. and Baratz, M. S. (1962). 'Two faces of power'. *American Political Science Review*, **56**, 947–52.

Braybrooke, D. and Lindblom, C. E. (1963). *A Strategy of Decision.* New York: Free Press.

Butler, R. J. *et al.* (1979). 'Strategic decision-making in organizations: concepts of content and process'. *International Studies of Management and Organization*, **9**, 5–36.

BUTLER, R. J. (1982). 'A transactional approach to organizing efficiency: perspectives from markets, hierarchies and collectives'. *Administration and Society*, forthcoming.

BUTLER, R. J. *et al.* (1982). 'Decision-making: technical and political explanations'. *Working Paper*, Organizational Analysis Research Unit, University of Bradford.

CAMPBELL, D. T. and STANLEY, J. C. (1966). *Experimental and Quasi-Experimental Designs for Research*. Chicago: Rand McNally.

CHERNS, A. (1980). 'Organizations as instruments of social change in post-industrial societies'. *Organization Studies*, **1**, 109–22.

CHURCHMAN, C. W. (1961). *Prediction and Optimal Decision*. Englewood Cliffs, N.J.: Prentice-Hall.

CLAWSON, D. (1980). 'Class struggle and the rise of bureaucracy'. In Dunkerley, D. and Salaman, G. (Eds.), *The International Yearbook of Organization Studies*. London: Routledge and Kegan Paul.

CLEGG, S. (1979). *The Theory of Power and Organization*. London: Routledge and Kegan Paul.

COHEN, M. D. *et al.* (1972). 'A garbage-can model of organizational choice'. *Administrative Science Quarterly*, **17**, 1–25.

COLIGNON, R. and CRAY, D. (1980). 'Critical organizations'. *Organization Studies*, **1**, 349–66.

CROZIER, M. (1973). 'The problem of power'. *Social Research*, **40**, 211–28.

CYERT, R. M. and MARCH, J. G. (1963). *A Behavioral Theory of the Firm*. Englewood Cliffs, N.J.: Prentice-Hall.

EVAN, W. M. (1971). 'The organization-set: toward a theory of inter-organizational relations'. In Maurer, J. G. (Ed.), *Readings in Organization Theory: Open System Approaches*. New York: Random House.

FREEMAN, J. H. (1978). 'The unit of analysis in organizational research'. In Meyer, M. and Associates (Eds.), *Environments and Organizations: Theoretical and Empirical Perspectives*. San Francisco: Jossey-Bass.

GOULDNER, A. W. (1959). 'Organizational analysis'. In Merton, R. K. *et al.* (Eds.), *Sociology Today*. New York: Basic Books.

HAGE, J. (1980). *Theories of Organizations: Form, Process and Transformation*. New York: Wiley.

HEYDEBRAND, W. (1977). 'Organizational contradictions in public bureaucracies: towards a Marxist theory of organizations'. *Sociological Quarterly*, **18**, 83–107.

HICKSON, D. J. *et al.* (1978). 'Decisive coalitions'. In King, S. *et al.* (Eds.), *Managerial Control and Organizational Democracy*. Washington: Winston, Wiley.

KARPIK, L. (1978). 'Organizations, institutions and history'. In Karpik, L. (Ed.), *Organization and Environment: Theory, Issues and Reality*, London: Sage.

KICKERT, W. J. M. (1979). *Organization of Decision-Making: A Systems Theoretical Approach*. Amsterdam: North-Holland Publishing.

LINDBLOM, C. E. (1959). 'The science of "muddling through"'. *Public Administration Review*, **19**, 79–88.

LINDBLOM, C. E. (1968). *The Policy Making Process*. Englewood Cliffs, N.J.: Prentice-Hall.

LUKES, S. (1974). *Power: A Radical View*. London: Macmillan.

MARCH, J. G. and OLSEN, J. P. (1976). *Ambiguity and Choice in Organizations*. Oslo: Universitet Sforlaget.

MARCH, J. G. and SIMON, H. A. (1958). *Organizations*. New York: Wiley.

MECHANIC, D. (1962). 'Sources of power of lower participants in complex organizations'. *Administrative Science Quarterly*, **7**, 349–64.

MINTZBERG, H. *et al.* (1976). 'The structure of unstructured decision processes'. *Administrative Science Quarterly*, **21**, 246–75.

NORMANN, R. (1971). 'Organizational innovativeness: product variation and reorientation'. *Administrative Science Quarterly*, **16**, 203–15.

PAHL, R. E. and WINKLER, J. T. (1974). 'The economic élite: theory and practice'. In Stanworth, P. and Giddens, A. (Eds.), *Élites and Power in British Society*. Cambridge: University Press.

PARKINSON, C. N. (1964). *Parkinson's Law*. New York: Ballantine Books.

PERROW, C. (1967). 'A framework for comparative organizational analysis'. *American Sociological Review*, **32**, 194–208.

PETTIGREW, A. (1973). *The Politics of Organizational Decision-Making*. London: Tavistock.

RAE, D. W. and TAYLOR, M. (1970). *The Analysis of Political Cleavages*. London: Yale University Press.

RODRIGUES, S. B. (1980). *Processes of Successful Managerial Decision-Making in Organizations*. PhD Thesis, University of Bradford, England.

SALAMAN, G. (1978). 'Towards a sociology of organizational structure'. *Sociological Review*, **3**, 519–54.

SALANCIK, G. R. and PFEFFER, J. (1974). 'The bases and uses of power in organizational decision-making: the case of a university'. *Administrative Science Quarterly*, **19**, 453–73.

SIMON, H. A. (1947). *Administrative Behavior*. New York: Free Press.

SIMON, H. A. (1962). 'The architecture of complexity'. *Proceedings of the American Philosophical Society*, **106**, 467–82.

SUMNER, W. G. (1906). *Folkways*. New York: Dover (republished 1959).

THOMPSON, J. D. (1967). *Organizations in Action*. New York: McGraw-Hill.

WEICK, K. (1969). *The Social Psychology of Organizing*. Reading, Mass.: Addison-Wesley.

WILSON, D. C. (1980). *Organizational Strategy*. PhD Thesis, University of Bradford, England.

WILSON, D. C. (1982). 'Electricity and resistance: a case study of innovation and politics'. *Organization Studies*, **3**, forthcoming.

WILSON, D. C. *et al.* (1982a). 'The selective embodiment of power'. *Working Paper*, Organizational Analysis Research Unit, University of Bradford.

WILSON, D. C. *et al.* (1982b). 'The limits of trade union power in organizational decision-making'. *British Journal of Industrial Relations*.

[4]
ORGANIZATION AS POWER

David J. Hickson, W. Graham Astley,
Richard J. Butler and David C. Wilson

ABSTRACT

Two perspectives of organizational power are presented. First, power as technique views organizational power as a means to coordinate people and activities to organizational ends. Second, power as domination views organizational power as a means for individuals and groups to pursue their own ends and interests. These two perspectives of power are threaded through a discussion of inter and intraorganizational power. Current research is described which takes strategic decision making as a situation especially appropriate for the examination of organizational power. The balance of power in an organization then becomes a matter of a dialectic between the technical and political perspectives worked out in a decision-making arena.

Research in Organizational Behavior, Volume 3, pages 151–196.

ISBN: 0-89232-151-2

Permeating the organizational literature, sometimes explicitly, sometimes implicitly, are two contrasting views of what constitutes the warp of organization. One view interprets organizations as rational instruments for achieving some goal or set of goals. Structural mechanisms act as tools deliberately established for the realization of collective purposes. This goal-oriented or instrumental view of organizations is referred to by Gouldner (1959) as the "rational model" and it directs our attention to those characteristics which distinguish organizations as entities in their own right: as something distinct from mere agglomerations of personnel with diverse purposes. Durkheim (1933) might have referred to the structural embodiment of such instrumental rationality as organization "sui generis."

But the distinctive features of organizations as social entities are not their only characteristic. Attention must be directed not only to collective purposes, but also to those features of organization which are reflections of the localized interests of actors who have a stake in collective organization but who are only "partially included" (Allport, 1933) in organizational life and also exhibit an autonomy which is derived from their partial exclusion. While Gouldner referred to this focus as the "natural system model," it is now common, in this vein, to talk of organizations as coalitions (Cyert and March, 1963) in which interests come and go, or are avoided, resulting in organizational activities removed from stated purposes (Pfeffer and Salancik, 1978).

Organizations, then, are at one and the same time instruments which serve collective purposes, and coalitions which respond to localized pressures and interests. Nowhere is this contrast illuminated more clearly than in the literature's treatment of the concept of power. On the one hand, power has been of interest in terms of its technical advantages, or instrumentality, for achieving collective purposes; on the other hand, power has been of interest in terms of its implications for political domination by some over others. The one is not independent of the other. Power as domination, as we will explore further in this paper, and as indicated by Crozier (1964) and Hickson *et al.* (1971), can be buttressed by task uncertainty which also impacts upon the kinds of control techniques appropriate in an organization.

POWER AS A TECHNIQUE

A technical interest in power is often indicated by usage of the terminology "control." In the sense used here, control refers to the technical necessity for the individual pieces of the jigsaw to cohere and to "circumscribe idiosyncratic behaviors" for the overall purposes of the organization (Tannenbaum, 1968). The need for control has led to the suggested ubiquitousness of hierarchy in Simon's (1960, 1962) parable of the two watchmakers. Hora, the successful watchmaker, makes his watches out of manageable subassemblies enabling him to deal with interruptions without having to restart from scratch. Tempus, the unsuccessful watchmaker, attempts to fit all the bits together in one go. Any involuntary interruption resulting in the watch having to be put aside means that upon resuming work the entire assembly has to be remade instead of only the immediate subassembly being worked on.

In a similar argument, Thompson (1967) sees hierarchy not only in the sense of authority relationships but as a more inclusive clustering. Thus, departmentalization is derived from technical considerations rather than from considerations of local interests, work being successively subdivided on the basis of dimensions homogenizing activities within subunits. For example, departmentalization might proceed first by specializing according to geographical area, then, within each area, according to product type, and, finally, within each product division according to functional expertise, producing a hierarchy of work-flow activities.

Each of the above refers to centralization of power as a technique of organization. But even when power is decentralized this may take place for technical reasons. Scott, Mitchell and Peery's (1980) review of American efforts in worker participation concludes that participation can be used as social technology to increase productivity, though it is probably less effective than its advocates like to think, certainly less effective than pay (Locke *et al.* 1979). Even so, participation, in the form of programs such as Management by Objectives, may make employees less defensive and increase their motivation to reach the explicit agreed upon goals (Drucker, 1964), ensure commitment to organizational changes and increase accuracy in decision making about complex problems since responsibility is delegated to those participants who have access to the relevant information (Argyris, 1972).

Despite politically charged appeals for "democratic" management in this literature, the basic supporting arguments for participation are primarily technical in origin. The four themes identified in Dachler and Wilpert's (1978) extensive review of the participation literature can be seen in this way. The "human growth" theme, as typified by Argyris (1957), McGregor (1960), Bennis (1966) and Likert (1967) and elsewhere more generally known as the "human relations" approach (Mouzelis, 1967) bears a direct link to the notion of participation as technique. So too does the "productivity and efficiency" theme, but the ethos of the "democratic" and "socialistic" themes would see participation as a value in itself. But the problem of putting these ideals into practice within large organizations still has to be solved. It has more than once been indicated how the practice of socialism leads to centralized planning mechanisms, the very antithesis of participation (Lindbeck, 1971; Kuc *et al.*, 1980).

Dachler and Wilpert (1978) correctly point to the importance of task content and complexity in promoting participation for technical reasons. Under complexity those at the top of a hierarchy cannot possibly understand all the conditions relating to a decision. Decision makers become constrained by cognitive limits to rationality (March and Simon, 1958) and one way of dealing with this is to call upon experts for information. These experts will, however, bring with them localized interests and power as domination returns to the picture.

POWER AS DOMINATION

Weber's (1947) interpretation of bureaucracy as an ideal type viewed it primarily as a rational and "technically superior" instrument. However, though he never fully developed the ideas theoretically, he also saw bureaucracy as a structure of political domination. He agreed, on the one hand, that bureaucracy was a form of administration based on knowledge and expertise, but he also saw that bureaucratic authority was always, in some measure, an expression of power. Weber's view of bureaucracy involved two sources of authority stemming from its overall rational-legal legitimation: authority based on expertise, and authority based on sheer incumbence in office. That is, bureaucratic organization requires some degree of obedience as an end in itself; obedience is due to a superior, not only because of his technical knowledge, but also because of the office he occupies. Authority, a form of power, therefore takes on political connotations over and above its technical *raison d'être*.

Mao Tse-tung was acutely aware of this. In his day recurrent criticisms were reported from China of the insidious assumption of power by bureaucrats in the hierarchies, a power which might accrue to them merely by virtue of expertly doing a good job. A factory manager is quoted as saying when recalling the 1966 "Cultural Revolution" in China: "When I was criticized by the workers I was aggrieved. Didn't I work hard, come early and leave late, carry out all my duties conscientiously?" (Robinson, 1973: 29). He was unaware of the power accruing to him day by day by which he gradually came to dominate the organization. The Maoist opposition to management by experts, summed up by King (1977: 367) as the dilemma of "redness versus expertness," comes from a recognition that experts can insidiously acquire power, whether by design or not.

Salaman (1978) has recently expounded on this issue, warning that "efficiency" and "rationality" are often inappropriately used as justifications for the inegalitarian nature of organizational structure. Such justifications explain hierarchy, and the asymmetrical distribution of rewards and deprivations associated with it, as the inevitable and inexorable consequence of the application of the criterion of efficiency to the achievement of generally beneficial societal tasks. In this way, power as technique supports power as domination, with ideologies of efficiency buttressing, disguising, or justifying organizational inequality.

Meyer and Rowan (1977) go further and argue that the formal structures of many organizations in modern society may be inconsistent with the technical demands of their work activities. Though these structures are often rationalized as serving technical purposes they are also in some degree myths representing social purposes and interests which have gained an institutionalized status. This argument suggests that organizations may incorporate structures which are prescribed by the institutional environment in order to gain legitimacy, even if this conflicts with efficiency criteria.

As we noted earlier, the conceptualization of power as a political phenomenon is consistent with the view of organizations as coalitions. Organizations as coalitions are settings in which groups and individuals with varying interests and preferences come together and engage in exchanges. In this sense "organizations are markets for influence and control" (Pfeffer and Salancik, 1978). Out of exchanges, and the interdependencies created by them, emerge differences in power among organizational participants. Such power can be used to further the ends of these participants; it thus is to be interpreted in terms of domination rather than in terms of a logic of technical prescription.

The distinction between power as technique and power as domination has been made elsewhere in different terminology. Lehman (1977) distinguishes between "systemic power," which is the capacity of agents of the system to overcome resistance to collective goals, and "intermember power," which focuses upon competition over scarce resources in a system. "Systemic power," as Lukes (1974) states, is conveyed through the expression "power to" and is thus a technical instrument in the pursuit of collective goals. "Intermember power," on the other hand, is conveyed through the expression "power over" and is thus the manifestation of relationships of political domination between actors.

Where should the balance be set? To return to the Chinese context, King (1977: 371) once more has a knack of stating things plainly:

> The Maoist critique of the so-called Liuist model as "seeing only organization but not men" may be correct, but the Maoists, too, can be criticized for "seeing only men but not organization."

This is a dilemma in no way peculiar to Chinese society alone, but one common to all "organizational societies," to use Presthus' (1979) term. Both faces of power, as technique and as domination, are omnipresent.

POWER WITHIN ORGANIZATIONS

In an attempt to map out empirically the essentials of organizational control and power Pugh *et al.* (1968) found that two sets of factors emerged which alone accounted for over half the variance in a principal-components analysis. Organizations could vary, first, in the degree to which they structured their activities, that is, by specialized functions, standardized procedures and formalized documentation, and secondly, in the degree to which they concentrated authority at the apex of the hierarchy. Both are means of controlling organizations, that is, of exerting power.

Plotting the widely representative sample of organizations in their study against the two dimensions (Pugh *et al.*, 1969), these researchers showed a broad scatter but within it a tendency to cluster into four types. These were full bureaucracies, work-flow bureaucracies, personnel bureaucracies, and implicitly structured organizations. Full bureaucracies exert control by specializing tasks and imposing control procedures, and by centralizing decisions. They use both control mechanisms to the full. These bureaucracies, typically, were smaller units within large private or public corporations. Work-flow bureaucracies by comparison rely rather more on specializing and on procedures, i.e., on structuring activities, and not so much on centralizing decisions at the top or waiting for "head office" to take them. This control strategy would be typical of big business. Personnel bureaucracies lean the other way. They control by centralizing decisions and by governing the selection and reward of personnel with detailed procedures, but much less by structuring the activities of those personnel once they are recruited. This strategy is followed by many governmental administrative organizations, and by those with large proportions of professionally qualified members. It relies on careful selection of pretrained members who can subsequently be left alone—comparatively speaking, to get on with the job, whereas the strategy of industrial workflow bureaucracies is close control of members who are not necessarily pretrained. The fourth type, the implicitly structured organization, tends to be smaller with concentrated ownership (e.g., family ownership) and for control purposes probably relies more on nonformalized custom, and "mutual adjustment" (Thompson, 1967).

So organizations may lean one way or the other in the patterning of power, toward centralizing decisions or structuring activities, or may make full use of both. The one can be seen as vertical power, the other as lateral power insofar as it affords power (within limits) to specialist functions. Are these in any way mutually exclusive alternatives? Is there a tendency to do one or the other rather than both? Are centralizing and structuring alternative control strategies, or can they be combined in a strategy in which they are complementary?

Discussion of this question has been prompted by the apparently contrasting results of successive Aston Programme projects, in which Pugh *et al.'s* (1969) taxonomy treated a small negative relation between the two dimensions as negligible and plotted them orthogonally, whereas Child (1972) reported a bipolar factor on which centralizing and structuring were opposed. The first study therefore appeared to allow a wide choice of strategies with complementary means combined in any proportions. The second appeared to limit choice to an emphasis one way or the other, implying, for example, that once a structured organizational machine had been set to run it had to be left to do so because authority could not simultaneously be centralized. However, differences of sample confuse the comparison, and in any case an improved centralization measure is needed (Greenwood and Hinings, 1976). Probably these extreme theoretical interpretations are both exaggerated. There is choice, but it is limited.

Further empirical research has left the question, if it is a real question, as open as ever. Results assembled from six countries (Hickson *et al.*, 1979) and subsequently also reported from Poland (Kuc *et al.*, 1980) show correlations between variables, representing the two dimensions, which range from negative through nil to positive.

If the relationship between the fundamental elements of organization underlying lateral power and vertical power remains obscure, this might well be the fault of research which fails to examine both dimensions within an encompassing framework. Studies of intraorganizational power have tended to focus on one aspect of power to the exclusion of the other. Those studies which attempt to explain power from the organizational division of labor have been interested in why different subunits vary in power laterally across the organization; these are discussed in the next section. Those studies more interested in division of authority, on the other hand, have concentrated on vertical distributions of power and are discussed in the subsequent section.

I. Lateral Power

It is not unusual for organizational actors to exert considerable power and influence not associated with their formally defined positions of power within the organization. Though an actor's personal characteristics and activities may contribute to such power, "no power relationship can be dissociated from the institutional system" (Crozier, 1973: 214) within which it is located.

Thus, Scheff (1961) explained the power of hospital attendants by reference to the ward physicians' dependence upon them. This dependence ensued from the large amount of administrative responsibility the physician had to assume. Attendants would take on some of this responsibility in return for increased power in decisions regarding the handling of patients. If the latter part of this exchange was not fulfilled the attendants would withhold information, disobey instructions, refuse to handle paperwork officially the responsibility of physicians, and fail to serve as a barrier between the physician and a ward full of patients demanding attention and recognition. Thus the attendants could wield influence by suddenly refusing to assume responsibilities which they normally assumed but which were not their legal responsibility to assume.

Similarly, Hickson (1961) described how a worker group in a British engineering factory exploited its position. Placed on a task which gave it control of what were new machines producing components needed for the biggest orders for the main customers, the group was able to regulate output in such a way as to protect its bargaining position. Its location in a sequentially interdependent work-flow (Thompson, 1967) gave it a power potential which it exercised effectively.

These examples suggest that a subunit's location within the division of labor places it in a more or less fortuitous position with regard to its ability to exert power. Such fortuity is usually labelled "strategic." Sayles (1958) attached this label to his "strategic groups," workers whose tasks were central to the functioning of the plant and required relatively high skill. Perrow (1970), using data from twelve American industrial firms, concluded that such firms would usually be dominated by their sales departments since these act as gatekeepers between these organizations and the customers on which they depend. Lawrence and Lorsch (1967) found the same result in container organizations, but found that, in food organizations, research departments were able to match sales in influence because they dealt with the most critical issue facing the organization: the need to innovate. Hinings *et al.* (1974), in contrast, found in the Canadian and American brewing and packaging industries that production departments predominated.

Woodward (1965) extended this idea of different critical functions in different organizations by suggesting that the cycle of manufacture places development, production and marketing in a different order in different technologies. In unit or jobbing systems, marketing precedes development and production follows last, since not until a customer requires a product and it is designed can production occur. In large batch and mass systems, the development and production of a new line precedes its mass marketing. In process systems, development of a possible product and marketing to assured customers must precede commitment of capital to special-purpose plants to produce it. In each system the most critical function is the central one which has the greatest effect on success. That is, in unit systems, development is dominant; in mass systems it is production; in process systems it is marketing.

In formal theoretical terms the power of subunits is explained by the organization's dependence upon them. Emerson (1962) proposed that:

> The dependence of actor A upon Actor B is (1) directly proportional to A's motivational investment in goals mediated by B, and (2) inversely proportional to the availability of those goals to A outside of the A-B relation.

In organizations, subunit B will have more power than other subunits to the extent that (1) B has the capacity to fulfill the requirements of the other subunits and (2) B monopolizes this ability. The notion of dependence as a source of organizational power is contained within the variable of the "strategic contingencies theory" of intraorganizational power (Hickson, *et al.*, 1971; Hinings, *et al.*, 1974), and has been elaborated further in "the resource-dependence" model of interorganizational power (Pfeffer and Salancik, 1978).

For Blau (1964), the mediation of goals within a dyad can be viewed in terms of an exchange between actors. Thus, B can establish power over A by supplying resources which A is dependent upon in the absence of alternative sources of supply. If A is unable to reciprocate with resources of equivalent value and thereby make B dependent upon him in return, the exchange relationship becomes unbalanced. However, in this situation A is still obligated to repay the debt in some manner, and an alternative way of doing this is to display obeisance by acceding to B's wishes, in which case B gains power over A. Power is thus derived from exchange in that it equalizes the imbalance of exchanged resources.

How, then, does a subunit fulfill the requirements of other subunits? What makes a particular function critical? What is the major source of dependence in organizations? Thompson (1967) has suggested that the central problem facing organizations is that of uncertainty. Those subunits which cope with the most uncertainty should therefore have the most power. Crozier's (1964) study of a French tobacco factory supports this notion. He found that maintenance engineers held considerable power because they controlled the one remaining uncertainty the organization faced—the repair of the machinery. The fact that the engineers possessed the knowledge to repair machinery when the production workers did not, meant that they wielded a large amount of influence over production supervisors.

But the possession of expertise in role performance, and its use in coping with uncertainty (Hickson *et al.*, 1971), is not enough. To fulfill the second requirement in Emerson's (1962) theory, this possession must be monopolized. Thus, the "functional importance" of an activity only confers power upon an actor if his performance of it is "functionally exclusive" (Dubin, 1963; Mechanic, 1962); that is, if other actors cannot easily replace his performance. Thus it was that Crozier's maintenance engineers took steps to resist the codification and standardization of maintenance procedures since this would have afforded production workers' knowledge of machine repair and enabled them to do it instead.

To Crozier's notion of a critical uncertainty and Dubin's and Mechanic's notion of "functional exclusiveness" (nonsubstitutability), Hickson *et al.* (1971) added Woodward's (1965) and Mechanic's (1962) notion of the centrality of a subunit's work activities. This notion they subdivided into "pervasiveness," the degree to which the work-flows of a subunit connect with the work-flows of other subunits, and "immediacy," the degree to which the cessation of a subunit's activities would quickly and substantially impede the primary work-flow of the organization. They argued that in combination these four dependency-generating factors, the ability to cope with uncertainty, nonsubstitutability, pervasiveness and immediacy, give a subunit a control of "strategic contingencies."

A limited test of this comprehensive theory by Hinings *et al.* (1974) on subunits in the brewing and packaging industries (already referred to) found its hypotheses to be firmly supported by a variety of data. In their words:

> Strongest support for the theory is from the evidence that only a combination of high values on all the variables postulated gave dominant first-rank power. With this combination, the activities of a subunit become contingencies for other subunits upon which they are critically dependent (Hinings *et al.*, 1974: 40).

Combinations of lower values yielded lesser power.

With the increasing popularity of resource-dependence approaches in organization theory (e.g., Pfeffer and Salancik, 1978) one can easily be led into thinking that everything can be explained by reference to dependence relationships. Indeed our discussion of lateral power has merely treated power as the obverse of dependence. However, not everything in organizations is dependence. Using data on subunit power in sixteen organizations, Astley (1978) found that subunit power was associated with dependencies arising from the flow of work between those subunits. But dependence was only a partial explanation. Holding subunit interdependencies constant, he also found that level of hierarchy was positively associated with subunit power. Level of hierarchy affected subunit power independently of work-flow dependence. This supports Weber's (1947) assertion that the authority of bureaucratic office-holders derives both from their technical indispensability and from incumbency of an office in itself.

To account for this situation we must consider the phenomenon of institutionalization. The power which adheres to bureaucratic offices from nonfunctional sources derives its efficacy from the institutionalized status which organizational structures evolve. As time passes, after the inception of a particular organizational structure, the characteristics of which derive from a functional rationale, that structure's existence becomes taken for granted. The now historical *raison d'êtres* might no longer logically apply to present organizational situations and "institutions are now experienced as possessing a reality of their own" (Berger and Luckmann, 1966). Power relationships, then, are played out within an apparent objectively given world defined by institutionalized rules (Clegg, 1975) as much as they are generated from interdependent relationships.

These rules will manifest themselves in many ways. The notion of rules as a means of organizational control is contained within the standardization and formalization, or structuring activities, of Pugh *et al.* (1969). This structuring exemplifies mainly the technical rule type suggested by Clegg (1979), setting the kinds of activities employees have to contribute. Three other categories of rules (Clegg, 1979: 122) are social regulative, typified by the human relations techniques of participative management, extra-organizational rules, typified by discriminatory practices of race or age, and strategic rules, typified by incomes policies.

Rules relating to ownership exemplify seldom questioned aspects of power as domination through institutionalization. Zeitlin's (1974) analysis of large American corporations shows domination by ownership interests, whereas in Great Britain, Dobbins and Briston (1978) point to an increasing concentration of corporate ownership into the hands of financial institutions, although in practice there is a marked reluctance to use this potential power. Baumgartner *et al.* (1977) see the institutions of private property with associated legal and judicial "support structure" as providing a general "normative pressure" to maintain existing social structures.

II. Vertical Power

Institutionalized rules will have both a lateral and hierarchical dimension in creating the context for organizational power relations. Technical rules concerning, for instance, specialization and departmentalization will derive in part from the technical requirements of the job and from the "construction of social reality" (Berger and Luckmann, 1966) that experts will bring with them, and in part from the hierarchically set context.

The manner in which a skillful operator can successfully intermingle both the lateral and vertical rules in power play is portrayed by Pettigrew's (1973) character, Kenny. He held a key position both in terms of expertness and in having special access to the board decision-making processes of the company, allowing him eventually to sway a major computer purchase decision his way.

Discussions of lateral power usually attempt to identify various sources of subunit power and, as such, treat power itself as a dependent variable. (An exception to this is the discussion of the effects of subunit power on decision making, a topic we shall come to later.) In contrast, discussions of the vertical distribution of power within organizations have usually treated power as an independent variable by focusing on the effects of this distribution upon individual psychological reactions and behavior.

The best example of this approach is the work of Tannenbaum on control (1968). Tannenbaum's basic ideas are expressed in a "Control Graph" (Figure 1).

If the horizontal base of this graph is taken to represent the hierarchical echelons of an organization, and the vertical scale the amount of control exercised by the respective hierarchical echelons, then a curve drawn on this graph represents the hierarchical distribution of control. It is immediately apparent that such curves may differ in their average height, suggesting theoretically that organizations may differ in their total amount of control, as well as in the relative amount of control exercised by the respective hierarchical echelons. This use of the control graph leads

Figure 1. Tannenbaum's Control Graph

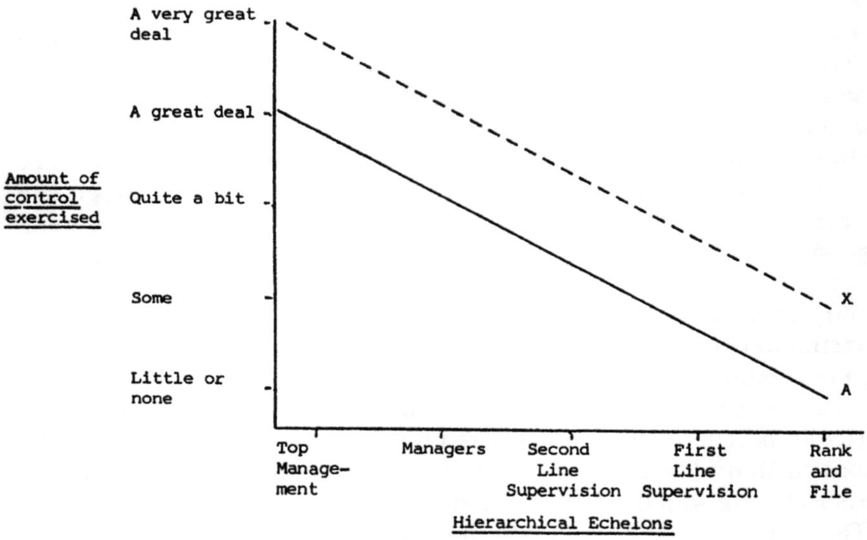

Tannenbaum to question the "fixed pie" or "zero sum" assumptions underlying traditional analyses of organizational power. Thus:

> By comparison with curve A, curve X is both more "democratic" in the sense of greater control by lower echelons, and more "oligarchic" in the sense of greater control by upper echelons (Tannenbaum, 1968).

The nature of the interest by Tannenbaum and his colleagues in control (or power) as an independent variable becomes apparent when he reviews the literature which has encouraged increases in the total amount of control, namely, the participative approaches of McGregor (1960), Likert (1961), Haire (1962), and Shepard and Blake (1961). These authors imply that participation which increases the total amount of control makes available for exploitation individual capabilities (resources) that are not otherwise exploited by the organization.

In theory, therefore, the distribution of power is open to deliberate variation. It could be more hierarchical, or less so. Contemporary societies usually pay lip-service at the very least to making it less so. That may be either as a technical means to other ends such as greater job satisfaction or productivity, manipulating power as an assumed independent variable; or to change the pattern of domination as a desirable end in itself. There may be differing emphases in this. Scott *et al.*'s (1980) contrast of approaches to participative management in Europe and America:

> In most American organizations, participation is introduced because management believes it will increase the effort, motivation and productivity of its employees, not because of concerns about equity, equality, or rights in allocation decisions. A vastly different emphasis is apparent in most European organizations. Europeans view participation in terms of the political redistribution of power. Socialists have indicated that it is desirable to use methods which increase the power of people over nature or which abolish the power of people over people. The proponents of power redistribution do not usually talk about participation; they speak of self management by workers as the means of eliminating arbitrary power from organizations.

In Dachler and Wilpert's (1978) terms, participation is a value in its own right and not simply a means to efficiency.

Whether either of these aims of participation is achieved is not the main issue to be pursued in this paper but rather whether, given the accepted and apparently technically imperative hierarchically structured form of organizations, any noticeable "power-equalization" (Strauss, 1963) is possible. It is indeed the Europeans who give most grounds for skepticism. Lund (1980) traces the extent of meaningful participation by employee representatives on the board of a small Danish company in three major decisions. He finds that they were overwhelmed by facts and figures beyond their normal everyday experience and so had little to say.

In power-base terms, their lack of expertise gave them very slight influence compared to that yielded to the executives on the board by their superior expertise. Reviewing the possibilities much earlier from The Netherlands, Mulder (1971) gave general support to the typical case detailed by Lund (1980), suggesting that this expert power base of managers is simply a result of their spending more time upon such major problems than subordinates can. To this we would have to add that their position in a hierarchy makes access to information easier.

Even in Yugoslavia, where an attempt has been made to redistribute power by structural devices such as a nominally controlling worker's council in each enterprise, the situation is much the same. Mulder (1971) reports Broekmeyer (1968) as finding that expert elites held the real power. Others contributed little to meetings and did not respond to invitations to comment on important issues. Dominant manager power in Yugoslavia is confirmed by the control graphs presented by Kavic *et al.* (1971). Laboratory experiments have found the same (Mulder, 1971: 34). In short, participation has little effect in changing the dominant distribution of power.

Nor is it at all certain to increase job satisfaction, if that is the intended result. The British authors Wall and Lischeron in an extensive review go so far as to suggest that whereas most authors assume a positive link, often implicitly, "the evidence obtained to date encourages a rejection of the participation-satisfaction thesis" (Wall and Lischeron, 1977: 147). Positive associations in correlational studies are not borne out by experimental investigations. Given that participation seems to make so little change in power it is perhaps not surprising that it then produces inconsequential change in other variables. The most employees want to do is to influence managers by direct interaction within an accepted power structure (Wall and Lischeron, 1971).

Reconsider the distinction between power as technique and power as domination. Increased control in the technical sense of tightening up coordination of work elements toward organizational goals is positive sum control. Hence Pugh *et al.* (1968) can see centralization and structuring of activities as two potentially complementary factors of control. But the positive sum view of control is not appropriate to the political realities of power play in which if one protagonist wins the other must lose. It is perhaps in this way that Child (1972) can see centralization and structuring as two opposed means of control a zero sum view. We would have to admit, though, that an alternative "efficiency" explanation is also available for this finding which is simply that it might be wasteful to over control an organization. Control has its cost and an efficiency oriented management would wish to weigh the costs and benefits of each additional quantum of control.

The control graph (Tannenbaum, 1968) method combines both the absolute (positive sum) and the relative (zero sum) views of power. But as Simon (1962) pointed to the ubiquitousness of hierarchy as a means of co-ordinating activities, so Tannenbaum's method shows up the ubiquitousness of hierarchical power differentials. Control graphs from countries spread across North and South America and Western Europe all reveal the same kind of picture. Hierarchical power differentials are the norm, and differ little if at all between continents or between what for simplicity's sake we may call capitalist and communist societies (Tannenbaum and Cooke, 1979). In Poland, for example, all the dysfunctions typical of centralized bureaucratic administration occur just as they have been found to do in equivalent situations in the West (Kiezun, 1977; Marawski, 1978). There is no clear evidence that the Mao regime in China changed power differentials and symbols (Whyte, 1973).

Control graphs display just a flicker of variation to the dominant pattern in respect of what might be called alternative organizations, namely, those who do not pay their main membership, such as trade unions and the American League of Women Voters, and Israeli kibbutzim. They rely relatively more upon normative power and moral commitment (Etzioni, 1961); with the kibbutzim in varying degrees also having management subject to election as do the voluntary associations.

This otherwise constant picture is not method-bound. It is not only a product of control-graph influence questions. It is supported by the results from the Aston Programme centralization measure in a number of countries (Hickson and McMillan, 1980). This measure uses nonpersonal data on formal decision levels. A broadly similar pattern of the levels in hierarchies at which decisions are authorized is broken only by Poland and Japan (Kuc *et al.* 1980). The high degree of centralization in Polish industrial units shows that central planning is able to concentrate decisions at an unusually high level, whereas the lingi formal consultative system in Japan may devolve some decisions, though this interpretation of the results is not certain.

Much greater variation occurs in the individual's socially conditioned response to power than in the distribution of power in itself. Hofstede (1979) opens a sweeping perspective by reporting power distance differences across no less than forty countries spanning the non-Communist part of the globe. Power distance is whether the individual sees himself as close to or far from hierarchical superiors in the sense of his readiness to question their use of their authority or his preference for a less authoritarian style. Latin and Asian nations show a wide power distance between superior and subordinate. In wealthier nations it is much less, and in addition may be lessening at a faster rate. The world seems to differ more in the way power is handled than in the way it is allocated. It is pure speculation, but possibly Maoist China succeeded primarily in changing the face of power by diminishing the symbols of differentiation, rather than in changing the nature of power.

In practice, lateral power and vertical power are not things apart. Organizations are made to work through combinations of both. Butler (1980) found that the degree to which research engineers engaged in advanced technical work could control the service given them by technicians upon whom they depended was a matter of successfully operating lateral relationships within a framework of bureaucratic rules. Vertical bureaucratically based sources of power were provided to the research engineers by institutional context in the form of rules governing the allocation of work, promotions, higher authorities who could be approached in the event of noncompliance by a technician, and the ultimate sanction of dismissal. But these rules only provided a background against which they had to act out their lateral bases of power such as special professional relationships with technicians, referring to a common set of values, assisting technicians to gain professional recognition, or allocating them especially interesting work. Although the match is not perfect, Butler (1980) suggests that in this case vertical power included the reward and coercive bases from the well-known classification of five bases of power by French and Raven (1959), and that lateral power included the expert and referent power bases.

POWER BETWEEN ORGANIZATIONS

I. Organizational Autonomy: Constraint and Choice

Aldrich (1979) has pointed out that the "environment" of organizations has been conceptualized in two contrasting ways, as an encompassing medium from which information is received and monitored by members, and as an interorganizational resource-exchange network.

Within the first approach there have been different emphases on the degree to which organizations react to or enact upon their environments. One view has emphasized an image of organizations adapting and responding to the constraints which their environments impose upon them. This view is at the heart of contingency theories of organization which suggest, for example, that certain degrees of "fit" are appropriate between internal organizational structure and the degree of environmental uncertainty facing the organization (Lawrence and Lorsch, 1967).

The other view emphasizes that organizations do not simply react to information in their environments but "enact" (Weick, 1969) their environments, since decision makers selectively attend to some parts of the environment while other parts become irrelevant since they are defined out of existence in an operational sense, as lying outside the organization's "domain" of legitimate activity (Levine and White, 1961). The notion of organizational domain derives from the specific goals which decision makers wish to pursue and the functions which they cause an organization to undertake in order to implement those goals. Thus the process whereby organizations, for example, come to select certain products and markets as their domain, is one of "strategic choice" (Child, 1972). Decision makers' frames of reference have to take into account some constraints on their activities, but there will normally be considerable leeway within these constraints for the expression of such strategic choices.

The problem with these two views is that they can appear to be mutually exclusive. The first sees environmental constraints as impinging on organizations, whereas the second sees organizations as impinging on their environments through the choices that are made by their decision-making members. On the face of it we are left to believe that either nothing is chosen or everything is chosen; either environment has immutable effects, or its effects are felt because decision-makers' preferences have directed attention toward it.

But such views are reconcilable. To begin with, the tendency to pose them as if everything happens at once overlooks time. Choices are made in sequence over time. Thus a choice made at time 1 may form an environmental feature which is a contingency for a choice at time 2. A commitment to a new product which is launched in an untried market means that subsequent choices take place in a more uncertain environment. Choices lead to situations which then directly constrain subsequent choices. Environments both are chosen and constrain choices.

Moreover, it becomes possible to replace mutual exclusivity by a continuum ranging from complete organizational autonomy to complete environmental constraint if we view the environment not solely in terms of information but in terms of a flow of resources. This is Aldrich's (1979) second conceptualization of "environment." Here the environment consists of scarce resources sought by organizations. Furthermore, the most important of these resources are supplied by the environment of other organizations. It now becomes possible, in this conceptualization, to view organization-environment relations in terms of relationships of power existing between different organizations. Through the use of the resource-dependence explanation of power, we can locate any particular organization as relatively autonomous, dominating other organizations in its environment, or relatively constrained by other organizations which dominate it.

An unusual example of organizations responding to environmental fluctuations is the longitudinal study of the behavior of miners' unions by

Butler (1976). Time series data on American and British unions permitted rigorous controls of the cross-national comparison and established that strike activity followed variations in the dependence of each nation upon coal. Strike activity followed this environmental variation, which determined potential power, rather than internal considerations of pay needs as indicated by relative deprivation in relation to other workers. This study using data over many years and from two nations suggests that unions are relatively constrained by the contingencies of an environment which for them is dominated by other organizations, those which use coal and those which employ mining labor. They are relatively less autonomous, less able to enact the environment in which they find themselves.

II. Interorganizational Interactions

Pfeffer and Salancik (1978) note that the interconnectedness of the environment in terms of resource interdependence between organizations is a dimension that is attracting growing research concern as empirical investigations of organization-environment activity move from analyzing the strategic actions taken by single organizations to consider the design of networks of organizations (Emery and Trist, 1965; Warren, 1967). This is particularly so in view of the indications that interdependence is increasing. Why is interdependence increasing? Pfeffer and Salancik (1978: 94) offer an answer:

> The density and interconnectedness of interorganizational fields today derives from adaptations to past problems. In a world characterized by competition for scarce resources, the predominant adaptations were developments to achieve control over the availability of resources. Technologies were developed to produce foodstuffs to improve the yield, and then to distribute and store them efficiently to guard against periods of unfavorable weather. The developments that provided more control over production and availability themselves created new interdependencies. The efficiency of production deriving from the use of chemical fertilizers and herbicides and insecticides made the agricultural industry dependent upon the chemical firms. Furthermore, as the fertilizers drain into the water supply, further dependencies are created with suppliers of drinking water and with those who fish the affected waterways. As these interdependencies become known, still other organizations are created to regulate and adjudicate the conflicts among the contesting interests.

Thus the motivation to create interdependencies with other organizations is based in the need to control and stabilize productive operations. But the reduction in uncertainty is achieved at a cost. The organization loses some of its autonomy since along with its increased dependence on other organizations it must accept their partial control over its operations. The organization must therefore find a tolerable point in the compromise between the desire for autonomy and the realities of interdependence. On the one hand, if it fails to safeguard itself through interdependence it may not survive; on the other hand, it may needlessly throw away autonomy by entering into relationships of interdependence which exceed the level necessary for a stabilization of operations.

With this trade-off in mind Thompson and McEwen (1958) identify four methods by which an organization can interact with other organizations. Like these authors, we order these forms of interaction in terms of the degree to which they afford external organizations control over the focal organization. The ordered forms of interaction are: competition, contracting, cooptation and coalition. Further, in response to Warren's (1967) typology of interorganizational interactions which is arranged along a similar dimension, we add to the end of this list a fifth form of interaction: combination or merger.

A. Competition. Competition refers to rivalry between two or more organizations which is mediated by a third party. In the case of the manufacturing firm the third party may be the customer, the supplier, the potential or present member of the labor force, or others. In each case the third party makes a choice among alternatives, two or more organizations attempt to influence that choice through some type of appeal or offering, and choice by the third party is a vote of support for one of the competing organizations and a denial of support to the others involved.

Albeit through indirect means, competition is one way through which organizations are controlled by their environments. Such control predominates where sources of dependence are relatively dispersed, that is, where there are many competitors. This lack of concentration of dependence, however, and its indirect mediation, tend to make the control relatively limited. If the organization chooses goals which are inappropriate for its environment, control will, sooner or later, be felt. But, at the same time, in contrast to each of the following forms of interaction, there is no direct controlling intervention by any one element of the environment in the actual process of choosing organizational goals itself.

B. Contracting. The term contracting refers to the negotiation of an agreement for the exchange of goods or services between two or more organizations. Such contracts need not be formal (Macaulay, 1963; Guetzkow, 1966) as when the university entices donations by bargaining away the name of a building or of a library collection, or by the conferring of an honorary degree.

Contracts are used to stabilize relations among organizations and to eliminate environmental uncertainty. Thus organizations can avoid having to anticipate external events by arranging a "negotiated environment"

(Cyert and March, 1963), that is, establishing long contracts with suppliers and customers, adhering to industry-wide pricing conventions, and supporting stable "good business practice."

Clearly, these practices reduce uncertainty for any one organization, but simultaneously impose constraints upon it since it must fulfill its part of the contract. To the extent that contracting sets limits on the amount of resources available or the ways they may be employed, it effectively sets limits on choice of goals. Furthermore, contracting involves direct interaction with, and thus direct control by, other organizations in the environment. These organizations constitute an "organization set" (Evan, 1966) consisting of organizations with which a focal organization has direct links and which exert pressures upon it. This direct interaction appears, therefore, to invade the actual decision process itself.

C. Cooptation. Cooptation has been defined (Selznick, 1949) as the process of absorbing new elements into the leadership or policy-determining structure of an organization as a means of averting threats to its stability or existence. Selznick found that in order to neutralize congressional opposition to the TVA, reclamation and social programs were handled in such a way that local power interests were not alienated. This was done by bringing into the TVA, as staff members, representatives of the "vested" interests in the area—the land-grant college system, the county-agent system, and the Farm Bureau Federation.

Though there are many varieties of cooptation perhaps, the most visible present-day example is the use of interlocking boards of directors. This practice provides a way of managing interdependence since the establishment of friendships, the exchange of information, and identification with the focal organization all facilitate stable relationships (Pfeffer and Salancik, 1978: 161–165).

However, while cooptation brings stability, it also brings loss of autonomy for the focal organization. For example, in the case of the TVA, the original aims of the organization became somewhat diverted as its socialistic aims were diluted by vested conservative interests.

Cooptation is a more constraining form of managing interdependence than contracting. To the extent that cooptation is effective it places an element from the environment in a position to raise questions and exert influence on aspects of the organization beyond those issues which originally prompted the outsider's cooptation.

D. Coalition. The term coalition refers to an expedient combination of two or more organizations for a common purpose. Thus it is widely used when two or more enterprises wish to pursue a goal calling for more support, especially for more resources, than any one of them is able to procure unaided.

One form of coalition is the Trade Association which forms to provide centralized information and coordination throughout an industry. Often, however, such associations go beyond merely sharing information by establishing such mechanisms as pricing systems and attempting to enforce them. For example, the American Bar Association regularly published fees and implied that charging less than the minimum prescribed fees might be grounds for discipline for professional misconduct. When such procedures become even more overt they are referred to as cartels or oligopolies.

A form of coalition which pools not just support but resources is the joint venture (Pfeffer and Nowak, 1976). A joint venture is the creation of a new organizational entity by two or more partner organizations. This new entity can incur debt, sign contracts, or undertake other activities in its own name, and without consequence to the financial or legal position of the parents, except to the extent of their investment in the joint venture.

Though a joint venture may be only a temporary alliance between organizations, the organizations involved must effectively act as one for the duration of the alliance. This temporary unification again highlights the nature of the trade-off between stability and autonomy. It is captured in Gamson's (1967) explanations of coalitions as involving mixed motivations. The short-term motivation of achieving joint ends conflicts with the long-term desire for organizational independence.

E. Combination. The distinction between total combination or merger and a joint venture is that in a merger, two or more organizations combine all of their assets to create a new entity, whereas in a joint venture they combine less than all of their assets to create a new entity. Additionally, in the case of a merger, combination is permanent, whereas in a joint venture the form of the arrangement signifies an intent to retain organizational identity.

Pfeffer (1972) has identified three types of merger, suggesting that each is a response to differing conditions of interdependence. First, companies may employ merger in order to vertically integrate operations. Thus they might merge backward to reduce uncertainties associated with suppliers or merge forward to reduce uncertainties associated with customers. Second, companies might expand horizontally in order to reduce competition and stabilize their markets. Third, companies can diversify, transforming their characters into that of the conglomerate. By diversifying into new product-markets an organization reduces dependencies associated with overconcentration of resources in limited areas.

Merger, then, represents an end point of Thompson and McEwen's continuum. On the one hand, uncertainty is dealt with by its complete absorption. On the other hand, merger substantially obliterates not just organizational autonomy, but its very identity, very often to the extent that completely new names are instituted for the merged organization.

INTRAORGANIZATIONAL AND INTERORGANIZATIONAL POWER

Can any theoretical link be made between intraorganizational and interorganizational distributions of power? Human ecology theory, as expounded by Hawley (1968), suggests such a link, since it focuses on the fundamental role of the environment in shaping social organization.

In this model organizational subunits are assumed to be functionally differentiated, performing diverse specialized functions for the organization. Those subunits which link the organization to its environment, and through which it obtains needed resources, are called boundary spanners. All other subunits are dependent on these boundary spanners for the resources they need, which gives the boundary spanners dominance over them. Boundary spanners consequently exercise functional dominance throughout the organization, influencing the activities of all other subunits that have only indirect links to the environment. Some amount of dominance can also be exerted by these other subunits, but only in inverse proportion to their distance from the boundary spanners. Of course, this explanation of power is consistent with that offered earlier as "strategic contingencies" theory. Boundary spanners in direct contact with environmental uncertainty have more opportunity to cope with uncertainty, and hence may exert more power.

Moreover, the distribution of power between boundary spanners and other subunits varies with system openness/closure. In a completely open system, all subunits have direct access to the environment, so that every subunit acts as its own boundary spanner. In a partially closed system, some of the units relate directly to the environment performing boundary-spanning roles, while others maintain only internal linkages with these boundary spanners and are dependent upon them for needed resources. In a system which has attained maximum closure only one subunit interacts with the environment and all other subunits are dependent on this single boundary spanner. Thus, with the movement from openness to closure, the organization experiences growing power centralization.

But what characteristics of the environment are likely to cause power to be either concentrated in a few boundary spanners or dispersed more widely? Pugh *et al.* (1969) suggest an answer to this. They found that a concentration of intraorganizational authority was associated with a concentration of focal organization's dependence on other organizations. Dependence was conceptualized as a measure of interorganizational relations, combining a series of small scales reflecting the period of contractual links with other organizations, the proportionate reliance on any major suppliers or customers, the use of any central services, and status in an owning group. The greater the dependence in these ways, the greater was the concentration of authority.

Pugh *et al.* (1969) results came from a widely representative stratified random sample of all types of organization, service and manufacturing, public and private, and are therefore likely to be generalizable. But are they generalizable beyond England where the sample was located? The answer is a fairly confident yes, given Hickson *et al.* (1979) report of consistently similar results obtained by themselves and others in the United States, Canada, Sweden, Japan, and West Germany. As they put it:

> In all countries, organizations dependent on others will take decisions centrally and in addition decisions will be taken for them outside and above them (Hickson *et al.*, 1979).

Why should this be? Consider a hypothetical but typical situation. A purchasing department arranges for supplies from various sources. The head of department is authorized to conclude all necessary contracts, and being an experienced man he does so without having to trouble the organization's chief executive over what are comparatively routine deals. Then an opportunity arises for the organization to reduce uncertainties associated with the supply of raw materials by arranging a long-term contract for its critical input with a single supplier. With supplies assured, production of lines which use the material can be confidently expanded, making this single contractual relationship even more critical. When the time comes to renegotiate the contract it has become so crucial to the whole firm that the chief executive deals with it himself. In this way the head of the purchasing department has, by his own success in originally securing supplies, inadvertently moved decision making out of his own hands to a higher level. Possibly even more common is the injection of capital (i.e., money supplies) by a large firm into a smaller one whose custom is useful to it, as might follow in the situation just described. This will be accompanied by assurances that no managerial control is intended. "You may be assured, Mr. Smith, that you will be free to run your company as you have always done." But whatever the intentions, the need for the larger firm to protect its investment means that before long the once independent Mr. Smith is being constrained by Head Office. Thus decisions become centralized first within the focal organization unit itself, and then beyond it. In such ways, closer links with external units steadily raise authority levels. Single crucial decisions become so important that relevant decisions are taken higher and higher up.

As Jacobs (1974: 53) writes: "Organizations are controlled by those who comprise or control the organization's most problematic dependence." The argument applies as readily to internal subunits for as Benson (1975) notes there is a close analytic resemblance between interorganizational and intraorganizational relationships.

Stated differently, we can therefore say that a concentration of authority in a few internal subunits is associated with a concentration of dependence upon a few external units. Just as with system closure and centralization, the intricacy of internal dependencies makes their fine tuning more crucial, so the establishment of specific exchanges which concentrate external dependencies makes their fine tuning more crucial. This need for fine tuning is what channels the flow of information and resources through a few boundary spanners. It seems possible to say, therefore, that as interorganizational dependencies become more concentrated, intraorganizational dependencies become more concentrated and power is centralized in those boundary spanners which act as nodes connecting the intraorganizational and interorganizational worlds.

There is some similarity between the above proposition and Coser's (1956) proposition that "Conflict with out-groups increases internal cohesion." This proposition is drawn from Simmel (1955), who suggests that outside conflict will strengthen the internal cohesion of the group and increase centralization:

> The group in a state of peace can permit antagonistic members within it to live with one another in an undecided situation because each of them can go his own way and can avoid collisions. A state of conflict, however, pulls the members so tightly together and subjects them to such uniform inpulse that they either must get completely along with, or completely repel, one another. . . . The fighter must "pull himself together." That is, all his energies must be, as it were, concentrated in one point so that they can be employed at any moment in any required direction.

Though Coser and Simmel refer to external conflict in particular, this can be taken as one instance of the generic category, cruciality of external relations. External dependence in terms of resources is another aspect of this cruciality. If this is so it seems plausible to say that the research on conflict supports our argument.

IN AND BEYOND DECISION MAKING

I. Power in Decision Making

Organization as partly conflictual is suggested by the notion of organization as a coalition of interests (Cyert and March, 1963) in which decision makers are "adaptively rational," rather than "omnisciently rational" economic people, adapting to the contingencies posed by the shifting and divergent interests of those actors having an interest in the organizations. These actors may be internal or external interests (Butler *et al.*, 1974) exerting whatever power they can. Again we find support for the view of organization not as a tidy monolith but as political coalition of localized interests which exhibits multiple and conflicting goals.

It is through decision making that power as dominance may be observed. Authors who emphasize the study of decision making as an approach to understanding power in organizations start by ridiculing for its naivety the straw model of rational decision making (for example, Pettigrew, 1973), which enshrines the notion of power as technique, derived especially from economic theory and portrayed in works such as Baumol (1959), Churchman (1961), and more recently Hague (1971) and Moore and Thomas (1976). But in order to cope with competing pressures from often conflicting interests trying to achieve dominance the organization is forced to use devices which "quasi-resolve conflict." This is partially achieved by the use of "acceptable level decision rules." Overall optimization by the firm might require each decision to be consistent with all the others; but in fact the acceptable level of consistency is made low enough to permit an outcome which is simply acceptable to all interests, rather than optimal to anything overall. "Sequential attention to goals" also helps to quasi-resolve conflict. Rather than commit itself to one goal or another, an organization attends first to one goal and then to another in sequence. For example, it resolves pressures for "smooth production" versus "satisfy customers" (with custom-made modifications) by doing first one and then the other. The rationality of the decision process is thus contaminated by political considerations deriving from localized interests rather than collective purpose.

Case studies such as Pettigrew's (1973) also reflect this kind of pluralism in the decision-making process. Pettigrew analyzed in detail the political goings-on between different organizational departments, each trying to influence the purchase of a computer according to its own preferences. Pettigrew's example is located in a private firm but the indications are that the public sphere is even more replete with political activity, as in Allison's (1971) "bureaucratic politics" model. The notion of bargaining looms large in these examples and is dealt with in a more formal manner by Abell (1975) who portrays organizations as a collection of "overlapping bargaining zones."

Taking a different approach to the analysis of decision making. Mintzberg *et al.* (1976) represented the decision-making process as a sequence of events, with the decision topic passing through separate "phases." The familiar "identify the problem," "search for alternatives," "evaluate possible solutions" and "select the optimum" phases of prescriptive models, however, did not capture the full complexity of the decision making process. Thus, his analysis of 25 strategic decisions revealed that multiple interferences, many of which were political in nature, slowed down the process, stopped it, sidetracked it or recycled it back to an earlier phase in a protracted, bewildering, and circuitous manner.

Further, Cohen *et al.* (1972) and March and Olsen (1976) ask us to consider "organized anarchies" in which ambiguity seems to obscure intelligible procedure in the decision-making process. Significantly, two of the defining characteristics of organized anarchies are "problematic preferences" and "fluid participation," notions which convey the political element in decision making. In organized anarchies, for example, there is no guarantee that the solutions which are adopted are generated logically from the nature of a problem. Indeed, solutions may exist independently in decision makers heads, for example as pet projects, and then be attached to problems as they arise, whether this is logically appropriate or not. Solutions are looking for problems in this case, rather than problems looking for solutions.

Finally, we are told that in complex decision situations we must "muddle through" (Lindblom, 1959) according to a "strategy of disjointed incrementalism" (Braybrooke and Lindblom, 1963), since a "synoptic" mode of decision making is impossible. For example, policy makers should continually redefine their problems, often adjusting ends to the means available rather than vice versa, thereby constantly compromising their choices, and gearing them more to the alleviation of the present, concrete social imperfections, rather than to the promotion of future goals. Of course, we know why decision making must be a disjointed process—it is always susceptible to intrusions from politically motivated parties. And incrementalism, a piecemeal inching forward step by step, is desirable in this circumstance, since it permits the flexibility needed for political compromise.

One problem with the above literature on power in decision making, however, is that it has been based on restrictive samples, often single cases, which give us little clue as to how typical these descriptions are. One suspects, for example, that politically charged aspects of organizational life are being played up to make the narratives more colorful. If so, we must treat the images they convey as caricatures only (which is not to say that we cannot learn from them). With this in mind Butler *et al.* (1977) deliberately set out to find two organizations which could be represented as contrasting caricatures, as extremes on a continuum. The empirical discovery of such variation was necessary in order to develop a set of concepts and variables by which comparisons could be made across a large number of organizations.

The first organization they studied was a university. Its structure was represented as a loosely coordinated set of subunits competing for common resources. They found it to be a prototype for Cohen *et al.'s* (1972) "garbage can model of organization choice," which caricatures universities as garbage cans in which participants grope around attempting to impose their preferred solutions on organizational problems. Decision making was racked by the infighting Thompson (1967) saw as typical of a system held together merely by the "pooled interdependence" of reliance on a common pool of resources. Small wonder that Butler *et al.* (1977) named their case "the politicking organization."

The university fitted the caricatures of the decision-making literature, but the second case, an energy utility, did not. The authors reported that the feature of the utility's decision making was its featurelessness. Meetings appeared routine, and "the possibility of alternatives seemed not to be raised." There was no noticeable pressing for new activities or competing for resources.

> Researchers found that prompts, probes, and ultimately direct questions about how resources are allocated produced puzzled and seemingly bland replies. For there was nothing much to tell.

The authors dubbed this case "paralytic" attributing its condition to the dominant power of external organizations which immobilized it.

II. Power and Modes of Decision Making

From these and other contrasting case studies Butler *et al.* (1980) have generated a set of variables and concepts for comparative research on the decision-making process. After an extensive review of the development of decision-making theory they conclude that, whilst Cyert and March's (1963) insights allow general descriptions of decision making to be made highlighting processes not in accordance with neat prescriptive models, and whilst Mintzberg *et al.* (1976) drew particular attention to the sequential nature of decision making, available concepts do not as yet allow comprehensive comparison of all dimensions of decision-making processes between organizations and between decision topics within organizations. To allow such comparisons, concepts must be formulated as variables.

Thus, drawing upon Cohen *et al.'s* (1972) metaphor of the garbage can, Butler *et al.* (1980) suggest that decision topics will *occur*, or drop into the garbage can, with varying *frequency* and *regularity*. Topics will have a particular *content*, the characteristics of which are conceived as *consequentially* or impact upon the organization, and as *equivocality*. Weick (1969) states that decision making has to do with the removal of equivocality which is taken to mean the contingencies posed by a topic to decision makers, and covers the complexity and dynamics of decisions distinguished by Axelsson and Rosenberg (1979), and the uncertainty identified by March and Simon (1958).

Once in the garbage can, topics are *scrutinized* and looked at with varying degrees of thoroughness and precision. Here is the notion of search for information inherent in the rational model of decision making. March and Simon (1958) distinguish between the all-pervading search programs of rational economic man, and the satisfying of decision makers operating under uncertainty. In searching for the needle in the proverbial haystack the satisfyer sets up an acceptable standard of sharpness and stops searching when a needle reaching this standard is found: the optimizer continues until he has found the sharpest.

Decisions are made within hierarchies and the point at which they are made is the *centrality* of decision making. Not only are some organizations more centralized than others but within an organization some decisions are more centralized than others.

Thus scrutiny and centrality are variables describing the *action* that an organization takes in decision making.

The performance of the decision-making process is expressed in the variables of *rapidity* and *continuity*. Performance is not here a normative concept but a description in the sense of saying that car A performs at 100 mph and car B at 60 mph. Whether one is better than the other depends upon the type of car required. Rapidity is perhaps the most commonly measured attribute of decision making as seen, for example, in Mintzberg *et al.'s* 25 case studies, or Cyert and March's (1963) four reported cases. Major decisions seem to take from a year or so to many years. Case studies tend to emphasize the discontinuous nature of strategic decision making, relishing reports of blockages or interruptions (Mintzberg *et al.*, 1976) induced by powerful interests, and the confusion caused by "organized anarchy" (March and Olsen, 1976: Ch. 6).

How do the notions of power as dominance and of power as technique come to bear upon the way in which decisions get made? In Pettigrew's (1973) case of a computer purchase, the manager Kenny was able to use his position to gain greater access to the decision-making apparatus than his opponents. But he was only able to do this because it was a decision involving uncertainty. If there had been a clear-cut and generally understood case for one computer above all others then Kenny's power would have been lost. It is in this way that power feeds off the uncertainty of unclear ends-means relationships and it is in this way that Hickson *et al.* (1974) were able to hypothesize, and Hinings *et al.* (1971) were able to confirm empirically, that the ability to cope with uncertainty, subject to conditions, leads to influence over a wide range of organizational decisions.

But this still does not enable us to connect the technical aspects of a decision and the interests of involved parties to the way in which decisions get made, as opposed to identifying the outcomes of specific decisions in the sense of who wins or loses (Pettigrew, 1973), or who has most influence over a range of decisions (Hinings *et al.*, 1974). Appropriate to making this connection are Thompson and Tuden's (1959) insights relating four kinds of organizational decision issues to two dimensions of the unit making the decision. Decision makers will have preferences about possible outcomes of the decision, the significant feature being the degree of agreement (or disagreement) about these outcomes. Decision makers will also hold beliefs about ends-means relationships, the significant feature being the degree of certainty (or uncertainty) about these causal beliefs (Thompson, 1967; 134).

A computational type of decision occurs when there are both agreement over possible outcomes and certainty about ends-means relationships. This type may be compared to the calculative decisions encountered in bureaucracies (Weber, 1947), or to the synoptic decisions of Lindblom (1959). Diagonally opposed to the computational decision is the inspirational decision which carries some of the connotation of satisficing (Simon, 1960) or muddling through decisions (Lindblom, 1959). Thompson and Tuden also identify the compromise decision, when decision makers are certain about ends-means relations but disagree about outcomes, and the judgmental decision when ends-means relationships are uncertain but there is agreement over preferences.

Extending Thompson and and Tuden's (1959) argument, it is not difficult to see how a preference, weighted by overwhelming power, could lead to the forcing of agreement upon other weaker troublesome interests, or to the ignoring of disagreement. Pursuing this line of thought further, it can be seen how interests feed off uncertainty about means-ends relationships and enhance their power if they cope with it (Hickson *et al.*, 1971; Crozier, 1964).

When more comprehensive concepts of decision making have been derived and empirically verified they should make possible a better understanding of how the power of interests, intermingled with technical aspects, have an impact upon decision making. It is to this end that Butler *et al.* (1980) have begun to define concepts of decision making, and that Astley *et al.* (1980) have further pursued these ideas to conceptualize decision-making mode, the manner in which solutions are chosen (e.g., quickly or slowly, incrementally or adventurously), as the product of activities in a decision-making arena. The decision-making arena is "a sphere of activity energized by the identification of a decision topic" and is represented by variables such as plurality, the number of actors involved in making the decision, and negotiability, the amount of to-ing and fro-ing, or arguing, that goes on, and so on. The exact manner in which the arena is energized depends on a) the content of the decision topic which acts as a stimulus for decision making to take place, and b) the nature of the constellation or coalition of interest units which surrounds and enters the arena (internal departments and external organizations), in terms of its distribution of power, congruence of interests, and so on (Astley *et al.*, 1980).

III. Some Research Findings

This section summarizes some preliminary empirical research findings which illuminate the above conceptual framework. These preliminary results are the outcome of current research by the authors and have emerged from a two pronged approach of research into decision making involving case studies and survey data.

a. Case Study Findings. Data gathered by attendance at some meetings, from interviews and from documents was used, in the first place, to assist in the development of the decision making concepts outlined above. Initially two organizations, a university (XU) and an electricity board (XEB), which is one of a network of distributing boards in the nationalized British electricity industry, were studied. This early data led to the caricatures of the "politicking" and the "paralytic" organization (Butler *et al.* 1977).

The term politicking was coined to refer to a decision-making process in which there is intrigue, a playing of political games, as much for its own sake as for any instrumental reason related to organizational goals. This was interpreted as a result of a power structure in which, partly because of the autonomy granted to universities through their charters and the associated method of financing, and partly because of an internal structure in which there are many competing interests for the common pool of resources. Each faculty and department is anxious to expand its own sphere of activities as resources accrue to areas of growth. This situation is exacerbated by the uncertain ends-means relationships (Thompson, 1967) and by the vagueness of educational goals.

In contrast, the paralytic organization (XEB) is one in which ends-means relationships are quite clear. The task is to distribute electricity, for which precise measurements of technical and economic efficiency exist. XEB and its evaluators in the environment (Rhenman, 1973) know when it is doing a good job, whereas XU does not. Hence there is little to argue about in XEB and decision making was observed as placid, with only an occasional ripple upon generally calm waters, with a willingness by individuals to apply themselves to routine tasks and decision making. Whereas in XU, for instance, there were fierce arguments between faculties concerning a proposal to introduce a new committee structure, in

XEB a decision to provide an improved maintenance program involved almost no argument and negotiation. As well as the comparatively routine nature of XEB's task are the external constraints imposed upon it by government rules and regulations, further adding to organizational paralysis.

Extension of the case study approach led to a more systematic examination of decision making in three organizations, XU, XEB and an additional chemical manufacturing firm, XL. In particular, some preliminary findings (Butler *et al.*, 1980) in which the decision processes for new "product" decisions in XU and XL are compared are summarized (see Table 1).

New products in XU means new teaching programs and courses, and for XL new chemical products. XU would, on the average, introduce one new course per year, whereas XL would introduce at least 20 products throughout the year. The occurrence, therefore, of new products in XL was considerably more *frequent* than in XU. The *consequentiality* of new course decisions were lower in XU than in XL because there is usually only a small increment of extra resources required and it is relatively easy to withdraw an unsuccessful course as opposed to a new chemical. But the equivocality of new course decisions is considerably higher than for new chemicals. In XU it is difficult to assess the market for new courses without test launching them. Precise technical data concerning the requirements of potential chemical product customers can, on the other hand, be obtained. Decision makers in XU tend to argue for a long time over the merits and de-merits of a new course and the outcome is usually a resistant, somewhat timid, approach to marketing a program. Such is the essence of muddling through (Lindblom, 1959).

The actual process of scrutinizing a new course decision in XU is somewhat off-hand and unsystematic (low *scrutiny*) compared to the thorough examination given to new product suggestions in XL. As well as a systematic committee procedure, which also exists in XU, proposals are subjected to scrutiny on rigorous technical and commercial criteria using calculative management techniques. Such procedures are completely lacking in XU, a fact which is undoubtedly linked to the relatively high equivocality, but low consequentiality, of new product decisions in the university.

The point at which new product decisions are made also varies between the two organizations. *Centrality* in XU was lower than in XL. In the university decisions to introduce new courses could, in effect, be made at faculty level, unless considerable further resources were required when higher-level discussions involving the Senate would be required. In the chemical firm the chief executive always became actively involved in new product decisions. Again, this finding on centrality indicates the greater

Table 1. **The University (XU) and the Firm (XL): a Comparison of Decision Making on the Same Topic: a New Output**

VARIABLE	*THE UNIVERSITY : New Courses*	*Estimated relative positions** *UNIVERSITY*	*FIRM*	*THE FIRM : New Chemicals*
Topic OCCURRENCE Frequency	About one per year, no more than two, in each faculty initiated internally, to take advantage of "market" opportunities.	LO	HI	20 or more per year usually initiated internally to take advantage of market opportunities: sometimes initiated by customer request.
Regularity	Annual.	HI	HI	Evenly distributed through year.
Topic CONTENT Consequentiality	A new course can begin with no fear of serious consequences if it fails and has to be dropped.	LO	HI	One among many outputs is not usually of major importance, but occasionally a completely new chemical has far-reaching consequences.
Equivocality	Only guides to prospects are applications for existing courses. Success eventually judged by demand figures.	HI	LO	Possible to obtain technical data from literature, from own tests, and from prospective customers who also estimate demand. Financial and (where appropriate) health and safety data available. Success eventually judged financially.

Process ACTION				
Scrutiny	Examination of proposed courses largely by committees, i.e., Faculty Committee or Academic Development Committee, sometimes with special Working Parties. Outside organizations such as secondary schools, research councils or professional institutions can be involved.	LO	HI	Groups/Committees within Research Department. New Products Committee, Capital Committee, and Company Board all consider proposals. Research Department and Development Department test them: Sales and Production Departments report. Customers and Government agencies may supply information. The departments for Sales, Production Research, Development are concerned, and sometimes Customers, etc., are consulted.
Centrality	Preparations may commence after Academic Committee approval, subject to Senate approval. Lowest grade in academic hierarchy (lecturer) will have been involved previously.	LO	HI	Managing Director decides. Production, Research, and Sales Directors will have been involved.
Process PERFORMANCE				
Rapidity	6 months to 5 years, average about 3 years.	LO	HI	6 months to 2 years, average rather less than 1 year.
Continuity	Usually recycles from committee to committee with blockages and bargaining, especially if conflict over departmental/faculty domains of work, when the customary committee consensus is unobtainable and the decision is by vote. Novel combinations of subjects into completely fresh courses are rare. Syllabus revisions evolve gradually.	LO	HI	Smooth progression, unless technical snags interrupt the process. Continual informal discussions in management offices. New products are usually within an accustomed range of chemicals and technology but novelties do occur.

*SCORING: HI/LO indicates the higher or lower of the two cases.

consequentiality of new product decisions to XL than to XU, and the greater equivocality in XU than in XL.

New course decisions in the university proceeded slowly, with an average duration of about three years, but rapidly in the firm. This undoubtedly reflects the discontinuous nature of university decision making with numerous stoppages while various interests have their say. In the firm the only reason for stoppages while considering new products appeared to be for technical reasons.

These findings came from systematic interviewing of informants in the two organizations concerning decision making. Naturally there are wide variations within each organization concerning the scores of each of these variables, some of which are reported in Wilson (1980), where one new product in the firm took thirteen years. But this was an aberration upon a process which was generally rapid.

Why the emergent patterns of decision making within an organization occur we suggest can be explained by the task and political perspectives. As XL operates within a highly competitive commercial environment it cannot afford the luxury of stops and starts in decision making. Ends-means relationships are comparatively clear and divergences of interests can be resolved more easily than in the university. Politicking in XL is limited to a comparatively small circle of senior managers (Wilson, 1980), whereas in the university interests are diverse, diffused throughout the organization and not easily resolved by reference to a common and definable rationality. In this situation local interests can feed off the cognitive limits to rationality (March and Simon, 1957) inherent in the task of a university and create the politicking type of decision making illustrated by the new course example.

b. Survey Findings. As Butler *et al.* (1980) point out most empirical studies of decision making have been based upon limited samples, with Mintzberg *et al.'s* (1976) 25 decisions being a notable exception. The authors' current research has a sample of nearly 150 decisions drawn from 30 organizations and has the aim of examining relationships between decision making variables, and between these variables and task and power variables at play in each decision and in each organization. Patterns in decision making across organizations, in the manner outlined above, and across decisions will be examined.

Although theoretical development and the case studies may have allowed fairly precise meanings and definitions to be assigned to concepts, the operational definition of decision making variables is less precise. Whilst some variables, such as rapidity, can be operationalized on *a priori* well-defined scales, other variables such as equivocality are coded into categories on a notional ordinal scale, later to be verified by techniques such as multidimensional scaling. Thus, data on equivocality for the sample of decisions can be ordered by the "hardness" of the criteria which the correctness of decisions are judged (Table 2). The hardest measure of correctness are output and cost measures and scales, and the softest, morale or feelings and image.

A dimension of the scrutiny variable is the ratio of internal sources of expertise and information to the external sources. This is assessed by the number of internal and external interest units providing information on a particular decision (Astley *et al.*, 1978).

From these and similar measures preliminary tests of interrationships between variables can be made. For instance, it was hypothesized that the number of interest units involved in a decision is directly proportional to the time taken on a decision, that is, there should be a negative correlation between the number of interest units and rapidity. However, this appears only to hold for internal units as a near zero correlation between number of external units and rapidity shows. It seems that the number of fingers in the pie only increases the time taken to make decisions when they are internal units.

Another finding suggests that organizational size is negatively correlated to rapidity; large organizations tend to take longer over decisions. This is hardly a surprising result as large organizations, for technical

Table 2. Indices of Decision Equivocality

Criteria	*Examples reported*
Output Measures	Output level, production volume
Cost Measures	Lower operating cost, cost effectiveness, economies.
Sales	Sales turnover, orders, actual sales against forecasts.
Profit	Profit targets, return on sales, earnings, financial criteria.
Quality Tests	Prototype reliability, performance of equipment, consistency of product, acceptability of outputs.
Return on Investment, etc.	Return on capital, discounted cash flows.
Efficiency Measures	Eases flow of work, staff more efficient, improved control.
Service Level	Market share, satisfies public, benefits to patients.
Personnel Measures	Better labor relations, favorable staff response, reduced labor turnover.
Image	Reputation, respect in market, identity.
Morale or Feelings	Feelings, attitudes, student opinion, lack of negative comments.
None	Difficult to judge.

Criteria by which the correctiness of a decision is reported to be judged.
Categories ordered from "*hard*" or least equivocal (numerical data directly responsive primarily to that decision) to "*soft*" or most equivocal (nonnumerical data indicative of other factors besides that decision).

reasons, bring in many specialists to deal with complex decisions. Slower decision making can therefore result from the time taken to collect and sift through the information generated. What is not emphasized in the existing literature based upon the technical nature of organization is that the mere presence of departmental interests increases the scope for internal politicking to appear in the guise of working on the task, but in fact to be the result of opportunistic self seeking behavior (Williamson, 1975). Stops and starts (low continuity) can emanate from technical problems or from political intrigue.

As already emphasized technical problems and opportunism find lush pastures in equivocality, hence, the negative correlation in our sample between rapidity and the time horizon ahead that decision makers are looking to in a decision, taken here as one indicator of equivocality.

Extending beyond the decision making processes elaborated here is the question of what happens "upstream" and "downstream" from these processes. Upstream lies the whole story of the origins of the values of interests and how they enact their environments (Weick, 1969) and of the corresponding background structure (Astley *et al.*, 1980). In this respect the population ecology model (Aldrich, 1979) may be useful in drawing our attention to the sources of variation for decision makers which will help form their causal maps (Bougon *et al.*, 1977).

Downstream aspects are to do with the outcomes of decision making. Pioneering studies of policy making (Chandler, 1962) and their successors (Stopford and Wells, 1972; Channon, 1973) have looked at outcomes in terms of the development of new structures. In fact, on closer examination, we find only one variable of outcomes contained within these studies, whether or not structure is divisionalized. Although there is a surfeit of descriptive business policy case material there is a paucity of concepts and variables of outcomes as strategy, although recent attempts have been made to fill in this gap (Child and Francis, 1976; Horvath and McMillan, 1978).

The predefinition of structure and its impact upon decision making becomes apparent in our cases and survey sample. The interests involved in a particular decision are a result of the particular internal division of labour and the external organizations, both largely outside the control of the decision makers involved in any one decision. The paralytic nature of decision making in XEB, inpart, emanates from its location within the total inter-organizational set (Evan, 1966). Similarly, the criteria used to evaluate an organization, whether a profit in XL, cost and reliability in XEB, or quality of education in XU, are a result of predefined structures. Again, these are generally unalterable with reference to an individual decision, although they may be changed when viewed over a longer time perspective. Although a model such as that used to guide the research described are capable of representing power and its effects in the decision-making process, they are not capable of taking into account the wider context within which the decision making occurs. This wider context also has implications for power, and this is the issue to which we now finally turn.

IV Power Beyond Decision Making

For political scientists such as Dahl (1958) power is synonymous with participation in decision making and can be analyzed only after "careful examination of a series of concrete decisions." Bachrach and Baratz (1970) criticize this approach on the grounds that it takes no account of the fact that power may be, and often is, exercised by confining the scope of decision making to relatively "safe" issues:

> Of course power is exercised when A participates in the making of decisions that affect B. Power is also exercised when A devoted his energies to creating or reinforcing social and political values and institutional practices that limit the scope of the political process to public consideration of only those issues which are comparatively innocuous to A. To the extent that A succeeds in doing this, B is prevented, for all practical purposes, from bringing to the fore any issues that might in their resolution be seriously detrimental to A's set of preferences.

Such a "mobilization of bias" which suppresses certain issues from the agenda so that they cannot be contested, is referred to as the "nondecision making process." Thus there are "two faces of power," one which is overt and manifested in decision making, and one which is less readily apparent since it resides in biases which escape public purview in decision-making arenas.

In a discussion which parallels that of Bachrach and Baratz in that power is exerted in unobtrusive ways outside of the process of decision making itself, Perrow (1972) draws extensively upon the work of Simon (1947) and March and Simon (1958). Here individuals in organizations are controlled not in the sense that they cannot make decisions about their organizational activities, since they do make decisions all the time, but in the sense that the decisions they make are engineered by the organization to be consistent with its requirements. Such control is unobtrusive since the organization achieves it not by constraining the actual decision making process, but by supplying the individual with premises on which the decision is made. As Perrow (1972) indicates:

> The superior has the power or tools to structure the environment or perceptions of the subordinate in such a way that he sees the proper things in the proper light. The superior actually appears to give few orders. Instead, he sets priorities and alters the flow of inputs and stimuli. The image of the order-barking boss is not there.

A major mechanism for achieving this effect is the placement of individuals in appropriate locations in the organization's channels of communication (i.e., its structure). These channels control the supply of information which the individual receives, focusing his attention in the proper directions by "screening out some parts of reality and magnifying other parts." The organization also develops a vocabulary based on "technical" categories and classifications. Anything that does not fit into these categories is not easily communicated, and so the premises on which decisions can be made are immediately limited. The selective stimuli which the individual is allowed to receive therefore effectively constrain the way in which he can define the situation. The organization thus controls behavior by immersing the individual in structural constraints which allow only "minor innovations within a complex network of established premises for action."

Blau and Schoenherr (1971) also eschew the idea that control in modern organizations is achieved primarily by virtue of superiors' power advantages over subordinates inside the decision-making situation. This kind of power, exercised through a chain of command in which superiors give orders subordinates are obligated to obey, is direct control, and is utilized only sparingly in the present day. Much more common are indirect controls which control behavior "insidiously" since they do not entail subjugation to the arbitrary will of a superior and so are not experienced as an exertion of power.

Indeed, the meaning in language itself is evidence of power (Silverman, 1970). As Hickson and McCullough (1979) put it:

> Suppose that a university staff group proposes to a committee that a new course on "Organizations" be offered. In the university many people think of sociology as a "soft" subject and of sociologists as "unreliable," whereas management is "hard-headed" and "sound"(!) If so, the first issue is not the proposed course itself, but the word(s) by which it will be known and the associated language in which it will be known and the associated language in which it will be discussed, and hence the concepts by which it will be construed. If the course should be called "Organizational Sociology" its fate may be different than if it is called "Organizational Analysis" in which case the negative associations of the word "sociology" disappear; or if (irrespective of its title) it is discussed in terms of being an exercise in theoretical sociology rather than as being a contribution to practical management. The several interest groups concerned may even spend more effort on the "language issue" than on the substantive syllabus. In such ways the whole "language" of an organization becomes an indication of its power structure, from its "cost consciousness" (or its "cheese-paring") to its "personal initiative" (or its "rat race"), with its "bosses," "pay packets" and "absenteeism." This is a major factor in the complexity and protractedness of many decision processes.

This same basic theme emerges again, in different terms, in the work of Baumgartner *et al.* (1976), who refer to it as the exercise of "meta-power''. Rather than focusing on specific relationships, administrators can design and control the total social context within which others are acting. They need not be concerned with influencing every particular activity, for they can be certain that the long-run course of events will benefit them. The exertion of meta-power, then, is:

> Attempts to structure or re-structure the social and cultural matrix within which power activities are to be played out. . . . That is control over relationships and social structure.

An example might be the arrangement of tasks in a manner that requires little interaction between individuals. Isolation of individuals in terms of workflow then inhibits communication between them and preempts their formation into political coalitions which might act as a challenge to management's position of power. Such preempting again represents an exercise of power outside of the decision making situation.

Consider the presumption that increased participation in decision making and discretion in work activity increase the power of lower participants. Earlier we discussed the paradox here. The increase in power may be more apparent than real. Evan (1976) has summarized the reasons why increased participation may even decrease the power of the participants. First, workers given a share in decision making frequently become sympathetic to management's point of view. Second, management's greater technical expertise sustains their ''expert power'' as we have already noted. Third, workers feel more committed to decisions in which they have participated with the result that their implementation is greatly facilitated and direct management control becomes unnecessary.

This notion of power beyond decision making, then, brings into focus the difference between an exertion of power and the experience of an exertion of power. It warns us not to be misled by the latter since power can be exercised in ways that are not easily recognized as acts of dominance. Indeed, if anything, the degree to which power can be successfully exerted is likely to be inversely related to the extent to which such an exertion is experienced by the dominated actor. This follows since actors will only countervail with recalcitrant moves if they realize they are engaged in a power struggle in the first place. As Blau and Schoenherr (1971) put it, ''slavedrivers went out of fashion not because they were cruel, but because they were inefficient.''

BALANCE OF POWER

With or without the velvet glove, the exertion of power in and between organizations rests on the institutionalization of those organizations as systems of power. We have already referred to the gradually evolving institutionalization of the structure of an organization. This process, the embodiment of values in organizational forms, is often termed institution-building (Ganesh, 1979, 1980). What is not so often recognized is that it is a construction of a balance of power. Ganesh (1980) admits that his analysis of institution-building does not cover power.

Yet an organization is at any one time a balance of power. A shifting one, perhaps, though the evidence we have reviewed implies that it shifts relatively superficially upon a stable basic pattern of differentiation. In turn that rests upon a similarly shifting legitimacy.

The legitimation of organizations as institutionalized systems of power is formally denoted by the acts and decrees and regulations of governments. In Britain, for example, there are the generic Companies Acts of Parliament which define how a corporation may be established and frame the powers of owners and employees and suppliers and customers. There are specific Acts which establish, for instance, the state Electricity Boards or the British Broadcasting Corporation. The Local Government Act establishes city and county governments throughout the land. And so on.

Yet:

> the acquisition and use of powerful resources by organizations does not go unquestioned. In most if not all "organizational societies" there are groups, large or small, blatant or concealed, which deny the legitimacy of the use of resources by certain organizations (Hickson and McCullough, 1979).

There are demonstrations in Europe and North America and Japan against those organizations developing nuclear energy. There is resistance to new airports and new airplanes (for example, the Franco-British Concorde). There is pressure against organizations which manufacture products such as cigarettes which are a health hazard. In Eastern Europe the press and other media convey complaining "voice" (Kolarska and Aldrich, 1980) some part of which may go beyond complaints to question the legitimacy of what is done.

Such anti-organization activities are just one example of the curious phenomenon that "who says power says counter-power." The balance of power may be tilted one way or the other but there is no such thing as complete and utter powerlessness. The positive power to induce an activity is offset by the negative power to resist it (Rus, 1980). Power is "a holistic dialectical process in which induction and resistance simultaneously condition and exclude each other" in a "cyclical relationship" (Rus, 1980). Thus organizations are at one and the same time jostling coalitions of diverse internal and external interests in which the power of one constrains the power of another, *and* institutionalized hierarchies in which power runs up as well as down. At first sight Michels (1949) and Mechanic (1962) cannot both be right. The one says there is in organizations a dominant oligarchy, a power elite, because of their unique administrative and political expertise: the other says that the lower participants in organizations have power because of their nonsubstitutable know-how. But both are right because both powers exist each constraining the other. Organizations are composites of what Rus (1980) would see as unending Hegelian contradictions.

This is so in power between organizations as much as in power within organizations. Galbraith (1967) sees giant manufacturing organizations giving rise to giant retail organizations which take their products and match selling power with buying power. Giant employer corporations give rise to giant trade unions, and so on. Power gives rise to countervailing power among the organizational colossi of contemporary economies.

We can begin to see such a scene taking shape decision by decision in organizations for any one major decision involves a series of interested parties, internal departments, sections, and committees, and external suppliers or buyers or governments, and so on, (Astley *et al.*, 1978, 1979). The influence they exert differs between different types of decision and also between different types of organization. There are comparatively self-sufficient organizations in which internal power matters most, and other dominated by external interests. There are decisions taken with scarcely a glance beyond the bounds of the organization and others taken very much under the influence of outside interests.

It is within the decision making arenas of organizations that we can see interests at work in a fine balancing act. Thrown into the arena are the technical problems concerned with working toward organizational goals, and also the power and nature of those interests representing both the collective purposes of organization and the localized purposes of specific groups. But we must be wary. Interested parties do not always flaunt their power nor their intentions for all to see. Organizational power can be a subterranean process, difficult to uncover, involving unobtrusive structuring of the rules, and plainly visible only at crucial moments.

REFERENCES

Abell, P. (1975) *Organizations as Bargaining and Influence Systems*. London: Heinemann.

Aldrich, H. (1979) *Organizations and Environments*. Englewood Cliffs, N.J.: Prentice Hall.

Allison, G. T. (1971) *Essence of Decision: Explaining the Cuban Missile Crisis*. Boston: Little Brown.

Allport, F. H. (1933) *Institutional Behavior*. Chapel Hill, N.C.: University of North Carolina Press.

Argyris, C. (1957) *Personality and Organization*. New York: Harper and Row.

——— (1972) *The Applicability of Organizational Sociology*. London: Cambridge University Press.

Astley, W. Graham (1978) "Sources of Power in Organizational Life." Unpublished Ph.D. dissertation, University of Washington.

Astley, W. Graham, Richard J. Butler, David J. Hickson, Geoffrey Mallory, and David C. Wilson (1978) "How Many Fingers in the Pie." Presented to Public Administration Committee of the Joint University Council for Social and Public Administration, York, England (September).

——— (1979) "Cross-Institutional Decision Making: Theory and Results." Paper presented at EGOS (European Group for Organizational Studies) Colloquium, Noordwijk aan Zee, The Netherlands (June).

Astley, W. Graham, Runo Axelsson, Richard J. Butler, David J. Hickson and David C. Wilson (1980) "Processual Concepts and Dialectics of Strategic Decision Making (in draft).

Axelsson, Runo and Lennart Rosenberg (1979) "Decision Making and Organizational Turbulence," *Acta Sociologica*, 22, 1 45–61.

Bachrach, P. and M. S. Baratz (1970) *Power and Poverty: Theory and Practice*. New York: Oxford University Press.

Baumgartner, T., W. Buckley, T. Burns and P. Schuster (1976) "Meta-Power and the Structuring of Social Hierarchies. In: Tom Burns and Walter Buckley (eds.), *Power and Conflict: Social Structures and their Transformation*. London: Sage Publications Ltd.

Baumol, W. J. (1959) *Business Behaviour, Value and Growth*. New York: Macmillan.

Bennis, W. (1966) *Changing Organizations*. New York: McGraw-Hill.

Benson, J. Kenneth (1975) "The Interorganizational Network as a Political Economy," *Administrative Science Quarterly*, 20: 229–249 (June).

Berger, P. L. and T. Luckmann (1966) *The Social Construction of Reality*. New York: Doubleday.

Blau, P. M. (1964) *Exchange and Power in Social Life*. New York: Wiley.

Blau, P. M. and R. A. Schoenherr (1971) *The Structure of Organizations*. New York: Basic Books.

Bougon, Michel, Karl Weick and Din Binkhorst (1977) "Cognition in Organizations: An Analysis of the Utrecht Jazz Orchestra," *Administrative Science Quarterly*, 4: 606–639 (December).

Braybrooke, D. and C. E. Lindblom (1963) *A Strategy of Decision*. New York: Free Press.

Broekmeyer, M. J. (1978) *De Arbeidsraad in Zuidslavie*. Meppel: Boom.

Butler, Richard J. (1976) "Relative Deprivation and Power: A Switched Replication Design Using Time Series Data of Strike Rates in American and British Coal Mining," *Human Relations*, 19 7: 623–642 (July).

Butler, Richard J. (1980) "User Satisfaction with a Service: Power, Task and the Personal Touch." Forthcoming in *Journal of Management Studies* (Winter).

Butler, Richard J. David J. Hickson and Arthur McCullough (1974) "Power in the Organizational Coalition." Paper presented to International Sociological Association, Toronto (August).

Butler, Richard J., David J. Hickson, David C. Wilson and R. Axelsson (1977) "Organizational Power, Politicking and Paralysis." *Organizational and Administrative Sciences*, 8(4): 44–59 (Winter).

Butler, Richard J., W. Graham Astley, David J. Hickson, Geoffrey Mallory and David C. Wilson (1980) "Strategic Decision Making in Organizations: Concepts of Content and Process." To appear in *International Studies of Management and Organization*.

Chandler, Alfred D. (1962) *Strategy and Structure: Chapters in the History of the Industrial Enterprise*. Cambridge, Mass.: MIT Press.

Channon, Derek F. (1973) *The Strategy and Structure of British Enterprise*. Boston: Division of Research, Graduate School of Business Administration, Harvard University.

Child, John (1972) "Organization Structure, Environment and Performance: The Role of Strategic Choice," *Sociology*, 6: 1–22.

Child, John and Arthur Francis (1976) "Strategy Formulation as a Structured Process." Working paper, University of Aston Management Centre, Birmingham, England.

Churchman, C. W. (1961) *Prediction and Optimal Decision*. Englewood Cliffs, N.J.: Prentice-Hall.

Clegg, S. (1975) *Power, Rule and Domination*. London: Routledge and Kegan Paul.

——— (1979) *The Theory of Power and Organization*. London: Routledge and Kegan Paul.

Cohen, Michael D., James G. March and Johan P. Olsen (1972) "A Garbage Can Model of Organizational Choice," *Administrative Science Quarterly*, 17(1): 1–25.

Coser, L. (1956) *The Functions of Social Conflict*. London: Routledge and Kegan Paul.

Crozier, M. (1964) *The Bureaucratic Phenomenon*. London: Tavistock.

——— (1973) "The Problem of Power," *Social Research*, 40(2): 211–228.

Cyert, R. M. and J. G. March. (1963) *A Behavioural Theory of the Firm*. Englewood Cliffs, N.J.: Prentice-Hall.

Dachler, H. Peter and Bernhard Wilpert (1978) "Conceptual Dimensions and Boundaries of Participation in Organizations: A Critical Education," *Administrative Science Quarterly*, 23(1): 1–39 (March).

Dahl, Robert A. (1958) "A Critique of the Ruling Elite Model," *American Political Science Review*, 52.

Dobbins, R. and R. J. Briston (1978) *The Growth and Impact of Institutional Investors*, Institute of Chartered Accountants in England and Wales.

Drucker, P. F. (1964) *Managing for Results*. New York: Harper and Row.

Dubin, Robert (1963) "Power, Function and Organization," *Pacific Sociological Review*, 6.

Durkheim, E. (1933) *The Rules of Sociological Method*, trans. Sarah A. Solovav and John H. Mueller. Glenco, Ill.: Free Press.

Emerson, P. E. (1962) "Power-Dependence Relations," *American Sociological Review*, 27.

Emery, F. E. and E. L. Trist (1965) "The Causal Texture of Organizational Environments," *Human Relations*, 18.

Etzioni, A. (1961) *A Comparative Analysis of Complex Organizations*. Glencoe, Ill.: Free Press.

Evan, W. (1966) "The Organization-Set: Toward a Theory of Interorganizational Relations." In *Approaches to Organizational Design*, James Thompson (ed.). Pittsburgh: University of Pittsburgh Press.

——— (1976) *Organization Theory*. New York: Wiley.

French, J. R. P. and B. Raven. (1959) "The Bases of Social Power. In D. Cartwright (ed.) *Studies in Social Power*. Ann Arbor: University of Michigan, pp. 150–167.

Galbraith, J. K. (1967) *The New Industrial Estate*. London: Hamish Hamilton.

Gamson, W. (1967) *Power and Discontent*. Homewood, Ill: Dorsey Press.

Ganesh, S. R. (1979) "From Thin Air to Firm Ground: Empirical Guidelines for a General Processual Model of Institution Building," *Human Relations*.

——— (forthcoming 1980) "Institution Building for Social and Organizational Change," *Organization Studies*.

Gouldner, A. W. (1959) "Organizational Analysis." In *Sociology Today*, Robert K. Merton, Leonard Broom, and Leonard S. Cottrell, Jr. (eds.). New York: Basic Books.

Greenwood, R. and C. R. Hinings. (1976) "Centralization Revisited" (Research Note), *Administrative Science Quarterly*, 21(1): 151–155.

Guetzkow, H. (1966) "Relations among Organizations." In R. V. Bowers (ed.), *Studies on Behavior in Organizations*. Athens: University of Georgia Press, pp. 13–44.

Hague, D. C. (1971) *Managerial Economics: Analysis for Business Decisions*. London: Longman.

Haire, M. (1962) "The Concept of Power and the Concept of Man." In G. Strother (ed.) *Social Science Approaches to Business Behavior*. Homewood, Ill: Dorsey Press.

Hawley, A. (1968) "Human Ecology." In David L. Sills (ed.), *The International Encyclopedia of the Social Sciences*. New York: Crowell-Collier and Macmillan.

Hickson, David J. (1961) "Motives of Workpeople Who Restrict Their Output," *Occupational Psychology*, 35(3): 111–121.

Hickson, D. J. and A. McCullough (1979) "Power in Organizations." In K. Thompson and J. G. Salaman (eds.), *Control and Ideology in Organizations*. Open University Press, London.

Hickson, D. J., C. R. Hinings, C. A. Lee, R. E. Schneck and J. M. Pennings (1971) "A Strategic Contingencies' Theory of Intraorganizational Power," *Administrative Science Quarterly:* 216–229 (June).

Hickson, D. J. and C. J. McMillan (forthcoming 1980) *Organization and Nation: The Aston Programme IV*. Lexington, Mass.: Saxon House/D.C. Heath.

Hickson, D. J., C. J. McMillan, K. Azumi and D. Horvath (1979) "Grounds for Comparative Organization Theory." In C. J. Lammers and D. J. Hickson (eds.) *Organizations Alike and Unlike*. London: Routledge and Kegan Paul.

Hinings, C. R., D. J. Hickson, J. M. Pennings, and R. E. Schneck (1974) "Structural Conditions of Intraorganizational Power," *Administrative Science Quarterly*, 19(1): 22–43.

Hofstede, G. (1979) "Hierarchical Power Distance in Forty Countries." In C. J. Lammers and D. J. Hickson (ed.), *Organizations Alike and Unlike*. London: Routledge and Kegan Paul.

Horvath, Dezso and Charles McMillan (1978) "Strategy, Structure and Performance: A Contingency Model." Working paper, Faculty of Administrative Studies, York University, Toronto.

Jacobs, D. (1974) "Dependency and Vulnerability: An Exchange Approach to the Control of Organizations," *Administrative Science Quarterly*, 19(1): 45–59.

Kavcic, Bogdan, V. Rus, and A. S. Tannenbaum (1971) "Control, Participation and Effectiveness in Four Yugoslav Industrial Organizations," *Administrative Science Quarterly*, 16(1): 74–86.

Kiezun, W. (1977) *Autonomization of Organizational Units*. Warsaw.

King, Ambrose Yeo-Chi (1977) "A Voluntarist Model of Organization: the Maoist version and its critique," *British Journal of Sociology* 28(3): 363–374.

Kolarska, Lena and Howard Aldrich (forthcoming 1980) "Exit, Voice and Silence: Consumer's and Manager's Responses to Organizational Decline," *Organization Studies*, 1(1).

Kuc, B., D. J. Hickson and C. J. McMillan (forthcoming 1980) "Centrally Planned Late Development: A Comparison of Polish Organizations with British, Japanese and Swedish Equivalents," *Organization Studies*.

Lawrence, P. R. and J. W. Lorsch (1967) *Organization and Environment: Managing Differentiation and Integration*. Cambridge, Mass.: Harvard Graduate School of Business Administration.

Lehman, E. H. (1977) *A Macrosociology of Politics*. New York: Columbia University Press.

Levine, S. and P. F. White (1961) "Exchange as a Conceptual Franework for the Study of Interorganizational Relationships," *Administrative Science Quarterly*, 5.

Likert, R. (1961) *New Patterns of Management*. New York: McGraw-Hill.

Lindbeck, Assar. (1971) *The Political Economy of the New Left: An Outsider's View*. New York: Harper and Row.

Lindblom, Charles (1959) "The Science of 'Muddling Through,'" *Public Administration Review*, 19: 79–88.

Locke, E. A., D. B. Feran, V. M. McCaleb, K. N. Shaw and A. T. Denny (1979) "The Relative Effectiveness of Four Methods of Motivating Employee Performance." Proceedings of NATO Conference on Changes in the Nature and Quality of Working Life. New York: Wiley.

Lukes, S. (1974) *Power: A Radical View*. London: Macmillan.

Lund, R. (forthcoming 1980) "Power and Indirect Participation: The Danish Experience," *Organization Studies*.

Macaulay, S. (1963) "Non-contractual relations in Business: A Preliminary Study," *American Sociological Review*. 28: 55–57.

Marawski, Witold (1978) *"Socialist Industrialization in Poland: The Doctrine, the System of Decision Making, Uncontrolled Phenomena."* Warsaw: Institute of Philosophy and Sociology.

March, J. G. and J. P. Olsen (1976) *Ambiguity and Choice in Organizations*. Norway: Universitetsforlaget.

March, J. G. and H. A. Simon (1958) *Organizations*. New York: Wiley.

Margulies, N., and A. P. Raia (1972) *Organizational Development: Values, Process and Technology*. New York: McGraw-Mill.

McGregor, D. (1960) *The Human Side of Enterprise*. New York: McGraw-Hill.

Mechanic, David (1962) "Sources of Power of Lower Participants in Complex Organizations," *Administrative Science Quarterly*, 7: 349–364.

Meyer, John W. and B. Rowan (1977) "Institutionalized Organizations: Formal Structure as Myth and Ceremony," *American Journal of Sociology*, 83(2).

Michels, R. (1949) *Political Parties*. Glencoe, Ill.: Free Press. 1949.

Mintzberg, Henry, Duru Raisinghani, and Andre Theoret (1976) "The Structure of 'Unstructured' Decision Processes," *Administrative Science Quarterly*, 21(2) 246–275 (June).

Moore, P. G. and H. Thomas (1976) *The Anatomy of Decisions*. Baltimore: Penguin. 1976.

Mouzelis, N. (1967) *Organization and Bureaucracy*. London: Routledge and Kegan Paul.

Mulder, M. (1971) "Power Equalization Through Participation?" *Administrative Science Quarterly*, 16(1): 31–39.

Perrow, C. (1970) "Departmental Power and Perspective in Industrial Firms." In Mayer N. Zald (ed.) *Power in Organizations*. Nashville, Tenn.: Vanderbilt University Press.

——— (1972) *Complex Organizations: A Critical Essay*. Glenview, Ill.: Scott, Foresman.

Pettigrew, A. (1973) *The Politics of Organizational Decision Making*. London: Tavistock.

Pfeffer, Jeffrey (1972) "Merger as a Response to Organizational Interdependence," *Administrative Science Quarterly*, 17.

Pfeffer, Jeffrey and Philip Nowak (1976) "Joint Ventures and Inter-organizational Dependence," *Administrative Science Quarterly*, 21.

Pfeffer, J. and G. R. Salancik (1978) *The External Control of Organizations: A Resource Dependence Perspective*. New York: Harper and Row.

Presthus, R. (1979) *The Organizational Society*, rev. ed. London: Macmillan.

Pugh, Derek S., David J. Hickson, Christopher R. Hinings and Christopher Turner (1968) "Dimensions of Organization Structure," *Administrative Science Quarterly*, 13: 65–105.

——— (1969) "The Context of Organization Structure," *Administrative Science Quarterly*, 14.

Rhenman, Eric (1973) *Organization Theory for Long Range Planning*. New York: Wiley.

Robinson, Joan (1973) *Economic Management–China 1972*. London: Anglo Chinese Educational Institute.

Rus, Veljko (forthcoming 1980) "Positive and Negative Power: Thoughts on the Dialectic of Power," *Organization Studies*, 1(1).

Salaman, Graeme (1978) "Towards a Sociology of Organizational Structure," *The Sociological Review*, 3(26).

Sayles, L. R. (1958) *Behavior of Industrial Work Groups*. New York: Wiley.

Scheff, Thomas J. (1961) "Control over Policy by Attendants in a Mental Hospital," *Journal of Health and Human Behavior*, 2.

Scott, William G., Terrence R. Mitchell and Newman S. Peery (1980) "Organizational Convergence." In Paul C. Nystrom and William H. Starbuck (eds.), *The Handbook of Organizational Design: Remodelling Organizations and their Environments*, Vol. 2. New York: Oxford University Press.

Selznick, P. (1949) *IVA and the Grass Roots*. Berkeley, Calif.: University of California Press. 1949.

Shephard, H. and P. R. Blake (1961) "Changing Behavior Through Cognitive Change," *Human Organization*, 21.

Silverman, D. (1970) *The Theory of Organizations: A Sociological Framework*. New York Basic Books.

Simmel, G. (1955) *Conflict*, trans, Kurt H. Wolff. Glencoe, Ill.: Free Press.

Simon, H. A. (1947) *Administrative Behaviour*. Glencoe, Ill.: Free Press.

——— (1960) *The New Science of Management Decision*. New York: Harper and Row.

——— (1962) "The Architecture of Complexity," *Proceedings of the American Philosophical Society*, 106: 467–482 (December).

Stopford, J. M. and L. T. Wells, Jr. (1972) *Managing the Multinational Enterprise-Organization of the Firm and Ownership of the Subsidiaries*. New York: Basic Books.

Strauss, G. (1963) "Some Notes on Power Equalization." In H. A. Leavitt (ed.), *The Social Science of Organizations*. Englewood Cliffs, N.J.: Prentice-Hall. pp. 39–84.

Tannenbaum, A. S. (1968) *Control in Organizations*. New York: McGraw-Hill.

Tannenbaum, A. S. and R. A. Cooke (1979) "Organizational Control: A Review of Studies Employing the Control Graph Method." In C. J. Lammers and D. J. Hickson (eds.), *Organizations Alike and Unlike*. London: Routledge and Kegan Paul.

Thompson, J. D. (1967) *Organizations in Action*. New York: McGraw-Hill.

Thompson, J. D. and Arthur Tuden (1956) "Strategies, Structures and Processes of Organizational Decision." In J. D. Thompson (ed.), *Comparative Studies in Administration*. Pittsburgh: University of Pittsburgh Press.

Thompson, J. D. and William McEwen (1958) "Organizational Goals and Environment: Goalsetting as an Interaction Process," *American Sociological Review*, 23: 23–31 (February).

Wall, T. D. and J. A. Lischeron (1977) *Worker Participation: A critique of the literature and some fresh evidence*. New York: McGraw-Hill.

Warren, Roland (1967) "The Interorganizational Field as a Focus for Investigation," *Administrative Science Quarterly*, 12.

Weber, M. (1947) *The Theory of Social and Economic Organization*, Trans. A. M. Henderson and Talcott Parsons. Glencoe, Ill.: Free Press.

Weick, K. (1969) *The Social Psychology of Organizing*. Reading, Mass: Addison-Wesley.

Whyte, M. K. (1973) "Bureaucracy and Modernization in China: The Maoist Critique," *American Sociological Review*, 38: 149–163.

Williamson, Oliver E. (1975) *Markets and Hierarchies: Analysis and Antitrust Implications: A Study in the Economics of Organization*. New York: Free Press.

Wilson, David C. (1980) "Strategic Decision Making in Organizations: Six Case Studies Illustrating the Role of Task, Power and Pace in Three Organizations." Unpublished doctoral thesis, University of Bradford Management Centre, Bradford England.

Woodward, J. (1965) *Industrial Organization: Theory and Practice*. New York: Oxford University Press.

Zeitlin, M. (1974) "Corporate Ownership and Control: The Large Corporations and the Capitalist Class," *American Journal of Sociology*, 79: 1073–1119.

Part II
Decision Making Processes

[5]

Journal of Management Studies 25:1 January 1988
0022-2380 $3.50

SPORADIC, FLUID AND CONSTRICTED PROCESSES: THREE TYPES OF STRATEGIC DECISION MAKING IN ORGANIZATIONS[1]

DAVID CRAY

GEOFFREY R. MALLORY
Carleton University, Ottawa

Richard J. Butler

David J. Hickson
University of Bradford

David C. Wilson
University of Warwick

ABSTRACT

Using 136 cases of strategic decision-making described by a number of variables drawn from the literature, three distinct types of decision-making processes are found. These are termed sporadic, fluid and constricted processes. They are parsimonious characterizations of decision-making processes which, given the variety of the 30 organizations from which the cases are drawn, should be generalizable to a wide range of contexts.

INTRODUCTION

For four decades the importance of decision-making for the study organizations has been recognized. Beginning with Simon's (1947) pioneering analysis of administration as a system for structuring decision-making, this process has been allotted a key place in organizational theory. More recently, the focus on the allocation of power in organizations and the use of organizational power in society has brought attention to the decision-making process as the means through which power is enacted (Hickson *et al.*, 1981; McNeil, 1978; Mintzberg, 1983; Pfeffer, 1981; Wilson *et al.*, 1982). At the same time the recognition of organizations as sources of social change has focused more attention on the way that decisions taken within organizations affect their surroundings (Clegg and Dunkerley, 1980; Colignon and Cray, 1980; Pfeffer and Salancik, 1978). Thus the process of making organizational decisions is important not just for the success or failure of the organization but for the allocation of resources in society.

Address for reprints: Professor David Cray, School of Business, Carleton University, Ottawa, Canada.

Much of the work on decision-making has considered the strategies that organizations pursue (Miles and Snow, 1978; Mintzberg and Waters, 1982). However, as Mintzberg and Waters (1982) have pointed out, strategy can be seen as a pattern in a stream of decisions. It seems likely, therefore, that the way decisions are made, the structure of the decision process itself, may fashion decision outcomes and hence strategies that organizations follow (Cray *et al.*, 1986). Mohr (1982, p. 158) has argued that the link between decision process and decision outcome is so intimate that 'the process is itself an outcome'. Because the way the decision is taken influences the information gathered, the options considered, and the arenas in which the action takes place, understanding the strategies of organizations inevitably requires a clearer comprehension of the process of decision-making.

Trying to comprehend the decision-making process analytically is frustrated by the convolutions and variety of the process. One needs only to consider the different sources of information, the groups involved, the possible disruptions *etc.* to see the combinations of events that may occur. Since these elements are combined in a sequence which is rarely linear, but repeats stages one or more times, the problem is compounded. When one tries to understand the process over a variety of organizations, topics and settings, the task of constructing a simplifying yet inclusive framework becomes formidable. As Astley *et al.* (1982) have argued, most researchers into decision-making have been forced to limit the scope of their investigations by focusing on a few cases and/or by concentrating on a few aspects of the decision-making process.

Early case studies such as those by Allison (1969, 1971), by Cyert, Simon and Trow (1956), and by Pettigrew (1973) provided insight into specific choice situations, but they have not been sufficiently expanded by comprehensive comparative research. There have been studies which have brought together larger numbers of cases which were recorded by different individuals such as the 25 cases analysed by Mintzberg, Raisinghani and Theoret (1976) or the 13 discussed by March and Olsen (1976). Axelsson and Rosenberg (1979) used structured interviews in their comparison of decision making in 20 Swedish organizations and Stein (1981a, 1981b) analysed 64 mailed questionnaires returned from an unspecified sample of managers and organizations. However, difficulties of comparison across cases remain, samples have been small, and the validity of data collected by mailed questionnaires for a process as complex as strategic decision-making has yet to be demonstrated. Drenth *et al.* (1979) increased the coverage of decisions in their study, examining 103 cases, but at the cost of a narrow focus on the influence of hierarchical levels. More recently Nutt (1984) collected 73 cases in health-related organizations to produce a typology. Quinn (1980) returned to the case study tack in acquiring in-depth information by interviewing managers in nine business corporations.

Of these studies, that by Mintzberg, Raisinghani and Theoret (1976) is one of the most ambitious in combining depth and breadth of coverage. Using data collected by teams of students, they analysed 25 strategic decisions, From these they identified seven distinct types of decision process and the order and frequency of their appearance. The seven derived types are based on a substantial sample of varied organizations and include several different aspects of the decision-making process rather than focusing on a single attribute. At the same time the proposed typology is made less useful because it is open-ended. Given that there are as many as seven decision types for just 25 cases, there are very few cases to substantiate each type. More importantly, the twelve elements that Mintzberg, Raisinghani, and Theoret employed distinguish the seven types basically by their appearance, repetition and ordering. This makes it easy to visualize a particular process, but without operationally defined concepts it is difficult to analyse other decisions in the same way. It also inhibits more general statements about the contribution of each element to the overall process or the influence of other factors on these elements. Even though the scope of this pioneering study is larger than most, and it pointed the way ahead, the road to a comprehensive model seems still to be a long one.

The Bradford studies (Hickson *et al.*, 1986) are an attempt to expand the study of strategic decision making in both depth and breadth. A large number of cases was examined using a consistent set of concepts. The data collection covered a wide variety of organizations and included more than one case per organization. Six of the cases were examined in great detail, and all provided descriptive narratives as well as information on numerous aspects of the decision-making process, thus avoiding one of the main constraints of earlier studies. These data are used to respond to Mohr's call for an adequate description of decision making processes as the first step toward a theory of decision making (Mohr, 1982, pp. 158–67) by distinguishing three analytically and empirically derived characterizations of the decision making process.

THE ELEMENTS OF THE DECISION-MAKING PROCESS

Decision processes are composed of a number of different elements. Over the years many such elements have been selected, singly or in combination, as the major variables for specific studies. As Astley *et al.* (1982) have argued, this selective emphasis on either the technical or the political view of the decision process includes not only elements of process but of decision outcomes and implementation. In this study we attempted to separate process, outcome and implementation and to focus only on the process of decision making.

When a decision opportunity arises one of the main activities is the collection of information about the issue and possible alternative solutions. This aspect of the decision-making process, which we call scrutiny, includes a number of routines that may be used by the organization (Cyert and March, 1963, pp. 79–80). It is similar to Hage's (1980, p. 117) variable, 'the extent to which the interest groups seek facts relevant to the decision issue' and to Mintzberg, Raisinghani and Theoret's (1976) idea of search. In this study it is characterized by four variables. The first of these is the number of sources consulted in the search for information. The amount of *expertise* thus called upon influences other aspects of the decision-making process by drawing interests into the decision arena whose contribution must be evaluated and integrated with that from other sources (Astley *et al.*, 1982).

When information comes from multiple sources, decision-makers' confidence in its reliability will vary. If there is great *disparity* in the confidence accorded to different sources, then the decision-making process may need some filter mechanism. The sources tapped by the scrutiny process may also differ by their position relative to the organization. For reasons of cost and control internal information is preferable, but organizations are often forced to turn to outside sources for information on competitors, financial arrangements, or simply for technical expertise which the organization lacks (Simon, 1947, pp. 167–8). The *externality* of scrutiny we measured as the ratio of the confidence in external information to that placed in all information.

Finally, information may be gathered with more or less *effort* (Cyert and March, 1963, pp. 79–80; Mintzberg, Raisinghani and Theoret, 1976). A search may involve no more than the recall of actions taken in similar circumstances or a quick search of the files. It may also, as it did in a number of the decisions examined in this study, go as far as the formation of working parties in order to collect specific information and subject it to evaluation and synthesis.

A further important aspect of the decision process is the interaction that occurs between decision-makers. Much of this is *informal interaction* during which the substance of the decision is discussed in hallway conversations, over lunch, or during brief visits to colleagues' offices. At some point in almost all strategic decisions, the process becomes more structured and *formal interaction* takes place, in meetings of committees, special purpose working groups or project teams (Mallory *et al.*, 1983). The balance between informal and formal interaction may differ widely according to the substance and setting of the decision, as March and Romelaer's (1976) study of four academic decisions illustrates.

Another feature of interaction is the scope of negotiations that occur when the decision is being taken. Numerous authors, including Abell (1975), Mintzberg, Raisinghani and Theoret (1976) and Pettigrew (1973), have pointed to negotiation as one of the central dynamics in decision making. The *scope for negotiation* may be so restricted that a single individual will make the decision on the basis of computations. In other cases there will be considerable latitude for discussion and dissension before an alternative is selected (Thompson and Tuden, 1959).

As Mintzberg, Raisinghani and Theoret (1976) point out, few strategic decisions are taken in a linear manner. There are delays, reconsiderations and interruptions. This aspect of decision making we call flow. One dimension of flow is the length and occurrence of *disruptions* in the decision process. A second dimension is *impedance* or the intractability of causes of delays. These can range from a delay caused by scheduling a meeting to those caused by the active opposition of interested groups.

During the process of arriving at a decision attention is frequently drawn to the time it is taking to get there. As the decision is seen to have wider ramifications for the organization, there is pressure to take more time so as to ensure a correct outcome (Thompson and Tuden, 1959). With this there is always the countervailing pressure to stop talking and make a decision. In measuring the duration of the decision process, we found it necessary to break decision time into two components. *Gestation time* is the interval from the first mention of the issue by someone in the organization until the beginning of specific action taken toward making a decision, *e.g.* a meeting called or information gathered. *Process time* is the interval from the initiation of specific action towards a decision to the moment when the final decision is authorized for implementation.

The final aspect of the decision-making process included in the study is the centrality of the decision or the *level* at which it was authorized. Although centralization has long been an important variable in the discussion of organization structure (Child, 1973; Pugh and Hickson, 1976) it has not received similar attention in the decision making literature even though centralization is most often measured by the level at which certain decisions are made (Blau and Schoenherr, 1971). Certainly the process of decision-making will look very different if the outcome can be authorized by a divisional manager than if it must be approved by the board of directors or superiors in a separate controlling company. For a complete description of the measures of the variables described above see the appendix.

Table I. Aspects of the strategic decision-making process

Scrutiny
Expertise
Disparity
Externality
Effort
Interaction
Informal interaction
Formal interaction
Scope for negotiation
Flow
Disruption
Impedance
Duration
Gestation time
Process time
Centrality
Level

The five aspects of the decision-making process with their associated variables shown in table I provide an extensive, but by no means exhaustive, characterization of the decision process. The proposed scheme allows us to categorize a given decision by the amount and type of search that went into providing information so that the decision could be taken. It provides three dimensions on which we may examine the interaction that takes place over the interpretation of this information as well as other, more political issues associated with the decision. The trajectory (Hage, 1980, pp. 116–24) of the decision process in terms of both the time it took and the disruptions that may prolong it, is captured in the flow and duration variables. Finally, the level to which the final outcome had to be referred before the decision process was completed rounds out our description.

Our characterization of the strategic decision-making process differs from those of two other large-scale empirical studies (Mintzberg, Raisinghani and Theoret, 1976; DIO International Research Team, 1983) in that it applies variables to the overall process. The methodological aim is to free the study of process from being further tied to the reiteration of single case narratives, going beyond the analysis of phases to attempt an overall characterization of historical narratives.

It tests the potential of using a series of variables to describe the processual features of each case as a means of synthesizing the character of process comparatively. Thus, who spoke to whom is summarized in the overall amount of interaction (some processes are busier than others), what interruptions and recycles occurred (Mintzberg, Raisinghani and Theoret, 1976) is summarized in the overall impedance (some processes are more delayed and repetitive than others), and so on.

SAMPLE AND METHODS

From the beginning of this project it was clear that results with a useful degree of generalizability dictated a large, heterogeneous sample rather than the small samples or single case studies previously found in the field. A large number of varied decisions from a diverse set of organizations was required, including more than one decision in each organization. Within the limits imposed by time and resources this eventually led to the collection of data on 150 decisions from 30 British organizations. Five cases were taken from each. The organizations were chosen to reflect the diversity of institutions in British society along two important dimensions, public *versus* private and manufacturing *versus* service. Within this general sampling plan some organizations were chosen so as to allow specific comparisons. For example, there are two universities (with quite different histories and characteristics) and two breweries (of quite different sizes) included. Two chemical manufacturers, one in the public sector and another in the private, allow another type of comparison. The organizations and the decisions investigated in each are listed in table II.

The sample included, besides the breweries, universities and chemical firms mentioned above, organizations ranging from an automobile parts manufacturer to an airline to a police force. Many of these are nationally or internationally prominent and all were of at least regional importance. They varied in size from 100 employees to over 50,000. There were seven organizations with between 100 and 750 employees, ten between 1,000 and 3,000 nine in the range from 4,000 to 9,000 and four with over 9,000.

The organizations were first approached by letter. Of those contacted two-thirds eventually agreed to co-operate. Participation in the study represented a considerable commitment of managerial time and signalled a willingness to discuss decisions which had considerable importance for the organization. Data collection took place in three overlapping phases moving from broader to more focused data gathering as experience showed the feasibility of doing so, in pursuit of as large a sample as limits to the research funding and time allowed. In phase one, two decisions were studied intensively in each of three organizations, a public utility, a university and a manufacturer. One case in each organization was followed as it unfolded, while the other was traced historically. Data were collected through interviews, lunchtime contacts and document searches by a researcher who spent many hours a week in the organizations over two or three years. All six cases are fully reported in Wilson (1980) and further explored in Wilson (1982) and Wilson *et al.* (1986). These six cases helped in the development of concepts and the refinement of data collection techniques. They also helped to validate the interview method used in subsequent phases when managers in the three organizations were again interviewed as if nothing were known of the previous cases and their accounts when checked against the very detailed histories that had been compiled.

Phases two and three of the data collection relied solely on interviews. Phase two covered 48 cases with two or more principal informants per process, usually interviewed separately. Phase three covered 96 cases with one principal informant per case when this was judged to be adequate for the data required. Other managers were often consulted during interviews to clarify or expand specific points. It was not necessary to discover every incident or who said what on every occasion in the detail recorded by intensive cases. A narrative of the main events and participants sufficed, though it should be said that very detailed accounts were frequently gathered.

Those who talked to the members of the research team did so as informants rather than respondents. They gave information as 'key witnesses' of events and not about themselves or their opinions, though this more personal element was accepted if it arose. Data collection aimed at compiling a consistent account of what had happened and not at a spread of opinion. Firstly, the collection of five cases in each organization not only made the researchers familiar with it and enabled them to check information on one case against information on another, it meant that the majority of cases formed part of ongoing organizational strategies and often overlapped in time. Obvious inconsistencies of recall could be corrected. Secondly, principle informants frequently had taken part in more than one decision-making process so that each could and did comment on more than just the case that was the main subject of the interview. Finally, the decisions under discussion were major events in the histories of the organizations concerned. They were not everyday matters. They stood out. The salient characteristics of the decision-making process, the possible alternatives, the evidence considered, and the positions taken by those involved were common currency among the upper echelon managers and administrators who had been there at the time.

An initial interview was held with the chief executive officer (CEO) in which information was gathered on the history of the organization, its outputs and structure, and its relation to other organizations. The chief executive was then asked to nominate a number of decisions within recall which were important for the organization. From this list five decisions were chosen to represent the spectrum of decisions made by that organization. As can be seen from table II, both the decision topics and the organizations from which they were drawn were exceptionally varied.

When asking the CEO to nominate decisions we did not provide him[2] with a definition of a strategic decision, merely asking about the most important decisions the organization had recently taken. We were reluctant to impose such a definition partly because of the current ambiguities over the meaning of 'strategic' (Wilson, 1980, pp. 10–13) and partly because we wanted CEOs to define the significance of decisions in their own terms. It might be thought that this latitude would allow the chief executive to focus only on relatively successful decisions which informants felt had been mistaken, others which had visibly negative consequences, in one case hastening the demise of a firm a short time after the interviews were completed, and instances in which, after long and

Table II. Organizations and decisions

Organizations	*Decisions*
Public Manufacturing	
Construction equipment	1. New line of trucks 2. Standard company name 3. Expand capacity 4. Production plan 5. Re-equip
Chemicals	1. Plant investment 2. Divisionalization 3. Plant in Sweden 4. Employment policy 5. Take over share in company
Private Manufacturing	
Metal components	1. Takeover bid 2. Open new plant 3. New components line 4. New components line 5. New components line
Textiles	1. New manufacturing premises 2. Not to make takeover bid 3. New manufacturing premises 4. Close factory 5. Resist takeover
Chemicals	1. New chemical 2. Generate own electricity 3. Land acquisition for expansion 4. Extend manufacturing plant 5. New source of material
Paints	1. Handle agency lines 2. Not to enter market 3. Direct distribution 4. Extend product range 5. New premises
Tool components	1. New material in product 2. New department 3. Expand premises and plant 4. Business plan 5. Data processing
Friction products	1. New plant 2. New line 3. Employee grading 4. Stock control mechanization 5. Business plan
Glass	1. Plant in Sweden 2. Novel product and material 3. New committee decision structure 4. Massive plant investment 5. Takeover bids

Table II. *continued*

Brewery	1. New division 2. New market 3. Not to launch new line 4. Labour deployment 5. Price structure
Public Services (commercial)	
Air transport	1. Larger capacity helicopters 2. Replace divisional with functional structure 3. Merge pilot forces 4. Reduce flights 5. Order new generation aircraft
Electricity	1. Massive new current supply 2. Complete transmission overall 3. Close selected retail showrooms 4. New retail sales line 5. Adapt transmission network
Water	1. Budget 2. Regional supply network 3. Financial appraisal of network 4. Joint service collaboration with customers 5. Direct billing
Public Services (non-commercial)	
Health Service	1. Budget 2. Close hospital 3. Physiotherapy service delivery 4. Strategic plan 5. Body-scanner purchase
Health Service	1. Geriatric hospital closure 2. Reallocate psychiatric services 3. Increase radiography service 4. Catering programme 5. Pathology services centralized
Municipality	1. New administrative premises 2. Housing project 3. Lottery 4. Merge departments 5. Joint financing of service for aged
Police	1. Close police stations 2. Staff appraisal 3. Police travel/mobility policy 4. Civilianization of work 5. Traffic division
Polytechnic	1. Overseas student policy 2. Staff development policy 3. Short course resources 4. New courses 5. Data processing

22 CRAY, MALLORY, BUTLER, HICKSON AND WILSON

Polytechnic	1.	Amalgamation with colleges
	2.	Plan
	3.	Location of schools
	4.	Boards of studies
	5.	Post-amalgamation allocation of resources
University	1.	Information service
	2.	Student residences
	3.	New department
	4.	Budget
	5.	Administrative job-grading
University	1.	Staff appointment system
	2.	Novel interdisciplinary form of degree
	3.	Departmental conflict
	4.	Collaborative programme with another university
	5.	Student intake
Private Services		
	1.	Cut costs to avoid merger
Insurance	2.	Expansion or merger
	3.	Centralization of claims
	4.	Data processing
	5.	Stay at existing site
Insurance	1.	Massive share issue
	2.	Overseas subsidiaries
	3.	Separate reinsurance work
	4.	Productivity agreement
	5.	Takeover bid
Bank	1.	Customer charges
	2.	Data processing
	3.	Centralization of operations
	4.	Changing from division to subsidiary
	5.	Joining London clearing house
Credit company	1.	New market
	2.	Takeover bid
	3.	Resist unionization
	4.	New service
	5.	Not to launch new facility
Housing loans	1.	Segment the market
	2.	New mini-branches
	3.	Regionalize structure
	4.	Interest rates
	5.	Head office to stay at existing site
Road transport	1.	Sell Italian trucks
	2.	Fit Italian vehicle bodies
	3.	Container repair section
	4.	Hire vehicles instead of buy
	5.	New depot for container repairs
Industrial research	1.	Training for industry firms
	2.	Type approval testing
	3.	Overseas market
	4.	Raise capital
	5.	New test facility
Entertainment	1.	Advertising strategy
	2.	Management structure
	3.	Budget
	4.	Staff allocation and availability
	5.	Plan programme

tortuous deliberation, the organization decided to do nothing. The final choice of five decisions out of those nominated was made jointly with the CEO and was based on the availability of informants, the importance of the decision for the organization, and the desire to obtain a distribution of different decision topics. It was not based on the success or failure of the decision outcome nor on the process by which it was reached.

For each of the five decisions the chief executive nominated one or more key informants who had been central to the decision process. Examples of informants include managing directors and directors of firms, vice-chancellors and deans in universities, management team members in hospital districts, and chief officers in local government. Each informant was interviewed at length, often more than once. Since the desired information was about the *processes* of decision making which take place at top management levels, employees at middle management levels and below were not approached as they would have little first-hand knowledge about how such decisions were made. Interviewees gave information about the events of the decision-making process, not their opinions about how decisions are made generally in the organization or their own orientation toward the process.

In the initial interview the chief executive gave a synopsis of each decision which served as a benchmark and guide for the detailed interview. Since many of the decisions overlapped in time or subject, cross-checking was often feasible. When an anomaly did arise it was settled by consulting the informants and/or the chief executive. In a number of cases in which the issue was unusually complex or the topic contentious, multiple informants were used, often at the suggestion of the chief executive or the principal informant.[3] When there was information from more than one individual, the separate accounts were consolidated through extensive consultation into a single description.[4]

Each interview began with an extended description of the decision process from the time the issue was first raised until the outcome, positive or negative, was authorized. In all cases therefore, analysis was based on narrative histories of what had happened. During the interviews, informants went on to answer a number of open-ended questions, which drew them to reiterate and expand upon certain aspects, such as the departments involved or the amount of interaction that had taken place. For a minority of the questions the respondents placed the decision on a five point scale (see the appendix for descriptions of the disparity and externality scales). This gave the advantage of both interview notes and scale ratings on the same feature. Answers to most questions, and material from the narratives, were content analysed and coded by the research team.

All data on decision making relies on memory. Even when a researcher is continually present in the organization, that researcher is not personally in every place at the moment when managers are talking or calculating. The story is pieced together from what they say about it later. Interview data is the same but the recall is over longer periods. The difference between shorter recall in concurrent cases and the longer recall tapped in interviews is that the story becomes less cluttered and relatively simpler, not that it changes. With longer hindsight, the main pathways of the process are recalled and less attention is given to the byways and dead ends.

RESULTS

To seek empirical patterns from which a typology of processes might arise, it was necessary to use a means of data analysis capable of handling a large number of cases described by a set of twelve process variables. Therefore the data were subjected to cluster analysis (Anderberg, 1973) to group decisions. A hierarchical clustering technique randomly assigned cases to a cluster and then relocated them to minimize the error sum of squares within the clusters. The result is a local optimization of the clustering, with a high probability of obtaining a global optimization, for a given number of clusters (Wishart, 1978, pp. 43–6).

The choice of the set of clusters that provides the best division of the data rests on substantive as much as on statistical grounds (Anderberg, 1973, p. 183; Everitt, 1974, p. 59). In this instance a three cluster solution provided a clear discrimination among the groups at the same time as it eliminated clusters which were largely dependent on a single variable. Because the cluster program requires complete data to operate and 14 cases had missing data on one or more variables, 136 of the 150 cases were used in this analysis. It is on these 136 cases that the results reported below are based.

The sizes of the three clusters were similar, with the clusters having 53, 41, and 42 cases respectively. Having derived the clusters it was necessary to determine what each represented. Although this could be done by examining the characteristics of the cases in each to see what they held in common, given the number of cases in each cluster and the variety of the decision-making processes, unaided inspection was difficult and liable to bias. Moreover, it had been an aim of the study from its inception to associate any typology with an estimate of the importance of each variable for the discrimination implied.

To estimate the contribution of each variable to the partitioning of the groups the three clusters were subjected to discriminant analysis using the same variables on which they were clustered. This technique of using discriminant analysis to evaluate clustering results, suggested by Howard *et al.* (1982), has three advantages. Firstly, it allows a more precise interpretation of the meaning of each cluster. Secondly, it provides an indication of the comparative importance of each variable for distinguishing among the clusters. Thirdly, it assists in establishing the substantive plausibility of the clusters as well as giving an indication of the reliability of the clustering process.

The discriminant analysis technique generated two functions which correctly classified 95 per cent of the cases indicating that the clusters derived represented a realistic partition of the cases. A holdout sample using 40 per cent of the cases to compute the coefficients gave a 96 per cent correct classification. Using these functions to classify the remaining 60 per cent produced 84 per cent correct classification indicating that the original functions were not reliant on the sample of the cases used.

The coefficients for the variables on the two functions yielded by the discriminant analysis technique are given in table III. It should be noted that two of the twelve variables that were used for the original clustering do not appear in the discriminant functions. Neither externality nor gestation time contributed significantly to the differentiation among the clusters.

Table III. Rotated, standardized, discriminant function coefficients

	Discontinuity (function 1)	*Dispersion (function 2)*
Expertise	0.35	−0.24
Externality	*a*	*a*
Effort	0.00	0.28
Disparity	0.51	0.03
Formal interaction	−0.35	0.29
Informal interaction	0.24	0.05
Scope	0.08	0.38
Disruption	0.36	0.04
Impedance	0.54	−0.05
Gestation time	*a*	*a*
Process time	0.33	−0.16
Level	−0.01	0.91

$N = 136$
a = variables which did not enter into the analysis due to lack of significant contribution to the functions.

Function 1 is dominated by positive loadings on disparity (0.51) and impedance (0.54). This means that the clusters are distinguished by the degree to which information collected for the decisions is of roughly the same reliability and by the sources of the delays that occur during the decision process. Clusters, and decisions within those clusters, which score highly on this function will be characterized by disparate sources of information and by more serious sources of delays, notably resistance by other parties in the decision-making arena.

At a lower level the number and seriousness of the disruptions to the process also contributes to the function (0.36). With the positive contribution of impedance, it is not surprising that process time for decisions scoring highly on this function tends to be longer (0.33). During the longer decision time, information may be gathered from more sources (0.35) and there tends to be more informal interaction among the parties (0.24) although with less formal interaction (−0.35).

This dimension of the decision-making process was named discontinuity. Its character can be seen most obviously in the greater number of more serious disruptions to processes. There is another element of this discontinuity in the provision and processing of information for the decision. The larger number of disparate sources leads to more informal interaction and, quite probably, to disagreements over interpretation of data by those responsible for delays. The negative coefficient for formal interaction indicates that the interaction, while relatively greater for discontinuous decisions, occurs in unstructured rather than structured settings. The overall picture of a decision scoring highly on this function is one which proceeds in a series of uneven steps separated by delays due to the need for securing, processing, or interpreting information, or, more seriously, by opposition from interests in the decision arena. The business of sorting out the data and settling disagreements tends to occur in informal rather than formal settings.

Function 2 is dominated by the extremely high coefficient for the level at which the decision was authorized (0.91). The second most powerful variable is the scope of negotiation (0.38) which is closely followed by formal interaction (0.29), scrutiny effort (0.28), and the inclusion of experts in the scrutiny process (−0.24). The first two coefficients indicate that while the final step in the decision process, authorization, is restricted to the higher levels of the organization, there is a fair amount of scope for negotiation before authorization takes place. There is an effort to gain and analyse information, but this information is provided by a relatively small number of experts. Both negotiation and information processing pass through more committees and working parties than they do for decisions characterized by positive scores on function 1, as formal interaction tends to increase with a higher score on function 2.

This second function was called dispersion because it reflects the distribution of decision-making activity through managerial or administrative levels in the extent of negotiation, the gathering of information, and the use of committees. At the wide end of the dispersion dimension, the decision is considered by the board of directors who represent not only a variety of internal views but often those of external interests. The wide focus is also seen in the greater scope of negotiation. There is more room for discussion of the decision, and more dissension may emerge. The greater effort used to collect information and the more frequent use of committees which bring together parties from different parts of the organization in a formal setting also indicates wider dispersion.

At the opposite end of this dimension a restricted field is indicated by authorization at a lower level with a concomitant limitation on the parties involved, reduced scope for negotiation, less effort made to gather information, and fewer committees used. This contrasts with wider ranging processes which take place in a setting structured by the use of formal mechanisms such as approval by the board of directors and committee meetings, ensuring that the decision process does not get out of control. With a more limited process the consideration may be less formal.

The two functions described here suggest fundamental dimensions on which strategic decisions can be grouped. Since the decisions were taken from a wide range of organizations, it seems likely that these dimensions will categorize most strategic decision making, although other dimensions may be discovered. It is difficult to imagine a decision making process the nature of which could not be summed up in terms of its discontinuity and its dispersion of activity through the organization. Whether it is more discontinuous with discrete, uneven episodes of activity or more smoothly continuous, whether it is more dispersed with wide-ranging activity or more confined, these concepts between them depict much of its essential character. They offer an economical means of describing what hitherto have seemed to be almost limitless variations in this fundamental form of managerial behaviour.

THREE TYPES OF DECISION PROCESS

While the two functions are themselves substantively interesting, they are but an intermediate step toward the goal of developing a typology of decision-making processes. Each of the three clusters can be characterized by a value on the two functions. The values given in table IV are those of the group centroids for each cluster. Scores on the variables which go to make up the functions are standardized so the resulting function values can be evaluated accordingly. The values given here, will, of course, be influenced by the composition of the sample. However, since the decisions come from a variety of organizations and cover many decision topics, they should represent a reasonable estimate for strategic decisions in general.

Table IV Function values for group means (centroids)

Cluster	*Discontinuity (function 1)*	*Dispersion (function 2)*
1 (sporadic)	1.49	0.88
2 (constricted)	0.19	-2.03
3 (fluid)	-2.06	0.87

Cluster 1 is denoted by a relatively high value on the discontinuity dimension (1.49) and a moderately positive value on dispersion (0.88). The processes in this cluster are discontinuous and have wide dispersion. This is *sporadic* decision making. It proceeds in short bursts of activity interspersed with delays while information is gathered and groups argue over the interpretation of data or merely restate opposing positions. The scope of negotiation is wider than usual, as indicated by the positive value of dispersion, but more of the interaction seems to take place in informal settings. The neutral value of level on discontinuity coupled with the strong positive value on dispersion indicates that there will be some tendency for the process to require authorization by the highest executive, however it is a moderate tendency. There is a certain latitude in the way that the decision is made and this leads to these decisions taking more time than most but the path that the decision takes is more like a narrowing valley than a broad field with few boundary lines. The players in the decision game may roam widely over the valley, backtracking and delaying the game, but in the end they must exit through the narrow pass of upper level authorization. It should be noted that sporadic refers exclusively to the interconnection of the processes within the decision and not the occurrence of decisions within the organization.

From among the 53 cases in the cluster of sporadic decision-making processes, an interesting and illustrative example occurred in a large nationalized industry.[5] This firm, in purchasing a subsidiary, had acquired the European rights to an industrial chemical process. Everyone concerned agreed on its potential as a profitable venture. The disagreement arose over the way in which it was to be exploited. Basically the decision to be made was two-fold. Firstly, where was the chemical to be produced, in Britain or on the Continent? Secondly, how was the product to be marketed? In order to assess the alternatives posed by these two questions a fair amount of information had to be gathered from internal departments, other organizations, and the government of the country in which a continental plant might be located.

The number and severity of disruptions was somewhat above the mean for the sample as a whole. These interruptions stemmed mainly from the need to gather information and the difficulties of co-ordinating action by a number of different internal and external units. There was also a delay while permission for the plan was obtained from the licensor. However, the most serious source of impedance was opposition from another nationalized organization which wanted the opportunity to exploit the process for itself. The managers of this organization delayed the final decision until some of their objections could be assuaged. Not surprisingly, the decision process was drawn out, taking three years to complete.

This decision is nicely described by the discontinuity dimension in that it had a large number of disruptions, some of which were serious, relied on several sources of expert information, and took a long time to make. It reflects the lesser loading on the dispersion dimension mainly through the high level at which the decision was authorized. When it was finally decided to locate the plant in Scandinavia, the board at first only gave approval in principle, causing another delay. When the board finally gave its approval the whole plan had to be ratified at yet a higher level of the nationalized industrial structure. The decision process had proceeded in an uneven, halting, and recursive manner until eventually it was approved by the highest level of organization. In this it was a typical case of sporadic decision making.

As can be seen in figure 1, cluster three makes an interesting contrast with cluster one which will be discussed before comparing both with cluster two. Clusters one and three are both moderately positive on the dispersion dimension, 0.87 for cluster 3 *versus* 0.88 for cluster 1. On the discontinuity function, however, cluster three is strongly negative (−2.06). In this sense clusters one and three form two ends of a continuum from discontinuity to continuity. If function 1 is the vertical axis and function 2 the horizontal, then clusters one and three are at opposite ends of a line a little less than one unit to the right of and parallel with the *Y* axis.

The decisions in cluster three, then, tend to have fewer interruptions and those that do occur are less serious. The decisions are taken more quickly with fewer experts providing more homogeneous information which is more likely to be processed through formal interaction. This use of committees reinforces the structuring implied by the positive value on function 2. The framework for decision making remains in place, but the process moves through it much more smoothly. For this reason these are called *fluid* decision-making processes.

The financial restructuring of a brewery was among the 42 cases which fell within this cluster. At the beginning of the process the brewery was a family owned enterprise which had just expanded by acquiring another small brewery. As a result the company was too highly geared and its lenders were exerting pressure on it to raise more equity capital. There were several possibilities, but they resolved themselves into two strategies. One was to sell off company assets, such as some of its pubs. The second was to seek new investors by issuing new shares. The decision was strategic in that the choice would result in a company considerably modified either at the operating or ownership level. It was strategic on another level because, until this time, all shares had been held by family members, most of whom felt that accepting outside investors would be an irreversible break with the past.

Despite the potential for disagreement among a number of parties, this decision moved quickly and smoothly to its conclusion. In only nine months the company found a group of outside investors, developed a proposal upon which they agreed

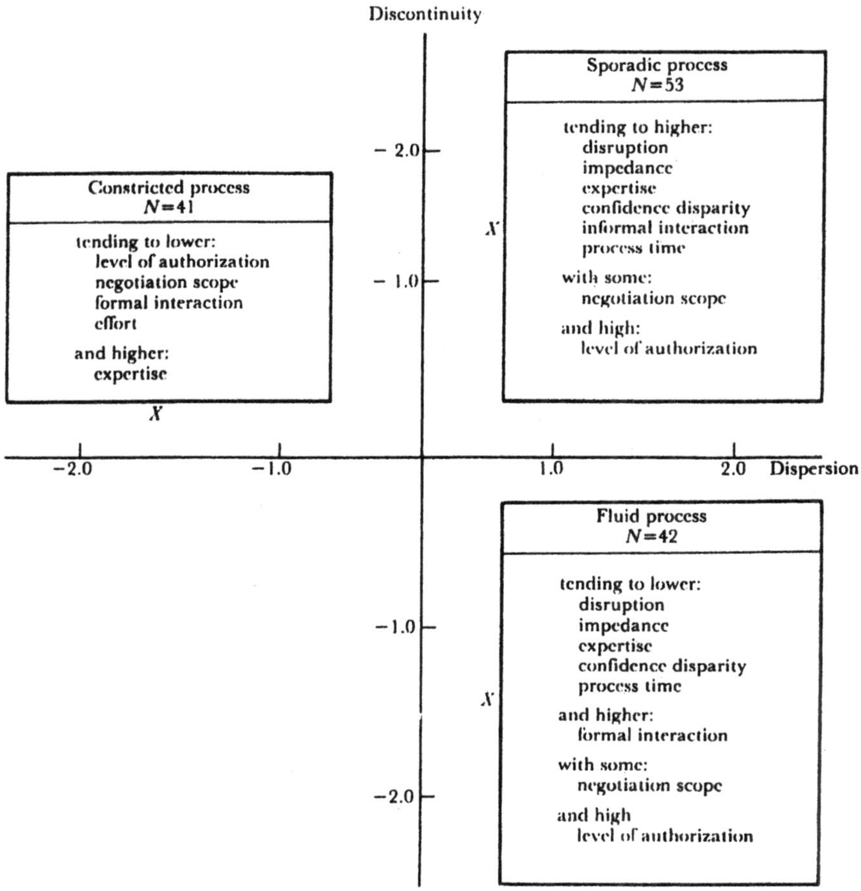

Figure 1. Location of group centroids on discontinuity and dispersion axes

and had it accepted by the financial institutions. The brewery had turned a historic corner with very few delays and surprisingly little opposition. In keeping with the positive loading of cluster 3 on the dispersion dimension, there had been considerable scope for negotiation but the search for an acceptable solution had narrowed quickly. It was finally authorized, as such an important decision must be, by the board of the brewery voting for the last time in its family-dominated form.

Cluster two is unlike both one and three in that it is nearly neutral on discontinuity, having a group mean of only 0.19. It is almost entirely defined by its strong negative group mean on the dispersion dimension (−2.03). These decisions tend to be authorized at relatively lower levels within top management, such as the CEO rather than the board of directors, and to offer little scope for negotiation. Experts are called in to provide information, but there is typically less effort to scrutinize the wider environment for information and committees are seldom convened.

The picture here is of decisions which emerge from lower levels of the senior management and do not have to travel to the top for ratification. However, since the sample is one of strategic decisions, the lower reaches at which these are approved are still very near the top of the organization. Of the 150 decisions, less than 5 per cent were ratified at the divisional level and none below it. This means that over 95 per cent were authorized by the chief executive and/or groups above him (see appendix for a complete description of the levels scale). Thus the decisions in cluster 2, while ratified at a relatively low level compared to those in the other clusters, are still taken within higher echelons of the organization.

Decisions in cluster two tend to use experts, but little effort is made to collect data that is not readily available. Formal interaction is not necessary because the narrowed range of the process allows it to be dealt with by a few individuals who are often in regular contact. The agendas, minutes and recorded votes which may be found at committee meetings are not required here. The lack of any sizeable contribution by the informal interaction variable to function 2 indicates that this type of decision will be made using the usual procedures that prevail in the organization rather than patterns of interaction made necessary by the decision topic or specific decisional procedures.

This type of process is called *constricted*. This term was used partly to reflect the definition of this cluster by its position on the narrow end of the dispersion dimension and partly because these processes often seem to be focused around the single decision-maker, frequently the CEO. Using information that is easily accessible, a minimum of formal committee work, and allowing little scope for negotiation, this individual oversees the process and approves the decision himself with higher ratification occasionally following. By focusing on one person, especially one who has a fair amount of authority, the decision is structured, but without much of the organizational impedimenta that is often associated with strategic decisions.

A prime example of the 41 cases in the constricted cluster was observed in an organization which provides services to the motor industry in Britain. This organization had previously had some minor contact with the automobile industry in an Asian country, mainly through British managers and engineers who had gone there to work. By chance, one of the top managers in the organization, who will be called Jackson here, discovered that a former colleague was selling machine tools in this country and had become convinced that there were attractive business opportunities there. After some preliminary investigation Jackson flew to Asia to talk with government and industry officials. What he learned there convinced him that his colleague's advice was sound. He in turn persuaded local managers that they needed his organization's services.

At this point no decision had been made except the fairly routine one of sending someone to investigate a possible opportunity. Now the organization's executives were faced with the strategic decision of whether to pursue an opportunity which would put a strain on lines of communication, take the organization into new territory, and commit resources that were, at this time, none too plentiful. The decision was taken to proceed and Jackson, along with his CEO, returned to Asia to attempt to negotiate an agreement, which they subsequently did.

The focused nature of this decision can be seen in Jackson's key role in both the procurement of information and the processing of it for the final decision. This example varies slightly from a typical constricted process in that more effort than usual was made in collecting information, but this was mainly due to the geographic separation from their sources of information of those who had to make the decision. It is more typical in its relatively low level of authorization. Once the CEO returned with the agreement he discussed it with his immediate subordinates and then approved it himself. No higher authority was needed. The scope for negotiations was limited since the CEO made the decision alone, aided mainly by Jackson's advice.

These three types of decision process have a standing similar to the dimensions which define them. They are basic ways in which organizations make strategic decisions. Sporadic processes tend to be interrupted, informal and drawn out. Fluid processes are much smoother, quicker, and more formally structured. Constricted processes are bound by few formal structures but proceed around a single individual and are authorized at a relatively low level in the organization. With its empirical justification this typology forms a new basis for understanding the way in which strategic decisions are made.

DISCUSSION

While the three types of decision processes described above offer a more parsimonious categorization than Stein's (1981a) sixteen hypothesized modes or the seven categories proposed by Mintzberg, Raisinghani, and Theoret (1976), they do reflect some of the same contrasts in types of decision-making. Among the types found by Mintzberg, Raisinghani and Theoret there were three basic search and design processes, all of which proceed with little interruption or deviation. These can be contrasted with the other four types which are more often blocked. This seems to echo the contrasts between the fluid and sporadic types of decision process and suggests that there may be varieties within the sporadic and fluid patterns. If Mintzberg, Raisinghani, and Theoret's (1976) classification is supported, there would be 'blocked' 'political' and 'dynamic' varieties of sporadic process and 'search' and 'design' varieties of fluid process. Indeed, fluid processes may proceed through several search or design cycles if these are not caused by unexpected checks or by political opposition, but are instead part of the normal decision process. For sporadic decisions delays are more serious because of their greater political content, as the plant location decision illustrates.

The contrast between sporadic and fluid processes also finds a parallel in Miles' (1980, p. 181) distinction between 'political' and 'rational' decision-making. The parallel is not exact because a basically political decision may move fluidly toward a compromise acceptable to all parties. An example of this was found in a decision taken by a municipal government to raise revenue through a lottery. Although it was one of the first British municipalities to adopt this method and although there was considerable doubt among some councillors about the political and moral implications of the scheme, it was proposed and ratified in not much more than a month and with few interruptions. Despite this exception it seems likely that many of the decisions that are rational in Miles' sense, those that are seen as problems with a largely technical content, will be decided by fluid processes, while those that are more political will tend to provoke a sporadic type of process. A similar distinction can be seen in Allison's (1971) contrast between the 'rational' actor and 'government politics' models.

A comparison with Stein's (1981b) sixteen categories of decision methods is more difficult. Stein factor-analysed 64 questionnaires to identify four dimensions of decision making. There is little match between Stein's dimensions of analysis, search, problem definition, and group behaviour and the two dimensions uncovered by this study. Discontinuity was reflected in one variable of the approach dimension and dispersion in the bargaining aspect of group behaviour, but the differences in the results are more striking than the similarities.

These differences undoubtedly are partly due to different methods of data collection, questionnaires *versus* interviews, and different samples. They are probably also due to quite different approaches to the problem of arriving at a categorization of decision types. Stein used his analysis to test nine hypothesized dimensions of the decision process. Three of these dimensions were retained and two others combined to make the fourth. This procedure resulted in dimensions which were roughly verified by the factor analysis, but were initially derived from theoretical justifications. In the Bradford study the choice of the original variables was influenced by theoretical considerations, but the analysis did not constrain them to any particular configuration. Similarly the three clusters of decisions, the three types, were seen to be the best empirically derived partioning of our cases into groups. Stein's 16 types were generated by separating the dimensions into high and low categories and crossing them to provide a 16 cell table. The Bradford results imply that Stein's categorization may be far more complex than necessary and may include dimensions that are not fundamental to understanding the process.

More recent work by Nutt (1984) also provides an interesting contrast with the present study. Using five stages in the decision-making process (formulation, concept development, detailing, evaluation and implementation) Nutt derives five categories of decision-making processes with 11 subcategories from a sample of 78 decisions. In an approach similar to that of Mintzberg, Raisinghani and Theoret (1976) the five categories depend on the utilization and ordering of the stages in the decision-making process. From the point of view of these two studies the specification of stages provides a framework that allows categorization of processes which, on the surface, are quite dissimilar. At the same time the results generated by these studies indicate that there is a great variety in the appearance and importance of these stages among organizations and quite probably within them. The Bradford studies make no assumptions about stages of the decision process. Rather, the process as a whole was characterized by variables without regard to a prescribed set or ordering of stages. This is not meant to imply that the approach of Nutt or Mintzberg and his colleagues was invalid, rather than the research objectives were different. The results reported here indicate that the types of decision making derived from an analysis of stages, in fact, may be more complex manifestations of a few basic decision-making processes. Whether or not there is a correspondence between the three types of decision-making processes reported here and the more structured systems of Nutt and Mintzberg *et al.* would require a thorough re-analysis of the data from all three projects, a task that is likely to prove difficult given problems of data comparability.

The three types also help to expand other themes in the study of strategic decision making. One of the most persistent of these has been the non-optimal behaviour of decision-makers. Because decision-makers are bound by their own cognitive limitations (March and Simon, 1958, pp. 136–9) and the resources of the organization, they are unable to identify an optimal alternative (Braybrooke and Lindblom, 1963, pp. 21–36). How then do they proceed? They choose decision-making strategies which narrow the choice of alternatives to a reasonable number and which allow some distancing from the effects of decision. Observation of this behaviour has given rise to descriptions of decision-making processes as 'the science of muddling through' (Lindblom, 1959), 'loosely coupled' (Weick, 1976), 'satisficing' (Simon, 1960) and even as 'garbage cans' (Cohen *et al.*, 1972).

The research reported in this study indicates that these characterizations of the strategic decision-making process, while important for the individual points they illuminate, may have actually obscured some very basic features of decision making which cut across a number of decision types. For example, sporadic decisions are characterized by delays and opposition which generally include reconsiderations of disparate data. Radical solutions are unlikely to survive this iterative process. This means that sporadic decisions exhibit the 'disjointed incrementalism' described by Braybrooke and Lindblom (1963, pp. 81–110). As Wilson (1982) has pointed out there is incrementalism of both process and outcome. The sporadic process specifies the description of the process and implies a similar incrementalism of both process and outcome. At the same time the satisficing concept explored by Simon (1960) also partakes of the sporadic character in its hesitant moves towards a decision. However, these results would indicate that the limited amount of information Simon indicates is collected may be overstated. Our research shows that as the sporadic process wanders toward its conclusion more information will be collected, if only to provide a reason for delay to those who are opposed to the probable outcome.

Fluid decisions raise another set of issues for decision-making research. Most of the theorizing about and much of the research into strategic decision-making highlights the difficulty of arriving at a strategic decision. Some of the decisions we have studied, indeed the majority of them, did encounter difficulties and delays that were significant. However, nearly a third of the decisions were made by a process which went smoothly to completion, with few disruptions. Moreover, it is clear that these were not trivial decisions. The brewery refinancing decision described earlier, despite its obvious importance to the firm and the family members who owned it, proceeded smoothly to its novel conclusion. This does not indicate that some of the reasons proposed for strategic decision-making difficulties were not present in this or other decisions that were made through fluid processes. In this example, the number of potential solutions was large and the amount of information potentially enormous, but the solution, the outcome, was arrived at through a very non-disruptive decision process.

Finally, the constricted cluster of decisions sheds some light on an early idea in the decision-making literature. Despite the early focus on a single decision-maker (Simon, 1947) later work (*e.g.* Cohen *et al.*, 1972) has focused more on group decision-making. The constricted decisions indicate that a single individual, even one at a comparatively lower level, can serve as the focus for a strategic decision, using only easily available information and little negotiation. This brings ideas neatly back to Simon's manager operating within bounded rationality. These results would imply that the idea of bounded rationality may apply not only to the manager's cognitive processes, but also to the organizational setting in which such constricted decisions are taken. Rationality is bounded by the limitations of the process as well as by the abilities of the manager.

CONCLUSION

The three types of decision-making processes described here are grounded on a broad empirical foundation supported by in-depth studies. Although all the organizations in which they took place are in Britain, and this might be a source of some peculiarities (Mallory *et al.*, 1983), the extent of national differences can only be determined by further research. Given that Mintzberg, Raisinghani and Theoret (1976) produced concordant results with Canadian data, the probability is that the broad picture is widely valid.

The three types demonstrate that it is possible to conceptualize the constituent elements of process so that a substantial number of diverse cases are encompassed with comprehensible results. Obviously there can be no claim that these three types cover all possible forms of strategic decision making, nor can there be any prediction as to how long these types will survive future research in their present form. However, it can be argued that they and their constituent elements are sufficiently fundamental that they will persist in one guise or another. This typology shows that an economical conceptualization of process is feasible, so that one need not resort to sweeping generalizations about tortuous, repetitive and ill-formed decision making, nor rely on particularistic descriptions of unique processes chosen from an infinite universe of decisions and organizations.

Mohr (1982, pp. 166–7) suggests that one of the first tasks necessary in developing a theory of decision behaviour is the adequate description of different 'modes' of decision making such as this article has attempted. A typology having been achieved, he suggests (Mohr, 1982, pp. 175–7) that the differences among modes must be explained. This raises two issues. First, what factors are linked with the location of decisions in one or another process type? The literature offers several possibilities including political pressures, the nature of the decision topic, environmental factors, and characteristics of the organization. Future papers from this project will investigate some explanations for types of process. The second issue is broader. To what extent is the typology proposed here useful in model and theory building? This issue must also be subject to the outcome of future research, but the results reported here provide some confidence in both its empirical justification and its theoretical potential.

APPENDIX: ORGANIZATION OF VARIABLES

Scrutiny

Expertise: Number of sources (internal subunits or specialists and external organizations and agencies) providing information or views (as distinct from having influence) during the decision process.

Disparity: Range between sources providing information or views, of five point ratings by informants of confidence ('little' to 'a very great deal') in what was provided.

Externality: Sum of confidence ratings by informants of information provided by external sources as a percentage of the sum of confidence ratings of all sources.

Effort: Data concerning information and expert judgement used for decision were coded into the following categories:

1. Available information: personal opinions, or knowledge
2. Obtained information: readily accessible from records
3. Researched information: generated by scanning or perceptual means such as a market survey
4. Synthesized information: integrating disparate information from diverse sources *via* a meeting to collate information, or a report.

Interaction

Informal interaction: The amount of discussion, to-ing and fro-ing or arguments encountered was coded on the following scale:

1. None
2. Little
3. Some
4. Quite a lot
5. A great deal
6. A very great deal

Each decision was scored by its highest rating.

Formal interaction: Number of committees of any kind involved in a decision process (committees may be general, *e.g.* boards, executives; specialized, *e.g.* sales committee; or special purpose, *e.g.* working parties).

Scope for negotiation: Data concerning discussion and dissent were coded on the following scale:

1. Decision was not open to negotiation
2. Negotiation only in the final stages
3. Negotiation possible on choices, but one man chooses the course of action (*e.g.* chief executive)
4. Collective decision
5. Negotiation including dissenting parties, but subsequent consensus
6. Negotiation resulting in limited consensus to the exclusion of dissenters
7. Decision reached with dissent remaining, such as in voting.

Flow

Disruptions: Data concerning the delays encountered during the decision process were coded on the following scale:

1. None
2. Intermittent
3. Continual
4. Prolonged

Each decision was scored by its highest coding.

Impedance: The reasons given by informants for delays in decision processes were coded on the following scale:

1. No impediments
2. Sequencing; awaiting priority in the order of attention to the decision
3. Co-ordinating; awaiting requirements becoming available
4. Timing; awaiting an opportune time
5. Searching; awaiting the obtaining or analysing of data, either by direct action or by the action of other agencies
6. Problem solving; awaiting investigation of what is not understood
7. Supplying; awaiting the availability of resources
8. Recycling; awaiting reconsideration of what has already been gone over
9. Resisting–internal; awaiting the outcome of active internal opposition
10. Resisting–external; awaiting the outcome of external opposition

Each decision process was scored by its highest coding.

Duration

Gestation Time in months from first recognition of emerging topic to the commencement of process time.

Process time: Time in months from first deliberate consideration of a topic to authorization of the implementation of a decision.

Centrality

Level: The level at which implementation was authorized, excluding any subsequent rubber stamping:

1. Below divisional level
2. Divisional level
3. Chief executive
4. Chief executive but later ratified by board
5. Board, or equivalent top governing body
6. Board, and later ratified outside organization
7. Outside organization.

NOTES

[1] This research has been supported by the British Social Science Research Council, the University of Bradford Management Centre and the Faculty of Graduate Studies, Carleton University.

[2] Of the more than 200 principal informants interviewed for this study only two were women. Neither of them was a CEO.

[3] The suggestion that data be checked with files or minutes of meetings is unrealistic. For most organizations such documents are sparse and, where they do exist, usually unavailable. Even where such documents are available, they generally only record the outcome of the decision-making process and not the process itself. Finally, as earlier work suggests, much of managerial interaction takes place in brief, informal exchanges which normally are unrecorded (Kurke and Aldrich, 1983; Mintzberg, 1973).

[4] When the discrepancies between accounts were minor, the responses were, where feasible, averaged (*e.g.* estimates of the length of a delay). Other minor discrepancies were resolved through a set of coding protocols (*e.g.* where estimates of conflict over

the decision differed slightly, the higher rating was used since managers generally downplay the existence of dissension with the organization). Where the discrepancies were major, other sources, such as internal evidence from the interview, the initial description by the CEO or further consultation with the interviewees were used to resolve the differences.

[5] A certain vagueness in the examples, *e.g.* lack of identification of a manager's position or the location and function of a subsidiary, is a result of preserving the anonymity of our informants and their organizations.

REFERENCES

ABELL, P. (1975). *Organizations as a Bargaining and Influence System*. London: Heinemann.

ALLISON, G. T. (1969). 'Conceptual models and the Cuban missile crisis'. *American Political Science Review*, **58**, 689–718.

ALLISON, G. T. (1971). *Essence of Decision: Explaining the Cuban Missile Crisis*. Boston: Little, Brown.

ANDERBERG, M. R. (1973). *Cluster Analysis for Applications*. New York: Academic Press.

ASTLEY, W. G., AXELSSON, R., BUTLER, R. J., HICKSON, D. J. and WILSON, D. C. (1982). 'Complexity and cleavage: dual explanations of strategic decision-making'. *Journal of Management Studies*, **19**, 357–75.

AXELSSON, R. and ROSENBERG, L. (1979). 'Decision-making and organizational turbulence'. *Acta Sociologica*, **22**, 45–62.

BLAU, P. M. and SCHOENHERR, R. A. (1971). *The Structure of Organizations*. New York: Basic Books.

BRAYBROOKE, D. and LINDBLOM, C. E. (1963). *A Strategy of Decision*. London: Collier-Macmillan.

CHILD, J. (1973). 'Predicting and understanding organization structure'. *Administrative Science Quarterly*, **18**, 168–85.

CLEGG, S. and DUNKERLEY, D. (1980). *Organization, Class and Control*. London Routledge & Kegan Paul.

COHEN, M. D., MARCH, J. G. and OLSEN, J. P. (1972). 'A garbage can model of organizational choice'. *Administrative Science Quarterly*, **17**, 1–25.

COLIGNON, R. and CRAY, D. (1980). 'Critical organizations'. *Organization Studies*, **1**, 349–66.

CRAY, D., BUTLER, R. J., HICKSON, D. J., MALLORY, G. R. and WILSON, D. C. (1986). 'Proactive and reactive decision making'. In Subramaniam, V. (Ed.), *Problem Recognition in Public Policy and Business Management*. Delhi: Ashish.

CYERT, R. M. and MARCH, J. G. (1963). *A Behavioral Theory of the Firm*. Englewood Cliffs, NJ: Prentice-Hall.

CYERT, R. M., SIMON, H. A. and TROW, D. B. (1956). 'Observation of a business decision'. *Journal of Business*, **29**, 237–48.

DIO INTERNATIONAL RESEARCH TEAM (1983). 'A contingency model of participative decision making: an analysis of 56 decisions in three Dutch organiztions'. *Journal of Occupational Psychology*, **56**, 1–18.

DRENTH, P. J. D., KOOPMAN, P. L., RUS, V., HELLER, F. and BROWN, A. (1979). 'Participative decision making: a comparative study'. *Industrial Relations*, **18**, 295–309.

EVERITT, B. (1974). *Cluster Analysis*. London: Heinemann.

HAGE, J. (1980). *Theories of Organizations: Form, Process and Transformation*. New York: Wiley.

HICKSON, D. J., ASTLEY, W. G., BUTLER, R. J. and WILSON, D. C. (1981). 'Organization as power'. In Cummings L. L. and Staw, B. M. (Eds.), *Research in Organizational Behavior*, 151–96. Greenwich, Conn.: JAI Press.

HICKSON, D. J., BUTLER, R. J., CRAY, D., MALLORY, G. R. and WILSON, D. C. (1986). *Top Decisions: Strategic Decision-Making in Organizations*. Oxford: Blackwell and San Francisco: Jossey-Bass.

HOWARD, K., MOSTAFA, A. M. M. and SHARP, J. A. (1982). 'Current issues in transfer pricing'. *Managerial Finance*, **8**, 3&4, 1–38.

KURKE, L. B. and ALDRICH, H. E. (1983). 'Mintzberg was right!: a replication and extension of *The Nature of Managerial Work*'. *Management and Science*, **29**, 975–84.

LINDBLOM, C. (1959). 'The science of muddling through'. *Public Administration Review*, **19**, 79–88.

MALLORY, G. R., BUTLER, R. J., CRAY, D., HICKSON, D. J. and WILSON, D. C. (1983). 'Implanted decision-making: American owned firms in Britain'. *Journal of Management Studies*, **20**, 191–211.

MARCH, J. G. and OLSEN, J. P. (1976). 'Ambiguity and choice in organizations'. Bergen: Universitetsforlaget.

MARCH, J. G. and ROMELAER, P. J. (1976). 'Position and presence in the drift of decisions'. In March J. G. and Olsen, J. P. (Eds.), *Ambiguity and Choice in Organizations*, 251–76. Bergen: Universitetsforlaget.

MARCH, J. G. and SIMON, H. A. (1958). *Organizations*. New York: Wiley.

MCNEIL, K. (1978). 'Understanding organizational power: building on the Weberian legacy'. *Administrative Science Quarterly*, **23**, 65–90.

MILES, R. E. and SNOW, C. C. (1978). *Organizational Strategy, Structure and Process*. New York: McGraw-Hill.

MILES, R. H. (1980). *Macro Organizational Behavior*. Glenview, Ill.: Scott, Foresman.

MINTZBERG, H. (1973). *The Nature of Managerial Work*. New York: Harper and Row.

MINTZBERG, H. (1983). *Power in and around Organizations*. Englewood Cliffs, NJ: Prentice-Hall.

MINTZBERG, H., RAISINGHANI, D. and THEORET, A. (1976). 'The structure of "unstructured" decision processes'. *Administrative Science Quarterly*, **21**, 246–75.

MINTZBERG, H. and WATERS, J. A. (1982). 'Tracking strategy in an entrepreneurial firm'. *Academy of Management Journal*, **25**: 465–99.

MOHR, L. B. (1982). *Explaining Organizational Behavior*. San Francisco: Jossey-Bass.

NUTT, P. C. (1984). 'Types of organizational decision processes'. *Administrative Science Quarterly*, **29**, 414–50.

PETTIGREW, A. M. (1973). *The Politics of Organizational Decision-Making*. London: Tavistock.

PFEFFER, J. (1981). *Power in Organizations*. Marshfield, Mass.: Pitman.

PFEFFER, J. and SALANCIK, G. R. (1978). *The External Control of Organizations*. New York: Harper and Row.

PUGH, D. S. and HICKSON, D. J. (Eds.) (1976). *Organizational Structure in its Context: The Aston Programme I*. Farnborough: Gower.

QUINN, J. B. (1980). *Strategies for Change: Logical Incrementalism*. Homewood, Ill.: Irwin.

SIMON, H. A. (1947). *Administrative Behavior*. New York: Free Press.

SIMON, H. A. (1960). *The New Science of Management Decision*. New York: Harper.

STEIN, J. (1981a). 'Contextual factors in the selection of strategic decision methods'. *Human Relations*, **34**, 819–34.

STEIN, J. (1981b), 'Strategic decision methods'. *Human Relations*, **34**, 917–33.

THOMPSON, J. D. and TUDEN, A. (1959). 'Strategies, structures and processes of organizational decision'. In Thompson, J. D. (Ed.), *Comparative Studies in Administration*, 195–216. Pittsburgh: University of Pittsburgh Press.

WEICK, K. E. (1976). 'Educational organizations as loosely coupled systems'. *Administrative Science Quarterly*, **21**, 1–19.

Wilson, D. C. (1980). *Strategic Decision Making in Organizations: Six Case Studies Illustrating the Role of Task, Power and Pace in Three Organizations*. Unpublished doctoral thesis, University of Bradford Management Centre, Bradford, England.

Wilson, D. C. (1982). 'Electricity and resistance: a case study of innovation and politics'. *Organization Studies*, **3**, 119–40.

Wilson, D. C., Butler, R. J., Cray, D., Hickson, D. J. and Mallory, G. R. (1982). 'The limits of trade union power in organizational decision making'. *British Journal of Industrial Relations*, **XX**, 322–41.

Wilson, D. C., Butler, R. J., Cray, D., Hickson, D. J. and Mallory, G. R. (1986). 'Breaking the bounds of organization in strategic decision making'. *Human Relations*, **39**, 309–32.

Wishart, D. (1978). *Clustan*. Edinburgh: Program Library Unit, Edinburgh University.

[6]

Journal of Management Studies 28:3 May 1991
0022-2380 $3.50

EXPLAINING DECISION PROCESSES

David Cray

Carleton University

Geoffrey R. Mallory

The Open University

Richard J. Butler

University of Bradford

David J. Hickson

University of Bradford

David C. Wilson

University of Warwick

INTRODUCTION

The study of strategic decision-making in organizations has given rise to a large body of theory and research. There are substantive reasons for this; strategic decisions affect not only the organizations in which they are taken, but have potential effects for large segments of society (Colignon and Cray, 1980). Strategic decisions also offer a research site for considering important theoretical questions regarding the way that individuals and organizations seek out and process information in situations of uncertainty (Zeleny, 1982). Because such decisions often carry high stakes for those involved, political processes which may otherwise be hidden are brought to the fore. The combination of substantive weight and theoretical interest has provided ample incentive for researchers to examine closely the processes by which organizations arrive at strategic decisions.

One of the main tasks in the study of strategic decision-making has been the accurate description of the decision-making process (Pennings, 1985), which has led naturally to attempts at categorization. A number of typologies of strategic decision-making process (*e.g.* Allison, 1971; MacCrimmon, 1985; Mintzberg *et al.*, 1976; Nutt, 1984; Stein, 1981a) have been constructed on various dimensions. While some of the underlying dimensions exhibit commonalities, there has been a general lack of agreement on what the basic types of strategic decision-making might be. This lack of consensus has both contributed to and resulted

Address for reprints: David Cray, Carleton University, Ottawa, Ontario, Canada K15 5B6.

from a corresponding absence of explanation as to how decisions come to be made in one way rather than another (Mohr, 1982, pp. 175–7).

The lack of explanation is due to the very qualities that have provoked such intriguing descriptive work. The intricate, convoluted nature of the process and the variety of contexts in which it occurs provide interesting anecdotes but make the development of a coherent, widely applicable explanation difficult. Researchers have attempted to deal with the twin issues of intricacy and variety in a number of ways. One tack has been to analyse a decision or series of decisions in a single organization. Pettigrew's work (1973, 1985) is the most developed example of this approach, but several others exist (*e.g.* Allison, 1971; Pinfield, 1986; Rowe, 1989; Wilson, 1982). The case study approach tackles the problem of intricacy directly, but at the expense of generalizability. Influences, both political and technical, which may loom large in one organization can be quite absent in another. A second approach has been to search for general dimensions on which one might locate any strategic decision. For the most part these exercises have been theoretical (*e.g.* Hage, 1980; MacCrimmon, 1985) although some have attempted to mate theoretical formulations with empirical support (*e.g.* Stein, 1981a, b). Strategic decisions have central importance in many fields of inquiry which has led to the development of numerous scholarly perspsectives, each with its own specific agenda and particular biases (Bass, 1983, p. 27).

In an earlier report on the Bradford studies (Cray *et al.*, 1988) three types of decision-making processes were described in terms of the variables shown in table I. Using clustering and discriminant analysis techniques, the three types, sporadic, fluid and constricted processes, were derived from a sample of 150 cases in 30 diverse organizations. Thus the three types should be widely generalizable, at least within the British context. The objective of this article is to explain as far as possible within the available data why these types of process occur.

Table I. Process variables

Information sources	— Expertise
Information sources	— Externality
Information sources	— Effort
Information sources	— Confidence disparity
Formal interaction (committees)	
Informal interaction	
Negotiation scope	
Disruption	
Impedance	
Duration	— Gestation time
Duration	— Process time
Authority	— Level

A brief description of each process type in terms of the relevant process variables is given in table II. Sporadic decision processes tend to encounter a larger number of more serious delays, to take longer than other types and to involve relatively more informal interaction along the way. The decision process lurches from one impasse to the next with individuals and groups debating alternatives in the halls and cafeterias so that the decision process is drawn-out. Fluid decisions move more quickly and steadily, encountering fewer and less important delays. This is facilitated through the work of more formal committees and working parties with more of the interaction taking place in these settings. Constricted decision processes are more focused than the other two types with most of the interaction taking place around a single individual or a small group. There are many sources of information but little extra effort made to gather less accessible data. Constricted processes tend to be limited in the information considered, the levels of the organization involved and the amount of formal interaction necessary.

Table II. Three types of decision-making processes

Process type	*Characterized by process variables*
Sporadic (informal, spasmodic and protracted)	More delays More impediments More sources of information More variability of information More informal interaction Some scope for negotiation More time to reach decision Decision taken at highest level
Fluid (steadily paced, formally channelled and speedy)	Fewer delays Fewer impediments Fewer sources of information Less variability of information Some scope for negotiation More formal interaction Less time to reach decision Decision taken at highest level
Constricted (narrowly channelled)	More sources of information Less effort to acquire information Little scope for negotiation Less formal interaction Decision taken below highest level

The decision process types described by the Bradford studies differed from earlier efforts in that the typology was derived from the analysis of specific variables. The data analysis provided estimates of the importance of individual variables for the differentiation of process types. For example, the amount of formal interaction did distinguish among three decision types, while the importance of information from outside the organization did not.

The Bradford studies differed from previous efforts in another way. If the intricacy and diversity of strategic decision processes has posed difficulties in creating usable typologies of strategic decision-making, then it has positively discouraged the development of explanations as to how particular decisions are made (Mohr, 1982, pp. 175–7). From their inception the Bradford studies were designed to distinguish between the process of decision-making and the factors which influence that process. The end product of the research which we wish to report in this article is not just another typology but an explanation of why decisions are made in one way rather than another. Using variables shown in table III which tap the technical and political conditions surrounding strategic decisions an explanation for the allocation of decisions to the three types can be constructed.

Table III. Explanatory variables

Complexity
Rarity
Precursiveness
Openness
Seriousness
Diffusion of consequences
Endurance
Radicality of consequences
Involvements
Diversity
Politicality
Contention
Pressure
Imbalance
Intervention

Operational definitions for the explanatory variables are given in Appendix A.

THEORY

In the four decades since Simon's (1947) seminal critique of the rational man model of decision-making, theorists have been trying to replace it with a systematic and coherent explanation of decision-making behaviour. Over the years a number of factors have been suggested as being important for understanding strategic decision-making. Hage (1980, p. 110), for example, argues that frequency of occurrence, costs, discontinuity with previous issues and risk are important factors. In a theoretical exposition MacCrimmon (1985) outlines four dimensions on which one may locate strategic decision processes. For MacCrimmon, the degree of rationality, informedness, social interest and degree of manipulativeness are the key dimensions of the decision-making context. Those beginning from empirical data have proposed more particular explanations of process, often alluding to external factors which influence the occurrence of stages in the decision-making process (*e.g.* Mintzberg *et al.*, 1976, Nutt, 1984).

In an effort to try to bring conceptual order from this plethora of explanations, Astley *et al.* (1982) proposed grouping explanatory factors under two general headings, problem complexity and political cleavage. These provide a dual explanation of decision processes, derived from both aspects of the matter under decision. Lyles' (1987) identification of politicality and complexity as two of the three subjective criteria managers use to classify strategic problems indicates that these headings have an experiential as well as theoretical grounding. Our purpose in this article is to examine a number of variables of problem complexity and political cleavage for their efficacy in allocating decisions to the three categories of decision process previously identified.

Problem complexity reflects the technical and informational aspects of the decision topic. The decision is viewed as a problem to be solved through the collection and analysis of data and the subsequent evaluation of alternative courses of action. The problem-solving rationality (Hickson *et al.*, 1985) invoked by this view is largely influenced by the nature of the problem itself as it passes through the established decision-making routines of the organization. This view has been criticized in its purely rational form as being hopelessly idealistic (Braybrooke and Lindblom, 1963), but in pointing out the difficulty of adequately analysing complex problems, these critics have underlined the importance of the complexity dimension. Non-optimal decision-making behaviour such as satisficing (Simon, 1960) is a reflection of the very difficulty that complexity presents.

Political cleavage, on the other hand, encompasses those explanations which focus on negotiation among interests in the decision-making arena. This approach is exemplified by those authors who emphasize the internal wrangling and external negotiation which is often present in strategic decision-making (*e.g.* Abell, 1975; Pettigrew, 1973; Pinfield, 1986). From this perspective the content of the issue is not nearly so important as the stakes that groups and individuals attach to probable outcomes. The most extreme version is found in the garbage can model (Cohen *et al.*, 1972; March and Olsen, 1976) in which the organization is seen as a collection of solutions looking for appropriate problems. The substance of the problem is, in a sense, irrelevant except for the stakes that can be attached to it by various interests.

The orchestration of decision processes, however, is far more than the sum of its parts in the guise of either technical or political explanations. As Astley and his co-authors (1982) argue, both complexity and political aspects should govern any integrated analytical approach to explaining decision process. Such a dual explanation allows the researcher to capture the collective social processes which are at play in the decision arena, thus avoiding focusing on individual managers (who may be idiosyncratic) or upon particular technical considerations (which may be decision-specific or which can only be understood in the context of a wider sphere of action). Reference to the collective and interactive processes of the technical and political factors establishes what might be called the culture of decision processes (Schwartz and Davis, 1981; Silverzweig and Allen, 1976). Culture in this context captures the collectivity of decision process characteristics, reflecting particular ways of proceeding and the routines which surround this.

Explanation requires the separation, for the purposes of causal argument, of the elements of explanation from what it is that these are believed to explain. That is an elementary and familiar step. Yet in research on decision-making process it is oddly unfamiliar. It is as if the fascinatingly intricate details of decision-making mesmerize onlooking researchers so that they cannot bring themselves to dissect each story. No attempt is made to sort out within the story what explains what. Description prevails, explanation fails.

We will examine in turn the complexity and the politicality inherent in what happens, treating each as part of the explanation.

Problem Complexity

The literature on strategic decision-making suggests a large number of factors which may contribute to the complexity of a problem. One set of factors is linked to how familiar the problem is. If the opportunity or problem is a common occurrence, say building a plant or launching a new product, then routines, or at least precedents, exist for the decision-making process. Unfamiliar topics raise the possibility of unforseen events. This dimension can be tapped most simply by *rarity*, the infrequency with which similar topics have arisen in the organization. Unfamiliar topics which occur less frequently will be more complex not only because alternatives must be sought, but because the mechanisms of search and evaluation will also have to be constructed (Butler *et al.*, 1979/80; DIO International Research Team, 1983; Hage, 1980). Situations which are perceived as unique, as many strategic decisions are, require considerable effort simply to construct the framework for considering the topic. The operationalization of this and all other explanatory variables is given in Appendix A.

The degree to which decisions fall into established organizational routines is also characterized by their place in a strategic stream (Mintzberg, 1978). If the decisions follow logically from an earlier decision, then some of the boundaries of the decision space are known and quite probably the orientations of organizational interests are known as well. If, on the other hand, topics are *precursive, i.e.* parameter-setting, they will be more complex than those which are not.

In a similar vein, not all decision topics have the same degree of *openness* in the search for possible alternatives. In some cases a solution will be virtually at hand, or at any rate, evident to those in authority; the decision to be made is simply whether or not to employ it (Mintzberg *et al.*, 1976). This may happen when a decision is reconsidered because of changing circumstances. In one of the cases collected for this study a particular alternative had been considered several times over the previous 15 years, but always rejected. When the circumstances of the firm changed, it was brought forward again and quickly adopted. Openness was low since only two alternatives, to adopt the proposal or not, were considered and the consequences of each had been discussed for years. The possibility of other alternatives was almost completely closed off.

While all strategic decisions are, by definition, about important issues, some are clearly of more importance than others. Yet there has been virtually no consideration in the literature on organizational decision-making as to how the possible consequences of a decision might affect the process by which it is made. This can be measured through the amount of funds committed, the degree of top management involvement or any number of other ways. In the Bradford studies the focus was on the *seriousness* of the decision topic, the degree to which the organization would suffer if the decision went wrong. This is somewhat akin to Hage's (1980, pp. 120–4) notion of risk, though, as will be noted below, with some important differences. Decisions which are seen as having more serious consequences for the organization demand careful attention to all factors so that the possible effects can be weighed more closely.

The breadth rather than the depth of possible consequences for the organization is indicated by the number of separate *criteria* used to evaluate success or failure (Campbell, 1988). Multiple, often conflicting, criteria greatly increase the number and content of possible tradeoffs (Landry, 1988). For Bronner (1986) the number and clarity of criteria is a key aspect of decision complexity.

The consequences of a decision also have a temporal component (Heller *et al.*, 1988, pp. 25–7). The longer it takes for the ramifications of a decision to appear, the more possible scenarios must be considered and the greater the period for which resources must be committed before corrective action can be taken. That is, the longer the *endurance* of the decision in the sense that the more years its consequences are likely to be felt and the further ahead the time horizon, the more complex it is.

Greater or lesser consequences are also indicated by the *radicality of consequences* that will result. Given the well-documented resistance to change that occurs in organizations, a radical change will give rise to a complex yet uncertain web of consequences which must be considered. Radicality of consequences differs from seriousness in that it charts the degree to which the decision outcome departs from the *status quo*, while seriousness reflects the difficulties that are likely to arise if the choice made is a wrong one.

Finally, the topic's complexity emerges from the variety of interests represented in the decision arena. The more there are and the more various they are, the greater the complexity to be faced. This is tapped in two ways. The sheer number of parties engaged is indicated by *involvements* and their variety of interests by the *diversity* of functional backgrounds represented. A problem which draws in experts with numerous perspectives and interests is liable to generate a process more sporadic in nature than one which relies on only a few functional groups for information and evaluation.

Politicality

Whatever the technical complexities inherent in a decision topic, the degree to which it raises political cleavage is the amount of *contention* that develops around a decision topic. For this study contention was seen as the existence of views opposing the eventual outcome. While contention denotes the opposition of aims, *pressure* refers to the total weight of influence brought to bear by the involved parties. Thus there could be a good deal of contention if two parties were bitterly divided over the course to follow, but if neither of the opponents were particularly powerful in the decision arena, or not interested enough to exert much influence, then the pressure would be low.

There may also be varying distributions of influence among the interests in the decision arena (Heller *et al.*, 1988, pp. 32–4). If the interests are made up of groups or individuals, some of whom are powerful and some weak, then the powerful should be able, if there is not contention among them, to impose a decision. However, if most of the interests have roughly the same amount of power, then bargaining and negotiation may complicate the decision process. Thus the *imbalance* of influence is an important aspect of politicality.

Finally, political cleavage is often intensified by the amount of *intervention* from outside the organization. Customers, competitors and regulatory agencies among many others, have the potential to disturb the decision process. This potential is even more pronounced when the external agent is a headquarters or owning group which may interfere directly.

Relating Process and Explantory Variables

For processes such as strategic decision-making which stretch over long periods of time, distinguishing between the variables which describe the process and those which influence it is not an easy task. The phase theorists (Mintzberg *et al.*, 1976; Nutt, 1984) attempt to avoid this difficulty by positing a series of steps in the decision process which may be accessed sequentially a number of times. Thus while the strategic decision-making process may be influenced by external considerations, in a very real sense each step of the process is the proximate cause for the next step. There is truth in this, of course, and this technique can provide a clear charting of specific decision processes and even allow identification of some similar processes. However, because process types are distinguished by the sequence of phases, decisions which are similar on underlying factors, *e.g.* the importance of external influence, but access phases in a different order, may be allocated to separate types. This limitation makes it very difficult to develop an overall explanation for decision process.

Another tack for explaining decision processes is to distinguish between independent and dependent variables and to relate one to the other. There have been a number of studies which have examined one or two independent variables and attempted to relate them to either decision types or to aspects of decisions embodied in independent variables. This approach can provide insights concerning the influence of particular factors or explanations of individual variables, but for a more general explanation the detail of multiple bivariate relationships obscures the overall story.

The Bradford studies were designed to draw on the strength of both approaches. Our aim was to discover and explain basic modes of decision-making derived from a large number of diverse cases. These modes were to be described in such a way that specific variables of process and explanation could be linked with general types. While accepting that processes may cycle many times through specific steps, we wished to examine the proposition that variables of complexity and politicality could explain the occurrence of decision processes of one type rather than another. Our interest was not in the relationships between particular process and explanatory variables but in the efficacy of the complexity and politicality variables collectively to distinguish among the three decision process types. We recognize that contained within the overall relationship there may be numerous phase-specific relationships, but we believe it is necessary to understand the overall relationship between explanatory and process variables before turning to specific bivariate relationships or particular sequences of activity. It is this basic relationship that is explored in this article.

SAMPLE AND METHODS

The data were collected from 30 diverse British organizations in both the public and private sectors, with each sector providing some which produced goods and some which delivered services. The organizations ranged in size from 100 to 50,000 employees. The 30 organizations included breweries, polytechnics, an automobile parts manufacturer, two public utilities and other similarly varied institutions. Many of the organizations studied have considerable national standing and a number are of international importance.

After being approached by letter, the chief executive officer (CEO) met with members of the research team to discuss the history of the organization, its structure and outputs and its position relative to other organizations in its environment. The CEO was then asked to nominate a number of important decisions made recently by that organization. Five decisions from each of the 30 organizations provided the 150 decisions which form the empirical base of this study. They included decisions to invest in new technology, reorganizations, corporate plans and budgets, market and image decisions, new products and services, personnel assessment and unionization, mergers and takeovers, financing and supplies and relocation decisions. A full description of the organizations and decision topics is given in a previous report (Cray *et al.*, 1988).

In the first phase of the fieldwork, the data on six of the 150 cases were gathered by a researcher who spent many months in each of three organizations, a university, a public utility and a chemical manufacturer. In each of these organizations two decisions were examined. One was recorded as it unfolded while the other was investigated retrospectively in detail by interviewing those centrally concerned. These six cases (Wilson, 1982; Wilson *et al.*, 1986) provided the methodological groundwork for the rest of the study. The remaining 144 narratives were collected through interviews with participants nominated by the CEO in the initial interview or suggested, in turn, by original informants.

Each interview began with an extended description of the decision process from the time the issue was first raised until the outcome, positive or negative, was authorized. This was followed by a series of open-ended questions in which the informant amplified and clarified certain aspects of the process. Some of these questions were supplemented by five-point scales on which the informant rated a particular feature. The most important of these were ratings of the influence of interests in the decision arena and the reliability of sources of information used in the decision. This method gave the advantage of a narrative provided by the interviewee in his/her own words with more specific information on selected points in line with the theoretical framework. Where multiple informants were employed, the separate accounts were consolidated into a single description. Details of this and other aspects of the research methodology can be found in earlier reports from the project (Cray *et al.*, 1988; Hickson *et al.*, 1986).

To appreciate fully the analysis reported in this article it must be placed in perspective with that reported in the companion piece (Cray *et al.*, 1988). The overall analytical process is described in summary in table IV. During stage 1 data was collected for both the process and explanatory variables. In the second stage data on the process variables were subjected to cluster analysis. This produced three distinct clusters of processes. Given the number of variables considered and the number of cases in each cluster it was difficult and potentially misleading to interpret the clusters merely through inspection. To add rigour to the description of each cluster they were subjected to discriminant analysis (stage 3) in order to provide an estimate (weight) of the importance of each variable for distinguishing among the different clusters. This procedure not only allowed the clear description of three empirically distinct types of decision process but also allowed us to characterize each type by means of the variable weights provided by the discriminant analysis.

In this article our purpose is to explain the occurrence of processes of each type. In stage 4 the three clusters were again subjected to discriminant analysis, but at this point the explanatory variables were used to discriminate. It should be noted that there is an important difference between the use of the discriminant analysis in the two papers. For the analysis reported in Cray *et al.* (1988) the process variables were first used to form the clusters and then to distinguish among them. Thus it was not the degree of discrimination which was of interest, since this must be high, but the weights of the individual variables which indicated the importance of each in producing the clusters.

Table IV. Data collection and analysis

Stage 1	Data collected for process (table I) and explanatory (table III) variables.
Stage 2	Data on process variables subjected to cluster analysis which produced three distinct clusters of processes, named as sporadic, constricted and fluid.
Stage 3	Discriminant analysis of the process variables used to determine the importance (weight) of each variable in distinguishing among the three process clusters thus providing a variable-based description for the three decision-making types.
Stage 4	Discriminant analysis again employed, now using the explanatory variables in order to determine which is important for allocating cases among the three process clusters.
Stage 5	The three process clusters, or types of decision processes are linked with the explanatory variables which distinguish them to constitute three decision modes.

The results of stages one, two and three are reported in Cray *et al.* (1988). The results of stages four and five are reported in this article.

For the second discriminant analysis, the results of which are reported here, the explanatory variables were employed to discriminate among the three clusters of processes. The discriminant analysis programme constructs functions by weighting the variables to reproduce as closely as possible an original allocation of cases among the categories. The procedure provides a global estimate of how well the explanatory variables collectively predict the allocation of the cases to clusters originally defined by the process variables, as well as providing estimates of the importance of each variable to that discrimination. If the explanatory variables were unrelated to the types of decision process, then neither the overall estimate nor the estimates for individual variables would discriminate.

This method of analysis follows from the theoretical task. While the relation ships between the individual variables (shown in Appendix B) are interesting, considering numerous measures of bivariate association tends to cloud rather than illuminate a discussion of the overall decision process and its explanation. The correlations indicate a number of possible connections, but they do not provide an explanation. Regression analysis was also rejected after some initial trials because the number and complexity of equations to be considered meant that conclusions about the decision process tended to be piecemeal and highly contingent. By using cluster and discriminant analysis the number of relationships to be considered was reduced and the required assumptions for the statistical techniques more nearly met.

RESULTS

On the whole, the results of the discriminant analysis bear out the claim that the variables of complexity and politicality can explain decision processes. The procedure generated two orthogonal functions which discriminated between pairs of groups with probabilities ranging from $p<0.0001$ ($F_{8,101} = 5.36$) to $p<0.003$ ($F_{8,101} = 4.12$).

Another way of judging the success of the partitioning exercise is by comparing the allocation of the cases by these two functions with the original groupings by process variables. If the explanatory variables were perfect predictors, then all the off-diagonal cells in a matrix of groupings produced from dependent process variables against those produced from independent complexity and politicality variables would be zero. As can be seen in table V this is not the case. While the relationship is very strong ($X^2 = 53.32$, $p<0.001$, df = 4) it is not perfect. Even so, it is strong enough to indicate that the explanatory variables do provide an efficient allocation. The evenness of the deviations from the diagonal suggests that there is unlikely to be another strong source of systematic variation which these concepts do not encompass.

Table V. Allocation of cases by explanatory variables

Groups predicted by discriminant functions	*Clusters derived from process variables*		
	1 Sporadic	2 Constricted	3 Fluid
1 Vortex	36	7	9
2 Familiar	12	20	7
3 Tractable	7	7	28

$n = 133$
$X^2 = 52.32$
dF = 4
$p<0.001$

Table VI shows the coefficients including the loadings of each variable on the functions which best discriminate between groupings of cases. The first noticeable result is that five variables, four of the nine complexity variables and one of the four politicality variables, do not contribute significantly to the discriminating functions. In a few cases sizeable correlations between variables (shown in Appendix B) made it unlikely that both would enter the equations. For most of the omitted variables, though, their absence simply means that they were not important in allocating decisions from this sample to process categories. For example, knowing whether a decision had radical or moderate consequences tells one little about whether it is likely to be made by a sporadic, fluid or constricted process.

The two functions shown in table VI are, by definition, dimensions on which the clusters can be located. The first function loads most heavily on imbalance, the negative coefficient (-0.77) indicating that those involved in the decision tend to be of roughly equal influence, with a relatively large proportion from outside the organization (intervention = 0.48). Precursiveness (0.57) is the most heavily weighted of the complexity variables indicating that decisions scoring high on this dimension may not generally be guided by pre-existing constraints, but tend to set parameters for future actions. The notion of moving into new areas is supported by the moderate positive coefficients for rarity (0.37) and the number of criteria used to evaluate the decision (0.32). Though this dimension is heavily loaded on two of the political variables, it does not involve a great deal of political conflict. It is dominated neither by politicality nor complexity factors.

Table VI. Rotated, standardized discriminant function coefficients

Variable	*Function 1*	*Function 2*
Complexity		
Rarity	0.37	0.02
Precursiveness	0.57	−0.34
Openness	*a*	*a*
Seriousness	−0.18	0.24
Diffusion of consequences	0.32	−0.11
Endurance	*a*	*a*
Radicality of consequences	*a*	*a*
Involvements	*a*	*a*
Diversity	0.11	0.67
Politicality		
Contention	0.01	0.79
Pressure	*a*	*a*
Imbalance	−0.77	−0.21
Intervention	0.48	0.32

n = 111
a = variables which did not enter into the functions

The second dimension is marked by high coefficients for contention (0.79) and diversity (0.67). Decisions scoring high on this dimension involve interests with opposing objectives and different functional backgrounds. There is also some intervention (0.32) by outside interests. While these decisions are seen as slightly (0.24) more serious than others, they tend to focus on fairly well-defined issues (precursiveness = −0.34).

The composition of these two underlying dimensions provides two important pieces of evidence for an explanation of decision process. First, a number of the variables of complexity and politicality do discriminate among the three types of decision process. Other variables might well improve such an effort, but the ones defined in this study are adequate for the task so that future efforts should take them into account. Second, for these organizations and decisions, the discriminating dimensions are not uniquely complexity and politicality but are comprised of aspects of each. The elegance of the two theoretical dimensions is reflected in a more complicated reality in which elements of each are found to be empirically significant.

THREE MODES OF DECISION-MAKING

We can now return to the possibility of holistic explanations for the occurrence of each type of process. Figure 1 shows the three types of decision process cases, sporadic, fluid and constricted, plotted on the two explanatory dimensions. The dimensions are a means of identifying the matter for decision that is most likely to generate each type of decision-making process. Three kinds of decision, vortex, tractable and familiar are identified.

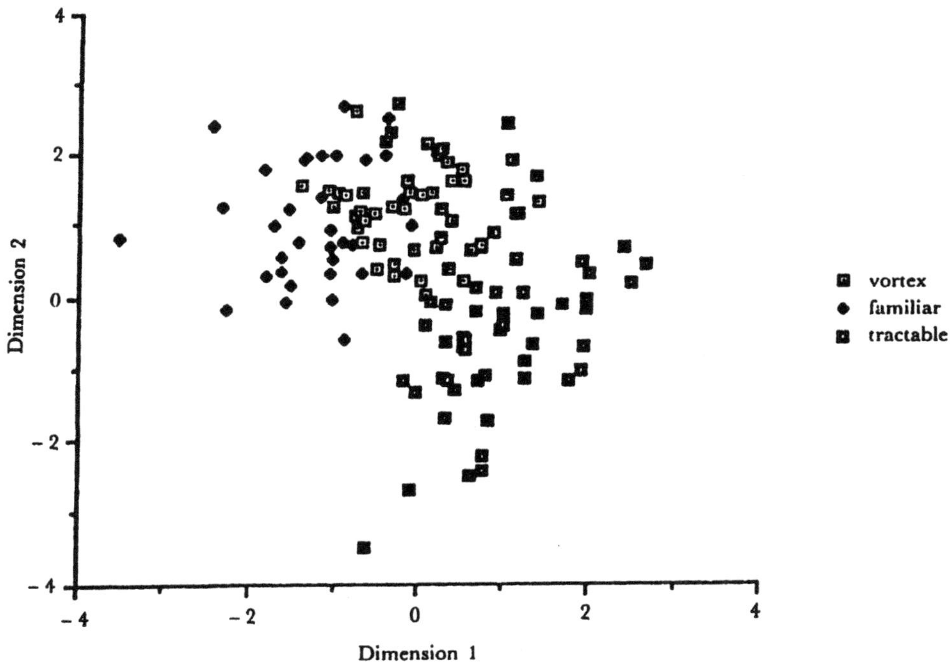

Figure 1. Distribution of three clusters

Table VII shows that the first process type, sporadic, which encounters numerous delays and interruptions and employs large numbers of experts to gather information, loads heavily on function 2 (0.72). Hence a sporadic process is most likely to occur when management is faced with a serious or weighty decision which involves a diversity of contending interests. Since there are contending groups involved in the matter, it is not surprising that such processes tend to take longer and to be frequently interrupted. These decisions are called *vortex* decisions because they tend to pull a large variety of different groups into the decision arena in energetic activity around a central issue. Because of the importance of the decision there is likely to be intervention by outside groups who also have their own interests to pursue.

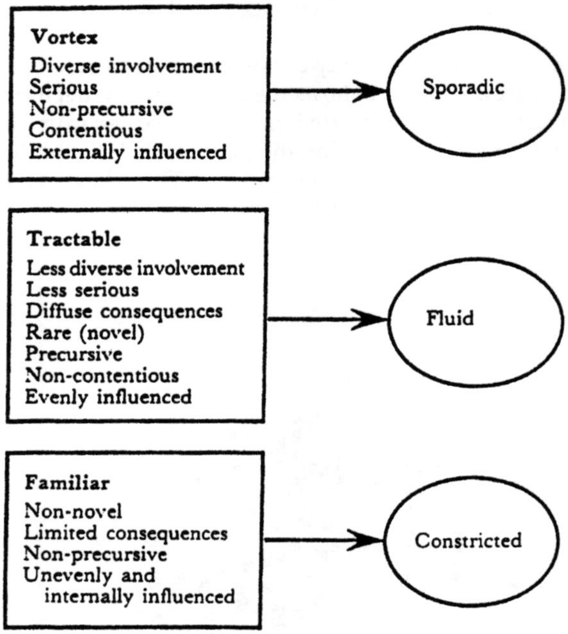

Figure 2. Three modes of decision-making

Table VII. Function values for group means (centroids)

Group	*Function 1*	*Function 2*
1 (Sporadic-vortex)	0.12	0.72
2 (Constricted-familiar)	– 0.90	– 0.21
3 (Fluid-tractable)	0.67	– 0.61

Putting together the concept of a vortex matter for decision and a sporadic type of process gives a *vortex-sporadic* mode of decision-making. An instance of this can be seen by examining a decision made in a nationalized chemical producer. The decision concerned the exploitation of a chemical process for which the firm had acquired a worldwide licence. All parties to the decision agreed that the process was likely to be profitable, perhaps very much so. The main issue was the location of the plant to utilize the chemical process. Since the main customers were other industries, many of them on the continent, there were arguments for locating the plant abroad. This brought the domestic and international divisions into the decision arena. Other groups, such as foreign governments, ministries of the national government and the company which licensed the process, were also very interested in the outcome.

This decision exhibited the characteristics of a sporadic process in that it encountered a number of delays for gathering information and obtaining approval. More serious delays were also experienced when some groups actively opposed it. It was a drawn-out decision, taking three years to complete. Finally, it had to be ratified at the top level of the organization and then ratified again by another level of the nationalized industry hierarchy.

The sporadic nature of this decision process seems due to the number and diversity of the interests involved. Each group could see that the plant would bring considerable resources to whoever controlled it. It would also offer a new profit opportunity for the controlling division at a time when such situations were in short supply. There were no less than 14 different interests which exerted influence in the decision arena at one time or another during the process. The bulk of the influence came from external parties including customers, the parent corporation and national governments. Contention was aroused as separate interests tried to gain control of the chemical process and the associated future investment. Other parties sought to protect their own interests. It was not a rare decision, since, despite the spirited discussion, it was a new product decision, a quite common type in the organization. However, this did not mean that the decision process moved quickly, quite the contrary. Since the stakes were high and apparent to everyone involved, and since the process was open, those interested took time to make sure that their arguments were as strong as possible. Information (*e.g.* shipping costs, demand location, tax incentives) had to be gathered to support opposing positions. The sheer number of individuals involved also meant that there were scheduling difficulties and delays while parties were consulted. A vortex decision with its diverse opposing interests led to a sporadic process which was intermittent, interrupted and drawn out.

Processes of the fluid type are located on the negative end of dimension 2 (– 0.61) and an almost equal distance along the positive axis of the other dimension (0.67). Hence this type of process tends to take place when decisions are not as serious as in the vortex-sporadic cases but are more precursive and rare. These decisions do not involve nearly as much political activity and are much less contentious. Even though they set parameters and do not occur all that often in the life of an organization, they can be smoothly processed through the usual framework of committees in a comparatively short time. These are the types of decisions, with low political involvement among a relatively evenly balanced group of interests, which we regard as *tractable*.

The *tractable-fluid* mode of decision-making can be illustrated by a decision in a large financial firm with worldwide operations. This was a topic which was unique for the firm both in its content and its implications. The issue was the status of the organization's many overseas units. Until this time they had been organized as branches of the firm, the usual arrangement in the industry. For both political and administrative reasons it was thought useful to consider changing these to subsidiaries. This was not a step to be taken lightly as it would have implications for taxes, for compliance with host country regulations, and most importantly, for the image that the foreign units would have of their place in the global organization. There were also the more familiar but no less important considerations of cost and efficiency.

The positive value on the first dimension is reflected in the long-term implications of the decision for the subsidiaries and the firm as a whole. The issue was regarded as quite serious and as such it was somewhat more contentious than most decisions in the tractable-fluid mode. However, most of the opposition came from a single foreign branch which resisted the change for purely local reasons. Among the other branches and in the home office there were no persistent dissenters.

The possibility of this change had been apparent for four years before actual deliberations started. Once consideration began, the decision was completed in nine months, a very short time for such an important matter. The process was simplified by having a single executive collect and synthesize most of the pertinent information. He was assisted by three others who had specialist knowledge in relevant business areas. Most of the consideration was done by one committee with its work approved by a second, the board of the firm. This tractable problem, for which a solution seemed apparent even if all the ramifications were not clear, was solved by a fluid decision process in which the parties came rapidly to a conclusion with little political bickering.

The remaining type of process, *constricted*, is loaded negatively on the second dimension (– 0.21) but much more so on the first (– 0.90). This type of process tends to occur when the decision topic has some recognizable features; something analogous has happened before. It has relatively few implications for later decisions, its consequences are limited, and those who are interested tend to be from within the organization itself. These are *familiar* decisions. Although strategic, they hold few surprises for those involved and are unlikely to be contentious. Whereas vortex decisions tend to pull in diverse and external interests with differing opinions, familiar decisions involve mainly internal departments which have been through it before and know what the score is. The decision moves through the hierarchy of the organization along an established path involving only those who are centrally concerned, since the guidelines for such a decision have already been established.

In this *familiar-constricted* mode of decision-making, authorization comes at a lower level (in the context of strategic decisions this usually means that the CEO makes the final decision without further authorization). There is little effort to gather information beyond what is normally available. The scope of negotiation is limited and the interaction that does take place is informal rather than in formally constituted committees. Familiar decisions are processed by moving over well-mapped terrain with a minimum of disruption.

The familiar-constricted mode is illustrated by a decision which took place in a British subsidiary of a giant American conglomerate. Since the subsidiary had recently been sold by its founder, who had then left the firm, the top managers were eager to produce good financial results. At the time the economy was slowing so it did not seem as if this could be achieved without some new initiative. The strategy finally settled upon was the reworking and expansion of their main product line, specialty paints. To some extent this was a familiar decision in that new products were introduced on a regular basis. However, such a major restructuring had not been undertaken for ten years.

As would be expected in a constricted decision, the CEO ratified the final choice with no further approval required. The scope of negotiation was limited to the CEO and his immediate subordinates. There were several internal influences but no outside intervention at all. The group that might logically be expected to intervene, the parent corporation, did not believe in direct interference in this type of business decision. The managers of the parent mostly limited themselves to exercising financial control (Cray, 1984). Whatever decisions the subsidiary managers took, the results would be judged through their impact on the profitability of the unit. For the British managers who made the decision it was familiar in most of its technical particulars. The only novel element was the fact that the effectiveness of the decision would be judged not by a colleague in the next office but by new masters several thousand miles away.

DISCUSSION

Writers on the study of strategic decisions have frequently commented on the confusing diversity of the field (Bass, 1983; Pennings, 1985). This study was designed to reduce rather than add to that confusion by developing from a large empirical base an explanation of how strategic decisions are allocated among three process types. To place the present study in its context it will be compared to a number of published theoretical and empirical efforts at explanation. Such a comparison cannot be exhaustive, of course, but it will serve to locate our efforts in this expanding field of inquiry.

Hage (1980, pp. 109–29), in an attempt to develop a comprehensive theory of decision-making argues that, 'a single decision can be characterized by its frequency of occurrence, its costs, its discontinuity with previous issues, and its risks' (Hage, 1980, p. 110). There is an encouraging congruence between Hage's theoretical argument and the results of the Bradford studies. We do find that frequency (the inverse of our rarity) is important for the first dimension in explaining decision processes (see table VI). Hage's discontinuity is paralleled by, but not identical to, our precursiveness, which contributes significantly to both dimensions. For these two factors the Bradford studies support Hage's contention that these are important determinants of the decision process.

It is harder to draw definite conclusions about the cost and risk factors. Hage defines risk as 'the predictability of outcome. . .' (1980, p. 110). This is clearly an important factor for managers. However, few managers of the over 200 interviewed appeared to think of risk only in terms of how predictable the end result might be. The more important consideration for the bulk of them was cost. Hage suggests the resources committed by a choice is the cost of the decision. For the managers in the Bradford sample cost was more commonly and immediately seen as the cost of failure. Should the decision be a wrong one, what would it cost the decision-maker and the organization. This was tapped in the Bradford studies by the variable seriousness of consequences, which did help distinguish, albeit marginally, among the three types of decision process.

A decision might very well be risky in that the outcomes could not be easily predicted, but it need not be serious because the occurrence of any of the outcomes, even negative ones, would not have important negative consequences for the decision-maker or the organization. This idea of seriousness also highlights the importance of the political aspect of decision-making which is missing from Hage's discussion of cost. Many of the most serious negative consequences that can emerge from a decision are political. A bad decision can cost a manager credibility, promotion, bonuses or even his/her job. Backing the wrong alternative can cost a department its political future. A serious error can hasten the demise of an organization, a circumstance observed in one of the cases in the Bradford studies. All this implies that Hage's development of separate models for high and low risk decisions (1980, pp. 110–24) may be based on a distinction that imperfectly reflects the reality of the decision-maker and his/her organization.

That these contrasting conceptualizations of risk are not simply a sematic quibble but a modification of a theory by empirical evidence can be seen in the three basic decision modes that emerged. Weighty and controversial matters which constitute vortex decisions are likely to be handled through sporadic processes. Unusual but not controversial tractable matters are usually processed in a fluid way. Normal and recurrent familiar matters, those which are frequent and continuous in Hage's terms, are processed in a constricted manner. For all three modes, the greater presence or relative absence of the political element is an important and distinguishing factor.

A further theoretical attempt to understand decision-making processes has been provided by MacCrimmon (1985). Using four dimensions of the decision-making context, degree of rationality, level of information, social interest and manipulativeness, he generates 36 possible types of decision-making process of which three are developed as holistic models. MacCrimmon defines these three as extreme instances which are intended to provoke discussion. The three types are the mechanistic model which is characterized by low rationality and low level of information, the super-rational model in which decision-makers have perfect information and operate in a highly rational manner, and the Machiavellian model in which high manipulativeness is coupled with a high level of information. Do these three hypothetical models in any way resemble the empirically derived modes presented above?

The Machiavellian model to some extent resembles our vortex-sporadic mode. Manipulativeness is high, though in our formulation it is not a single princely manager who has political interest in the decision, but virtually all those involved. The two also resemble each other on the high level of informedness. The political content of the decision drives the participants to seek information from many possible sources for use as ammunition in the political arena. Since the information is processed from a political rather than a technical perspective, it is seen as having variable reliability. Our research would also suggest that rationality is high in this case, but it is a political rationality (Hickson *et al.*, 1986; Rowe, 1989) rooted in the calculus of control and influence rather than an abstract logical rationality.

For the other two models the fit is less good. The super-rational model has some similarities with the familiar-constricted mode. For MacCrimmon the super-rational model depends on perfect knowledge of potential outcomes. In our study this situation is most nearly approximated when the matter is familiar, not very complex and least political. A single manager and his/her advisers are the fulcrum for the decision-making process. The certainty seems to stem from experience with similar problems, or at least problems that seem familiar. Difficulties arise when a manager mistakes a new problem for a familiar one (see MacCrimmon's discussion of Allison's (1971) analysis of the Cuban missile crisis).

The mechanistic model has little connection with any of the modes of decision-making emerging from the Bradford studies. Such behaviour could sometimes be seen in the routines that decision-makers used, for example in the use of a familiar committee structure or in soliciting opinions from often-used sources, but seldom in the way that routines and information were put together. Managers would, therefore, be unwise to assume standard procedures are a dominant pathway for process at the strategic level. Collective decision utilizes but usurps such pre-established routines. It takes place above and beyond them.

Our results and those of Mintzberg *et al.* (1976) do show some important parallel findings. The political aspect, far from being a myth as Klein (1988) maintains, is a central element of both typologies. Internal and external opposition to alternatives serve to lengthen, complicate and redirect the decision process. Where the Bradford studies go further is in providing a more generalizable explanation of the kinds of processes so vividly described by Mintzberg and his colleagues (1976).

Similarly the emphasis on complexity is reflected in both typologies. This leads to two important but more subtle points of agreement. Both sets of studies insist on the importance of both politicality and complexity. The ways in which the ideas are brought into the studies differ, but the evidence for dual explanation is clear. The Bradford studies make it clear that these are not orthogonal factors. Both of the discriminating functions drew on elements of both politicality and complexity to allocate the decision types in the three categories. Thus it is the interaction of the two rather than the simple action of one or the other which is important. Finally, since the Mintzberg *et al.* (1976) decisions were taken from a Canadian context, to the extent that there is congruence, these studies show common features for decision processes in two separate national settings.

Finally, Nutt (1984) reports evidence from a study conducted in the USA although, unlike the Canadian and British studies, it is limited to a single industry. Using 78 decisions in organizations related to medical practice, Nutt identifies five types with eleven subtypes. The study utilizes a phase approach to categorization.

Nutt goes beyond most other empirical investigations in that he does attempt to link his process types to the stimuli that prompt them. Unfortunately when the eleven subtypes are spread across the three types of stimulus (problem, opportunity and crisis) the number of cases in each cell becomes small, making it difficult to draw firm conclusions.

There are two basic differences between the approach of Nutt and that taken by the Bradford group. First, Nutt categorizes process largely by the type of search and the origin of alternatives. While taking these into account as important factors, the Bradford typology of process includes other important variables tapping, for example, interaction, negotiation and flow. For explanation Nutt relies mainly on the origin of the stimulus. The Bradford group did not include this *per se*. Rather we tried to characterize the stimulus in terms of its rarity, its seriousness, *etc*. The consequences of the two differing approaches can be readily seen in the typologies that result. The Bradford typology is broadly based, more general and includes both process and the explanation of that process. The Nutt typology is more specific, possibly more limited in its application, and more tenuous in the link between process type and stimulus.

CONCLUSION

Since decision-making lies at the heart of the collection of processes we know as organization, a full appreciation of its elements are vital to theorist and practitioner alike. In this article we have put forward an empirically derived explanation for a threefold typology of process. Such an approach characterizes the rich details of each case as a whole so as to link specific contexts with collective processual action. It separates, within the intricacies of decision-making, those variables which describe the matters under decision from those which describe the process of decision. The one is used to explain the other. It is shown that particular types of process tend to happen because of the particular kinds of decision being made. Vortex kinds of decision most often generate sporadic types of process, tractable kinds of decision most often generate fluid types of process and familiar kinds of decision most often generate constricted types of process.

The research described in this article is an attempt to replace single case descriptions and collections of rules-of-thumb with a rigorous and systematic analysis of the processual aspects of decision-making. In this way managers can understand past actions as well as predict the likely course of future efforts. The specifics of issues will differ, but much of the collective organizational context of decision-making is, we suggest, substantially captured in the three distinct modes which have been outlined here. Such a modal approach would seem appropriate in the current climate of corporate change and organizational renewal.

In this study we have avoided imposing a linear, phase-bound structure on the analysis of process. Thus we have avoided the often erroneous assumption (by theorists and practitioners alike) that the decision process moves in distinct steps. The modal approach to process adopted here makes no such assumption. Rather than encouraging the manager to think in steps or phases, it emphasizes the importance of recognizing the general nature of the process holistically, and recognizing the kind of decision likely to activate it. Sporadic, fluid and constricted processes reflect the impact of managerial action on vortex, tractable and familiar decisions against the background of the corporate context. We argue that primacy should be given to the understanding of the whole before analysis of the detail. Until now it would seem that the reverse has been true of decision theory.

As always much work remains to be done. This article has dealt with how the matter for decision may explain the kind of process that ensues, but has not considered how far the process may also result from the form of organization in which it takes place. We ourselves have discussed this elsewhere (Hickson *et al.*, 1986), but only as a beginning to answering a very open question. Cross-national comparisons with more specific comparative intent are needed to determine the extent to which results are applicable to other cultural settings. Individual behaviours within the overall process, such as the activation of influence and the use of information in the decision arena clearly call for their own detailed study. What we hope to have accomplished through the work presented in this article and other publications of the Bradford group (*e.g.* Cray and Mallory, 1987; Cray *et al.*, 1988; Hickson *et al.*, 1986; Mallory *et al.*, 1983; Wilson *et al.*, 1986) is to provide an empirical benchmark from which this research may proceed.

APPENDIX A
OPERATIONALIZATION OF EXPLANATORY VARIABLES

Complexity of Problems

Rarity. The negative of the frequency with which similar matters recur, indicated by the number of times per year that such a topic occurs.

Radicality of consequences. How far the decision changed things, indicated by a score on a five-point rating (1 = not at all; 2 = a little; 3 = quite a lot; 4 = substantially; 5 = radically).

Seriousness of consequences. How serious it would be for the organization if things went wrong, indicated by a score on a five-point rating (1 = not all; 2 = slightly; 3 = quite; 4 = very; 5 = extremely).

Diffusion of consequences. How widespread were the decisions effects, indicated by the number of categories of criteria used to judge its correctness from 11 categories (profit, quality, output, costs, sales, return on investment, service rendered, morale, personnel benefits, image, market share).

Endurance of consequences. How far ahead people looked when making the decision, to the nearest tenth of a year.

Precursiveness. How far a decision was likely to set parameters for subsequent decisions (non-precursive = the alternatives considered followed parameters within an overall strategy; precursive = any or all of the alternatives had no such parameters and therefore themselves set parameters for subsequent decisions).

Number of interests involved. The number of internal units/departments and external units/organizations named as having been involved.

Diversity of interests involved. The variety of interest, indicated by the number of categories of internal and external interests involved from 14 categories of interest.

Openness to alternatives. How far there was a feeling that the decision had already been made (4 = no feeling of this kind; 3 = partly, yes and no; 2 = yes, clear to some interest groups; 1 = yes, obvious to all interest groups).

Politicality of Interests

Contention of objectives. How far the interest units that exerted influence did so in opposite directions, indicated by the range of scores on a five-point scale of opposition to, or support for, the eventual decision (−2 = strong opposition; −1 = qualified opposition; 0 = neutral; +1 = qualified support; +2 = strong support).

Pressure of influence. How great a weight of influence was exerted, indicated by the mean for all interest units of ratings by informants of the influence of each interest involved (1 = little; 2 = some; 3 = quite a lot; 4 = a great deal; 5 = a very great deal).

Imbalance. How far the total pressure was uneven across interest units, indicated by the range of the influence ratings between them (narrow range = balanced influence, wide range = imbalance).

Intervention. How far external influence was exerted, indicated by the percentage of the sum of influence ratings for all interest units that was due to external units.

Appendix B – Correlations among variables of process and explanation

		(1)	*(2)*	*(3)*	*(4)*	*(5)*	*(6)*	*(7)*	*(8)*	*(9)*	*(10)*
Expertise	(1)										
Externality	(2)	– 14									
Effort	(3)	– 05	04								
Disparity	(4)	23	14	– 02							
Formal interaction	(5)	14	03	– 15	– 03						
Informal interaction	(6)	15	17	16	21	01					
Scope	(7)	– 06	05	– 01	– 16	12	25				
Disruption	(8)	15	– 01	11	17	09	25	07			
Impedance	(9)	22	06	14	28	03	36	08	71		
Gestation time	(10)	– 06	– 06	14	– 14	– 01	04	– 01	06	– 01	
Process time	(11)	14	07	11	10	10	18	06	27	22	07
Level	(12)	– 01	00	11	– 07	18	19	20	15	14	20
Rarity	(13)	– 04	– 12	– 01	– 05	15	06	03	06	03	04
Precursiveness	(14)	– 17	– 02	03	– 19	– 02	09	15	– 22	– 19	15
Openness	(15)	– 07	– 14	09	– 03	– 10	– 26	03	– 14	– 14	– 01
Seriousness	(16)	– 04	01	– 02	15	– 03	28	19	16	25	03
Diffusion of consequences	(17)	20	03	02	00	22	13	09	06	02	– 06
Endurance	(18)	– 02	– 03	14	– 11	06	13	20	14	07	35
Radicality of consequences	(19)	– 03	05	08	05	– 10	19	15	09	05	13
Involvements	(20)	54	12	11	14	31	19	01	19	25	03
Diversity	(21)	29	16	19	16	09	15	– 07	12	16	– 09
Contention	(22)	05	11	06	15	– 12	28	21	14	18	18
Pressure	(23)	– 16	– 02	14	– 13	– 02	10	23	– 15	– 20	18
Imbalance	(24)	25	02	– 13	24	09	04	– 14	08	10	– 10
Intervention	(25)	– 03	52	18	11	– 02	24	– 03	09	17	05
		(1)	*(2)*	*(3)*	*(4)*	*(5)*	*(6)*	*(7)*	*(8)*	*(9)*	*(10)*

For openness $N = 127$; for all other variables N ranges from 140–150

(11)	*(12)*	*(13)*	*(14)*	*(15)*	*(16)*	*(17)*	*(18)*	*(19)*	*(20)*	*(21)*	*(22)*	*(23)*	*(24)*
01													
08	28												
-06	25	16											
-01	-05	-01	13										
08	14	05	07	00									
-01	-02	06	01	-02	15								
10	11	15	12	01	13	09							
12	15	06	28	10	38	15	14						
16	13	09	-09	-03	08	30	01	10					
12	-03	03	-01	-01	20	32	-02	10	67				
10	10	-06	-06	-06	07	04	10	16	09	-04			
-01	12	-05	-16	-16	03	-01	23	13	-28	16	-09		
12	-07	01	19	19	09	11	-14	-01	39	28	23	-55	
23	30	-01	03	03	15	06	-01	21	36	22	17	-08	25
(11)	*(12)*	*(13)*	*(14)*	*(15)*	*(16)*	*(17)*	*(18)*	*(19)*	*(20)*	*(21)*	*(22)*	*(23)*	*(24)*

REFERENCES

Abell, P. (1975). 'Organizations as bargaining and influence systems: measuring intra-organizational power and influence'. In Abell, P. (Ed.), *Organizations as Bargaining and Influence Systems*. London: Heinemann; New York: Halstead Press-Wiley.

Allison, G. (1971). *Essence of Decision*. Boston: Little, Brown.

Astley, W., Axelsson, G. R., Butler, R. J., Hickson, D. J. and Wilson, D. C. (1982). 'Complexity and cleavage: dual explanations of strategic decision making'. *Journal of Management Studies,* **19**, 357–75.

Bass, B. M. (1983). *Organizational Decision-making*. New York: Irwin.

Braybrooke, D. and Lindblom. C. (1963). *A Strategy of Decision*. New York: Free Press.

Bronner, R. (1986). 'Perception of complexity in decision-making processes: findings of experimental investigations'. In Witte, E. and Zimmerman, H.-J. (Eds.), *Empirical Research on Organizational Decision Making*. Amsterdam: North-Holland.

Butler, R. J., Astley, W. G., Hickson, D. J., Mallory, G. R. and Wilson, D. C. (1979/80). 'Strategic decision making: concepts of content and process'. *International Studies of Management and Organization,* **9**, 5–36.

Campbell, D. J. (1988). 'Task, complexity: a review and analysis'. *Academy of Management Review,* **13**, 40–52.

Cohen, M. D., March, J. G. and Olsen, J. P. (1972). 'A garbage can model of organizational choice'. *Administrative Science Quarterly,* **17**, 1–25.

Colignon, R. and Cray, D. (1980). 'Critical organizations'. *Organizaton Studies,* **1**, 349–66.

Cray, D. (1984). 'Control and coordination in multinational corporations'. *Journal of International Business Studies,* **15**, 85–98.

Cray, D. and Mallory, G. R. (1987). 'A comparative examination of organizational decision making'. *International Business,* **8**, 42–50. Proceedings of the Annual meeting of the Administrative Sciences Association of Canada, Kingston, Ontario, ASAC.

Cray, D., Mallory, G. R., Butler, R. J., Hickson, D. J. and Wilson, D. C. (1988). 'Sporadic, constricted and fluid processes: three types of strategic decision making in organizations'. *Journal of Management Studies,* **25**, 13–39.

DIO International Research Team (1983). 'A contingency model of participative decision making: an analysis of 56 decisions in three Dutch organizations'. *Journal of Occupational Psychology,* **56**, 1–18.

Hage, J. (1980). *Theories of Organizations: Form, Process and Transformation*. New York: Wiley.

Heller, F., Drenth, P., Koopman, P. and Rus, V. (1988). *Decisions in Organizations: A Three-County Comparative Study*. London: Sage.

Hickson, D. J., Butler, R. J., Cray, D., Mallory, G. R. and Wilson, D. C. (1985). 'Comparing one hundred fifty decision processes'. In Pennings, J. M. (Ed.), *Organizational Strategy and Change*. San Francisco: Jossey-Bass.

Hickson, D. J., Butler, R. J., Cray, D., Mallory, G. R. and Wilson, D. C. (1986). *Top Decisions: Strategic Decision Making in Organizations*. San Francisco: Jossey-Bass; Oxford: Blackwell.

Klein, J. (1988). 'The myth of the corporate political jungle: politicization as a political strategy'. *Journal of Management Studies,* **25**, 1–12.

Landry, M. (1988). 'Les problemes organisationnels complexes et le defi de leur formulation'. *Canadian Journal of Administrative Sciences,* **5**, 34–48.

Lyles, M. A. (1987). 'Defining strategic problems: subjective criteria of executives'. *Organization Studies,* **8**, 263–80.

MacCrimmon, K. R. (1985). 'Understanding strategic decisions: three systematic approaches'. In Pennings, J. M. (Ed.), *Organizational Strategy and Change*. San Francisco: Jossey-Bass.

Mallory, G. R., Butler, R. J., Cray, D., Hickson, D. J. and Wilson, D. C. (1983). 'Implanted decision making: American owned firms in Britain'. *Journal of Management Studies*, **20**, 192–211.
March, J. G. and Olsen, J. P. (1976). *Ambiguity and Choice in Organizations*. Bergen: Universitetsforlaget.
Mintzberg, H. (1978). 'Patterns in strategy formation'. *Management Science*, **24**, 934–48.
Mintzberg, H., Raisinghani, D. and Theoret, A. (1976). 'The structure of "unstructured" decision processes'. *Administrative Science Quarterly*, **21**, 246–75.
Mohr, L. B. (1982). *Explaining Organizational Behavior*. San Francisco: Jossey-Bass.
Nutt, P. (1984). 'Types of organizational decision processes'. *Administrative Science Quarterly*, **29**, 414–50.
Pennings, J. M. (1985). 'Introduction: on the nature and theory of strategic decisions'. In Pennings, J. M. (Ed.), *Organizational Strategy and Change*. San Francisco: Jossey-Bass.
Pettigrew, A. (1973). *The Politics of Organizational Decision-Making*. London: Tavistock.
Pettigrew, A. (1985). *The Awakening Giant: Continuity and Change in ICI*. Oxford: Blackwell.
Pinfield, L. T. (1986). 'A field evaluation of perspectives on organizational decision making'. *Administrative Science Quarterly*, **31**, 365–88.
Rowe, C. (1989). 'Analysing management decision-making: further thoughts after the Bradford studies'. *Journal of Management Studies*, **26**, 29–46.
Schwartz, H. and Davis, S. M. (1981). 'Matching corporate culture and business strategy'. *Organizational Dynamics*, Summer, 30–48.
Silverzweig, S. and Allen, R. F. (1976). 'Changing the corporate culture'. *Sloan Management Review*, **17**, 33–49.
Simon, H. A. (1947). *Administrative Behavior*. New York: Free Press.
Simon, H. A. (1960). *The New Science of Management Decision*. New York: Harper.
Stein, J. (1981a). 'Contextual factors in the selection of strategic decision methods'. *Human Relations*, **34**, 819–34.
Stein, J. (1981b). 'Strategic decision methods'. *Human Relations*, **34**, 917–33.
Wilson, D. C. (1982). 'Electricity and resistance: a case study of innovation and politics'. *Organization Studies*, **2**, 119–40.
Wilson, D. C., Butler, R. J., Cray, D., Hickson, D. J. and Mallory, G. R. (1986). 'Breaking the bounds of organization in strategic decision making'. *Human Relations*, **39**, 309–32.
Zeleny, M. (1982). *Multiple Criteria Decision Making*. New York: McGraw-Hill.

[7]

Electricity and Resistance: A Case Study of Innovation and Politics*

David C. Wilson[1]

David C. Wilson
Organizational Analysis Research Unit,
University of Bradford Management Centre,
Bradford, England

Abstract

This article presents a case study of decision making in a British chemical organization. The initial problem is one of whether the generation of electricity is a feasible proposition in addition to the production of chemicals. This issue acts as a platform for protracted political debate as soon as questions of career succession and career interests are aroused. The focus shifts from economic criteria to those of career aspirations. The decision spans four years, from 1964 to 1968, and data for the case study were collected over a three-year period, from 1976 to 1979. Existing notions of decision making are examined for their adequacy in explaining the events that took place and modifications to these concepts are explored in the analysis of the case study. It is found that both the effects of the organization and the specific individuals within it, combine simultaneously to produce the events of this decision. The article begins with a short introduction of existing decision making theories, follows with an account of the case study, and concludes with an analysis of its decisional characteristics.

Functional and Political Criteria in Organizational Decision Making

One account of decision making portrays organizations as managerially contrived, subsuming a logic of managerial effectiveness which encompasses decision making in the dictates of technical criteria derived from immutable algorithmic precepts. Hence, decision making is flavoured with 'techniques' (Ellul 1964), and evokes planned responses to all possible contingencies (Luce and Raiffa 1957; Baumol 1959; Moore and Thomas 1976). Decisional criteria governing the choice of one alternative from a set of multiple alternatives are based upon utility maximization, relying on the rational choice processes of economic theory.

Despite Simon's attempt to finally seal the demise of rational economic man (Simon 1947), subsequent concepts of decision making still adhere to economic principles, displaying a modified economic rationality. As Astley et al. (1981) point out, the rationality which is applied in decision making is in fact severely bounded, whereby search procedures are truncated long before theoretically optimal alternatives can be identified. The result is incremental decision making with solutions typically close to existing routines (Lindblom 1959), and satisficing decision making, where what is felt to be adequate for the circumstances results in satisfactory rather than optimal solutions (March and Simon 1958). However imperfect its execution, decision making is still seen as an

Organization Studies
1982, 3/2:119–140

0170–8406/82/
0003–0007 $1.00

intendedly rational process purposefully directed towards the solution of problems.

Beyond the conventional wisdom of this rationality there is an alternative account of organizational decision making. This view portrays decision making less as product of organizational functioning and more as the result of power exertion which serves localized interests, often at the expense of other conflicting interests (Cyert and March 1963; Axelrod 1970; Abell 1975; Allison 1969). Case studies such as those of Pettigrew (1973) and those in Bachrach and Baratz (1970) provide colourful illustrations of the way in which political purpose facilitates access to information by two actors but excludes a third, or where preferential location in a communication network enables the selective filtering of what constitutes 'relevant' information (Leavitt 1972).

Similarly, March and Olsen (1976) de-emphasize goal-directed rationality in favour of an image of spontaneous and purposeless decision making, wherein political activity has primacy and goals are discovered through it. Outcomes are not always devised congruent with specific problems. Indeed, a solution may exist prior to the problem arising. Cohen et al. (1972:2) thus depict an organization as a collection of 'choices looking for problems'.

The focus for this article is provided by these two mutually exclusive perspectives on decision making. On what occasions does decision making subscribe to a goal-directed, utility-maximizing economic rationality — albeit a modified rationality — and when is decision making beset with interest, ambition, and political intrigue? The following section develops an account of a new product decision in Toxicem, a leading British chemical producer.

Methodology and Access

The data for the study were collected over a three-year period from 1976 to 1979, during which the author was a member of the Organizational Analysis Research Unit at the University of Bradford. Initial access was gained by discussions with the Chief Executive. The author was working as a researcher involved in a wider comparative study of decision making (see Butler et al. 1981 for the details of this research). An opportunity to conduct extended research came fortuitously. Toxicem was acting as 'host' to a senior manager from a large banking concern. It was intended that he should get a bird's eye view of how Toxicem functioned as a chemical company and, at my request I was allowed to accompany the banker for the following week.

Virtually all senior and middle managers were observed and interviewed during this time and through this I discovered that Toxicem was just about to decide whether or not to launch a new product. I asked the Chief Executive whether I could follow this new product through its decision process and he agreed to let me have access to all senior and middle managers and all documentary evidence. During the ensuing extended contact time with Toxicem, the Chief Executive developed an interest in the research itself and, over lunch, we identified four major areas that had, in his opinion, contributed significantly to the overall strategy of Toxicem. After talking through each of these areas I decided upon the decision to generate electricity as the best documented topic with ready access to verbal information from those who had participated in the decision-making process.

As Toxicem had a relatively small number of functional departments, and as the decision topic invoked readily identifiable sides for and against the generation of electricity, it was a relatively simple task to unravel who were the key decisional participants. These are shown in Figure 1. Identification of participants was a process of chain reactions. Those members of the organization who were obviously involved directly in the decision were interviewed in the first instance. Their accounts of the events of the decision process led to the identification of other members who were less directly involved in the decision. Subsequent discussions with these informants led to the identification of further participants and thus extended the gradually increasing number of informants.

Figure 1
The Key Participants in the Case Study

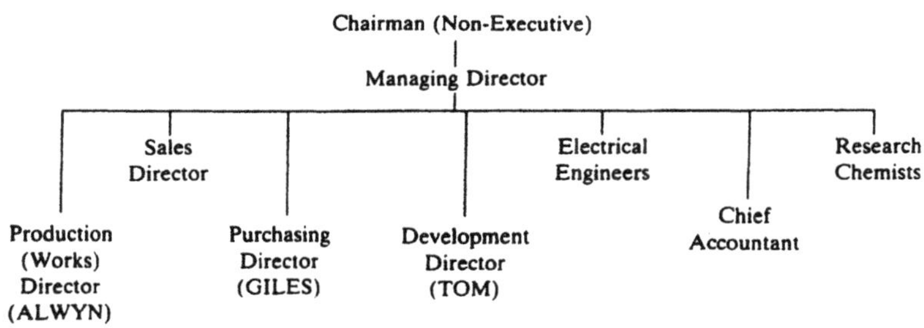

Interviews with each informant were open-ended and multiple, usually occurring once per week. As Dalton (1958:275–277) experienced, the formalities of interviewing lessened with the passing of time. Many of the informants subsequently became friends and acquaintances as a result of the extended contact time. One significant consequence of such relationships was that information about the topic, the people in the organization, and about the organization itself, was readily available and was culled from a wide variety of settings. Often, lunchtimes in the managers' dining room proved useful sources of information as did lunch in the staff social club. In addition, the creation of informal relations meant that many 'casual' conversations were possible, taking place in corridors, foyers, or reception rooms. Indeed, the experience of the present study concurs with Dunn and Swierczck (1977:142) whereby 'research data properly described as "anecdotes" are important sources of information'.

In addition, minutes of meetings, memoranda, personal letters, and other documents were scrutinized at length. Not only did this activity help to identify key participants in the decision, but also it highlighted specific points of ambiguity or vagueness that served as useful cues for discussion with informants. Like many case study analysts, I soon developed my own shorthand which enabled almost verbatim statements to be recorded either at the time of their occurrence, or shortly afterwards (see, for example, the developing of 'intimates' and the writing of accounts, in Dalton 1958:273–285).

The present case study was conducted alongside five other extended cases of decision making in other organizations (Wilson 1980). In an attempt to alleviate some of the criticisms of researcher bias and subjectivity in case study methods (Weick 1969:18–21; Campbell and Stanley 1966:6–12; McClintock et al. 1979:627), these five other cases were resubmitted to key respondents in an early draft form. The result was that no change of stories or events was requested by any of the key respondents beyond small alterations in numerical data such as costs or estimates. These were duly altered in the final reconstruction of the decision. In the present case, however, it was not possible to resubmit the case study for the same process of 'validation' as the present Managing Director (Alwyn) had figured strongly as a political figure in the decision. Over lunch, towards the end of the research he told me how he felt he had been extremely tolerant in allowing extended research in Toxicem, but now felt that 'I was overdoing things to the point of becoming a political embarrassment'. Bitterness over his appointment as Managing Director (which stemmed from the outcome of the present decision) was still quite marked among some other directors. This was especially true of Giles, the Purchasing Director, and as my continued presence in the organization would bring me into contact with Giles and others who were sympathetic to his views, Alwyn argued that I would only re-open what were comparatively recent wounds and exacerbate an already delicate situation. I was asked to leave, with which I duly complied, fortunately having collected sufficient data for the compilation of the present case study. Resubmission, under the circumstances, would have been undesirable, but it was felt that as the present case had been conducted in a similar method to the five other 'validated' cases, the likelihood of subjective bias significantly distorting the portrayal of events was substantially reduced.

Background to the Case Study

Prior to 1960, Toxicem was using a single, low pressure boiler in order to supply steam for various chemical processes at pressures of 80 to 150 pounds per square inch (psi). The rapid rise of steam demand in Toxicem necessitated the purchase of a new and larger boiler. Although there were a few dissenters, the majority of those concerned favoured the purchase of a boiler capable of operating at 400 psi. Higher pressure boilers were generally thought to be required to cope with the steady increase in demand experienced by the British chemical industry.

The higher pressure boiler was duly purchased in 1962 and, although capable of operating at 400 psi, most of the usage of the boiler was in producing low pressure steam at 80 psi. The demand for high pressure steam had not accelerated as quickly as had been predicted. In order to get a pressure of 80 psi, this boiler first had to be fuelled to raise 400 psi. The loss caused by having to reduce pressure from 400 to 80 psi meant little at the time in financial terms, but it stimulated the idea in some of the engineers' minds that this spare pressure capacity could be used in a productive way, particularly to facilitate the generation of electrical power.

Early Days: The Germ of an Idea

A suggestion to use the spare pressure capacity began to crystallize around the idea of electrical power generation. The chemists and engineers in Toxicem started to experiment with the notion of using steam pressure to drive a turbine and alternator which could theoretically provide Toxicem with enough electricity to supply their own requirements. Many informal discussions were held between the people interested in the concept of electricity generation. Small-scale experiments and hypothetical calculations were worked out, often on the backs of envelopes and scrap paper. Gradually, a small group of chemists, electricians, and engineers were coming to thinking that not only was electricity generation a feasible proposition, but also that it should be given priority in the policy of Toxicem.

The main problem at this time was that Toxicem had little spare money available for such projects. Thus, although the idea of electricity generation became more and more fixed in the minds of its proponents, it had to remain a hypothetical project. The Capital Control Committee, a standing committee which makes decisions on expensive projects such as this, would never have entertained the idea of spending some £150,000 on generation equipment.

However, encouraged by Alwyn, the energetic Welsh Works Director, the proponents of electricity generation invited the National Industrial Fuel Efficiency Service (N.I.F.E.) to conduct a general survey of efficiency in Toxicem. This visit was a standard procedure in Toxicem and occurred every two or three years, but on this occasion Alwyn was determined to ask their opinion on the question of electricity generation, in order to add weight to his argument. The report came back to Alwyn, suggesting that N.I.F.E. considered that savings of up to £39,000 per annum could be saved by Toxicem generating their own electricity. Alwyn submitted an informal report to his colleagues who were in favour of the project. It read as follows:

'1) We are large consumers of steam, and so the steam required for power generation has already been raised. The cost of giving it the extra energy to 600 psi to put it through a turbo-alternator is relatively small. The steam passes out from the turbo-alternator at the pressure of 85 psi which we use for most of our plants, and we are able to use all the

remaining energy in the steam, including its latent heat. The fuel efficiency of a back-pressure generator set such as ours would be 75%. The efficiency of modern power stations is of the order of 35%, and the average efficiency of all power stations is 28%.
2) Our electrical power demand, and the amount of power our steam usage enables us to generate, correspond quite closely. We shall need to continue to purchase a small portion of electricity requirements.
3) The Central Electricity Generating Board is required to earn sufficient profit on its sales of electricity to finance new power stations. We would prefer to retain this money to finance our own expansion.
The average cost per unit of electricity purchased from the Local Electricity Board over the last 12 months (i.e. before the new increases take effect on October 1st) has been 1.2d. The fuel, labour and maintenance cost of the electricity we can generate ourselves will be 0.2d. per unit, so the margin left for overheads and profit is considerable.'

There was, however, still little chance of such a project being allowed to come to fruition. There were still problems of economics to sort out leaving little spare money for projects of this nature.

The Purchase of a Boiler

Despite Toxicem's lack of funds, it was clearly evident that a second boiler would have to be purchased. The demand for steam had risen steadily throughout the previous three or four years and number one boiler was being used to its capacity. The question of the purchase of this second boiler was to be taken at Board level due to its high capital cost. The Board asked for information about the requirements for steam and about the various available boilers from the Works Director, the Purchasing Director, and the Development Director. It was here that Alwyn saw a glimmer of hope:

> Obviously it was not possible to tackle the question of electricity generation head on. This second boiler was important for us, however. If generation was to become a reality then the purchase of this boiler was critical. Here was an opportunity to take a step in the right direction.'

In order to run a turbo-alternator it is necessary to have a boiler capable of raising steam to a pressure of 600 psi. Anything less than this is useless as far as driving a turbine is concerned. Alwyn realized that the number two boiler to be purchased must have this 600 psi capability. He could then consider his next move with the knowledge that electricity generation was technologically possible.
Alwyn gathered his supporters together and informed them of the intended purchase of a new boiler and its necessary high pressure capability. They began to search for information about the projected requirement for steam usage, plus the various boilers that were on the market at the time, determined to secure the purchase of a high pressure boiler. Although the projected demand for steam over the next few years was sufficient to warrant a high pressure

boiler, the price of the boiler was not. They were substantially more expensive than the lower pressure boilers. The additional cost of a high pressure 70,000 lbs. per hour Water Tube Boiler was in the region of £15,000. There seemed no solution to this problem, so Alwyn and the engineers could move no further. They sat back and waited.

Meanwhile, Giles, the Purchasing Director, had also been gathering information about the specification of new boilers. Giles had the reputation as something of a 'whizz-kid' in Toxicem. He had reached his directorship comparatively rapidly through his apparently infallible ability to secure favourable and successful contracts with major suppliers and he was well respected in Toxicem as well as in the chemical industry as a whole. Giles was not a man to play about with ideas such as electricity generation.

I really thought that this project was ludicrous. No-one could give any facts and figures which supported electricity generation. Nobody knew enough about the problems and the technology of electricity production to be able to say anything worthwhile.'

He considered such ideas wasted time and effort, at the expense of hard facts and figures. Consequently he favoured the purchase of the cheaper, low pressure boiler on economic grounds, although he did admit that the higher pressure boiler was probably a better investment in the long term. 'It was just too expensive'.

At this time, purely by coincidence, the National Coal Board circulated an information sheet around manufacturing industries which used coal as a source of energy. In this document they stated that they had large stocks of pulverized, low quality coal stockpiled in a local pit. They could supply such fuel at a very low cost for at least the next ten years. Giles was not one to miss such an opportunity, and arranged a meeting of himself, Alwyn, and the Managing Director with the National Coal Board. The calorific value of this fuel was very low (8750) and most boilers would not be able to raise steam with such coal. However, this fuel could be used to fire a Water Tube Boiler using superheated steam, raising its pressure capability to 600 psi.

On financial criteria, it was more economical for Toxicem to purchase a higher pressure boiler using this new found cheap fuel, than it was to buy a low pressure boiler which needed higher quality coal. In December 1964 Toxicem bought a high pressure boiler, on Giles' recommendation. Alwyn and his engineers were overjoyed: 'This boiler was certainly capable of eventually producing electrical power with the addition of an alternator. The idea was, at least, a feasible reality in the future.'

They had kept very quiet about the possibility of generating electricity, never mentioning the fact in the meeting with the National Coal Board. They appeared to fully support the purchase of the high pressure boiler on economic criteria only. The boiler was duly installed and began working at 400 psi (reduced to 80 psi) to supply Toxicem's steam requirements.

The Case for Higher Pressures

The new boiler worked without problems for a year. However, as a result of Toxicem's continued expansion in the production of chemicals, it was being used to its full capacity by early 1966. It was now that Alwyn and his supporters made their move. Alwyn argued:

'Obviously, by increasing the pressure of the boiler the total output of steam could be substantially increased. But it seemed a waste to reduce this high pressure steam to the required 80 psi for the chemical plant. It was like boiling a kettle when you only wanted lukewarm water. The spare steam capacity could be used to drive a turbine and thus generate electricity.'

Armed with the information from N.I.F.E., Alwyn and his supporters submitted their proposals to the Managing Director. These proposals were circulated around top and middle managers and they immediately brought protests from Giles and from Tom, the Development Director, who were both totally opposed to the idea of electricity generation. The Managing Director proposed that debate on this issue should take place in the Capital Control Committee in order to provide a forum for all interested parties to present their case. In March 1966, Tom and Giles submitted a short report to the Committee in which they spelled out their objections to the concept of electricity generation. These were three-fold:

'1) that Toxicem's proper business was manufacturing chemicals, and that they should leave generating electricity to bodies like the Central Electricity Generating Board which were set up to do so;
2) that technical staff would not be competent to run the system, and that breakdowns in the boiler plant or generation house would lead to costly shut-downs;
3) that in order to raise sufficient high pressure steam on the 70,000 lbs/hr coal fired boiler to run the Generator, Toxicem would have to purchase a better and more expensive grade of coal.'

Alwyn, the engineers and chemists immediately countered these three objections by arguing that Toxicem could, in fact:

'produce electricity more economically than the Central Electricity Generating Board. In any case, existing staff were more than competent, and the existing supplies of low quality coal were not going to last forever and alternative sources would have to be found even at 400 psi pressures.'

The Capital Control Committee met a further three times in April, May, and June 1966, but no progress was made on this issue. The Chairman and the Managing Director suggested that deadlock had been reached because of lack of specific information about the technological and economic aspects of electricity generation. They suggested that both the opponents and proponents of the debate should clarify in more specific detail their positions. Accordingly, Alwyn and the proponents and Giles and Tom (with full support from their respective departments) went out to seek information to substantiate their cases. Giles and Tom approached the Accountancy Department to try and work through their figures, confirm their calculations and thus lend support to their view. However, Accountancy was noncommital, also suggesting that further figures were necessary in order to present a convincing case. Alwyn and his supporters attempted the same strategy with the same result. It was clear that Accountancy had no real interest either way in the outcome of this argument.

The Diseconomies of Electricity Generation

Both Giles and Tom realized that if Toxicem was to produce their own electricity, then this would mean negotiating with the Electricity Supply Industry which presently supplied them. There would need to be arrangements about release from the national grid and about any standby arrangements with the local Electricity Board, should any failures or breakdowns occur in the boiler or the turbo-alternator. In particular Tom, who had dealt with the Electricity Supply Industries in the past, felt that they would be totally against private electricity generation in industry:

> 'I. knew from experience that the electricity boards were hostile to any firm which attempted to become independent of the national grid. I knew of a couple of firms which had tried it and gone back to the national grid within a year because of all the problems they had with generators breaking down and intermittent supply of electricity ruining their production processes.'

Giles contacted the Industrial Section of the Electricity Council for their opinion on private generation. Tom was correct in his assumptions. The Electricity Council were most certainly not in favour of the private generation of electricity by organizations. Basically, the Electricity Council's attitude was that an organization's finances could be better directed than towards private generation, that it would prove a costly exercise and that the job of supplying electricity should be left to the specialists, that is, the local Electricity Boards.

In particular, Giles and Tom emphasized the point that standby charges for reconnection to the national grid in the event of the failure of the private system would be expensive. They wrote to the local Electricity Board asking for a specific figure for standby charges if Toxicem was to embark upon private generation. The local Electricity Board was hostile to the whole idea. At first they refused any information at all, suggesting that reconnection to the national grid would be impossible anyway for various technical reasons and that no precise figures could be given. They also refused to meet with Toxicem representatives to discuss the issue of private generation.

Alwyn was now beginning to fear that he had lost the battle in the light of both the Electricity Council's and the Electricity Board's hostile attitude to private generation. Even so, he had contacted two suppliers of turbo-alternators in order to find out how much they would cost to buy, install, and run.

In order to produce a realistic purchase price these suppliers needed to know the cost of standby charges from the Electricity Board, which they duly contacted. They received a curt reply stating that standby charges would be £5 per kVa per annum. This figure was then submitted along with the price of the turbo-alternator to Toxicem. Giles was more than satisfied: 'I knew that, given standby charges of this magnitude, the Capital Control Committee would never consider the purchase of a turbo-alternator.' The figures were submitted, and were rejected by the Committee as Giles predicted. Despondently, Alwyn retreated to consider his next move.

A Re-awakening: Career Issues and Interests

The Managing Director of Toxicem announced his impending retirement. It was clear that, within the organization itself, Giles and Alwyn would be prime candidates for the vacated directorship. More important, however, was that from Alwyn's point of view Giles had in a sense 'won' the battle over the issue of electricity generation. This would put Giles in an advantageous position in the promotions stakes especially combined with his 'whizz-kid' image. Energetic though Alwyn might be, charisma he did not have.

It was felt, especially by Giles and Alwyn, that success in gaining the managing directorship would be primarily determined by the track record of each candidate in the debate about private electricity generation. Although this was never expressly stated by the outgoing Managing Director, it was commonly thought among senior managers to originate from him.

Alwyn was well aware of his so-called failure. He thus set out to scrutinize all the memoranda, mathematics, and documents that the debate had produced. In a month he had found an important error in the figures given to Toxicem by the turbo-alternator suppliers concerning standby charges. Alwyn asked Toxicem's electrical engineers for their advice on a charge of £5 per kVA for standby supplies. They told him that such a charge was ridiculously high and was obviously an error that had not previously been identified by anyone. In the light of the Electricity Board's policy of noncooperation on this issue, Alwyn was not convinced that this mistake for standby charges was as innocent as it seemed.

Alwyn first informed the Capital Control Committee of the errors and, second, wrote to the Federation of British Industries concerning the excessive standby charges. Informing the Capital Control Committee had the effect of re-opening the debate on the issue and also cast doubts over the information given by the electricity supply organizations in general. Alwyn also received the following reply from the Federation of British Industries:

'I cannot understand how the £5 per kVa per annum has arisen. I attach a copy of a

reply to my enquiry to the Electricity Board concerning the Board's charges for stand-by and parallel-running supplies. From this you will note that the annual charge for standby supplies is £1.5.0d per k Va for high voltage supplies or £1.15.0d per kVA for low voltage supplies. Supplies actually taken are charged for at more or less standard rates.
If it should appear that the Board are attempting to impose charges otherwise than those stated in the attached copy letter, I would be very pleased to hear the details from you.'

The debate was re-opened. Giles felt the ground shifting beneath his feet. The figures upon which he had based his case had been proved to be more than a little erroneous. The whole argument against private generation was now open to question.

Months of Conflict

There followed nearly a year of disputes between Alwyn and his supporters and Giles and Tom and their supporters. These disputes concerned the economics of electricity generation, but because the majority of figures and calculations were computed on hypothetical measures of steam pressure, generator output and so on, no agreement about the 'real' cost of private generation could be reached on either side. The only firm figure that could be obtained during this period was the cost of standby charges from the Electricity Board.
Feuding between the proponents and opponents of electricity generation became bitter, reflected in heated discussions in the dining room every lunch-time and in the sheer volume of memoranda produced stating the cases for or against. Giles also realized:

'that the original plan of getting standby facilities only once per year was inadequate. We should have to have standby facilities during all holiday periods in case any breakdowns occurred.'

The following two months were spent negotiating such terms of standby with the Electricity Board. By January 1968, these charges had been agreed on all sides. Giles and Tom circulated a memorandum to the Capital Control Committee in which they stated all their objections to the private generation issue.
In this document they listed and expanded old arguments but introduced a new argument concerning the practice of other chemical companies on electricity generation. According to Giles, this document was the definitive statement about the pitfalls of electrictiy generation and showed the folly of embarking upon such an enterprise. A very long and involved document, it may be crystallized into the following points:
1) At least six well-known British chemical manufacturers had tried and rejected private generation.

2) The projected forecast of electricity usage in 1969 for XLtd was too high.
3) The Electricity Board has the right to radically increase the negotiated standby charges should the generator be unable to supply electricity for more than five days.
4) Steam pressure variation would radically affect electricity output. In order to minimize such variation, a higher quality coal would have to be purchased from the National Coal Board. Additional costs could therefore be as much as £12,000 for this item alone.
5) The turbo-alternator manufacturers would not accept liability if their machine was not supplied with clean steam. Toxicem could not guarantee such clean steam. In addition, this would mean an increase on chemical control or supervision on water supply and boiler conditions.
6) The cost of increasing the boiler operating pressure from 400 to 600 psi was too high, and would also reduce boiler reliability.
7) Existing maintenance staff was unable and unqualified to look after the proposed high pressure set-up.

Cases For and Against Generation Are Sharpened

Alwyn and his supporters from engineering and electrical services countered each of these arguments in turn. These counterarguments were also contained in a detailed memorandum which was submitted to the Capital Control Committee. In effect, each of the points made bv Giles was refuted in this document in an equally convincing manner.

Alwyn's main argument was that private generation was an economic proposition and that Toxicem stood to make a substantial profit in the generation of its own electricity. He submitted a breakdown of estimated costs to the Capital Control Committee showing that by August 1969 the total cost would be £135,000 (less than half the figure estimated by Giles and Tom). Each of the major arguments against private generation were shown in fact to be economic according to Alwyn. The only argument he accepted was that maintenance staff would involve an extra cost due to the need for increased supervision. Alwyn, however, emphasized that Giles' figure of £250 for this extra cost was ridiculously low, and consequently allowed £800 for this item. This report increased the antagonism between the proponents and the opponents of private generation. Giles explained:

> 'I saw the allowance of extra money for maintenance staff as a personal insult. It implied that Alwyn had no faith in Tom's and my calculations. He was trying to make us look incompetent in the eyes of the Capital Control Committee.'

These assumptions were correct.

Alwyn and his supporters never missed an opportunity to be derogatory to their opponents on this issue, the main occasion for mutual insults being lunchtime in the dining room. Missing such lunchtime 'debates' was considered an admission of failure or defeat and consequently no-one missed any of these sessions. Fired by the competition for the upcoming managing directorship, the arguments became increasingly personal. Controversy still raged concerning the accuracy of financial calculations and projected estimated costs for private generation. The Managing Director called another meeting of the Capital Control Committee. In this meeting he informed the Committee that since it was apparent that no decision or even compromise could be achieved on this issue, then a vote would be taken among all the senior managers to finally resolve the debate one way or the other. Giles comments: 'This played straight into Alwyn's hands. We knew that he had very strong support from the engineers and the electricians.' Giles and Tom had no determined support from other areas of the organization apart from themselves. As a result, Alwyn's case won the vote by using the extra muscle, and the case was finally presented by the Capital Control Committee to the Board of the company in September 1968.

As was the norm in Toxicem, the Board merely acted in a rubber stamping capacity, and the decision to purchase a turbine was approved. The first turbine was purchased exactly one year later in August 1969.

The Aftermath

The turbine was proving very successful in its operations. Very few of the problems posed by Giles and Tom appeared in practice. In the six-month period since its purchase, the turbine was estimated to be saving Toxicem some £60,000 per year. Just over a year later Alwyn was promoted to the position of Managing Director.

Over the next three years, the turbine operated at a steady profit, having effectively paid for its capital cost in two years. There had been problems of the turbine blades becoming salted and the necessity of having research chemists on night shifts in order to look after the purification of water, but overall such problems had been minimal in contrast to the apparently substantial financial saving. Giles and Tom were not, however, to be silenced so easily. Giles in particular was very bitter at not securing the managing directorship, and he continued to oppose private generation. Although a financial profit was undoubtedly being achieved, he argued that it was not really the result of any foresight or expertise on the part of Alwyn:

> 'Since 1969, the price of electricity purchased from the Electricity Boards has risen dramatically and, coupled with the effects of economic inflation, the turbine only appears to be making a profit. If it hadn't have been for inflation, then the success of the project would have been questionable.'

The Case for Another Boiler

The demand for electricity and process steam had risen in Toxicem to a level where a third boiler was certainly required. In view of a recent strike by the coal miners it was decided to purchase a new gas-fired boiler.

When estimates for the new boiler and attached turbine and alternator were submitted to the Capital Control Committee, the purchase of all items was automatic. The Board accepted the figures without question and the new boiler and turbo-alternator set were acquired in July 1974. Alwyn, as Managing Director, submitted the case to the Committee and to the Board, which, in the light of his previous participation in the issue, authorized the purchase without question.

Yet, Giles had had some success in persuading previous supporters of electricity generation that perhaps it was only due to the effects of inflation that the project had been seen to be so successful. Had a vote been taken, as in the purchase of the first turbo-alternator, it was possible that the vote would have gone against the purchase of a second turbine. Giles' influence, however, came too late. Both boilers and number two turbo-alternator were working successfully. The first turbo-alternator was now used as a standby. The following extract from one of Alwyn's memoranda indicates the profitability of private generation:

'1) What the total costs of electricity, including purchased fuel will be this year (turbo-alternator No. 2 now in use).
The figure comes to £80,452. It includes the cost of standby charges to the Electricity Board.
2) What the total costs of meeting our electrical demand this year would have been, had ve never embarked on power generation.
The figure would have been £325,135.
3) What the total costs would have been had we not invested in a second turbo-alternator, but continued using the first one, supplemented by substantial purchase from the Electricity Board.
The figure would have been £198,358.
It will be seen from the above that the financial savings from generating power ourselves are amounting to some £245,000 per annum. The first turbo-alternator is currently in "moth-balls" and will be brought into service again when the demand for electricity has grown beyond the capacity of Unit No. 2.'

Yet when last in touch with Toxicem the issue was still contested. The feeling among the 'losers' (Giles and Tom) was still that the so-called profitability of electricity generation was solely due to subsequent information and the rising price of electricity rather than to any strategic foresight on the part of Alwyn and his supporters. Some months later, Tom had suffered a mild heart attack and now only worked part-time as Development Director. Giles was still actively opposed to private generation and was waiting for the time when the demand for steam and electricity dropped, so that he can again point to the folly of private electricity generation which is no part of a chemical company's business.

Analysis: The Electricity Generation

The Issue as a Strategic Decision

Following Mintzberg et al. (1976) and Normann (1971), strategic decisions are those which are considered important to the organization, are novel to the organization, and consequently incur a large degree of uncertainty for decision makers.

Much of the literature concerning strategic decisions focuses on new product decisions as the more important issues of organizational decision making. Pettigrew (1973), for example, shows how the new computer issue assumes a critical level of importance in the Brian Michael organization, and Normann (1971) argues that new product decisions are invariably uncertain and troublesome.

The danger here is that, as Normann (1971:205) points out, not all new product decisions in all organizations represent uncertain and important issues. Indeed, new product decisions were the most numerous types of topics occurring in Toxicem between 1960 and 1978 (Wilson 1980:262). In this way, the new product decisions become 'programmed' and the organization develops specific, institutionalized procedures for handling these routine decisions (Simon 1947). The justification for treating the electricity generation issue as a strategic decision lies in its novelty to Toxicem.

As Walker (1969:881) argues, a strategic decision is one which is 'new to the organization adopting it, no matter how old the program or policy may be or how many other organizations may have adopted it'. Strategic decisions are thus made about issues previously unencountered or unexplored in an organization. Such is the case with the present study; from this perspective, the electricity generation issue becomes a strategic decision for Toxicem.

The Case as an Incremental and Satisficing Decision

The most striking aspect of the electricity generation issue is that the decision-making process cannot be described as *wholly* incremental or satisficing. It is possible to depict the decision-making process as comprising two distinctly different 'phases' (Mintzberg et al. 1976). Figure 2 summarizes the two stages and their more important constituent events.

Stage 1 of the decision represents the antithesis of either satisficing or incrementalism. Here, decision making is portrayed as founded upon a basis of 'technical rationality' (Thompson 1967:14). Although there are disagreements between Alwyn, Tom, and Giles concerning electricity generation, each course of action is fully scrutinized by the interested parties. Each decisional participant attempts to gain support for their point of view by enumerating the full range of alternatives, clearly defining objectives, and attempting to achieve the maximization of utility functions in the consideration of the alternative ways of producing electricity from turbines and alternators. The decision represents almost a stereotype of the 'synoptic' mode of decision making described by Lindblom (1959) and Braybrooke and Lindblom (1963:37) and is flavoured with little of the 'satisficing' activities proposed by March and Simon (1958:140).

Figure 2
The Generation of Electrical Power in Toxicem Figurative Representation

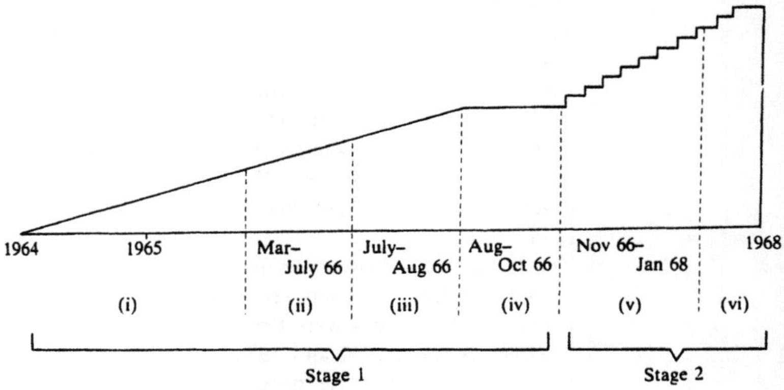

Stage 1 (smooth line)
(i) Initial thoughts of electricity generation
(ii) Formal proposals and objections to electricity generation
(iii) Scrutiny of facts and figures concerning private generation. Approaches made to the Electricity Board.
(iv) Figures produced. Rejected by Capital Control Committee. Toxicem decides *not* to generate its own electrical power.

Stage 2 (stepped line)
(v) The Managing Director announces his impending retirement. The debate on private generation is re-opened. Some 15 months of debate and negotiation ensue.
(vi) In the face of a deadlock situation, a vote is taken. On the strength of this result, Toxicem decides to *go ahead* and generate its own electrical power.

Stage 1 of the decision-making process (see Figure 2) is characterized by an extremely detailed search for an optimal solution, with Alwyn and Giles each indulging in the detailed scrutiny of the decisional implications such as the cost of an alternator and its upkeep, the types of fuel that would be required, and the possible action of the Electricity Board, the nationally owned monopoly supplier of British electricity. Between March and August 1966, the decision-making process displays none of the inadequacies described by March and Simon (1958:140–144) but instead is marked by an energetic search for information. Indeed, in March 1966 the Chairman and the Managing Director suggested that deadlock in the debate had been reached because of the lack of specific information and suggested that the opponents and proponents of the issue should clarify and justify in greater detail their respective positions.

However, in October 1966, the decision-making process becomes subject to delays as in Stage 2 (Figure 2) and functional criteria make way for the political manoeuvrings of localized interests. The conflicts of interest are not concerned with the primary issue of electricity generation, but focus instead upon career succession and the winning of the recently vacated Managing Directorship. Decision making becomes protracted and circuitous as political negotiations ensue (Abell 1975; Mintzberg et al. 1976; Pettigrew 1973). Information becomes employed as a political lever in an attempt to provide ready-made solutions to the problems being confronted (March and Olsen 1976; Jamous and Peloille 1970:149). Political activity gains primacy, the decision-making process loses its previously sharp goal-directed focus, and seemingly purposeless and irrelevant events occur between the proponents and the opponents of the electricity generation issue (Cohen et al. 1972). Consequently, the decision-making process becomes fragmented and incremental with the concommitant rise in political activity (Braybrooke and Lindblom 1963; Mintzberg et al. 1976; Butler et al. 1981). Some 15 months of debate and negotiation ensue (see Figure 2), resulting in the eventual purchase of a first turbine in August 1969.

This interpretation of the case study decision as neither wholly an incremental nor a satisficing decision has some implications for theories of decision making. The one decision-making process displays *both* characteristics of incremental and synoptic decision making. Beginning as a synoptic decision the case study decision develops into a hesitant, discontinuous, and incremental mode for a further two years. The decision-making process is only emergently incremental. In a similar vein, the satisficing behaviour of Alwyn and Giles, who restrict their scrutiny to information which will fully support their career interests but perhaps merely adequately support the issue of electricity generation, only emerges in the later stages of the decision. This behaviour is additionally facilitated by the relative lack of any concrete information on likely costs, in addition to the passive roles of the Accountancy Department and of the former Managing Director. As Astley et al. (1981) point out, the notions of satisficing and incremental decision making are, in themselves, inadequate concepts by which the characteristics of a decision-making process may be described. They explain only a partial aspect of part of a complex process (Butler et al. 1981).

Moreover, Lindblom's concept of incrementalism also appears to confuse the degree of change at the *outcome* of the decision-making process and the *piecemeal process* by which the outcome may be reached. The purchase of electricity generating equipment was a big step, or a large change from the status quo. It was the first time any such project had occurred in the organization and it represented a radical departure from the primary tasks of chemical production. Nonetheless, this nonincremental outcome (as defined by Lindblom 1959) was reached by an incremental, discontinuous decision-making process. It is suggested, therefore, that processual incrementalism be distinguished from outcome incrementalism (Wilson 1980). The degree of change from previous conditions may vary independently of the piecemeal quality of the decision-making process itself (Astley et al. 1981).

Power, Institution, and the Individual in Decision Making

One of the striking features of the case study is the role of Alwyn as an individual, superimposed against the fabric of Toxicem, as a political actor in the decision, and as a successful contender for career succession. His dominant presence, like that of Debré in the reform of the medical profession in France (Jamous and Peloille 1970:144), merits some discussion.

In Toxicem, one of the overriding institutional norms was one of quick action on highly quantifiable, accurate data:

> 'We pride ourselves on generating quantifiable data and making fast decisions on the basis of this information. When we go for something we all go together from the Managing Director right down to the gardener.' (Managing Director, Toxicem, in Wilson 1980)

The organization becomes a decisional system, developing repertoires of activities such as standard procedures, formal rules, and clearly established routines for handling decision-making processes (Pugh et al. 1968, 1969; Normann 1971; Simon 1947; Thompson 1967). Thus, faced with any problem, an organization will submit decisions to these predefined mechanisms for their solution.

Following Clegg (1979), power itself becomes institutionalized within the organizational structure, and as Crozier (1973:214) concurs: 'from a structural point of view, no power relationship can be dissociated from the institutional system or systems within which it develops'. Viewing the organization as a decisional system attempts to show how every power relationship is mediated by a whole array of structured conditions and constraints within the organization (Hickson et al. 1971). Indeed, Giddens (1976) points to the neglect of such 'structuration' in the conceptualization of power by Wrong (1968) and White (1971), who argue that power may be separated from the relationships within and the composition of the organization. Toxicem is clearly aware that it is substitutable in the production of chemicals, and consequently takes steps to ensure that it is innovative (creating uncertainty for others in the same business) and central (what it does immediately affects other chemical companies). Hickson et al. (1971) present dynamic models of such contingent power, concentrating upon the nature of power structures. However, it is in the *activation* of this power structure that the individual may take precedence over institutionalization (Pettigrew 1973:265).

> 'Strategies are formulated on the basis of perceptions. Accuracy here is critical. Those who correctly understand how a structure operates are in a much better position to make it work to their advantage.'

It is this activation of a power structure that reflects an individual's 'persona' (De Waele and Harré 1976:192).

'The powers of human beings are both actively exercised, often monitored, and always potentially under the control of a person through the organized structure of his cognitive and other resources, his nature, and so on are both variable and modifiable by self-intervention. They cannot therefore be traits.'

The term persona is used to distinguish it from personality characteristics. For example, entrepreneurial personality is invariably described as a trait, where the powerful leader takes adventurous, perhaps risky, decisions towards his vision of the organization's future (Collins and Moore 1970; Mintzberg 1978). The entrepreneurial personality pervades all decisions from new product to personnel topics. Persona, on the other hand, describes the variable characteristics of behaviours by individuals whereby the same individual may display one type of behaviour at one time, and another type of behaviour at a different time.

In the case study, Alwyn in the early stages displays little of the individualistic intervention that comes to the fore in the later stages of the decision. He develops a different persona as soon as career succession becomes the primary issue. His aspirations set on the managing directorship, Alwyn intervenes in the decision by finding an apparent mistake in some critical calculations. He does this in the knowledge that the debate will be re-opened. By questioning the competence of Giles and the Purchasing Department, he undermines their credibility in coping with uncertainty for Toxicem's supply of raw materials. Alwyn effectively undermines the delicate interdepartmental balance of power.

Toxicem's decisional system fails to accommodate the new issues and interests that arise from Alwyn's intervention. Individual activities come to the fore and the institutionalized Capital Control Committee is unable to function as a forum for debate between the various departments. The arousal of Alwyn's persona acts as the spark which forces a surfacing of awareness in other organizational members of how the system of decision making functions. It lays bare the balance of power between organizational departments. Personae are entities, called forth by the recognition of situations, whereby individuals have the capacity to endow the world with meaning and so negotiate with others who hold conflicting interpretations. From a Machiavellian perspective, the creation of such a situation may be a deliberate and conscious act (Secord and Backman 1961; Jamous and Peloille 1970; De Waele and Harré 1976). Although Alwyn himself may not necessarily be endowed with such Machiavellianism, the situation created by the passive role of the old Managing Director certainly is. His behaviour is to play off his two possible successors against each other in a situation where specific information was scarce and a decision one way or another was consequently difficult.

Summary

The analysis of the case study has led to the following speculations. First, notions of satisficing and incrementalism fail to adequately describe the essential features of this strategic decision. Distinctions are required between the particular characteristics of both decision-making processes and decision-making outcomes. Second, the case study gives evidence of the effect of institutionalization upon decision-making activities which simultaneously makes decision making predictable and yet facilitates the political manoeuvrings of Alwyn, resulting in a highly negotiable and protracted decision. The case is, therefore, argued for future theories of decision making to accommodate the organizational effects of institutionalized procedures with the individualistic manoeuvrings that such procedures may invoke.

Although this study is based upon a single case study and runs the risk of the accusation of 'making so much of so little' (Weick 1969:18), it has served to illustrate that existing notions of decision making can only partially describe the characteristics of this particular decision. Broader and more detailed concepts are required (Hage 1980), which can be applied across a large sample of organizations (Astley et al. 1981), and future work already well under way (Butler et al. 1981) should serve to confirm or modify the present interpretation of strategic decision making in Toxicem.

Notes

* In accordance with O.S. policy that the Editor-in-Chief should not influence decisions upon manuscripts with which he has a personal concern, Cornelis Lammers of the Editorial Board acted in his stead taking responsibility for the reviewing process and acceptance of this article because of the Editor-in-Chief's close working relationship with the author.

1. Acknowledgements are due to the following members of the Organizational Analysis Research Unit in Bradford for their comments and criticisms on this and earlier drafts of the paper. Richard J. Butler and David J. Hickson are, respectively, Research Lecturer and Professor and David Cray and Geoff Mallory are Research Fellows in the Unit. This research was supported by the Social Science Research Council, England.

References

Abell, P.
1975 *Organizations as bargaining and influence systems*. London: Heinemann.

Allison, G. T.
1969 'Conceptual models and the Cuban missile crisis'. *American Political Science Review*, September.

Astley, W. G., R. Axelsson, R. J. Butler, D. J. Hickson, and D. C. Wilson
1981 'Decision making: theory III'. Working paper, Organizational Analysis Research Unit, Bradford.

Axelrod, R.
1970 *Conflict of interests: a theory of divergent goals with applications to politics*. Chicago: Markham.

Bachrach, P., and M. S. Baratz
1970 *Power and poverty: theory and practice*. Oxford, Oxford University Press.

Baumol, W. J.
1959 *Business behaviour, value and growth*. New York: Macmillan.

Braybrooke, D., and C. E. Lindblom
1963 *A strategy of decision*. New York: Free Press.

Butler, R. J., D. Cray, D. J. Hickson, G. R. Mallory, and D. C. Wilson
1981 'Complexity and cleavage in decision making: an empirical investigation'. Working paper. Organizational Analysis Research Unit, Bradford.

Campbell, D. T., and J. C. Stanley
1966 *Experimental and quasi-experimental designs for research*. Chicago: Rand McNally.

Clegg, S.
1979 *The theory of power and organization*. London: Routledge and Kegan Paul.

Cohen, D. M., J. G. March, and J. P. Olsen
1972 'A garbage can model of organizational choice'. *Administrative Science Quarterly* 17/1:1–25.

Collins, O., and D. G. Moore
1970 *The organization makers*. New York: Appleton–Century–Crofts.

Crozier, M.
1973 'The problems of power'. *Social Research* 41/2:211–228.

Cyert, R., and J. G. March
1963 *A behavioral theory of the firm*. Englewood Cliffs, N.J.: Prentice–Hall.

Dalton, M.
1958 *Men who manage*. New York: Wiley.

De Waele, J.-P., and R. Harré
1976 'The personality of individuals' in *Personality*. R. Harré (ed). London: Basil Blackwell.

Dunn, W. N., and F. W. Swierczck
1977 'Planned organizational change: towards a grounded theory'. *Journal of Applied Behavioural Science* 13/2:135–157.

Ellul, J.
1964 *The technological society*. New York: Knopf.

Giddens, A.
1976 *New rules of sociological method*. London: Hutchinson.

Hage, J.
1980 *Theories of organizations: form, process and transformation*. New York: Wiley.

Hickson, D. J., C. R. Hinings, C. A. Lee, R. E. Schneck, and J. M. Pennings
1971 'A strategic contingencies theory of intra-organizational power'. *Administrative Science Quarterly* 16/2:216–229.

Jamous, H., and B. Peloille
1970 'Professions or self-perpetuating systems? Changes in the French university-hospital system' in *Professions and professionalization*. J. A. Jackson (ed). Cambridge: Cambridge University Press.

Leavitt, H. J.
1972 *Managerial psychology* (3rd edition). Chicago: University of Chicago Press.

Lindblom, C. E.
1959 'The science of "muddling through"' *Public Administration Review* 19:79–88.

Luce, D. R., and H. Raiffa
1957 *Games and decisions: introduction and critical survey*. New York: Wiley.

March, J. G., and H. A. Simon
1958 *Organizations*. New York: Wiley.

March, J. G., and J. P. Olsen
1976 *Ambiguity and choice in organizations*. Oslo: Universitet Sforlaget.

McClintock, C. C., D. Brannon, and S. Maynard-Moody
1979 'Applying the logic of sample surveys to qualitative case studies: the case cluster method'. *Administrative Science Quarterly* 24/4:612–629.

Mintzberg, H., D. Raisinghani, and A. Theoret
1976 'The structure of "unstructured" decision processes'. *Administrative Science Quarterly* 21/2:246–275.

Mintzberg, H.
1978 'Patterns in strategy formation'. *Management Science* 24/9:934–948.

Moore, P. G., and H. Thomas
1976 *The anatomy of decisions*. Harmondsworth: Penguin.

Normann, R.
1971 'Organizational innovativeness: product variation and reorientation'. *Administrative Science Quarterly* 16/2:203–215.

Pettigrew, A.
1°73 *The politics of organizational decision making*. London: Tavistock.

Pugh, D. S., D. J. Hickson, C. R. Hinings, and C. Turner
1968 'Dimensions of organization structure'. *Administrative Science Quarterly* 13/1:65–105.

Pugh, D. C., D. J. Hickson, C. R. Hinings, and C. Turner
1969 'The context of organization structures'. *Administrative Science Quarterly* 14:91–114.

Secord, P. F., and C. Backman
1961 'Personality theory and the problem of stability and change in individual behaviour: an interpersonal approach'. *Psychological Review* 68:21–32.

Simon, H. A.
1947 *Administrative behavior*. New York: Free Press.

Thompson, J. D.
1967 *Organizations in action*. New York: McGraw Hill.

Walker, J.
1969 'The diffusion of innovation among the American States'. *American Political Science Review* LXIII:879–893.

Weick, K.
1969 *The social psychology of organizing*. Reading, Mass: Addison–Wesley.

White, D. M.
1971 'The problem of power'. *British Journal of Political Science* 2:479–490.

Wilson, D. C.
1980 Organizational strategy. Ph.D. thesis. University of Bradford.

Wrong, D. H.
1968 'Some problems of defining social powers'. *American Journal of Sociology* 79/5:673–681.

[8]

Journal of Management Studies, **21**, 4, 1984
0022–2380 $3.50

THE INTERDEPARTMENTAL INFLUENCE OF MANAGERS: INDIVIDUAL AND SUB-UNIT PERSPECTIVES

GRAHAM K. KENNY
Department of Organizational Analysis, University of Alberta, Canada
DAVID C. WILSON
Organizational Analysis Research Unit, University of Bradford Management Centre

ABSTRACT

This paper examines the extent to which managerial influence over group-interdepartmental decisions is derived from sub-unit contingencies or is due to more individualistic characteristics of the manager. Both individual and sub-unit perspectives are presented in a framework composed of seven power factors each of which is investigated empirically. The major finding from a survey of 142 departmental managers is that individual managerial expertise is more important than sub-unit-based power with access to and control of information being of equal importance. We suggest that the investigation of managerial influence from a sub-unit perspective alone may be insufficient and that, in certain circumstances, both individualistic and sub-unit perspectives should be taken into account.

INTRODUCTION

CENTRAL to studies of intraorganizational power have been two distinct levels of analysis. On the one hand, are studies focusing on the exercise of power by individuals whereby the possession of certain qualities and resources endows power. The work of French and Raven (1960) typifies such an approach. On the other hand, are studies which embrace a more structural analysis, emphasizing the division of labour as a causal base of power. The level of analysis here is concerned with sub-units (usually specific departments) some of which are more essential to the organization than others by their ability to control resources, their central function in a system of task interdependence and their lack of ready substitution (Dubin, 1957; Thompson, 1956; Hickson *et al.*, 1971).

Each of these approaches (the individual and the sub-unit) is concerned

Addresses for reprints: Dr. G. K. Kenny, Department of Organizational Analysis, Faculty of Business Administration and Commerce, Central Academic Building, University of Alberta, Edmonton, Canada T6G 2GI.

Dr. D. C. Wilson, Organizational Analysis Research Unit, University of Bradford Management Centre, Emm Lane, Bradford, West Yorkshire, BD9 4JL.

with the possession of certain resources as constituents of a power base. French and Raven listed five examples of power sources [1] the possession of which affords control to an individual over certain issues and situations. Sub-unit analyzes of power equally emphasize the possession of certain resources as constitutive of a power base. Differential power exists between sub-units in organizations, however, because some are able to deal successfully with 'strategic contingencies' faced by an organization or because they are 'central' and 'pervasive' to its effective functioning (Hickson *et al.*, 1971). This base of power rests less on formal hierarchy than it does on the control of certain strategic resources [2].

Despite the similarities of the individual and sub-unit approaches to power (the control and the possession of valued resources) there has been little integration of the two levels of analysis. Some integration has taken place in the works of authors who attempt a more historical and macro-approach to power. For example, Scott (1979) differentiates between control, ownership and possession as separate but interdependent facets of power. Pahl and Winkler (1974) point toward similar distinctions highlighting the differences between 'operational' and 'allocative' control. Again, Clegg and Dunkerley (1980) attempt an integrative approach of individual power *via* 'skill possession' with the overall control of resources. All these integrative approaches, however, share a common theme of power analyzes which are grounded less in individualistic reputation amongst managers, for example, and more in long term and gross changes. In this paper, we are concerned with such reputational power amongst managers and we are less specifically concerned with macro, historical issues. From this reputational perspective Schein (1977, p. 65) notes:

> Despite the conceptual work in this area (intraorganizational power), there has been little integration of the interpersonal and sub-unit bases of power as they are utilized by the head of the functional unit. To what extent does the head draw power from that of the unit and to what extent from his or her personal base? Unknown also is the differential importance of these bases and the ways in which they are used in combination as sources of power to the powerholder.

The present paper addresses precisely this question. The structural and contingent location of a sub-unit is seen as an initial power base, whereby sub-unit managers are able to accrue power and, in addition, such sub-unit power acts as a platform from which individual managers have the capacity to embody varying degrees of power. Power, in this context, is seen to be the extent to which individuals have the capacity to influence the processes and outcomes of decision-making in a relative and variable manner (Butler *et al.*, 1979; Hinings *et al.*, 1974). Such influence, therefore, constitutes the basis of differing intra and extra-organizational conditions embodied in a range of different skills. Power is viewed as a relative phenomenon amongst managers, the balance of which is likely to change given variable organizational conditions. A summary of existing sub-unit and individual levels of analysis of power appears below, leading to the development of an integrated theoretical framework.

THEORETICAL FRAMEWORK

Sub-Unit Analyzes of Power

The control of strategic resources endows sub-units with power (Hickson *et al.*, 1971) and such power facilitates a degree of influence by some individuals over organizational decision-making. This thesis has been empirically examined by Hinings *et al.* (1974, p. 24) for a number of organizational sub-units. They found correlations between sub-unit control of strategic resources and sub-unit influence. A broadly similar perspective and set of findings may be found in Pfeffer and Salancik (1974) and Salancik and Pfeffer (1974). Their investigation, which parallels the strategic contingencies approach of Hickson *et al.* (1971) [3] focused on 'sub-unit horizontal power differences' and horizontal power is argued to be the 'use of influence among co-acting peers to obtain benefit for themselves' (Salancik and Pfeffer, 1974, p. 453). As part of this research, managers were asked to rate the differential influence of various sub-units and to rate sub-unit importance to the organization as a whole.

In an anaylsis of two U.S.A.F. bomber wings, Thompson (1956) examined power from a similar angle and found that the power of certain sub-units stemmed ultimately from the division of labour. This was because certain tasks became of central importance to organizational functioning and the specialized technical requirements of task fulfillment endowed those sub-units in this domain with greater power than other, less essential sub-units. Following the same theme, Crozier (1964) illustrated how essential were those sub-units which could control and cope with uncertainties in an organization. In his analysis of a French tobacco organization, the maintenance sub-unit accrued a useful power base from a position of coping with uncertainty (in this case created by machine breakdowns).

Despite the number of empirical studies of sub-unit power described above, the sub-unit perspective remains a partial model of power in organizations. It predicts those conditions in which, *ceteris paribus*, sub-units ought to accrue power (Child, 1973; Clegg and Dunkerley, 1980). Those sub-units that are less dependent, or contingent, upon other sub-units in an organization are deemed to have power. This power is, however, only accrued in relatively stable conditions of non-substitutability and where the sub-unit is central to the organization. The actual exercise of power in organizations (as opposed to where power is predicted to reside) is, however, most manifest in individual activity. Individual managers bargain over decision-making, negotiate over issues and defensively protect their own domain (Abell, 1975; Dalton, 1959; Pettigrew, 1973). This poses the question of to what extent individual managers derive their influence from the contingent nature of the sub-unit of which they are the head, or whether there are further sources of influence endowed upon these individuals beyond the importance or centrality of their respective sub-units. This is not to assume that managers of strategically contingent sub-units will necessarily always be endowed with power in their 'representative' capacity. Rather, we examine in this paper to what extent variable resource acquisition and control (as indicative of power) is derived from primarily sub-unit or more individualistic characteristics.

Individual Analyzes of Power

Although not specifically concerned with organizational settings, French and Raven's (1960) five types of power remain a pervasive theme in any study of individual power. Closer examination of French and Raven's typology reveals that each type of power is not conceptually congruent with the others. Sometimes, as in the case of reward and coercive power, power is seen to derive from the resources available to the individual, often from an existing sub-unit power base. At other times, as in the case of referent and legitimate power, individual power is less a derivation of sub-unit contingencies than it is a function of 'the characteristics and motivations of the target' in power relationships (Patchen, 1974, p. 196). Furthermore, where expert power is concerned, a blend of both individual characteristics and sub-unit contingencies are interwoven. Expert power depends, in part, on certain individual characteristics of the influencer – his standing or credibility in the eyes of peers – and, in part, on the possession of certain organizational resources such as ready and fast access to reliable information and facts.

Power is, therefore, both derived from organizationally based factors (sub-unit centrality, for example) and from the individual characteristics of sub-unit representatives. Nonetheless, it is not an easy task to distinguish whether individual managers have power because of their ability to reward, punish or be obeyed, or because organizational hierarchy and coordinating the division of labour endow them with formal authority. In which case, power may be as much an individual characteristic as it is derived from sub-unit contingencies. Whilst a substantial amount of power may accrue to an individual manager on the basis of his or her personal characteristics, it is unlikely that such power will be derived solely from such individual qualities. Influence in these cases is drawn from a power base founded upon the importance of the manager's sub-unit to the organization (Butler *et al.*, 1979).

Additional influence over decision-making may, however, accrue to the manager *via* certain individual characteristics. Wilson (1982) termed these characteristics 'personae' which may vary independently of any sub-unit power base. Personae may be brought into play over some issues and not over other issues as variable individual characteristics whilst a manager's position in a sub-unit remains relatively invariate. In this case, individual characteristics resulted in one manager having preferential access to information and senior management as well as to powerful others both inside and outside the organization. Raven (1974) calls the first 'informational power' as managers can influence decision-making by their access to and control of information (Pettigrew, 1973). Access to influential others – cynically summarized as who you know, not what you know – has been stressed by Zalesnik (1970) and McMurray (1973). The case study by Kenny and Palmer (1980) illustrated how an individual's access to senior management can undermine the formal authority of those who supervise him.

Integrating Individual and Sub-Unit Analyzes

Our examination of both individual and sub-unit analyzes of power reveal three distinct bases of power for a sub-unit manager which may be summarized as (see also Kenny and Palmer, 1980):

(a) The manager's person
(b) The manager's position
(c) The manager's sub-unit

Preliminary interviews for the present study lent support to the existence of the three power bases listed above [4]. A manager's power to influence decision-making appears to be derived from all three bases and we further suggest that the bases are additive. A high score on each of the power bases endows an individual with greater power than a manager who has, for example, a senior position but is head of a peripheral and substitutable sub-unit.

We further suggest that from these power bases a number of power factors are derived. Power factors are the specific features that empower a manager with the ability to influence decision-making. One such power factor is expertise. A manager's person-based power may be manifest as expertise or the ability to influence decisions because of 'superior knowledge or ability' (Raven, 1974). The managers interviewed preliminary to the present study tended to distinguish between technical expertise and managerial expertise. Technical expertise was concerned with knowledge of a technical process whereas managerial expertise was concerned with knowledge of organization and people. Thus an engineering manager may have considerable technical expertise, *i.e.* knowledge of engineering, but have little managerial expertise, *i.e.* knowledge of the 'workings' of the organization and an understanding of people. A manager's person-based power may also be manifest as, what managers refer to as, 'personality' (referent power, the ability to get on with and persuade people). A manager's position-based power may be manifest as formal authority (reward, coercive and legitimate power), as access to and control of information, and as access to senior management and other influential people. A manager's sub-unit based power may be manifest as the importance of his department to the organization – the extent to which the department (sub-unit) is strategically contingent (Hickson *et al.*, 1971). Figure 1 outlines the full theoretical framework.

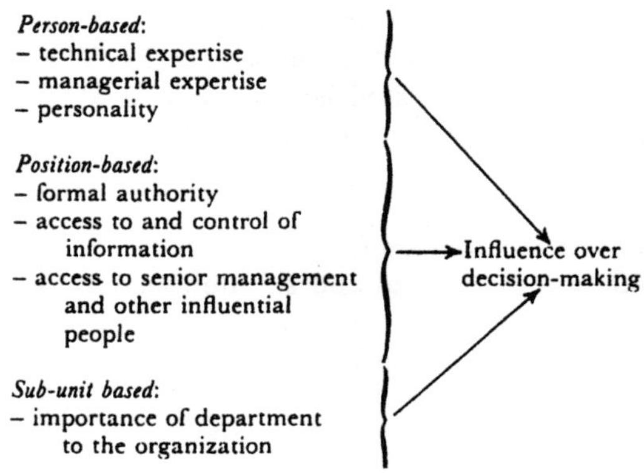

Figure 1. Power factors and departmental managers' influence

Influence Over Decision-Making
Although the majority of studies concerned with intraorganizational power have concentrated on decision-making, there has been little evidence of an attempt to build a classification of decision types. Such a classification is necessary if we are to examine the differential power of departmental managers, for we need to know over what ranges of decision types are managers influential. Existing studies have looked at non-repetitive purchasing decisions (Patchen, 1974), resource allocation (Pfeffer and Salancik, 1974; Manns and March, 1978), new products (Norman, 1971), equipment purchase (Salancik, Pfeffer and Kelly, 1978) and a number of hospital issues (Comstock, 1980).

If we are to examine this range of decisions in which managers exert some influence, then some classification is necessary. We suggest that these decisions may be categorized by two dimensions. The first, *decision method*, examines whether the decision is made by the manager alone or in conjunction with others (individual *versus* group decisions). The second, *issue domain* distinguishes between those issues that are exclusively concerned with decisions internal to the department and those issues which involve and concern decisions external to the department (intradepartmental *versus* interdepartmental issues). Combining these two dimensions yields a four way classification of decisions. These are shown in figure 2.

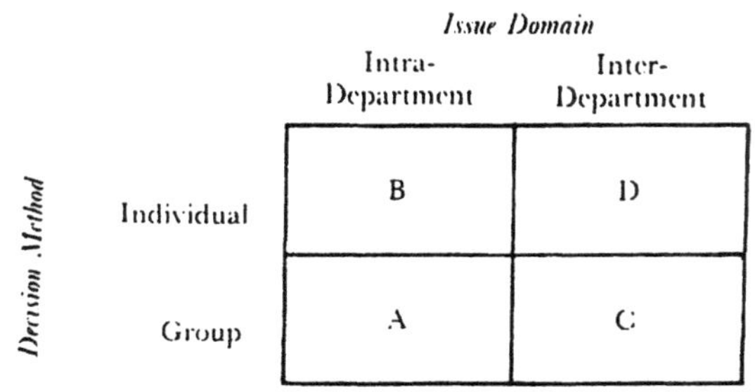

Figure 2. Classification of Intraorganizational decisions

An individual-intradepartmental decision (cell B) is the type of decision made by a manager alone and which is concerned solely with issues internal to the manager's department. Examples include decisions over delegation and the allocation of specific tasks to departmental members. Work procedures and decisions over planning departmental affairs are examples of group-intradepartmental decisions (cell A) where the domain of the issues focus on one department but are decided upon by a group composed of the departmental manager and members of his department. Individual-interdepartmental decisions (cell D), whilst theoretically possible, are unlikely to exist in practice. Departmental managers are unlikely to take alone decisions which centre upon issues external to their departments and hence are partially the concern of other departments and their managers [5].

The focus of our attention in this paper lies with those decisions in cell C. The domain of issues is interdepartmental and decisions are made between groups of managers. Examples of this type of decision would be the allocation of resources between departments and the determination of policy, planning and forecasting decisions. For the purposes of this research, these decisions allow us to examine the relative impact of sub-unit and individual factors on managerial influence over decision-making [6]. Although we recognize that managers at different hierarchical levels will have correspondingly different amounts of formal authority, they will still, nonetheless, have considerable influence over specific local decisions. This implies that the chief executive will have more global influence over decision-making than the more junior departmental manager, but both may have considerable influence over specific local decisions (Patchen, 1963). Further, when managers become involved in group-interdepartmental decisions they are likely to be interacting with managers of equal, or near equal, formal authority.

Following this reasoning, we might expect the perceived importance of the seven previous power factors to remain constant for all managerial levels in a hierarchy but that there will be some difference in perceived importance of the power factors across functional specialities. That is, some departments are regarded as being more strategically contingent than others within an organization. For example, where organizational emphasis is upon expansion and growth, the department which copes with this strategic contingency (usually marketing) is likely to be regarded as a highly important and influential sub-unit (Hickson *et al.*, 1971).

In general, line departments, such as marketing and production, are regarded as being more strategically important than staff departments such as personnel or research and development (Dalton, 1959; Golembiewski, 1967). From the perspective of this paper, we would expect that line managers would, therefore, perceive that departmental importance would be more salient to their influence over decision-making than would staff managers. On the other hand, because staff managers are the technical experts in an organization (Thompson, 1967), it would be expected that they would perceive that technical expertise (a person-based power factor) is more salient to their influence over decision-making. Nonetheless, the importance of *other* factors, such as personality or formal authority, is likely to be perceived as being equal by both line and staff managerial groups.

METHOD

This research is based on the responses of 188 departmental managers from sixty Australian organizations. Of these responses, 148 came from business organizations and 40 came from government organizations. The mean size of the managers' departments was 38.03 employees (S.D. 66.51). Data were gathered from each manager *via* a questionnaire which was completed during an interview session. Each of the seven power factors in figure 1 were examined in the questionnaire and the managers were asked to rate each on a seven point scale which assessed the importance of the factors to their influence over decision-making. (The relevant extract from the questionnaire is shown in appendix I).

The phrasing of the questionnaire and the division of expertise into technical and managerial were a result of preliminary interviews conducted prior to the present study in which managers themselves suggested the terminology. The term 'personality' was used to cover what French and Raven (1960) termed referent power because preliminary interviews indicated that this was the way the majority of managers referred to such power. 'Formal authority' included coercive, reward and legitimate power and was chosen again because the majority of managers used the term in this way.

As each manager was asked to indicate the importance of each of the factors to the amount of influence that he or she had over organizational decision-making, there was obviously *no* attempt to ask respondents to rate the importance of the factors for managers in general across a range of organizations. The aim of this approach was to establish the relative impact of the power factors as they contributed *to the managers' own influence* in decision-making. In this respect, the present study differs markedly from the methods employed by Hinnings *et al.* (1974) and Pfeffer and Salancik (1974) in which managers were asked to rate, among other things, the influence of sub-units and, independently, certain contingency factors. Their method was then to correlate the two sets of results. In the present study, data were also gathered concerning specific details, the most relevant of which were the level in the organization occupied by the respondent (chief executive is level 1 and so on) and the type of department managed. The departments were classified into five broad functional areas plus a sixth 'other' category. The classification scheme is shown in appendix II.

Because the study is based upon individualistic perceptions of the importance of power factors, some consideration of consistency must be made. To what extent were the managers studied consistent in their interpretation of the power factors? Because there was only one item examined for each power factor, a reliability coefficient such as Cronbach Alpha could not be employed. Therefore, we tested respondent consistency by examining the unimodality of the distribution of responses. This examination was to determine whether or not some respondents repeatedly interpreted an item differently from other respondents. A non-unimodal distribution would show up the case of differential interpretation. Reference to appendix I reveals that there is no significant multimodality in the distributions of the responses. In consequence, we conclude that the power factors were not interpreted significantly differently by two or more sub-groups of managers.

RESULTS

Of the 188 departmental managers interviewed, 142 indicated that they took part in group-interdepartmental decisions (taken in the company of others outside their own departments). Examples of such decisions were, new systems design, industrial relations issues, investment and accounting policies. Results for the power factors over this range of decisions are shown in table I and the distribution of respondents by departmental type is shown in appendix II.

Respondents rated managerial expertise (knowledge of organization and people) as the most important power factor in securing influence over decision-making, and deemed formal authority to be the least influential factor. Hierarchically endowed power, it seems, is regarded by departmental managers as of little significance in providing a political lever in group-interdepartmental decision-making. This finding concurs with much of the recent literature which focuses upon the extent to which hierarchical location endows power to individuals in decision-making processes. Clawson (1980)

Table I. Importance of power factors

Power Factor	*Importance* [Rank]*	*Mean and (S.D.)*
***Person-based*:**		
technical expertise	[4]	5.08 (1.48)
managerial expertise	[1]	5.39 (1.25)
personality	[6]	4.87 (1.50)
***Position-based*:**		
formal authority	[7]	4.40 (1.43)
access to and control of information	[2]	5.14 (1.39)
access to senior management and other influential people	[5]	4.96 (1.48)
***Sub-unit-based*:**		
importance of department to the organization	[2]	5.14 (1.65)

* n = 142

argues that bureaucratic structures (which distinguish between hierarchical levels) are a result of the need to create management as a separate, controlling category. Once created, however, the formal authority thus accrued is of little value in providing a power base for individuals at this managerial level. Where managerial interests diverge in the decision-making process, formal authority is the least powerful lever to secure those interests, for logically, it seeks to homogenize rather than to differentiate management (Boreham, 1980).

Our results indicate that the most important power factor in managerial decision-making is the knowledge of organization and people (managerial expertise). This factor was consistently rated the most important in securing influence over decision-making. In the light of the emphasis on sub-unit power in intraorganizational decision-making (Hickson *et al.*, 1971; Hinings *et al.*, 1974), this result is surprising. Closer examination of Hickson *et al.* (1971) does, however, reveal a recognition that such individualistic rather than sub-unit power may come to the fore. They cite the 'qualities of interdepartmental relationships' (p. 227) and suggest that:

> Finally, but perhaps most important, individual differences must be accepted, that is, differences in the intelligence, skills, ages, sexes, or personality factors such as dominance, assertiveness, and risk-taking propensity, of personnel in the various subunits (p. 227).

Although contingencies may change and endow different sub-units with power on different occasions, knowledge of how the organization operates and of the individuals who comprise the organization seems an overriding and enduring power factor. This corresponds with what Wilson *et al.* (1981, p. 25) suggest, 'that knowledge of how the "system" operates becomes a key factor in the securing of power by individuals'.

The finding that managerial expertise is an important factor to managerial influence over decision-making is reinforced by other studies. Rasmus (1974) argues that although the trend is to give non-managerial groups greater responsibility for workflow operations and internal processes, they are denied control of such processes as they are not commensurately endowed with managerial expertise. The denial of managerial expertise to these groups could be seen as an implicit or explicit recognition by management of its efficacy as a power factor.

Managers rated 'access to and control of information' equal second in importance as a power factor alongside 'importance of department to the organization'. Hage (1980) emphasizes the role of information in any analysis of managerial power and argues that a predominant characteristic of decisions involving management is that of high information search. Control over this information, therefore, endows individuals with the capacity to influence decisions one way or another. Arguing along the same lines, Norman (1971) illustrates the importance of information control as a managerial power factor. Those individuals who can elicit and monitor not only from within but also from outside and can feed such information into decision-making processes, become influential as a result. These individuals become potentially the most influential in what he terms 'innovative' or 're-orientation' new product decisions, which are characterized by a lack of readily available and easily interpreted information.

In a study of 150 cases of strategic decision-making, Butler *et al.* (1982) have also emphasized the role of information in moulding the politics of decision-making. In situations where managerial interests conflict over specific issues, information search activity is sharply increased as each interest group tries to amass data which can substantially add to the defence of a particular point of view. This finding again points to the pervasive role of information as a power factor. The use of information control as a political lever is also graphically illustrated in two case studies of decision-making by Pettigrew (1973) and Wilson (1982).

The contingent nature of the manager's sub-unit must not be overlooked, however. The importance of the sub-unit to the organization was rated equal second by the respondents as a power factor. This result provides empirical justification for the theoretical stance of Hickson *et al.* (1971). The contingent nature of a manager's sub-unit *is* of concern in securing a power base, and presumably an individual's control over information is also made easier from a position of being located in a strategically contingent sub-unit. Those sub-units which cope with uncertainty for the organization will be arguably privy to information not as immediately available to other, less contingent, sub-units. Managers in a sub-unit which copes with uncertainty are, therefore, in a preferential position to gain access to and effect control over information. One implication of this reasoning is that power begets power. Those managers who are in a position to control information as a result of their location in a strategically contingent sub-unit are simultaneously in a preferential position to secure the perpetuation of this power by selectively controlling information input into decision-making processes. Clegg and Dunkerley (1980, p. 444) illustrate this effect by reference to a chess game, wherein 'a piece like the Queen would start in a more privileged position than a Pawn' as a result of the structural basis of the games. Although they develop this line of reasoning into a discussion of rules, the differential power upon which the Queen and Pawn can draw is made explicit.

In the face of the emphasis that has been placed in the management literature and in management training on a manager's interactive skills for 'success', the result for the factor 'personality' (the ability to get on with people) – being rated second last as an important power factor – is somewhat surprising (see table I). Unlike the result for formal authority, there seems to be no immediate situational or structural explanation for this finding. It appears that the effects of being personable or not are overridden by both sub-unit contingencies and managerial expertise. Apparently to be personable is not very important in influencing decisions.

Table II. Relationship between hierarchical level and importance of factors*

Power Factor	*Correlation Coefficient*
***Person-based*:**	
technical expertise	0.04
managerial expertise	−0.08
personality	0.00
***Position-based*:**	
formal authority	−0.04
access to and control of information	−0.02
access to senior management and other influential people	−0.02
***Sub-unit-based*:**	
importance of department to the organization	0.01

* Hierarchical level measured from chief executive, '1', down the organization. However, level 1 managers (chief executives) were excluded from the study as they were not regarded as 'departmental managers'. Mean hierarchical level was 3.04 (S.D., 1.10).

The sample was examined to reveal whether hierarchial level had any association with ratings of importance of the power factors. Similarly the sample was divided into line and staff managers in order to examine whether this would result in different ratings of the power factors. The line manager group was composed of sales/marketing and manufacturing/production managers, while the staff manager group comprised personnel/training, finance/accounting and research and development managers (see appendix II). The results for hierarchical level are shown in table II and table III shows results for line and staff differentiation.

Table III. Importance of factors for line and staff managers

Power Factor	*[Rank], Mean and (S.D.)*	*Line*		*Staff†*
Person-based:				
technical expertise	[6]	4.71 (1.73)	[1]	5.32* (1.29)
managerial expertise	[1]	5.59 (1.16)	[2]	5.28 (1.23)
personality	[5]	5.05 (1.59)	[6]	4.68 (1.32)
Position-based:				
formal authority	[7]	4.50 (1.41)	[7]	4.42 (1.26)
access to and control of information	[4]	5.13 (1.36)	[3]	5.14 (1.26)
access to senior management and other influential people	[3]	5.14 (1.48)	[4]	5.00 (1.36)
Sub-unit-based:				
importance of department to the organization	[2]	5.41 (1.37)	[5]	4.88* (1.73)

* $p < 0.05$ (One-Tailed test)
† Line = sales/marketing and manufacturing/production (n = 62); Staff = personnel/training, finance/account, research and development (n = 50). The mean hierarchical levels for the line managers and staff managers were 2.90 and 3.14 respectively – they do not differ significantly.

Taking hierarchical levels first, there were no significant correlations between level and the perceived importance of the power factors (see table II). This result suggests that although managerial echelons are differentiated hierarchically, managers at all levels have influence over group decisions that are local to them. The fact that formal authority varies over these hierarchical levels is of little consequence when departmental managers engage in decision-making with other departmental managers of equal, or near equal, status. Formal authority, here, is roughly equal between managers and, therefore, serves to integrate rather than to differentiate between them. The consistently low rating of formal authority coupled with the consistently nigh rating of managerial expertise and information control does tempt the conclusion that management represent a coherent and distinctive sub-group within organizations.

Although there are no differences in perceived importance of the power factors over hierarchical levels, differentiating between line and staff managers does reveal two differences. These are in the rating of 'technical expertise' and 'importance of department to the organization' (see table III). Each variation is, perhaps, predictable, with staff managers rating the importance of technical expertise significantly above that of the line managers. Similarly, line managers rate the importance of department to the organization significantly above that of the staff managers. This is evidence of the nature of functional differentiation. Faced with environmental uncertainty, for example, line managers (such as marketing) cope with such contingencies more immediately than do their staff counterparts (such as personnel). Both Golembiewski (1967) and Hickson *et al.* (1971) point toward this tendency. In the same way, these results concur with Thompson's (1967) prediction that as staff managers are the technical experts in organizations (they comprise part of the 'technical core') they will consequently be buffered from the immediate effects of environmental uncertainty and that they will, therefore, perceive knowledge of specific technical processes as of paramount importance in influencing decisions.

CONCLUSION

The data presented in this paper show to what extent managers perceived each of seven power factors to be important in securing influence over decision-making. Somewhat surprisingly, the contingent nature of the managers' sub-unit did not rate as supremely important. Managers consistently perceived managerial expertise (knowledge of the organization and people) and access to and control over information as more and of equal importance respectively to sub-unit based power. The variation of this rating over different levels in the managerial hierarchy was not significant and there was only a predictable variation between line and staff managers. Even here, both line and staff managers rated managerial expertise above sub-unit based power. Formal authority and interactive skills in the form of being personable were perceived as of little importance in wielding influence over decision-making. If power is seen to accrue from the possession of resources, we suggest that the dominantly sub-unit view of power is misplaced and that we should, therefore, incorporate more individualistically based resources into any analytical scheme. Such a modification of sub-unit perspectives is in line with the theoretical predictions of Hickson *et al.* (1971) who argued the case for a dominantly sub-unit view of power but also suggested that individual characteristics may well override structural contingencies.

Our findings are also supported by much of the recent work concerning worker participation and the delegation of responsibility (see for example Boreham, 1980 and Wood, 1980). The delegation of responsibility and collective decision-making schemes arguably erode existing managerial power when examined from a solely sub-unit perspective. Such participative exercises between manager and worker reduce the uniqueness of managerial sub-units rendering them less central and more substitutable – in the vocabulary of strategic contingencies theory. What this sub-unit perspective misses, however, is that overall knowledge of the system and access to and control over information is reserved for management alone. These are not areas in which workers participate and share. This serves to emphasize the importance of these power factors above the contingent nature of managerial sub-units. For the denial of managerial expertise and information control to labour may be seen as the implicit or explicit recognition by management of its efficacy as a power base. Our results seem to confirm this view.

Of course, exactly on which occasions this individual power supercedes sub-unit power is of importance and we suggest that further analysis is required across different types of decisions. The present paper has only examined group-interdepartmental decisions, but the results displayed here may not be consistent in individual-intradepartmental decisions. We approach this aspect of the research in a future companion paper.

NOTES

[1] French and Raven (1959) listed five examples:
Expert power: 'The strength of the expert power of O/P varies with the extent of the knowledge or perception which P attributes to O within a given area' (p. 620).
Referent power: 'The referent power of O/P has its basis in the identification of P with O. By identification, we mean a feeling of access of P with O, or a desire for such an identity' (p. 618).
Reward power: 'Reward power is defined as power whose basis is the ability to reward. The strength of the reward power of O/P increases with the magnitude of the rewards which P perceives that O can mediate to him' (p. 613).
Coercive power: 'Coercive power is similar to reward power in that it also involves O's ability to manipulate the attainment of valences. Coercive power of O/P stems from the expectation of the part of P that he will be punished by O if he fails to conform to the influence attempt' (p. 614).
Legitimate power: 'Legitimate power of O/P is here defined as that power which stems from internalized values in P which dictate that O has a legitimate right to influence P and that P has an obligation to accept this influence' (p. 616).

[2] Crozier's (1964) analysis of the considerable power of maintenance men in a French tobacco factory is evidence of a contingent rather than a hierarchical power base.

[3] Pfeffer has recently replicated this study, (see Pfeffer and Moore, 1980).

[4] Preliminary interviews were conducted with 208 departmental managers. Among the questions asked was: 'What factors contribute to your influence over decisions in your organization?'

[5] The preliminary results of this study confirm this.

[6] Analysis of the remaining cells in figure 2 is therefore *not* the central concern of this paper. We intend that such analyzes will be carried out in subsequent papers.

REFERENCES

ABELL, P. (1975). *Organizations as Bargaining and Influence Systems*. London: Heinemann.

BOREHAM, P. (1980). 'The dialectic of theory and control: capitalist crisis and the organization of labour'. In Dunkerley, D. and Salaman, G. (Eds.), *The International Yearbook of Organization Studies*. London: Routledge and Kegan Paul.

BUTLER, R. J., ASTLEY, W. G., HICKSON, D. J., MALLORY, G. and WILSON, D. C. (1979). 'Strategic decision-making: concepts of content and process'. *International Studies of Management and Organization*, **IX**, 4, 5–36.

BUTLER, R. J., ASTLEY, W. G., CRAY, D., HICKSON, D. J., MALLORY, G. and WILSON, D. C. (1982). 'Strategic decision-making: a large scale study'. *Working paper*, Organizational Analysis Research Unit: University of Bradford Management Centre.

CHILD, J. (1973). 'Organization: a choice for man'. In Child, J. (Ed.), *Man and Organization*. London: George Allen and Unwin.

CLAWSON, D. (1980). 'Class struggle and the rise of bureaucracy'. In Dunkerley, D. and Salaman, G. (Eds.), *The International Yearbook of Organization Studies*. London: Routledge and Kegan Paul.

CLEGG, S. and DUNKERLEY, D. (1980). *Organization, Class and Control*. London: Routledge and Kegan Paul.

COMSTOCK, D. E. (1980). 'Dimensions of influence in organizations'. *Pacific Sociological Review*, **23**, 67–84.

CROZIER, M. (1964). *The Bureaucratic Phenomenon*. London: Tavistock.

DALTON, M. (1959). *Men Who Manage*. New York: Wiley.

DUBIN, R. (1957). 'Power and union management relations'. *Administrative Science Quarterly*, **2**, 60–81.

FRENCH, J. R. P. and RAVEN, B. H. (1960). 'The bases of social power'. In Cartwright, D. and Zander, A. (Eds.), *Group Dynamics: Research and Theory*. London: Tavistock.

GOLEMBIEWSKI, R. T. (1967). *Organizing Men and Power: Patterns of Behavior and Line-Staff Models*. Chicago: Rand McNally.

HAGE, J. (1980). *Theories of Organizations: Form, Process and Transformation*. Wiley: New York.

HICKSON, D. J., HININGS, C. R., LEE, C. A., SCHNECK, R. E. and PENNINGS, J. M. (1971). 'A strategic contingencies theory of intraorganizational power'. *Administrative Science Quarterly*, **16**, 216–29.

HININGS, C. R., HICKSON, D. J., PENNINGS, J. M. and SCHNECK, R. E. (1974). 'Structural conditions of intraorganizational power'. *Administrative Science Quarterly*, **19**, 22–44.

KENNY, G. K. and PALMER, I. (1980). 'Individual power bases in organizations: a case study'. *Management Forum*, **6**, 227–231.

MANNS, C. L. and MARCH, J. G. (1978). Financial adversity, internal competition and curriculum change in a university'. *Administrative Science Quarterly*, **23**, 541–52.

McMURRY, R. N. (1973). 'Power and the ambitious executive'. *Harvard Business Review*, **51**, 140–5.

NORMANN, R. (1971). 'Organizational innovativeness: product variation and reorientation'. *Administrative Science Quarterly*, **2**, 203–15.

PAHL, R. E. and WINKLER, J. T. (1974). 'The economic élite: theory and practice'. In Stanworth, P. and Giddens, A. (Eds.), *Elites and Power in British Society*. Cambridge: Cambridge University Press.

PATCHEN, M. (1963). 'Alternative questionnaire approaches to the measurement of influence in organziations'. *American Journal of Sociology*, **69**, 41–52.

PATCHEN, M. (1974). 'The locus and basis of influence on organizational decisions'. *Organizational Behavior and Human Performance*, **11**, 195–221.

PETTIGREW, A. M. (1973). *The Politics of Organisational Decision-making*. London: Tavistock.

PFEFFER, J. and MOORE, W. L. (1980). 'Power in university budgeting: a replication and extension'. *Administrative Science Quarterly*, **25**, 637–53.

PFEFFER, J. and SALANCIK, G. R. (1974). 'Organizational decision-making as a political process: the case of a university budget'. *Administrative Science Quarterly*, **19**, 135–51.

RASMUS, J. (1974). 'Why management is pushing "job enrichment" '. *International Socialist Review*, **35**, 22–5 and 43–4.

RAVEN, B. H. (1974). 'A comparative analysis of power and power preference'. In Tedeschi, J. T. (Ed.), *Perspectives in Social Power*. Chicago: Aldine.

SALANCIK, C. R., PFEFFER, J. and KELLY, J. P. (1978). 'A contingency model of influence in organizational decision-making'. *Pacific Sociological Review*, **21**, 239–56.

SALANCIK, G. R. and PFEFFER, J. (1974). 'The bases and use of power in organizational decision-making: the case of a university'. *Administrative Science Quarterly*, **19**, 453–73.

SCHEIN, V. E. (1977). 'Individual power and political behavior in organizations: an inadequately explored reality'. *Academy of Management Review*, **2**, 64–72.

SCOTT, J. (1979). *Corporations, Classes and Capitalism*. London: Hutchinson.

THOMPSON, J. D. (1956). 'Authority and power in "identical" organizations'. *American Journal of Sociology*, **62**, 290–301.

THOMPSON, J. D. (1967). *Organizations in Action*. New York: McGraw-Hill.

WILSON, D. C., BUTLER, R. J., CRAY, D., HICKSON, D. J. and MALLORY, G. R. (1981). 'The selective embodiment of power'. *Working paper*, Organizational Analysis Research Unit, University of Bradford Management Centre.

WILSON, D. C. (1982). 'Electricity and resistance: a case study of innovation and politics'. *Organization Studies*, **3**, 119–40.

WOOD, S. (1980). 'Corporate strategy and organizational studies'. In Dunkerley, D. and Salaman, G. (Eds.), *The International Yearbook of Organization Studies*. London: Routledge and Kegan Paul.

ZALESNICK, A. (1970). 'Power and politics in organizational life'. *Harvard Business Review*, **48**, 47–60.

Appendix I. Relevant Section of Questionnaire and Distribution of Responses

(1) Section of Questionnaire:
Respondents were asked to rate the importance of the factors below to *their* influence over group-interdepartmental decisions on a seven point scale from 1, 'no importance', to 7, 'very great deal of importance'. Factors, as stated on the questionnaire were:
my technical expertise (*e.g.* knowledge of a technical process)
my managerial expertise (*e.g.* knowledge of organization and people)
my formal authority
my access to and control of information
my access to senior management and other influential people
the importance of my department to the organization

(2) Distribution of responses across rating scale:

Power Factors	*Percent Responses* *Scale Points*							*Total* %
	1	2	3	4	5	6	7	
Person-based:								
technical expertise	2.1	7.1	3.6	16.4	23.6	32.9	14.3	100.0
managerial expertise	0.7	2.9	2.9	15.7	22.9	37.9	17.1	100.0
personality	5.0	2.9	7.9	22.9	25.7	22.9	12.9	100.0
Position-based:								
formal authority	2.9	7.1	14.3	30.0	22.1	17.1	6.4	100.0
access to and control of information	1.4	4.3	5.0	19.3	25.0	29.3	15.7	100.0
access to senior management and other influential people	1.4	3.6	12.1	22.9	16.4	28.6	15.0	100.0
Sub-unit-based:								
importance of department to the organization	5.7	1.4	8.6	16.4	15.0	32.1	20.7	100.0

Appendix II. Distribution of Respondents by Type of Department

Department	Number of Respondents
Sales/Marketing	42
Manufacturing/Production	20
Personnel/Training	12
Finance/Accounting	32
Research and Development	6
Other	30
Total	142

[9]

Human Relations, Volume 39, Number 4, pp. 309–332

Breaking the Bounds of Organization in Strategic Decision Making

David C. Wilson,[1] Richard J. Butler, David Cray, David J. Hickson, and Geoffrey R. Mallory
University of Warwick

This paper examines the exercise of power in organizational decision making. Four case studies are presented in the text and are analyzed in terms of the power plays of senior managers who were centrally involved in the decision-making process. In particular, the analysis distinguishes between bounded and unbounded decisions. In the former case the power plays of interests are constrained by preestablished organizational rules and procedures, while in the latter case unbounded decisions are relatively free from such organizational parameters and allow actors to exercise power selectively to secure their own interests. The data suggest that decisions may become unbounded in four ways: through unaccustomed forms of data, individual conflict, and novel topics for decision and where the problem is initiated from an unexpected or unusual source. Where decisions become unbounded the data suggest that those actors who are existing power holders through the control of critical contingencies are also able to take advantage of the rules and procedures of the institution to further their own interests.

INTRODUCTION

Theoretical speculations on the sources and exercise of power in organizational decision making are represented in abundance in the various texts which may be loosely classified as addressing the sociology of power.[2]

[1]Requests for reprints should be sent to David C. Wilson, School of Industrial and Business Studies, University of Warwick, Coventry, England.

[2]Although a large body of literature has grown around the concept of power, the theoretical debates most pertinent to this study are summarized by Clegg (1979), Lukes (1974), Clegg and Dunkerley (1980), and Giddens (1973).

Much of the literature remains speculative and largely theoretical, for little evidence is offered in support to show how such power is manifested and exercised, although there are some notable exceptions in the areas of both organization theory and industrial relations. Pettigrew (1985), for example, illustrates the interconnectness of content, context, and process with respect to various exercises of power within Imperial Chemical Industries, while Batstone, Ferner, and Terry (1983) present an analysis of power through an experiment in industrial democracy on the Board of the Post Office. Both studies attempt to account for the manifestation of power and to show its exercise against the backcloth of specific organizations.

Nevertheless, a large part of the literature on power progresses little beyond problems in the conception of power itself. In some cases this subscribes to the individual power of A over B and, in other cases, examines the power of elite domination exercised in institutions and their inbuilt biases over great numbers of individuals. Such a wide lens precludes a sharp focus on the nature of power, and it is notable that when empirical evidence is sought to defend the various theoretical standpoints, power has been characterized largely by subgroup and individualistic studies (for example, Hinings, Hickson, Pennings, & Schneck, 1974; Bachrach & Aiken, 1976; Blau & Schoenherr, 1971; Kenny & Wilson, 1984; Wilson & Kenny, 1985).

The intention of this paper is to illustrate the ways in which power is embodied in organizations, chiefly through an examination of their strategic decision making processes. Following Hickson, Butler, Cray, Mallory, and Wilson (1986), an organization is viewed as an institutionalized system of procedures and rules through which strategic decision topics are processed. Decision topics are subjected to a stream of events, such as committee meetings, working parties, consultative groups, and interdepartmental negotiations, until final authorization takes place. It is argued in the present paper that these events represent decision rules or procedures which submit the power relations of individuals and subgroups within the organization to constraints. Their power is bounded by what have become the "normal channels" of decision-making process to which strategic decision topics are submitted.

In addition, this paper examines in what circumstances these bounds may become strained and eventually broken, enabling actors with a political stake in the outcomes of a decision to exercise power more selectively to secure their expressed interests. In this way, a resolution is sought between individualistic and organizational perspectives of power. Examples from four case studies are given of how the one interacts with the other. First, a brief overview of existing perspectives on power and decision making is outlined in order to illustrate and locate the analytical focus of the present paper.

PERSPECTIVES ON POWER AND DECISION MAKING

Exemplars of the exercise of power in organizational decision making characterize the choice process as one in which the domain or direction of a decision is contested and finally resolved. Broadly, the domain of a decision focuses upon which topics are available for decision and which are not. In their study of the Post Office organization, Batstone *et al.* (1983, p. 166) illustrate that while unions had free access to the strategic decision arena (the board), this was with the tacit understanding that certain topics, such as the basic corporate policies of the organization, were not open to debate. Wilson, Butler, Cray, Hickson, and Mallory (1982) reach similar conclusions in their study of decision making and union power. The direction of a decision, on the other hand, emphasizes that once a topic is open to debate, power plays between subgroups or individuals can lead to problem redefinition or to substantial modifications to the original intended outcomes (see, for example, Pettigrew, 1973; Quinn, 1980; Hickson *et al.*, 1986).

The most obvious exercise of power in decision making lies firmly within what Lukes (1974) has called the one-dimensional view of power. It is here that the expressed interests of A and B are both in conflict and mutually exclusive (Gouldner, 1971, p. 294). A has power over B to the extent that A, by acting in a particular manner, can affect B in a way that is contrary to B's interests. A "wins" and B "loses" in the contest. Examples of overt conflict over preferences and wants are well illustrated in Dahl's (1961) study of New Haven, where contests between A and B center on open and conflicting issues.

Subsequently espoused by organizational theory, A and B became synonymous with functionally differentiated subgroups within various specialisms in accordance with Weber's bureaucratic model. Coalitions developed between subgroups that held similar preferences, and antagonistic attitudes were embraced by them in response to other subgroups that held conflicting preferences. Their existence secured by the division of labor, coalitions battled out their differences in an attempt to secure their own preferred outcomes over various issues.[3]

[3]Leading exponents of coalitions and the bargaining that occurs between them are Cyert and March (1963), who argue the case for a dominant coalition that, by dint of preferential access to resources of all kinds in an organization, creates and maintains a position of power. Again, Hickson *et al.* (1971) proposed a contingency theory of subgroup power, arguing that the division of labor produced subgroups which could accrue differential influence over decision making, depending upon their strategic location in organizational processes. This was empirically demonstrated by Hinings *et al.* (1974).

In contrast to this pluralistic analysis, Bachrach and Baratz (1970) argue that conflict over overt issues is only one aspect of the exercise of power. It is one dimensional in Lukes' terminology. In order to add perspective and depth, an analysis of power must be two dimensional and take note of those issues and potential conflicts that are suppressed and that are, hence, precluded from debate. These are nondecisions. Yet Lukes argues further that even nondecisions are located in an inherently pluralistic analysis, for their eventual empirical focus assumes nondecisions to be observable events in their own right. Benton (1981, p. 163) notes that "nondecisions are a species of decision, thereby restoring at one remove the behavioural and individualistic focus of one-dimensionalism."

Adding a third dimension to the analysis of power, Lukes (1974) argues that power may be exercised to the extent that institutions may reflect culturally patterned norms and that power is consequently exercised by the enduring bias of such institutionalised frameworks. Lukes (p. 38) terms this "the sheer weight of institutions." A precursor of this three-dimensional approach may be found in the notion of the "mobilization of bias" proposed by Schattsneider (1960). According to Schattsneider, such a view of power represents a "realist's" perspective of institutional domination wherein inherent systematic biases fashion the range of emergent issued and circumscribe possible solutions and strategies. As both Benton (1981) and Clegg and Dunkerley (1980) note, the exercise of power by institutional bias presents something of a problem. Definitions of exactly when the power is exercised hang on the questions of whether A would normally affect the behavior of B and of whether A and B, if left alone, would behave differently in line with some asserted rationality had power not been exercised. These problems remain, as yet, unanswered and it is not the intention of this paper to address these questions.[4] The present paper accepts a priori the potency of collective structures and their fashioning of relative spheres of influence for both groups and individuals. The concern over real interests and its associated debates does not, therefore, constitute the central theme of the present argument.

What is of central concern, however, is to identify the coexistence of institutional or organizational power (embodied in decisional rules and procedures) and how individual power may or may not gain primacy over organizational procedure in the decision-making process.

[4]The problematic of real interests and of whether Lukes' (1974) proposal that such interests are "empirically applicable" is discussed in Alan Bradshaw's critique of Lukes in *Sociology*, Vol. 10, No. 1, 1976. Critical problems abound in Lukes' collective assumptions from what is essentially an individualistic analysis of interests.

ORGANIZATION AND THE BOUNDING OF POWER

Our concern with organization in this context focuses on the nature of organization itself and to what extent its institutional character constrains or enhances the ability of individual interests both to represent their case and to influence decision making. Neglect of the role of the institution has been termed "psychologism" by Mills (1959). He states.

> Psychologism refers to the attempts to explain social phenomena in terms of facts and theories about the make-up of individuals. Historically, as a doctrine, it rests upon an explicit metaphysical denial of the reality of social structure. (p. 67)

It is the reality of organization itself which is argued to shape and create the representation of interests. As Clegg (1975, p. 51) observes, the creation of organization is synonymous with the creation of rules which "are not simply a property of actors exercising power, but are constitutive of relations between them." The ways in which organizations are structured have a pervasive influence on the ways in which relations between interests are fashioned and how they are manifested in decision-making processes. The interdependencies created between subgroups and individuals (Crozier, 1964; Hickson, Hinings, Lee, Schneck, & Pennings, 1971) are themselves shaped by the existence or organization.

Recent theories of organization have begun to emphasize the political nature of the structuring of activities. Clawson (1980, p. 1), for example, argues that the structuring of private business organizations, far from being an ad hoc development, was a conscious attempt by capitalists to gain control of the production process and, thereby, to establish a position of hegemony. In this way, the greater influence over decision making is reserved for those who represent "the leading group in the decisive nucleus of economic activity" (Gramsci, 1971, p. 161). The exercise of power in decision making cannot be divorced from the "sedimented" rules which are embodied in the structure of various organizations. As Offe (1972) recognizes, rule and structure are often congruent, whereby structure creates the facility for rules to be embodied and espoused by interests which are in managerial, authoritative positions. In addition, Walsh, Hinings, Greenwood, and Ranson (1981) have noted that the structuring of organizational activities operates to the benefit of some rather than others in the decision-making process.

In decision-making theory, too, recent work has begun to acknowledge the power of the institution to "both create and maintain dependencies and disparate perspectives between various interests" (Astley, Axelsson, Butler, Hickson, & Wilson, 1982, p. 361). This view of institutional power is removed analytically from the rather abstract "formal rules of the game" described by Dahrendorf (1959, pp. 225–226) to a more concrete concept whereby rules and procedures reflect a relatively enduring balance of power and which may also "in turn shift that balance" (Batstone, 1984, p. 301). In his study of Imperial Chemical Industries, Pettigrew (1985, p. 292) illustrates this kind of institutional power by means of describing the prevailing "mood" of the organization reflected in the main board which promoted the status quo, feared change, and resulted in inadequate committee decision-making processes. In this case, individual power plays by managers who were seeking organizational change met with a stronger institutional power which smothered their demands.

Ranson, Hinings, and Greenwood (1980) also point to the coexistence of overt power plays and the context within which they are enacted. They point to the importance of institutionalized power as an essential processual component, in particular in the mobilization or activation of individuals and subgroups. Furthermore, these authors emphasize the more overtly structural elements of organizational power such as centralization, differentiation, and the division of labor which equally constrain or enhance the power plays of actors and interest groups.

An organization, therefore, represents a structured decision-making system with clearly developed repertoires of established rules and routines for handling decision topics. The power relationships between interests which participate in decision-making processes are mediated by this network of routines (Hickson *et al.*, 1986). Four case studies of strategic decision making are presented in order to establish, first, what constitutes these institutionalized procedures and, second, what unanticipated events might strain such procedures until they can no longer cope, allowing power plays between interests to be relatively "unbounded" by institutional pressures.

METHODOLOGY AND THE DATA

The data were collected between 1976 and 1979 from two British organizations, a university in the north of England and a privately owned chemical manufacturer. They are referred to as Unix and Toxicem, respectively. Intensive case studies of strategic decision making were conducted in each organization, four of which are examined in this paper.[5] These four

[5]The term "strategic decision" is used in this paper in order to distinguish these decision topics from more routine operating decisions. Strategic decisions are, therefore, those which are important to the operation or survival of an organization as a whole. Such decisions are relatively rare in relation to operating decisions (rolling budgets or product modifications, for example) and, once implemented, invariably set precedents for subsequent decision processes. J. Q. Wilson (1966) and D. C. Wilson (1980) outline in detail the nature of strategic decisions, and empirical work on strategic decisions is given by Mintzberg, Raisinghani, and Theoret (1976), Cray *et al.* (1984), and Hickson *et al.* (1986).

decision topics are part of a larger sample of 150 cases of strategic decision making examined by members of the Organizational Analysis Research Unit, University of Bradford Management Centre. Empirical analyses of the 150 cases are given by Cray, Mallory, Butler, Hickson, and Wilson (1984) and Hickson *et al.* (1986); comparative analyses of the four intensive cases in the present paper have not been previously published elsewhere.

Over the 3-year data period, two case studies were studied contemporaneously (one in each organization) and the remaining two cases were reconstructed from extensive discussions with multiple informants who had been central participants in the decisions and from documentary evidence. All cases involved informants from primarily senior and middle management, although a number of informants from other hierarchical positions were also interviewed. In addition, there were observations of meetings and the minutes of meetings, memoranda, personal letters, and other documents were scrutinized at length. Not only did this help to identify the key participants in the decisions, but also it highlighted specific points of ambiguity or vagueness which served as useful cues for subsequent discussions with informants.[6]

The four cases were chosen for analysis in the present paper because they illustrate those decision topics which strain and eventually break the bounds of organizational decision procedures and also illustrate decision topics which are processed totally within these parameters. In each organization, one decision process breaks the bounds, while the other is contained within institutional rules and procedures. All four topics are, nevertheless, strategic decisions.

CASE 1. TOXICEM. THE NEW PRODUCT BLUESTUFF: A BOUNDED DECISION

As Meyer and Rowan (1977) suggest, decision making in organizations is pursued in predictable and largely systematic ways. Toxicem is no exception to this tendency. The Bradford data show quite clearly that shared perceptions among Toxicem's managers were "quick action on quantifiable data." Information search was invariably at a pitch which generated a great number of data about likely demand, fiscal limits, government regulation,

[6]This kind of case-study methodology follows closely the approach utilized by Dalton (1958) and theoretically espoused by Van Velsen (1967, p. 140). In addition, such data collection methods allow for any serendipity factor to be incorporated, whereby many of the data that prove to be analytically useful are often gathered in an unexpected and unplanned manner. For a detailed exposition of this kind of method see Hodgson, Levinson, and Zaleznick (1965, p. 20).

and overseas markets. These data were then quantified and submitted to the board of the holding company for a reaction and a quick decision (Wilson, 1980). The strategic decision to produce and market BLUESTUFF is an almost "ideal-type" process which conforms to Toxicem's formal decision rules and procedures.

In the early 1960s, Toxicem had been asked to manufacture BLUESTUFF by many of their customers. This kind of request was usual practice. Toxicem maintains very close contact with its customers, often manufacturing custom-made products for particular customers when this is mutually profitable. As usual, these requests landed on the desk of Dick (the sales director), having been directed to him by Alwyn (the chief executive). A standard market survey was enough to convince Dick that, at the time, the demand was too small to be worth embarking upon manufacture. By the late 1970s, however, there had been a marked change of emphasis in the chemical markets away from inorganic products and toward organic compounds such as BLUESTUFF. This trend was especially noticeable in the dyestuff industries, which comprised one of Toxicem's major group of customers. Coupled with the growth in demand for pigment dyes which are based upon BLUESTUFF, Dick suggested that Toxicem ought to consider its manufacture. As was standard practice, the sales department employed a market survey in order to discover the likely level of demand for the product, should Toxicem manufacture it. Response from their regular customers was favorable this time. Demand was likely to be high.

Dick presented the tabulated results from the market survey to the board, which authorized pilot manufacture. At this point, the research department became involved in the decision-making process, for the development of pilot manufacture approved by the board was their primary function. They, too, had developed standard repertoires of action. If other manufacturers produced the same or similar products, then the research department would gather samples of these products and analyze their composition. This was the case with BLUESTUFF. Despite some initial difficulties, research was able to recommend that Toxicem should build a new production plant to manufacture BLUESTUFF. The location of the plant was not a problem, for it was organizational policy always to maintain space for projects of this nature. The design of the plant was not quite so clear.

There began to be disagreements between individuals and departments concerning the likely design of the plant. In order to accommodate both expertise and interests, a new special committee was formed by the board. The composition of the committee was from production, sales, and research departments as well as comprising four experts in chemical engineering from outside Toxicem. According to informants, the formation of the committee was to maintain the momentum of product development by containing potentially antagonistic interests in a common project (Wilson, 1980).

The committee resolved that the new plant would require the use of a high-pressure autoclave. This was the first time that Toxicem had used such high-pressure technology and, characteristically, a further information search was instigated in order to gather data concerning high-pressure production. Despite a small delay in securing insurance coverage for the high-pressure plant, the only remaining preproduction problem was financial. Standard financial limits imposed by the accountancy department would preclude an appropriately aggressive marketing exercise in North America. However, there was provision in the financial assessment of projects for special cases (such as this) to reduce the stringencies of financial control and it was a simple matter for Alwyn, the chief executive, to negotiate special terms. The product was launched only 3 months later than the estimated target date and was immediately profitable and successful.

The sequence of decision process in the case summarized above conforms almost exactly with the formalized statements of policy in Toxicem. Each decision was to be subjected to a predetermined flow chart of sequence and process, and the BLUESTUFF example conforms to these procedures very closely indeed. Built into Toxicem's formal policy statements was the facility for what Cyert and March (1963) have termed "organizational learning," whereby activities deemed to have been successful in the past are retained in the organizational system of procedures to be applied in subsequent decision-making processes. In line with this policy, the special committee, formed for the first time in the BLUESTUFF decision, was retained as a standing committee for future decisions in Toxicem.

The extent to which the BLUESTUFF decision was bounded by organizational repertoires can be seen only by a comparison with another case in the same organization which broke these same bounds. Such a case is summarized below.[7]

CASE 2. TOXICEM. THE GENERATION OF ELECTRICAL POWER: AN UNBOUNDED DECISION

Between 1960 and 1970, the demand for chemical products from Toxicem grew at an unprecedented rate. This growth in demand meant that the existing boiler housed in a Victorian boiler house was totally inadequate. The proposal was that Toxicem should purchase new, high-pressure boilers which

[7]This particular case study is also described by Wilson (1982) in an analysis of incrementalism. The remaining three case studies are not published in comparative form anywhere else.

were capable of coping with the rising demand for output. A suggestion for using the spare pressure capacity of the boilers began to focus around the idea of electrical power generation. The chemists and engineers experimented with the notion of using steam pressure to drive a turbine and an alternator which could, they argued, provide enough electricity to make Toxicem self-sufficient. They conducted small-scale experiments and convinced Alwyn, who was then Works Director, that the proposal was feasible and should be pursued. The Purchasing Director, Giles, was not sure that the project was a very good idea. He thought that the main concern of Toxicem should be the production of chemical products and that it was no business of a chemical company to generate electricity.

In accordance with organizational procedure, both Alwyn and Giles began to search out information about the likely cost of such a project. Giles chose to concentrate on the costs of running, buying, and maintaining turboalternators, while Alwyn approached the National Industry Fuel Efficiency Council, which lent support to the generation of electricity. A wealth of data was submitted by Alwyn and Giles to the Capital Control Committee of the board for a decision. The proposal was rejected on the grounds of its being uneconomic.

So far, the decision process has all the characteristics of the previous BLUESTUFF decision: a quick and thorough information search for quantifiable data, with a committee (the board) to contain any conflicts of interest and to make a final decision. Subsequent events were to strain these organizational procedures to the breaking point, however, and to pave the way for open conflict between individual actors.

The current chief executive announced his impending retirement. It was clear that both Alwyn and Giles were prime candidates for the position. More important, however, was that from Alwyn's point of view, Giles had won the power generation issue, especially as it was felt by both candidates that the success or not of securing the job would be determined primarily by the track record of each candidate in this issue.

Aware of this, Alwyn set out to reopen the debate about power generation. He scrutinized in great detail all the memoranda, calculations, and documents that the debate had produced. In a month he had found an error in the figures concerning the charges for standby connection to the National Grid, and he duly informed the Capital Control Committee. Now Giles felt uneasy. The figures upon which he had based his case were being portrayed as more than a little erroneous. He felt personally slighted and began researching his existing data and seeking out new information about the cost of electricity generation. Alwyn also embarked upon a new wave of data collection. Open conflict and hositility grew between the two senior managers (and between their respective departments) until arguments were intensive, frequent, and emotional. These antagonisms could no longer be contained by the Capital Control Committee, for such were the discrepancies about the "real" cost of electricity generation and such was the volume of data that the committee could not make a decision one way or the other. Open conflict lasted over a year and the decision was no nearer a resolution. Since it was apparent that no decision could be achieved by normal procedures, the retiring chief executive resorted to a novel move not provided for in any rule or by any precedent. He proposed that a vote be taken among all the managerial staff to resolve the issue finally one way or the other. This move also favored Alwyn, who had majority support from the engineers and electricians. Alwyn won the vote, Toxicem now produce their own electrical power, and some months later, Alwyn was promoted to chief executive.

BREAKING THE BOUNDS IN THE CHEMICAL FIRM

While both processes in Toxicem may be characterized by their relatively high degrees of search activity for information relevant to the decision topic, they differ markedly in the level of overt political activity between constituent interests. The decision process of the new product, BLUESTUFF, is notable for its lack of conflict between interests. In addition, information search is seemingly all goal directed in the manner described by rational theories of decision making (see, for example, Cyert & March, 1963; Moore & Thomas, 1976; Astley *et al.*, 1982). Indeed, the early stages of the decision to generate electricity are also characterized by similar rational search procedures within the customary bounds. Decisions are initially subjected to a preestablished network of organizational rules and procedures. While interests between Alwyn and Giles (the leading figures) differ, they are not in outright conflict, for neither is sure of his position until sufficient information has amassed around the technicalities of the topic. Information becomes a vehicle for the political aspiations of careerism.

Both Alwyn and Giles become gatekeepers for this particular decision, for they are both central to communication channels and are thus "in a position to regulate the flow of demands and potentially control decisional outcomes" (Pettigrew, 1972, p. 190). Furthermore, both actors are "technical gamekeepers" by virtue of having almost sole access to the suppliers of turbo-generating equipment (Pettigrew, 1972, p. 197). They are the two individuals through whom all such technical information must pass in order to be disseminated to the wider organization. Two gatekeepers presenting conflicting versions of technical information create an extreme situation of decision upheaval in Toxicem given the predisposition toward unambiguous, qualitative information which had, until now, been the prevailing context of decisional action within Toxicem (Ranson *et al.*, 1980; Pettigrew, 1985, pp. 288–290).

Yet there is also a simultaneous bounding of this potentially ambiguous and unpredictable situation which is embodied in the prevailing organizational ethos of predictable and systematic decision-making processes (Wilson, 1980, 1982). This creates what Zald (1970) and Karpik (1978) have termed "regime maintenance." In the case of Toxicem, such a regime of predictability is maintained by the insistence on acting only on hard facts and figures. Both decisions display this logic of precedure, illustrating constant recourse to empirical evaluation criteria.

One gatekeeper, however, was able to circumscribe this logic. Alwyn's strategy of questioning what were previously considered "hard" facts and figures ensured that the debate was reopened (having been rejected initially on fiancial grounds), kept boiling, and eventually, resolved in his favor.

The ensuing renewed decision-making process became so protracted and complex that existing procedures for conflict resolution proved ineffective. Designed on the criterion of processing hard facts, existing procedures could not cope with assessing two sets of contradictory and equally defensible or indefensible quantifiable data. Alwyn turned the scrutiny of information into a political ploy. Facts were no longer hard and action was no longer swift. The decision process broke through the usual institutionalized procedures and became *unbounded,* with no clear guidelines from which resolution could be sought. As a result, resolution was in the form of a vote, the first in the documented history of Toxicem. This gave Alwyn his final level in securing his own political success, for he was in a position to cull a majority of votes from both engineering and electrical staff.

The data from the two Toxicem cases suggest two reasons why the regime of procedures which bound decision making may be broken or circumscribed. They are as follows.

(1) Where crucial data are fed into the decision process in an unaccustomed form or amount. Both aspects occurred in Toxicem. Data became too qualitative for the organizational decision-making system to operate effectively, and it was also subject to overload as increasing amounts of conflicting information were amassed by all parties.

(2) Where there are overt conflicts between personalities which emphasize the interests of political stakeholders in a functionally differentiated organization. In the case of Toxicem, this was most manifest in the career struggles between production and purchasing directors.

We now examine two cases of strategic decision making in a middle-sized British University (Unix) and examine to what extent the above conclusions from Toxicem may be relevant to decision making in a university organization. Again, the first case presented is a bounded decision and the second topic is unbounded.

CASE 3. UNIX. A NEW COURSE: A BOUNDED DECISION

The initial idea originated from a one-time professor of botany who had been considering the possibilities of designing and running a broadly based interdisciplinary course focused upon the subject areas of botany, geology, and geography. Exploratory papers were circulated from botany to the other departments, and some enthusiasm was evident from geography, although at this stage the course was just an outline sketched on the back on an envelope. Geology, however, was totally opposed to the course, preferring to concentrate upon its specialist subject areas and not produce students who were shared among three separate departments. Little then happened for several years. Even botany was not as united as it initially appeared to be in its support of the course. The idea had divided loyalties in the botany department between the academic specialists, who gave priority to a pure discipline, and the relatively applied conservationists, who were concerned with interdisciplinary work on ecology. Continuing disagreements occurred both withn and between the departments but little progress was made.

With Unix experiencing rapid expansion (along with most other British universities), a current report from the Senate suggested that the future strategy of the university should be, as far as possible, to support areas of interdisciplinary study. This boosted the morale of those who supported the idea of the new course, but all that occurred were countless meetings among the heads of the three involved departments, who countless meetings among the heads of the three involved departments, who consistently failed to agree.

Then during the next 18 months, two new professors, of botany and geography, were appointed. They were both strong environmentalists. Upon discovering the couse proposals, the new professor of botany began to promote the course, following the lead of his predecessor. This served to divide the loyalties of the botany department even further, especially when the professor changed the proposed title of the course. Geography was now supportive, however, and as both the professor of botany and the professor of geography were active members of the Planning Committee of the

University (which decides upon educational policy), they were able to gain a favorable view from the committee toward the course.

Geology still resisted. It wanted to remain a specialist department and also had no extra space or financial support to provide laboratory and teaching facilities for such a course. Undeterred, the professor of botany drafted out an outline proposal for it, involving the department of architecture, which was also supportive. Two further years of negotiation followed, with the professor of botany offering to provide substantial financial backing for the course (from Research Councils) as well as to provide any extra teaching staff which might be required.

Coincidentally, the Geography Department was due to move into a newer and larger building and the additional students that would come from the new course were seen as instrumental in maximizing the usage of the building. Geography, therefore, proposed a formal meeting among the departments concerned. Faced with three departments which wholeheartedly supported the proposed course, plus a committed Senate, geology finally capitulated, although its professor still expressed doubts about the limited career prospects of students who took such a course. By this time, resources were beginning to be less readily available at the university, resulting in the professors of botany and geography designing and implementing the course in a very short time. Any additional financial restrictions on the course would be fatal to its chances. As a result, the course began as a very ill-defined and ad hoc blend of subjects. However, the three departments persevered and within 2 years they had won some recognizable "identity" for the course, which subsequently became a model for other British universities which were considering implementing similar cross-disciplinary courses.

While this case of a decision-making process may appear at first sight to be manifestly political (and slow), it is, nevertheless, a bounded decision. The decision was processed within the parameters of university organization, where the "bias" of the organization is able to contain the conflicts among the various interests in the decision (Lukes, 1974). University procedures which accommodate debate and conflict mean that the decision process of the new course was bounded in comparison to Toxicem's electricity generation issue. Data for this new university course were in an accustomed form and conflict among participating interests was contained within accustomed organizational procedures. The following case of university decision making, however, illustrates how and why the bounds of university organization may become strained and, eventually, broken.

CASE 4. UNIX. THE NEW COMMITTEE: AN UNBOUNDED DECISION

Over the last 50 years Unix had employed a method of hiring, firing, and promoting staff that consisted of an ill-defined and relatively disorganized collection of standing and ad hoc committes. Complaints about the arbitrary nature of this process, plus its unfairness, led the Association of University Teachers (AUT) to request formally that the university should do something about the problem, especially about the huge backlog of complaints and unresolved issues that had built up over a long period. Nobody on the academic staff was enthusiastic about tackling these problems, and all said that such matters should be dealt with by the administration. Nothing happened. Senior administrators felt unable to sort out the long-standing problems of inconsistent and arbitrary decision making by the academic staff.

Internal dissatisfaction and outside pressure from the AUT forced the council to take action over the staffing crisis. A working party was organized with a wide brief to consider all aspects of staffing policy and to suggest a solution to the present unacceptable state of affairs. John, a previous Pro Vice-Chancellor, was nominated the head of the working party. Shrewdly, John chose individuals for the party whom he knew were vociferous and held conflicting viewpoints. In this way he knew that the working party would be seen to be doing its job by giving the fullest possible debate to all the issues, while he could take a low level of participation in the debates. Nevertheless, the working party could not reach any solution despite endless debates, and the unprecedented move of calling in the administration was embarked upon. Recognizing that this request gave them carte blanche, the administration accepted the offer to advise the working party. Within 2 weeks, four alternative structures of new and existing committees had been devised and submitted to the working party.

Each suggestion included the formation of a new umbrella committee which would handle all staffing matters. This committee was to be located just below the Senate and would effectively preclude much of the Senate's previous autonomy in these issues. The debates that followed were long and tortuous. Finally the working party had to approach the barristers, who were employed by the university and who were empowered to make any changes in the statute involving the delegation of powers in staffing procedures. During the ensuing discussions, John suggested that in order to test the efficacy of the proposed committee, the working party should consider and act upon an actual staffing problem. He had in his department a troublesome member of the staff whom he wanted to move, although previously he had not had the power to do this and the Senate would have to authorize any such action. John recognized that if he could get the working party to consider this test case and if it were empowered to take action, then he could rid himself of the troublesome staff member. John suggested to the Senate that this should be considered as a test case (and a difficult one) and the Senate agreed. In consequence, the member of the staff was removed from the department.

However, the test case created more problems than it solved, for it brought to light more and more problems of staffing procedures and ethics. Other departments, such as finance, felt that they were being overlooked and should have been consulted and have participated in this decision. The Senate, too, felt uneasy that such actions could occur in the future without their approval and direct involvement. Despite all these problems the new committee was born. Within 2 years it was a manifest failure. Unwilling to relinquish any of their powers, the faculties, Senate, council, and finance all contrived to interfere. Even with the changes in the statutes (which still persist today), the committee exists in name only.

BREAKING THE BOUNDS IN UNIVERSITY ORGANIZATION

Some care should be exercised in the comparison of the university cases with those of Toxicem. For if a subgroup perspective of political activity were to be taken from which to analyze, it would be easy to conclude that both decisions in Unix were comparably more political in nature than those in Toxicem. The new cross-disciplinary course is an almost "classic" example of subgroup bargaining (Hinings *et al.,* 1974), with each department head taking a different stance toward the decision, depending upon how they predicted the new course would enhance or impinge upon their present and likely future interests.

However, at the organizational level of analysis, such a conclusion would be untenable. The nature of the bounds or the rules of the decision-making game are very different in commercial organizations and universities (Clegg, 1975, 1979). Commercial organizations espouse a logic of rationality which aims to suppress conflict in favor of profitable activity in the market, while universities are organized around a logic which espouses and may even encourage debate. University organizations embody procedures which are designed to contain any conflicts of interest between subgroups.

Conflict between departments does not imply that decision making is basically any more political in university organizations than in commercial firms. It is, rather, that the university system is designed to express it. It would be unwise, therefore, to take solely some total measure of conflict as an indicator of political decision processes. Something more than that has to occur. In particular, the process has to be viewed against the organizational context within which it takes place. Context, content, and process thus become interlinked to the extent that variation in any one factor is likely to impinge upon the others (Crozier, 1973, p. 214).

The enduring different contextual "biases" (Lukes, 1974) of the two organizations may be summarized by two exemplary quotes from two of the key participants in the case studies:

> We're a competitive, profit making organization. When we decide to manufacture, say, a new product then everyone from the Director to the gardener is aware of it. We all pull together to make the best, most profitable product so we can compete in the cut-throat chemical market. (Alwyn, Toxicem; Wilson, 1980)

> In the university situation, inevitably there are many conflicting views on how we should tackle any problem to be resolved. The problem is that the pros and cons get debated to such a protracted and high level that the pros begin to resemble the cons and vice-versa. Then we can go no further until the next issue comes along.

If the new course decision represents a bounded decision in Unix, then in which ways does the new committee decision break these bounds? Furthermore, are the bounds strained and broken in the same ways as were evident in Toxicem?

Certainly, the form of the data fed into the new committee decision was not as radically different as that surrounding Toxicem's electricity generation issue. Nevertheless, the inability of the working party to make any decision at all on the information at their disposal bears comparison with the inability of Toxicem's Capital Control Committee similarly to make a decision. Just as Toxicem resorted to a vote, Unix resorted to the unprecedented step of calling in administration departments to take an active part in the design of the new committee and its place in the organization. Their involvement in the decision process radically altered the usual "trajectory" for university decisions (Hage, 1980). Indeed, legal advice had to be sought in order to reorganize the rules of decision procedure, particularly with respect to the formal power of the Senate.

One aspect in which the form of the information was different in the new committee decision was its locus of origin. As Cray, Butler, Hickson, Mallory, and Wilson (1983) argue and Hickson *et al.* (1986) empirically demonstrate, decision making in the sample of university decisions studied by the Bradford research team (two universities, 10 strategic decision topics) is proactive except for the new committee decision. This was initiated by an effort from the AUT, which originated outside the university and forced it to react on the issue of staffing policy. Of course, recent events in university financing (which occurred after the present data were collected) have pressured university policy making into an increasingly reactive stance toward the fiscal restrictions imposed by the central government. The reorganizations and reformulations undertaken by British universities in the face of these recent external pressures lend additional support to the present thesis that reactive decision making in previously proactive university organizations is likely to result in unbounded decision making. Empirical support (from American data) is provided by Manns and March (1978).

The university cases, therefore, add to the list of potential factors of context and content which are likely to thrust decision-making processes through the bounds of organizational procedure. We have seen from Toxicem that particular forms of decision *content* and *context* can result in unbounded decision processes. In particular, unaccustomed types of information, novelty of topic, and overt conflict among political stakeholders were argued to lead to unbounding. While the university cases suggest that a measure of conflict alone is unlikely to predict whether or not a decision

Table I. Four Factors Leading to Unbounded Decision Processes

Factors: content/context	Organization	Decision
(1) Unaccustomed forms of data	Toxicem (primarily) Unix (secondarily)	Electricity generation New committee
(2) Personality conflicts or a personal stake in the outcome of the decision	Toxicem	Electricity generation
(3) Topic novel to the organization, i.e., never been a problem before or issue never raised previously	Toxicem (primarily) Unix (secondarily)	Electricity generation New committee
(4) Locus of issue generation is unusual or unexpected	Unix	New committee

process becomes unbounded, issues which require the university organiation to react to external pressures are one way in which unbounding can take place. Putting the factors from the case studies together gives four situations which are capable of contributing to the unbounding of the decision process. They are summarized in Table I.

This is unlikely to be a complete list, of course, since it represents only those factors which were identifiable from the present case studies. A wider sample of organizations and decisions would be required to identify, for example, whether an unexpected locus of issue generation is likely to unbound organizational procedure in the case of a commercial firm or in other kinds of nonuniversity organizations. No data were available for this in the present study. An enduring methodological problem is likely to be that data which reveal the unbounding of the decision process seem necessarily to be of the in-depth case-study variety, so that the accumulation of examples will be hindered by the practicalities of conducting research of this nature.

SUMMARY AND CONCLUSIONS

This paper has examined to what extent senior managers who participate in strategic decision making are ultimately constrained themselves and are bounded by organizational repertoires of decision procedures. From the analysis of four case studies of strategic decision making, it has been proposed that these bounds become strained and then broken for a number of reasons which allow conflict and negotiation to occur outside the usual organizational repertoires of action. Four of these reasons have been identified in the present paper, namely, data in an unaccustomed form, conflict among stakeholders, a novel topic for decision, and an unusual or unexpected locus of issue generation.

Bounds are broken in both the university and the chemical firm by the occurrence of novel topics and unaccustomed forms of data. However, the process by which the bounds are broken differs in each organization. In the chemical firm, it is the inability of managers and the Capital Control Committee to accommodate the technical complexity of electricity generation which allows unbounded conflict to occur between participants. In the university, it is less the technical complexity of the new committee decision that breaks the bounds and more the threat to political stakeholders which the novel topic was likely to pose. Professional autonomy was one of the aspects of university organization under threat from the impending decision. From this perspective, the counterpoint of complexity and the political face of decision making described by Astley *et al.* (1982) is highlighted.

The differences between the two organizations (in the process by which bounds become broken) may be due to the very different domains within which each organization operates (Thompson, 1967). Toxicem sells its products in a worldwide commercial market place which, as Thompson (1967) and Perrow (1972) observe, puts pressures upon competing organizations to emphasize efficient and economically effective task accomplishment. Unix, like most British universities, is comparatively less influenced by such a direct imposition of the market place. Rather than achieve coherence through task efficiency, university organizations tend to emphasize more qualitative characteristics such as professional achievement, status, and autonomy. Breaking the bounds in such an organization requires that these rules of organization are put to the test rather than questions of economic efficiency (see, for example, Hickson *et al.*, 1986). A novel topic, therefore, or unaccustomed forms of data strain and break organizational bounds initially in different directions in the firm and the university. The technical and political are put to the test, respectively, as the factors for unbounding come into play. Nevertheless, there is a commonality of factors in both organizations which contributes to the unbounding of organizational procedure (see Table I).

This is not to suggest that university decision making which is bounded is commensurately apolitical. While this is implied in Simon's (1947) distinction between programmed and nonprogrammed decision processes, evidence from the data in the present paper suggest, rather, that politicality itself may become part of accustomed organizational procedures. The politicality of process is recognized and is largely contained in university organizations within a system of committees designed to cope with conflicting interests (Astley *et al.*, 1982; Hickson *et al.*, 1986).

It should be emphasized that while decision processes may become unbounded, it is only the managerial elite who are free to negotiate unfettered by organizational repertoires. The rest of the organization is still subject to continuing domination by formal structure, hierarchy, and its attendant norms (in addition to a lack of relevant information on the decision in question). Only Alwyn and Giles, for example, could possibly benefit from the uncertainty that surrounded the electricity generation issue. Other employees on the shop floor and as far up the hierarchy as middle management were not in a position to influence the debate in ways congruent with their own interests. The bounding of decision-making processes reinforces the effects of formal structure whereby only those who hold power in the first place can further their interests by manipulating what is considered legitimate in the organization (Habermas, 1974; Meyer & Rowan, 1977; Offe, 1972). The bounding of decision making offers existing power holders the opportunity to *multiply* the potency and extent of their power by circumventing, breaking, or modifiying the bounds which endowed them with power in the first place.

Finally, the present data have examined the decision processes only from initiation to final authorization. No data have been presented concerning the implementation of these decisions. As Wilson *et al.* (1982) note, the implementation phase of decision processes may allow new interests to emerge and become powerful, whereas their power to influence the decision prior to authorization was relatively weak. The four factors which are here argued to strain and break the bounds of decision making may be relevant solely to the process of decision making prior to authorization. While implementation is equally likely to be bounded by organizational procedures and repertoires, the reasons why these bounds break may differ from the four factors outlined in the present paper. It is for future research to uncover to what extent this is the case and to what extent the four factors delineated in the present study may be equally useful in examining the question of organizational bounding in a number of different organizations.

REFERENCES

ASTLEY, W. G., AXELSSON, R., BUTLER, R. J., HICKSON, D. J., & WILSON, D. C. Complexity and cleavage: Dual explanations of strategic decision making. *Journal of Management Studies,* 1982, *19,* 357-375.

BACHRACH, S. B., & AIKEN, M. Structural and process constraints on influence in organizations: A level-specific analysis. *Administrative Science Quarterly,* 1976, *21,* 623-642.

BACHRACH, P., & BARATZ, M. S. *Power and poverty: Theory and practice.* Oxford: Oxford University Press, 1970.

BATSTONE, E. *Working order: Workplace industrial relations over two decades.* Oxford: Blackwell, 1984.

BATSTONE, E., FERNER, A., & TERRY, M. *Unions on the board: An experiment in industrial democracy.* Oxford: Blackwell, 1983.

BENTON, T. "Objective" interests and the sociology power. *Sociology,* 1981, *15,* 161-184.

BLAU, P., & SCHOENHERR, R. *The structure of organizations.* New York: Basic Books, 1971.

CLAWSON, D. Class struggle and the rise of bureaucracy. In D. Dunkerley & G. Salaman (Eds.), *The international yearbook of organization studies.* London: Routledge and Kegan Paul, 1980.

CLEGG, S. *Power rule and domination.* London: Routledge and Kegan Paul, 1975.

CLEGG, S. *The theory of power and organization.* London: Routledge and Kegan Paul, 1979.
CLEGG, S., & DUNKERLEY, D. *Organization, class and control.* London: Routledge and Kegan Paul, 1980.
CRAY, D., BUTLER, R. J., HICKSON, D. J., MALLORY, G. R., & WILSON, D. C. Proactive and reactive decision making. Working paper, Carleton University, Ottawa, Canada, 1983.
CRAY, D., MALLORY, G. R., BUTLER, R. J., HICKSON, D. J., & WILSON, D. C. Sporadic, constricted and fluid processes: Three empirical types of strategic decision making in organizations. Working paper, Organizational Analysis Research Unit, University of Bradford Management Centre, Bradford, England, 1984.
CROZIER, M. *The bureaucratic phenomenon.* London: Tavistock, 1964.
CROZIER, M. The problem of power. *Social Research,* 1973, *40,* 211-228.
CYERT, R. M., & MARCH, J. G. *A behavioural theory of the firm.* Englewood Cliffs, NJ: Prentice Hall, 1963.
DAHL, R. A. *Who governs? Democracy and power in an American city.* New Haven, CT: Yale University Press, 1961.
DAHRENDORF, R. *Class and conflict in an industrial society.* London: Routledge and Kegan Paul, 1959.
DALTON, M. *Men who manage.* New York: Wiley, 1958.
GIDDENS, A. *The class structure of the advanced societies.* London: Hutchinson, 1973.
GOULDNER, A. W. *The coming crisis of western sociology.* London: Heinemann, 1971.
GRAMSCI, A. *Selections from the prison notebooks of Antonio Gramsci.* London: Lawrence and Wishart, 1971 (translated by Q. Hoare & G. N. Smith).
HABERMAS, J. *Theory and practice.* London: Heinemann, 1974.
HAGE, J. *Theories of organizations: Form, process and transformation.* New York, Wiley, 1980.
HICKSON, D. J., HININGS, C. R., LEE, C. A., SCHNECK, R. E., & PENNINGS, J. M. A strategic contingencies theory of intra-organizational power. *Administrative Science Quarterly,* 1971, *16,* 216-229.
HICKSON, D. J., BUTLER, R. J., CRAY, D., MALLORY, G. R., & WILSON, D. C. *Top decisions: The process of strategic decision making in organizations.* Oxford: Blackwell/San Francisco: Jossey-Bass, 1986.
HININGS, C. R., HICKSON, D. J., PENNINGS, J. M., & SCHNECK, R. Structural condition of intraorganizational power. *Administrative Science Quarterly,* 1974, *19,* 22-43.
HODGSON, R. G., LEVINSON, D. J., & ZALEZNICK, A. *The executive role constellation.* Cambridge, MA: Harvard University Press, 1965.
KARPIK. L. Organizations, institutions and history. In L. Karpik (Ed.), *Organization and environment: Theory issues and reality.* London: Sage, 1978.
KENNY, G. K., & WILSON, D. C. The inter-departmental influence of managers: Individual and sub-unit perspectives. *Journal of Management Studies,* 1984, *21,* 409-429.
LUKES, S. *Power: A radical view.* London: Macmillan, 1974.
MANNS, C. L., & MARCH, J. G. Financial adversity, internal competition and curriculum change in a university. *Administrative Science Quarterly,* 1978, *23,* 541-552.
MEYER, J., & ROWAN, B. Institutionalized organizations: Formal structure as myth and ceremony. *American Journal of Sociology,* 1977, *83,* 340-363.
MILLS, C. R. *The sociological imagination.* New York: Oxford University Press, 1959.
MINTZBERG, H., RAISINGHANI, D., & THEORET. A. The structure of "unstructured" decision processes. *Administrative Science Quarterly,* 1976, *21,* 4 246-275.
MOORE, P. G., & THOMAS, H. *The anatomy of decisions.* Harmondsworth: Penguin, 1976.
OFFE, C. Political authority and class structures—an analysis of late capitalist societies. *International Journal of Sociology,* 1972, *2,* 73-105.
PERROW, C. *Complex organizations: A critical essay.* Glenview, IL: Scott Foresman, 1972.
PETTIGREW, A. M. Information control as a power resource. *Sociology,* 1972, *6,* 187-204.
PETTIGREW, A. M. *The politics of organizational decision making.* London: Tavistock, 1973.
PETTIGREW, A. M. Examining change in the long-term context of culture and politics. In J. Pennings *et al.* (Eds.), *Organizational strategy and change.* San Francisco: Jossey-Bass, 1985.

QUINN, J. B. *Strategies for change: Logical incrementalism*. Homewood, IL: Irwin, 1980.
RANSON, S., HININGS, C. R., & GREENWOOD, R. The structuring of organizational structures. *Administrative Science Quarterly*, 1980, *25*, 1-17.
SCHATTSNEIDER, E. E. *The semi-sovereign people: A realist's view of democracy in America*. New York: Holt, Rinehart and Winston, 1960.
SIMON, H. A. *Administrative behaviour*. New York: Free Press, 1947.
THOMPSON, J. D. *Organizations in action: Social science bases of administrative theory*. New York: McGraw-Hill, 1967.
VAN VELSEN, J. The extended case method and situational analyses. In A. L. Epstein (Ed.), *The craft of social anthropology*. London: Tavistock, 1967.
WALSH, K., HININGS, B., GREENWOOD, R., & RANSON, S. Power and advantage in organizations. *Organization Studies*, 1981, *2*, 131-152.
WILSON, D. C. *Organization strategy*, Ph.D. thesis. Bradford, England: University of Bradford, 1980.
WILSON, D. C. Electricity and resistance: A case study in innovation and politics. *Organization Studies*, 1982, *3*, 119-140.
WILSON, D. C., & KENNY, G. K. Managerially perceived influence over intradepartmental decisions. *Journal of Management Studies*, 1985, *22*, 155-174.
WILSON, D. C., BUTLER, R. J., CRAY, D., HICKSON, D. J., & MALLORY, G. R. The limits of trade union power in organizational decision making. *British Journal of Industrial Relations*, 1982, *20*, 322-341.
WILSON, J. Q. Innovation in organizations: Notes toward a theory. In J. D. Thompson (Ed.), *Organizational design and research*. Pittsburgh: University of Pittsburgh Press, 1966.
ZALD, M. N. Political economy: A framework for comparative analysis. In M. N. Zald (Ed.), *Power in organizations*. Nashville, TN: Vanderbilt University Press, 1970, pp. 221-261.

BIOGRAPHICAL NOTES

RICHARD J. BUTLER is Senior Lecturer in Organizational Analysis at the University of Bradford Management Centre. He received his Ph.D. degree in organizational behavior from Northwestern University (1973). His main research activities are in decision making, voluntary organizations, and the government regulation of industries, and he has published widely in a number of journals about these topics. He has also held positions in industry and at the University of Otago, New Zealand.

DAVID CRAY is Assistant Professor of Human Resource Management in the School of Business at Carleton University, Ottawa, Canada. He received his Ph.D. degree in sociology from the University of Wisconsin. He is currently involved in studies of the allocation of control between Canadian subsidiaries and their American parents and the impact of new data handling techniques on decision making in the pension fund industry.

DAVID J. HICKSON is Professor of International Management, and was formerly Professor of Organizational Analysis, at the University of Bradford Management Centre, England. His principal research has been on organization structure, intraorganizational power, and strategic decision making. He is founding Editor-in-Chief of *Organization Studies* and was a founder of EGOS (European Group for Organizational Studies).

GEOFFERY R. MALLORY is Assistant Professor in the School of Business, Carleton University, Ottawa, Canada. He is completing his Ph.D. on elapsed time in decision making. Before graduating as a mature student he held industrial positions in timber marketing and systems analysis, and he subsequently joined the decision making project at Bradford. His current research interests are the development and impact of expert systems in organizations.

DAVID C. WILSON is a Lecturer in Organizational Behaviour at the University of Warwick and was formerly Senior Research Fellow in Organizational Analysis at the University of Bradford Management Centre, England. His principal research activities have been on strategic decision making and power in organizations, and he has concentrated in particular on longitudinal methodologies in the study of decision processes. Currently, he is the joint director of a research project investigating strategy and structure in British voluntary organizations which forms part of his future research efforts in the areas of corporate strategy and organizational change. He is a member of EGOS and is Editorial Assistant of the journal *Organizational Studies*.

[10]

THE LIMITS OF TRADE UNION POWER IN ORGANISATIONAL DECISION MAKING[1]

DAVID C. WILSON, RICHARD J. BUTLER, DAVID CRAY, DAVID J. HICKSON AND GEOFFREY R. MALLORY*

UNION PARTICIPATION IN STRATEGIC DECISION MAKING

If we are to accept at face value the image of British industry that is portrayed by the popular national press and by the network news media, then we inevitably conclude that unionised labour is now a major influence to be contended with in the process of organisational decision making. Once the sole province of managers and directors, strategic decisions appear to be increasingly influenced by the interests and bargaining power of a unionised workforce. By strategic decisions, we mean those higher-level decisions which concern the running and the future planning of the whole organisation.[2] The popular image of trade union dominance as yet, however, has limited foundations or support from empirical research. Edwards[3] has examined the relative power of unions in the coal industry and Heller, Drenth, Koopman & Rus[4] have examined union participation in a cross-national framework. Both studies pointed out the relative lack of union influence in decision making. Edwards illustrated that certain types of decision, such as those concerning pay and conditions, were often reserved for Management to make alone, whilst Heller, Drenth, Koopman & Rus highlighted the scepticism of unions toward worker participation in decision making. They pointed to the prerogative of Management to control the agenda of decision making and to decide which issues were open to participation and which were not. The present research addresses these questions, examining the influence of trades unions in one hundred and fifty cases of strategic decision making. The aim is to provide a systematic and comparative study of union influence over a wide range of decision types and over a wide range of organisations.

The data employed are part of a large scale investigation by the Organizational Analysis Research Unit (OARU) in the University of Bradford Management Centre. The research was primarily aimed at uncovering the characteristics of strategic decision making processes by examining factors which fashion their main features.[5] For example, a decision to launch a new product may become hesitant and discontinuous due to the technological problems of product design, or this discontinuity may be due to the incompatible perspectives of different interests such as trade unions or function managers, each holding a different view of what the new product should comprise, or whether there should be a new product at all. One result of this research was that a considerable amount of data were gathered concerning who was involved in each decision, what each interest wanted and whether those objectives were fulfilled in the final decision. As trades unions were involved in a number of the decision topics in our sample, we were able to assess their influence over the decision making process relative to managerial power. It must be stressed here that this research examines decision making at the company or organisation unit level and does not attempt to distinguish the influence of trades unions over "own work" decisions, such as job content, which are confronted by individuals.[6]

Despite the popular image of powerful unions, such tangential evidence that does exist suggests that the actual power of trades unions over organisation level decisions is

*Organizational Analysis Research Unit, University of Bradford.

relatively low, irrespective of desired or actual participation in the decision making process. Both Holter[7] and Ramsay[8] present substantial data showing that although individual workers in their respective unions approve *in principle* of participation in company level decisions, they are *in fact* unlikely to take an active or an influential part. These findings are supported by Banks & Jones'[9] study of employee directors in the British Steel Corporation, which exemplified the non-involvement of each employee director's trade union in decision making processes (the unions were deeply suspicious of employee directors). Indeed, as Banks & Jones[10] point out, '...certain policy decisions in the British Steel Corporation are beyond the employee directors' control'.

In an analysis of trade union power in Western Germany, Kirkwood & Mewes[11] similarly suggest that the apparent power of British trades unions is, in fact, an illusion. What power they have stems from a limited capacity to obstruct or impede an otherwise smooth running economy, but this power, although apparently cumulative, is insufficient for them to attain much of the administrative and strategic control of organisational activities. As Kirkwood & Mewes[12] point out, the ability of a union to impede smooth functioning '...does not stand in any positive relationship to its proficiency in attaining professed goals'. It may be that trades unions merely hamper managerial decision making at their own cost. Additionally, Heller, Drenth, Koopman & Rus analyse the role of trades unions in decisions involving direct participation by the workers and comment that:

> These unions welcome the idea of a genuine redistribution of power to the workers on the shop-floor. However, they suspect that the introduction of "participation" may be manipulative and that, far from leading to a sharing of power, it is intended to consolidate those already in control.[13]

This paper addresses these issues. When unions are involved in strategic decision making what level of influence do they possess and how is this reflected in the decision making process; and is union involvement in decision making dominated by managerial control and ideologies?

The Data

The data for the present research are on 150 decision making processes selected from a sample of thirty British organisations. Five decisions were studied in each organisation. These organisations were chosen primarily to reflect the broad diversity of existing organisations and, consequently, the sample consists of organisations from both the public and private sectors which together produce a wide range of goods and services. Seventeen organisations were from the private sector and the remaining thirteen organisations were in the public sector. Decisions were defined by the chief executive and top management as those which were important to the organisation as a whole. In addition, six intensive cases (three of which were traced contemporaneously) expanded the data available on the 150 decision making processes in the study.[14]

Data on the 150 decisions were collected by lengthy interviews with senior executives who had been centrally involved in the decision making process. The organisations were first approached by letter and, subsequently, the chief executives were interviewed to obtain background information on the history, products and structure of the firm. The aim was to produce a list of major decisions which had been taken within the recent memory of senior managers. The chief executive suggested as many such decisions as could be readily recalled and, from these, a selection was made to include as broad a spectrum of decision topics as possible.

The hundred and fifty decisions so produced were then classified into eight types of topics and these are shown in Table 1. No attempts were made to force informants to select decisions within pre-defined categories and, as a result, coverage of topics was uneven. For example, if no inputs or domain topic could be recalled, informants were not encouraged to find one in order to fit the topic categories.[15] The chief executive then nominated one or more key informants to discuss each decision. Informants were senior executives who had been centrally involved in the decision making process. There was an average of six informants per organisation, plus some documentary data: the six intensive case studies had multiple informants including senior executives, administrative staff and trade union representatives. The results from several interviews were consolidated into a single detailed description of each process.

Every interview elicited an initial historical description of the decision making process from the time the issue was first raised until the time the decision, positive or negative, was authorised. This information was then followed by a standard series of questions to which responses were either open-ended only, or were open-ended together with a rating by the informant on a short scale.

A substantial amount of this data was concerned with identifying which interests were actively involved in the decision making process. These interests could be internal departments, such as production or sales; could be individuals, such as Managing Directors and Chairmen of the Board; or could be external organisations-in-contact such as suppliers, customers or government departments. Data were collected on the influence of each interest, together with a statement of their expressed preferences about how decision making should proceed. Finally, data were gathered identifying the way in which each interest made its wants known (in committees, informally, in memoranda, etc) in the decision making process. Trades unions were one of the many interests identified as being involved in decision making.

With these data at our disposal, the paper is divided into two parts. Firstly, we examine the influence of trades unions on decisions. Are trades unions powerful arbiters of organisational strategy, or are their countervailing powers for shaping such strategy in line with their own preferences severely restricted? Secondly, we examine the role that trades unions play in influencing the ways in which these decisions are made.

The Nature of Strategic Decisions

The range of topics which comprise the sample of 150 strategic decisions is shown in Table 1. The decisions are categorised into eight types of topic ranging from those concerned with outputs (such as new products or services), through inputs (such as changing suppliers of raw materials or securing substantial financial resources), to topics concerned with the organisation itself, focusing on mergers between firms or reorganisation. They are all strategic decisions by the nature of their importance in the organisation as a whole. All thirty organisations are unionised to the extent that unions are at liberty to become involved in the strategic decision making process.[16]

As Blackburn and Mann[17] imply, we would predict that some of the decisions examined would be more pertinent to union interests than would other decisions. We would expect, *a priori*, that new equipment, location, personnel and reorganisation decisions would be most likely to affect the interests of union members, for it is likely that these topics would have direct consequences for them. Less immediate would be decisions over inputs, outputs and domain, which are traditionally seen as the province of managerial expertise and have consequences primarily for such managerial concerns as the negotiation of contracts for supplies, marketing policy and inter-organisational relationships generally.[18]

TABLE 1

Strategic Decisions: Managerial and Union Involvement (n = 150 decisions) Percentage of Total Sample shown in brackets

Decision Topic Category	*No. of decisions overall*	*No. of decisions involving trade unions*	*No. of decisions involving solely non-union interests*
	per cent	per cent	per cent
1 Outputs	28 (19)	4 (3)	24 (16)
2 Equipment & Plant	23 (14)	7 (5)	16 (11)
3 Domain	18 (12)	0 (0)	18 (12)
4 Personnel	12 (8)	6 (4)	6 (4)
5 Inputs	9 (6)	0 (0)	9 (6)
6 Location	8 (6)	2 (1)	6 (4)
7 Control & Planning	19 (13)	2 (1)	17 (11)
8 Organisation	33 (22)	8 (5)	25 (17)
Total	150 (100)	29 (19)	121 (81)

Reference to Table 1 shows the distribution of topics in the overall sample and the number of decisions in which trades unions are actively involved. The largest category of decision topics overall are those concerned with organisation itself. These comprise thirty-three topics of the total sample. Organisation topics, similarly, are the largest category of decisions in which unions are involved. Unions are involved in eight of these thirty-three decisions. Organisation topics arguably impact upon the interests of union members, for such decisions often radically change the status quo by reorganisation internally (such as setting up new departments or merging existing ones), or by reorganising externally (such as buying and selling subsidiaries).

Equipment and plant decisions are the second largest category of topics in which unions are involved, followed by personnel topics (see Table 1). Unions are involved in seven equipment decisions out of twenty-three such topics overall and in six personnel topics out of the total of twelve in our sample. In personnel decisions jobs may be lost or created, or the terms of employment may be altered and, in the case of equipment decisions, old and trusted shop floor and administrative operations may have to be radically altered with the advent of new machinery. Historically, the introduction of assembly lines was a striking example of new equipment decisions and their subsequent effects on the labour force.[19] The advent of computerised and micro-chip technologies possibly heralds equally substantial consequences.

Although we suggest that the number of decisions in which unions are involved acts as an initial indicator of their importance (as perceived by the various trades unions which are at liberty to become involved), an essential caveat must be made here. Participation in the decision making process neither presupposes nor endows any interest group or individual with power to influence a decision one way or another. Unions which have been identified as being involved in the decision making process are not necessarily powerful. The same is true, of course, where managerial interest groups are involved in the process of decision making. They may have little power to sway the outcome of decision making in their favour. In the terminology of Astley *et al*, the unions are 'involved in the decision making arena'[20] having been identified by informants as an interest group with a degree of influence. Unions are, hence, localised interests,[21] but their actual power to influence decision making processes in which they are involved is constrained by the conditions or rules that surround the exercise of power, the nature of the organisation in which the decision occurs and the amount of resources at the unions' disposal.[22] Established power structures may effectively preclude unions from actively participating in the decision making process.

However, the number of strategic decisions in which unions are involved as an interest group is remarkably low. From a hundred and fifty examples of what managerial echelons consider are strategic decisions, trades unions were present in only twenty-nine cases. As already indicated, the two larger areas of union involvement are in decisions concerning organisation itself and new equipment or plant. In these decisions, however, only eight and seven topics respectively displayed unions as an interest group. This may indicate that either unions consider such decisions as not impinging on their members' interests or, conversely, do not become involved because they do not consider such decisions as strategic in the same way as management.

It is notable, however, that trades unions are involved in six of the twelve personnel topics in the sample. These decisions are explicitly those which touch upon the areas of working conditions, levels of pay and grievance procedures. Union anxieties would, arguably, be pre-eminent here. Thomson & Murray, for example, find that union involvement is virtually without question in decision topics of this type.[23] Again, Brown finds that the dominant theme of union-management decisions is the level of pay (irrespective of the type of bargaining structure that may exist).[24]

The finding that unions are not identified as interest groups in more than half of the personnel decisions (when it might be anticipated that they would participate in every one) may arise from the types of topics within the category. Not one of the 150 examples of strategic decisions was solely about pay. No distinctly typical personnel decision emerged from the data, with topics ranging from a job evaluation scheme in a chemical producer to training and appraisal schemes in a police force. The case that is probably nearest in our sample to being a decision about pay is the introduction of a productivity deal in an insurance company. This hinged on the question of whether to break governmental 10 per cent increase guidelines or to opt for a productivity deal which would be linked to overall profit and the rate of growth of income from premium. In the end, the productivity route was chosen.

This examination of personnel type decisions tempts two possible interpretations. Given that the sample of decision topics arose from managerial definitions of strategic decisions, it is possible to conclude firstly that decisions over pay are considered comparatively unimportant by managers compared with decisions to launch new products, expand domain or to invest in new equipment. Therefore, cases of pay decisions are not included among examples of strategic decisions. Alternatively, we may conclude that decisions over pay and conditions are essentially non-decisions in the sense that they are routinised, well-established and carry little risk of real change.[25] Existing empirical and theoretical justifications provide greater support for the latter interpretation.

In an analysis of decisions over pay and conditions, overtime distribution and union consultation, Edwards notes that:

> ...half of the decisions were seen by both sides to be the prerogative of management to make alone. Few, if any, of the decisions were seen to be the prerogative of the union to make alone, and very few were considered 'mainly' a union decision.[26]

Brown produces data to show that organisations reflect the institutionalisation of industrial relations and related issues.[27] Managements utilise employers' associations, for example, to get industry-wide agreements on the terms and conditions of employment. Furthermore, the larger the organisation the more likely it is that there will be a director with industrial relations as his sole responsibility leaving the rest of the management and directorate to get on with the 'real' business of strategic decision making — launching new products or expanding domain — confident in the knowledge that they have provided for the contingency of workforce antagonism.

Theoretically, the two assumptions that decisions are either defined as not concerning unions or that they are seen as marginal changes to be routinely processed are supported by Boreham.[28] He suggests that succeeding changes brought about by the Human Relations School or the Industrial Democracy Projects[29] are in reality, aimed at legitimating the dominance of labour by management. Industrial democracy, he argues, instills a unitary, but essentially managerial, view of organisation in a participatory workforce.[30] Far from being an inevitable facet of organisational structure, bureaucracy is actively utilised and maintained by management because it favours and fuels the interests of managerialism and control. Strategy and managerialism thus become inseparable.[21] The balance of power between management and unions would appear not to have shifted in the direction predicted by Flanders who suggested that we should see a trend heralding the increased power of employees via trades unions.[22] Rather our data support the case for portraying modern forms of organisation as mechanisms which delimit union power and channel the collective voice of employees. Unions challenge the existing power structure of managerial hegemony, privilege and resources only at the margins. As Fox argues:

> Labour often has to marshall all its resources to fight on these marginal adjustments; capital can as it were, fight with one hand behind its back and still achieve in most situations a verdict that it finds tolerable. What many see as major conflicts in which labour seems often now to have the advantages are conflicts only on such issues as management deems it realistic to contest, and these never touch the real roots of ownership, inequality, hierarchy and privilege. Only if labour were to challenge an essential prop of the structure would capital need to bring into play anything approaching its full strength...[33]

Involvement of the unions in only twenty-nine of the 150 decisions in our sample seems to support this argument. However, the question remains concerning the position of unions in this minority of decisions in which they *do* appear as interest groups. We now assess the extent of union power relative to that of management in these issues which evoke active union interest. The following section examines the relative levels of union power across the twenty-nine decision topics.

The Union-Management Balance of Power

An indication of the relative power of unions and management was given by a five point scale ranging from 'a very great deal' of influence to 'little' influence. Informants on each of the 150 decision topics were asked to rate the influence on the decision of each of the separate interests which were involved. These interests were, for example, trades unions, internal departments, external suppliers and customers, or the chief executive.

Ratings were obtained from managerial informants only, because access to union officials or members was unnecessary for the wider study of decision making processes. The key figures were always senior executives as only they experienced the entire process and could, therefore, rate the *relative* influence of all involved interests. Union representatives could have rated their own influence but this would have had no meaning without simultaneous ratings of all other interests; and their view is one confined to those points in the process when they were drawn in, thereby excluding the greater part of what occurred. In any case, it was the senior executives who, in taking the decision, were the subjects of union influence and their assessment of it upon them

Where possible, information about the decision was built up before the interviews with managers took place. Documentary evidence, such as the minutes of meetings and internal reports, was examined prior to interviewing and where the influence ratings produced by the respondent appeared to conflict with that we had read or knew about the decision, the respondent was asked to expand further the reasons for his ratings.

Where unions appear as interest groups, their impact is mostly slight. They impose little restriction on the scope of choice available. Of the twenty-nine cases of major decisions where unions received any mention, their influence was 'little' or merely 'some' in seventeen cases. In only one case is the maximum score 'a very great deal' achieved by a trade union. In all these decision topics, internal functions such as finance or production, or external interests such as suppliers, had a greater influence on the decision process. Their power was to constrain the parameters of the decision, such as the locus of the initial idea, the number of alternative courses of action and of equipment design that were considered, the number and type of committees that were employed in the decision making process and the level at which the decision was finally authorised.[34]

In Figure 1, an example of this relative lack of influence of the unions is illustrated in a decision which occurred in an engineering firm. The aim was to achieve a cheaper product which was always in regular demand. This was to be achieved by the opening of a new plant in order to manufacture a component which was previously bought from an external supplier. Figure 1 is in the form of a Tannenbaum control graph.[35] This graph was originally employed by Tannenbaum to identify the relative power of each level of hierarchy in an organisation. The hierarchical levels were arranged on the lateral axis. In Figure 1, this technique is adapted by arranging the interests on the lateral axis, ordered from highest to lowest influence within interests internal to the organisation such as finance or production, and those that are external such as suppliers and customers.

It can be seen immediately that departments such as manufacturing, finance and purchasing had a good deal of power as did the Managing Director and, externally, the supplier of the new equipment and the competitor firm which spurred on the decision process and set its pace.[36] It was these interests, rather than the union (AUEW) which delimited the course of the decision and the final action, for the union takes its place at the end of the line as one of the two least influential interests. This is a surprising result, for where a substantial part of the workforce is to work on new equipment in a new plant, the union would be expected to be concerned about labour conditions and threfore to wield a commensurate amount of influence over the decision; but this finding is typical.

The profile of union influence over all the twenty-nine decisions in which they were involved is shown in Table 2.

The organisations in which the decisions occurred ranged from an engineering company, through a local authority to an insurance company and a police force. All were unionised (see note 16). The decisions covered a wide range of topics ranging from new plant decisions, through reorganisations, to productivity agreements and plant closures. Usually a single union participated, but in the NHS decision on radiographers there were two, and in the Polytechnic decisions three and four respectively. The topic category (as in Table 1) is given for each decision and they are numbered appropriately.

The most noticeable feature in the table is the heavily skewed distribution of union influence to the lower end of the five point influence rating scale. Fifteen of the total of thirty-five unions were rated one (a little influence) and a further six were merely two (even if an under assessment) is the appropriate data for our purpose, rather than union assessments of what they believe their influence might have been.

FIGURE 1
A Rating of the Influence of Interest-units in a Decision to Open a New Plant in an Engineering Firm

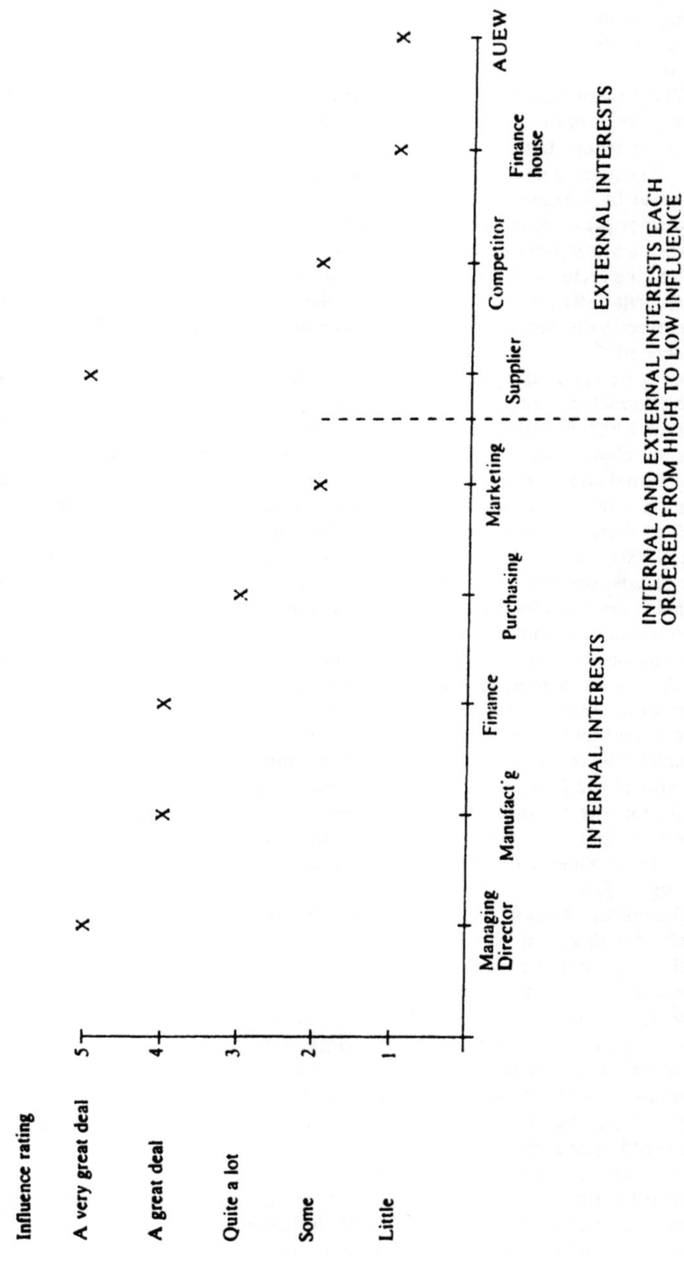

TABLE 2

Union Influence in Twenty Nine Decisions

Organisation	*Decision Topic*	*Topic Code**	*Influence Ratings***
Engineering Company	New plant, new equipment	2	1
	New product	1	2
	New product	1	1
Contractor's Equipment Manufacturer	Purchase of new equipment	2	1
Airline Company	Reorganisation of Pilot Force	8	4
Textile Company	Expansion of product line	2	1
	Closure of a Plant	2	1
Chemical Company	Reorganisation into divisions	8	2
	Future Employment Policy	4	2
Chemicals and Paint Company	Rent a Factory	2	1
Precision Small Tool Company	New product	1	1
	Expansion of plant	2	1
	Business Plan	7	3
	Expand Data processing	7	1
Local Authority	Merger of Departments	8	4
National Health Service District	Increase radiographers	1	5,1
	New catering programme	4	4
	Reorganisation of Pathology	8	2
Polytechnic	Amalgamation of Departments	8	4,3,3
	Creation of Boards of Studies	8	1,4,1,2
Ceramics Manufacturer	Location of New Plant Abroad	6	1
	Investment in U.K. Plant	2	1
Finance Company	Resist Unionisation	4	4
Insurance Company	Productivity Agreement	4	1
	Purchase of a Company	8	2
University	New Committee	8	3
Police Force	Change Staff Appraisal	4	4
	Policy on Travel	4	4
Electricity Board	Showroom Closure	6	3

* Numbered by category of decision type as in Table 1
** On the scale: 1. A little
2. Some
3. Quite a lot
4. A Great Deal
5. A Very Great Deal

(some influence). Even in the few cases where unions scored quite a lot of influence (scale point three), this was in decisions where there were also multiple and highly influential managerial interests which counteracted union power.

Union influence is, however, greater in nine cases of decision making and these cases merit some discussion. Concentrated in organisation and personnel decisions, eight cases show unions scoring a great deal of influence (scale point 4) and, in the ninth case, unions have a very great deal of influence (scale point 5). The nine decisions are shown in Table 3.

TABLE 3

Nine Cases of Decisions in Which Union Influence was High

Organisation	*9 Decision Topics*	*Union Influence Ratings*
Airline Company	Reorganisation of Pilot Force	4
Local Authority	Merger of Departments	4
National Health Service District	Increase Radiographers	5
	New Catering Programme	4
Polytechnic	Amalgamation of Departments	4
	Creation of Boards of Studies	4
Finance Company	Resist Unionisation	4
Police Force	Change Staff Appraisal	4
	Policy on Travel	4

In three cases, in an airline, a health district and a police force, the unions were both influential and positive towards the decision. They got what they wanted. In the airline, an increase in organisational size by amalgamation was followed by a merging of pilot complements in which BALPA, the pilots' union, used its influence to push the decision along as some union members stood to benefit by the merger. Most of the pushing was accomplished by active participation in meetings, making constant reference to comparability with other airlines.

In the two other instances in which union influence helped to bring about a decision, ASTMS pressed for more jobs for radiographers in a National Health Service District and got them; in a police force the Staff Association pressed for changes in the methods of staff appraisal and was instrumental in effecting an entirely new appraisal system. As in the airline, union influence was backed by comparability studies, in this case with the Army and Civil Service.

In the other six cases of high influence, the union stance was negative. The two polytechnic decisions are examples of the inevitable consequences of previous decisions aimed at creating one large polytechnic from several small colleges. One decision was to amalgamate various schools under a single banner, the other was to set up boards of studies to facilitate staff representation in the new organisation structure. Unions were active participants in each decision with a view to protecting the interests of their members. In the board of studies decision, the teaching union (NATHFE) and the technical and administrative union (NALGO) were influential (and successful) in trying to preserve representation of their members in the new structure.

As in the polytechnic, the increase in size of a local authority, brought about by national reorganisation in 1974, was followed by a decision to amalgamate some departments. Union concern, in this case from NALGO, was that amalgamation could cause redundancies, and the union wielded its influence throughout the organisation with representatives in attendance in the Management Team, the Chief Executive's Working Party and the Joint Staff Consultative Committee.

In the three remaining cases, unions attempted outright resistance to the decision being made. In one case, the Staff Association of a police force attempted to secure travel allowances for lower ranks in the belief that this would bring them into line with practice elsewhere. Their influence on this issue, although seen as considerable, was no match for that of an economy-minded Police Authority. Similarly, unions were unsuccessful in resisting the introduction of a new catering system in a National Health Service District even though this meant an inevitable loss of jobs in order to keep down costs.

FIGURE 2

A Rating of the Influence of Interest-units in a Decision to Introduce a New Technology in a Finance Company

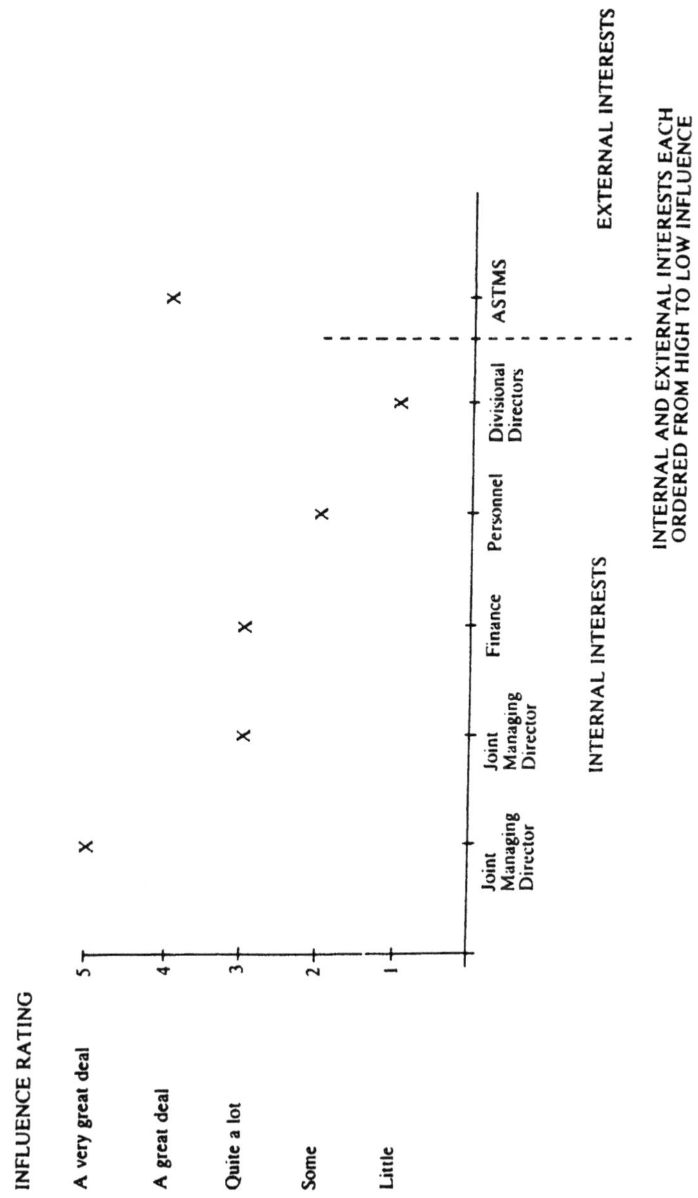

In the final case, ASTMS also failed to reach its objectives. It fought the reduction of jobs in a finance company incurred by the introduction of tele-processing which would enable branch offices to dispense with some staff. A long and bitter struggle ensued but, in spite of this resistance by the union, tele-processing eventually went ahead. Figure 2 depicts the pattern of influence, perceived by managerial respondents, of each interest group in this particular decision. It is in the same form as Figure 1. In this case, the union (ASTMS) has a great deal of influence but, in the final analysis, the combined influence of the Head Office Directors and departments is the greater.

There are two striking features of these nine cases where union influence is reported at its highest. First, if the unions are in any degree negative toward the decision, their influence achieves little or nothing. Unions only get their way when this is congruent with Management's way. Second, their part is wholly *reactive* to Managerially defined topics. Strategic decisions are initiated by senior management and, if seen to have advantages or disadvantages for union members, are subsequently supported, or more usually opposed, by union activity; senior management then makes and authorises the decision. Unions appear to have little influence in the formulation of strategic decisions, such as whether the launch of a new product is, for example, the means to solve a problem of falling profits (and ensure future employment), or whether reorganisation or reduction of staff and administrative departments would be an alternative solution for the same problem.[37]

Among the twenty-nine cases where unions are involved, there is only one in which the union initiated the decision making process. This was a proposal to set up a new committee for handling all staffing problems in a university (Table 2). In 1975 the Association of University Teachers (AUT), faced with a rising number of complaints about the unfairness of hiring and firing staff and the arbitrary nature of many personnel decisions, submitted a letter to the University Council in which they outlined specific weaknesses in existing procedures and suggested that immediate action be taken. Recommendations were made that a new committee should be formed which could formulate policy on all staffing matters. This constituted a substantial erosion of Council's existing powers and, not surprisingly, they argued against the new committee proposal. The net result was the formation of a committee which was not, however, allowed any effective influence on staffing policy. This remained with Council. The over-arching power of Council served to emasculate union influence.

In summary, three main points have emerged out of the discussion so far:

1. In those decisions that management define as strategic, union participation is low Unions actively participate in only twenty-nine out of a sample of 150 decisions.
2. Where unions do participate in the decision making process, their influence in relation to management is low.
3. Unions almost always react to managerially defined topics. Only in one case does a union initiate a decision making process.

These results may not give the complete picture. Does management arrange the process of decision making to sustain its power position? Does union involvement, or the anticipation of involvement, make any difference to the characteristics of the decision process itself?[38]

Effects of Unions on the Process of Making the Decision

Six concepts which describe the characteristics of decision making processes were examined and these are displayed in Table 4.[39] The concepts encompass four main characteristics of decision making processes, namely, the overall time the decision takes (gestation time and process time), the use and availability of information

TABLE 4

Decision Making Process Features: Comparison of Decisions With and Without Union Participation
(Student t test of difference between means)

Concept	*Definition*	*Operational Variables*	*Means*		*t Value*
			Solely Managerial (n = 121)	*Trades Unions in (n = 29)*	
Gestation Time	Any period from first inception of an issue during which awareness builds up but nothing is done towards arriving at a decision	Time in months from first recognition of a continuing issue to the commencement of process time	19.2	8.9	2.29*
Process Time	The temporal extent of that process which arrives at a decision	Time in months from first deliberate consideration of a topic to authorisation of the implementation of a decision	12.7	13.9	−0.38
Scrutiny	(i) The extent to which the topic is processed through committees	(i) The total number of committees of any kind that are used	2.3	2.2	0.03
	(ii) The extent to which effort is expended in the collection of information	(ii) Four point rating from Information Available to Disparate Information Input needs Synthesising	2.8	2.7	0.56

Interaction volume	The extent to which the process generates interaction among its participants	Five point rating from None to A Very Great Deal	4.1	4.6	−1.88
Discontinuity	(i) The extent to which delays are encountered in the process	(i) Four point rating from No Delays to Prolonged Delays	2.4	2.5	−0.50
	(ii) The extent to which the process is impeded	(ii) A ten point scale assessing the severity of any stops and starts ranging from No Impediments, through Impediments due to Searching for Information, to Impediments due to Awaiting the Outcome of External Resistance	4.9	5.6	−0.90
Centrality	The extent to which the process occurs at the summit of the organisational hierarchy	The level in the hierarchy at which a decision is authorised. Seven levels ranging from Outside the Organisation through the Governing Body to where the hierarchy divides below the Chief Executive	4.7	4.6	0.11

*Significant at 0.05 level

(scrutiny), the level of interaction (interaction volume) and the occurrence of delays and interruptions (discontinuity). In addition, the level at which the topic is finally authorised is examined and this marks the end of the process. In all, eight operational variables were employed and their results are shown in the table. Having identified two discrete samples (those topics where unions were interest groups and those where they were not) it was possible to examine whether union participation had any significant effect on the process. Table 4 gives the mean scores of the two samples and the t value of the Student comparison of means significance test.[40]

Of the eight operational variables in Table 4, only gestation time is significantly different between the two samples (at the 0.05 level of significance). Leaving this difference aside for a moment, the remaining variables show no significant difference between the two samples.

Process time measures the time taken by active decision making up until authorisation (as opposed to gestation time which measures the inactive months of decision making where problems and issues build up but no identifiable topic can be determined). Given the popular image of the supposedly high bargaining power of trades unions, it might be thought that process time would be longer in those topics where unions were involved. Their involvement in the decision making process, however, makes no significant difference to the time required to reach authorisation of a final solution. Both managerial and union samples take around thirteen months of decision process time. Neither do unions seem to induce the setting up of committees by management either to get together to decide how to cope with union activities or to incorporate and discuss union views. Decision making processes in which unions are involved go through no greater number of committees than do other decision processes: the existing committee system functions unchanged. The difficulty of collecting information is also the same in both samples.

Again, it might be thought that influential unions would interrupt the smooth course of decision making processes, but there is no suggestion of this in our results. There are no more delays and severe stoppages in decision making processes where trades unions are involved than when they are not. There are delays in both samples with mean scores of 2.4 and 2.5 for managerial and union samples respectively, corresponding to there being 'some' intermittent delays in the decision making process: and it would seem that unions as an interest group do not significantly increase the amount of interaction in the decision process with both samples scoring a mean of around 4 (a great deal of interaction between participants). Nor are union influenced decisions seen to warrant higher authority; the level at which the decision is authorised is unaffected.

The significant difference between the two samples is in the gestation time of decision making. This is the time where issues and problems build up until, finally, a decision topic is identified (such as to launch a new product) and active decision making takes place. Where solely managerial interests participate in the decision, the gestation time is more than twice as long (19.2 months for the managerial sample and 8.9 months for the union sample). The difference here seems crucial. Where unions are likely to be involved in decision making it appears that an issue becomes an identifiable topic for decision more quickly than if solely managerial interests are concerned.

In order to examine whether these means conceal differences between topic types, gestation time was compared between the solely managerial and the union samples for each of the eight decision types. The results are shown in Table 5.

Where unions are involved in output, equipment, location, control and organisation decisions, gestation time is indeed shorter and is consistent with the summated results in Table 4. If it is perceived by management that unions will become involved in the ensuing decision making process, gestation time is significantly shorter than when

TABLE 5

Gestation Time for Decisions With and Without Union Involvement Analysed by Decision Type

Decision Topic Category	*Mean Score in Months: Solely Managerial*	*Mean Score in Months: Trades Unions in*
1. Outputs	11.8	3.8
2. Equipment & Plant	28.7	11.3
3. Domain	16.1	Unions not participants
4. Personnel	0.7	7.0
5. Inputs	39.7	Unions not participants
6. Location	23.8	5.0
7. Control & Planning	12.2	0.5
8. Organisation	22.8	14.3

unions are absent from the process. This tendency is, however, not reflected in personnel decisions where the reverse situation holds true. Where it is perceived by management that unions will become involved in personnel decisions, gestation time is not shorter but longer (in our sample from 0.7 to 7 months, see Table 5).

This result is taken to mean that, generally, managerial recognition of impending union participation spurs action in order to avoid speculation and rumour but, more importantly, to prevent the hardening of positions which could lead to conflict. Within the reactive posture evidenced earlier in this paper, unions do have some inadvertent and unawares power to trigger decision processes faster. They cannot determine the content of the topic, nor how it is processed once decision making has begun, but their pending presence does hoist its priority on the agenda of decisions.

In the case of personnel decisions, the unique extension of gestation time in the union sample may be interpreted from the same perspective. Brown[41] points out that decisions over pay and conditions are of central concern to trades unions. Half our sample of personnel decisions are concerned specifically with pay and conditions, whilst the rest are concerned *inter alia* with manning levels via the creation of new divisions or the closure of departments. In these decisions, too, unions are organised in to the decision making arena and their influence will be felt to some degree. Our data indicate that where personnel decisions are concerned, management does not appear to spur on the preliminaries in order to begin the actual decision making process (as in the case of other types of decisions). Rather, management treads carefully and slowly through the issues, knowing that such topics are the central interest of unions and that collective bargaining will often be a feature when overt steps are taken towards a decision.

CONCLUSIONS AND SUMMARY

Analysis of the data overall paints a picture of strategic decision making in which management has a firm and dominant grip. As Coates & Topham emphasise: 'Trades unions have to take on an adaptive stance towards established managerial control.'[42] Even in the case of nationalised industries, four of which form part of the sample, it appears that management still holds the greater sway over decision making. In an analysis of the board composition of nationalised industries since the second world war, Coates & Topham note that:

> In the absence of either a successful political struggle or a determined trade union fight for workers' control in nationalised industry since the war, the boardrooms and the policies of public industries have been dominated by the needs of private interest.[43]

This perpetuation of managerial dominance over decision making places unions in the defensive position of having to react to already announced topics, or in a position of extreme uncertainty whereby unions must anticipate correctly the decisions to be made by respective managements. The relative impotence of union power, vis à vis managerial influence and control, is unavoidable under these circumstances.

These findings suggest that if unions want a greater say in the decision making process, then present modes of union participation in strategic decisions are ineffective to this end. Not only do trades unions merely react to strategic decisions, but also they have little effect on the information that is sought out or generated in the decision making process (see Table 4, scrutiny). Information is critical to influence in the decision making process as it is closely associated with the level of political activity in the decision. Information can become a political lever and powerful interest groups can limit or collect relevant information to support their own perspective on how decision making should proceed and on what issues.[44]

Further, union involvement is largely confined to certain customary kinds of decisions even though this means that they ignore others which could implicate their interests. For example, they are not represented in any domain or input decisions in our sample (see Table 5). Yet, although these decisions appear not to have any direct effect on employees' pay and conditions, union acquiescence to managerial prerogative in these decisions can only further erode their potential influence. For example, union involvement in domain decisions could be crucial, as the implications of expanding or contracting markets permeate throughout the organisation. Domain decisions may have direct consequences for the type and number of jobs that employees undertake as well as having implications for the continued profitability of the organisation and hence its ability to provide and maintain a consistent level of employment. The apparent non-involvement of trades unions in these decisions reflects their general impotence in influencing strategic decision making processes, the results of which impinge directly or indirectly on their members' interests.

Even where unions *are* an active interest, their perceived influence in the decision making arena is, from a managerial perspective, very little, and it is excercised only in a reactive manner. Nor do unions have any significant effects on the decision making process itself, serving neither to prolong nor to disrupt it.

The implications of these findings are pervasive. They reflect the persistence of management as a relatively autonomous, elite echelon of strategic decision makers. Decisions on domain, inputs, control and planning are taken with virtually no union representation at all. Where unions are an interest group (such as in personnel or new equipment decisions), they must firstly react to these decisions as they emanate from management and secondly, they then find that, to a great extent, well established parameters already exist in areas of pay and conditions.

It is remarkable that no case of 150 shows industrial labour unions to be influential. (In addition, eight of the nine cases where unions are more influential are in the public sector.[45]) Yet unionised industry does not feel like that to the managers involved. Here one of us remembers discussions with the Personnel and Technical Directors in a large Division of a national company. They had been interviewed about a decision on siting and building a new plant. During this they had assessed the influence of the unions. Some weeks later at a feedback session they were presented with what they themselves had said, (in particular, with a rating of union influence as 'little'). They laughed. 'Rubbish', they said, 'Where did you get that idea from?' They would not believe it had come from them. An absorbing discussion ensued. Half an hour later they agreed the assessment was correct. Their own constant preoccupation with union questions, the time taken by union matters, the never-ending intrusion of union affairs into their daily lives was not the same, they agreed, as unions having great influence over major decisions. No instance could be recalled where such a decision had been different or had not been taken because of unions. What unions *did do* was to shape, stretch and delay the detailed *implementation* of decisions.

The influence of organised labour over the implementation of our 150 decisions was not a concern of the research. However, it is not too speculative to suggest that the influence of unions may be greater at this stage of the decision, rather than during the decision making process itself. Reflections of this influence may be found in the restriction of outputs, disputes over productivity deals and inflationary pay increases that feature in British industrial relations. The seemingly deliberative way that management deals with personnel topics in our sample does suggest that unions have power to impede management over these issues.

Whilst this may be so, a power limited to impeding implementation remains a power that is on the fringe of decision making. It is a power with little chance of deflecting or influencing the decisions themselves. An ability to block or impede decisions which have already been made delimits such influence within a solely reactive stance. In comparison with management, who can initiate and influence decision topics, union power appears to remain comparatively insubstantial in the process of strategic decision making.

REFERENCES

1. We acknowledge the contributions of Dr. Runo Axelsson and Dr. W. Graham Astley to this research. They are respectively Associate Professor, University of Sundsvall, Sweden, and Assistant Professor, The Wharton School, University of Pennsylvania, U.S.A. This research was supported by the Social Science Research Council and the University of Bradford Management Centre.
2. H. Mintzberg, D. Raisinghani and Andrew Theoret, ('The Structure of "Unstructured" Decision Processes', *Administrative Science Quarterly*, Vol. 21, No. 2, June 1976, pp. 246–75), point to the pervasiveness of strategic decisions throughout an organisation in terms of 'the actions taken, the resources committed, or the precedents set' (p. 246). C. Pateman, ('*Participation and Democratic Theory*', Cambridge U.P., 1980, p.70) suggests that such strategic decisions are at a level where they 'relate to the running of the whole enterprise'.
3. C. Edwards, 'Measuring Union Power: A Comparison of Two Methods Applied to the Study of Local Union Power in the Coal Industry', *British Journal of Industrial Relations*, Vol. XVI, No. 1, 1978.
4. F.A. Heller, P.J.D. Drenth, P. Koopman and Veljko Rus, 'A Longitudinal Study in Participative Decision-Making', *Human Relations*, Vol. 30, No. 7, 1977, pp. 567–87.
5. For examples of initial papers from this research see R.J. Butler, W.G. Astley, D.J. Hickson, G. Mallory and David C. Wilson, 'Strategic Decision Making in Organizations: Concepts of Content and Process', *International Studies of Management and Organization*, IX, 4, 1979/80, pp. 5–36, and R. Axelsson, R.J. Butler, D.J. Hickson and David C. Wilson, 'Organizational Power in Organizational Decision Making', in M. Warner (ed.), *Organizational Choice and Constraint*, Saxon House, Farnborough, 1977. Under review by journals are R.J. Butler *et al*, 'Strategic Decision Making: A Large Scale Study', and W.G. Astley *et al*, 'Complexity and Cleavage: Dual Explanations of Strategic Decision Making'. Copies are available from the Organizational Analysis Research Unit, University of Bradford Management Centre.
6. H. Ramsay, ('Participation: The Shop Floor View', *British Journal of Industrial Relations*, Vol. XIV, No. 2, pp. 128–41, 1976), makes the distinction clear between decisions concerned with individuals' own work and company level decisions.
7. H. Holter, 'Attitudes Toward Employee Participation in Company Decision-Making Processes', *Human Relations*, No. 18, 1975, pp. 297–321.

8. H. Ramsey, *op cit.*, pp. 129–35.
9. J. Banks and Ken Jones, '*Worker Directors Speak*', Gower Press, Farnborough, 1977.
10. J. Banks and Ken Jones, *op cit.*, p. 58.
11. T. Kirkwood and Horst Mewes, 'The Limits of Trade Union Power in the Capitalist Order: The Case of West German Labour's Quest for Co-Determination', *British Journal of Industrial Relations*, Vol. XIV, No. 3, 1976, pp. 295–305.
12. T. Kirkwood and Horst Mewes, *op cit.*, p. 297.
13. F.A. Heller, P.J.D. Drenth, P. Koopman and Veljko Rus, *op. cit.*, p. 581.
14. The six case studies can be found in D.C. Wilson, '*Organizational Strategy*', Ph.D. Thesis, University of Bradford. One of the case studies, showing how the career interests of a senior manager can dictate the characteristics of decision making, is in D.C. Wilson, 'Electricity and Resistance: A Case Study of Innovation and Politics', *Organization Studies*, Vol. 3, No. 2, 1982.
15. The eight topic categories are derived from an open-systems view of organisations and focus on the procurement of inputs, their transformation to outputs and on other organisation/environment factors. See D. Katz and Robert L. Kahn, '*The Social Psychology of Organizations*', Wiley, New York, 1966, pp. 71–109.
16. The comparative level of unionisation of the thirty organisations is data not collected in the present research. However, each organisation has more than one recognised union at liberty to participate in the decision making process. The unions are acknowledged by management for negotiating pay and conditions in each organisation.
17. R.M. Blackburn and Michael Mann, 'Ideology in the Non-Skilled Working Classes', in M. Bulmer (ed.), *Working-Class Images of Society*, Routledge and Kegan Paul, London, 1975.
18. For example see D. Katz and Robert L. Kahn, *op. cit.*, p. 86. They point to the need for organisations to develop sub-systems for maintenance of the working structure leaving management free for 'resolving conflicts between hierarchical levels, coordinating and directing functional sub-structures, coordinating external requirements and organizational resources and needs'. See also R.M. Cyert and James G. March, '*A Behavioral Theory of the Firm*', Prentice Hall, Englewood Cliffs, New Jersey, 1963 and J. Child, '*Organization: A Guide to Problems and Practice*', Harper and Row, London, 1977.
19. See, for example, C.R. Walker and R.H. Guest, '*The Man on the Assembly Line*', Harvard U.P., Cambridge, Massachusetts, 1952 and C. Merz, '*And Then Came Ford*', Doubleday-Doran, New York, 1929.
20. W.G. Astley *et al, op.cit.*, p. 11.
21. For a full exposition of the concept of localised interests see R.M. Cyert and J.G. March *op. cit.*, Ch. 1–3 and D.J. Hickson, W.G. Astley, R.J. Butler and David C. Wilson, 'Organization as Power', in L.L. Cummings and B.M. Staw (eds.), *Research in Organizational Behavior*, Vol. 3, 1981, pp. 151–96.
22. The explicit or implicit constraints upon the exercise of power in organisations have been examined at great length. Central texts would be, for example, S. Clegg, '*Power, Rule and Domination*', Routledge and Kegan Paul, London, 1975 and '*The Theory of Power and Organization*', by the same publisher, 1979. P. Bachrach and M.S. Baratz, ('*Power and Poverty: Theory and Practice*', Oxford U.P., 1970), focus on non-decisions whereby adherence to the status quo may be, in reality, consensus enforced through the established power structure in which certain issues are taken for granted and seldom questioned. In the same vein, S. Lukes, ('*Power: A Radical View*, Macmillan, London and Basingstoke, 1974), points to the inherent contradiction' ...between the interests of those exercising power and the real interests of those they exclude. These latter may not express or even be conscious of their interests...' p. 25.
23. A.W.J. Thomson and V.V. Murray, '*Grievance Procedures*', Saxon House, Farnborough, 1976.
24. W. Brown (ed.), '*The Changing Contours of British Industrial Relations*', Industrial Relations Research Unit, Unpublished Paper, Warwick University, 1980.
25. P. Bachrach and M.S. Baratz, *op. cit.*, Ch. 3. See also W. Wesolowski, '*Classes, Strata and Power*', Routledge and Kegan Paul, London, 1979, who cogently argues the case of the domination of labour by capital via the sedimentation of accepted values especially over 'the means of production, the process and the product and labour' and by the legal norms of capitalism which guarantee the control of labour conditions by capital, pp. 50–64.
26. C. Edwards, *op. cit.*, p. 8.
27. W. Brown (ed.), *op. cit.*, Ch. 2.
28. P. Boreham, 'The Dialectic of Theory and Control: Capitalist Crisis and the Organization of Labour', in D. Dunkerley and G. Salaman (eds), *The International Yearbook of Organization Studies*, Routledge and Kegan Paul, London, 1980.

29. The term Industrial Democracy Projects is used to cover the many studies aimed at transforming the workplace into a participatory and efficient organisation given the constraints of specific technologies. For example, see E.L. Trist, G.W. Higgin, G. Murray and A.B. Pollock, *'Organizational Choice: The Loss, Re-discovery and Transformation of a Work Tradition'*, Tavistock, London, 1963. See also IDE International Research Group, Industrial Democracy in Europe: Differences and Simulation Across Countries and hierarchies' *Organization Studies*, Vol. 2, No. 1981, pp. 113–29.
30 P. Boreham, *op. cit.*, p. 25
31 S. Wood, 'Corporate Strategy and Organizational Studies, in D. Dunkerley and G. Salaman (eds), *The International Yearbook of Organization Studies*, Routledge and Kegan Paul, London, 1980.
32. A. Flanders, *'Management and Unions'*, Faber, London, 1970.
33. A. Fox, *'Beyond Contract'*, Faber, London, 1974, pp. 276–80.
34. R.J. Butler *et al.*, 1982, *op. cit.*, pp. 22–30.
35. A.S. Tannenbaum, *'Control in Organizations'*, McGraw-Hill, New York, 1968.
36. D.C. Wilson, 1980, *op. cit.*, pp. 70–2.
37. J. Banks and Ken Jones, *op. cit.*, p. 66, accord with these findings. In the British Steel Corporation, employee directors only expressed views on issues that had already been decided upon, such as cutting 30,000 jobs and closing down plants, and they were not allowed to initiate or 'to pick up on controversial matters' of policy information.
38. R.J. Butler, *et al.*, 1982, *op. cit.*, distinguish between issues, topics and decisions by arguing that an *issue* is a continuing problem/opportunity faces by an organisation, a *topic* is a label attached to an issue when it is the subject of a decision making process (such as a new product or reorganisation topic) and a *decision* is a choice arrived at by the processing of an issue.
39. These six concepts are drawn from Butler *et al.*, 1979/80, *op. cit.*, pp. 26–9. For a full range of concepts and variables used in the decision making research project see Butler *et al.*, 1982, *op. cit.*, pp. 8–13.
40. For a full discussion of this test of significance see F.N. Kerlinger, *'Foundations of Behavioural Research'*, Holt, Rinehart and Winston, New York, 1973.
41. W. Brown (ed.), *op. cit.*, Chapter 2.
42. K. Coates and T. Topham, *'The New Unionism: The Case for Workers' Control'*, Owen, London, 1972, p. 89.
43. K. Coates and T. Topham, *op. cit.*, p. 110.
44. See D.C. Wilson, 1982, *op. cit.*, p. 25.
45. See G.K. Kenny, R.J. Butler, D. Cray, D.J. Hickson, G. Mallory and David C. Wilson, 'Public and Private Organizations: Influence Patterns', forthcoming, for an extended discussion and empirical analysis of trades union involvement and influence in both public sector and private sector organisations. Copies are available from the Organizational Analysis Research Unit, University of Bradford Management Centre.

[11]

Journal of Management Studies 28:4 July 1991
0022-2380 $3.50

STRATEGIC INVESTMENT DECISION-MAKING: COMPLEXITIES, POLITICS AND PROCESSES*

RICHARD BUTLER

The Management Centre, University of Bradford

LES DAVIES

Bodø Graduate School of Management, Norway

RICHARD PIKE

The Management Centre, University of Bradford

JOHN SHARP

Canterbury Business School, University of Kent

ABSTRACT

This article is a preliminary report on an investigation into the processes of investment decision-making. Three case studies from three firms are presented which show disparities in a number of aspects of process, for example, the length of time taken to arrive at a decision, the number and intensity of disagreements and uncertainties encountered. Data were collected for these cases through semi-structured interviewing from multiple informants in the three organizations, thereby permitting the use of analysis of variance techniques of the different perspectives given by informants. Perceptions of the effectiveness of the decisions were also gathered. One finding from the study is that the decisions with the lowest perceived effectiveness (in firm HE) also lost support from those involved in making the decision during the process, although the decision was eventually implemented. This decision also had the least agreement amongst informants as to the main sources of disagreements. Informants of all three decisions saw effect upon product quality and productivity, fit with business strategy and competitive position of the company as the most important factors to take into account in evaluating the decisions. In firm CG, however, there were disagreements as to how the investment should be evaluated. In the conclusions to the article a disucssion is given as to the nature of evaluation procedures in relation to the developing theory of information systems.

THE QUESTION

As a roving consultant you have become familiar with three companies and, over the past few years, with their struggles to make important investment

Address for reprints: Richard Butler, Accounting, Information and Decision-Making Unit, The Management Centre, University of Bradford, Emm Lane, Bradford, West Yorkshire, BD9 4JL.

decisions. All three companies are sophisticated organizations apparently well up-to-date with modern management techniques for appraising investments and in other areas of management. The particular decisions that have caught your attention were all seen as important to their respective organizations in the sense that they had strategic long-term implications and involved significant levels of expenditure.

Yet there are some obvious differences in various aspects of these decisions. The first thing that strikes you is the variation, between 1 and 7 years, in the length of time taken to make the decisions. You also note that as time progressed support for the investment proposal waned somewhat in the firm taking the longest time, whereas in the other two companies support was increased amongst the managers concerned.

You also sense a number of other significant differences in the way in which things happened in the three companies; so, as a consultant with a sound social science training you decide to investigate more closely and in a more systematic way. As a social scientist you wish to understand and explain what went on; as a consultant you wish to draw some conclusions with implications for making investment decisions more effectively.

We, of course, did not come across our companies in quite this haphazard way; but our question is essentially as described above. This study sets out to observe and explain the actual investment behaviour of managers engaged in capital budgeting decisions. Particular attention is given to how complexity and politics may influence and, ultimately, be effective. Studies of particular strategic investment decisions, for example, Bower (1972), suggest that capital investment should be investigated as an organizational process. Investment decision-making is viewed as an incremental activity, involving many people and groups at various levels, often over lengthy time periods. This process is typically described in terms of a series of stages whereby, although top management retains final approval, the real decisions take place much earlier in the process (*e.g.* Bower, 1972; King, 1975).

THEORETICAL FRAMEWORK

The dual explanations of strategic decision-making processes proposed by Hickson *et al.* (1986) are those of complexity and politicality. In this model, making a decision can be seen to involve two fundamental problems; a *technical* problem of attempting to calculate the best solution, given a number of parameters, and the *political* problem of resolving divergent interests. As regards the technical problem, Simon (1960) emphasized that under complexity (or uncertainty) decision makers will 'satisfice', *i.e.*, will accept incomplete search, often use post-rationalization of the decision and exhibit a number of other aspects of behaviour which 'good' managers are not supposed to endorse. Here, following Thompson and Tuden (1959) the problem is that of uncertainty about cause/effect relations.

Even so, the technical model takes for granted 'intended rationality' (Simon, 1960) in the sense that managers will strive to achieve organizational goals even though accepting that they may not perfectly articulate them or reach them. But organizations are made up of multiple interests in which people may be pursuing local rather than organizational goals. It is because of this, Astley *et al.* (1982) argue, that the notion of the *political cleavage* associated with a decision is needed for a fuller explanation of decision processes. Here, following Thompson and Tuden, the decision-making problem is that of uncertainty about the ends or objectives that are being sought. The notion of a control system underlies much of conventional management accounting. Top management are supposed to set targets, budgets *etc.*, following a planning process which involves lower management's views. The problem now becomes that of ensuring, through feedback, that the organization and its constituent parts remain on course.

Large organizations often exhibit quite distinct identifiable investment planning systems but there is dispute over the effect of formal planning systems upon economic performance. For instance, Stagner (1969) found that profitable firms tended to use fairly formal planning and control procedures, although these were augmented by considerable informal contacts. Klammer (1973) and Pike (1984), on the other hand, found little relationship between the existence of formal investment systems and profitability although they did not consider the interaction between formal and informal aspects of planning.

Investment Decisions Behaviour

The aim of an investment decision system (IDS) is to decide, in the first place, whether a project proposal should be accepted or rejected; there may be an in-between, modify and accept category.

Although a project proposal has, in the end, to be accepted, rejected or modified, different managers in different positions will have different perceptions of the uncertainties and the attendant risks. For each project proposal there will, therefore, be a degree of risk incongruence. Acceptance of a low degree of risk congruence in an organization may be a form of 'satisficing' behaviour, enabling an investment to proceed. The control and reward systems are not sufficient to ensure that all levels of management view risk in the same way.

Problems may exist in the investment decision and in the organization as a whole if there is lack of risk congruence. For instance, investment decisions are likely to be difficult to analyse and may lead to excessive bargaining. Some managers, especially those at a lower level, may be less prepared to take risks (Itami, 1975; Swalm, 1966), indicating perhaps a fear of career repercussions if they later become associated with failure. Here we may see 'scapegoating' (Bonazzi, 1983), with lower managers as a more likely target. Staw (1976) suggests that the degree of personal responsibility for the outcome of a particular decision is a critical factor in determining whether the risk managers are prepared to accept high risk associated with low personal responsibility.

We also consider the *mode* in which the decision is made based upon the framework proposed by Thompson and Tuden (1959). First, *computational* decision-making is where the decision essentially falls out of the various calculations that can be done; for investment decision-making this might involve the use of techniques such as discounted cashflow, return on investment and the like. Second, *judgemental* decision-making occurs when, although facts and figures might be referred to, the decision ultimately involves the weighing up of intangible factors not easily quantifiable. A third, *bargaining* type of decision occurs when the decision is made by weighing up the views of the various involved parties and by compromise. The fourth decision type occurs when there is an impasse, nobody knows what to do and ultimately the situation is only resolved by a fortuitous event or by somebody seizing hold of the situation and by some kind of *inspiration* making the decision.

Decision Characteristics

Investment decisions do not exist in isolation. They evolve out of the organizational context and have particular characteristics of their own. It is here that we see Cohen *et al.*'s (1972) notion of an organization as a 'garbage can' coming to life. According to this, issues drop into the decision area (garbage can) for consideration but they come labelled with certain characteristics leading to certain types of treatment. As noted earlier, however, lower levels of management may delay the surfacing of an investment proposal until it is adjudged to be acceptable to higher tiers of management.

Organizational Context

Particular decisions derive from the wider organization context within which investments are made. A number of factors are relevant here.

First are the characteristics of the investment decision itself. Scapens *et al.* (1982; 1985) distinguish between the setting of pre- and post-decision controls. Pre-decision controls involve the corporate capital expenditure budget and specification of projects suitable for investment. Here we see a likely impact upon characteristics of decisions that eventually find their way into the investment decision arena. Post-decision controls involve periodic reports of divisional performance, project accounts and post audits. Again these will set the performance parameters connected with a decision. At the organization level the investment planning systems sets the overall 'rules of the game' (Crozier, 1964) within which decisions are made.

Technical ambiguity is also likely to impact upon decision characteristics and uncertainty. When technical ends/means relations are unclear and the end itself variable (Perrow, 1970) investment decisions pertaining to plant and equipment are difficult to evaluate and are surrounded by many uncertainties. *Strategic ambiguity* for an organization can result from the demands of a number of publics with conflicting views on what that organization should be doing. Often this is seen in public organizations.

The argument presented above is summarized in figure 1 which indicates the relationships between the major variable groupings.

SAMPLE

Our research aim was to describe and investigate the process of capital investment projects of a strategic nature in UK companies. The three companies chosen for this study form the first phase of a wider investigation into the process of decision-making. They were selected for their diversity, representing different industries, technologies, markets and sizes.

Within each firm selected one recent investment decision was chosen which managers concerned regarded as 'strategic' as defined by Hickson *et al.* (1986), namely those decisions which were concerned to have a significant impact on the firm and its long-term performance. Semi-structured interviews were held

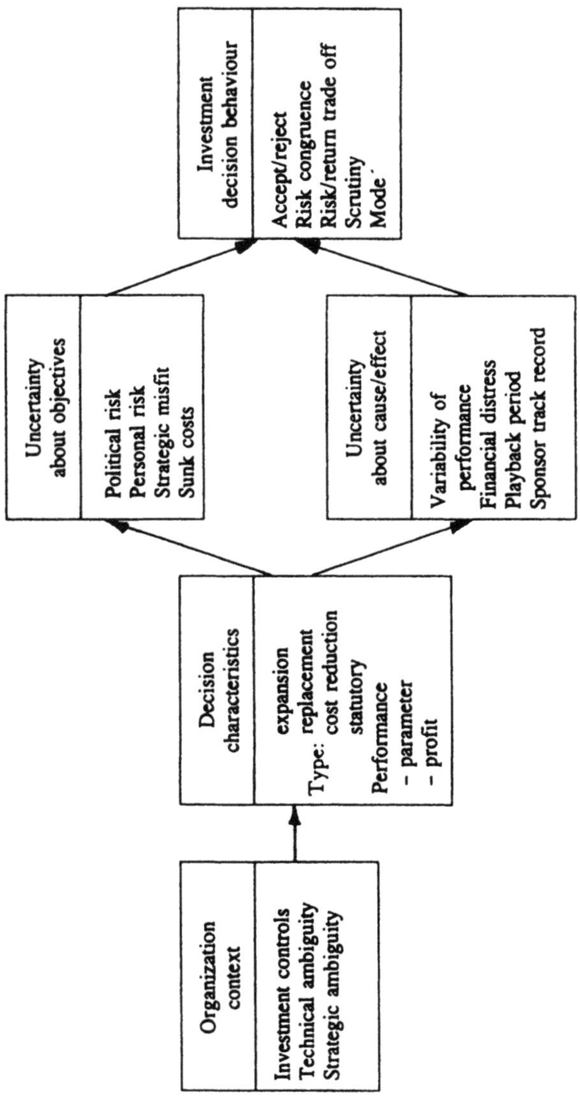

Figure 1. Determinants of investment decision behaviour

with all managers seen to have some reasonable degree of influence in shaping, evaluating and approving those proposals. These discussions followed a common pattern based on a questionnaire involving 32 questions on the investment process and its outcome, most variables being measured on a 5-point scale.

Our aim was to get the perspectives of a number of different informants using structured interviewing, thereby building up three intensive case studies which would, nevertheless, be amenable to statistical analysis. In this method, differences of perception of informants become part of the data, not an inconvenience to be explained away in the search for some objective truth. Seven, six and six informants were extensively interviewed in companies EC, CG and HE respectively.

Some of the differences in the decision-making processes noted above can undoubtedly be interpreted in terms of the different organizational contexts provided by the three companies. One firm (EC) is a relatively small electronics company. Turnover for 1984–5 was approximately £25m in a dynamic, fairly high technology market based upon the manufacture, installation and servicing of the one central product line of electronic equipment. The capital investment here was concerned with the replacement of this single product with a new but closely related product involving the expenditure of about £400k. Consideration of the investment followed the appointment of a new managing director, ECmd, whose remit was to improve the competitive position of the company. At this time the company had little in the way of formal procedures for investment appraisal and, in spite of the magnitude of the investment, the whole decision was completed in the relatively short time of one year. During interviews the informants were asked to rate their support for the investment proposal before and after the decision; average support across informants increased from a high initial score of 1.83 to the maximum of 2.00 denoting total support (the minimum point on the scale was – 2.00 denoting total opposition).

The second firm is a division of a major engineering capital goods manufacturer, CG. It is also essentially a one product line company and has five or six major competitors both in domestic and international markets. The impetus for its major capital investment of £4m was to improve competitiveness by reducing substantially manufacturing lead times and annual costs of about £4m by purchasing a new machining centre; this would also have a major impact upon the firm since it introduced a change in manufacturing technique. As part of a large international corporation, this organization has extensive procedures for the evaluation of investment proposals and the decision was completed in about three years; support for the project from all the managers concerned was still fairly high at the start (but not as high as for EC) at 1.0 but as in EC support increased significantly across all managers to 1.83 by the time of the decision, a greater increase than seen in EC.

The third company (HE) is a health equipment supplier and is a subsidiary of a large multinational corporation. Of the three decisions this involved the least expenditure (initially £75,000 but rising to £150,000) but was strategic in the sense that it introduced a new manufacturing process, fundamentally altering the way in which the product was made, enabling improved efficiency and potential price reduction, higher quality and some possible benefits for the user, although user acceptance of these benefits remained unproved at the beginning of the decision process. This firm also had extensive formal evaluation procedures for capital investment projects. Of the three companies it took by far the longest time to reach a decision (7 years) with the proposal initially receiving a great deal of support from involved managers, the average level of support declined significantly from 1.4 to 1.2 although the decision to invest was eventually approved.

It might be argued that the differences so far noted between EC and CG can be explained in terms of quite conventional contextual variables that organizational analysis uses (Pugh *et al.*, 1968), of which size and complexity are the most prominent. As a relatively small tightly-knit organization with low formalization of procedures EC would be expected to reach decisions rapidly and harmoniously. On the other hand CG is spending a much bigger sum of money, is in itself a bigger organization and is embedded within a larger corporation. Major investments are accountable to head office and in order to achieve comparability across many business units head office will impose a standard appraisal system across divisions.

Another explanation might be sought in the differences which managers ascribe to the importance of different factors: perhaps for one company the need to fit the investment with existing business strategy was more important than in another. To test this idea we asked the managers in our sample to rate the importance of 19 different factors that might be used to form their views of an investment proposal; these factors could be broadly classified under the headings of strategic factors, quantitative performance factors, qualitative performance factors and risk factors. Each factor was scored by our informants in each organization and table I shows the five most important and the two least important factors mentioned.

Table I. Importance of factor to investment decisions

Factor	*Average score (min = 0, max = 4)*
Most important	
Effect on product quality	3.33
Fit with business strategy	3.28
Effect on productivity	3.00
Type of project	2.89
Competitive position of company	2.83
Least important	
Impact upon current year's earnings	1.22
Effect upon industrial relations	1.06
Overall average, all companies	
All informants	2.33

Kendall's W on within-company rating shows agreement within companies (W sig < 0.0014). ANOVA shows no difference between average company ratings.

We can see that product quality, fit with business strategy and improving the competitive position of the firm were the most important factors considered by all informants in all three companies. In this respect, in spite of the different contexts, managers demonstrate a remarkable unanimity about what is important in investing. Our, admittedly limited, sample of British management gives optimistic support for the notion that implementation of competitive strategies (Porter, 1985) is filtering through to investment decisions.

For EC, the new product line was being introduced entirely for market reasons and at the behest of the new managing director. For the middle managers this was seen to be of great importance in their careers, a chance to make a mark. Current earnings and industrial relations factors were overridden by these strategic considerations. For CG, the investment was to provide a change in manufacturing techniques and reduction in lead times, the opportunity being the need to replace existing plant and hence this project would have an effect on product quality; cost reduction and productivity were key motivators and from this the gaining of competitive advantage in the market. Again, current earnings were unimportant and so too were personnel matters. The new manufacturing method at HE was to provide an improved product, therefore attractive to customers, at a cost reduction initially estimated at 30 per cent. Against the benchmark of a gross profit margin of 20–25 per cent required to break even on new projects the proposed investment in HE was attractive.

Quantifiable financial performance factors (whether measured by discounted cash flow techniques, payback period, or impact on sales and profits) were viewed as of secondary importance by most respondents. This confirms the impressions of Haynes and Solomon (1962), King (1975) and Pike (1983) that the emphasis in the capital budgeting literature on formal investment appraisal using discounted cash flow methods is misplaced. Equally apparent is the relatively low priority given to risk and uncertainty factors. This is not altogether unexpected given that far less attention is generally devoted to analysing project risk than to formal financial evaluation (Pike, 1983).

The Effect of Hierarchy

Hierarchy is an important concept within organizations since it is one important method of directing resources and effecting co-ordination. In developing a measure of hierarchy we adapted the scale established by Pugh *et al.* (1968) to fit the organizations in our sample and to give a greater sensitivity to the divisionalized structures now more prevalent. Starting with the highest level, the scale proceeds as follows with score followed by a generic name:

> 25, group board; 30, group chief executive officer (CEO); 35, group director; 40, headquarters technical expert or functional head; 45, divisional board; 50, divisional CEO: 55, divisional director; 60, functional heads, divisional general manager or expert reporting to level 55 or above; 65, divisional technical expert; 70, department head, factory or unit manager; 75, departmental technical experts. Committees are rated as the level to which their recommendations have to go for approval.

This we call the Hierarchy Scale (HS); the scoring system adopted gives us scope to extend the scale in either direction and to insert intermediate levels as our experience of different organizations develops. Recalling the Aston scale of Pugh *et al.* we can still convert scores on HS to an Aston score and we can also accommodate the possibility of extending the scale to above group board in the case of decisions involving, for instance, a multinational.

It is useful to present the application of the US to our three companies in table II. This shows abbreviated job titles with code for the major actors involved in the decisions, allows us to make direct comparisons across the organizations and preserves anonymity.

Table II. Hierarchical location of major actors

		EC	*CG*	*HE*
Group level				
25.	Board			
30.	CEO		Grp mgr dir CGgmd	
35.	Director		Grp fin dir	Exec mgmt comm HEemc
40.	Expert/functional nead			Ops mgr HEopm Purch mgr HEprm
Company/divisional level				
45.	Board			
50.	CEO	Mgr dir ECmd	Div gen mgr CGmd	
55.	Director	Fin dir ECfd Tech dir ECtd Mktg dir ECmkd	Manf dir CGmnd Co fin dir CGcfd	
60.	Functional head/ General manager/ Expert reporting to level 55	Prd mgr ECprm R&D mgr ECrdm	Site gen mgr CGsgm	Div mtg mgr HEdmm Plant mgr HEplm R&D mgr HErdm
65.	Expert	Prj ldr ECpjl	Prj eng mgr CGpem	Prj scien HEpsc
70.	Department manager			
75.	Department expert			

Analysis of variance of importance factor by HS shows that overall importance across all factors assigned by informants at different levels varies with level as shown in table III.

Table III. Effect of hierarchy (HS) on overall importance

HS level	50	55	60	65	70	75
Average importance	2.16	2.08	3.00	2.31	2.46	2.22

From these scores we can see a significant curvilinear relationship between level and the overall importance scores with greater importance being assigned by middle levels in the organization. This pattern is noted across the three organizations and supports the view that middle management (level 60, functional heads or general management) are the people who get most involved in the implementation of investment decisions (Bower, 1972; Carter, 1971). Higher management will tend to see a given project against a background of a number of other projects; lower-level people will tend to be experts offering advice but without direct responsibility for the decision.

COMPLEXITIES AND POLITICALITIES

While the contextual explanation adds to our understanding of what happened in these decisions there is obviously a great deal still to be explained. More specifically, if size is to be the only explanation for the differences in decision duration and for the change of support, why does firm HE significantly vary from CG since both of these companies are large relative to EC? In their extensive analysis of 150 strategic decisions across 30 organizations Hickson *et al.* (1986) pointed to the far greater importance factors especially associated with a decision issue or topic in explaining decision processes than of organizational contextual factors. They argue that an organization provides a framework of rules of the game within which topics arise, become issues about which a decision is required, each topic presenting uncertainties (or complexities) to be resolved. During this process different interests will become involved, each pushing a point of view; making a decision in an organization becomes, in the end, a matter for bargaining between these interests. These are the politicalities of decision-making. Arriving at a decision in an organization becomes a matter of coping with these complexities and politicalities.

What were these complexities and politicalities for our companies? Informants were asked to rate from 0 to 4 each of the factors on a standard listing covering possible sources of uncertainty likely to be met in organizational decision-making. These factors reflected the standard list of importance factors already described above covering market, supplier, production and cost, financial, technical, industrial relations, personnel and regulatory considerations and were derived from the literature and from pilot interviews in the firms. Table IV presents the average scores given to a source of greater than 2 or less than 0.5 by informants.

Table IV. Sources and strength of uncertainty

Source of uncertainty *Type of consideration*		*Average score*
High		
Production and cost		2.28
Market		2.22
Financial		2.19
Technical		2.06
Low		
Personnel		0.33
Overall average		1.50
By company		
	EC	1.19
	CG	1.58
	HE	1.80

Company differences significant $p<0.0001$. Inter-informant scores agree Kendall's W $p<0.007$

From these figures we see a picture that in some ways reflects the factors that managers take to be important in considering investments. Hence we see production and cost, and market factors coming out as causing major uncertainties. As all three investments had a considerable technical element this also creates uncertainties while the uncertainty of seeing a sufficient financial return is also a cause for concern for all three firms. Again we note the low concern given to personnel matters; markets, technology and finance are undoubtedly the main concerns for these companies (Hickson *et al.*, 1986).

Looking across companies the analysis of variance shows a significant increase in total uncertainty in moving from EC through GC to HE (scores 1.19, 1.58 and 1.80 respectively) although the sources of uncertainty for each remain in the same order. When we examine our data more closely we can see the reasons for this. The major areas of uncertainty for EC were external to the firm: market reaction, suppliers' quality, prices and reliability. The managing director (ECmd) gave import and export policy the highest rating, indicating that such matters can often have a greater concern for a chief executive than can more direct customer relations. The marketing director (ECmkd) highlighted variable market information and future government spending since this affected whether various public institutions would buy their electronic systems. The research and development manager (ECrdm) emphasized the problems of buying-in components from Japan while ECprm, the production manager, concentrated upon uncertainties in the manufacturing processes, the highest source of uncertainty across the three decisions. Market factors scored high for CG because of an inelastic demand curve, intense competition in export markets and the buying policy of the main British buying organizations.

Production and cost factors were the major sources of uncertainty seen by all informants in HE except the plant accountant, HEpa, for whom market factors were the most uncertain; generally market factors did not score highly as a source of uncertainty for other informants. The analysis of variance shows that there is a statistically significant lack of disagreement between informants in the ratings given to the various sources of uncertainty. It is here that seeds of the highly political nature of this decision in HE may be seen.

A similar approach was taken to assembling politicality. Informants rated a standard list of eight possible sources of disagreements to be met in decision-making, derived from the literature and the pilot interviews, from 0 to 4. Analysis of the strength of various sources by company are given in table V. Here we can see that HE experienced approximately 2½ times the disagreement strength of the other two companies; CG shows a slightly higher level of disagreement than EC.

Table V. Strength and sources of disagreement

	Company		
	EC	*CG*	*HE*
Disagreement source			
Objectives of decision	0.20	0.67	1.00
Overall objectives	0.40	0.33	1.20
Procedures	0.60	1.50	1.40
Personality clash	0.00	0.50	3.20
Pace	1.80	1.17	2.20
Ethics	0.80	0.17	1.00
Average for all sources	0.60	0.67	1.60

ANOVA of disagreement strength × source × company: differences between companies $p<0.001$; differences between sources $p<0.005$; interaction effect $p<0.025$.

Inter-informant agreement over sources of disagreement within companies: EC $p<0.09$; CG $p<0.006$; HE $p>0.5$

When we examine disagreement strength by level we note a highly significant tendency towards a greater awareness of disagreements at lower levels as shown in the following figures of disagreement strength by HS as shown in table VI.

Table VI. Effect of hierarchy (HS) on average disagreements

HS level	40	45	50	55	60	65
Average disagreement	0	0.75	0.57	1.71	1.02	1.86

These figures show a highly significant tendency for more disagreements to be seen at lower levels in the organization ($p<0.0001$) reflecting the notion that higher managers can stay relatively aloof from the day to day politics of such practical matters as to whether a new production technique is introduced.

The investment in the new product line in EC shows a high consensus amongst the involved managers as to what should be done (the objectives), the procedures to be used in evaluating the investment, any questions of ethics or responsibility and a zero level of personality clash. This finding is supported by the in-depth interviewing, in which all managers spoke of the obvious need for the investment as determined by the overall long-term strategy of the company. The only area in which there was major disagreement concerned the pace at which the decision should go. This reflects the urgency which was felt in the organization as to the need to replace an ageing product upon which the company was solely dependent.

The outstanding feature of the still relatively minor disagreements within CG concerns the procedures to be used in evaluating the investment. The root of this disagreement involved the extent to which conventional financial measures of assessment, such as payback period, internal rate of return (IRR), or other, should be used or whether wider strategic issues were more important. Of all participants the company managing director, CGmd, emphasized the strategic aspect by raising the question as to whether CG should stay in this particular market. Other participants were emphasizing the financial return and the use of a particular capital investment decision support tool called BORIS to evaluate projects. This debate was also conducted against a corporation myth that the chairman of the group board (CGcm) favoured the simple payback measure; the quotation attributed to the chairman being: 'Don't tell me its return, tell me how long it is before I get my money back'.

CGspm got his way in the sense that the project appraisal report of several hundred pages long only contained a few pages concerning financial justification. This comparative lack of concern with financial measures was undoubtedly exacerbated by the fact that there was doubt in the minds of managers as to the expected rate of return required by the company for new projects of this type. It is here we can see how uncertainty can lead to disagreements which in turn can lead to politicking in the organization. Also this case shows how a serious disagreement of this nature can lead to disagreements over the pace at which things should proceed. The hold-up in CG was of a different nature to that in EC, where there was urgency to get the new product onto the market and the decision was made very much faster anyway; in CG the method of evaluation to use was the predominant area of disagreement.

If we look at the overall pattern of disagreements in CG by level we see the following:

HS level	50	55	60	65	70
Average disagreement	0	0.57	0.57	1.71	0.57

One manager at level 65 was particularly associated with trying to get figures to match the expectations of higher management, which explains the much higher average scores for disagreements seen at this level.

The outstanding feature of disagreements in HE is not just the higher overall score but that it scores higher than the other two organizations on nearly all sources (the exception is for procedures where CG scores 1.50 against 1.40 for HE) and particularly the very high score of 3.20 for personality clash, a factor that is notable for its absence from the other two organizations; this was rated number one source of disagreement amongst all six informants. To understand the nature of these disagreements we need to recall that the impetus for this decision was cost reduction and product improvement through the introduction of a new type of process involving the purchase of a new machine. The idea had been around for quite a long time but the present phase of interest was started by a junior person, the project scientist at Plant A, HEpsc and was enthusiastically embraced by the research and development manager (HErdm) and the marketing manager, HEdmm.

Compared to the other decisions this one started low down in the organization. Research and development then provided a major driving force for the decision. Trial runs and costings were carried out based on a 60 per cent machine utilization; these costings were later based upon a 10 per cent utilization following concern from product managers that market forecasts were too optimistic. In spite of the now unfavourable costings the decision to purchase the machine was made in 1984 and the purchasing manager (HEprm) was appointed as project leader; HEprc and HErdm were disgruntled at this since both thought that they had prior claim upon this project.

A major problem came to light concerning the location of the machine when it was found that conditions were not suitable in Plant A due to lack of a suitable hygienic location. Consequently, the machine was left unused in a warehouse for over one year. A possible solution to this problem considered was to move production from plant A to another part of the country, which nobody there wanted (*i.e.* HEpsc, HErdm, and others). The alternative was to use a subcontractor, whereby the machine would be operated by a subcontracting company on their site but the production would still count as part of Plant A. It was suggested by others that this was favoured by HEprm partly because, as purchasing manager, the operation would then come under his control.

A prominent feature of our data concerning disagreements and politicality at HE is our inability to get a uniform story from the informants, an aspect that is shown up in the lack of statistical significance in inter-informant ratings over the source of disagreements. Although personality clash rated highly there was no unanimity over who was clashing with whom and why; personal objectives remain submerged in this case but the methodology used has been vindicated, since without systematic inter-informant scores such views would never have surfaced. Further, the emphasis upon personality clashes at HE should not allow us to ignore the fact that our sources of disagreement also rate highly at HE. In common with the other organizations, pace was reported as a problem due to the delay in getting the machine into operation. Similarly, people were having problems in agreeing over the objectives of the decision in HE compared to the other organizations. The lack of inter-informant consistency is perhaps even more notable since most of the informants were located on the same site, unlike CG, where high inter-informant agreement was found in spite of relatively high geographical dispersion.

DECISION PROCESSES

Case by case data of this nature can give a lot of richness and detail as regards what happens in decision-making. In order to provide more of an overall measure of the decision processes we operationalized Thompson and Tuden's (1959) four types of decision process discussed earlier. This typology provides a useful way of summarizing the overall processes as seen to this point. Average scores for each organization were computed as to the extent to which informants saw their particular decision conforming to the four types. From table VII we can see that the decisions in EC and CG are viewed as predominantly computational and judgemental with only a small amount of bargaining and hardly any inspiration; CG was noticeably more judgemental than computational.

Table VII. Process type

Company	*Computational*	*Judgemental*	*Bargaining*	*Inspirational*
EC	2.83	2.83	1.33	0.17
CG	3.00	3.50	1.17	0.33
HE	2.40	2.20	2.00	2.80

minimum = 0, maximum = 4

HE shows its highest score on the inspirational decisions process at 2.80 although it should also be noted that it scores fairly highly on the other three decision types and is by far the highest (2.00) on bargaining. Analysis of variance shows that within EC and CG informants are in agreement as to the type of decision process (Kendall's W, $p < 0.004$) but that in HE this agreement is not achieved; different people have different perceptions of the process in HE.

Overall, the problems faced by EC and CG were to cope with the main sources of uncertainties, although in different ways. For EC the problem was to respond quickly to the prospect of a declining market through quickly bringing in a new product; in CG the investment was embedded in a much larger organization and the biggest single problem concerned the balance between strategic fit and cost reduction. The judgemental processes were to do with working out the appropriate method of assessment to use. The decision processes in HE, where there was little evidence of a corporate view of what happened, were driven much more by the aspirations of individuals.

Patterns of Influence and Information

The patterns of influence achieved by the various participants is an important aspect of decision-making. Here we need to make the distinction between involvement and influence in decision-making. People can be involved in the sense that they provide information or their views are sought or in some more general way they are in the decision arena. Involvement does not necessarily lead to influence, however. To investigate this aspect of the three decisions our informants were asked to identify the people who were involved and then to rate the influence of these people (including themselves) on a scale from 0 to 4 thereby giving a matrix on inter-informant scores.

Analysis of variance on a company by company basis follows; in this analysis any person is rated as having influence if that person is assigned a score of more than zero by any informant:

EC: The number of people rated as having influence by one or more informant was 11; none of these was external to the organization. An average inter-informant score was computed for each involved person. These scores ranged from the highest of 3.57 to the lowest of 0.14 giving an overall average of 1.61. There was no significant difference between informants as to their ratings of the 11 people.

The new managing director (ECmd) was very influential in the early stages of the decision process but once the need for the new product had been established he took little direct part. The company had started on a road towards formalizing a process which had previously been non-formalized and a product strategy group was formed to consider new proposals in relation to overall strategy. New documentation was created by the finance department (the product approval sheet or PAS). An aspect of this thrust to greater control is the growth strategy of the company which has recently acquired a number of subsidiaries.

CG: Sixteen people or organizations were seen as having influence, considerably more than in EC and probably reflecting the greater organizational size. The one external organization was the Department of Trade and Industry, involved due to CG's obtaining a government grant. Average inter-informant scores for influence ranged from 3.17 to near 0 with an overall average of 1.40. Here we see a significant difference ($p < 0.024$) in assigned influence which occurs because one person's allocation of overall influence is more than twice the average (2.38) suggesting that he sees much more influence around in this decision than the others. The key person in getting a project approved is CGspm who is based at divisional headquarters, 150 miles from the manufacturing plant; the general view is that all projects have to be accepted by him. In this organization there are well-established procedures for dealing with new proposals but in this case it was a matter of doing the calculations knowing what the decision was. Financial data here fulfil a highly symbolic role.

HE: Twenty people had influence in this decision ranging from an average of 3.00 to 0 with an overall average of 1.43; four of these were external suppliers and subcontractors. There was no significant difference between informants as to influence assigned. This organization also has a formalized system for assessing projects. The project in question started low down in the organization following a meeting between HEdmm, HErdm and HEspm in a roadside hostelry and it generally maintained this low trajectory (Hage, 1981) throughout its course. The decision to purchase the machine was made by the executive management committee (EMC). There was certainly considerable confusion amongst managers about the precise cost of the project, an aspect which is reflected in the analyses of variance presented, indicating lack of agreement between participants over the main sources of disagreements. In documentation presented to EMC Research and Development gave a cost of £23k but another cost in the same summary gave £72k with a total capitalization of £104k. To this had to be added extra costs due to the need to change production facilities up and down stream from the new machine, particularly bleaching, drying and finishing processes, giving a total cost of circa £200k. Whatever the actual figures believed by the various participants it is certainly difficult to get a corporate view of what the costs were expected to be.

One conclusion that we may draw from this result is that low overall influence and lack of a single dominant influence centre tends to increase decision time and lead to negative change in support for the decision. In HE our statistical and interview data support the view that the investment decision in HE lacked a clearly defined influence centre.

EFFECTIVENESS OF DECISIONS

Understanding and explanation are necessary pre-conditions of improving decision-making but on their own are not enough. In order to move towards improving the effectiveness of decision-making we also need concepts of effectiveness. As decision-making is about making choices, the notion of intention and the extent to which those original intentions are met must be represented in the concept of effectiveness. A range of general questions was asked of our informants (at this stage we can only report data for CG and HE) capturing various aspects of effectiveness. These are first summarized in table VIII.

Table VIII. Aspects of decision effectiveness

Criterion of effectiveness	*CG*	*HE*
Right choice made	3.00	1.80
Decision process satisfactory	2.75	0.80
There was an unexpected outcome	1.00	2.40
Useful learning as a result of the decision	2.60	3.40

From the above analysis we can see that HE scores lower than CG on the choice made and satisfaction over the process all factors except learning. We should note that the unexpected outcomes for HE tended to be negative, a feature which reinforces our initial observation that dissatisfaction grew as the decision proceeded. The precise unexpected outcomes for HE were to do with the additional expenses incurred in the finishing processes, in not realizing that there was already a subcontractor with the same machine which could have been used, and in not achieving the premium on the product which their analysis of customer reaction had anticipated. But significantly, HE records greater learning than does CG although we have yet to find out why this is. Could it be, for instance, that under appropriate organizational conditions a poor process leads to improvements in procedures being adopted?

One aspect emphasized in HE was the poor communication between different parts of the organization. In particular, communication was seen to be poor between marketing, research and development and production. Further investigation revealed an important organization structural aspect to this poor communication. Turnover amongst product managers on the marketing side would follow a two-year cycle since this fitted the greater consumer product orientation that had become more prevalent as a matter of company strategy. The decision process lasted for seven years, during which time product managers changed at least three times, thereby making the transmission of information about changes in market conditions into the decision process difficult. Indeed, each change of product manager meant that market forecasts were reworked from scratch. These varied widely, as already noted.

More detail was sought on the matter of the choice made in the decision. Here we asked our informants whether the decisions attained their objectives, these being categorized as to whether strategic, quantifiable performance, qualitative performance and risk factors were attained; with respect to risk factors this question was aimed at discovering whether, with hindsight, the decision process was successful in assessing the riskiness of the project. Overall, CG recorded 2.63 and HE 1.45 on this question, a difference which is highly significant as shown by analysis of variance ($p < 0.002$). Again, informants in HE were unable to agree as to the degree of attainment of objectives. Overall, both organizations rated their attainment of strategic and qualitative factors much higher than (2.71 and 2.29 respectively) their attainment of quantitative factors (0.86) and their success in assessing risk.

More information was collected on whether the process was regarded as satisfactory. An important aspect of process is the extent and severity of delays. Here again we note significantly fewer problems in CG than in HE, each recording respectively 1.5 and 3.0. There was a detectable effect of the hierarchy scale on this.

CONCLUSIONS

Our comparison of three investment decision processes started with some general observations about their performance; the decision in HE took a long time and lost much support during the process compared to the decision in EC and CG which were much quicker and generally well supported afterwards. In attempting to understand and explain our initial observations we have drawn upon the general framework laid down by Thompson and Tuden (1959) and further elaborated by Earl and Hopwood (1980). Thompson and Tuden used two principal dimensions of decisions to explain the processes that are likely to occur. These dimensions are uncertainty about ends/means relationships and disagreements over the ends to be achieved. Hence, the inspirational decision mode would be seen as a result of attempting to cope with uncertainties and disagreements, a feature which is prominent in the HE decision, but we should note that this inspiration is also accompanied by computation, judgement (the predominant modes for the other two decisions) and bargaining.

If we relate our findings to other studies of decision-making processes, we can see that HE is exhibiting many of the features of the sporadic process reported by Hickson *et al.* (1986) in that there are many stops and starts, a long process time, a drawing in of many interests and bargaining. As Hickson reports, the outstanding features of decisions attracting sporadic processes are contentiousness and complexity, aspects which we see in the HE decision. What differs somewhat from the ideal sporadic process is the relatively low level at which it started and even final authorization only occurred at a middle level. This however might be explained in terms of the relatively low sum of money involved. EC displays many of the characteristics of the fluid process also reported by Hickson *et al.* (1986), that is, the decision proceeded with few delays, relative confidence in the information used, little negotiation, initiation of the decision occurring at the top of the organization but then being worked out in its details and implementation lower down. The decision proceeded smoothly, thereby illustrating what Hickson *et al.* (1986) describe as an essentially tractable problem, with little contentiousness due to the apparent obviousness of the need to move away from reliance on a single and ageing product. For CG the decision showed some features of Hickson *et al.*'s intermediate type of decision, the constricted decision, in that this type is worked out fairly low down in the hierarchy, involves some delays but is generally non-contentious.

Although we may be seen as broadly supporting an already established contingency framework of decision-making, our examination of the concept of effectiveness also highlights the limitations of this approach. The limitations are well illustrated by what happened in HE. In a sense we can argue that managers in HE did the right thing; the decision was complex and political and they used a great deal of inspiration and we see many of the characteristics of the sporadic process. This fits the contingency theories of Thompson and Tuden (1959), and of Hickson *et al.* (1986). Yet involved managers' own rating of this decision's effectiveness exhibits a poor opinion for the decision eventually made and of how they went about making it.

Part of the answer to this problem is that complexity and politicality are not necessarily independent variables but are part of the process itself. Hence, we see that disgreements arise as part of the contriving of individuals; we also see that uncertainties arise as part of that same contriving, in a similar way that Crozier (1964) described how the maintenance engineers in a French tobacco enterprise ensured the continuance of uncertainty by refusing the routinization of maintenance procedures. In order to improve effectiveness, we would not only have to work on trying to match process to conditions, but would also have to change those conditions themselves. This point is perhaps most clearly illustrated by CG, where problems arose from middle managers trying to fit the decision into established assessment procedures; we might argue that this also is an unnecessarily contrived uncertainty, one solution to which would be simply to remove that procedure.

Such an approach would perhaps come close to Lindblom's (1959) notion of 'muddling through' decision-making as appropriate for very complex decisions due to the difficulty of introducing formalized procedures. Simon's (1960) approach was to emphasize the need for heuristic decision-making procedures under conditions of uncertainty, to allow new information to be absorbed as decision-making proceeds. More recent suggestions emphasize the need to adapt information systems to individual decision-making styles, although research by Nutt (1985) has cast doubt on this idea, showing that personal attributes had no impact upon information required in decision-making. The question of matching procedures and decision support systems to management decision-making requires much greater research.

A significant methodological point is that the generally high agreement between informants over many questions asked provides partial confirmation for those approaches to the study of organizational decision-making which have relied upon comparison between cases collected from studies with larger samples but using predominantly single informants (*e.g.* Mintzberg *et al.*, 1976; Hickson *et al.*,

1986). Generally, one suitable chosen person can often give a good overall insight into some of the processes of a decision but we would have to provide a strong caution and point out that a high level of agreement was not obtained in our politically charged decision. Further studies of decision-making must take into account the need to cross-reference with multiple informants when it comes to these kinds of issues.

Finally, we return to where we began, to our roving consultant and his question. With what kind of systematic social science knowledge can we provide him to help improve investment decision processes in organizations. It would seem no accident that the two organizations which achieved a high consensus between managers on the various questions also gave high ratings for effectiveness. In HE, on the other hand, this consensus was lacking on questions to do with objectives of the decision, who had influence, perceptions of the overall process and in some other areas as reported above. This finding would put a premium on developing common views in organizations about how decisions ought to be tackled. To assist in this we would point out that decision-making research is now beginning to develop a methodology for mapping out the various uncertainties and disagreements that organizations encounter in their decision processes, with the aim of trying to improve those processes. Further areas of research should include investigation of the types of procedures and information systems used by decision-makers.

NOTE

* Richard Butler is Reader in Organizational Analysis at the University of Bradford Management Centre; Les Davies is Professor at the Bodø Graduate School of Management, Bodø, Norway; Richard Pike is Provident Finance Group Professor of Finance at the University of Bradford Management Centre; and John Sharp is Professor at the Canterbury Business School, University of Kent at Canterbury. The research is supported by grants from the Economic and Social Research Council, the Institute of Cost and Management Accountants, and the University of Bradford.

REFERENCES

Astley, W. G., Axelsson, R., Butler, R. J., Hickson, D. J. and Wilson, D. C. (1982). 'Complexity and cleavage: dual explanations of strategic decision-making'. *Journal of Management Studies*, **19**, 4, 357–75.

Bonazzi, G. (1983). 'Scapegoating in complex organizations: the results of a comparative study of symbolic blame-giving in Italian and French public administration'. *Organization Studies*, **4**, 1, 19–38.

Bower, J. L. (1972). *Managing the Resource Allocation Process*. Homewood, Ill.: Irwin.

Carter, E. (1971). 'The behavioral theory of the firm and top level corporate decisions'. *Administrative Science Quarterly*, **18**, 4, 413–27.

Cohen, M. D., March, J. G. and Olsen, J. P. (1972). 'A garbage can model of organizational choice'. *Administrative Science Quarterly*, **17**, 1–25.

Crozier, M. (1964). *The Bureaucratic Phneomenon*. London: Tavistock.

Earl, M. J. and Hopwood, A. G. (1980). 'From management information to information management'. In Lucas, H. C., Jr. *et al.* (Eds.), *The Information Systems Environment*. Amsterdam: North-Holland.

HAGE, J. (1981). *Theories of Organizations: Form, Process and Transformation*. New York: Wiley.

HAYNES, W. and SOLOMON, M. (1962). 'A misplaced emphasis in capital budgeting'. *Quarterly Review of Economics and Business*, February, 39–46.

HICKSON, D. J., BUTLER, R. J., CRAY, D., MALLORY, G. R. and WILSON, D. C. (1986). *Top Decisions: Strategic Decision-Making in Organizations*. Oxford: Blackwell; San Francisco: Jossey-Bass.

ITAMI, H. (1975). 'Evaluation measures and goal congruence under uncertainty'. *Journal of Accounting Research*, **13**, 1, 73–96.

KING, P. (1975). 'Is the emphasis on capital budgeting misplaced?', *Journal of Business Finance and Accounting*, Spring, 69–82.

KLAMMER, T. (1973). 'The association of capital budgeting techniques with firm performance', *Accounting Review*, **48**, 2, 353–64.

LINDBLOM, C. (1959). 'The science of muddling through'. *Public Administration Review*, **19**, 79–88.

MINTZBERG, H., RAISINGHANI, D. and THEORET, A. (1976). 'The structure of "unstructured" decision processes'. *Administrative Science Quarterly*, **21**, 2, 246–75.

NUTT, P. C. (1985). 'Behavioral bases for the design of a MIS: managerial ability to specify'. Working paper 85-25, Administrative Science Research, College of Administrative Science, Ohio State University.

PERROW, C. (1970). *Organizational Analysis: A Sociological View*. London: Tavistock.

PIKE, R. H. (1983). 'A review of recent trends in formal capital budgeting processes'. *Accounting and Business Research*, **51**, Summer, 201–8.

PIKE, R. H. (1984). 'Sophisticated capital budgeting systems and their association with corporate performance'. *Managerial and Decision Economics*, **5**, 2, 91–7.

PORTER, M. E. (1985). *Competitive Advantage*. New York: Free Press.

PUGH, D. S., HICKSON, D. J., HININGS, C. R. and TURNER, C. (1968). 'Dimensions of organizations structure'. *Administrative Science Quarterly*, **13**, 1, 65–104.

SCAPENS, R. W. and SALE, T. J. (1985). 'An international study of accounting practices in divisionalized companies and their association with organizational variables'. *The Accounting Review*, **60**, 2, 231–47.

SCAPENS, R. W., SALE, T. J. and TIKKAS, P. A. (1982). *Financial Control of Divisional Capital Investment*. London: Institute of Cost and Management Accountants.

SIMON, H. A. (1960). *The New Science of Management Decision*. New York: Harper & Row.

STAGNER, R. (1969). 'Corporate decision-making: an empirical study'. *Journal of Applied Psychology*, **53**, 1, 1–13.

STAW, B. M. (1976). 'Knee-deep in the big muddy: a study of escalating commitment to a chosen course of action'. *Organizational Behavior and Human Performance*, **16**, 1, 27–44.

SWALM, R. O. (1966). 'Utility-insights into risk-taking'. *Harvard Business Review*, **44**, November–December, 123–36.

THOMPSON, J. D. and TUDEN, A. (1959). 'Strategic structures and processes of organizational decision'. In Thompson, J. D., Hammond, P. B., Hawkes, R. W., Jurker, B. H. and Tuden, A. (Eds.), *Comparative Studies in Administration*. Pittsburgh: University of Pittsburgh Press, 195–216.

Part III
Organizational Features

[12]

Human Relations, Volume 40, Number 9, 1987, pp. 613-632

Strategic Decision Making: Influence Patterns in Public and Private Sector Organizations [1]

Graham K. Kenny [2]
San Diego State University

Richard J. Butler and David J. Hickson
University of Bradford

David Cray and Geoffrey R. Mallory
Carleton University

David C. Wilson
University of Warwick

This paper pursues the question of whether differences exist between influence patterns in decision making in public and private sector organizations. Results are reported from an analysis of the interest units appearing in 150 strategic decision-making processes studied in 30 British organizations. We conclude that, while there is an overall similarity in the involvement of types of interest units in the two sectors, there are notable differences in the influence exerted.

INTRODUCTION

Previous empirical studies of influence patterns in organizations have focused upon those units that are internal to an organization (Hinings, Hickson, Pennings, & Schneck, 1974; Salancik & Pfeffer, 1974; Hambrick, 1981) and have not investigated the relative impact of internal vs. external units upon organizational decision making. Further, with the exception of Hambrick

[1] This research was undertaken when all the authors were at the Organizational Analysis Research Unit, Management Centre, University of Bradford, England.
[2] Requests for reprints should be sent to Dr. Graham Kenny, Department of Management, San Diego State University, San Diego, California 92182.

0018-7267/87/0900-0613$05.00/1

(1981), these studies have not considered how these influence patterns might vary by organizational type and environment.

The purpose of the present paper is to extend these previous studies through an investigation of the influence that both internal and external units have upon strategic decision making undertaken in public and private sector organizations. We have chosen to compare organizations in these sectors because of the differences that public ownership may be presumed to make to the patterns of influence (Dewey, 1927; Murray, 1975; Rainey, Backoff, & Levine, 1976). We anticipate differences in the composition as well as the influence of these units in decision making.

THEORETICAL FRAMEWORK

The influence of the environment upon organizational structure and processes has been much emphasized in the literature (Lawrence & Lorsch, 1967; Thompson, 1967; Katz & Kahn, 1978; Aldrich, 1979) such that some authors see environments as potentially controlling organizations (Pfeffer & Salancik, 1978). Subunits and procedures are created to cope with the uncertainties that arise. The strategic contingencies theory (Hickson, Hinings, Lee, Schneck, & Pennings, 1971) argues that this is fundamental to the influence that subunits exert. Thus, Crozier (1964) found in French tobacco factories that the maintenance subunit had power beyond what could be expected from its formal position in the organization. Similarly, from Perrow's (1970) study of industrial firms we see that the sales subunit "dominated" other subunits. The study by Hinings et al. (1974) of manufacturing organizations confirmed that subunits are influential to the extent that they control contingencies that are strategic to the organization of which they are a part.

From this perspective, the internal differentiation of organizations may be seen as a response to uncertainty or other environmental pressures (Thompson, 1967; Lawrence & Lorsch, 1967; Duncan, 1972; Aldrich, 1979). Yet, organizational environments are themselves differentiated. This had led some authors (Pennings & Goodman, 1977; Cameron, 1981; Jobson & Schneck, 1982) to propose that such environments are composed of "strategic constituents" such as customers, owners, and suppliers. Viewed this way, organizational differentiation may be seen as a response to pressure from differentiated constituents within an organization's environment. Thus, we see certain types of organizations paying heed to certain strategic constituents while others do not (Cameron, 1978, 1981; Jobson & Schneck, 1982), and we notice certain types of subunits placing emphasis upon certain strategic constituents while others do not (Hayes, 1977; Hitt & Middlemist, 1979; Kenny & Dunk, 1986). Consequently, variation in the internal differentiation of organizations may be thought of as arising from variation in the external differentiation of organizational environments and from pressure placed upon organizations by the differentiated segments within these environments. Do public and private organizations differ in these regards? There appear to be two lines of argument on this question.

One suggests that there are deep and fundamental differences between organizations in the public and private sectors (Dewey, 1927; Murray, 1975; Rainey et al., 1976). One of these differences is in external control. There are those who argue that public ownership leads to governmental control and that public sector organizations are inevitably more subject to this than are private sector organizations (Dewey, 1927). Thus, the managements of public sector organizations are held more "publicly accountable" (Dahl & Lindblom, 1953; Woll, 1963; Millett, 1966; Golembiewski, 1969; Mainzer, 1973). Rainey et al. (1976) appear to support this when they note that public sector organizations "tend to have their purposes, methods, and spheres of operation defined and constrained by law and legally authorized instructions to a much greater degree" (p. 238) than do private sector organizations. Following the strategic contingencies argument, we could expect the emergence of differences internal to the organizations of both sectors in response to these external differences. Again, Rainey et al. (1976) provide support here when they suggest that "there are a number of propositions to the effect that government (public sector) organizations tend to be characterized by cautiousness, inflexibility, and lack of innovativeness" (p. 241). Thus, public sector organizations may become characterized by formalization (written rules, procedures, instructions, and communications) and centralization (nondelegation of decision making) (Blau & Scott, 1963; Pugh, Hickson, Hinings, & Turner, 1969; Samuel & Mannheim, 1970; Heydebrand, 1973; Holdaway, Newberry, Hickson, & Heron, 1975; Mintzberg, 1979; Rainey, 1983). However, empirical support for how far differences exist in the influence patterns that occur in public sector and private sector organizations is lacking.

There is some support, though not a great deal, for the opposing line of argument, which concludes that public and private sector organizations are basically the same (Murray, 1975; Aharoni & Lachman, 1982; Lachman, 1983). Murray (1975), for instance, concludes that "theoretically similar principles of hierarchical control, comprehensive coordination, the rule of merit and line of authority apply to both the public and private sectors" (pp. 369-370). Similarly, Aharoni and Lachman (1982) conclude that "management is a general process irrespective of the type of organization or its goals" and suggest that in both public and private sector organizations "the undifferentiated managerial orientation. . .may justify and perhaps legitimize executives' uniformity in operation and management practices" (p. 44).

There is an apparent divergence in the conclusions that the two lines of argument reach. It is our purpose in this paper to shed some empirical light on the question of whether differences exist between public and private sector organizations in the patterns of influence exerted on their decisions by both internal and external interest units.

METHOD

Data on the 150 cases of strategic decision processes, which form the empirical base for this study, were collected from 30 British organizations. Five cases were examined in each organization (a full account of further analyses undertaken is given in Hickson, Butler, Cray, Mallory, & Wilson, 1984; Hickson, Butler, Cray, Mallory, & Wilson, 1985). Decisions at this senior executive strategic level are crucial to the future state of an organization since they involve considerable resource commitment and risk (Mintzberg, Raisinghani, & Theoret, 1976; Butler, Astley, Hickson, Mallory, & Wilson, 1979; Hage, 1980). During the process of making such decisions, therefore, a wide range of interest units will be drawn in, both internal and external to an organization.

Selection inevitably depended on cooperation as the managements approached had to be willing to give considerable information about specific instances of decision-making processes. The organizations were first approached by letter. Of those approached, two-thirds eventually agreed to cooperate. Organization sizes ranged from 100 employees to over 50,000. Many were national and international leaders in the public and private sectors, and almost all were of considerable prominence. Data collection took place from 1974–1980 but was concentrated from 1978–1980. The shortest decision was one that was rushed through a polytechnic in approximately 1 month, the longest decision, in a private manufacturer, took over 4 years to process.

In each of three organizations, a utility, a university, and a manufacturer, two decisions were studied in a greater depth by intensive case study methods, and these helped to develop concepts and data collection methods. They are reported in Wilson (1980, 1982).

An initial interview as conducted with the chief executive about the history of the organization, its outputs and structure, and its relation to other organizations. He thought back over major decisions, those that had widespread consequences for the organization, and after discussion five of these were chosen to include as far as possible one each concerning inputs, outputs, core technology, personnel, and reorganization. Not every organization had made within recall a strategic decision in every one of these areas, but all were well represented overall (Hickson et al., 1986). They had to have occurred sufficiently recently to be within the recall of executives who were still with the organization and who could talk about what had happened from personal experience.

For each of the five decisions, the chief executive suggested principal informants who had been central to the decision process. Examples of informants are managing directors and directors in firms, vice-chancellors and deans in universities, management team members in hospital districts, and chief officers in local government.

The research interviews centered on one or more of these "key witness" informants, with other managers and administrators informally enlarging upon what the principal informant(s) could say. After recounting the story of the decision chronologically, informants were asked to pick out those internal and external interest units that had been involved. Internal departments and sections by whatever name became involved in many ways, and some more, some less. For example, in industry, sales departments prepare surveys, accounting departments supply cost estimates, research and development committees make recommendations, and the personnel managers talk to the managing director about morale. In a health service district, doctors from different hospitals sit on a committee with nursing, medical ancillary, and administrative representatives, and each argues their case. External organizations may become involved because they are suppliers who are telephoned to see if they can make a component for a new product, or because they are major customers who are asked whether they will order the new product if it is launched, or because as trade unions or banks or government departments they are concerned with what is to be done.

Interest units were counted as involved if mentioned by informants as being so. Units were specified departments or other organizations (usually named) except in a handful of instances where an informant wished to include "competitors" or "customers/clients" generally.

Internal units and external organizations were categorized by the research team into 14 types plus general management, e.g., chief executive, according to their interest in the decision-making process and its outcome (see Table I). The types were grouped into "internal," "external," and "general management." The classification of the internal units originates in the systems model of Katz and Kahn (1978), and follows the units extant interests that arise from their function within the organization. These interests are shown in Table I along with typical interest units. For example, production and equivalent workflow departments are typical of those units whose interest in the decision-making processes in the organizations studied was in the "transformation" of an input to an output. Similarly, the interests of external organizations such as suppliers, or customers, or government departments arise from their function in relation to the organization in which the decision is being made.

Principal informants rated the influence on the decision of each internal and external interest unit on a 5-point scale from 1, "little influence," to 5, "a very great deal of influence." These were not generalized abstract

Table I. Classification of Interest Units

Typical interest unit	Primary interest
Internal	
Production and equivalent "workflow" departments	Transformation
Maintenance, personnel, etc.	Stability
Accounting, quality control, and inspection	Conformity
Compliants and claims departments	Adjudication
Research and design departments	Innovation
Purchasing	Acquisition
Sales and marketing	Domain
Self-sufficient divisions, etc.	Autonomy/devolution
External	
Supplier firms	Inputs
Customers and clients	Outputs
Trades unions	Employment
Government departments and agencies	Public standards
Auditors, trade associations, and shareholders	Private standards
Competitors	Comparative performance
General management	
Chief executive and policy committees	Direction and coordination

ratings, but assessments of the influence exerted by those subjected to it during a specified decision-making process that had been freshly brought to mind.

The 150 decisions were classified into eight topics types (Table II). Decisions concerned with supplies and finance, for example, were classified as

Table II. Decisions and Organizations Studied

	N
Decisions[a]	
Organization (internal reorganizations, mergers, and takeovers)	33
Outputs (new products or services)	28
Equipment/plant (major re-equippings and factory expansions)	23
Control/planning (business plans, budgets, and major data processing rearrangements)	19
Domain (market segmentations, price, and image)	18
Personnel (grading schemes, productivity deals, and employment policies)	12
Inputs (financial sources, supplies, and suppliers)	9
Location (re-siting head offices and overseas operations)	8
Total	150
Organizations[b]	
Public sector organizations (local government, universities, health service districts, airways, utilities, chemical manufacture, and earthmoving equipment)	13
Private sector organizations (banks, housing finance corporation, insurance, trucking, metal components, glass, chemicals, and breweries)	17
Total	30

[a]The strategic decisions studied were classified under eight topics (examples of particular decisions are in parentheses).

[b]Five decisions were studied in each of 30 organizations (examples of particular organizations are given in parentheses.

"inputs" topics, those decisions concerned with new products and services were classified as "outputs," and those concerning with markets and prices were classified as "domain" topics. Decisions concerned with throughputs and control were variously classified as "equipment/plant," "personnel," and "control/planning," and those concerning restructuring or site were classified as "organization," e.g., reorganization and amalgamation, and "location," e.g., relocation of factory or administrative headquarters.

Of the 30 organizations from which the 150 cases were drawn, 13 were public sector and 17 were private sector. They ranged from universities and districts of the health service and nationalized industries in the public sector, to financial service and manufacturing firms in the private sector (Table II).

The public sector organizations were constituted under state ownership in a variety of ways, all of which allowed their managements to make strategic decisions. This can be seen in Table III where the cases in the public sector cover the same topics as those in the private sector.

RESULTS

Pervasive Involvement

Table IV presents the results for the pervasive involvement of types of interest units across the range of decision topics researched for both private and public sector organizations. Pervasive involvement is indicated for each interest unit type by calculating the mean number of involvements by units of that type of interest (Table I) in all the decisions in each of the eight categories of decision topics (Table II), and then taking the mean of the eight means. Taking the mean of the means dampens down any effects due to there being varying numbers of decisions from one category of topic to another, and indicates the extent to which each type of interest is involved across the array of decision topics. Hence, the use of the term "pervasive."

Table III. Number of Decision Topics: Private and Public Sectors

	Number	
Decision topic	Private	Public
Organization	18	15
Outputs	16	12
Domain	13	5
Control/planning	11	8
Equipment/plant	11	12
Inputs	7	2
Personnel	5	7
Location	4	4
Total	85	65

Table IV. Involvement of Interest Units: Private and Public Sectors

Typical interest unit[a]	Involvement (mean, rank in parentheses)[b] Private	Public
Accounting, quality control, and inspection (conformity)	1.24 (1)	1.43 (1)
Production and equivalent "workflow" departments (transformation)	0.91 (2)	0.75 (4)
Auditors, trade associations, and shareholders (private standards)	0.81 (3)	0.48 (5)
Sales and marketing (domain)	0.64 (4)	0.15 (11)
Supplier firms (inputs)	0.57 (5)	0.45 (6)
Maintenance and personnel, etc. (stability)	0.47 (6)	0.28 (7)
Government departments and agencies (public standards)	0.43 (7)	1.14 (2)
Customers and clients (outputs)	0.39 (8)	0.14 (12)
Self-sufficient divisions, etc. (autonomy/devolution)	0.37 (9)	0.87 (3)
Competitors (comparative performance)	0.21 (10)	0.24 (8)
Trades unions (employment)	0.20 (11)	0.23 (9)
Research and design departments (innovation)	0.17 (12)	0.09 (13)
Purchasing (acquisition)	0.14 (13)	0.06 (14)
Complaints and claims departments (adjudication)	0.08 (14)	0.20 (10)
Overall involvements	6.63	6.51

[a]External interest units underlined, primary interests in parentheses.
[b]Rank correlation coefficient = 0.64, which is significant at the 0.05 level.

Although the table contains some differences in the placings of certain interest units, overall there is considerable similarity between both sets of rankings ($r = 0.64, p < 0.05$). This supports the argument presented earlier (Murray, 1975; Aharoni & Lachman, 1982) that the involvement of interest units in the organizations of both sectors is similar. Irrespective of ownership there is a degree of bureaucratic homogeneity whereby the range of interest units (both internal and external) that becomes involved in decision is independent of organization type in ownership terms.

However, in spite of this overall similarity there are notable individual differences. The most noteworthy differences between the public and private-sectors is in the rankings for the interest category "government departments and agencies." Ranked seventh in the data for the private sector organizations and second in the data for the public sector organizations, these interest units become much more involved in strategic decision making in public sector organizations than in private sector organizations. This concurs with much of the literature on this issue, which suggests that public ownership does oblige managers to advise, to consult, and to seek assistance from departments of state much more often and, thereby, to submit to their scrutiny (Dahl & Lindblom, 1953; Woll, 1963; Millett, 1966; Golembiewski, 1969; Mainzer, 1973; Rainey et al., 1976).

Table V. Influence of Interest Units: Private and Public Sectors

Typical Interest Unit[a]	Influence (mean, rank in parentheses)[b] Private	Public
Sales and marketing (domain)	3.44 (1)	2.92 (4)
Production and equivalent "workflow" departments (transformation)	3.02 (2)	3.28 (3)
Customers and clients (outputs)	3.01 (3)	2.92 (4)
Government departments and agencies (public standards)	3.01 (3)	2.44 (8)
Accounting, quality control, and inspection (conformity)	2.96 (5)	2.27 (7)
Auditors, trade associations, and shareholders (private standards)	2.93 (6)	1.84 (13)
Purchasing (acquisition)	2.83 (7)	1.75 (14)
Supplier firms (inputs)	2.76 (8)	1.98 (12)
Self-sufficient divisions, etc. (autonomy/devolution)	2.68 (9)	3.30 (2)
Research, design departments (innovation)	2.65 (10)	2.00 (11)
Competitors (comparative performance)	2.59 (11)	2.13 (10)
Maintenance, personnel, etc. (stability)	2.52 (12)	2.80 (6)
Complaints and claims departments (adjudication)	2.50 (13)	3.69 (1)
Trades unions (employment)	1.55 (14)	2.19 (9)
Overall mean	2.75	2.57

[a]External interest units underlined, primary interests in parentheses.
[b]Rank correlation coefficient = 0.10, which is not significant.

However, both public and private sector organizations are subject to pressures from regulatory agencies, whether these are governmental in nature such as the factory inspectorate, or are independent professional bodies (as in accounting and medicine). This shows clearly in the continual involvement of "accounting, quality control, and inspection," whose interest is in conformity to financial, quality, and safety standards in decision making in *both* sectors.

Pervasive Influence

Table V shows the pervasive influence of interest unit types, again comparing decisions in private and public sector organizations. Because of the relatively low number of influence ratings on some decision topics, the eight categories of topic were collapsed to four. Inputs, equipment/plant, and personnel all became "input" decisions, control/planning became "throughput" decisions, outputs and domains all became "output" decisions, and location and organization became "organizational" decisions. The mean of the influence ratings of units of each type of interest (Table I) for each of these four categories of decision topic was calculated, and then the mean of the four means was taken. This again minimizes any effects due to there being varying numbers of decisions from one category of topic to another, and indicates how far the influence of each type of interest pervades decision making across all kinds of topics, hence, the use of the term "pervasive" once more.

The notion of pervasive influence can be seen, either implicitly or explicitly, in several previous studies. In Perrow's (1970) comparison of subunit influence, a measure of influence was sought that was nonspecific to decision topics. Thus, when Perrow reports that sales is dominantly influential, this is across a range of unspecified decision topics. More recently, in Hambrick (1981), we see an investigation of influence "over the full array of strategic decisions that an organization faces" (p. 262). Hambrick specifically averages functional executives' influence over four decision topics. The existence of what we call "influence extension," i.e., the extension of an interest unit's influence beyond its functional domain, was also noted by Hinings et al. (1974), wherein production departments especially were found to have considerable influence over a range of decision topics beyond those that were *prima facie* their concern.

There are major differences between the private sector and public sector organizations in the influence exerted by types of interest, whereas with the involvement of interest units, the overall patterns were similar. The rank order correlation between the pervasive influence means in Table V is a mere nonsignificant 0.,10. There are differences due to ownership and, at the same time, an apparently dissimilar overall response to environment.

In both private and public sectors, the internal scales and equivalent departments, as well as the customers and clients with which they deal, jump up Table V as compared to Table IV. In influence, they are first and joint third, respectively, in the prviate organizations in Table V, and jointly fourth in the public organizations. This means that, although they are not involved in every decision, when they are involved their influence is considerable. This seems to be so whether an organization is publicly owned or privately owned. In other words, this is a clear indication that organizations can be market responsive irrespective of their ownership. Even in public sector organizations the making of major decisions is heavily influenced by customer or client considerations. In those that are substantially customer funded, such as public utilities that charge for energy supplies, or public industries that sell their manufactures, this may be especially so; but, after all, universities continually change their range of degree courses in response to student demand, and hospitals adopt new ways of dealing with the diseases of the day. State ownership does not stop an organization responding to the influence of those whose demands it serves and on whom it depends (Pfeffer & Salancik, 1978). Customer and clients are more pervasively involved in the affairs of private organizations, it is true (Table IV), but when involved in public organizations they are quite influential (Table V).

As expected, the differentiating effects of ownership on the source of external control (Rainey et al., 1976; Rainey, 1983) make for pronounced differences in pervasive influence. Predictably, auditors, trade associations, and shareholders exert much greater influence on private sector than public sector organizations (ranked, respectively, sixth and thirteenth). In private firms, the financial checks made by auditors are routine, but nevertheless on occasion the standards they embody do influence what is decided. Similarly, the demands of shareholders for dividends and growth are recurrent and in that sense routine, but on occasion they can be paramount, as in takeover bids and major financial restructurings.

In the public sector organizations, the most immediately obvious feature of Table V is that "adjudication" interest units, the complaints and claims departments as they are called, leap to first place on influence as compared to their tenth place on involvement (whereas in the private sector organizations there is no such shift in ranking). This implies that in those situations where they are involved they can be crucial. Essentially, in the public sector organizations the cases in point are of committees rather than departments as such, committees that "adjudicate" insofar as they determine resource allocations or critical policies. For example, a university development committee heavily influenced a budget decision, and a health service district priorities committee heavily influenced the allocation of equipment and personnel.

The most surprising feature of Table V is the low influence of government departments and agencies in *public* sector decision making. These government units are only eighth of 14 interests in influence. Since the ideological underpinning to public ownership is the assumption that it confers influence on the major topics that come up for decision, it is startling to find no overt evidence for this. Indeed, rather the opposite, for the government units exert greater influence, if anything, on decisions in private sector organizations. While too much should not be made of small differences in averages, nevertheless the result is provoking. Is government in Britain out of control of its own?

Not entirely, of course. First, it should be recalled that Table IV showed high government involvement. That is, government is more involved than influential. To put it another way, government departments and the like are often involved in public sector decision making, but when involved they are not outstanding influential. Even so, this modicum of governmental influence is frequently exerted, and moreover, there is a small number of particular circumstances when state intervention is more decisive (see Hickson et al., 1986).

Second, directly exerted influence as reported by public sector managers is unlikely to be the whole story. Much state power is enshrined in taken-for-granted regulations and rules of conduct (Clegg, 1975) by which public sector managements abide at a level that is semi-unawareness. Thus, the influence of government in private sector decision making may be more direct and, therefore, more often reported in the recall of decision-making processes, whereas in the public sector it is less overt, more latent.

Having recognized that, it remains undeniable that this result questions the power of the state to affect managerial choices in the organizations the state itself owns, and calls for further research on exactly what influence it does exert and when.

Trade unions fare a little better in the state-owned sector (nineth place in the public sector ranking in Table V as compared to bottom place, fourteenth, in the private sector ranking), but they are nowhere a real force to be reckoned with during the making of strategic decisions as distinct from the implementation of such decisions (see also Wilson, Butler, Cray, Hickson, & Mallory, 1982; Hickson et al., 1986).

Differences between Decision Topics

The research focused upon not only the involvement and influence of interest units in public and private sector organizations, but it also investigated differences between decision topics. Some topics involve many interest units while others involve comparatively few. Some are heavily influenced, others less so.

Very little has been written on which decision topics involve most interests, and on which topics are subject to most influence or "pressure" (as indicated by the mean of the influence ratings of all interest units in decision cases in any one topic category). There has been no empirical study that has specifically covered this, although Comstock (1980) has examined what we call pressure in order to assess decision importance. Comstock defines, in our terms, high pressure decisions as organizationally important decisions.

Table VI shows the results on involvement for the eight categories of decision topics included in this paper. Of overall interest is the lack of correspondence in the rankings of topics for the private and public sector organizations ($r = -0.01$). This indicates that there is a general disparity in the mean number of interest units drawn into particular decision topics in private and public sector organizations. Of special interest here are the organizational decisions topics, i.e., "location" and "organization," since it is these that set the context for other strategic decisions. In Table VI these are ranked, respectively, first and second in the public sector organizations, and fifth and eighth (last) in the private sector organizations. This illustrates

Table VI. Involvement by Decision Topic: Private and Public Sectors

Decision Topic	Involvement (mean, rank in parentheses)[a,b]	
	Private	Public
Equipment/plant	8.55 (1)	7.00 (4)
Outputs	8.06 (2)	7.83 (3)
Control/planning	7.18 (3)	6.63 (5)
Personnel	6.40 (4)	4.29 (7)
Inputs	6.00 (5)	3.50 (8)
Location	6.00 (5)	8.25 (1)
Domain	5.62 (7)	6.60 (6)
Organization	5.17 (8)	8.07 (2)
Total	6.62	6.52

[a]Involvement includes internal and external interest units.
[b]Rank correlation coefficient = −0.01, which is not significant.

the widely held view that these most critical decisions of all draw in a larger set of interests in public sector organizations where the form of the organization itself and its siting are exceptionally political issues. In private sector organizations, it is decisions on outputs and equipment that come first and second, demonstrating the greater attention paid to these.

Table VII shows that, while there is some accordance between the private and public sector organizations in the rankings of the pressure exerted on the decision topics, this agreement is not total ($r = 0.44$, not significant). To adopt Comstock's (1980) terminology, this result suggests that there are organizational dissimilarities in the "importance" of decision topics between public and private sectors.

The identical first and second places of location and control decisions are striking. Because these affect a range of interest units, they are the focus

Table VII. Pressure by Decision Topic: Private and Public Sectors

Decision topic	Pressure (mean, rank in parentheses)[a,b]	
	Private	Public
Location	3.75 (1)	2.97 (1)
Control/planning	2.99 (2)	2.94 (2)
Domain	2.92 (3)	2.88 (5)
Inputs	2.86 (4)	1.57 (8)
Organization	2.85 (5)	2.90 (4)
Outputs	2.84 (6)	2.80 (6)
Equipment/plant	2.84 (6)	2.94 (2)
Personnel	2.63 (8)	2.57 (7)
Total	2.96	2.70

[a]Pressure includes internal and external interest units.
[b]Rank correlation coefficient = 0.44, which is not significant.

of considerable influence irrespective of the organization in which they occur and even though fewer interest units are involved in these decisions in the private sector. Few are not concerned sooner or later with whether to move company or corporate headquarters, and with the implications of where to place a major new plant. Few escape the consequences of controls decisions, i.e., plant and budgets. So, there are many influences upon the choices.

"Organization" decisions are ranked fifth in the private sector organizations and fourth in the public sector organizations. These relatively low rankings are surprising as higher rankings could have been anticipated in both systems for decisions to reorganize. However, a closer inspection of the results shows that, in the case of the public sector organizations, very little separates the highest ranking (2.97) from the fourth ranking (2.90), so at least in public sector organizations the organization decision seems to be regarded as "important" (Comstock, 1980) as well as highly involving. This claim cannot be made in the case of private sector organizations. The highest ranked decision topic, location, at 3.75 seems appreciably distanced from the organization decision topic, which is fifth ranked and rated at 2.85.

CONCLUSIONS

This research suggests a way of comparing the decision-making processes that occur in private and public sector organizations. It suggests a classification of decision topics (we used eight for this study) and a classification of interest units (we used 14). These classifications permit a comparison between organizations of diverse interest units and decision topics. Although their surface differences, including nomenclature, are at first sight wide from one form of organization to another, they can be classified and compared in terms of their function-derived interests.

This approach has also made it possible to encompass both internal and external interest units. Past studies of influence patterns (Hinings et al., 1974; Salancik & Pfeffer, 1974; Hambrick, 1981) have focused upon internal interest units only. This has been in part because such studies have been grounded in the strategic contingencies theory of Hickson et al. (1971) and have been very much concerned with testing this theory. It specifies the conditions under which internal interest units accrue power by coping with environmental contingencies. While there has been an historical development of ideas along this line, there has been no similar development of ideas regarding external influence *conjointly* with internal influence in organizations. Maybe this is one reason for the lack of empirical attention to this issue. It might also account for the lack of empirical attention given to comparisons of interests between organizations in the public and private sectors.

This paper takes up the issue of whether differences do or do not exist between private and public sector organizations. Our evidence suggests that, while there is an appreciable similarity in the pattern of pervasive involvement of interest units, a bureaucratic homogeneity that pervades both sets of organizations within this overall similarity, some interesting exceptions occur (Murray, 1975; Aharoni & Lachman, 1982; Lachman, 1983). Government departments and agencies are more highly involved in public sector decisions than in private sector decisions.

Being involved in a decision is not the same as being influential. A particular example is the "accounting, quality control, and inspection" units, which were the most highly involved in both sets of organizations but were only moderately influential. It will be recalled that, although there was an appreciable relationship between the rank ordering of private and public sector organizations on involvement of interest units, there was no significant relationship between the rank ordering on influence.

We suggest that an interest unit, once involved, will be influential over a decision topic in proportion to the criticality of the resources supplied by it relative to the criticality of the resources supplied by other involved interest units (Kenny & Wilson, 1984; Wilson & Kenny, 1985). Thus, influence is more difficult to predict than is involvement. However, on the basis of this argument we would expect the result we have observed for sales and marketing, which was more influential in private sector organizations than in public sector organizations, and for the complaints and claims departments that were more influential in the public sector organizations. Two unanticipated results occur with customers and clients, and government departments and agencies. Both are external interest units. Is there something peculiar in the situation of external interest units to produce these effects? We can only speculate on this score, but we think yes. In the case of customers and clients we suspect that their influence is limited to specific decision topics that they are "invited" to influence. On the other hand, in the case of their internal counterparts, sales and marketing, their influence is more extensive across decision topics as they are part of the internal organization system. After all, customers and clients are unlikely to be influential over decisions beyond those on the outputs of the organizations concerned. Because for the private sector organizations customers and clients pose a greater strategic contingency than they do for public sector organizations, those internal interest units that cope with this contingency are more pervasively influential. The customers and clients themselves, however, are no more influential in private than in public organizations.

In the case of government departments and agencies we find what appears to be an anomaly in that they are more pervasively influential in private sector organizations than in the public sector organizations that they own.

Are government departments and agencies a special case? We suspect, and we can put it no stronger, that managers in the public sector may tend to underestimate the influence of government departments and agencies since their influence is enshrined in rules and regulations and taken-for-granted codes of conduct (Clegg, 1975) and, therefore, not so manifest sanctions of function and of legal enactment. In contrast, the influence of government departments and agencies is more overt in private sector boundaries, i.e., from the public into the private sectors. Thus, government departments and agencies are ranked relatively higher on direct influence in private sector organizations than in public sector organizations.

The primary question pursued in this study has been: are public sector and private sector organizations similar in the pattern of involvement and influence of different internal and external interests in their decision making? We conclude that there is a degree of basic similarity or "bureaucratic homogeneity" between organizations in function-derived involvement, which affirms the views of Murray (1975) and Aharoni and Lachman (1982), even though within this there are some marked differences. But, as we said earlier, being involved is not the same as being influential. There are types of interest units that, although involved at some stage or stages in decision making, exert little influence upon it, and others that, although rarely involved, are highly influential when that involvement occurs. There are greater differences here between public sector and private sector organizations. Hence, while the "bureaucratic homogeneity" of public and private organizations produces a similarity of interest-unit involvement in strategic decision making, ownership appears to change the pattern of influence exerted.

REFERENCES

AHARONI, Y., & LACHMAN, R. Can the manager's mind be nationalized? *Organization Studies,* 1982, *3,* 33-46.

ALDRICH, H. E. *Organizations and environments.* Englewood Cliffs, Prentice-Hall, 1979.

BLAU, P. M., & SCOTT, W. R. *Formal organizations.* London: Routledge and Kegan Paul, 1963.

BUTLER, R. J., ASTLEY, W. G., HICKSON, D. J., MALLORY, G. R., & WILSON, D. C. Strategic decision-making: Concepts of content and process. *International Studies of Management and Organization,* 1979, *9,* 5-36.

CAMERON, K. S. Measuring organizational effectiveness in institutions of higher education. *Administrative Science Quarterly,* 1978, *23,* 604-632.

CAMERON, K. S. Domains of organizational effectiveness in colleges and universities. *Academy of Management Journal,* 1981, *24,* 25-47.

CLEGG, S. *Power, rule and domination.* London: Routledge and Kegan Paul, 1975.

COMSTOCK, D. E. Dimensions of influence in organizations. *Pacific Sociological Review,* 1980, *23,* 67-84.

CROZIER, M. *The bureaucratic phenomenon.* Chicago: University of Chicago Press, 1964.

DAHL, R. A., & LINDBLOM, C. D. *Politics, economics and welfare.* New York: Harper and Row, 1953.

DEWEY, J. *The public and its problems.* New York: Swallow, 1927.

DUNCAN, R. B. Characteristics of organizational environments and perceived environmental uncertainty. *Administrative Science Quarterly,* 1972, *17,* 313-327.

GOLEMBIEWSKI, R. T. Organization development in public agencies: Perceptives on theory and practices. *Public Administration Review,* 1969, *29,* 367-368.

HAGE, J. *Theories of organizations: Form, process and transformation.* New York: Wiley, 1980.

HAMBRICK, D. C. Environment, strategy and power within top management teams. *Administrative Science Quarterly,* 1981, *26,* 253-276.

HAYES, D. C. The contingency theory of managerial accounting. *The Accounting Review,* 1977, *52,* 22-39.

HEYDEBRAND, W. V. Autonomy, complexity, and non-bureaucratic coordination in professional organizations. In W. V. Heyderbrand (Ed.), *Comparative organizations: The results of empirical research.* Englewood Cliffs: Prentice-Hall, 1973, pp. 158-189.

HICKSON, D. J., HININGS, C. R., LEE, C. A., SCHNECK, R. E., & PENNINGS, J. M. A strategic contingencies theory of intraorganizational power. *Administrative Science Quarterly,* 1971, *16,* 216-229.

HICKSON, D. J., BUTLER, R. J., CRAY, D., MALLORY, G. R., & WILSON, D. C. Comparing one hundred and fifty decision processes. In J. M. Pennings (Ed.), *Organizational strategy and change.* San Francisco: Jossey-Bass, 1984.

HICKSON, D. J., BUTLER, R. J., CRAY, D., MALLORY, G. R., & WILSON, D. C. *Top decisions: Strategic decision-making in organizations.* San Francisco: Jossey-Bass, and Oxford: Blackwells, 1986.

HININGS, C. R., HICKSON, D. J., PENNINGS, J. M., & SCHNECK. R. E. Structural conditions of intraorganizational power. *Administrative Science Quarterly,* 1974, *19,* 22-24.

HITT, M. A., & MIDDLEMIST, R. D. A methodology to develop the criteria weightings for assessing subunit effectiveness in organizations. *Academy of Management Journal,* 1979, *22,* 356-374.

HOLDAWAY, E. A., NEWBERRY, J. F., HICKSON, D. J., & HERON, R. P. Dimensions of organizations in complex societies: The educational sector. *Administrative Science Quarterly,* 1975, *20,* 37-58.

JOBSON, J. D., & SCHNECK, R. Constituent views of organizational effectiveness: Evidence from police organizations. *Academy of Management Journal,* 1982, *25,* 25-46.

KATZ, D., & KAHN, R. L. *The social psychology of organizations.* New York: Wiley, 1978.

KENNY, G. K., & DUNK, A. S. Evaluative differences for production and marketing subunits: Australian managers' perceptions. *Asia Pacific Journal of Management,* 1986, *3,* 99-109.

KENNY, G. K., & WILSON, D. C. The interdepartmental influence of managers: Individual and subunit perspectives. *Journal of Management Studies,* 1984, *21,* 409-427.

LACHMAN, R. Perception of role-environment among public and private sector executives. *Academy of Management Proceedings,* 1983.

LAWRENCE, P. R., & LORSCH, J. W. *Organization and environment.* Homewood: Irwin, 1967.

MAINZER, L. C. *Political bureaucracy.* Glenview: Scott, Foresman, 1973.

MILLETT, J. D. *Organization for the public purpose.* Princeton: Van Nostrand, 1966.

MINTZBERG, H. *The structuring of organizations.* Englewood Cliffs: Prentice-Hall, 1979.

MINTZBERG, H., RAISINGHANI, D., & THEORET, A. The structure of "unstructured" decision processes. *Administrative Science Quarterly,* 1976, *21,* 246-275.

MURRAY, M. A. Comparing public and private management: An exploratory study. *Public Administration Review,* 1975, *35,* 364-371.

PENNINGS, J. M., & GOODMAN, P. S. Toward a workable framework. In P. S. Goodman and J. M. Pennings (Ed.), *New perspectives in organizational effectiveness.* San Francisco: Jossey-Bass, 1977, pp. 146-184.

PERROW, C. Departmental power and perspectives in industrial firms. In M. N. Zald (Ed.), *Power in organizations.* Nashville: Vanderbilt University Press, 1970, pp. 59-89.

PFEFFER, J., & SALANCIK, G. R. *The external control of organizations.* New York: Harper and Row, 1978.

PUGH, D. S., HICKSON, D. J., HININGS, C. R., & TURNER, C. The context of organization structures. *Administrative Science Quarterly,* 1969, *14,* 91-114.

RAINEY, H. G. Public agencies and private firms: Incentive structures, goals and individual roles. *Administration and Society,* 1983, *15,* 207-242.

RAINEY, H. G., BACKOFF, R. W., & LEVINE, C. H. Comparing public and private organizations. *Public Administration Review,* 1976, *36,* 233-244.

SALANCIK, G. R., & PFEFFER, J. The bases and use of power in organizational decision-making: The case of a university. *Administrative Science Quarterly,* 1974, *19,* 453-473.

SAMUEL, Y., & MANNHEIM, B. F. A multidimensional approach toward a typology of bureaucracy. *Administrative Science Quarterly,* 1970, *15,* 216-228.

THOMPSON, J. D. *Organizations in action.* New York: McGraw-Hill, 1967.

WILSON, D. C. *Organizational strategy.* Unpublished doctoral dissertation, University of Bradford, 1980.

WILSON, D. C. Electricity and resistance: A case study of innovation and politics. *Organizations Studies,* 1982, *3,* 119-140.

WILSON, D. C., & KENNY, G. K. Managerially perceived influence over intradepartmental decisions. *Journal of Management Studies,* 1985, *22,* 155-174.

WILSON, D. C., BUTLER, R. J., CRAY, D., HICKSON, D. J., & MALLORY, G. R. The limits of trade union power in organizational decision making. *British Journal of Industrial Relations,* 1982, *XX,* 322-341.

WOLL, P. *American bureaucracy.* New York: Norton, 1963.

BIOGRAPHICAL NOTES

GRAHAM K. KENNY is Visiting Professor in the Department of Management at San Diego State University. In 1978 he received a PhD in Management from the University of New South Wales, Australia. The focus of his research interests is upon organizational decision making which leads him to take interests in influence patterns in organizations and the decentralization of decision making. He teaches business strategy and organization design.

RICHARD J. BUTLER is Senior Lecturer in Organizational Analysis at the Management Centre, University of Bradford, England. He received his BSc in 1962 from the University of Southamptom in Engineering and spent a number of years working in industry as an engineer. He then received his MSc in 1968 from the Loughborough University of Technology in Management Studies and his PhD in 1973 from the Graduate School of Management at Northwestern University in Organizational Behavior.

DAVID CRAY is Assistant Professor of Human Resource Management in the School of Business at Carleton University, Ottawa, Canada. He received his BA from New College and his MS and PhD from the University of Wisconsin, all in Sociology. He is currently involved in studies of the allocation of control between Canadian subsidiaries and their American parents and the impact of new data-handling techniques on decision making in the pension fund industry.

DAVID J. HICKSON is Professor of International Management, formerly of Organizational Analysis, at the University of Bradford Management Centre, England. He qualified professionally as a corporation administrator (ACIS) in 1954 and in personnel management (AIPM) in 1958. He received a master's degree by research (MSc Tech) from the University of Manchester Institute of Science and Technology in 1960, and in 1974 he was awarded an honorary doctoral degree by the University of Umea, Sweden. His primary research has centered on the structures of organizations, intraorganizational power, and the processes of strategic decision making. He is Editor in Chief of *Organization Studies.*

GEOFFREY R. MALLORY is Assistant Professor of Human Resource Management in the School of Business at Carleton University in Ottawa, Canada. He received his BSc in 1975 from the University of Bradford and his MA in 1976 from the University of Leeds, and he is currently completing a PhD thesis at Bradford on speed of decision making.

DAVID C. WILSON is Lecturer in Organizational Behaviour in the School of Industrial and Business Studies at the University of Warwick, England. He is currently conducting research into the strategies and structures of British voluntary organizations. He is a member of the European Group for Organizational Studies (EGOS) and is also editorial assistant of *Organization Studies*. He received his BA in 1974 and MA in 1975 from the University of Leeds in Management Studies and his PhD in 1980 from the University of Bradford in Organizational Strategy.

[13]

Governmental Influence Upon Decision Making in Organizations in the Private and Public Sectors in Britain

David J. Hickson in association with Richard J. Butler, David Cray, Geoffrey R. Mallory and David C. Wilson

Introduction

The 20th century is remarkable for many things, not the least among them being the attempts by governments from East and West, from North and South, to control economies. Some succeed sometimes, some succeed hardly at all. In Europe, the sharpest divide is between the varieties of direct control practised in the East, and the varieties of indirect control practised in the West. But the aim of governments on both sides of this sad divide is to influence the managements of organizations.

Usually this is discussed in the West in terms of generalized policies such as taxation policy or export subsidies or market protectionism, and of generalized indicators such as inflation rates or balances of payments or government borrowing. Much less is known, often nothing is known, of how government influence – if any – is brought to bear. How is it done?

To go to the heart of the matter requires investigating whether or not managements are affected in what they do by government and its agencies. That means getting beneath the abstractions about state and economy to ask whether or not major strategic decisions by managers and administrators are influenced. And are these decisions influenced more in some organizations than in others, notably in the government's own public sector organizations as compared to the "free" enterprise private sector organizations? It is these critical decisions which in the aggregate determine what the condition of the economy shall be.

The Bradford studies of strategic decision-making in organizations were designed on a large scale to analyse types of decision process, and explain the differences between types by features of the decision and the organization. They include information on the influence exerted by all interests on each decision studied. These interests are both internal, such as the sales (and equivalent), finance, and research departments; and external such as suppliers or trade associations or trades unions (the influence of unions is analysed in detail in Wilson et al., 1982).

A quite unanticipated by-product of the research was information on the influence exerted on strategic decisions by government departments and agencies, as reported by the top managers and administrators who had experienced it. This paper examines that influence, based on extracts from the full accounts of the Bradford studies published elsewhere (Hickson et al., 1984, 1986).

Sample and Data Collection

A data base was built up of 150 cases of strategic decision-making obtained by interviewing, and six of the same cases traced by intensive case-study methods. Data collection, all in Britain, took place from 1974 to 1980, especially in the years 1977 to 1980. The decision-making processes described often reached back in their origins, and most were concluded by the time of the data collection, so that they occurred over periods from the mid 1960s to the late 1970s.

Organizations were first approached by a letter to the chief executive, supplemented by telephone calls as necessary. Of those approached, two thirds, that is 30 organizations, cooperated. They range in size from 100 to over 50 000 employees; there are 17 privately owned (manufacturers, financial institutions, road transport etc.), and 13 publicly (state) owned (health service districts, universities, utilities etc.); there are 11 manufacturing (metal components, glass, chemicals, breweries) and 19 service (banking, insurance, airways, local government etc.). Most were relatively prominent, a large proportion being national or international leaders in the private or public sectors and household names, which prevents publication of some details in case histories. They were taken from published directories with the aim of getting as even a coverage as possible over a selection matrix which offset private and public ownership categories against manufacturing and services categories to reflect as far as practicable the diversity of contemporary organizations. However, the resulting set of organizations depended upon personal managerial collaboration because those at the top who were centrally involved in cases of decision-making had to be willing to give considerable information about decisions that to them were still important and had occurred sufficiently recently to be readily recalled. They also had to be willing and able to give time to researchers. As in all this sort of research, any biases introduced by self-selection are beyond knowing.

In an initial interview the chief executive reviewed the history of the organization, its outputs and basic structure, and external relationships. He was asked to nominate major decisions involving more than just one department or section and with widespread effects, five of which were chosen to include when possible one each concerning inputs, outputs, core technology, personnel and reorganization, but there was no hard and fast sticking to these categories.

Centrally involved 'eye-witness' informants were then interviewed about each case, for example managing directors and function directors in firms, vice-chancellors and deans in universities, management team members in health districts, and chief officers in local government. Since what was wanted was information about *processes* of decision-making which take place at top managerial levels, middle management or lower employees or unions were not approached as they would know nothing first hand of the inner workings at this level. Interviewees were informants giving information about events, not respondents talking about themselves; each was interviewed at length, often more than once. There was an average of six informants per organization; in one third of the cases there were two or more informants but when the direct account was from one informant only, then as otherwise many interviews were joined by managerial colleagues who were asked to come in and add to what the informant(s) could say.

Each interview began with an historical narrative of the sequence of events as they unfolded. This was followed by numerous open-ended questions about particular aspects of the story which led the informant to elaborate on certain features of what had happened, seven of which were then in addition rated on five point scales (for example, of influence and of prevalence of delays). These ratings provided precise summings up, whilst the narrative notes gave them meaning.

In each of three organizations – a public utility, a university, and a private manufacturer – two cases were studied in far greater depth by intensive methods. Three were followed concurrently as they happened, and three were treated historically, by interviews, casual discussion, lunchtime contacts, and document searches throughout management across departments by a researcher who spent hours or days weekly in the organizations over two to three years. These six case studies are fully reported by Wilson (1980, 1982).

Governmental Influence

On the whole, government is surprisingly weak (see also Hickson et al., 1986). In Britain, its national departments and agencies, and also city and county local governments, average only a low place towards the bottom of five point influence rating scales running from 'little influence' to 'a very great deal'. Here is the symptom of government in a pluralistic society wrestling with a recalcitrant economy whose decision-makers do not leap to do its bidding. The influence it exerts on what they decide is on average less than that of most of their internal departments, implying that an organization's own interests are very much first among the considerations, governmental interests taking a back seat. Among the external pressures, the influence of customers or clients is again well ahead of governmental interests, implying that marketplace survival, success in the field of operation whatever it may be, takes priority over any governmental desires.

An efficient totalitarian government relying less on cajoling and more on force will be in a stronger position, of course, and organizational decision makers will find themselves much more hemmed in. A change in a society in that direction will slice away their alternatives as the giant Dutch firm Philips found under totalitarian German rule during the Second World War. Its alternatives in what it could make and what people it could employ were reduced until it was collaborating in military production and in using forced labour, whatever may have been intended to begin with (Teulings, 1982).

However, the normal Western European government relies on subsidies and regulations and propaganda and nationalization and the like. It may also sponsor work that has long-term indirect effects. In a leading private manufacturer which dominated its market, a decision was made to commit huge sums to the development and testing of a radical new product that could not have occurred but for government action years previously. A state research laboratory had been established where an employee, who incidentally was not British, found the solution to a technical problem that for decades had baffled researchers and firms throughout the world. The manufacturer bought the patent rights and decided to develop the product. Private enterprice exploited what public initiative had opened up.

This case was unusual. The 150 Bradford cases show that in Britain governmental influence is usually exerted through the appropriate channel among a set of channels evolved to connect government with particular sectors of activity. Strategic decisions in the health service are influenced by the Department of Health, in the universities by the University Grants Commission, in industry by the Department of Industry, and in public utilities by the Departments of Environment or Agriculture and by local governments with interests in the services provided. Intervention other than through these specialized channels is rare, and conspicuous personal moves by a Prime Minister such as those by James Callaghan who visited an American airline to support British airplane parts manufacturers are rarer still.

Though government in a state such as Britain does not have the influence to order everything to its own liking, it can still have fingers in a great many pies.

Influence from governmental sources was reported in as many as 40% of the decisions studied (60 out of 150). The first impression, therefore, is a weak but intensive influence. However this general impression is superficial and rather misleading. There are more subtle features which are more notable.

Since an ideological reason for state ownership is to subject organizations to greater governmental influence, differences would be anticipated between the decision-making of nationalized (state-owned) industries and services and those which are privately owned. Is decision-making a public industries and services beset – or maybe stimulated – by governmental influence, whereas private enterprise decision-making is blithely free of it?

Before the findings are examined, it must be remembered that the nationalized organizations depend on the state for their financing, a power base that is latent behind every decision made. It gives government an ultimate stranglehold. Government can sell off parts of them, or close parts of them down.

Thus though it is surprising it is not wholly surprising to find that the amount of governmental influence reported in the decision-making of the state-owned business organizations is no greater than in those that were private. If anything, it could have been less, though the difference if any appears negligible and nothing much should be read into it. The mean rating of the influences of national government departments, and of agencies such as the Health and Safety Executive and the Monopolies Commission, was 2.5 (on a 5 point scale) for 9 instances of influence in the decision-making of three state-owned organizations, against 3.0 for 17 instances in 13 privately owned organizations. The three public organizations were an autonomous division manufacturing products different to that of its parent corporation, a subsidiary company also making products different to those of a parent that had been reluctantly taken into a form of public ownership because of its economic difficulties, and a large service organization that was a household name in Britain and beyond. The 13 private organizations ranged from manufacturing to brewing and financial services.

The comparison is of the influence ratings of all reported instances of government department of governmental agency involvement in the decision-making in comparable business organizations. This excludes three private firms where there were no such involvements in any of their five cases of decision-making and therefore no ratings of governmental influence: it was not meaningful to equate no rating with nil rating numerically. Also excluded are eight non-commercial public services in health, education, the police, and local government; and two public utilities and an industrial research association.

However, although the *amount* of influence exerted by any one department or agency upon any *one* decision does not differ on average between public and private business, government influences a much *greater proportion* of the decisions of nationalized concerns. Switching from the influence of interest units to the number of decisions influenced (irrespective of amount exerted), fifteen cases of decisions were studied in the three state-owned organizations, five in each, and among these eight showed governmental influence, that is 53%. Eighty decisions were studied in 16 privately owned organizations (the 13 where governmental influence was reported, and 3 where there was none), only 15 of these decisions showing any governmental influence, that is 15/80 or 19%. Hence there was governmental influence on nearly three times the proportion of decisions in nationalized industries and services as in private business. Again caution must prevail, since the numbers in the nationalized industries are small, but the proportionate difference strongly supports the assumptions and periodic complaints of public sector managements that they encounter government at every turn whatever they do. *In nationalized businesses, government does not exert a greater amount of influence on any one decision, but it exerts influence on more decisions.*

A striking example of intrusive but ineffectual governmental influence in the public sector is two decisions that coincidentally were virtually the same and so make an apt comparison, one in a nationalized manufacturer and one in the leading private manufacturer that has been mentioned before. Each chose to cite a substantial new plant in Sweden and committed the required financial investment. The private firm went ahead with this major commitment which created employment in Sweden and not in Britain with no interference from government. From the British government that is, for the Swedish government was of course positively influential (ratings of 2 for Swedish national government and 5 for local government). Whereas the nationalized corporation was caught between two governments pulling in opposite directions. The Swedes were again very positive (with an influence rating of 4), but on the other side were the British Treasury and Department of Industry (both rated 5) striving to retain capital investment and employment in Britain. The state owned business had to contend with them whereas the private business did not. Yet the decision also shows that once the financing and terms of operation of nationalized organizations are arranged the British government influences but does not determine even their strategic moves, for in this case the investment went to Sweden despite the efforts of the Treasury and the Department of Industry to stop it. A similar case where the French government delayed but eventually did not stop foreign investment by the nationalized Elf oil corporation is reported by Bauer and Cohen (1983).

The obverse to this should not be missed. If government influences any one decision in a state business no more than in a private business, that also means there are times when it *can* influence a decision in a private business just as much! Private business cannot exclude government from its deliberations.

So public/private differences are relatively small. Indeed, they are by no means the feature of governmental influence. There is a much more vivid contrast which cuts across the decision-making of both. Governmental influence is far greater when its departments and agencies intervene or threaten to intervene specially, than when routine subsidies and regulations are applied in the ordinary way. This goes equally for the public and private sectors (see Table 1).

In the Table, the 9 instances reported of governmental interest units exerting influence in the decision making of state owned businesses are compared with the 17 instances in private businesses, both divided into instances of routine support and regulation versus particular interventions. If every decision in each organization was influenced by one governmental interest unit then, for example, the Table might show ten units influencing ten decisions in two organizations (all five cases studied in each of the organizations), and the entries would neatly correspond along the rows in an immediately self-evident way. As life is not so tidy, there is no such correspondence since first, not all decisions are influenced by a government department or agency, and second, some decisions are influenced by more than one such unit. So for example in the first row under the heading Routine Support and Regulation, there are *five instances of influence* (the Department of Trade influenced two decisions, and the Department of Industry, the Health and Safety Executive, and the National Enterprise Board influenced one each), which give a *mean of 1.2* (on a five point scale), in *five decisions* (here it does happen that each decision was influenced by one unit only) among the ten cases studied in *two state-owned* business organizations.

Comparing first these routine instances, the influence attributed to the five departments and agencies involved in the decision-making of the two state-owned businesses was weak, the mere 1.2 rating, and that of the 12 units involved in the larger number of decisions in nine private businesses was no higher than a mean of 2.4. It is again noticeable that when decisions are classified in this way, government may even have less overt influence in the decision-making of state organizations than in private business, if there is any material difference at all, but that is not the significant point. The conspicuous feature is the relatively low influence *irrespective of ownership* of the Department of Industry when giving grants towards new industrial and commercial developments, of the Department of Trade when a nationalized service it was concerned with purchased equipment abroad, of the Health and Safety Executive concerned with pollution, and of the National Enterprise Board which at the time held shares in firms on behalf of the state and in one case approved expansion in the firm's manufacturing capacity. All these are instances of relatively routine subsidizing and regulating of business. Whilst for state policy they are evidence that governmental action of this kind does have some effect, they show that it is far from decisive. It is merely a contributory level of state action.

Beyond it is a further and more vigorous level of action. The instances of particular intervention shown in the lower section of Table 1 average very high

Table 1: Governmental Influence in Public and Private Business

Government Department or Agency influencing a decision	Influence Rating	Decisions Influenced	Organization
	Overall Means		
	State Owned Businesses:		
9 interest units	Mean 2.5	8 decisions	3 organizations
	Private Businesses:		
17 interest units	Mean 3.0	15 decisions	13 organizations
	Routine Support and Regulation		
	State Owned Businesses:		
5 i. e. Departments of Trade (twice) and Industry, Health and Safety Executive, National Enterprise Board	Mean 1.2	5 decisions, i.e. new products and factories, massive re-equipment	2 organizations
	Private Businesses:		
12 i.e. Departments of Industry (10 instances), Health and Safety Executive (twice)	Mean 2.4	11 decisions, i.e. new products, buildings and plant, and one factory closure	9 organizations
	Particular Interventions		
	State Owned Businesses:		
Specialist Ministry	5	Major reorganization by merger	Transport Service
Specialist Ministry	4	Reorganization of personnel	Transport Service
Treasury	4	Siting of plant in Sweden	Manufacturer
Department of Industry	4	Siting of plant in Sweden	Manufacturer
	Mean 4.2		
	Private Businesses:		
Treasury	5	Change in interest rates	Financial Institution
Department of Environment	5	Change in interest rates	Financial Institution
Department of Employment	5	Productivity agreement	Insurance Company
Arts Council	4	Budget and programme	Entertainment Service
Monopolies Commission	3	New credit service	Finance Company
	Mean 4.4		

influence indeed in both state and private businesses, the means being respectively 4.2 and 4.4. These are occasions when a department or agency deliberately influences a particular decision in a particular organization as far as it can. Among the state businesses, major reorganizations with repercussions beyond Britain were successfully influenced; and influential efforts were made to prevent investment in Sweden though these were unsuccessful, as already described. Among the private businesses, key interest rates were successfully influenced in the direction of government policy, and the Department of Employment influenced an unusual 'white-collar' productivity agreement in a world leader insurance company at a time when government was attempting to push such agreements in the direction it wanted. The Arts Council directly affected an entertainment organization's programme by the terms and size of its financial grant, and the threat of Monopolies Commission action constrained a finance company's move into a new credit service (Hickson et al., 1986).

The case of the unsuccessful effort to prevent a nationalized manufacturer investing in Sweden rather than in Britain shows that it is necessary to interpret these cases of high attributed influence in conjunction with the outcome of the decision-making. It is possible for a decision to go against highly influential government interests, either because they lack absolute power or because they come to accept or tolerate the opposite view. Influence on this scale appears to be of two kinds:

(a) *constraining*, where the influence of the government department or agency is taken into account in framing an alternative or alternatives acceptable to them, as for example with the insurance company's productivity agreement approved by the Department of Employment, and the entertainment organization's programme shaped to fit likely Arts Council financial support.
(b) *indicatory*, where their influence is exerted in favour of a specific alternative. Although they have a high probability that this alternative will be decided upon, they can be unsuccessful as they were over the Swedish investment.

However, it is clear that specific non-routine governmental interventions can and do have an effect; and that this can be just as great in the private sector as in the public sector. Though at first sight government looks weak and though its influence may at all times be outweighed by all the other influences upon a decision of which it is only one, it can be a force to be reckoned with when its departments and agencies intervene in particular situations.

From this comparison of public and private sectors three remarkable inferences can be drawn. First, government does not have any special ability to 'call the tune' for any one decision even in its own nationalized corporations, though it does influence a larger proportion of their decisions. Second, government influence does penetrate the privacy of private enterprise, albeit as a lesser influence among greater internal managerial influences. Third, government is most effective in this form of influence, both in public and private sector organizations, when its departments and agencies intervene in particular circumstances beyond the usual run of subsidizing and regulating.

References

Bauer, Michael, Cohen, E. (1983) The Iron Law of 'Private Governments' in the French Industrial System. Paper presented at the *6th EGOS Colloquium*, Florence.

Hickson, David J., Butler, Richard J., Cray, David, Mallory, Geoffrey R., Wilson, David C. (1984) Comparing one Hundred and Fifty Decision Processes. *Organizational Strategy and Change.* J. M. Pennings (Ed.), San Francisco: Jossey-Bass.

– (1986) Top Decisions: Strategic Decision Making in Organizations. Blackwells (Britain) and Jossey-Bass (USA).

Teulings, A. (1982) Interlocking Interests and Collaboration With the Enemy: Corporate Behaviour in the Second World War. *Organization Studies*, 3/2, pp. 99–119.

Wilson, David C. (1980) *Organizational Strategy*. PhD Thesis, University of Bradford, England.

Wilson, David C.., Butler, Richard J., Cray, David, Hickson, David J., Mallory, Geoffrey R. (1982) The Limits of Trade Union Power in Organizational Decision Making. *British Journal of Industrial Relations*, XX/3, pp. 322–341.

[14]

Journal of Management Studies 23:5 September 1986
0022–2380 $3.50

VOLUNTARY ORGANIZATIONS IN ACTION: STRATEGY IN THE VOLUNTARY SECTOR[1]

David C. Wilson

and

Richard J. Butler
Organizational Analysis Research Unit,
University of Bradford Management Centre

ABSTRACT

Organizations in the voluntary sector have received relatively little attention from researchers in the field of organizational analysis. In particular, the strategy of organizations in the voluntary sector has been assumed to be passive, concentrating on a co-operative role with commercial or public agencies. This article argues that such a picture is not necessarily accurate and examines the strategies of four leading British voluntary organizations. Data suggest that co-operation is but one of many strategies pursued by some voluntary organizations. Two of the sample organizations deviate markedly from the stereo-typical image of co-operation, and variation in their strategy choice is argued to emanate from dependence relations created by organizational links. The paper argues that the influences which shape the choice of strategy in voluntary organizations are primarily those created by inter-dependence, and that aspects of task and ambiguity are secondary sources of influence.

INTRODUCTION

Recent work in the field of organizational analysis has shown an increasing interest in the collective or voluntary organizational form, especially as it represents an alternative to bureaucratic service organizations or to those firms in the commercial business world (Butler, 1983a). Taking efficiency and economy in transaction costs, for example, Ouchi (1980) argues that the collective is likely to be the most suitable organizational form for mediating transactions where performance measures are ambiguous and individual and

Address for reprints: Richard J. Butler, Organizational Analysis Research Unit, University of Bradford Management Centre, Emm Lane, Bradford BD9 4JL.

organizational interests are highly congruent. Similarly, Williamson and Ouchi (1981) and Rothschild-Whitt (1979) argue that non-profit voluntary organizations represent a unique combination of internal organization and external conditions which together serve to create and maintain particularistic organizational behaviours. Shapiro (1973, p. 124) has demonstrated such unique features specifically in the marketing and product decisions of organizations in the voluntary sector, whilst Zeitz (1980) points toward the unique qualities of voluntary associations in facilitating successful resistance to governmental agencies in the areas of mental health planning (based on data from Aiken et al. (1975)).

Simultaneously, the field of social policy and public administration, both in North America and Western Europe, has witnessed increasing concern with the role of voluntary organizations in the mixed economy (e.g. Leat, Smolka and Unell, 1981; Hatch and Mocroft, 1979; Hegner, 1980). Often set against a background of a decreasing level of service from public welfare and health agencies, such studies point toward the alternative provision of services by voluntary organizations and the increasing need for their role in health, education and welfare services (Butler and Wilson, 1983).

Despite such trends, however, we know little of the prevailing characteristics of voluntary organizations and the processes through which they formulate strategies and interact with their environments. Existing references to voluntary organizations from an organizational perspective are largely theoretical rather than empirically based (Ouchi, 1980; Butler, 1983a, b). These argue that, under certain conditions of goal congruence or performance ambiguity, the voluntary form of organization is likely to be the most effective and efficient (compared with public agencies or private firms). Miles and Snow's (1978, p. 215) analysis of the strategies of voluntary hospitals represents a rare exception to this kind of analysis. Data on 19 voluntary hospitals were examined to highlight the process of organizational adaptation to the environment. In the present article we utilize Miles and Snow's (1978) initial framework, developing it to meet the requirements of our own research focus.

Social policy and administration research, on the other hand, has a sizeable empirical base in the voluntary sector, but this tends to be focused either upon specific types of voluntary organization (such as those which are largely extensions of public agencies) or upon the individual characteristics of volunteer labour (Titmuss, 1970; Kanter, 1968). The picture of voluntary organizations as they interact with their environment is, therefore, necessarily incomplete.

The present article aims to provide a framework for the analysis of voluntary organizations. Four British voluntary organizations are examined. In each case, data concerning strategy, structure and environmental characteristics are presented and compared with prevailing theories in organizational analysis in order to highlight differences and similarities in the voluntary sector organizations. In particular, this paper counterposes two broad streams of theory which may be employed to explain variations in the strategy of voluntary organizations. One of these theoretical approaches is based upon the notion of transaction costs (Williamson, 1975). Here, organizational strategy is aimed largely toward securing efficient and equitable exchange between parties, given particular environmental and organizational conditions. As we shall examine in a later section, such a theoretical approach has important implications for voluntary organizations in that they are considered appropriate organizational forms for achieving efficiency under conditions of performance ambiguity, unique tasks and low opportunism. In other circumstances, commercial or bureaucratic forms of organization become appropriate.

A second theoretical approach places less emphasis on a strategy of securing efficiency in transactions and, rather, suggests that interdependencies between a focal organization and its network of external contacts are the primary influences upon shaping strategy (Emerson, 1962; Pfeffer and Salancik, 1978). In this article we shall examine each theoretical strand analytically in the extent to which organizational strategy is shaped by concerns of transactional efficiency or by interdependencies in the organizational network (Aldrich, 1979).

Before this analysis, however, it is necessary to define what we mean by the term 'voluntary' organization.

Voluntary Organizations: Key Elements

Differing terminology abounds in existing work concerning voluntary organizations. Ouchi (1980, p. 136) uses the term 'clan' to describe collective labours which lack market and bureaucratic mechanisms but which are characterized by high levels of 'organic solidarity' (Durkheim, 1933, p. 365). Rothschild-Whitt (1979, p. 519), however, refers to 'collectivist-democratic organizations' to describe those organizations which display a value-rational orientation to social action, encompassing values for their own sake, independent of any prospects of financial success (Weber, 1968). Hegner (1980) prefers the term 'solidarity' organizations, whereas Kramer (1979) somewhat ambiguously uses the term 'voluntary agency' to distinguish between collective action and 'public agencies', whilst Butler (1983b) refers to 'communes' or to 'collectives' (Butler, 1983a).

The present article refers to voluntary organizations as a discrete and readily identifiable population of organizational types, although within this population is a wide range of organizations with commensurate variations in many of their characteristics (McElvey and Aldrich, 1983, pp. 110–11). The key elements of a voluntary organization are defined here:

(1) A considerable proportion of the labour force is voluntary and, hence, unpaid. A voluntary organization does not lose its title, however, if some of its members are paid, or if it receives financial aid from government agencies. Membership of a voluntary organization is not inherited

through familial or societal connections. Neither is membership specifically aimed at securing economic benefit for its individuals.

(2) Such organizations are engaged in the non-commercial provision of goods or services. Voluntary organizations do not specifically seek profit from the selling of goods or services in the market although, as we shall see, many voluntary organizations set up profit-seeking subsidiary trading companies, but with the purpose of providing funds for that voluntary organization.

These criteria necessarily narrow down the potential range of organizations in our sample. For example, it would not include professions or labour unions. Although such organizations may operate on a high degree of congruence between constituent individuals holding common values and beliefs, this sense of community is, nonetheless, directed at successful business behaviour (Ouchi and Jaeger, 1978; Kanter, 1972). The voluntary organizations discussed in the present article provide non profit-making services to a community and are financed to varying degrees by donations given to the organization largely under the banner of altruistic behaviour (Titmuss, 1970).

The Strategy of Voluntary Organizations: A Typology

It is not the intention of the present article to discuss the conjectural areas of strategy *per se* (see, for example, Braybrooke and Lindblom, 1963; Norman, 1963; Cyert and March, 1963; Thompson, 1967; Hickson et al., 1985). Rather, the aim is to expand a typology suitable for illustrating the strategies of voluntary organizations. This is attempted by drawing upon existing descriptions of strategic types. Whilst these have been derived from organizations which are not voluntary in form, nevertheless the typologies may be adpated to the voluntary context.

In order to achieve this, the typology derived is here related to the work of Bowman (1976), Miles and Snow (1978), Mintzberg (1979) and Miller and Friesen (1984), who view strategy as emanating from a continuing stream of decisions aimed at an organizational domain (Thompson, 1967), from the nature of domain-organization interaction and from commensurate strategic profiles which last over time. For purposes of analytical convenience at the illustrative level of the case-study data presented in this paper, a three-way classification of strategy types is adopted which captures, in broad terms, the predominant stances adopted by voluntary organizations toward their domain. These are outlined in table I.

Three broad strategy types are classified into innovatory, consolidatory or co-operative stances toward domain (Thompson, 1967). Each strategy type represents a broad attitude toward domain in general and characterizes the predominant strategic stance taken by an organization (Snow and Hrebiniak, 1980). At a more detailed level of course, *multiple* strategies may be evident in any one organization with, for example, an innovatory stance toward services

Table I. Typology of strategies and typical decision topics

Strategy	*Stance toward domain*	*Typical decision topics*
Innovatory	Domain prospectors	New products; diversification of inputs and outputs; prestige seeking decisions aimed at securing distinctive competence
Consolidatory	Domain defenders	Continued survival decisions; pruning; retrenchment; economic efficiency decisions, e.g. dropping services and products thought to be loss-making
Co-operative	Domain reactors	Decisions aimed at securing environmental support; co-opting, joint ventures; a focus on trust and goodwill

provided, coupled with a consolidatory strategy toward securing inputs (such as finance and personnel). This level of analysis, however, is examined in future research publications and not in the present article.

(1) *Innovatory strategies* are pursued by organizations which are domain prospectors. Such organizations typically launch new products in both existing and new markets, or diversify both outputs and sources of inputs. These innovatory strategies correspond to Miller and Friesen's (1984, p. 122) 'assertive', 'niche' and 'expansion' strategies, all of which involve prospecting the domain in order to secure either opportune adapations to environmental conditions, or are attempts to modify the immediate environment itself to secure more congenial conditions.

(2) *Consolidatory strategies* reflect organizations which are domain defenders (Snow and Hrebiniak, 1980, p. 310). Strategic emphasis is placed upon securing general efficiency, ensuring the continued survival of the organization often by careful pruning and retrenchment where appropriate. As Miller and Friesen (1984) point out, consolidatory strategies may be pursued because it is apparent that the organization is facing a changing, possibly more competitive, environment ('adaptive or incremental') or may largely ignore environmental conditions in an attempt to produce yesterday's product more efficiently (p. 102).

(3) *Co-operative strategies* are pursued by organizations which react to their environment typically in an attempt to reduce domain uncertainty. Joint ventures, often on a temporary basis and decisons aimed at securing greater environmental support are typical of such a strategy (Engwall, 1985). Co-optation represents another avenue of co-operative strategies. As Pfeffer and Salancik suggest (1978, pp. 162–3), co-opting can draw in previously lacking skills and expertise to the organization, allowing the representation of external interests and, hence, increasing the chances of gaining external support for organizational activities. Each of the three broad strategic types is characterized by a particular pattern of decision topics which represent an organizational response to the demands and opportunities presented by the external environment. We

shall explore in the following sections whether this broad strategy is an attempt to achieve minimized transaction costs given specific tasks, or is aimed largely at managing interdependencies.

Organization and Strategy: A Task and Transactions Perspective

Following Ouchi (1980), Butler and Wilson (1983) and Butler (1983a), each of the three categories of strategies are argued to have broadly corresponding organizational forms associated with them. Underlying this argument is the recognition that organized co-operative action incurs certain transaction costs (Williamson, 1975). Ultimate goals of prospecting organizational domain for both prestige and profit are facilitated more easily by commercial firms operating in competitive markets where the price mechanisms ensure greater efficiency in transaction costs coupled with equitable exchange between transacting parties. Recent governmental policies in the United Kingdom, aimed at removing state support from selected areas of the economy (privatization), are largely based on the assumption that the commercial market organization is more efficient in effecting such transactions than are state owned agencies (see, for example, Millward, 1982, p. 83; Murray, 1975 and Rainey et al., 1976). In the discipline of economics, also, it is argued that the market will foster innovation, since outdated products and working practices will be constantly replaced under the conditions of inherent competition (Hayek, 1945; Kirzner, 1980).

Such conditions, however, are only appropriate, or possible, where some relatively precise value can be placed upon exchanged commodities. Galbraith (1967), Arrow (1974) and Weber (1947) have all argued as to the inability of market organizations to provide adequate levels of service in the areas of health, welfare or education. To achieve such adequacy would mean abandoning economically motivated activity aimed at manufacturing products for which there is a great demand and simultaneously restricting supply. Hence, the bureaucratic form of organization comes into being where market forces are largely absent. Bureaucracies in the health and welfare sectors try to ensure adequate provision of their services to all who require them. Strategy is consolidative, trying to achieve both efficient internal organization and the provision of adequate services to the community.

Implicit in much of the theoretical discourse on voluntary organizations is that they represent the most appropriate organizational form for operating under certain specific conditions. As Ouchi (1980, pp. 134–5) notes:

> When tasks become highly unique, completely integrated, or ambiguous for other reasons, then even bureaucratic mechanisms fail. Under these conditions, it becomes impossible to evaluate externally the value added by any individual . . . the clan, which is the obverse of the market relation . . . achieves efficiency under the opposite conditions: high performance ambiguity and low opportunism.

Given these conditions, coupled with the inherent trust and goodwill both within and between voluntary organizatons and their domain, it is likely that such organizations will be most suited to pursuing co-operative strategies. Emphasis will be on gaining support for organizational activities (often by co-opting) or on working alongside other organizations to achieve a common goal. Each requires a good deal of trust and goodwill amongst participants.

Paradoxically, ambiguity of task may also act as the impetus for pursuing innovatory rather than co-operative strategies within voluntary organizations. Where ends–means relationships are unclear, or criteria of evaluation are imprecise, the less likely it becomes that decision-making will be sufficiently routine or predictable to support co-operative activity (Hage, 1980, pp. 120–4; Hickson et al., 1985). The choice process becomes largely independent of substantive outcomes (March and Olsen, 1976) and reduction of ambiguity is likely to take the form of diversifying services and seeking prestige in an attempt to secure 'distinctive competence' (Snow and Hrebiniak, 1980). Whilst innovation in the face of ambiguous tasks is theoretically possible, however, it is a far from safe strategy toward long-term survival should the niche of distinctive competence not be secured. Miller and Friesen (1984, pp. 91–103) graphically illustrate how attempts at innovatory strategies in situations of high task ambiguity can lead to 'over-extension' of the organization or to 'grafting and groping' where risky, unplanned and often over-simplistic innovatory strategies have led to organizational demise. We suggest that co-operation is a safer and, hence, more likely strategy from the perspective of task and transaction costs, even though this may be difficult to achieve in the short term.

Organization and Strategy: A Resource Dependence Perspective

Voluntary organizations are no different from their commercial or statutory counterparts in that they face a number of external contingencies which must be taken into account during the process of strategy formulation. These contingencies take the form of other organizations which may be suppliers, customers, competitors or regulatory agencies. As Pfeffer and Salancik (1978) argue, interdependence relations between these external contingencies and the focal organization are crucial for its autonomy to achieve desired outcomes (p. 41).

Butler et al. (1977) and Hickson et al. (1985) illustrate that organizations can become so dependent upon a few customers, suppliers and or on a dominant headquarters that their autonomy of strategy is completed 'paralyzed' in cases of extremely powerful external contingencies. Wilson and Butler (1985) have shown empirically the importance of interdependencies in the voluntary sector for strategy formulation with a specific focus upon regulatory agencies. It is likely that suppliers, customers and competitors will equally have an impact upon strategy in voluntary organizations.

As far as competition is concerned, we limit our level of analysis to specific industries of voluntary organizations. By industry, we mean the family of organizations which operate in the same domain (Levine and White, 1961). Domain definition refers to relatively broad industries such as aerospace or the steel industry (Grinyer and Spender, 1979). In the voluntary sector, this means identifying those organizations which act as 'commensals' and strategy thus becomes a response to these competitors within a given industry (Aldrich, 1979, p. 266) rather than toward the voluntary sector as a whole (which would require a more 'meso' inter-economic-sector level of analysis). Four different industries are represented in this article – emergency sea rescue, public transport, child welfare and disaster relief. These are described in detail in a later section.

Competition in the voluntary sector is focused primarily upon securing financial resources from a constituency of givers (Titmuss, 1970) although competition for clients can also occur both between voluntary organizations and statutory agencies where alternative or complementary services are provided (Leat, Smolka and Unell, 1981). When competition for support is high, we would expect to find strategies aimed at seeking prestige which, as Thompson (1967, p. 38) notes, is a way of 'gaining power without increasing dependency'. This would preclude the risky innovatory strategy under these conditions, but would promote consolidatory strategies in order either to achieve or to appear more efficient to present and potential supporters. Indeed, much of the recent (and relatively new phenomenon) of advertising by voluntary organizations reflects this concern with presenting an image of an administratively efficient service organization (Shapiro, 1973; Wallberg, 1982).

In industries where there is little competition, voluntary organizations are likely to pursue innovative strategies aimed at securing distinctive competence which also, to some extent, precludes the intrusion of subsequent competitors (Selznick, 1957). Empirical justification for this assertion can be found in the same (commercial) organizations studied by Snow and Hrebiniak (1980) who found that, whilst several feasible strategies existed for many organizations, those in industries with few competitors are more likely to seek high performance through domain prospecting strategies (see table I). But this strategy of innovation attempts to avoid competition by constantly anticipating and moving ahead of potential competitors, as opposed to a consolidatory strategy which attempts to shut competitors out.

Financial support also presents a powerful external contingency for most voluntary organizations. In particular, strategy is constrained when money is received from state agencies which, justifiably from their perspective, wish to see their financial support utilized in a manner congruent with their interests and which does not always coincide with the preferences of the voluntary organization (Leat, Smolka and Unell, 1981; Wilson and Butler, 1985; Saxon-Harrold, 1985). Except in very specific circumstances (such as research) it is unlikely that a state agency will grant financial support to a voluntary organization in order that it can innovate. It is far more likely that the funding agency will expect a co-operative relationship to be established either between itself and the voluntary organization, or between a number of voluntary organizations operating in the same domain.

Furthermore, voluntary organizations face a particular kind of dependence, absent from other forms of organization, termed the 'gift relationship' (Titmuss, 1970). This relationship examines the interdependencies between clients, the organization and givers of resources. In many voluntary organizations, the clients and the givers of resources are the same group of people. Such is the case in what Kanter (1968; 1972) and Butler (1983b) call 'communes' or mutual help organizations. In other voluntary organizations, individuals give resources to the organization in the expectation that these will be used to give services to an anonymous group of clients, who may even reside in another country. In these cases, the voluntary organization must ensure that it creates and maintains identification between clients and suppliers. This social psychological process of achieving a *Gemeinschaft* (Tonnies, 1955, p. 20) between client and supplier requires a considerable effort on the part of the voluntary organization to maintain such congruence.

The extent to which clients and suppliers *overlap* is likely to have crucial implications for the strategy of a voluntary organization. The less the degree of overlap (clients are remote from suppliers), the more strategic emphasis will have to be placed on securing support for organizational activities from voluntary suppliers. In open systems terminology, much strategy will be oriented toward the input side of the organization. The greater the degree of overlap, the less likely it will be for strategy to be geared to receiving support from suppliers. As suppliers are clients anyway (in the pure case of total overlap), the organization is assured survival as long as there is a demand for its services. Strategy, here is likely to be output oriented toward consolidatory services provided.

From a political perspective, overlap has implications for the influence of any dominant coalition. If overlap is complete, then it becomes less likely for a dominant coalition to influence choice over strategy, for specific interests will have less of a power base from which to secure strategic advantage (Abell, 1975; Butler et al., 1979; Pfeffer and Salancik, 1978). We suspect that the reverse may be true of a voluntary organization which acts in a mediating role between remote clients and suppliers. A dominant coalition is likely to reside within the focal organization, largely sustained by its success in securing and furthering support for organizational activities. Here an innovative strategy is theoretically possible in the absence of powerful external contingencies.

SAMPLE AND METHOD

The study was based on data collected from four leading voluntary organizations in the United Kingdom. They were chosen primarily to reflect variation in organizational type and domain and are outlined in the sampling framework in table II.

Table II. The sample of four voluntary organizations

Organization	*Task ambiguity*	*Resource dependence*
1. National Society for the Prevention of Cruelty to Children (NSPCC)	*Relatively low*: a specific and measurable task (child abuse statistics, successful cases, etc.)	*Relatively high*: some money from central government. Some competition both from statutory and voluntary organizations.
2. Metropolitan Community Transport Service (MCT)	*Very low*: easily measurable criteria surrounding transport and bus service operations.	*Very high*: one third of annual income in the form of government grants. Two thirds from service charges which are often from local government departments.
3. Royal National Lifeboat Institution (RNLI)	*Medium*: measurable data available upon number of persons rescued. On other activities such as international co-ordination, research into boat design and the necessity to co-ordinate with other bodies during rescue, the task becomes less precisely quantifiable.	*Relatively low*: no income from government sources. Some competition from the Royal Air Force, but unique as a sea-born life-saving service.
4. OXFAM	*Relatively high*: the relief of poverty, distress and suffering is innately unquantifiable and, at best, ambiguous.	*Very low*: almost no income from government grants. Bulk of service is aimed outside the UK, but income comes from British sources through voluntary donations and profit from trading activities.

Data were collected in three ways. Firstly, data were gathered by extended open-ended interviewing, usually with one or two senior managers. Secondly, data were gathered by a 36-point interview schedule which included structured and open-ended questions in approximately equal proportions. Finally, a great deal of documentary evidence was collected for each organization. Both OXFAM and NSPCC have their own library facilities (OXFAM publishes material as well) and a wealth of data detailing the history and present-day activities of the organization were available in all cases.

Respondents for the interview schedule were all from the senior echelons of each organization. One respondent per organization was asked to fill in the questionnaire in conjunction with the researchers. Such interviews typically lasted between two and three hours. Senior personnel were chosen to be respondents in the belief that such 'top managers' are in the best position to assess the organization's strategic orientation toward its environment. These kind of data can usually only be obtained from individuals in relatively senior positions who are responsible for monitoring the environment and for formulating appropriate strategies (Hickson et al., 1985).

The Organizations

OXFAM is an organization dedicated to relieving poverty, distress and suffering, particularly in the Third World. Specifically, the organization aims to provide food, heating, clothing, shelter, training and education to those in need. A second task of the organization is to provide research data and to publish the results thereof. Very little funding comes from central government and this is decreasing year by year. Forty per cent of the funds come from OXFAM's own retail trading outlets and a wholly-owned trading company which produces Christmas cards, handicrafts and so forth: the remaining income is from voluntary donations. The organization is unique in allocating funds to finance programmes and other groups who are working in the field. Recently, however, OXFAM has been employing doctors, nurses and engineers in emergencies and in helping refugees, which will erode some of its unique qualities since other relief charities are also operational in this scene.

OXFAM's central tasks are relatively ambiguous. The service it offers to clients is difficult to evaluate especially by any readily quantifiable data. Both Jones (1965) and Gill (1970) detail the difficulties of assessing the quality of overseas aid by any tangible criteria. Assessments of poverty relief lend themselves more readily to qualitative analysis or moral judgements rather than to statistical support.

The Royal National Lifeboat Institution, RNLI, has as its sole task the saving of life at sea up to 30 miles off-shore and in national in-shore waters. RNLI receive no financial support from the British central government (0.25 per cent of total funds come from the government of the Irish Republic). Sixty-seven per cent of funding comes from legacies and from individual donations, often from fishermen, merchant seamen and, to a limited extent, from private boat-owners, all of whom are potential beneficiaries of RNLI's rescue services. The remaining funds come from collections and from sales revenue through a wholly-owned trading company which markets gifts, clothing and so forth, all bearing the RNLI insignia. RNLI co-ordinates with the governmental Search and Rescue Committee, in which the Royal Air Force and the Coastguard Service are participants. In addition, RNLI is the co-ordinating body for other lifeboat organizations located, for example, in Holland, Sweden, North America, Spain and Portugal.

RNLI (like OXFAM) displays some ambiguity in its central tasks. Not only is rescue at sea a technologically complex operation, it is also full of ambiguities over what constitutes a rescue service. For example, RNLI's brief is to rescue individuals from peril at sea, but most of those rescued also need immediate medical care. Decisions concerning the level of medical care provided (minimal or remedial) have to be made on the spot with little guidance from the central organization. Medical care offered by RNLI often goes unpaid by many merchant shipping lines. In addition, RNLI has to liaise at each rescue with the Coastguard Service and the Royal Air Force, which increases the complexity of the operation. RNLI do try to evaluate rescue success by a simple ratio of number of launches of lifeboats to the number of reported incidents at sea, but respondents admitted that this is a very unsatisfactory criterion.

The National Society for the Prevention of Cruelty to Children, NSPCC, is an organization aimed at preventing the corruption of morals of minors and to prevent cruelty to children. This can be achieved through legalistic devices (NSPCC has the power to prosecute) or through more supportive means (such as through case-work or through education). Central and local government provide money for administrative costs and for specific projects, usually split 75–25 per cent respectively for projects of up to 5 years' duration. NSPCC is not wholly unique in the services it provides. The social services departments of local government also provide a very similar service, whilst charities such as Dr Barnardo's and the National Children's Homes provide residential care for mal-treated children. NSPCC does boast a 24-hour service, unlike any statutory provider of similar services, but in all other respects it operates in an industry comprising a number of other similar organizations.

Presently, the bulk of NSPCC's task falls into the legalistic category. As Parton (1981, p. 392) notes, 'removal of a child from its parents is now seen far more as a first rather than a last resort'. Such removal is often followed by the prosecution of parents or guardians and task ambiguity is thus lessened, with criteria of evaluation (number of removals, prosecutions and re-abuse data) easier to specify.

The Metropolitan Community Transport Service, MCT, is closely linked to local government through the Council for Voluntary Services. These Councils are intermediary bodies aimed at creating and maintaining liaison between statutory local government and voluntary organizations in the area. MCT provides a service to all who require transport in the community. It purchases, maintains and runs a fleet of minibuses. It receives 32 per cent of funding from government grants and some 60 per cent from charges for services, although clients are often local government departments (such as Child Development Centres). MCT operates alongside few competitors (public transport and private bus companies operate in a different domain and have different client groups), but its central task is relatively less ambiguous than that of OXFAM or RNLI. Financial criteria, availability of vehicles, maintenance data, vehicle down time and operating costs all serve to reduce ambiguity in the operation of the bus services.

RESULTS AND DISCUSSION

Heeding Kanter's (1979) assessment of measures in the voluntary sector being inherently 'intangible' and necessarily 'soft and subjective', the present data nevertheless show reported variations in the strategies of the four organizations studied. The documentary evidence which was examined also supported the variation of strategic orientations which we shall outline in this section. We take this to be a substantial reinforcement to the reported data from our interview schedule. Following Kanter's (1972) study of 'successful' voluntary organizations, the sample consisted only of those organizations which had been in operation for sufficient time to show evidence of flexibility, weathering crises, adapting to environmental circumstances and attracting sufficient resources. In addition, we assumed that the continued survival of the organization meant that individuals who supported the organization, suppliers and clients, at least had their wants satisfied to a satisfactory (March and Simon, 1958) if not optimal level by the particular choice of strategy adopted by a voluntary organization (Kanter, 1972).

The strategic stances of each of the four organizations are outlined in table III. They are classified according to types of decisions made in each of the organizations.

For example, decisions in RNLI to liaise with other voluntary organizations aimed at changing current tax laws, to maintain an advisory and information-giving service to private commercial shipping lines and to liaise with governmental agencies and foreign rescue services are taken to characterize an overall strategy of co-operation for, like Mintzberg (1979), we infer strategy type from a stream of strategic decision topics.

Both RNLI and MCT are depicted as pursuing primarily co-operative strategies, although accounting for their strategies appears to be different in each case. RNLI appears to pursue a strategy of co-operation largely through its task considerations (Ouchi, 1980) whilst MCT is rather pressured into co-operation through being resource dependent upon the state not only for income but also as a client. Each case is discussed in turn.

In order to accomplish its task, RNLI needs to collaborate with other organizations (both voluntary and publicly owned). Task knowledge of sea rescue is shared across these collaborating organizations (for example, the Coastguard Service, the Royal Air Force and other overseas sea rescue organizations). However, there are no direct competitors to RNLI which offer a national lifeboat service. Neither is RNLI dependent upon central government for financial support. In addition, annual income appears to be growing steadily (from voluntary donations and trading profits) increasing by almost £2 million each year (rising from £12 million in 1980 to around £17 million in 1983–4).

The creation of clubs for private boat-owners who contribute to RNLI, plus the establishment of a trading company which covenants all profits to RNLI have all served to bolster this economic success. As Miles and Snow (1978,

p. 215) predicted in their study of voluntary hospitals, organizations such as RNLI which are subject to relatively few contingent demands from the task environment are likely to adopt a prospective attitude toward their domain. Such organizations have the facility to pursue innovative strategies (in the terminology of this article). Although RNLI fits such a picture, it is largely constrained from taking an innovatory strategic stance by virtue of its task complexity.

Table III. The strategic stances and typical decision topics of the four voluntary organizations

Organization	*Strategy*	*Typical decision topics*
RNLI	Co-operative	To liaise with other voluntary organizations to lobby for tax reforms: co-operate with private commercial shipping lines and to act as co-ordinating body for other sea rescue services world wide: to liaise with government agencies to provide a better standard of service: to work alongside the Royal Air Force and apportion the rescue task accordingly.
OXFAM	Innovative	To maintain flexibility of service by increasing the role of skill and expertise in authority to make decisions: to increase the range of decision-making topics from those concerned immediately with relief to those concerning public works, roads, energy supplies, all aspects of agriculture and legal work: to change the image of retail outlets from one of a second-hand shop to one of a more up-market craft shop: to employ commercial design agencies in advertising such shops.
NSPCC	Consolidative	To change the structure of the organization and the execution of its task from a national to a regional service: to integrate with government agencies, the Police and the Health Authorities in child care: to increase organizational efficiency especially in the successful prevention of the occurence of rebattering of children.
MCT	Co-operative	To work in tandem with other voluntary organizations to assist and advise on the running of vehicles: to collaborate temporarily with vehicle manufacturers and the Department of Transport over vehicle use and design: to collaborate with local government to secure and justify financial aid: to collaborate with clients, especially with the aim of setting up a users' committee to achieve a better standard of service.

Not only does sea rescue require the collaboration of at least three different organizations (usually the Royal Air Force, the Coastguard Service and RNLI), it also demands high levels of investment in technology. Lifeboats are relatively expensive commodities to purchase and maintain, whilst crews, coxswains and engineers require considerable investment in their training. In Thompson's (1967) terms, the task environment of sea rescue imposes contingencies on the focal organization which preclude regular innovative decisions to launch new products or to diversify outputs, for example (see table I).

Typical decisions in RNLI, therefore, are to liaise with government agencies in formulating rescue strategies, to co-operate with seamen and commercial shipping lines and to act as world-wide co-ordinator for other sea rescue organizations (see table III). In addition, interdependencies created by the overlap of suppliers and clients also act as an external constraint on organizational autonomy (Pfeffer and Salancik, 1978), although these are less pressing than the considerations of task accomplishment. Fishermen, private and merchant seamen all donate funds to RNLI and are also receivers of its services should they require them. Such overlap increases the influence of suppliers and clients in the focal organization and any decisions are subject to taking their interests into account. Any radical shift of strategy would have to take notice of their desire (and those of central government) for a universalistic rescue service around the British shoreline, thus also reducing the likelihood of RNLI's pursuing innovative strategies (Lindblom, 1959; Astley et al., 1982) quite apart from task considerations.

MCT also pursues a co-operative strategy, but respondents indicated that this was largely a result of the organization's position of extreme dependence upon government agencies both as suppliers of finance and as receivers of services. In addition, because MCT is so closely interlinked with government agencies, the organization is subject to pressures to comply with bureaucratic procedures and decision-making processes which, as Leat, Smolka and Unell (1981) suggest, stifles innovation and makes consolidation a difficult strategy to pursue as the often changing political climate of local government provides no consistent or stable environment for the voluntary organization. Hence, MCT is forced into a reactive stance toward its domain as governmental policies oscillate between favouring and disfavouring voluntary activities.

Unlike RNLI, however, the voluntary transport organization has attempted to make decisions which we would take as being indicative of pursuing an innovative strategy. One such decision was called 'dial-a-ride' whereby clients could telephone for a bus service. This would create a host of clients wanting 'one-off' transport facilities and would require MCT to implement a much strengthened administrative support structure, and install a larger capacity telephone exchange, plus a mini-computer to handle scheduling problems. However, such a scheme also meant that more money would have to be provided by local government, which turned down the scheme when approached by MCT.

Our data suggest that the autonomy of MCT to pursue innovative strategies is curtailed firstly by their financial dependence upon the state. Secondly, their central task of providing bus transport is highly regulated by external organizations both governmental (Department of Transport, local government) and private (insurance companies). Nevertheless, MCT conform closely to those organizations studied by Snow and Hrebiniak (1980, p. 325) which operated successfully in a highly regulated external environment. Like Snow and Hrebiniak's organizations in the semiconductor and air transportation industries, MCT is a domain reactor and is also successful in financial and operational terms. The kind of interaction between MCT and its regulators, however, does not allow room for an innovative strategy. It seems that when this is attempted, the dependencies created by such close regulation serve to resist the pursuit of proactive strategies (MCT had also tried to shift domain into the furniture removal business, but this was again discouraged).

Both NSPCC and OXFAM pursue strategies other than that of co-operation. We describe NSPCC as primarily a consolidator, whilst OXFAM is characterized as an innovator (see tables I and III). Again, each organization is discussed in turn.

Whilst NSPCC operates in a highly interdependent network of governmental agencies and medical organizations, it defends its domain by adopting a consolidative strategy. In particular, this is most manifest in strategic decisions to reorganize from a national to a regionally based structure (in the pursuit of efficiency and to ensure equality of treatment across the nation) and in the recent embarkation upon computerization of administrative support systems at headquarters. Our data suggest that a consolidative strategy is facilitated by both keeping dependencies to a manageable level and also reducing task ambiguity. Other research concerning NSPCC also supports this analysis (for example, Shearer, 1972; Parton, 1981).

Task ambiguity is reduced by pursuing a unitary policy toward child abuse which Parton (1981) describes as legalistic, NSPCC defends its rights in law to bring prosecutions and to remove a child from its parental home. This reduces the ambiguity which is faced by other organizations in the child-care field which favour much less precise casework-oriented relationships between organization and family. Whilst financial dependence upon the state has increased over the last 15 years (in terms of percentage of annual income) government money is usually earmarked for specific projects undertaken by NSPCC and is not an integral part of organizational survival. Indeed, NSPCC is currently examining the possibilities of securing corporate donations in order to supplement its income from voluntary sources. This follows a drive during NSPCC's centenary year (1984) aimed at attracting corporate finance. Coupled with relatively little overlap between givers of funds and receivers of services, NSPCC has been able to secure sufficient organizational 'slack' (Cyert and March, 1963) to be concerned with its internal organization to a greater extent than any other organization in our sample.

Paradoxically, this concern with efficiency and task accomplishment has resulted in dissention between two factions within the organization. There are those who believe that the legalistic approach should be maintained, whilst there is also a growing faction who believe that child-care should be conducted by setting up a consistent trusting relationship with the family. The paradox lies in the increase of task ambiguity which would be caused by taking a more casework-oriented approach. Other organizations in the child-care field would become competitors, for social services and health authority departments also operate on a casework approach. Instead of operating on a complementary basis, NSPCC would become a competitor and is likely, we suggest, to be pressured toward pursuing a co-operative rather than its present consolidative strategy.

OXFAM is the only organization in our sample with a dominant innovative strategy. Independent of state finance and with almost no overlap between givers of funds and receivers of services, OXFAM has consistently strived to increase the size and flexibility of its services. Typically, OXFAM has moved from a 'pure' relief organization to a more macro-approach of providing energy supplies, concern with the environment and supplying specialist knowledge on agriculture or the law, for example. Immediate relief is but one of many of the services offered by the organization. In addition, strategic action has been most strongly aimed at the input side of the organization. As OXFAM is wholly supported by funds from voluntary donors and profits from its retail outlets, it does experience some competition from other voluntary organizations which also lay claim to voluntary donors' money. Evidence of decisions which are oriented toward securing funds is the aggressive marketing of OXFAM shops as high street competitors (with commercial retail outlets) for items such as greeting cards, handicrafts, pottery, stationery and clothing. The cultivation of an up-market image is thought to be crucial in securing prestige for OXFAM in the eyes of the giver (40 per cent of OXFAM's funds come from trading activities) and, as such, is a relatively cheap way of coping with competition.

Although OXFAM has more comparable organizations in its industry than RNLI (for example, Christian Aid, Save the Children Fund, CAFOD, etc.), competition is limited to securing funds rather than in providing a service, although Christian Aid offer a partially similar service in relief aid overseas. Again, OXFAM seeks distinction from these competitors by being the only organization amongst them to provide research into disasters and relief aid and to publish the results. Respondents defined this as an important subsidiary task for the organization.

Decisions increasingly to decentralize decision-making represents an active attempt to remain flexible in the face of environmental demands and to remain unique in the kind of service provided overseas. Our data suggest that the diversity of services offered is likely to increase, although it is equally recognized that such flexibility requires increased funding which may have to be sought from other sources. Indeed, OXFAM is presently considering turning its attention to developing an education programme within Britain which represents a further novel venture for this traditionally overseas operator.

SUMMARY AND CONCLUSIONS

A lack of data-based research on voluntary organizations from the perspective of organizational analysis has acted as the impetus for the present article. Voluntary organizations have been given some *theoretical* consideration by those authors who espouse the transactions cost paradigm such as Williamson (1975) and Ouchi (1980). From this theoretical perspective, which focuses upon the achievement of efficiency in transactions, voluntary organizations represent the most appropriate organizational form for handling highly ambiguous tasks which, in turn, lead to their adopting strategies of co-operation in order to manage their inter-organizational network.

Like Perrow (1985, pp. 22–50), we felt that this approach posed some important questions, hence our inclusion of task and task ambiguity for the analysis of the sample. Equally, we were also aware that such a theoretical approach may hide more than it may reveal and that, in particular, neglect of the political face of voluntary organizations was likely to lead to a distorted view of their strategic operations. Hence, we have also examined the framework of dependencies within which the sample of four voluntary organizations operate.[2]

Certainly, the data from the sample organizations present some surprises if we were to take solely a 'transactions cost economics' perspective. Only one of the organizations pursues a task at a level of ambiguity we would expect (OXFAM). Two organizations pursue tasks which respondents described as *un*ambiguous (NSPCC and MCT) whilst RNLI appears to be a mixture of both. Given that we had also noted variation in strategic orientation across the four organizations, and that this also seemed to have little to do with task ambiguity, it seemed that we could account for the strategic behaviour of voluntary organizations by criteria which lie outside the scope of the transactions cost framework (see table III).

From the present data, it appears that strategic behaviour may be more accurately explained by reference to organizational dependencies. We have categorized MCT and NSPCC as being very highly and relatively highly dependent respectively. Respondents in MCT cited dependencies upon local government finance and government agencies as clients for the large part of shaping their co-operative strategies. Other empirical work on voluntary organizations which is emerging in North America and Australia supports this analysis by means of dependencies (see, for example, Scott, 1982; Moyer et al., 1983). Similarly, NSPCC's strategy is more open to fruitful interpretation if we take into account the dependencies with which it is faced. Government money, earmarked for specific projects, or aimed at financing joint projects with government departments, pressures NSPCC toward being co-operative. Yet, NSPCC are sufficiently independent of financial support from government in general to be concerned more with aspects of organizational efficiency, structure and integration (see table III) and to be primarily a consolidator.

In addition to dependencies created by interorganizational relations, the present research argues that voluntary organizations also have to manage a very special mode of interdependence between givers of finance and receivers of services. This is termed overlap, where high overlap describes the situation of givers and receivers comprising the same group of individuals. Variation in the degree of overlap is argued to contribute toward shaping organizational strategy. Where overlap is low (OXFAM) then organizations are likely both to be more input-oriented and to have the autonomy to choose their strategy. In OXFAM's case, such a choice is to pursue an innovative strategy. Certainly, analysis of OXFAM's strategic behaviour solely through considerations of its task ambiguity would only lead to an over-simplified and an erroneous conclusion (Perrow, 1985). Choice of strategy is explained by respondents primarily through reference to dependency relationships rather than to any considerations of task.

RNLI is the one organization in the sample where it is tempting to equate a strategy of co-operation with task ambiguity. To some extent, RNLI may represent a model case of the transaction's cost perspective. A deeper analysis of dependencies, however, would reveal that RNLI (like MCT) operates within a highly regulated industry. Whilst RNLI is the whole industry (no other national sea rescue organizations exist) its operators are closely monitored and regulated by central government to the extent that if RNLI were to deviate markedly from its present strategic behaviour, the state may be persuaded to bring pressure to bear upon the organization to resume its co-operative stance (see Wilson and Butler, 1985, for a more detailed discussion of RNLI's relations with the state).

Of course, these findings are based on a sample of only four organizations (although all are leaders in their field). Nevertheless, our data generally support the findings of existing research in the voluntary sector (much of which is tangential to organizational analysis). For example, as dependence on the state for finance increases, the likelihood of pursuing other than co-operative strategies is reduced (Leat, Smolka and Unell, 1981). Voluntary organizations also seem to respond in similar ways to external contingencies as their commercial counterparts, described, for example, in Pfeffer and Salancik (1978) and Butler et al. (1977). Each tries to reduce uncertainty, but decisions aimed at securing environmental support involve largely the pursuit of co-operative strategies.

This article has scratched the surface as far as any systematic analysis of the voluntary sector is concerned. However, the preliminary results from the four sample organizations indicate the importance of considering aspects of organizational task and inter-dependencies simultaneously if we are to examine strategic behaviour in any meaningful way. The present authors intend to extend the analysis of organizations in the voluntary sector in future research which should go some way to informing this much neglected area of organizational research.

Appendix I: A listing of the questions in the interview schedule

The following list of questions represents a summary of the original interview schedule. Respondents had space to answer each question at length and data were recorded on the schedule.

1. *Organization and Structure.*
1.1 Draw the organization chart, showing major functional areas.
1.2 Specify the geographical area serviced by the organization.
1.3 Does the organization have local branches either nationally or internationally? If yes, how many and how are they distributed?
1.4 Local branches are (i) fully responsible to H.Q.; (ii) autonomous within limits (specify); (iii) fully autonomous from H.Q.
1.5 Define the primary task of the organization.
1.6 What are the subsidiary tasks of the organization?
1.7 Number of paid full-time, paid part-time and unpaid voluntary individuals.
1.8 Is the organization a pioneer, a pressure group, a provider of unique servies, a provider of services also supplied by other organizations (specify), other?
1.9 Have there been any changes in the above characteristics in the past, or are there any changes anticipated in the foreseeable future? Describe any changes fully.

2. *Organizational Strategy*
2.1 Does the organization have a stated policy? What is it?
2.2 Has this policy been (i) planned; (ii) evolved over time; (iii) a mixture of both?
2.3 At what level in the organization are strategic decisions finally authorized?
2.4 Does this level of authorization vary with types of decision or with other factors? How?
2.5 Fully outline your general policies toward: resource givers, clients, regulatory bodies, other competing voluntary organizations, any other agencies.
2.6 To what extent are agencies outside the organization involved in decision-making?
2.7 Name these external agencies.
2.8 In what ways do each of these agencies hinder or facilitate organizational decision-making?
2.9 What criteria of evaluation do you use to evaluate the success or effectiveness of your strategies?
2.10 Which one or more of the following strategic profiles tests fit the overall strategic stance of the organization?
 (i) diversify the kinds of services offered, diversify sources of funding, innovate services and funding, seek prestige, compete to offer services alongside other voluntary organizations;
 (ii) merge with or integrate with other organizations; acquire other organizations; concentrate on efficiency, cost-effectiveness or internal organization generally;
 (iii) join with other organizations temporarily or permanently to provide services or to engage in research and development; invite individuals or other organizations to serve on the executive bodies of the organization.

2.11 How is the organization's strategy affected by changes in government policies such as cuts in public sector spending or grants to the private sector?

2.12 Same as question 1.9.

3. *Task Environment*

3.1 List all sources of finance for the organization. Detail the amount of money, the percentage of total input and give percentage increase or decrease over the last five years.

3.2 List all clients of the organization.

3.3 To what extent are the providers of financial resources also the receivers of service from the organization? Identify such providers.

3.4 List all other resource inputs to the organization, not including finance.

3.5 Name all other statutory, private and voluntary organizations which provide services similar to your own.

3.6 Which of these organizations satisfy the same needs of the same clientele?

3.7 To what extent do each of these other organizations draw upon the same fund of resources?

3.8 Same as question 1.9.

4. *Institutional Environment*

4.1 What is the status of the organization?

4.2 Why was this status chosen?

4.3 List all major regulatory agencies which have an interest in or impinge upon organizational activities. Detail each agency and the nature of its regulation.

4.4 List all other organizations with which you have links (e.g. political parties, research bodies, other voluntary organizations).

4.5 Apart from financial aid, what is the nature of your organization's relationship with central government, local government, commercial firms (or other)?

4.6 Does the organization work independently, belong to a co-ordinating body, work in tandem with other voluntary organizations alongside statutory or commercial organizations? Detail each mode of operation.

4.7 Same as question 1.9.

NOTES

[1] The research reported in this article was partly supported by SSRC grant no. 7960/2 and by the Leverhulme Trust.

[2] The choice of dependencies as indicative of organizational power relations was chosen for analytical convenience at this stage in the research process. It represented a primary attempt to provide a theoretical and empirical counterpart to the transactions cost and task analysis of voluntary organizations. We recognize that, in order to study the question of power in voluntary organizations, resource dependencies are only a partial approach to the problem and that theories of institutionalization, the regulatory powers of the state and the structuring and sedimentation of power relations must be examined. These are questions which will be addressed in future work on the voluntary sector by the authors of the present article.

REFERENCES

Abell, P. (Ed.) (1975). *Organizations as Bargaining and Influence Systems*. London: Heinemann.

AIKEN, M., DEWAR, R., DITOMASO, N., HAGE, J. and ZEITZ, G. (1975). *Coordinating Human Services*. San Francisco: Jossey-Bass.

ALDRICH, H. (1979). *Organizations and Environments*. Englewood Cliffs, N.J.: Prentice-Hall.

ARROW, K. J. (1974). *The Limits of Organization*. New York: W. W. Norton.

ASTLEY, W. G., AXELSSON, R., BUTLER, R. J., HICKSON, D. J. and WILSON, D. C. (1982). 'Complexity and cleavage: dual explanations of strategic decision making'. *Journal of Management Studies,* **19**, 3, 357–75.

BOWMAN, E. H. (1976). 'Strategy and the weather'. *Sloan Management Review,* **17**, 2, 49–58.

BRAYBROOKE, D. and LINDBLOM, C. E. (1963). *A Strategy of Decision*. New York: Free Press.

BUTLER, R. J. (1983a). 'A transactional approach to organizing efficiency: perspectives from markets, hierarchies and collectives'. *Administration and Society,* **15**, 3, 323–62.

BUTLER, R. J. (1983b). 'Control through markets, hierarchies and communes: a transactional approach to organisational analysis'. In Francis, A., Turk, J. and Willman, P. (Eds.), *Power, Efficiency and Institutions*. London: Heinemann.

BUTLER, R. J. and WILSON, D. C. (1983). 'Profiteers and givers: perspectives on privatization'. Working paper, University of Bradford Management Centre.

BUTLER, R. J., HICKSON, D. J., WILSON, D. C. and AXELSSON, R. (1977). 'Organizational power, politicking and paralysis'. *Organization and Administrative Sciences,* **8**, 4, 45–60.

BUTLER, R. J., ASTLEY, W. G., HICKSON, D. J., MALLORY, G. and WILSON, D. C. (1979). 'Strategic decision making: concepts of content and process'. *International Studies of Management and Organization,* **IX**, 4, 5–36.

CYERT, R. M. and MARCH, J. G. (1963). *A Behavioral Theory of the Firm*. Englewood Cliffs, N.J.: Prentice-Hall.

DURKHEIM, E. (1933). *The Division of Labor in Society*. (Trans. G. Simpson) New York: Free Press.

EMERSON, R. E. (1962). 'Power-dependence relations'. *American Sociological Review,* 27, 31–41.

ENGWALL, L. (1985). 'Organizational drift as a response to resource dependence'. Paper presented at the 7th EGOS Colloquium: Challenges to Organizational Authority, Saltsjobaden, Sweden, 12–14 June.

GALBRAITH, J. K. (1967). *The New Industrial Estate*. London: Hamish Hamilton.

GILL, P. (1970). *Drops in the Ocean: The Work of Oxfam 1960–1970*. London: MacDonald.

GRINYER, P. H. and SPENDER, J.-C. (1979). 'Recipes, crises and adaptation in mature businesses'. *International Studies of Management and Organization,* **IX**, 3, 113–33.

HAGE, J. (1980). *Theories of Organizations: Form, Process and Transformation*. New York: Wiley.

HATCH, S. and MOCROFT, I. (1979). 'The relative costs of services provided by voluntary and statutory organizations'. *Public Administration,* **57**, Winter: 397–406.

HAYEK, F. (1945). 'The use of knowledge in society'. *American Economic Review,* **35**, September, 519–30.

HEGNER, F. (1980). 'Solidarity, hierarchy and market exchange'. Preprint Series, Institute of Management, Berlin.

HICKSON, D. J., BUTLER, R. J., CRAY, D., MALLORY, G. and WILSON, D. C. (1985). *Top Decisions: Strategic Decision Making in Organizations*. San Francisco: Jossey-Bass.

JONES, M. (1965). *Two Ears of Corn: Oxfam in Action*. London: Hodder and Stoughton.

KANTER, R. M. (1968). 'Commitment and social organization: a study of commitment mechanisms in Utopian communities'. *American Sociological Review,* **33**, 4, 499–517.

KANTER, R. M. (1972). *Commitment and Community: Communes and Utopias in Sociological Perspective*. Cambridge, Mass.: Harvard University Press.

KANTER, R. M. (1979). 'The measurement of organizational effectiveness, productivity, performance and success'. Program on Non-Profit Organizations: Yale University.

KIRZNER, I. (1980). 'The primacy of entrepreneurial discovery'. In *The Prime Mover of Progress: The Entrepreneur in Capitalism and Socialism*. London: Institute of Economic Affairs.

KRAMER, R. (1979). 'Voluntary agencies in the welfare state: an analysis of the vanguard role'. *Journal of Social Policy*, **8**, 4, 473–88.

LEAT, D., SMOLKA, G. and UNELL, J. (1981). *Voluntary and Statutory Collaboration: Rhetoric or Reality?* London: Bedford Square Press/NCVO.

LEVINE, S. and WHITE, P. E. (1961). 'Exchange as a conceptual framework for the study of interorganizational relationships'. *Administrative Science Quarterly*, **5**, 583–610.

LINDBLOM, C. E. (1959). 'The science of "muddling through"'. *Public Administration Review*, **19**, 79–88.

MCKELVEY, B. and ALDRICH, H. (1983). 'Populations, natural selection, and applied organizational science'. *Administrative Science Quarterly*, **28**, 1, 101–28.

MARCH, J. G. and SIMON, H. A. (1958). *Organizations*. New York: Wiley.

MARCH, J. G. and OLSEN, J. P. (1976), *Ambiguity and Choice in Organizations*. Bergen: Universitetforlaget.

MILES, R. E. and SNOW, C. C. (1978). *Organizational Strategy, Structure and Process*. New York: McGraw-Hill.

MILLER, D. and FRIESEN, P. H. (1984). *Organizations: A Quantum View*. Englewood Cliffs, N.J.: Prentice-Hall.

MILLWARD, R. (1982). 'The comparative performance of public and private ownership'. In Lord Roll of Ipsden (Ed.), *The Mixed Economy*, London: Macmillan, 58–93.

MINTZBERG, H. (1979). 'Patterns in strategy formation'. *International Studies of Management and Organization*, **IX**, 3, 67–86.

MOYER, M. S. (Ed.) (1983). *Managing Voluntary Organizatons*. Toronto: York University Voluntary Sector Program.

MURRAY, M. A. (1975). 'Comparing public and private management: an exploratory study'. *Public Administration Review*, **35**, 364–71.

OUCHI, W. G. (1980). 'Markets, bureaucracies and clans'. *Administrative Science Quarterly*, **25**, 1, 129–41.

OUCHI, W. G. and JAEGER, A. M. 'Type Z organization: stability in the midst of mobility'. *Academy of Management Review*, **3**, 305–14.

PARTON, N. (1981). 'Child abuse, social anxiety and welfare'. *British Journal of Social Work*, **II**, 391–414.

PERROW, C. (1985). 'Economic theories of organizations'. Paper presented at the University of Uppsala, Sweden. 15 May 1985, to form ch. 7 of the forthcoming 3rd Ed. of *Complex Organizations*.

PFEFFER, J. and SALANCIK, G. R. (1978). *The External Control of Organizations: A Resource Dependence Perspective*. New York: Harper and Row.

RAINEY, H. G., BACKOFF, R. W. and LEVINE, C. H. (1976). 'Comparing public and private organizations'. *Public Administration Review*, **36**, 233–44.

ROTHSCHILD-WHITT, J. (1979). 'The collectivist organization: an alternative to rational-bureaucratic models'. *American Sociological Review*, **44**, 509–27.

SAXON-HARROLD, S. K. E. (1985). 'Strategy in Voluntary Organizations'. Ph.D. dissertation, University of Bradford Management Centre.

SCOTT, D. (1982). *Don't Mourn for Me – Organise: The Social and Political Uses of Voluntary Organizations*. London: Allen and Unwin.

SELZNICK, P. (1957). *Leadership in Administration*. New York: Harper and Row.

SHAPIRO, B. P. (1973). 'Marketing for non profit organizations'. *Harvard Business Review*, **51**, 5, 123–32.

SHEARER, A. (1972). 'The NSPCC – in search of a new identity'. *World Medicine*, 8 March, 147–74.

SNOW, C. C. and HREBINIAK, L. G. (1980). 'Strategy, distinctive competence, and organizational performance'. *Administrative Science Quarterly*, **25**, 2, 317–36.

THOMPSON, J. D. (1967). *Organizations in Action*. New York: McGraw-Hill.

TITMUSS, R. M. (1970). *The Gift Relationship: From Human Blood to Social Policy*. Harmondsworth: Penguin.

TONNIES, F. (1955). *Community and Association (Gemeinschaft and Gesellschaft)*. (Trans. and supplemented by C. P. Loomis). London: Routledge and Kegan Paul.

WALBERG, A. (1982). 'Market decisions in voluntary organizations'. M.B.A. dissertation, University of Bradford Management Centre.

WEBER, M. (1947). *The Theory of Social and Economic Organization*. (Trans. A. M. Henderson and T. Parsons). Glencoe, Ill.: Free Press.

WEBER, M. (1968). *Economy and Society*. (Trans. G. Roth and K. Wittich). New York: Bedminster Press.

WILLIAMSON, O. E. (1975). *Markets and Hierarchies: Analysis and Anti-Trust Implication*. New York: Free Press.

WILLIAMSON, O. E. and OUCHI, W. G. (1981). 'The markets and hierarchies and visible hand perspectives'. In Van de Ven, A. H. and Joyce, W. F. (Eds.), *Perspectives on Organization Design and Behavior*. New York: Wiley.

WILSON, D. C. and BUTLER, R. J. (1985). 'Corporatism in the British voluntary sector'. In Streeck, W. and Schmitter, P. C. (Eds.), *Private Government as Agents of Public Policy*. London: Sage.

ZEITZ, G. (1980). 'Interorganizational dialectics'. *Administrative Science Quarterly*, **25**, 1, 72–88.

Part IV
National Features

[15]

Journal of Management Studies, 20, 2, 1983

IMPLANTED DECISION-MAKING: AMERICAN OWNED FIRMS IN BRITAIN [1]

GEOFFREY R. MALLORY, RICHARD J. BUTLER, DAVID CRAY, DAVID J. HICKSON AND DAVID C. WILSON

Organizational Analysis Research Unit, University of Bradford Management Centre

ABSTRACT

DECISION-MAKING processes are compared in American and British subsidiaries in Britain to investigate how far processual characteristics as distinct from structural features, may be implanted in subsidiaries abroad. Managements in the British owned subsidiaries tend to route their biggest decisions through the formalities of standing committees in conformity with customary procedures, taking a comparatively long time to do so. Managements in the American owned subsidiaries tend to rely on informally assembled working groups which help to arrive at a decision comparatively rapidly through a process which does not ostensibly follow any recognized procedure. The British mode is formal within a non-formalized customary pattern, the American mode informal within a formalized frame.

IMPLANTING PROCESSUAL CHARACTERISTICS

CONVERSATIONS between those who contend with the practical and theoretical obstacles of cross-national comparative research sometimes refer wistfully to an ideal study in which the organizations to be compared are perfectly matched. One ideal is where in comparing, for instance, firms in Japan, the United States, and other countries there would be an exact correspondence of Japanese firms in Japan and Japanese owned subsidiaries in the United States with American firms in the United States and American owned subsidiaries in Japan, and so on. In successive analyzes the apparent effects of national location, and of ownership, could then be controlled and anything due to elements in the national ways of life be more clearly exposed.

Pending such ideals, published research consists of piecemeal accumulation of results from samples each of which contributes only one piece to the picture. But even piecemeal accumulation during the 1970's did begin to put that picture together: '. . . there is gradually increasing understanding, and Child's (1981) review at the end of the decade does not have the despair that Roberts (1970) felt "on looking at an elephant" (as she put it) at the beginning of the decade' (Hickson and McMillan, 1981, p. 187).

Address for reprints: G. R. Mallory, Organizational Analysis Research Unit, University of Bradford Management Centre, Emm Lane, Bradford BD9 4JL.

The research reported here offers one such piece, the results of a comparison of American owned subsidiaries and British owned subsidiaries *all* with British managers and located in Britain. This has the advantage of controlling for any effects of national location, raising the question whether firms adjacent territorially can differ just because some of them are owned from the territory of another nation. Can the managements of multi-national corporations project national characteristics, which in this case would be 'Americanisms', across the oceans to their subsidiaries?

Since *prima facie* the answer is 'yes' for structural specialization and formalization, for obviously headquarters can require the setting up of specialist departments (*e.g.* insist on a marketing department being established by the subsidiary where there was none before) or conformity to corporation rules (*e.g.* monthly financial returns by the subsidiary in a standard form), what then if the question is asked of processes? This paper examines how far a multi-national's management can project characteristics in the processes of making decisions *even* though those making the decisions are of a *different* nationality, in this case British managers in American-owned subsidiaries where no American manager is personally present. Do the British managements in the subsidiaries tend towards decision-making processes with American characteristics?

Negandhi (1979) showed that the subsidiaries abroad of American multinationals, even if located in culturally different and economically 'developing' societies, do take over all the more formal paraphernalia of modern management normal to the parent corporation. They have comprehensive planning procedures, formalized budgetary controls, effective personnel and training functions *etc.*, whereas similar locally owned firms do not. He compared American owned subsidiaries with locally owned firms in South American and Asia.

In Africa, Ajiboye's (1980) comparison of two locally owned firms with a French subsidiary and a British subsidiary in Nigeria is suggestive in the same direction, but for hierarchical relationships. The two locally owned firms differed from the French and British owned subsidiaries in their employees' responses to questions on hierarchical influence, as plotted on a Tannenbaum (1968) control graph, but even more significantly the French and British owned subsidiaries differed from each other, the British being the less hierarchical. These owning corporations seemed able to stamp their own imprint on the managements of their overseas subsidiaries.

In both the Negandhi (1979) and Ajiboye (1980) studies the means used by the owning corporations appeared to be the export of expatriate top managers to the subsidiaries. Although this may be effective for management systems and the approach taken to subordinates, the national norms of behaviour in which arise the decision-making processes examined in this paper could be resistant to influences from foreign headquarters even when expatriates bring their own customary approach with them. Preliminary impressions of research by Kidd and Teramoto (1981) indicate that although expatriate Japanese managers bring to their European subsidiaries typical Japanese practices such as the widely participative *ringi* decision-making process and the *ringi sho* document which all involved managers sign to signify their assent, such practices do not include nor transfer to their European colleagues (in the particular instance of the *ringi sho* this is virtually impossible by it being in Japanese script). In the same way, the prolonged *nemawashi* process of informal, indeed casual, discussion which precedes the drawing up of the *ringi sho* rarely includes European colleagues who do not have time for it, neither literally nor temperamentally. Thus although the European managers appreciate what they find to be a more communicative organizational climate, despite the normative barriers, their own ways are little affected by the Japanese practices even though their senior colleagues are Japanese.

Given this resistance to the adoption of foreign ways when they are introduced by the presence in person of foreign nationals, the question is whether the decision-making processes of managements in far off subsidiaries show characteristics representing the ways of their foreign owners even when there are no expatriates among them? How influential in this respect are multinational corporations at, so to speak, one remove?

The importance of local conditioning is evidenced by Kelly and Worthley (1981) who show that Japanese-American managers in Hawaii are more like the Caucasian-American managers with whom they interact, and whose national outlook they share, than they are like Japanese managers in Japan. The implication is that it is difficult to implant characteristics from afar to managements of another nationality. Whilst it is commonplace for multinationals to introduce prescribed information and control systems, it is less likely that they are able to shape the processes by which major decisions are arrived at within their subordinate élites.

CASES COMPARED

The twenty cases of decision-making processes compared in this paper took place over various periods ranging from months to years during the ten years 1969–1979 in two American subsidiaries in Britain with wholly British managements (there were no American expatriates among them at any time), and two British owned subsidiaries in Britain. The selection of American owned subsidiaries parallels that made by Jamieson (1980a; 1980b) who argues that:

> The majority of studies which have attempted to investigate the effect of socio-cultural factors on business behaviour have tended to compare indigenous firms operating in country A with indigenous firms operating in country B. The design of this study is different in that all firms are located in one country, England. I would argue that in two distinct ways

> this is a more rigorous test of hypotheses about the effect of culture on business organizations. In the first place the operating environment of the firms is held constant and this is of vital importance. Secondly, if if can be shown that American firms, despite operating in England and employing English nationals, still exhibited the effects of American culture upon their structure and operation, then it can be safely assumed that cultural variables are relevant in the explanation of business behaviour (Jamieson, 1980a, p. 219).

Whilst agreeing with Jamieson's (1980a) point that such a sample can show how far 'culture' can be implanted abroad, it has to be recognized that the case of American firms in Britain is a less rigorous test than he here makes out, for despite fascinating American/British differences the two nations share an Anglo-Saxon cultural heritage that could make the implanting of American characteristics more likely than implanting, for example, from Japanese multi-nationals. This qualification will be referred to again in the interpretation of the result.

This paper also takes the same point of comparison for decision-making processes in the American owned subsidiaries as Jamieson (1980b) took for his comparison of structural, ideological, and organizational climate features, namely British owned subsidiaries. Any differences which may be attributable to American influence are exposed by comparing ten decision-making processes in the two American subsidiaries with ten processes in the two British subsidiaries.

For those who are concerned with cross-national research, this kind of comparison of subsidiaries within the one country might be exploited more than it has been so far. Whilst its interpretation must differ from those of country by country studies, where it is appropriate to research aims it brings the advantage of completely avoiding the costs in travel and time and coordination which those studies incur.

The comparison originated when it was noticed that a sample of thirty diverse organizations in Britain studied for an extensive project over 150 cases on the making of strategic decisions (Butler *et al.*, 1979/80; Butler *et al.*, 1982; Wilson, 1982) included two American subsidiaries. Since there is little or no empirical cross-national comparison of such processes this aroused immediate curiosity. The two most similar British subsidiaries in the same sample were compared. The results of the comparison were of sufficient interest to lead to the writing of this paper. However, an analysis of twenty cases of decision-making in only two pairs of organizations taken from a set chosen primarily for other purposes is strictly limited. This paper is bound by these limits, and its claims to validity rests primarily not on the sampling but on the correspondence of results with the implications of published research. It fulfils these implications in an area previously not directly investigated: decision-making processes.

The Firms

The four firms from which the twenty cases of decision-making are taken are denoted as US–H, US–J, UK–A, UK–M.

Firm US–H is a wholly owned subsidiary of a major U.S. food and chemical corporation. Its principal manufactures are chemicals and paint which it markets together with other agency products through a large and well established distribution network. The company was essentially a family business from its founding in the early 1900's until it went public in the mid-60's, since when it has continually and successfully added to its product range, eventually being taken over by the U.S. corporation in the early 1970's.

Firm US–J is a wholly owned subsidiary of a U.S. engineering group. It specializes in the manufacture of precision tools and also markets a variety of agency products. The company in its present form grew from an initial association of a subsidiary of the U.S. parent with a well established engineering group in the immediate post-war period. Two years later both were combined as a wholly owned subsidiary. It has a U.K. board of directors who are working executives of the company and it is this group, particularly the chairman, who are responsible for dealings with the parent group.

Firm UK–A is a wholly owned subsidiary of a major U.K. engineering group: it manufactures a standard range of construction engineering equipment. The company has gone through many stages of growth and mutation since its foundation in the late 19th century, particularly in the late 1960's when its existing organizational form and pattern of ownership was set, changing from being independent to a wholly owned subsidiary. Manufacturing is at two sites with the company's headquarters located at the major one. Group Head Office is in London.

Firm UK–M is a wholly owned subsidiary of a U.K. textile and engineering group, specializing in the manufacture of friction products which it markets on a worldwide basis to both manufacturer and *via* its own distribution network to replacement customers. The firm's task is difficult to characterize as the product requires an unusual amalgam of both chemical and engineering technologies. The production unit and Head Office function are located on the same site, which also houses the owning group's worldwide headquarters. There is a product division form of organization so that between the board of directors of UK–M and the holding group board, a divisional board is interposed, providing a complex pattern of interlocking directorates. The company began operations in the late 19th century and moved into its present product line in the 1920's; its current organizational form was the result of a succession of amalgamations and reorganizations in the late 1960's.

All four firms have a distinct corporate identity, marketing products under their own name. All had similarly functionally differentiated top manage-

Table I. Four American owned and British owned subsidiaries

	American owned		British owned	
Firm:	*US–H*	*US–J*	*UK–A*	*UK–M*
Ownership:	Wholly owned	Wholly owned	Wholly owned	Wholly owned
Owning group:	Chemical and food group	Engineering group	Engineering group	Engineering and textile group
Technology/ product:	Large batch chemicals and paint	Large batch precision small tools and their components	Small batch building contractors' equipment	Large batch automotive components (non-metal)
Size: (employees):	350	700	2000	2000

ments, the chief executives' spans of control ranging between six and eight. Table I lists some of their more obvious features, in addition to nationality of ownership, by which differences in decision-making might be explained. The factor on which there is a substantial disparity is size, the British being the larger. This makes some results difficult to interpret, where possible effects of size cannot be distinguished from those of nationality of ownership. This is referred to in the discussion of results.

But the firms themselves are not the primary unit of analysis. This is the decision-making process, of which there are five *per* firm. All but one fall into four categories of decision topics, product decisions, plant/equipment decisions, domain (marketing) decisions, and planning decisions, as shown in table II. There are new product and plant/equipment decisions in all four firms, and marketing and planning decisions in three out of four. This reflects the tendency for given kinds of organization to be preoccupied with certain categories of decision as reported by Hickson *et al.* (1982) in their analysis of the full sample of 150 cases in thirty organizations from which these twenty cases are drawn. Manufacturing firms are typically mostly concerned with product, plant, and marketing issues.

Data Collection

Data on twenty decision-making processes were collected by lengthy interviews with senior executives who had been centrally involved. The firms were first approached by letter, and the chief executives interviewed both to obtain background information on the history, products, and structure of the firm and to obtain a list of decisions defined by the management as major which had been taken within the recent memory of senior managers. The chief executive nominated as many such decisions as could be readily recalled, and from these a selection of five was made to include as far as possible one in each category of topic concerned with inputs, outputs, core technology, personnel and reorganization. Since the research dealt only with

Table II. Twenty decision cases

	American owned		*British owned*	
Firm:	*US-H*	*US-J*	*UK-A*	*UK-M*
Decision Topic Category:				
Products:	1. Extend product range 2. Become agents for German company's products	1. New product	1. New product	1. New product
Plant/equipment:	3. Expand production capacity (rent additional factory)	2. Expand production capacity (new building and plant) 3. Expand data processing facility	2. Expand production capacity (new building and plant) 3. Purchase new lathes	2. New plant 3. Computerize inventory control
Domain (marketing):	4. Stay out of a market 5. Direct sales to retail outlets	4. Create marketing specialism	4. Standardize company name	
Planning:		5. Business plan	5. Production plan	4. Business plan
Personnel:				5. Staff re-grading, using consultants

actual processes within recall the coverage was uneven, as table II shows, for if no reorganization case could be recalled, for example, no attempt was made to strain memory into the distant past to find or 'invent' one. The chief executive nominated one or more key informants from among his colleagues to discuss each decision. The twenty cases discussed in this paper were derived from interviews with from one to three informants *per* case, usually two, ranging from function heads through directors to managing director and chairman: the separate accounts were consolidated into a single process description of each case.

Each interview began with an historical description of the decision-making process from the time the matter was first raised until the decision, positive or negative, was reached. This was followed by a series of standard questions to which responses were either open-ended only or open-ended together with a rating on a short scale.

PROCESS FEATURES COMPARED

A set of concepts of strategic decision-making processes formulated by Astley *et al.* (1982) were used to guide the larger empirical project referred to earlier. From among these concepts, American/British differences were looked for in those listed in table III. It is not implied that the eight listed describe all aspects of decision-making, but they do represent aspects all through the process, from its initiation proactively or reactively, through the horizon of vision and the number of alternatives considered, to the amount and formality of interaction, the level at which the authorized decision was taken, and how long the process went on. It was these eight which carried the strongest presumptions of American/British differences.

These presumptions are succinctly put by McMillan *et al.* (1973, p. 157):

> Predominant American values of rugged individualism, a frontier spirit, a revolutionary character conducive to change and mobility, and a preference for pluralistic authority patterns are all part of a normative cultural mosaic. The much longer history of British society, its traditions and its stability, give it a legacy of normatively legitimized adherence to established institutions and behavioural patterns.

Jamieson (1980a) sees the American values as more fully in keeping with the interests generated by capitalism, so that the greater managerial dedication to all that is implied by 'scientific management' which Inkson *et al.* (1970) found reflected in their empirical results is to be expected.

Hence the 'Impressions of a Visiting Professor' put forward by Dubin (1970) have a ring of truth about them when they accord with these basic societal differences, even though Jamieson (1980a) is inclined to be dismissive about 'impressions'. Impressions are impressive when they accord with so much else, and they have a depth of understanding that is often

Table III. Decision-making process features

Concept	*Definition*	*Operational variables*
Proactivity:	The extent to which the process is an initiative.	Six point scale from No Initiative (decision predefined) through Constrained Initiative to Opportunistic Initiative (unexpected event triggers decision beyond any previous ideas).
Horizon:	The extent to which the process generates future resource commitment.	The period for which process participants looked ahead.
Scan:	The extent to which the process surveys available choices.	The number of alternatives considered (doing nothing being counted where it was a viable alternative).
Interaction volume:	The extent to which the process generates interaction among its participants.	Five point rating from None to A Very Great Deal.
Interaction formality:	The extent to which interaction generated in the process is predefined.	The number of working groups, special committees, and standing committees used (a committee being a body formally established, in the case of a special committee for the particular issue being processed).
Standardization:	The extent to which the process follows pre-existing routines.	The number of unwritten or written procedures followed.
Centrality:	The extent to which the process occurs at the summit of the hierarchy.	The level in the hierarchy at which a decision was authorized.
Duration:	The temporal extent of the overall process.	*a* Gestation time: the period in months from the first mention of an issue to the time identifiable action took place on a specific topic. *b* Process time: the period in months from the time of first action towards decision on a topic to the time the decision is authorized (*i.e.* approved choice is made).

missing from survey-type comparisons. So when Dubin (1970) suggests, as did Granick (1962) before him, that American managers are willing to try something out despite risks, whereas their British counterparts demand that proposals for innovation be proved before they are applied, this does create a presumption that decision processes in American owned firms are more likely to be initiated proactively rather than to be reactive, to go ahead on a shorter view (*i.e.*. time horizon) of possible consequences with less concern for the farflung future, and to scan more alternative possibilities. These features, proactivity, horizon, and scan are the first, second, and third concepts in table III.

Dubin (1970) makes much of the personal trust in subordinates that British management style emphasizes, a trust which requires reciprocal conformity from those subordinates, in contrast to the openness of American management style. This latter might well stimulate a greater interaction volume (table III) since more is open to discussion, and Jamieson (1980a, p. 226) did find 'more meetings of managers' in American owned subsidiaries. In contrast, British style interaction may not only be less but may have more formality (table III) about it, for Jamieson (1980a) found American owned firms comparatively informal in personal relationships. If that is so in American firms it is an intriguing combination with American bureaucratic formalization (pointed to by Inkson *et al.* (1970), McMillan *et al.* (1973), and to a lesser degree by Jamieson (1980b). It leads to a presumption that American-influenced managerial decision-making processes will combine informal interaction with formalized standard procedures (table III: Standardization).

All comparative statements are relative, and although Clark (1979) finds British management more decentralized than equivalent French management, and Budde *et al.* (1982) find some tendency in the same direction on some decisions only in a comparison with West German managements. Jamieson (1980a) suggests that American owned firms are even further decentralized. So their decision processes should culminate at a lower authority level (table III) than do those in British owned firms.

Eggars (1977) asserts that American managers like to get a move on. Comparing them with their French counterparts, he writes:

> An American will probably lose his typical enthusiasm for a project before a Frenchman gets over his typical reservations (Eggars, 1977, p. 137).

This caricature may be overdone just for effect, but it fits well with Jamieson's (1980a) finding that managers in American owned subsidiaries rated forcefulness relatively highly as a characteristic, and with the tendency for his data to support Child and McMillan's (1972) finding that American managers not only work longer than British managers but use leisure time as an 'extension of work' into which work related activities intrude. This pattern of characteristics implies that American-influenced managements may take decisions faster, *i.e.* the duration (table III) of major decision-making processes will be shorter.

In summary, on variables representing the concepts of decision-making process in table III, American influenced subsidiary firms might be anticipated to show greater proactivity, interaction volume, standardization, and scan, and British subsidiaries not so influenced might be anticipated to show longer horizon and greater interaction formality, centrality, and duration. The twenty processes dealing with the decision topics listed in table II are now compared, ten in each pair of subsidiaries. The comparison is on the operational variables in table III, these being taken from those devised by Butler *et al.* (1982) for the larger project.

RESULTS

The differences between decision-making processes in the American owned and British owned subsidiaries are not extensive. It would be surprising if they were. Even comparing firms located in the United States and in Britain, Inkson *et al.* (1970, p. 363) suspected there were . . . 'more differences among managers and organizations within both U.S. and G.B. cultures than between these cultures'; and comparing subsidiaries located in Britain, as this paper does, Jamieson (1980a, 1980b) reported few differences.

Across the twenty decision-making processes, the U.S/U.K. proactivity, horizon, scan, interaction volume, and centrality are much the same. There is nothing to suggest that the decisions in the U.S. owned firms were more often launched proactively; nor that the decision-makers in the British owned firms looked further ahead since in both sets of decision processes the horizon averaged about six years (ranging from the very short term to many years); nor that American influence encourages a wider scan of alternatives for in both sets of processes two, three, or four possibilities were usually considered, such as investment in equipment *versus* product rationalization *versus* buying in supplies as alternative ways of circumventing bottlenecks in future plans (table II, US–J5) or several company image names (table II, UK–A4). Thus American ownership did not appear to spur British managements into the more risk-taking mode of proactive, short term, alternative scanning decision-making that Dubin's (1970) impressions suggest.

Likewise, all the decisions in both pairs of subsidiaries were reported as having stimulated comparably busy interaction, a to-ing and fro-ing which rated similarly on a scale of interaction volume. The sheer amount of interaction did not differ.

Finally, centrality of authorization of the decision, either to go ahead or more rarely not to do so (table II, US–H4), was at similar levels. In both pairs of subsidiaries, some decisions were authorized by the chief executive alone (such as the new product decisions in US–J and UK–M: table II), some by the top governing body (such as direct sales to retail outlets decision in US–H), some by that body but subject to ratification by headquarters (such as UK–A's new company name and US–J's data processing expansion). The American owned subsidiaries were not noticeably more decentralized in this respect, despite the anticipation that they were likely to be so.

So on these aspects of process there is no hint of any difference which might be due to American influence. It is in the kinds of interaction and routines that differences stand out, and in the time it takes to take a decision. These differences are apparent in overall comparisons across all the decision topics in table II, and even more clearly if decision topic is controlled for by comparing across only the new product/extend product range topics or expand production/new plant topics that are common to all four subsidiaries (table II: topics 1 and 3, US–H, and topics 1 and 2, US–J, UK–A, UK–M).

Interaction formality (table IV) is indicated by the use of management working groups, special committees, or standing committees during a decision-making process. The working group is informal in origin and composition, and temporary, arising in the course of the particular decision process. For example, senior managers may get together several times although no one sets terms of reference, or agenda, or plans the meeting. Special committees, frequently called task forces or project teams, are formally constituted to accomplish a certain task, but they too are finite. Standing committees are positioned well within the formal institutional framework, being both formally constituted and of infinite life. They meet at regular intervals, with agenda and minutes, and have a comparatively static membership: examples are Management Meetings, Finance Committees, and Boards of Directors.

Table IV compares the decision processes in these terms. The contrast is plain to see. The processes in UK–A and UK–M have all the standing committees and all but two of the special committees. Those in US–H and US–J have all but one of the working groups. The contrast is especially clear if like decision topics only are compared, the four new product cases (all topic 1) and the new plant cases US–H3, US–J2, UK–A2, and UK–M2.

It is tempting to conclude that American influence breaks down the formality of decision-making in British management. The social customs of British society which require a time and a place for everything, including predictable meetings of predictable composition for predictable purposes, give way to informally gathered working groups. Indeed, this is a likely and tenable interpretation, but it has to be held alongside an alternative interpretation that gives primacy to size. As the British owned subsidiaries are larger it can also be argued that interaction has to be more formally pre-planned and regulated to avoid confusion. Probably the influences of American ownership and of size are both operative, but if so and both are working in the same direction their effects cannot be separated in this sample of decision-making processes.

Table IV. American/British differences in decision-making

		Interaction formality			*Standardization*		*Duration*	
		Number of:			*Any procedures:*		*Number of months:*	
Firm	*Decision topic*	*Working Groups*	*Special Committees*	*Standing Committees*	*Unwritten*	*Written*	*Gestation*	*Process*
US–H	1. Extend product range	1	0	0	0	0	0	5
	2. Become agents for German company's product	0	1	0	0	0	0	10
	3. Expand production capacity	1	0	0	0	0	0	1
	4. Stay out of a market	1	0	0	0	0	96	18
	5. Direct sales to retailers	1	0	0	0	0	180	3
US–J	1. New product	1	0	0	0	0	0	2
	2. Expand production capacity	1	0	0	0	1	0	3
	3. Expand data processing facility	1	0	0	0	0	0	12
	4. Create marketing specialism	1	0	0	0	0	0	12
	5. Business plan	0	1	0	0	1	0	8
UK–A	1. New product	0	1	2	1	0	6	6
	2. Expand production capacity	0	1	3	0	1	0	30
	3. Purchase new lathes	0	1	1	1	0	0	18
	4. Standardize brand name	0	1	0	0	0	1	6
	5. Production plan	0	0	2	1	0	12	1
UK–M	1. New product	0	0	1	1	0	0	27
	2. New plant	0	1	1	0	1	72	24
	3. Computerize inventory control	1	1	0	1	0	22	18
	4. Business plan	0	0	2	1	0	0	2
	5. Staff re-grading, using consultants	0	0	2	0	0	0	11

However, it is possible that within the four firms there is some apparent size effect in the opposite direction, favouring formal committees in the American owned pair and in some degree offsetting any direct size effect in the British owned pair, since the parent corporations of the American pair are somewhat larger.

Other evidence also helps to sustain the interpretation that American ownership is a strong influence. Even though the sizes of the subsidiaries differ their top management echelons do not. It is these echelons whose members generate and take part in the processes of deciding what they regard as major matters, and it is these processes that are the subject of comparison here. It was mentioned earlier that in both pairs of subsidiaries the numbers at the top reporting direct to the chief executive and making up his span of control were similar, as were the functions they represented. Thus UK–A and UK–M did not have greater numbers of immediate participants to coordinate through their standing committees than did US–J and US–H.

Standardization, the second variable in table IV, indicates whether any part or parts of a decision-making process followed a standard procedure, that is a recognized routine existing prior to the particular topic arising and applying also to other decision processes. It can be seen that only two procedures were reported in the processes in US–H and US–J, whereas eight out of the ten processes in UK–A and UK–M followed procedures. Of these eight, most were unwritten rather than bureaucratized: one did follow a written procedure predominantly, but another did so in part only and the others followed what were termed unwritten procedures.

Among the instances of written procedures, US–J5, the business plan decision, had to conform to a procedure imposed by the American owning corporation, a procedure conspicuous in the stack of estimates and supporting data in a standard form which the chief executive heaved from his desk drawer. The other three instances of written procedures all apply to new plant/expand production capacity decisions, and suggest a tendency for this type of decision to be governed by written procedures, whatever the firm. In any firm the renewal or expansion of plant and equipment is likely to be a recurrent topic so that written procedures are evolved for it. Here the topic could be a factor as well as the U.K. bias. But that bias is much the most distinctive in *un*written procedures. They are referred to by the managers in the British owned subsidiaries alone.

These unwritten procedures are the tacit taken-for-granteds such as that this kind of matter is always looked at first by Department X before ever it gets to Committee Y, but of course it must always be considered by Committee Y before anyone can take it on further—yet nowhere is all this written down. Everyone is supposed to know. After all, how else could it be done?

So the decision processes in the American owned subsidiaries were not encrusted with formalized rules to the extent anticipated; it was the British owned subsidiaries which mostly followed procedures, but these were unwritten customary ones. Taken together with the possibility that the British tend to make more use of formal committees, this implies that decision-making in the British owned subsidiaries was more institutionalized in general, following comparatively unvarying custom and practice both in meetings and in the sequence of things to be done and who must be involved, which was sufficiently known and accepted as not to require formalized documentation.

Recalling that the processes in US–H and US–J used working groups whereas those in UK–A and UK–M used special and standing committees, it can be suggested that in UK–A and UK–M the authority over a decision was formally institutionalized into the process by these committees. Special committees (task forces *etc.*) reported to standing committees directly or through managers who reported their results, the function of the standing committee then being collectively to legitimate action. In contrast, the working groups in the American owned subsidiaries did no more than collect and pool information and make recommendations.

But does traditional formal institutionalization slow things down? Table IV compares the duration of the twenty processes, in months, being the period from the first remembered inception of the topic, however casually introduced, to the authorization of a decision, whether to go ahead with implementation or to abandon the idea. The table follows Butler *et al.* (1982) in splitting duration into gestation time and process time. Gestation time is any period from the first inception of an issue (*e.g.* when someone said something about it, or information came in indicating a coming problem), during which nothing is done towards arriving at a decision, but awareness builds up towards the process time. A case does not necessarily have a discernable gestation period (see table IV). Process time follows, being the time period in which an issue becomes a recognized topic for decision, from the first step in the process of moving to a decision (*e.g.* an arranged discussion, or the appearance of the matter on an agenda) to approved choice (*i.e.* authorized decision). For example, the feasibility of bypassing wholesalers and selling direct to retailers had been informally discussed in US–H (topic 5) among various members of management, who came and left, for a gestation period of no less than fifteen years before eventually a working party initiated a rapid process period which led to the decision.

It can be been in table IV that in UK–A and UK–M the process periods far exceed those in US–H and US–J, indeed they are twice as long (mean 14·3 months against 7·4 months). This is very stark when the equivalent topics are compared. In US–H and US–J, new products are decided upon in 5 months and 2 months respectively as against the 6 months and 27 months it took to arrive at decisions in UK–A and UK–M (table IV: topic 1 in each case). New plant decisions also were far faster in US–H and US–J at 1 month and 3 months (table IV: topics 3 and 2) as against 30 months and 24 months in UK–A and UK–M (table IV: topic 2 in each case).

Moreover, gestation periods occur more often in the British owned subsidiaries. Although there are two exceptionally prolonged gestation periods in US–H4 and 5, both were due to the specific difficulties in overcoming or circumventing strong external opposed interests. The decision to stay out of a certain market was reaffirmed despite persistent American head office pressure to go in, and the decision to bypass wholesalers had to await it becoming possible to ignore them and their long connections with US–H. These two decisions are the exceptions. Far more often there are no gestation periods in the American owned subsidiaries, and they not only go right ahead with a decision process once the matter is raised but they then despatch it twice as fast, as Eggars (1977) surely believed they would.

The British owned subsidiaries more often contemplate the matter for months or years before moving in on it, and then take much longer to arrive at a decision. The unmodified institutionalization of their decision-making does seem to slow them down. Everyone knows anecdotes about committee procrastination, and these have never been summed up better than in the couplets published by Downs (1967, p. 160):

Committees of twenty
Deliberate plenty.

Committees of ten
Act now and then.

But most jobs get done
by committees of one.

The comparison in table IV suggests that this is true much more of the formalities of standing and special committees, especially the former, than it is of working groups.

It is interesting to wonder how far the gestation period serves for the British the same integrative function as their *nemawashi* phase serves for the Japanese. Does it enable fears to fade away, resistance to remove itself, communication to counsel understanding? Both societies are homogeneous with immemorial traditions and so may have aspects in common in their decision-making. Perhaps so, but if so then in the British case the gestation period does not speed up the action afterwards as the Japanese is believed to do. Is it more likely to reflect hesitancy, the reluctance to embark upon change noticed by Dubin (1970)?

As has already been said, the influences of American ownership and of organization size cannot be separated in the available sample. Samples of manufacturing subsidiaries of approximately the same sizes would be required for this. Among the thirty organizations of the larger study from which the subsidiaries examined here are drawn, there are four that are British owned and similar in size to the two American owned subsidiaries, and at first sight they give hopes of such a controlled comparison. Unfortunately, they are different in their outputs from the American owned subsidiaries, being a road transport firm, an insurance company, an industrial research association, and a brewery, and different in ownership status, three being independent firms and not subsidiaries. Thus the most controlled comparison available is the one made in this paper in which products and ownership statuses are similar, even though sizes are not. The interpretation that the differences found are due more to the influence from afar of corporation headquarters than to size is encouraged not only by their congruence with the implications of published research but by a lack of correlation between features of decision processes and organization size in the larger study.

SOME COMMENTS

This paper does not conclude with a section headed 'conclusions' for the small scale of the comparison leaves it with clues rather than conclusions.

There are clues to American ownership from afar having little or no influence on the way that decisions arise, the planning horizon, the range of possibilities that are looked at, the straight amount of interaction (as distinct from it forms) that is engaged in, and the level in the hierarchy at which the decision is ultimately authorized. In the terminology of tables III and IV, the ten decision-making processes in the two American owned subsidiaries differ hardly at all from the ten in the two British owned subsidiaries in their proactivity, horizon, scan, interaction volume, and centrality. Differences are less widespread than inferences from existing literature suggested.

But when it comes to the form and length of interaction, the ways in which the processes are typically arranged and conducted between those involved, differences are sharp enough to prompt further research. These are the differences in *interaction formality*, *procedural standardization*, and *process duration*.

In brief, the clues hint that British managements in British owned subsidiaries are prone to route their biggest decisions through the formalities of standing committees in conformity with pre-existing customary procedures and taking a comparatively long time to do so, often presaged by a prolonged gestation before anything at all is deliberately done. That is, high interaction formality, procedural standardization (unwritten), and duration.

Whereas British managements in American owned subsidiaries tend to rely on informally assembled working groups which help to arrive at a decision comparatively rapidly through a process which does not ostensibly follow any recognized procedure. That is, lower interaction formality, procedural standardization, and duration.

These results add to those of Jamieson (1980a, 1980b) on the informality and openness of personal relationships and managerial meetings, and begin to fill in a possible picture of process characteristics alongside what has often been reported on American/British structural differences. As with the probable process differences, these structural differences are not radical, but they do consistently show American organizations to have more formalized documentation than their British equivalents (*e.g.* Inkson *et al.*, 1970; Jamieson, 1980b; Richardson, 1956). This is commonly argued to be functionally equivalent to British traditionalism in effecting coordination and control, because the American ethnic miscellany requires more deliberate measures to hold it together whereas until very recent years those who had over centuries past contributed to the British mix had merged their differences into long evolved common traditions.

Overall, then, the American mode of making major decisions could be characterized as informal within a formalized frame, the British mode as formal within a non-formalized customary pattern.

Seen like this, the British mode is the more comprehensive in what it covers. No one in the firm, not the managing director nor the chairman, escapes control by custom. All must accept and conform. However, the formalization examined in the literature on bureaucratization (*e.g.* Blau, 1974; Hage, 1981; Hall, 1977; Pugh and Hickson, 1976) is of rules and procedures that govern lower echelons, including middle and senior managers, but do not, if the results in this paper are to be believed, govern the decision-making of the topmost élites themselves. They and their working groups pursue decisions untrammelled.

The argument has now ventured beyond the confines of this paper's coverage, subsidiaries in Britain, to expose the inference that the distinctive characteristics of decision-making in the American owned subsidiaries are indeed American (for they do plausibly accord with the other published research referred to) and that they will be found in the decision-making of American managements in the United States. This, of course, can only be confirmed by a processual study of U.S. firms in the U.S.A. Further, a fully controlled test of differences between subsidiaries would require a comparison of U.S. and U.K. subsidiaries both in a third country, as Jamieson (1980a) points out in assessing his data.

Nevertheless, it appears that multinational corporations can reach beyond the horizon to affect some at least of the interpersonal elements of decision-making processes. In the subsidiaries investigated in this paper they did so even without using their own expatriates, and without any special training of the local managers who only visited the owning corporation very briefly once in years, if ever. The American voice on the phone, the American stamp on the envelope, the telex print-out, the form to be completed, were sufficient. Possibly plus one other factor. Both the American owned subsidiaries had forceful chief executives, a judgment shared by the researchers who met them as well as conveyed by their managerial colleagues. They were men with a capacity to push things along if they wished to. It cannot be determined whether individuals with this characteristic were accidental in these positions, or developed it in response to what they perceived as the style looked for by the firm's owners, or were accurately selected for it. But selection of local managers in their own management image is obviously one means of control available to multinationals.

Of course, any effects brought about by the multinationals in these cases were in the most receptive setting, subsidiaries within the broad Anglo-Saxon English speaking culture, whatever the differences between the two societies. Given this, and that the distinctiveness of the American owned subsidiaries whilst important and interesting was far from total, then it is safer to assume that multinationals can affect only limited features of processes, particularly in societies with more contrasting cultures. Even expatriate representatives on the spot then face greater linguistic and normative barriers.

If process is relatively resistant, what about the decisions themselves? This paper has been wholly concerned with the ways in which decisions are made rather than with what the decisions are. However, it ends by turning to the question of the multinational's influence on what is decided.

Cray (1981) in an extensive study of American multinationals in Europe found that national preferences of the managements of the subsidiaries 'operate within a framework of structure, coordination, communication and control dictated by the American parent'. In the subsidiaries compared in this paper, US–H and US–J, they too worked within broad parameters set by headquarters. Their chief executives said so, and in US–H it was focused in the annual 'end of March panic' when their results for the first quarter of their year became available and remedial action to redress budget imbalances had to be taken as these became exposed to the eyes across the Atlantic. But the American parent attended primarily to budget parameters rather than getting involved in multifarious matters.

Was this borne out by the influence the American parents exerted on the ten major decisions in US–H and US–J? Their specific influence on each decision was commented on by those subject to it, the informants in the subsidiaries, and rated by them on a five-point influence scale (from 'a little influence' to 'a very great deal') which served to focus their perceptions. In both subsidiaries, multinational headquarters was seen as exerting its greatest influence on decisions which committed money, namely those on plant and equipment or the business plan (table II: US–H3; US–J2, 3, 5), and its least influence on those concerning products and marketing (table II: US–H1, 2, 4, 5; US–J1, 4). This supports the view that American multinationals do not enter into operating decisions, even those regarded as major, but rely primarily on financial controls.

Thus both in decisions and in decision-making the multinational permits wide scope to its subsidiary managements. It sets ultimate limits to decisions but within these grants considerable freedom, and it affects some aspects of decision-making but probably most are typically indigenous. But whereas its effects on decisions are deliberate and known to managers in headquarters and subsidiaries alike, its probable effects on decision-making have gone unseen.

NOTES

[1] This research was supported financially by the British Social Science Research Council and the University of Bradford Management Centre.

REFERENCES

Ajiboye, Gbenga Y. (1980). *Control in Nigerian Organizations: Hierarchy and Functional Differentiation.* Master of Business Administration Dissertation. University of Bradford.

Astley, W. Graham, Axelsson, Runo, Butler, Richard J., Hickson, David J. and Wilson, David C. (1982). 'Complexity and cleavage: dual explanations of strategic decision-making.' *Journal of Management Studies*, **19**, 4, 357–75.

Blau, Peter M. (1974). *On the Nature of Organizations.* New York: Wiley.

Budde, Andreas, Child, John, Francis, Arthur and Kieser, Alfred. (1982). 'Corporate goals, managerial objectives, and organizational structures in British and West German companies'. *Organizational Studies*, **3**, 1.

Butler, Richard J., Astley, W. Graham, Hickson, David J., Mallory, Geoffrey R. and Wilson, David C. (1979/80). 'Strategic decision-making: concepts of content and process'. *International Studies of Management and Organization*, **IX**, 4, 5–32.

Butler, Richard J., Astley, W. Graham, Cray, David, Hickson, David J., Mallory, Geoffrey R. and Wilson, David C. (1982). 'Strategic decision-making: a large scale study'. (forthcoming).

Child, John (1981). 'Culture, contingency and capitalism in the cross-national study of organizations'. In Cummings, L. L. and Staw, B. M. (Eds.), *Research in Organizational Behavior*, Vol. 3. Greenwich, Conn: JAI Press.

Child, John and Macmillan, Brenda (1972). 'Managerial leisure in British and American contexts'. *Journal of Management Studies*, **9**, 2, 182–193.

Clark, Peter (1979). 'Cultural context as a determinant of organizational rationality: a comparison of the tobacco industries in Britain and France'. In Lammers, C. J. and Hickson, D. J. (Eds.), *Organizations Alike and Unlike.* London: Routledge and Kegan Paul.

Cray, David (1981). 'Control in multinational corporations'. Paper presented at the meetings of the American Sociological Association, 1980: to appear in Bacharach, S. B. (Ed.), *Yearbook of Organizational Sociology.*

Downs, Antony (1967). *Inside Bureaucracy.* Boston: Little Brown.

Dubin, Robert (1970). 'Management in Britain: impressions of a visiting professor'. *Journal of Management Studies*, **7**, 2, 183–198.

Eggars, E. Russell (1977). 'How to do business with a frenchman'. In Weinshall, T. D. (Ed.), *Culture and Management.* Harmondsworth: Penguin.

Granick, David (1962). *The European Executive.* London: Weidenfeld and Nicolson.

Hage, Jerald (1981). *Theories of Organizations: Form, Process and Transformation.* New York: Wiley.

HALL, RICHARD, H. (1977). *Organizations: Structure and Process.* (2nd edition). Englewood Cliffs, N.J.: Prentice-Hall.

HICKSON, DAVID J. and MCMILLAN, CHARLES J. (1981). *Organization and Nation: The Aston Programme IV.* Farnborough: Gower.

HICKSON, DAVID J., BUTLER, RICHARD, J., CRAY, DAVID, MALLORY, GEOFFREY R. and WILSON, DAVID C. (1982). 'Decisional differences in decision-making: subject and process'. (forthcoming).

INKSON, J. H. K., SCHWITTER, J. P., PHEYSEY, D. C. and HICKSON, D. J. (1970). 'A comparison of organizational structure and managerial roles: Ohio, U.S.A. and Midlands, England'. *Journal of Management Studies*, **7**, 3, 347–363.

JAMIESON, IAN (1980a). Capitalism and culture: a comparative analysis of British and American manufacturing organizations'. *Sociology*, **14**, 2, 217–246.

JAMIESON, IAN (1980b). *Capitalism and Culture: A Comparative Analysis of British and American Manufacturing Organizations.* Farnborough: Gower.

KELLEY, LANE and WORTHLEY, REGINALD (1981). 'The role of culture in comparative management: a cross-cultural perspective'. *Academy of Management Journal*, **24**, 1, 164–73.

KIDD, JOHN B. and TERAMOTO, YOSHIYA (1981). 'Japanese production subsidiaries in the United Kingdom: a study of managerial decision-making'. *Working Paper*, No. 203, University of Aston Management Centre.

MCMILLAN, C. J., HICKSON, D. J., HININGS, C. R. and SCHNECK, R. E. (1973). 'The structure of work organizations across societies'. *Journal of Academy of Management*, **16**, 4, 555–69.

NEGANDHI, ANANT R. (1979). 'Convergence in organizational practices: an empirical study of industrial enterprises in developing countries'. In Lammers, C. J. and Hickson, D. J. (Eds.), *Organizations Alike and Unlike*, London: Routledge and Kegan Paul.

PUGH, DEREK S. and HICKSON, DAVID J. (1976). *Organizational Structure in its Context: The Aston Programme I.* Farnborough and New York: Saxon House and D. C. Heath.

RICHARDSON, S. A. (1956). 'Organizational contrasts in British and American ships'. *Administrative Science Quarterly*, **1**, 3, 189–207.

ROBERTS, KARLENE (1970). 'On looking at an elephant: an evaluation of cross-cultural research related to organizations'. *Psychological Bulletin*, **74**, 5, 327–50.

TANNENBAUM, ARNOLD, S. (1968). *Control in Organizations.* New York: McGraw-Hill.

WILSON, DAVID C. (1982). 'Electricity and resistance: a case study of innovation and politics. *Organization Studies*, **3**, 2.

[16]

British Journal of Management, Vol. 2, 67–79 (1991)

Decision Style in British and Swedish Organizations: A Comparative Examination of Strategic Decision Making

Runo Axelsson, David Cray*, Geoffrey R. Mallory†, and David C. Wilson‡

University of Uppsala and SENSIA Consultants Ltd., Lund, Sweden, *Carleton University, Ottawa, Canada, †The Open University, Milton Keynes, UK, ‡University of Warwick, Coventry, UK

SUMMARY **In this paper results from parallel large scale studies of strategic decision making in Sweden and the United Kingdom are reported. Swedish decision makers are found to employ a decision making style which emphasizes negotiation within a restricted group. This style, which involves considerable information search, leads to very long decision times. Strategic decisions in Britain are made among groups which include fewer strongly committed participants. Delays are common and often serious, but do not lengthen the process unduly. Decision styles in both countries include contrasting tendencies which produce a dynamic tension in the decision arena.**

Introduction

Research on strategic decision making processes has seen steady development over the years, growing both in the sophistication of the models examined and the size of the empirical samples employed, yet it has remained predominately rooted in single nation studies. Mintzberg, Raisinghani and Theoret (1976) describe strategic decisions in Canadian organizations. March and Simon's (1958) keynote studies of satisficing, the descriptions of incrementalism by Lindblom (1959) and Quinn (1980) and the investigation of phase theory by Nutt (1984) are all based on organizations in the USA. Hickson *et al.* (1986) based their analytical clustering of decision processes on a sample of organizations from the UK. With the notable exception of Heller and his colleagues (DIO International Research Team, 1979; Heller *et al.*, 1988) there have been very few cross-national comparisons of strategic decision making processes and almost none on a large scale.

From one perspective it would seem that whether decisions are made in Canada, the US or the UK is almost irrelevant. The results look additive and surprisingly consistent. Incrementalism or politically charged discontinuous processes can be found, for example, in the works cited above as well other major studies of decision making (e.g. Pettigrew, 1973, 1985), again located in a single nation. It appears that the factors with the most immediate impact on the character of decision process are the topic for decision (a new product or a reorganization, for example) (Hickson *et al.*, 1986), the particular role taken by key individual managers (Pettigrew, 1973, 1985) or the predominantly conservative influences of historical precedent and fear of uncertainly on the part of

Many thanks to Richard J. Butler and David J. Hickson for their help. Correspondence should be addressed to David Cray at School of Business, Carleton University, Ottawa, Ontario, Canada.

1045–3172/91/020067–13$06.50

Received 10 April 1990
Revised 3 December 1990

management decision making teams (Braybrooke and Lindblom, 1963).

Such consistency is, we believe, misleading, if it is taken to imply that decision processes generally occur in a context in which questions of national culture play a relatively minor part. Reference to research outside the specific area of strategic decision making indicates that the impact of national culture, however defined, is likely to colour the apparent homogeneity of strategic decision processes. The two relevant literatures are, first, that concerned with strategic management in a global context (e.g. Prahalad and Doz, 1987; Kogut and Singh, 1988; Lorange and Probst, 1990) and second, that concerned with the general effects of national culture on organizations (e.g. Hofstede, 1980; Bottger, Hallein and Yetton, 1985; Tayeb, 1988). Both of these substantial literatures point toward variance among national cultures as the norm.

The issue of universality versus particularism across national and regional cultures has long been a concern of organizational theory. In the first instance this led to attempts to document and explain variations in managerial practice (e.g. Granick, 1962; Haire, Ghiselli and Porter, 1966; Dore, 1973). Despite considerable theoretical and methodological difficulties (Roberts, 1970; Hickson *et al.*, 1979; Adler, 1984; Roberts and Boyacigiller, 1984) comparative research using a variety of approaches and instruments has flourished (e.g. Lammers and Hickson, 1979a; Hofstede, 1980; Hickson and McMillan, 1981; Mansfield and Poole, 1981; Joynt and Warner, 1985; Martin and Glisson, 1989). Much of this work has centred on the degree of influence exerted by national culture on the structure of organizations and the behaviour of their members.

On one side of this debate are the culture-free theorists (Horvath *et al.*, 1976; Hickson, *et al.*, 1981; Hsu, Marsh and Mannari, 1983) who argue that behaviour is constrained through the medium of organizational structure which is, in turn, dependent on the familiar contingencies of size, environment and technology and the managerial imperatives of control, co-ordination and communication. While the behaviour of individuals within the organization clearly differs due to national or regional culture, these deviations are of less interest than the regularities that occur due to the universal demands of industrial organization. For the culture-free camp the issue is not so much explaining differences across national and cultural boundaries, but revealing the regularities among organizations from countries in similar stages of economic development.

Those who subscribe to the culture-bound approach (Hofstede, 1980; Lincoln, Hanada and Olson, 1981) see organizational form emerging from human preferences and decisions which are shaped by the values of society refracted through individual personalities. Therefore, the organization and the behaviour of those associated with it must reflect the characteristics of the surrounding culture. There may be structural regularities across national cultures, but they are relatively unimportant in the face of the substantial differences in the ways that individuals interact and in the views they hold of the organization's place in its environment.

The debate between culture free and culture bound explanations has reached the stage at which it is more constructive to regard them as complementary than competing explanations (Lammers and Hickson, 1979b; Child, 1981). Instead of regarding the contextual imperatives found in every society as proof that culture is unimportant, one should ask to what extent does culture affect behaviour within the limits of contextual constraints. To address this question it becomes necessary to focus on specific organizational behaviours rather than general views of organizational structure. In this paper the style of strategic decision making is examined in two countries, Sweden and the UK, as a step toward understanding how such behaviours may diverge.

To make this comparison, the concept of decision making style (Hellriegel and Slocum, 1975; Rowe and Mason, 1987) is adapted. In its original formulation the idea of decision making style describes the preferences of managers for certain types of situations which allow them to exercise their problem solving skills and to gain satisfaction through their successful exercise. Rowe and Mason (1987) arrived at four archetypes of decision making style through observation and evaluated individuals through a psychological inventory. For the purposes of this paper the elements of a decision making style are related not to individual psychological characteristics, but to common patterns of behaviour which differentiate group decision making in contrasting cultures. The profile of such a national style cannot be constructed merely through observation, though of course experience provides a useful guide. By building a picture of decision making style for each country based on specific behavioral variables, the advantages of close comparisons of specific variables can be coupled with the contrast of overall styles.

Strategic decision making in contrasting cultures

Given its centrality for organizational success, strategic decision making is an obvious choice for investigation in a cross-national study. Since strategic decisions must take into account environmental conditions, including government policies, the activities of competitors and general economic climate, they will be influenced by the sedimentation of cultural values represented by these factors and found in the institutions in which they are embedded. Since strategic decisions tend to be novel, ill-structured (Mintzberg, Raisinghani and Theoret, 1976) and rare (Hage, 1980), managers will be forced to revert to generalized problem-solving techniques (Simon, 1960). Cultural values should be more clearly exposed here than in routine activities which might reflect factors which are more task specific.

While the use of Sweden and the UK for this comparison stems more from the dynamics of international team research (see below) than a specific plan, the cultural differences between the two countries provide the background for a useful test of the assertion that different cultures make for contrasting decision styles. According to McMillan *et al.* (1973) many of the dominant values in Britain are rooted in the stability of parliamentary democracy, the monarchy and an unwritten constitution which emphasize traditional, normative methods of control. More recently Tayeb (1988) found that the English are a people wedded to tradition with a marked reluctance to change.

In organizational terms this means that roles are given and that innovation is unlikely to be valued. In a comparison between decision making in British and US organizations, Mallory *et al.* (1983) found that in Britain strategic decisions took place within established arenas, i.e. formal and standing committees, but were guided by unwritten procedures. Granick (1972) in comparing managers in the UK with those in the US, France and Russia, found that British firms did little planning beyond what was necessary for co-ordination. As a consequence British managers operated in a decentralized system bounded by broad policy, but often accompanied by arbitrary constraints. While the intervening years and increased international competition may have forced some changes, more current work by Baier, March and Saetren, (1986) found that the intrusion of several functional areas into the decision space leads to more ambiguity. Given the proclivity of British managers for functional solutions, they are likely to find their jobs and the associated complex decisions ambiguous. Control in the British context is based less on formal rules and more on reciprocal, personal trust relationships.

The received stereotype of Sweden pictures a nation with a very strong commitment to social equality and human welfare. While critics both within Sweden and from abroad have argued that this picture is misleading (Korpi, 1975; Jepsson and Agren, 1979), their debunking approach underlines the power of the image. One of the points often made by critics is the strength of privately-owned companies within the Swedish economy. Although the government often intervenes in corporate affairs, relatively few Swedish firms are government owned or dominated (Fry, 1979, p. 1). The welfare state coexists with an aggressive, export-oriented private sector.

In terms of management these values are expressed in a tendency toward negotiation as a means of decision making. This is found in the notion of *förhandlingsrätt*, the right to negotiate, which is entrenched in Swedish law, especially as it applies to industrial relations (Lawrence and Spybey, 1986, pp. 50–51). When compared to German practice, the Swedish emphasis on the right to negotiate over, rather than the right to decide about, certain issues becomes clear (Lawrence and Spybey, 1986, pp. 90–93). The value placed on human rights and democratic procedures exists in tension with the vesting of ultimate power in the hands of top managers.

Differences between the United Kingdom and Sweden emerged in Hofstede's (1980) large-scale investigation of cultural differences. Using data collected from employees of a single organization located in 40 countries, Hofstede situated them along four cultural dimensions. For two of these, the perceived distance between superiors and subordinates and the need to avoid conditions of uncertainty, Great Britain and Sweden were in the same cluster, showing no important differences. On the individualist-collectivist dimension Great Britain had a more individualist character. The

British score on this scale was only exceeded by those of Australia and the United States. The greatest difference was observed on what Hofstede termed the masculinity index. The Swedes, who were found at the feminine end of the scale, espoused values of interdependence, quality of life and service. The British were to be found nearer the end of the scale dominated by independence, performance and ambition.

From these brief descriptions certain outlines of the two decision making styles can be anticipated. Each would be expected to exhibit distinctive features, but each also contains its own contrasting elements. The British style of decision making should be marked by conservatism. Decisions take place within formal settings, but proceed by using unwritten rules which are maintained through personal connections. At the same time the individuals in the decision arena will tend to be more individualistic, task oriented and ambitious than their counterparts in other countries, specifically Sweden. Personal ambition within a conservative framework and the use of unwritten rules in formal setting ought to characterize the decision making style of British managers.

The tension in the Swedish decision making style stems from a belief in negotiation and compromise coupled with aggressive corporate strategies. A tendency toward this type of decision making, especially a concern with the individuals involved, fits with the behavioral style described by Rowe and Mason (1987, pp. 49–50). Managers who use this style of decision making focus on the people aspects of decision making and operate best when ambiguity is low and the task relatively clear. Since strategic decisions are often characterized by the opposite conditions, it seems likely that demands of a competitive environment would require some deviation from the archetype.

The general hypothesis which governs this paper was generated after the data were collected, but before the analysis was carried out. It can be stated quite simply. Given the contrasting values underlying the cultures of the United Kingdom and Sweden, styles of decision making should exhibit substantial differences. The Swedish decision making style will be characterized by the use of negotiation and compromise as means of making important choices, which will be limited by the demands of strategy formulation and execution. The British decision making style will reflect a conservative approach to business decisions coupled with a tendency to rely on personal rather than institutional connections. A conservative approach will be balanced by a relatively higher level of personal ambition among the participants.

Samples and Methods

The empirical section of this paper is based on two studies, one of which was conducted in the UK with data collection taking place mainly during the period 1978–80 (Hickson, *et al.*, 1986; Cray *et al.*, 1988). The second study was conducted in Sweden in 1981 by a member of the original Bradford research team (Axelsson, 1982; Axelsson, Mallory and Wilson, 1987). The two studies were not designed as a cross-national research project. Rather, the second emerged from the first as an application of a successful methodology in a new setting. Professor Axelsson, who helped articulate the theoretical basis for the studies (Astley *et al.*, 1982) and develop the data collection methods, applied the methodology to a sample of firms in his native country. Since they are parallel in intent and nearly identical in methodology with a collective data base which is considerably larger than any other available in the area, the data are more suited to cross-national research than much that has been previously employed.

The British work, known as the Bradford Studies, yielded a data set which includes 150 strategic decisions taken from 30 organizations in Britain each of which provided five decisions for the sample (Hickson *et al.*, 1986). The 30 organizations were selected to represent the variety of organizations found in British society. The second study drew on a sample of ten Swedish organizations with each again providing five decisions (Axelsson, 1982). The distribution of organization types for both samples is shown in Table 1.

In both studies a wide variety of decisions was studied including decisions concerning floating new shares, investing in new equipment, launching new products and services, negotiating union agreements, internal restructuring and external acquisitions and mergers. As can be seen in Table 2, there is some discrepancy in the distribution of decision topics encountered. The greater incidence in the Swedish study of technology decisions involving heavy financial commitments is particularly marked and its possible effect on decision pace will be discussed below. While one cannot rule out

Table 1. Types of Organizations

Type	UK	Sweden	Examples
Public service	11	3	local government, health care, police university, electricity board
Public manufacturing	2	2	construction equipment, chemicals, telecommunication equipment
Private service	8	2	insurance, bank, entertainment, industrial research, transport
Private manufacturing	9	3	chemicals, paints, brewery, paper and pulp, aluminium, textiles
Totals	30	10	

the possibility that the contrasting distributions could affect results, a meticulous examination of differences between decision topics for the Bradford study (Hickson *et al.*, 1986, pp. 131–164) showed that there were few systematic differences across ten categories of topics although there were marked differences for some specific comparisons. In any case the two samples are comparable in that they reflect the types of strategic decisions that were being made at the time by a variety of organizations in the two countries.

Table 2. Decision Topics

Topics	UK	Sweden	Examples
Technology	23	15	new equipment, new buildings
Organization	33	12	restructuring, mergers
Location	8	8	siting of plants, offices
Controls	19	7	business plans, data systems
Outputs	28	4	new products, services
Domain	18	2	marketing, distribution
Personnel	12	1	unions, job assessment
Inputs	9	1	finance, raw materials
Totals	150	50	

The data for both studies were collected through personal interviews with participants in the decision making process. After an initial interview with the chief executive officer of the organization which provided structural and historical background, five strategic decisions were chosen in consultation with the researchers for further study. No attempt was made to define strategic for the respondents unless they requested elaboration. In this case they were told that decisions which led to important, long-term consequences for the organization should be considered strategic. Few requested such clarification.

Each interview began with an extended description of the decision process from the time the issue was first raised until the outcome, positive or negative, was authorized. This was followed by a series of open-ended questions in which the informant amplified and clarified certain aspects of the process. Some of the questions were supplemented by five point scales on which the interviewee rated a particular feature. The most important of these were ratings of the influence of interests in the decision arena and the reliability of sources of information used in the decision. This method gave the advantage of a narrative provided in the interviewee's own words augmented with more specific information on theoretically important variables. Where multiple informants were used, the separate accounts were consolidated into a single description. Operational definitions of individual variables are provided in the Appendix. Further methodological details can be found in earlier reports from the projects (Axelsson, 1982; Hickson *et al.*, 1986).

Results

Participation and Influence

The data from the two studies were analyzed using a one-way analysis of variance in order to tap directly the contrasts between the two cultures (Lammers and Hickson, 1979b). The results provide a clear picture of the differences and similarities that exist in the Swedish and British styles of making strategic decisions. As Table 3 shows, making strategic decisions typically involves the same number of interests (units or individuals who have influence on the decision outcome) in both countries. There is no significant difference between the British mean of 8·25 and the Swedish mean of 7·36. The number of types of interests (diversity) showed even less difference.

There is a significant difference, however, in the range of views that players bring to the decision arena. The objective of each interest in relation to the final outcome was measured on a scale from +2 (strong support) to −2 (strong opposition). Thus the range of objective scores for a decision is a measure of contention or the extent to which the views of those involved diverge. Participants in strategic decisions in Britain are significantly more likely (mean = 2·57) than their Swedish counterparts (mean = 2·14) to hold strongly opposing views.

Table 3. Analysis of Variance: Participation and Influence

Variable	UK Mean	Swedish Mean	F	Sig.
Number of interests	8·25	7·36	2·17	n.s.
Diversity	5·17	5·46	0·89	n.s.
Contention	2·57	2·14	4·49	0·035
Total impact	23·58	32·56	12·08	0·001
Pressure of influence	3·12	3·33	4·51	0·035
Conviction	1·23	1·54	26·27	0·000
Intervention	28%	32%	1·23	n.s.
Negotiation scope	4·24	2·90	32·37	0·000
Authorization level	4·74	5·18	4·63	0·033

For UK N = 150; for Sweden N = 50.

There is also an important difference in the extent to which parties try to sway the eventual outcome of the decision making process. In an attempt to gauge the force that interests exerted in the decision arena, a measure of total impact was constructed which weighted the influence of a participant (measured on a five point scale) by the absolute value of his/her objective. Thus a highly influential player with a strong preference for a particular outcome would receive a high impact score, while one with little influence or who was indifferent to the outcome would receive the minimum score. As can be seen in Table 3, the total impact of the players was considerably higher in the Swedish arena than in the British.

Part of this effect comes from the significantly higher Swedish mean on the pressure of influence measure. The substantive difference is, however, small. The more important contrast, both statistically and theoretically, is that shown by the mean absolute value of the objectives scores on conviction. Those who participate in strategic decision processes in Sweden are likely to have strong opinions, whether negative or positive, about the eventual outcome. In Britain the decision arena is more likely to include those who are only mildly interested or even indifferent to the alternative chosen. To put it in a slightly different way, the British manner of making strategic decisions includes a greater proportion of those who do not feel strongly about the outcome.

The explanation of the difference in the impact scores highlights a general contrast in decision making between the two samples. While the British managers show greater range in the objectives they desire so that there is more likely to be opposition to any alternative, the Swedish managers tend to hold less divergent views more strongly. One explanation of this could be the intervention of a strong party from outside the organization which causes managers to pull together. As the results in Table 3 indicate, there is no support for this explanation. The percentage of influence from outside the organization is nearly the same for both samples.

There are three other possible explanations for these findings which deserve consideration. First, it is possible that the importance of external influence for Swedish decisions is underestimated by our measure. The state in Sweden plays a powerful and intrusive role in decisions relating to industrial policy (Lawrence and Spybey, 1986, pp. 50–51). Knowing that the state may intervene might cause Swedish managers to hold strong, but not very divergent positions despite the absence of the state as an active participant. Its potential role would be enough to influence managerial behaviour.

The contrasting role of trade unions in the two countries might also provide an explanation. The British research (Wilson *et al.*, 1982) demonstrated that trade unions seldom exerted important influence in strategic decisions and were often absent from the decision arena entirely. In the Swedish study nearly every decision investigated involved union representation under the nation's co-determination law (Axelsson, Mallory and Wilson, 1987). The introduction of a specific, strongly held point of view into virtually every strategic decision might account, at least in part, for the higher level of influence shown in the Swedish decisions.

The third possible explanation, which may complement the first two, is the existence of a strong tradition of negotiation in Sweden (Axelsson, Mallory and Wilson, 1987). Entering the decision arena knowing that the end result is likely to be a compromise taking into account all proposals rather than a clear choice among alternatives, has clear behavioral implications. First, when a negotiated compromise is the most likely outcome, a player with an extreme position risks losing effective influence. The contrast between the two samples on the variable negotiation scope supports the idea that there are perceived limits to acceptable positions. This variable measures the degree to which there was room for negotiation and dissent in the decision. The British managers reported significantly more scope for negotiation (mean = 4·24) than the Swedish (mean = 2·90). This does not mean that less actual negotiation took place, but that it occurred within narrower boundaries.

A second behavioral effect implies that one might be willing to risk greater commitment to a position when the psychological and political risk of having it completely rejected is lower. Third, a strongly held position is more likely to have weight in any negotiation than one which is weakly held. Taking these three points together it would appear that a position which is not extreme in its orientation but strongly held would yield the optimal bargaining position in the Swedish context.

There is also indirect support for this view in the significant difference between the level at which decisions were finally authorized. Swedish strategic decisions typically go to a board for authorization while those in Britain fall, on average, somewhere between the CEO and a board. Final authorization by a group rather than an individual underlines the importance of group processes in decision making. Given the small absolute difference between the two means shown in Table 3 one would not wish to put too much stress on this result, nevertheless it is consistent with an interpretation which stresses the importance of negotiation for Swedish managers.

Decision Pace

The differences in the extent and nature of managerial participation are intriguing in themselves, but they are only part of the overall contrast in decision making between the two countries. One of the most striking differences occurs in the pace of decision making. As shown in Table 4, British managers reported that on average, an issue was apparent in the organization (gestation time) for 17·41 months before specific action was taken to reach a decision. The corresponding period in the Swedish sample was 36·54 months. Once the actual decision making process began it took an average of 12·95 months (process time) to reach a decision in Britain versus 23·02 months in Sweden. The result for Sweden is all the more striking since reports from Canada (Mintzberg, Raisinghani and Theoret, 1976), the US (Nutt, 1984) and the Netherlands (DIO International Research Team, 1983) were all congruent with the British findings. While these differences may be exaggerated by the large number of Swedish decisions involving sizeable investments in technology, it seems likely that Swedish managers do take longer to make strategic decisions. Lawrence and Spybey (1986, pp. 50–51) concluded that decision making in Sweden tended to be lengthy compared to other countries. Although strategic decision making is known to be time-consuming, an average of five years from the first appearance of an issue to final approval does seem rather leisurely given the pace of change in most environments.

Table 4. Analysis of Variance: Decision Pace

Variable	UK Mean	Swedish Mean	F	Sig.
Gestation time (months)	17·41	36·54	11·12	0·001
Process time (months)	12·95	23·02	12·51	0·001
Informal interaction	4·24	4·30	0·09	n.s.
Formal interaction	2·25	1·78	3·42	n.s.
Delay occurrence	2·45	1·92	7·72	0·006
Delay importance	2·21	1·88	4·34	0·039
Impedance	5·06	7·62	24·86	0·000

For UK N ranges from 148 to 150 (see appendix); for Sweden N = 50.

Why should this difference exist? The explanation can be sought in three general areas; the interaction among the decision makers, the delays they face and the search for information used in making decisions. The data concerning interaction yields some interesting results although mostly in a negative sense. As can be seen from the values given in Table 4, the measure of informal interaction shows virtually no difference between the two samples. Despite the prediction of more concern for group interaction and cohesion by Swedish managers, the level of informal interaction in casual meetings and lunchroom conversations was nearly the same for both samples. The number of committees and working parties used, the measure of formal interaction, showed some difference. The British averaged about half a committee more per decision, but again this was not statistically significant. Those who regularly sit on committees might argue that the presence of even half a committee extra could well extend the time taken to make a decision, but this explanation, while intuitively appealing, is not supported by the data.

An examination of the delays encountered in the decision process shows more clear-cut distinctions. Even though the British tend to be much quicker than their Swedish counterparts in making decisions, they report significantly more delays and ascribe greater importance to them. Yet on the third measure of delay, impedance, the Swedish sample showed a significantly greater mean. The impedance scale taps the tractability of delays, that is, the degree to which they were under the control of those making the decision. The British managers perceived that the delays they encountered were serious and more frequent, but reckoned that they had relatively greater ability to deal with them. The Swedish managers evaluated the delays as less serious, but also felt that they had less control over manipulating these blockages. As the top two points on the impedance scale are resistance by internal and external forces, it seems plausible that the Swedish managers encountered more resistance from those in the decision arena, but did not regard this as a serious source of delay. Resistance, as part of the ethos of negotiation, is regarded as part of normal decision making in Sweden. It is in accordance with the rules of the game. This interpretation fits with the findings discussed above, that Swedish managers tended to have more strongly held objectives and greater average influence. This seems a reasonable interpretation in light of Hofstede's (1980) findings.

The most powerful explanation for the differences in the speed of decision making is found in the contrast of search processes illustrated in Table 5. The number of participants in the decision arena who contributed information was much higher for the Swedish sample than for the British. Indeed the average number of parties providing information for Swedish decisions is marginally higher than those exerting influence, indicating that some individuals or groups provided information without exerting influence. In the British decisions this was a rare occurrence; it was much more common for individuals to exert influence without providing information. This would seem to indicate some prohibition on the exercise of influence without information to buttress one's position in Sweden. It also points up the strong commitment to rationality by Swedish managers. More information is thought to improve the quality of decisions.

Table 5. Analysis of Variance: Information Search and Evaluation

Variable	UK Mean	Swedish Mean	F	Sig.
Expertise	4·82	7·38	52·01	0·000
Search effort	2·76	3·94	87·84	0·000
Alternatives considered	2·88	4·84	3·37	n.s.
Criteria	2·16	6·32	277·50	0·000

For UK N ranges from 145 to 150 (see appendix); for Sweden N = 50.

The central role of information in the Swedish decision making processes is also reflected in the search activities undertaken. On a four point scale of search effort, on which the simple recall of similar decisions was the lowest point and the integration of diverse research efforts the highest, the Swedish managers averaged nearly a full point higher. This reflects a Swedish tendency to appoint commissions or special working groups to investigate particular aspects of complex problems. Such a search strategy would naturally bring more interests into the decision arena as a consequence of including more providers of information.

A wider search for information does not seem to be associated with the consideration of more alternatives. Although the Swedish decision makers did examine nearly two additional alternatives per decision, the difference is not statistically significant. The higher number of criteria that Swedish managers employed may be interpreted either as a stimulus for gathering more information or as a result of more information being available. The most likely explanation is that it is related both as cause and effect to search effort.

Discussion

The results of this study support the hypothesis that Sweden and Britain display contrasting styles of strategic decision making. To a great extent the styles which emerge from the examination of differences on particular variables are in line with the expectations outlined above. The Swedish style of strategic decision making is marked by higher levels of influence and conviction, but lower levels of contention. Those in the arena negotiate within a narrower scope, but each individual participant tends to have more impact on what is eventually decided. Not unnaturally this is a slow moving process in which delays are seen as inevitable and not particularly serious. The negotiation process is fuelled by a greater emphasis on searching out more information and comparing alternatives on a larger number of criteria.

British strategic decision making involves more parties who are only a marginally interested in the outcome. On average there is less effort expended in the British decision arena, but what is there is concentrated in fewer hands. The picture that emerges is the inclusion of a number of individuals or groups who monitor the decision process with little influence and no information to contribute. These interests may be acting out of personal ambition, as a means of keeping abreast of the informal distribution of power, or simply out of a concern for the status quo. This results in less effort to uncover new information and a much quicker pace of decision.

These results indicate how important it is to focus on specific variables in building an image of managerial style. If one were to examine, for example, only the obvious variables of interests and diversity, the number and types of actors in the decision arena, one would conclude that the level of participation did not differ significantly between the two nations. Closer examination of the process through additional variables discloses a quite different pattern of interaction by the individuals and groups involved. Most of those participating in a strategic decision in Sweden have both influence and input. In Britain there appears to be an inner group which exerts proportionately more influence and provides most of the information. The outer group merely monitors developments and perhaps protects local interests. When levels of influence and commitment are distinguished from mere participation, the apparent similarities disappear.

Though there is little in the literature which bears directly on strategic decision making cross-culturally, there is some support for these findings. As discussed above, Lawrence and Spybey (1986, pp. 50–51) also observed very long decision times in Sweden and attributed it to basic democratic values of the society. To this they added the intervention of the state. This is important in strategic decisions because government approval, formally or informally given, is often necessary. If such approval requires the same type of slow discussion and search as the decisions studied here, then the overall effect will be a very slow decision process indeed.

Lawrence and Spybey (1986, pp. 42–46) also refer to the high technical qualifications of Swedish managers when compared with their British counterparts. Greater technical competence would, at least in part, explain the tendency for search to be much more important in Swedish decisions. First, each individual, given the negotiation framework, would expect his/her special interests to be considered. Second, greater technical expertise would allow participants to access more sources of information. For the British managers, with their narrower, functionally-based outlook, search for new information is apparently less important than protecting the interests of the department. From the evidence gathered in this study we cannot demonstrate that Swedish decision making is more technically oriented and the British more politically oriented, but this would seem a reasonable hypothesis for future investigation.

The placement of Sweden and Britain in Hofstede's (1980) worldwide comparison reinforces the findings of this study. Britain's location at the individualist end of the individualist-collectivist continuum is congruent with a decision making style which focuses decision making influence while the Swedish style disperses it more uniformly. This is underlined by Hofstede's finding that Sweden and Great Britain differed little on the perceived power distance between superiors and subordinates. The narrower focus in British decisions is not due to the existence of a smaller elite, but to more selective entry, perhaps based on the relevance to functional interests, into the heart of the decision making process.

Great Britain and Sweden also show an important contrast on Hofstede's (1980) 'masculinity-femininity' scale. The Swedes are more feminine in the espousal of values of interdependence, quality of life and service. British managers were placed toward the masculine end of the scale which is characterized by values of independence, performance and ambition. The findings reported in this paper help provide further interpretation of this contrast. The negotiation-based Swedish style is feminine in the sense that full participation is encouraged, but this does not mean that opinions are more weakly held or expressed less forcefully. Contention is lower, but the difficulties arising in terms of impedance are greater than for the British managers. What seems to be 'feminine' about the Swedish style is its tolerance of these costs rather than any reluctance to enter fully into the decision process.

A study by Horvath *et al.* (1976) compared a matched sample of organizations from Sweden, Great Britain and Japan on a number of structural dimensions. Swedish organizations scored lowest on formalization but highest on both specialization and centralization. The British firms scored lowest on specialization and centralization but were between Sweden and Japan on formalization. Because the three countries are at roughly the same stage of development and because the organizations were closely matched on industry and size, the authors argue that these differences are 'culturally conditioned'.

The findings on formalization and specialization do not contradict the findings from this study, but the placement of Sweden as most centralized and Britain as least does not at first glance fit with the picture developed here. However, the measures of centralization used in the Horvath *et al.* study cover mainly routine decisions. Thus it would seem that a group at the top of Swedish organizations makes a greater proportion of all kinds of decisions than in British organizations, but for strategic decisions in particular, the inner circle in Britain has a narrower compass.

Conclusion

The results reported in this paper demonstrate that the consistency in strategic decision making processes found by comparing previous, single country work masks very different practices. We have no reason to believe that the cultural differences that exist between Sweden and the United Kingdom are more dramatic than those between other countries. Therefore, contrasts that are similar in scale if quite different in character can be expected when other countries and other cultures are compared.

In addition to the specific conclusions about the decision making styles in Britain and Sweden, there are two more general conclusions to be drawn from this research. First, there is the substantive issue of complexity and tension within decision styles. While both decision styles discussed above fit with what was known about the underlying values of the societies, neither is a simple function of a single value or even a cluster of values. Each style is formed by the action of several basic values with contradictory implications. Attempts to characterize national cultures or their effects on managerial behaviour through a focus on single values are bound to be of little empirical or practical use.

The second point is the methodological implication of the first. No one who has studied organizations could seriously advocate the primacy of a particular methodology. Modern organizations are too complex and operate at too many levels in both hierarchical and theoretical terms to be encompassed by a single approach. The findings reported here, based on the measurement of specific variables taken in the context of narratives of managerial experience, illustrate the equal necessity of rigorous measurement and a holistic approach to managerial experience. Comparative work, if it is to be anything more than a series of disjointed vignettes, must marry the virtues of these two approaches.

Appendix

Number of interests The number of internal units/departments and external units/organizations named as having been involved.

Diversity of interests The variety of interests, indicated by the number of categories of internal and external interests involved from 14 categories of interest.

Contention of objectives How far the interest units that exerted influence did so in opposite directions, indicated by the range of scores on a five-point scale of opposition to, or support for, the eventual decision (−2 = strong opposition; −1 = qualified opposition; 0 = neutral; +1 = qualified support; +2 = strong support).

Total impact The total potential effort made to effect the outcome of the decision, indicated by multiplying the absolute value of the conviction score by the influence score and summing over all the interests present in the decision arena.

Pressure of influence How great a weight of influence was exerted, indicated by the mean for all interest units of ratings by informants of the influence of each interest involved (1 = little; 2 = some; 3 = quite a lot; 4 = a great deal; 5 = a very great deal).

Conviction The overall strength of feeling toward the final decision indicated by the mean of the absolute values of ratings on the contention of objectives scale (see above).
Intervention How far external influence was exerted, indicated by the percentage of the sum of influence ratings for all interest units that was due to external units.
Negotiation scope How far there was room for negotiation and dissent, indicated by a score on a seven-point scale (1 = decision not open to negotiation; 2 = negotiation only in final stages; 3 = negotiation possible on choices but one person chooses the course of action; 4 = collective decision; 5 = negotiation including dissenting parties, but subsequent consensus; 6 = negotiation resulting in limited consensus to the exclusion of dissenters; 7 = decision reached with dissent remaining such as in voting).
Authorization level How high in the hierarchy did the process culminate, indicated by a score for the level at which implementation was authorized and could commence (1 = below divisional level or equivalent; 2 = divisional level or equivalent; 3 = chief executive; 4 = chief executive and ratified by board; 5 = board or equivalent top governing body; 6 = board and ratified at higher external level; 7 = outside and above the organization).
Gestation time How long it took for a topic to emerge, indicated by the number of months from first recognition of a potential topic to the commencement of process time.
Process time How long it took to arrive at the approved choice (or process outcome), indicated by the number of months from first deliberate consideration of a topic to an authorized decision.
Informal interaction How much discussion, toing and froing, or arguments took place, indicated by the highest score for the process on a six-point scale (1 = none; 2 = little; 3 = some; 4 = quite a lot; 5 = a great deal; 6 = a very great deal).
Formal interaction How many kinds of pre-arranged meetings were included in the process, indicated by the total number of general committees/boards/councils, etc., specialized committees, e.g. finance or sales, and special purpose working parties/project teams.
Delay occurrence To what extent were there interruptions, delays or reconsiderations during the decision process, indicated by the score on a five point scale (1 = not at all; 2 = a little; 3 = some; 4 = quite a lot; 5 = a great deal).
Delay importance To what extent were the delays encountered perceived as serious, indicated by ranking on a four point scale (1 = no delays; 2 = delays were minor; 3 = delays were moderate; 4 = delays were serious).
Impedance How far the process encountered impediments, indicated by the highest score for the process on a ten-point scale (0 = no identifiable impediments; 1 = sequencing; 2 = coordinating; 3 = timing; 4 = searching; 5 = problem solving; 6 = supplying; 7 = recycling; 8 = internal resistance; 9 = external resistance).
Expertise How many sources of data were drawn upon, indicated by the number of internal and external units providing information or views.

Means, Standard Deviations and N'S for British and Swedish Samples

	Britain			Sweden		
Variable	Mean	SD	N	Mean	SD	N
Number of interests	8·25	3·22	150	7·36	1·72	50
Diversity	5·17	1·97	150	5·46	1·49	50
Contention	2·57	1·17	150	2·14	1·40	50
Total impact	23·58	15·40	150	32·56	17·05	50
Pressure of influence	3·12	0·62	150	3·33	0·57	50
Conviction	1·23	0·37	150	1·54	0·38	50
Intervention	28%	0·18	150	32%	0·18	50
Negotiation scope	4·24	1·37	150	2·90	1·63	50
Authorization level	4·74	1·30	150	5·18	1·08	50
Gestation time	17·41	36·06	148	36·54	31·89	50
Process time	12·95	11·70	149	23·02	28·42	50
Informal interaction	4·24	1·24	150	4·30	1·31	50
Formal interaction	2·25	1·48	150	1·78	1·73	50
Delay occurrence	2·45	1·16	150	1·92	1·92	50
Delay importance	2·21	0·96	149	1·88	1·04	50
Impedance	5·06	3·29	148	7·62	2·63	50
Expertise	4·82	2·34	150	7·38	1·69	50
Search effort	2·76	0·86	150	3·94	0·42	50
Alternatives considered	2·88	1·74	145	4·84	12·55	50
Criteria	2·16	1·25	150	6·32	2·16	50

Search effort How readily information was accessible, indicated by a score on a four-point scale (1 = information available from personal knowledge or opinions; 2 = information obtained readily from records; 3 = information researched by scanning, for example by a market survey; 4 = information synthesized by integrating disparate information from diverse sources).

Alternatives considered The number of distinct options considered in the course of the decision process.

Criteria The number of categories of criteria used to judge the correctness of the decision from 11 possible categories (profit, quality, output, costs, scales, return on investment, service rendered, morale, personnel benefits, image, market share).

References

Adler, N. J. (1984). 'Understanding the Ways of Understanding: Cross-cultural Management Methodology Reviewed', *Advances in International Comparative Management*, **1**, pp. 31–67.

Astley, W. G., R. Axelsson, R. J. Butler, D. J. Hickson and D. C. Wilson (1982). 'Complexity and Cleavage: Dual Explanations of Strategic Decision Making', *Journal of Management Studies*, 19, pp. 357–375.

Axelsson, R. (1982). 'Strategiska Beslut och Strategiskt Beslutsfattande', *Erhvervsokonomisk Tidsskrift*, **46**, pp. 173–182.

Axelsson, R., G. R. Mallory and D. C. Wilson (1987). 'Bureaucracy, Decision-Making and Leadership in Private and Public Organisations', *Scandinavian Journal of Management Studies*, **3**, pp. 185–195.

Baier, V. E., J. G. March and H. Saetren (1986). 'Implementation and Ambiguity', *Scandinavian Journal of Management Studies*, **2**, pp. 197–212.

Bottger, P. C., I. H. Hallein and P. W. Yetton (1985). 'A Cross-National Study of Leadership: Participation as a Function of Problem Structure and Leadership Power', *Journal of Management Studies*, **22**, pp. 358–368.

Braybrooke, D. and C. Lindblom (1963). *A Strategy of Decision*. Free Press, New York.

Child, J. (1981). 'Culture, Contingency and Capitalism in the Cross-National Study of Organizations', *Research in Organizational Behaviour*, **3**, pp. 303–356.

Cray, D., G. R. Mallory, R. J. Butler, D. J. Hickson, and D. C. Wilson (1988). 'Sporadic, Fluid and Constricted Processes: Three Types of Strategic Decision Making in Organizations', *Journal of Management Studies*, **25**, pp. 13–39.

DIO International Research Team (1979). 'Participative Decision Making: A Comparative Study', *Industrial Relations*, **18**, pp. 295–309.

DIO International Research Team (1983). 'A Contingency Model of Participative Decision Making: An Analysis of 56 Decisions in Three Dutch Organizations', *Journal of Occupational Psychology*, **56**, pp. 1–18.

Dore, R. (1973). *British Factory-Japanese Factory*. George Allen and Unwin, London.

Fry, J. A. (1979). 'Introduction', pp. 1–9. In J. A. Fry (ed) *Limits of the Welfare State: Critical Views on Post-War Sweden*. Saxon House, Farnborough.

Granick, D. (1962). *The European Executive*. Doubleday, New York.

Granick, D. (1972). *Managerial Comparisons of Four Developed Countries: France, Britain, United States and Russia*. MIT Press, Cambridge, Massachusetts.

Hage, J. (1980). *Theories of Organizations: Form, Process and Transformation*. Wiley, New York.

Haire, M., E. E. Ghiselli and L. W. Porter (1966). *Managerial Thinking: An International Study*. Wiley, New York.

Heller, F. P. Drenth, P. Koopman and R. Veljko (1988). *Decisions in Organizations: A Three-country Study*. Sage, London.

Hellriegel, D. and J. W. Slocum, Jr. (1975). 'Managerial Problem-Solving Styles', *Business Horizons*, **18**, no. 6, pp. 29–37.

Hickson, D. J., R. J. Butler, D. Cray, G. R. Mallory and D. C. Wilson (1986). *Top Decisions: Strategic Decision Making in Organizations*, Blackwell, Oxford and Jossey-Bass, San Francisco.

Hickson, D. J., C. R. Hinings, C. J. McMillan and J. P. Schwitter (1981). 'The Culture-Free Context of Organization Structure', pp. 3–17. In D. J. Hickson and C. J. McMillan (eds.) *Organization and Nation: The Aston Programme IV*, Gower, Farnborough.

Hickson, D. J. and C. J. McMillan (eds.) (1981). *Organization and Nation: The Aston Program IV*, Gower, Farnborough.

Hickson, D. J., C. J. McMillan, K. Azumi and D. Horvath (1979). 'Grounds for Comparative Organization Theory: Quicksands or Hardcore?', pp. 25–41. In C. J. Lammers and D. J. Hickson (eds.) *Organizations Alike and Unlike*, Routledge and Kegan Paul, London.

Hofstede, G. (1980). *Culture's Consequences: International Differences in Work-Related Values*. Sage, Beverly Hills.

Horvath, D., C. J. McMillan, K. Azumi and D. J. Hickson (1976). 'The Cultural Context of Organizational Control', *International Studies of Management and Organization*, **6**, pp. 60–86.

Hsu, C. K., R. M. Marsh and H. Mannari (1983). 'An Examination of the Determinants of Organizational Structure', *American Journal of Sociology*, **88**, pp. 975–996.

Jepsson, O. and G. Agren (1979). 'Work Milieu-Part II', pp. 204–15. In J. A. Fry (ed.) *Limits of the Welfare State: Critical Views on Post-War Sweden*, Saxon House, Farnborough.

Joynt, P. and M. Warner (eds.) (1985). *Managing in Different Cultures*. Universitetsforlaget, Bergen.

Kogut, B. and H. Singh (1988). 'The Effect of National Culture on the Choice of Entry Mode', *Journal of International Business Studies*, **19**, pp. 411–432.

Korpi, W. (1975). 'Poverty, Social Assistance, and Social Policy in Post-War Sweden', *Acta Sociologica*, **18**, pp. 120–141.

Lammers, C. J. and D. J. Hickson (eds.) (1979a). *Organizations Alike and Unlike*, Routledge and Kegan Paul, London.

Lammers, C. J. and D. J. Hickson, (1979b). 'Are Organizations Culture-Bound?', pp. 402–19. In C. J. Lammers and D. J. Hickson (eds.) *Organizations Alike and Unlike*, Routledge and Kegan Paul, London.

Lawrence, P. and T. Spybey (1986). *Management and Society in Sweden*. Routledge and Kegan Paul, London.

Lincoln, J. R., M. Hanada and J. Olson (1981). 'Cultural Orientations and Individual Reactions to Organizations', *Administrative Science Quarterly*, **26**, pp. 93–115.

Lindblom, C. (1959). 'The Science of Muddling Through', *Public Administration Review*, **19**, pp. 79–88.

Lorange, P. and G. Probst (1990). 'Effective Strategic Planning Processes in the Multinational Corporation', pp. 144–163. In C. A. Bartlett, Y. Doz and G. Hedlund (eds.), *Managing the Global Firm*, Routledge, London.

Mallory, G. R., R. J. Butler, D. Cray, D. J. Hickson and D. C. Wilson (1983). 'Implanted Decision Making: American Owned Firms in Britain', *Journal of Management Studies*, **20**, pp. 191–211.

Mansfield, R. and M. Poole (eds.) (1981). *International Perspectives on Management and Organization*, Gower. Farnborough.

March, J. G. and H. A. Simon (1958). *Organizations*, Wiley, New York.

Martin, P. Y. and C. Glisson (1989). 'Perceived Structure: Welfare Organizations in Three Societal Cultures', *Organization Studies*, **10**, pp. 353–380.

McMillan, C. J., D. J. Hickson, C. R. Hinings and R. E. Schneck (1973). 'The Structure of Work Organization across Societies', *Academy of Management Journal*, **16**, pp. 555–569.

Mintzberg, H., D. Raisinghani and A. Theoret (1976). 'The Structure of "Unstructured" Decision Processes', *Administrative Science Quarterly*, **21**, pp. 246–275.

Nutt, P. (1984). 'Types of Organizational Decision Processes', *Administrative Science Quarterly*, **29**, pp. 414–450.

Pettigrew, A. (1973). *The Politics of Organisational Decision-Making*. Tavistock, London.

Pettigrew, A. (1985). *The Awakening Giant: Continuity and Change in ICI*. Blackwell, Oxford.

Prahalad, C. K. and Y. L. Doz (1987). *The Multinational Mission: Balancing Local Demands and Global Vision*. Free Press, New York.

Quinn, J. B. (1980). *Strategies for Change: Logical Incrementalism*. Irwin, Homewood, Illinois.

Roberts, K. H. (1970). 'On Looking at an Elephant: A Review of Cross-Cultural Organizational Research', *Psychological Bulletin*, **74**, pp. 327–350.

Roberts, K. H. and N. A. Boyacigiller (1984). 'Cross-national Organizational Research: The Grasp of the Blind Men', *Research in Organizational Behaviour*, **6**, pp. 423–475.

Rowe, A. J. and R. O. Mason (1987). *Managing with Style*. Jossey-Bass, San Francisco.

Simon, H. A. (1960). *The New Science of Management Decision*. Harper and Brothers, New York.

Tayeb, M. (1988). *Organizations and National Culture: A Comparative Analysis*. Sage, London.

Wilson, D. C., R. J. Butler, D. Cray, D. J. Hickson and G. R. Mallory (1982). 'The Limits of Trade Union Power in Organizational Decision Making', *British Journal of Industrial Relations*, **20**, pp. 322–341.

[17]

Sensitivity to societal culture in managerial decision-making: An Anglo-Brazilian Comparison

Carlos Alberto Arruda and David J Hickson

INTRODUCTION

Although calls for more, and more carefully thought out, cross-societal cross-culture research continue to be justified, during the last quarter of a century work of this nature has expanded apace. It has progressed from a stage when there was a mere handful of publications to survey, to a stage where sophisticated syntheses and appraisals become not only possible but necessary. Those by Boyacigiller and Adler (1991), Triandis (1982–3), Lachman, Nedd and Hinings (1994), Redding (1994) and Smith (1992) all testify to this, in themselves and in the substantial lists of references they encompass.

The reasons are both practical and theoretical. The advent of the jet engine made travel easy and, for those in richer lands, affordable. Hence more Westerners could study other Westerners and more Westerners could study non-Westerners, the latter a virtual one-way flow due not only to the ability to pay the air fare but perhaps also to less affinity by some non-Westerners with Western research methods and thought ways. A second practical stimulus was the economic rise of Japan and subsequently of other nations of the Asian Pacific rim, which drew to itself the attention of Westerners generally and Americans especially.

Theoretically, some conceptual commonality was needed which, even though disputed – as it properly should be – offered a point of departure for research. Here the vital impetus was given by the work of a single Dutch individual, Hofstede (1980; 1991). Until he brought into organizational analysis four sociologically derived concepts of 'work-related values' there was no widely recognized conceptual means of comparison across societies. Like them or not like them, these concepts – power distance, individualism-collectivism, uncertainty-avoidance, masculinity-femininity (and a fifth added later, 'confucian dynamism' (Hofstede and Bond, 1988) or long-term-short-term), showed how necessary it is to have concepts of culture pertinent to this field of research that run across societies. Others have tried to follow Hofstede's lead (e.g. Trompenaars, 1993 – see Chapter 17 in this book).

The point has been reached where it is even becoming possible to attempt to portray world-wide the cultural linkages with management and organization. 'World-wide' is the term used by Hickson and Pugh (1995) for their series of succinct portrayals of the approaches to management which typify the Anglos, the Latins, the Northern Europeans, the East-Central Europeans, the Asians, the Arabs and developing countries generally. Though sometimes the evidence is thin and the portrayals precarious, such an attempt exemplifies the current rapid widening of perspective to encompass the many 'mindscapes of management' (Maruyama, 1994).

It is an enthralling perspective, partly because it reveals so many conceptual puzzles. It shows how the cultures of societies enter unevenly into features of management and organization. Management and organization-relevant characteristics of societal cultures make more of an impression in some directions in some societies, in other directions in other societies. This is well illustrated by Tayeb:

> Take three collectivist nations – Japan, India and Iran, for example. These societies are characterized by, among others, a strong sense of the group and the community. A typical Japanese, Indian or Iranian person is very loyal to his or her own group or team and places the interest of the group before his or her own interests. On the face of it, one would expect to see this characteristic – collectivism – carried over into their work organizations in the form of, for instance, hard work and a high degree of commitment, dedication and emotional attachment to the company. However, a close examination of societal cultures, employees' attitudes and values and the management structure of work organizations in these countries (Tayeb, 1979; 1988; 1990) reveals that it is only in Japan where the collectivism of Japanese culture has been carried over into its companies. The Iranians and Indians as employees are as detached from their work organizations and have as individualistic a relationship with their work places as any individualistic nation. There are, of course, several cultural and non-cultural reasons for this, but the reasons will reveal themselves only through a careful and detailed study of these nations and their organizations.
>
> *Tayeb (1994: 38)*

The puzzle is, into which features of management and organization do societal cultures enter most? In other words, how uneven is organizational culture-sensitivity? This is a question put in a different way by Redding (1994: 341) when he asks the seventh of seven questions about 'cross-cultural OB': 'Which aspects of organizing and managing may be said to be universal and which are most affected by culture (that is, if there is such a construct as managing which can be disembedded at all)?'

CASES IN POINT: BRAZIL AND ENGLAND

This puzzle was brought out by a comparison of top management decision making in Brazil and England. Decision making at this level involves a number of individuals, sometimes just a few, sometimes many and the weighing of the interests involved, which again may be few or many (across 150 British cases reported by Hickson *et al.* (1986) the number of interests ranged from two to twenty, a mean of almost seven). It is a sociopolitical process, of a kind which a priori would be thought to be highly susceptible to the influence of societal culture.

It was decided to compare such processes among Brazilian and English managers because of the sharp contrast between a Latin New-World culture and an Anglo Old-World culture. The lead given by Tayeb (1987; 1988; 1994) was followed as far as possible. Cross-national research had been criticized both for failing to separate clearly the characteristics of a culture from those of management and organization that they were supposed to explain and, even more, for retrospective explanation – that is, for finding differences between organizations in different societies and attributing them to 'cultural effects' with no direct evidence for that (for example, Child, 1981). In response, Tayeb (1987; 1988) gave a remarkable demonstration of how societal cultures could be defined and operationalized separately from and before studying organization structural and behavioural features, and only then interrelating the two.

To operationalize cultures, she used published sociological research results, histories and literatures together with an original questionnaire administered personally by her to other respondents outside the work situation. Our time and funding did not permit the latter, but prior to defining and operationalizing the variables of decision making on which managements in Brazil and England were to be compared, portrayals of each culture were independently composed from sociological, historical and literary sources (for example, for Brazil: Azevedo 1963; Da Matta 1983; Faoro 1975; Hollanda 1969; Marshall 1966. For England: Commager 1974; Gorer 1955; Lytton 1833; Orwell 1947; Priestley 1973; Tayeb 1988; Terry 1979). In addition, unstructured interviews, which concluded with the completion of questionnaire scales largely taken from Terry (1979), were conducted with six Brazilian (English speaking) managers working in England and six English (Portuguese speaking) managers who had worked in Brazil and/or with Brazilian managers. These interviews explored the experience each had of the other and their views of the other, as a small but separate verification. The results accorded closely, indeed perfectly, with the cultural portrayals that had been built up (Oliveira, 1992).

Management is society and it is culture, of course. The one is part of the other. But they can be separated analytically for explanatory purposes and this is what is done here.

Throughout this research and this chapter we again follow (Tayeb (1987; 1988) in referring specifically to England and the English, not to Britain and the British. All published research deals only with the English, not with the Scottish, Welsh or Irish nations within the United Kingdom and we make no presumptions concerning them.

In brief, the composite cultural portrayals of the Brazilians and the English depicted them as follows:

The Brazilians

The culture of the Brazilians is influenced by a rural plantation past and by recent urbanization and industrialization. This society, which in 1940 found 60% of its population in rural areas, now finds 76% of it in urban centres with several cities of over one million inhabitants each. So its culture is made up of a blend of rural traits, colonial in origin, with urban values. For most sociologists and anthropologists (Azevedo 1963; Da Matta 1983; Faoro 1975; Hollanda 1969) two of the most representative features are legacies from long ago rural Brazil: a strong respect for authority, from the old patriarchal family structure and *personalism* from a highly collectivist rural society. Respect for authority is, quite possibly, the most traditional trait. Brazilian history is rife with examples: the long incumbency of a Portuguese as the first Brazilian ruler, the great number of military coups, two long periods of authoritarian rule and, in all matters, the importance of the paternalistic family in the make-up of society.

Personalism, which means relating to other people by means of personal knowledge of them rather than in terms of impersonal rights and duties, is accompanied by other characteristics such as informality and cordiality. Thus extensive networks of people who know each other involve almost all Brazilians (Da Matta 1983). These networks limit the privacy and outcomes of individuals and shape their personal development. This emphasis on direct informal relationships has as an attractive consequence the cordiality which is one of the most positive features of these people, in the opinion of both Brazilians and of foreigners visiting the country (Hollanda 1969; Marshall 1966).

Other less traditional, but not less significant, characteristics are immediacy and peacefulness. Brazilian immediacy has been observed by several authors (Amado and Brasil 1991; Faoro 1975; Hollanda 1969; Marshall 1966) who, whilst perceiving Brazil as the country of the future, find

Brazilians mainly concerned with the here and now. Things are needed now and ought to be done now. This is the most criticized feature of this culture since it tends to overcome consideration of future consequences. It may be an escape from uncertainty. It comes together with a propensity for the multification of rules and decrees which, according to Hofstede (1980), create a façade of apparent certainty.

Brazil is seen as a peaceful society, non-aggressive and non-assertive. There is an aversion to violent situations and a strong belief in the efficacy of mediating interventions, of personal negotiations, of the quest for a common solution which will benefit all.

The interviews with Brazilian and English executives reinforced this profile. They saw Brazilians as characterized by a personalized emotional involvement with work and, at the same time, flexibility. Brazilian executives tended to perceive themselves as open to argument and discussion through having a strong respect for all in positions of authority. However, English executives discussing Brazilians, perceived them as capable of taking risks to the extent of daring, but inefficient in transforming decisions into action.

Table 11.1 summarizes this picture in terms which are relative to the English, as in the English portrayal relative to the Brazilian. It uses the expressions 'power distance' and 'uncertainty avoidance' as they are used by Hofstede (1980; 1991).

The English

Historically, being English meant being at the apex of an empire on which it was said the sun never set. And many of the English, secure on their island, still think in this manner. England was the country where the Industrial Revolution began, where capitalism has its deepest roots and

Table 11.1: Brazilian culture profile (in relative terms)

Broad traits	*Some associated characteristics*
High power distance	Political authoritarianism, autocracies Need for strong leadership
Medium uncertainty avoidance	Need for formalized rules
Immediacy	Risk-taking capacity
Personalism	Strong interpersonal networks Informality and cordiality
Peacefulness	Low assertiveness

where tradition plays an important role. It is the land of time honoured unwritten law, where class differences are still carefully preserved. Visually, it is the land of ancient ceremony, historic buildings, gardens and parks. It is a land where leisure and life beyond work are important in the lives of every citizen.

English society has been studied over and over by many authors from different angles. Social investigators (Gorer 1955; Terry 1979; Tayeb 1988) as well as novelists and travellers (Commager 1974; Lytton 1983; Priestley 1973; Orwell 1947; Santayana 1922) have written numerous books about this society and its people. In a few words, being English means being a member of a society where due respect for authority is never misunderstood as submission; where the future is not controlled by written laws and rules but by caution, by the belief that changes are a part of a natural and continuous, not abrupt, process. Where relatively reserved behaviour and individual autonomy, together with a law-abiding honesty, and personal development and liberalism are taken as the basic rules of life. But also where the ego can prevail over the social and aggressive assertiveness is a component of daily life.

These aspects are not exclusively English, but this is a particular combination which can be summed up, in Hofstedian terms, as low power distance, low uncertainty avoidance and high individualism associated with personal assertiveness and conservatism under the rule of law. When interviewed, the Brazilian and English executives agreed with these characteristics. Both said that English managers and executives are much too inflexible. Brazilians emphasized their conservative and cautious ways, their slowness in decisions, the lack of emotivity in their business relationships and their arrogance. English executives added that English society is still too tied to traditional class structures with low mobility at the highest levels.

Table 11.2 sums up these characteristics.

Table 11.2: English culture profile (in relative terms)

Broad traits	*Some associated characteristics*
Low power distance in a finely layered society	Political liberalism Deference in accepting authority
Low uncertainty avoidance	Low formalization (fewer written rules)
Conservatism	Less risk-taking capacity Gradualism
Individualism	Reserved behaviour Less emotional involvement in the work organization
Assertiveness	Greater personal competitiveness

SAMPLE AND DATA COLLECTION

Equipped in advance with these cultural portrayals, of which the above are just a summary of salient aspects, the research then moved on to the empirical comparison of managerial decision making to investigate how far it might accord with them and be held to be explained by them.

In both countries, the chief executives of organizations selected from business directories and/or business association lists were approached by letter and by phone, beginning with those most easily accessible geographically. Co-operation was far harder to obtain in England than in Brazil. In England mangements are now besieged by researchers and students, whereas they are still a relative curiosity in Brazil, much as the second author recalls they were in England in the 1960s. In a neat demonstration of Brazilian immediacy and the English longer (gradualist) conception of time, when phoned for an appointment two or three weeks ahead Brazilians often laughed and asked to be contacted a few days beforehand, whereas the English routinely fixed dates many weeks or even months in advance.

The English sample, listed in Table 11.3, was built up first and it was hoped to match the Brazilians as closely as possible to it. This ideally required matching of both organizations and decisions, that is, finding similar organizations in which similar decisions had recently been or were being taken. That ideal was a very stringent requirement and was achieved in only three pairs of organizations, two universities, two textile firms and two newspapers (these are examined later in this chapter). One obstacle was that the range of business organizations is less varied in Brazil than in England so there were not many to choose from to effect matching. But irrespective of that, the chances of happening upon a similar decision in a similar organization were low.

The Brazilian sample is listed in Table 11.4. In all there are 20 Brazilian cases and 20 English, a total of 40. The decisions to be studied were chosen during the preliminary interview or conversation with the Chief Executive or other senior director, choosing those that were major in relation to the organization and recent enough or current so that memory would be fresh. There is no alternative to relying on memory if more than perhaps one case is to be studied, for the observation of the entirety of even a single decision making process is impossible and this cannot even be attempted on larger numbers. In this kind of research, memories of the main happenings are surprisingly clear and mutually corroborating, for as Cray *et al.* (1988: 23) found from the experience of 150 cases in 30 organizations, 'the difference between shorter recall in concurrent cases and the longer recall taped in interviews is that the story becomes less cluttered and relatively simpler, not that it changes'.

Tables 11.3 and 11.4 show that the 20 English cases of decisions occurred

Table 11.3: English sample of organizations and decisions

Code	Decision	*Organizations' Main Characteristics* Activity	Size (Employees)	Ownership	Number of informants
E1	Rationalization of expenditure	Retailing	3,000	Co-operative	3
E2	Introduction of franchises	Dairy Company	5,500	Private	1
E3	Rationalization and reorganization	Food Manufacturer	2,500	Private	2
E4	Re-equipment	Textile	2,000	Private	2
E5	Diversification	Textile	1,500	Private	1
E6	New presses	Daily Newspapers *	1,200	Private	2
E7	Computerization	Daily Newspapers *	1,200	Private	2
E8	Rationalization of expenditures	University *	430	Public	5
E9	Disposal of division	Construction	3,250	Private	1
E10	Reorganization	Chemical *	1,740	Private	3
E11	Budget	University *	430	Public	2
E12	Merger	Chemical *	1,740	Private	3
E13	Acquisition in The Netherlands	Games Manufacturer	4,200	Private	1
E14	New divisions in the USA	Road Transporter	1,600	Private	2
E15	New service	Finance	3,450	Building Society	2
E16	Acquisition of competitors	Construction	1,300	Private	1
E17	Closure of division	Textile	4,800	Private	1
E18	Re-equipment	Textile	900	Private	1
E19	Budget	University	1,050	Public	2
E20	Move the company's headquarters	Retailing	3,500	Co-operative	1

* Organizations with two decisions studied

Table 11.4: Brazilian sample of organizations and decisions

Code	*Decision*	*Organizations' Main Characteristics* *Activity*	*Size (Employees)*	*Ownership*	*Number of informants*
B1	Modify existing structure	Retailing*	1700	Private	2
B2	New branch in Brasilia	Retailing*	1700	Private	2
B3	New presses	Daily Newspapers	1110	Private	2
B4	Merger	Transporter	1650	Private	2
B5	Modify and rationalize structure	Steel Industry *	13400	Public	4
B6	Divisionalization/professionalization	Retailing	2100	Private	3
B7	Computerization	Daily Newspapers	900	Private	3
B8	Budget	Unversity *	2880	Public	1
B9	Increase in the number of staff	University *	2880	Public	2
B10	New division	Retailing *	1700	Private	1
B11	Closure of division	Retailing *	1700	Private	1
B12	Divisionalization	Construction	24300	Private	1
B13	New furnace technology	Steel Industry	1300	Private	1
B14	Introduction of information technology	University	4600	Public	1
B15	Merger	Construction	2200	Private	2
B16	New line of products	Steel Industry *	13400	Public	2
B17	Re-equipment	Textile	1800	Private	1
B18	New image	Banking	2700	Private	1
B19	Takeover bid	Textile	4600	Private	1
B20	Takeover a Portuguese firm	Construction	21900	Private	2

* Organizations with two decisions studied

in 17 organizations (one each in 14 organizations, two each in 3 organizations), the 20 Brazilian decisions in 16 organizations (one each in 12 organizations, two each in 4 organizations). Though there is no claim to exact matching, the organizations overall are not unlike in their broad diversity. The English include 13 manufacturing, 7 service, the Brazilians respectively 10 and 10. The English include 17 privately owned, 3 governmental, the Brazilians respectively 15 and 5. At first sight there is a sharp disparity in mean size, the English 2,264 employees and the Brazilians 5,426 and this does seem to represent a difference in economies, the older British economy having more middle-sized firms, whereas in Brazil there is a greater gap between small businesses and newer large corporations superimposed, so to speak, by recent industrialization. However, if three exceptionally large units are removed from the Brazilian calculation – the nationalized steel business (13,400) and two huge construction firms – sustained partly by lucrative state contracts (24,300 and 2,1900) – then the remaining organizations average out on a par with the English at 2,220 employees.

The tables show that there were one, two or three informants per case (and four in one of the Brazilian cases). There is no question that more would have been desirable, had they been available and had time and funding been available. The practical issue is how great the marginal addition to data would have been. These are informants, giving information about when a decision was reached (the authorized go-ahead for implementation), the kinds of information used, the main interests involved and so on, not respondents talking about details of who had said what or about their own feelings (though they may do so) or psychological processes. This study confirmed again the experience of Hickson *et al.* (1986), reported also by Cray *et al.* (1988), that a second or third informant added remarkably little to what a single centrally involved informant could recount. In any case, employees below the top echelon, even those immediately below, know little of what took place in the making of major decisions, so the number of useful informants is a handful at most. (Data collection took place in 1990 and 1991.)

THE MEANS OF COMPARISON

More than a decade of basic research in England, known as the Bradford Studies since it was (and continues still to be) based at Bradford Management Centre, provided the conceptual and operational means for the research reported here. This is the second cross-national extension of this work, the first having been in Sweden (Axelsson *et al.*, 1991). There is no known previous Brazilian/English study because variables of decision making which could be used for comparison were not available and no data collection experience on relatively large numbers of cases had accumulated, until the publications by Hickson *et al.* (1986) and Cray *et al.* (1988; 1991).

Interviews followed what these precursors had done by being a mixture of narrative case histories, open questions and rating scales (here 5 point scales), so numeral (rating) answers could be understood in the context of case knowledge. Oliveira (1992) contains full results, forty case histories, the interview schedule in English and in Portuguese.

The schedule was designed and tested first in English, guided by that used by Hickson *et al.* (1986). It was then translated into Portuguese by another Brazilian but in co-operation with the Brazilian author of this chapter, Arruda de Oliveira, then independently translated back by a Portuguese speaking Englishman and finally minor discrepancies of meaning were reconciled by all three together.

The salient variables are defined in Table 11.5. They are taken from those devised by Hickson *et al.* (1986), in some instances with improved definitions, except for Meandering Meetings, Meetings Completion, Informal Interaction Off Job, Interpersonal Facilitation and Organizational Innovativeness. These were added to extend the coverage of managerial decision making appropriate to the Brazilian setting. Since the variables used by Hickson *et al.* (1986) had been formulated in the English setting, it was recognized that they would include neither all the characteristics of interest in Brazil nor, therefore, all those pertinent to the comparison. The additional variables were defined so as to detect any reflection in decision making of the Brazilian cultural propensities for sociable personal relationships and for taking risks. Working within a single society, Hickson *et al.* (1986) had had no thought of covering these aspects. If they had not been included in this study the chances of revealing different culture effects would have been markedly lessened. Conversely, their inclusion added some bias towards detecting such effects.

CULTURE-LINKED CONTRASTS

Before any fieldwork had commenced, the two culture portrayals were used to predict what the Brazilian and English positions would be on every variable of decision making, assuming every variable to be highly, and to a similar degree, culture-sensitive. In a few words, predictions from the more leader-seeking, at times authoritarian, cordial, immediatist, optimistically risk-taking, Brazilian culture were that managerial decision making processes would be comparatively centralized, even autocratic, interpersonally interactive, fast and receptive to novel proposals. Whereas predictions from the deferential yet participative, personally reserved, gradualist, cautious English culture were that decision making would be comparatively less centralized, impersonal, slow and wary of innovation.

Table 11.5: Definitions of variables

Influence in favour, influence ratings of those who are favourable to the decision, from (1) a little to (5) a very great deal.
Number of active interests, the number of individuals, or groups (e.g. departments, committees, other organizations) who have influence on the process, not including any participant who although involved had not actively influenced the course of the decision.
Information diversity, a count of the variety of sources of information used (e.g. plans, internal documents, personal knowledge).
Meandering meetings, how far meetings meandered before becoming decisive, from never (1) to very often (5).
Meetings' completion, how far meetings finished the agenda, from never (1) to very often (5).
Overall informal interaction, how much discussion and toing and froing took place, in addition to pre-arranged meetings, from little (1) to a very great deal (5).
Informal interaction in breaks, how far people continued chatting about the decision during breaks in the working day, from never (1) to very often (5).
Informal interaction off the job, how far people continued chatting about the decision after normal working hours, from never (1) to very often (5).
Interpersonal facilitation, how far the right people knowing each other personally beforehand helped in coming to a decision, from not at all (1) to a great deal (5).
Negotiation scope, how much negotiation and compromise there was during the process, from little (1) to a very great deal (5).
Duration, the length of time from the first identifiable action which began movement towards a decision, to the moment when implementation was authorized or, in some cases, when the implementation began.
Perceived pace, how rushed was the decision, from not at all (1) to a great deal (5).
Organizational innovativeness, the extent to which decisions, in general, in the organization are novel, from not at all (1) to a great deal (5).

The main results are given in Tables 11.6 and 11.7. It must be stressed that in these tables and in the text, all results are relative. That is, indications of magnitude, of more or of less, are of Brazilian managements by reference to the English, of the English by reference to the Brazilian.

Table 11.6 contains those variables in which the strongest differences

Table 11.6: Culture-linked contrasts in decision making

	BRAZIL*	ENGLAND*	One Way: F	Sig.
Authority				
Influence in favour:	Hierarchical (smooth) slope	Participative (layered) slope	–	–
Active interests permitted:	5.5 (2.5)	6.8 (2.1)	2.9	087
Information diversity admitted:	3.0 (1.6)	4.6 (1.5)	11.3	001
Interpersonal Interaction				
Meandering meetings:	4.4 (0.9)	3.2 (1.1)	11.8	002
Meetings completion:	3.6 (1.1)	4.2 (0.5)	3.6	067
Informal interaction off job:	3.7 (1.7)	2.7 (1.6)	4.9	034
Interpersonal facilitation:	3.8 (1.7)	2.7 (1.6)	4.0	052
Temporal				
Duration (months):	8.2 (9.3)	12.2 (11.0)	1.5	ns.
Innovation				
Organizational innovativeness	3.9 (1.4)	2.9 (1.1)	5.1	030

* Mean scores, standard deviations in parentheses

Table 11.7: Common managerialism

In making major decisions, both Brazilian managements and English managements:
Confine the process, to the top élite.
Squeeze out opposition.
Interact and negotiate informally among themselves, on the job, about the matter on hand.
At least prepared to handle internal reorganization decisions.

were found between the two societies. The impact of their cultures is plain to see.

First, there is a marked difference in how authority is used. Forty 'control graphs' were drawn from the influence ratings given to those actively involved, excluding those opposed, following Tannenbaum (1968). All are reproduced in Oliveira (1992), together with their grouping in terms of angle and smoothness of slope. At the extremes, there were six Brazilian cases of steep, unbroken hierarchical slope, that is, dominant chief executive influence unrivalled by any other. There were no such English cases. But there were nine English cases of a 'double-zed' type, that is, a layered slope with successive Z shapes in which each layer or step represents influence by others, lesser influence but nevertheless strong influence. There were fewer Brazilian examples of this, namely five. Overall, Brazilian cases inclined towards the more hierarchical slope, English cases towards the more layered slope.

Figure 11.1 shows contrasting examples. Brazilian Case 2 is a typically opportunistic fast president-only decision (president's influence 5) to launch a retail chain cross-country out of its accustomed regional market into the capital Brasilia. Only the corporation's bank manager (influence 3) and a consultant acquaintance of the president (1) figured at all. Whereas the English decision, by coincidence also numbered Case 2, involved a series of others. It switched retail doorstep distribution from employees to a franchise form of operation, involving the managing director (president), operations director and production director, all of whom had an equal say (all influence 4), the sales director (3), the marketing director, with his deputy and staff, the finance director with his deputy and staff (all 2), and holding company's chairman and a colleague director (1). During interviews, many Brazilian managers remarked that this was 'the President's decision', whereas the English cases did not identify a single pre-eminent personage.

The two cases in Figure 11.1 also illustrate vividly the difference in the

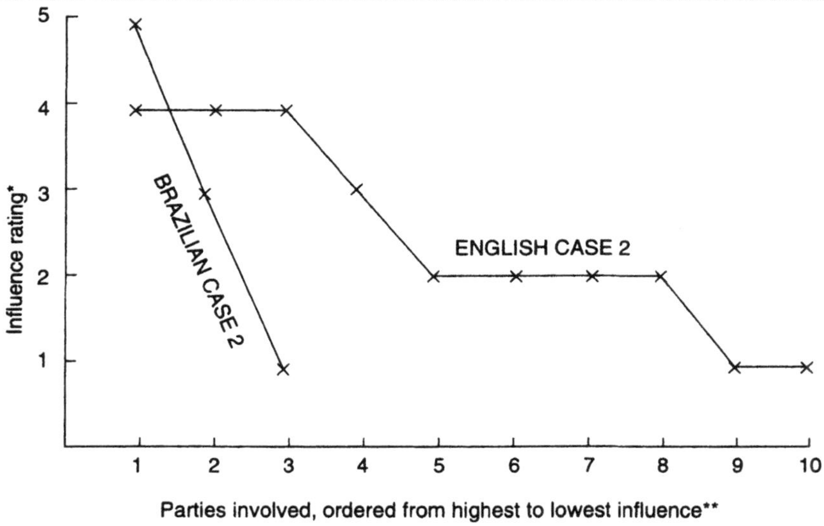

* from 1 = little to 5 = a very great deal

** informants were allowed to name whomever they perceived as being involved, individuals, departments, other organizations, etc.

Figure 11.1 Patterns of influence among the élites

number of active interests drawn in that appears in Table 11.6. The short sharp Brazilian slope encompasses only three, whereas the way in which authority is used in the English cases involves more – and more diverse – in this instance ten. The diversity extends, also, to the diversity of sources of information used. The less authority-focused, more involving, English processes draw on more sources.

The greater Brazilian readiness to exploit personal relationships and face to face contacts, in a cordial manner, compared to which English social inhibitions produce an aloof façade, shows plainly in the variables grouped in Table 11.6 under Interpersonal Interaction. In Brazilian decision making, meetings are more inclined to meander on to other subjects, including personal matters, whereas the English more often stick to the point. In consequence, whereas the English are likely to complete the agenda, the Brazilians are more likely to leave matters unfinished and, one of the most distinctive differences, to talk things over after work or in sociable situations at weekends, such as barbecues. To the English, sullying the social scene by 'talking shop' is, as another English expression has it, 'not done'. At the end of the working day, Brazilian executives could be found chatting over coffee in designated lounge corners: not so the English, who went home with a bulging briefcase or worked on at a solitary desk. Not surprisingly, the English more impersonal style pays less attention to knowing the right people (interpersonal facilitation), whereas the well-known 'jeitinho brasileiro', the Brazilian little way, uses contacts to find a way around.

The difficulty of interpreting statistical signficance arises with duration, the time taken to reach a decision (counting from the first identifiable action which set off the overt process, for example, discussions leading to placing the matter on an agenda, a presidential phone call, the preparation of a report). The spread of times taken by both Brazilian and English cases is wide. Either can take a long time or be quick. The difference between them is not numerically significant. Yet five Brazilian decisions were accomplished in only a month, under the impulse of presidential direction, as in the example in Figure 11.1, whilst no English decision was that fast. Table 11.6 shows an English mean of 12.2 months, which is extraordinarily close to the 12.4 and 12.5 obtained at different times from different samples by Hickson *et al.* (1986) and Mallory (1987), as also is the distribution (a finding which tends to validate the methods used). By comparison, the Brazilian mean is less, just over eight months, as would be expected. So Hickson *et al.*'s (1986) presumption that strategic decisions most often take around a year would seem to have been culture-bound. As is Eisenhardt's (1989) finding of fast decision making, which must be accelerated by the American cultural setting as well as by its occurring in small electronic firms.

Did Brazilians feel stampeded, rushed off their feet? Did the English feel impatient? Not at all. If anything, the inclination was the other way around. Few Brazilians suggested that they felt hurried along, whereas many English managers felt there should have been more time to consider information, with less pressure from competitiors, customers or shareholders. Hence an intriguing contrast. Where the Brazilians and the English differed in this respect, the immediatists felt their shorter time had been enough, the gradualists felt their longer time had rushed them!

Finally, in Table 11.6, the English saw themselves as running organizations less receptive to novel decisions. The Brazilians more often saw theirs as innovations. Other interview data implies that Brazilian managers see risk in a lack of information rather than in innovation itself and are willing to accept that risk and welcome an innovative disposition in their organizations. The English however, whilst they may well innovate no less than Brazilians when they have to, do so more as a necessity and are less inclined to regard innovativeness as attractive in itself.

The contrasts in Table 11.6 therefore bear out predictions of culture effects. Here is societal culture at work within work. In these respects, managerial decision making is culture-sensitive. Brazilian élites are relatively authority-centred, personal and sociable, wanting to get a move on and open to innovation. Not so the English. Their élites are relatively receptive to wider influences, impersonal with a clear separation of work and play, patiently slow-moving, cautious about innovating.

Common managerialism

Table 11.7 shows the opposite to Table 11.6. It presents those ingredients of managerial decision making in which there are no noticeable differences between the way the Brazilians go about it and the way the English do. In these managerial ingredients they are, more or less, the same.

In organizations in both societies, the major decisions are taken above the heads of those below. Mostly they are unaware of what is going on, certainly of exactly what is being discussed among the élite and of how that discussion, if there is much discussion, is going. This means that those fully in the know are a topmost group of just a few, maybe up to a dozen or so, but hardly more. Analysis of what happened in the Brazilian and English cases to those who did get to know and did not like what they heard, shows that they were in all instances effectively squeezed out. These were occasional middle managers, technical or financial staff, unions and shareholders. Their unfavourable views were of little effect, their influence minimal. In two Brazilian and three English cases where one of the élite (a director) disagreed, the consequences for him and usually his department were adverse. Either the individual subsequently lost his job or his future prospects deteriorated.

For example, in Brazilian Case 1, the Commercial Director opposed a decision to reorganize the management structure, following a proposal by American consultants to decentralize retail operations. During two difficult years the atmosphere in the executive suite worsened, until the Commercial Director realized he had to go. This he did, at an emotional meeting. He was succeeded by one of the President's sons. It may be wondered how this proposal stemming from American values may have been carried out in so Brazilian an organization.

In English Case 3, opposition to a decision to drastically rationalize the traditional varieties produced by a biscuit (cookie) manufacturer led to a diminution of the responsibilities of the Sales Director and his department. Loyal to longstanding customer retailers who had always had custom-designed lines, they resisted the change, but lost out and lost position.

In the organizations in both societies, the most immediate effect of such opposition was usually an increase in discussion and negotiation, as might be expected.

In any case, informal interaction and negotiation, in the sense of talks in the corridors or, more likely, the offices of power, was the norm for both Brazilian and English managers, over and above anything that took place in arranged meetings of committees or task groups. This is task-oriented talking with not, for the English, the degree of sociability woven in by the Brazilians.

Table 11.7 indicates that the inherent complexity of whatever is being decided also transcends societies. Both in Brazil and in England, decisions over internal reorganizations or external mergers and takeovers were experienced as the most complex, that is in essence most unusual, radical and serious. Decisions about new products or services and especially on budgets or personnel questions, were less so. In these latter decisions, managers (irrespective of whether they were Brazilian or English) appeared to know what they were about, whereas with reorganizations, either internal or external, they faced the indefinable. These were decisions the dimensions of which were not quantifiable, nor the consequences calculable.

Indeed, these unknowable matters could have strange effects. In some respects they seemed even to reverse the usual culture-imbued contrasts. Faced with such an issue, Brazilians seemed to become more cautious, using more information and taking longer over the decision, English style. Conversely, the English case histories contained more instances of off-the-job getting together and inconclusive meetings on-the-job, as if they coped by adding some interaction Brazilian style.

Here then is the kernel of a common managerialism in the handling of major decisions which is little, if at all, sensitive to differing societal cultures. It cuts across them, the way of the world managerially speaking, which Brazilians and English share equally. It is the mutually most readily recognizable content of what transpires. Each would take for granted, and be right to take for granted, that this kind of decision making by the other would be an élite process within the highest two echelons, reaching beyond or below only for information inputs, brushing doubters aside, continually alive in talks around the office desk in addition to any committee work (brief and limited though this may sometimes be in a Brazilian hierarchy), groping with the unfathomable when the issue is changing the organization itself. In these respects, it would be a process just like their own.

TESTING THE RESULTS

It will be recalled that these results are from samples that are not exactly matched. This defect can be partly overcome by making comparisons of decisions in organizations of as near as possible equivalent sizes, purposes and ownership.

First, two sub-samples in the same size bands were compared: eight decisions each in Brazilian and English organizations from 1,050 to 1,800 employees, plus five Brazilian and six English decisions in organizations from 2,000 to 3,500. Second, decisions were compared in service organizations (ten Brazilian, seven English) and in manufacturing organizations (ten Brazilian, thirteen English). This included some degree of simultaneous control for size, services in both countries being smaller and manufacturers larger. Third, private owner-managed firms were compared (thirteen and seven respectively) and government owned undertakings (five and three).

The outcomes were overwhelmingly and reassuringly the same as on the full samples. There were two variations, most probably showing common organizational effects.

In the largest organizations, especially manufacturers, the number of interests involved in the Brazilian cases reached English levels and this, together with the greater numbers of senior colleagues, placed more restraints upon the president as impersonalism began to intrude.

In the public sector universities, English informal interaction and decison times were close to the Brazilian. These speedy English decisions, around six months in duration, supported the finding by Hickson *et al.* (1986) within their British sample that university decision making is not unduly slow, as often averred, something which they attributed to smooth flow-through committee systems. Decision making in universities, as in other public services, has been found to be more concerned with process than with resources, relative to manufacturers (Rodrigues and Hickson, 1995).

These tighter tests compare kinds of organization, but still do not compare like with like in decisions. For this, the three matching pairs mentioned earlier were used. These were two regional newspapers, the managements of both of which had decided to re-equip with new computer-controlled presses, two textile manufacturers where it had been decided to expand and modernize production capacity and the corporate budget and business plan decisions of the universities (cases B3 and E6, B17 and E18, B8 and E19 in Tables 11.3 and 11.4).

Comparison of these cases feature by feature, combining numerically expressed variables and narrative case histories, was both the most stringent and most exhaustively detailed test. It too accorded with the results given so far in this chapter. In summary, the Brazilians were again seen to have taken more risks in more of a crisis atmosphere, interacting in a smaller clique around the president, failing to finish within meetings and continuing outside working hours, off the job. Once more the English appeared more cautiously defensive, but kept matters within working hours despite involving more participants. Both had in common the same holding of the interactive process within the bounds of the top echelons alone.

There was one exception to the accordance with the results from the full samples. The chairman of the English textile firm took things into his own hands and pushed the decision through quickly, in a manner that could be described as Brazilian-style. For some time the production and marketing directors had been pressing for new equipment, anxious about requests from their main customers for improved quality to equal that obtainable from competitor suppliers. Once capital became available, the chairman short-circuited the proper procedure laid down for an investment decision which required double scrutiny, from a steering committee and from an implementation committee both specially constituted. He himself acted alone in the capacity of 'steering committee' to approve the detailed proposal drawn up by the implementation committee, and ensured its rapid rubber stamping by the main board. In such ways do organizational imperatives for survival, faced in common by managements everywhere, override what may be the more accustomed approach.

CONCLUSIONS

How far can this study be construed not only to have posed the puzzle 'into which features of management and organization do societal cultures enter most', but to have fashioned a part of the solution?

Certainly, managements in a variety of organizations in Brazil and in England have been shown to differ sharply relative to one another in how they take major, indeed strategic, decisions. These differences have been attributed to differences in societal cultures, the more confidently because those cultures were portrayed prior to collecting data on decision making and predictions made of what differences they would make to it so that cultural explanations could not be put down to ex post facto wishful thinking. These cultures themselves originate in Latinesque Portuguese colonization of a New World still expansive and spacious and in the Anglo-Saxon takeover a thousand years earlier of an island where even then Old World traditions were taking shape.

So, in making decisions the Brazilians weave patterns of effusive interaction around dominating authority figures, ever hopeful but unwilling to wait long for a future that in an unsettled continent may not come. The English move coolly and cautiously, respecting but not over-needful of an authoritative lead, in time which for them stretches from a long settled past into an equally long future so that, as they say, patience is a virtue. Of course, these are stereotypical summaries. Not every Brazilian manager, not every English manager, is like this in all things all the time. There is widespread variation and these are, in effect, statements of differing central tendencies.

They are central tendencies which envelope but do not suppress a common managerialism that belongs to both. A managerialism at the top, moving decisions through an élite coterie who talk them over again and again inside meetings and out. What else is to be expected? Only the chief executive sees an organization whole, whole as far as the view downwards can scan and only his (there was no her in this study, anyway) nearest colleagues can see enough from their more partial perspectives, to talk with him and each other about matters so weighty. Others have neither the authority nor the outlook at that level to be able to take part in the same way. Once a pyramidal purposive organization has been set up, this is its effect on decision making whatever the society and whatever the politico-economic system.

Which then has the greater consequences, cultural difference or common managerialism? On the face of it, Table 11.6, which concerns the former, has more variables than Table 11.7 which concerns the latter. But counting variables must be nonsense. They and their effects cannot be added and weighed. Yet taken together, these tables and their elaboration in the text, could be interpreted to mean that those aspects of management which are interpersonal (that is, the use made of authority over others and of personal relationships with them) and philosophical (that is, the view taken of time and of change) are the most susceptible to cultural variation. How each deals with and responds to their fellow humankind and conceives of the temporal situation of humankind, are at the heart of societal culture. Fundamentally they define the nature and progression of life. Small wonder, then, that they imbue managerial behaviour and distinguish by it the organizations of one society from those of another. Ultimately, the decision making that is at the core of management is itself 'social representation' (Laroche, 1995).

Whereas the more formal structural features of organization design, in those aspects which are everywhere much the same, engender the same structure-linked responses everywhere. They give rise to internally interactive élite processes. It may be some part of the solution to the puzzle as to which managerial and organizational features are most and least societal culture-sensitive. It is, however, derived from a Brazilian–English comparison only, of decision making processes only.

REFERENCES

Amado, G. and Brasil, H.V. (1991) Organizational behaviors and cultural context: the Brazilian 'jeitinho'. *International Studies of Management and Organization*, **21**, 3, pp. 38–61.

Axelsson, R., Cray, D., Mallory, G.R. and Wilson, D.C. (1991) Decision style in British and Swedish organizations. *British Journal of Management*, **2**, pp. 67–79.

Azevedo, T. (1963) *Social Change in Brazil*, University of Florida Press.

Boyacigiller, N. and Adler, N.J. (1991) The parochial dinosaur: organizational science in a global context. *Academy of Management Review*, **16**, 2, pp. 262–90.

Child, J. (1981) Culture, Contingency and Capitalism in the Cross-

National Study of Organizations, in *Research in Organizational Behavior* (eds L.L. Cummings and B.M. Staw) JAI Press, pp. 303–56.

Commager, H. (1974) English Traits One Hundred Years Later, in *Britain Through American Eyes* (ed H. Commager) Blackwell, Oxford.

Cray, D., Mallory, G.R., Butler, R.J., Hickson, D.J. and Wilson, D.C. (1988) Sporadic, fluid and constricted processes: three types of strategic decision-making in organizations. *Journal of Management Studies*, **25**, 1, pp. 13–40.

Da Matta, R. (1983) *Carnavales, Malandras y Héroes*, Zahar.

Eisenhardt, K. (1989) Making decisions in high-velocity environments. *Academy of Management Journal*, **32**, 3, pp. 543–76.

Faoro, R. (1975) *Os Donos do Power*, Globo.

Gorer, G. (1955) *Exploring the English Character*, Crosset Press.

Hickson, D.J., Butler, R.J., Cray, D., Mallory, G.R. and Wilson, D.C. (1986) *Top Decisions: Strategic Decision Making in Organizations*, Jossey-Bass.

Hickson, D.J. and Pugh, D.S. (1995) *Management Worldwide: the Impact of Societal Culture on Organizations Around the Globe*, Penguin.

Hofstede, G. (1980) Culture's Consequences: International Differences in Work-Related Values, Sage (summarized in D.S. Pugh and D.J. Hickson *Writers on Organizations*, 4th edition, Penguin, 1989).

Hofstede, G. (1991) *Cultures and Organizations: Software of the Mind*, McGraw-Hill.

Hofstede, G. and Bond, M.H. (1988) The Confucius Connection. *Organizational Dynamics*, **16**, 4, pp. 4–21.

Hollanda, S.B. (1969) *Raíces del Brasil*, José Olympio.

Lachman, R., Nedd, A. and Hinings, R. (1994) Analysing cross-national management and organizations: a theoretical framework. *Management Science*, **40**, 1, pp. 40–55.

Laroche, H. (1995) From decision to action in organizations: decision-making as a social representation. *Organization Science*, **6**, 1, pp. 62–75.

Lytton, Edward (1833) *England and the English*, Berkley.

Mallory, G.R. (1987) The Speed of Strategic Decision-Making. PhD thesis, University of Bradford.

Marshall, A. (1966) *Brazil*, Thames and Hudson, London.

Maruyama, M. (1994) *Mindscapes in Management: the use of Individual Differences in Multi-cultural Management*, Dartmouth.

Oliveira, C.A.A. (1992) Societal Culture and Managerial Decision Making: The Brazilians and the English. PhD thesis, University of Bradford.

Orwell, G. (1947) *The English People*, Collins.

Priestley, J.B. (1973) *The English*, Heinemann.

Redding, S.G. (1994) Comparative management theory: jungle, zoo or fossil bed? *Organization Studies* **15**, 3, pp. 323–59.

Santayana, G. (1922) *Soliloquies in England and Later Soliloquies*, Constable.

Smith, P.B. (1992) Organizational behaviour and national cultures. *British Journal of Management*, **3**, pp. 39–51.

Tannenbaum, A.S. (1968) *Control in Organizations*, McGraw-Hill.

Tayeb, M. (1979) Cultural Determinants of Organizational Response to Envionmental Demands: an Empirical Study in Iran. M Litt. Thesis, Oxford.

Tayeb, M. (1987) Contingency and culture: a study of matched English and Indian manufacturing firms. *Organization Studies*, **8**, 3, pp. 241–61.

Tayeb, M. (1988) *Organizations and National Culture: A Comparative Analysis*, Sage.

Tayeb, M. (1990) Japanese management style, in *Organisational Behaviour*, Pitman, London.

Tayeb, M. (1994) Organizations and national culture: methodology considered. *Organization Studies*, **15**, 3, pp. 429–46.

Terry, P.T. (1979) An Investigation of Some Cultural Determinants of English Organization Behaviour. PhD thesis, University of Bath.

Triandis, H.C. (1982/83) Dimensions of cultural variation as parameters of organizational theories. *International Studies of Management and Organization*, Winter, pp. 139–69.

Trompenaars, F. (1993) *Riding the Waves of Culture: Understanding Cultural Diversity in Business*, Economist Books.

Part V
Successfully Managing Implementation

[18]

Journal of Management Studies 32:5 September 1995
0022-2380

SUCCESS IN DECISION MAKING: DIFFERENT ORGANIZATIONS, DIFFERING REASONS FOR SUCCESS

Suzana Braga Rodrigues

University of Minas Gerais, Brazil

David J. Hickson

University of Bradford Management Centre

ABSTRACT

In an attempt to elucidate some possible conditions for success in managerial decision making, data were analysed from 53 cases of decisions in eight British organizations, five business firms and three non-business organizations (two universities and a District of the National Health Service). No clear relationships between features of the processes of making the decisions, and their successfulness were found until the business firms and the non-business organizations were separated. Clear differences then showed up, relatively speaking, in the conditions conducive to success. In the business firms, a successful decision was more likely to result from a decision-making process in which resources were available. In other words, in business a successful decision is most likely when sufficient information and sufficient means of implementation are to hand. By contrast, in the universities and the Health District, a successful decision was associated more with the *social qualities* of the decision-making process itself. In other words, in non-business organizations a successful decision is most likely when the right people participate and the people at the very top do not interfere too much.

ORGANIZATION DIFFERENCES?

Are the conditions conducive to a successful decision in one kind of organization the same as those appropriate in another kind, or are they different? Probably they differ, for no one argues that managerial decisions are made the same way and for the same reasons in every organization. It is taken for granted that what happens in different kinds of organization must differ, given differing conditions. Though Hickson et al. (1986a) firmly conclude from their extensive data that 'the matter for decision matters most', meaning that processes of decision making are patterned primarily by what is being decided, they emphasize that there are also considerable differences according to type of organization. This is because for the making of decisions an organization is the ruling framework governing how a

Address for reprints: David J. Hickson, University of Bradford Management Centre, Bradford, West Yorkshire BD9 4JL, UK.

decision can be arrived at. If organizations are regarded as 'ensembles des jeux', collections of power games (Crozier, 1964; Crozier and Friedberg, 1980), then each constitutes the 'rules of the game' for those involved. An organization is, in effect, a 'mobilization of bias' (in the much used phrase: Lukes, 1974) before decision-making 'games' begin. Explicitly or implicitly, it is a roster of subjects for decision, premises on which they may be decided, and conditions governing their success. As March and Olsen (1976, p. 31) put it: 'Organizations regulate connections among problems, choice opportunities, solutions and energy by administrative practice.'

Curiously, this assumption of organization-induced differences does not have much empirically demonstrated support. Mintzberg et al. (1976) covered 25 diverse manufacturers, services, public, private, commercial and non-commercial organizations in their pioneering study of how decision-making processes twist and turn, but there do not appear to be any features typical of one kind of organization rather than another, and the authors do not deal with this question. Nor does Pettigrew in his in-depth historical accounts of a retail business (Pettigrew, 1973) and a large manufacturer (Pettigrew, 1985). This research, like almost all research on decision making, is for this purpose hampered by being '"one-in-one", that is, one case of decision making in one organization. This prevents any comparison of different decisions in the same organization or of the same kinds of decisions in different organizations' (Hickson, 1987, p. 188). It virtually rules out the detection of differences between types of organization.

So do single industry studies. Nutt (1984) concentrated on health related service organizations, which included hospitals, governmental agencies, insurance companies and consulting firms, and did not aim to contrast their decision making with that in other kinds of organization. Cohen et al. (1972) were similarly limited. They postulated a greater tendency to 'garbage-can' type decision making in 'organized anarchies', where preferences are inconsistent or unclear, where technology rests on trial and error, and where participants change capriciously. Therefore, they suggest, 'public, educational and illegitimate organizations' are especially prone to decision making of a 'garbage-can' nature, in which temporal sequence, the coincidence of participants, solutions and problems, is more important than logical causal sequence. But they were not in a position to show this empirically by contrast with, say, private business firms. Nor did Axelsson and Rosenberg (1979) go further than showing that among small Swedish colleges the issues arising in those training lawyers and physicians were seen as less complex and dynamic than those arising in the education of architects, journalists and social workers – another manifestation of the stabilizing effects of more clearly defined and accepted paradigms of knowledge.

Even so marked an assumed difference as that between publicly (state) owned and privately owned organizations has little to substantiate it. In an effort to synthesize such assumptions Rainey et al. (1976) list the most commonly held views of public organizations in the United States, partly empirically derived, and in a lengthy catalogue mention only 'less decision making autonomy and flexibility' as pertinent to decision processes. With samples of five cases of decision in each of 30 varied organizations, Hickson et al. (1986a) are able to make a tentative distinction, however, showing that publicly owned organizations are more prone to a 'sporadic' type of process when dealing with strategic decisions. This is relatively 'informally spasmodic and protracted' compared to more 'fluid' or 'constricted' processes, and public accountability seems to make it more frequent. This tendency may well be partly due to government departments and agencies being more often involved in the decision making of public organizations, even though they do not necessarily exert any more influence on the direction taken by the decision than they sometimes exert on private sector organizations (Hickson et al., 1986b; Kenny et al., 1987).

But no attempt is made by these authors to link these differences with *success*, or with the *reasons for it*. That is, to explore whether features of decision-making processes and resources which may be associated with better or worse decisions, vary between different kinds of organization. If there are sets of conditions associated with differing degrees of success, do these patterns differ between organizations? This question is pursued in the present paper. Patterns in what leads to a successful decision are compared in both business and non-business organizations, with the premise that commercial aims set different criteria for success in decision making than are pursued in non-commercial organizations.

The paper is not primarily about similarities or dissimilarities in the characteristics of these two categories of organizations. That is, it is not about levels of scores on variables, though the similar successfulness of decisions in the two categories is mentioned, as are a few process differences. The paper is about the different conditions likely to lead to success. That is, it is about differing patterns of relationships among variables.

CASE DATA BASE

Business organizations pursue commercial success. This means profit, but not only profit. With varying priorities, the pursuit of profit is weighed along with growth, achieving the desired market share, reputation in the industry, customer satisfaction, even employee satisfaction and development, and so on. Yet profit and its associated financial indices do provide numerate standards at which to aim, and these might be expected to figure prominently (the pun is intended) in the managerial activity prior to a decision. Non-business organizations by comparison have less clarity in what they are about, and no accepted lead indicator of performance. Although universities attempt to balance their books, or better, so as to be financially viable, their goals in research and teaching are multifarious, and much less visibly linked to financial outcomes than are those in the business sector. Similarly with health service organizations, where there is continual tension between patient care, regardless of cost, and cost restraints; and so too with municipalities or police forces or churches or charities or any organization of this nature.

This is exacerbated if the organization is one of those held together merely by 'pooled interdependence' (Thompson, 1967). That is where internal subunits depend on a common pool of resources which has to be divided between them, but depend relatively little on each other. The work of one department does not form the input for the work of another, as it does in the 'sequential interdependence' of manufacturing, and so all are free to compete with each other for shares of the pool. Universities and hospitals are prime examples where common funding has to be shared out on imprecise criteria of performance and future needs.

To study the possible reasons for success in decision making, a variety of decisions and of organizations was therefore sought, since there was no obvious set of hypotheses to focus choice, and variety was most likely to expose unforeseen differences. But care was taken to include both business and non-business organizations since this seemed a likely contrast to draw. An attempt was made to find organizations of both kinds whose managements were willing to collaborate. An ideal might have been equal numbers of each kind, perhaps controlling for size, exact form of ownership, and the precise business engaged in. But in the empirical study of organizations, perfect project designs and samples to perfectly test them are elusive ideals. Managers have other things to do than talk to researchers. In this instance, the most that could be achieved was an assortment of eight British organizations, five of which were business and three non-business. This puts a question mark against generalizability, which is discussed in the conclusions to this paper.

Letters were sent by the Brazilian first author of this paper (who undertook all the fieldwork) to the chief executives of 20 organizations in the North of England, 16 business firms and two universities and two National Health Service Districts. Of these latter public sector organizations, both the universities and one health district agreed to collaborate, though not without some persuasion. Private business was even more reluctant to volunteer executive time, and more suspicious that enquiries might encroach on financial information or trade secrets. Partly in the hope of eventual cross-national research, partly as a possible aid to access, half the firms were chosen for their commercial links with Brazil, and this did ease access, for ultimately four of the five firms which collaborated did have such links and were therefore more responsive to the researcher personally.

The result was two engineering firms (800 and 1500 employees), one firm in electronics (12,000), one in chemicals (100) and one in confectionery (600): and two universities (4400 and 4200 students) and one Health District (7800 employees).

Once access was obtained, there was greater success in the overriding aim of obtaining data on a large number of decisions, 53 in all. These are listed in table I. There are 19 in the non-business organizations and 34 in business. There are respectively, in order of number of cases, five, six, seven, seven and nine decisions in the five firms, seven each in the two universities and five in the health district. These numbers per organization are in line with the numbers of decisions which other large-scale research has found can be recalled by executives (e.g. Hickson et al., 1986a). In this instance, each chief executive, or an immediate senior colleague, was asked to list decisions which he (all were male) saw as important and had committed resources and/or were organization-wide in their effects.

An attempt was made to cover unsuccessful as well as successful decisions, and therefore executives were also asked to suggest examples of each. Not surprisingly, there were more successful cases than unsuccessful. Perhaps the less successful decisions are more readily forgotten; or perhaps organizations in which the majority of decisions are unsuccessful are no longer around to be studied.

Table I. Fifty-three decisions studied

Organizations		*Decisions*
University A	D1	A policy on vacation catering facilities
	D2	A review of the vacation catering facilities
	D3	Reorganization of computer offices
	D4	The introduction of new disciplinary procedures in the halls of residence
	D5	A new building for a new discipline
	D6	Expansion in the sports centre
	D7	The increase of fees for the halls of residence
University B	D8	The increase of fees for the halls of residence
	D9	Reorganization of the university's basic structure
	D10	Reorganization of the halls of residence administration
	D11	Introduction of an administrative computer
	D12	To change the university's administrative computer
	D13	To launch the university's development programme
	D14	The introduction of a system of a centralized timetabling for university examinations
Hospital	D15	Closure of a ward
	D16	The closure of social clubs in a district hospital
	D17	Rationalization of patient's meals
	D18	Organization of work of school nurses
	D19	Centralization of stores
Firm A	D20	The introduction of a new printing press
	D21	A new business in Germany
	D22	Reduction of inventory
	D23	Reorganization and manning reduction
	D24	A new business in India
	D25	Reorganization of factory lay-out
	D26	The introduction of an American product design
Firm B	D27	The manufacture of new electronic equipment
	D28	A new contract in São Paulo
	D29	The opening of a new factory
	D30	To terminate a development programme
	D31	Reduction of workforce
	D32	The closure of a factory
	D33	The manufacture of a new product
Firm C	D34	Introduction of a profit share scheme
	D35	A new business in France
	D36	To reduce workforce
	D37	Selection of a managing director
	D38	To move into the export business
Firm D	D39	To establish a new factory in Venezuela
	D40	Negotiation with two rival unions
	D41	Development of a new product
	D42	The termination of a development programme
	D43	A new business in Libya
	D44	Introduction of a new shareholder
	D45	Centralization of stores
	D46	Computerization of the clerical work
	D47	Acquisition of new equipment
Firm E	D48	Extension of depot
	D49	Changing factory layout
	D50	The introduction of computer terminals in distribution sites
	D51	The building of a new depot
	D52	Staff transference to a new site
	D53	The introduction of new technology

However, a range was achieved which did include unsuccessful cases, demonstrating that while these may be difficult to unearth, they can be found and studied.

Moreover, a range of topics was covered. These include product development decisions (e.g. launching new manufactures), marketing (e.g. new export markets), finance (e.g. fees for university halls of residence, capital from a new shareholder), personnel (e.g. reducing the workforce), reorganization (e.g. reshaping university structure, centralizing health district stores) and expansion decisions (e.g. university development programmes, extending factory premises).

DATA COLLECTION

Interviewees who had taken part in making a particular decision were nominated by chief executives, who were also interviewed themselves. Each was notified beforehand what was to be discussed and so most were prepared with minutes, memoranda and other documents, and many contacted colleagues to check points during interviews. The interviews took from one to one and a half hours to work through 18 open-ended descriptive questions on the importance of the decision, the main sequence of events, who was involved, and what benefits or problems ensued.

Each interviewee was also left a questionnaire of 40 items, mostly fixed-choice, which had been derived from prior theory (wordings were occasionally slightly adapted to be meaningful in particular settings: questions were pre-tested on a small number of MBA students who had work experience). Fifty-three questionnaires were completed satisfactorily, together with the basic interview, yielding the 53 cases analysed. The data given was informational, not personal or attitudinal. In 24 instances the full data was obtained from a second informant also, either to enlarge upon some points or to enable the most informed of the two to be used for final analysis. Any differences were in the depth of information given, not of substance.

Data collection extended through the years 1978 and 1979.

CONCEPTS AND OPERATIONALIZATION

Figure 1 gives nine conditions for success and four indicators of success, arranged according to the theoretical argument, which were the empirical basis for analysis. How they were arrived at is now described. Full definitions and operationalizations are given in the Appendix.

One of the most difficult concepts to define and operationalize is the successfulness of a decision. This is especially so if criteria are sought which can apply to any kind of major decision on any topic in any organization. Financial criteria, for example, may apply to the outcomes of a decision to launch a new product but they can hardly apply to the consequences of a structural reorganization. Indeed, even with a new product it is usually debatable whether its subsequent apparent financial earnings are due to the decision itself, the skill of the engineers and managers who implemented the decision, fortuitous subsequent

Conditions for success			*Successfulness*
Means:			
	Resources and Information:	Availability	
	Resources and Information:	Criticality	
Process:			Realization
	Interests:	Diversity	Propitiousness
	Influence:	Specialists' involvement	Non-Disturbance
		Top management's influence	Perceived Success
	Conflict:	(Dis)agreement	
		Compromise	
	Time:	Duration	
		Tardiness	

Figure 1. Successfulness and hypothesized conditions for it

favourable market changes, or whatever else. The causal connections seem multiple and ambiguous.

Therefore, in order to compare successfulness across topics and across organizations, indicators had to be devised which were not specific to either. They must not be limited to a certain form of decision topic (e.g. return on investment) nor to a certain form of organization (e.g. length of patient stay). They had to apply generally. So assessments were used of performance relative to each decision in the setting of the organization where each was taken, as in the judgement of the executive informants who had themselves been involved.

Exploratory interviewing led to the formulation of five variables of decision performance. Between them they described how far a decision had solved the problem(s) and made the most of the opportunity or opportunities, had gathered additional advantages and avoided raising further difficulties, and was taken to be a success overall.

'Closure' is the degree to which the problem(s) which evoked the decision was (were) solved, and is represented by a rating of problem solving. More positively, 'realization' is the degree to which the opportunity(ies) which evoked the decision was (were) realized, or taken, and is represented by a similar rating. Whether the decision gave rise to favourable or unfavourable circumstances is indicated by propitiousness and disturbance: 'propitiousness' is the degree to which unforeseen advantages arose, and 'disturbance' is the degree to which unforeseen problems arose.

As an overall assessment, and potential validation of the previous four measures, informants were also asked to give a simple overall rating of 'perceived success'.

To ascertain how far these five variables represented merely different facets of a common concept of success, they were factor analysed. A rotated factor matrix yielded a first factor accounting for 73 per cent of the variance, on which realization loaded 0.46, propitiousness 0.60, and disturbance −0.55. Since the overall perceived success rating loaded at approximately unity this strongly supported the interpretation of the factor as meaning general 'successfulness', perceived success serving to validate these three variables as success indicators (as did corrected item – total correlations which yielded reliability coefficients of respectively 0.40, 0.46, 0.45 and 0.84, with a standardized item alpha of 0.73).

However, the remaining variable, closure, was isolated with no loading on this successfulness factor, accounting alone for most of a second factor. Further, its Pearson correlation coefficient with perceived success was virtually zero (0.05). It was therefore dropped from further analysis. This poses the question whether managers do not see closing issues off by problem-solving as inherent in the *successfulness* of a decision, despite the constant allusion to it in academic writing as a decision-making activity. Is success or failure judged in more positive terms such as taking full advantage of a situation, as realization, propitiousness, and (non)disturbance imply?

We make no pretence that the four successfulness variables employed cover every criterion by which the worth of a decision might be judged. And their operationalizations may be considered rudimentary. In their favour, however, is their interlocking which demonstrates that they do catch at least something of the general managerial appraisal of a decision, grounded in managerial experience of what happened. They do enable some comparability between the performances of different kinds of decision in different kinds of organization.

What *conditions* or reasons might be adduced for successfulness appraised in these terms? What might make a highly realized, propitious and undisturbing decision, which people see as successful, more likely or less likely? Among the conditions could be the adequacy of resources and information, the way in which the interests involved in the making of the decision interacted, and the time it took. The research being reported here is an evaluation of these sorts of reasons only, and in particular an analysis of the way they differ between types of organization, and does not purport to encompass all or even most possible reasons and thereby essay a complete explanation of successfulness. Other reasons why things go well or go badly could include the personalities concerned, interpersonal relationships, managerial style, communication patterns, procedures such as committee systems, and overall patterns of movement towards a decision (such as the sporadic, fluid and constricted patterns identified by Hickson et al., 1986a, b, which have been referred to): none of these are dealt with in this research.

Of the possible conditions for successfulness that are dealt with, *resources* are the *means* to the end(s) in view. The availability of money, time, pertinent knowledge, customers or users for what might be done, labour and technology to do it, were all enquired about, and ratings summed to produce a quantity of resources score. Similarly, their timeliness was rated from 'well in time' to 'very late'. Information is always taken to be vital to a successful decision, so again both its quantity and its timeliness were reported on, and also its accuracy, covering a range of matters on which information might be needed. During interview, informants were asked how well search activities gathered the requisite information, and their answers rated 1–5.

But resources and information might be available and timely, and the information accurate and full, yet neither be of any great consequence. So in addition their *importance* was enquired about and rated, again across a range of resources (money, time, labour, etc.), and a range of information (on the money and the time in prospect, a competitor's strategies etc.).

A factor analysis of scores on these eight variables, all but one itself a mean of ratings on a range of resources and information and so representing a substantial amount of data, produced with a varimax rotation a first factor interpreted as *availability*, accounting for 76 per cent of the variance with loadings from 0.44 to 0.87 on six of the variables; and a second factor accounting for 24 per cent of the variance and virtually loaded only on importance of resources, 0.60, and importance of information, 0.54, which was interpreted as *criticality*. A single score for each factor was derived from weighted scores for the appropriate variables, and used in subsequent analysis.

The other operationalized reasons for successfulness are some of the more social *process* characteristics of decision making. First, the ways in which the interests interact. Their sheer diversity was listed in order to rate their influence, including both internal departments and sections of all kinds and also external interests such as competitors or suppliers or government departments and so on, all of which were seen as having influenced the decision. From among the many possible measures that can be extracted from influence ratings, only the two found to be most linked to successfulness are included here. These are specialists' involvement and top managements' influence. To obtain them, the managerial interests which were listed by informants were classified into those at the level of any parent organization (e.g. corporation Head Office, the Health Service Area Authority above the District), at top management level (e.g. company board, university senate and Vice-Chancellor), and at middle or upper middle management level (the specialized functions such as accounting, engineering, sales and personnel in the business firms, and accounting, resident architect, medical staff and gynaecology staff in the universities and health district). The measure of specialists' involvement indicated relative participation by the ratio of number of specialized functions involved from middle and upper middle management levels (as listed among the interests) to number of interests at top management and parent organization levels. Top management's influence similarly represented the balance of influence of the top versus that of the middle in management.

Two variables of conflict were also operationalized in relative rather than absolute terms. Disagreement is indicated by a summation of ratings in ratio to the theoretical ultimate potential disagreement score. Compromise is indicated similarly, by a summation of ratings in ratio to the theoretical ultimate potential compromise score.

The time the process took to get to a decision is represented by the period which elapsed and the delays which affected it. Duration is the actual time-lag from when the need for a decision was first recognized to when the decision was made. Tardiness indicates whether that duration was seen as needlessly prolonged, being the perceived delay in recognizing the need for a decision to be taken, and in the process of taking it.

RESULTS

Though this paper focuses upon the relations between conditions or reasons for successfulness and success itself, there are relationships among these conditions (or independent variables) themselves, on the left of figure 1, which should not be overlooked. Resources, and top managements' influence, figure prominently. There is some tendency for resources to be more available for those decisions where top managements' influence is greater (*r* resources availability . top managements' influence = 0.30; coefficients are calculated on n = 53 decisions, and have a confidence level of 95 per cent or greater) and there is more diversity of interests ($r = 0.30$). Hence it can be argued that the influential commitment of directors and their equivalents to an issue which draws in numerous interests tends to ensure that there is no shortage of resources for whatever is contemplated. Further, if resources are critical then people are more inclined to get on with the decision without delay (*r* criticality of resources . duration = −0.35; with tardiness = −0.30). Wasted time may mean wasted resources.

Most striking, however, is the mutual exclusion of top management and the specialist departments (*r* top managements' influence . specialists' involvement = −0.75). This is by far the strongest relationship. It could be partly an artefact of the measure of specialists' involvement being a ratio with number of top management, as described earlier, since more top managers might be expected to exert greater total influence between them, but that is not necessarily so. But which causes which? If top management treads heavily, exerting strong influence on the decision, does this cause the specialists to hold off – even allowing the top people to blunder on without specialist advice? Or does the non-involvement of specialists lower down, allowing matters to drift indecisively, bring in top management to force the issue to a conclusion? Probably both, of course, but whichever way it goes, there does not seem to be enough room in the decision-making process for both the top and the specialists.

Turning now to our main concern, the explanation of successfulness, the results were at first disconcerting and discouraging. There appeared to be hardly any links between the possible reasons covered by the research and the successfulness variables. The reasoning summed up in figure 1 seemed largely erroneous. True, disagreement looked likely to divert attention from possible advantages (*r* disagreement . propitiousness = −0.32), and a diversity of interests looked as if it provided the capability, or talent, to take all the opportunities that presented themselves (*r* diversity . realization = 0.44). These interpretations made sense. But beyond that nothing much could be said. It was this paucity of positive results which spurred the search for differences between kinds of organization that came to be the main finding.

The 19 decisions in the two universities and the Health District were separated from the 34 in the five business firms. The means and standard deviations for each are given in table II. These showed an overwhelming similarity between the two sets of organizations. There was merely a tendency for people to feel that the decision processes in the business firms were quicker in getting under way, and less needlessly delayed. But with hindsight, this was seen to have signalled the characteristic pressures of the business milieu, a clue to the explanation of the notable difference in correlations (as distinct from scores) which then appeared and showed that the conditions for the success or otherwise of a decision, in the terms defined here, differed markedly between the non-commercial and commercial worlds.

Table II. Means and standard deviations

Variables	*Non-business organizations (n = 19)* Mean	SD	*Business organizations (n = 34)* Mean	SD
Successfulness				
Closure	2.1	1.2	1.9	1.2
Realization	1.4	1.4	1.6	1.2
Propitiousness	1.5	1.3	1.9	1.5
Disturbance	1.0	1.2	1.1	1.5
Perceived success	3.3	1.4	3.4	1.4
Conditions for success				
Quantity of resources	3.5	1.0	3.4	0.8
Timeliness of resources	2.3	1.2	2.6	1.3
Quantity of information	4.2	0.8	3.9	0.6
Timeliness of information	2.8	1.7	2.8	1.4
Accuracy of information	0.7	0.2	0.7	0.2
Generation of information	4.6	0.7	4.2	1.1
Resources importance	3.3	1.3	3.4	0.9
Information importance	3.2	0.9	3.1	0.8
Diversity of interests	3.8	1.5	4.3	1.7
Specialists involvement	0.5	0.4	0.6	0.3
Top management's influence	0.4	0.3	0.4	0.3
Disagreement	0.4	0.3	0.3	0.2
Compromise	0.2	0.2	0.3	0.2
Promptness	3.3	6.4	2.1	6.7
Length	14.0	16.0	12.0	10.0
Delay in recognition	4.0	8.0	1.0	3.0
Delay in process	12.0	25.0	7.0	8.0

NON-BUSINESS ORGANIZATIONS

In the non-commercial world of universities and the Health Service, it seems that how things are done can matter more than what is to be done or even whether it is feasible. Here it is the politics of the process that is of primary importance for success in decision making. This interpretation is prompted by impressions given by informants when describing what happened, and by the correlations in table III.

The table gives the coefficients between the nine means and process variables, and the four successfulness variables, in other words between success and the postulated reasons for it. While 19 cases is an appreciable number given the access problems that confront data collection in this field, it is inadequate for correlational purposes, and therefore only the implications of coefficients of 0.40 or above are specifically considered.

In these 19 decisions in three non-business organizations, full; accurate and timely information appeared to be of little consequence. Nor did the adequacy of resources such as funds or client demand or equipment have much to do with success (columns a and b, table III). So the means to a decision were not important for that decision. Nor did it matter how long the decision took (column h).

Table III. Non-business organizations (n = 19 decisions)
Pearson correlation coefficients of means and process variables with successfulness variables

	a	*b*	*c*	*d*	*e*	*f*	*g*	*h*	*i*
Successfulness:									
Realization (v)	30	−04	54	.36	−32	−44	−30	00	−40
Propitiousness (w)	−08	−30	47	.28	−35	−32	07	13	−32
Disturbance (x)	-20	13	−33	−.53	45	70	−23	21	02
Perceived success (y)	00	−23	65	61	−70	−60	−07	−09	−33

Note:
Means and *process*
(independent variables)
a. Availability of resources and information
b. Criticality of resources and information
c. Interests diversity
d. Specialists' involvement
e. Top management's influence
f. Disagreement
g. Compromise
h. Duration
i. Tardiness

What mattered more was who became involved, the direction of influence, and agreement. Too much top management presence did not help things. That is, if top management (e.g. vice-chancellors or higher level Health Service officials) exerted much influence it increased the difficulties (*r* e.x = 0.45, table III), and certainly did nothing to improve realization and propitiousness, in other words the taking of opportunities and finding advantages (negative relationships). Of course, this interpretation could be reversed to suggest that rather than top management increasing the difficulties, problems arose which drew them in to try to deal with the situation, but this is the less likely interpretation. For disagreement also tended to make things worse (*r* f.x = 0.70) and disagreement was exacerbated if top management trod heavily (*r* disagreement (f) . top management's influence (e) = 0.51). Further, their influence tended to exclude specialists from the process (−0.45), which was the pronounced effect in both non-business and business organizations referred to earlier. So a heavy-footed top management could provoke difficulties and disagreements and push others aside.

That inference fits with the conditions that positively helped success. For the specialists did help. Failure to effectively involve them – the accountants, the planners, the engineers, the architects, et al. – could be particularly injurious in this kind of organization, where their participation warded off or coped with any problems or difficulties that cropped up (a negative relationship with disturbance: *r* d.x = −0.53) and, if anything, tended to boost realization and propitiousness (smaller but positive associations). Involving a diversity of interests also helped the organization to take full advantage of whatever opportunities opened up, and indeed to find unforeseen advantages (r c.v = 0.54; c.w = 0.47). Moreover, that diversity did *not* provoke disagreement ($r = -0.50$), unlike top management influence (though tardiness could still 'miss the bus': r i.v = −0.40).

Those concerned appeared themselves to see the outcome in these terms. They were inclined to see decisions as having been more successful when the fullest range of interests and specialists had been involved (r c.y = 0.65 and r d.y = 0.61), and when top management had stayed out and disagreements had been avoided (r e.y = −0.70 and r f.y = −0.60).

If these same four variables, diversity of interests, involvement of specialists, top management's influence, and disagreement, are factor analysed they reveal a pronounced common element (factor loadings 0.48, 0.66, −0.72, and 0.60 respectively). This has what might be termed a political nature, focusing on who is best in and who is best out of the decision making. Prima facie, getting this right is vital in non-business organizations since it is so strong a feature (the factor yields a standardized item alpha of 0.73, and when put into analysis of variance by MANOVA with the four successfulness variables, factor scores yield Beta coefficients with them of 0.47, 0.45, −0.62, and 0.80 respectively). However, it must immediately be pointed out that, consistent though this pattern is, the number of cases is insufficient to allow it to rest upon factor analysis as such. Fortunately it does not do so, but upon the overall pattern of relationships which is merely heightened in factor analysis.

It seems likely, therefore, that in a non-business setting it is important for successful decision making that the appropriate specialist departments are fully brought in and the entire range of interests likely to be affected have their say and know what is on the way, while top management are, at the least, discreet. In short, that the politics of participation are handled effectively. Which is exactly what the British National Health Service was attempting with a consensus-oriented structure during the previous two decades (Harrison, 1982).

Certainly an analysis of *desired* influence supports such an inference. A comparison of most successful with least successful decisions on answers to a question about how much influence each interest *should* have had showed less satisfaction with the distribution of influence in the least successful cases. In these, respondents were more likely to perceive an over-influential top to the hierarchy, and less than their due influence for the others.

One example was a unilateral decision by a university's administration to raise the charges for halls of residence. This met firm resistance from the Students' Union. A rent strike was called, and students paid their rents to the union, not to the university. After considerable turmoil, a compromise was reached whereby the university agreed to freeze rents for one more year in return for the union passing the accumulated funds to it. Fairly obviously, this was not regarded as a successful decision. The crucial interests (students) had not participated.

Similarly, in the health district an administrator's proposal to close a gynaecology section in which bed occupancy was low and waiting lists were disappearing, in order to save money, provoked a sharp reaction from the gynaecology department and doubts among other teaching units. It was a classic clash of bureaucrats and professionals. The medical staff felt that a decision had been taken over their heads, and that consultation had been inadequate. The dispute had to go to the higher regional level of the health service to be resolved, the

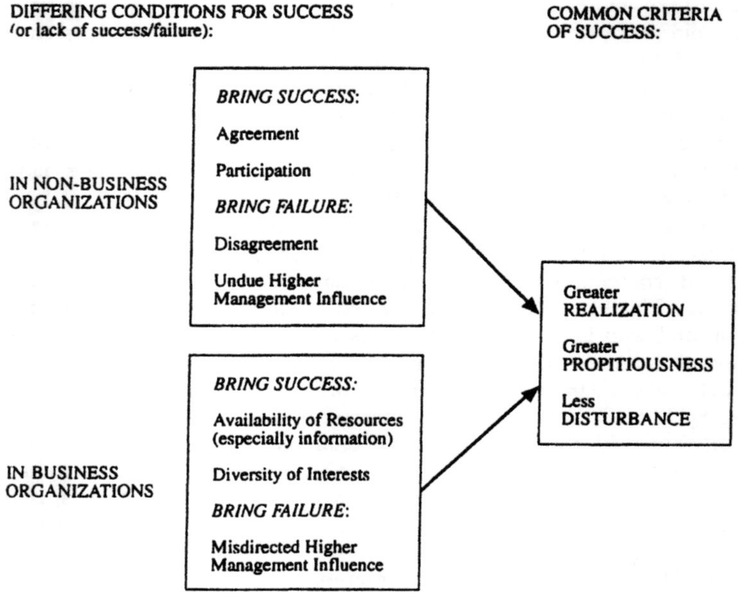

Figure 2. Different organizations, differing conditions for success

advent of a new professor whose work required more gynaecological places eventually settling it with a compromise that kept beds available. This is typical of less successful decisions which were revised, withdrawn, or not implemented.

In figure 2 the reasons for success are separated diagrammatically from those which hinder success or, at the extreme, lead to failure. For non-business organizations, the positive contributions of agreement and participation are separated from the negative effects of disagreement and undue top-down influence. As Braybrooke and Lindblom (1963) point out, in the decision making of organizations whose goals can only be stated abstractly, and in which there is no commonly accepted numerate criterion such as profit, agreement has to act as a substitute. Thus the participation conditional for agreement, and agreement itself, are valued, and become criteria of success, irrespective of whether more explicitly definable elements such as resources are available. Success becomes associated with process characteristics. Hence if in such organizations priority is given to, say, financial criteria, and political considerations are neglected, conflict ensues and decision making is jeopardized.

BUSINESS ORGANIZATIONS

Successful decision making looks different in the commercial world of the business firms. There it is relatively means-oriented. The wherewithal for deciding and implementing is comparatively important, and what is more, top management plays a larger part with better effect. Professional groupings such as academic faculty or medical consultants are not so prominent, or do not exist, and are in no position to dislocate the single, relatively unitary, hierarchy.

This interpretation, like that for the decisions in the non-business organizations, comes from the case descriptions and from correlations. The coefficients are given in table IV for the 34 decisions in the five firms. Two features, but only two, are the same. In the commercial milieu, too, tardiness can 'miss the bus' by missing opportunities, though the correlation is smaller (r i.v = −0.32 compared to −0.40 in the non-business organizations). More significantly, here again the political processes in decision making were not adversely affected by a diversity of interests, any more than they were in the universities and hospital administration. Indeed a greater diversity of interests again appears to have been beneficial, since it was associated with greater realization (r c.v = 0.45). The more that internal departments and sections, and connected external organizations, are drawn in, the more opportunities are brought to attention and are grasped. Therefore, to make the most of any potential that is opened up, managers and administrators should not lose time needlessly, should avoid delays, and should make sure that all interests are taken account of.

However, in contrast to what was reported from the non-business organizations, decision making in the firms was *not* hampered when disagreement arose, nor when top management stepped in. Neither disagreement nor top management's influence had any strong links with the three aspects of successfulness,

Table IV. Business organizations ($n = 34$ decisions)
Pearson correlation coefficients of means and process variables with successfulness variables

	a	*b*	*c*	*d*	*e*	*f*	*g*	*h*	*i*
Successfulness:									
Realization (v)	40	08	45	05	20	08	12	08	−32
Propitiousness (w)	26	−20	31	−30	13	−30	−20	41	33
Disturbance (x)	10	−08	01	14	−06	13	−09	−20	−12
Perceived success (y)	40	−20	24	−30	20	−20	03	24	20

Note:
Means and *process*
(independent variables)
a. Availability of resources and information
b. Criticality of resources and information
c. Interests diversity
d. Specialists' involvement
e. Top management's influence
f. Disagreement
g. Compromise
h. Duration
i. Tardiness

unlike the non-business setting where they reduced the chances of success (columns f and e in tables III and IV). Most strikingly, they did not create disturbance, that is they did not raise fresh unforeseen problems. Nor was it a necessary condition for success that the specialists participated (column d).

So, in business, top management can play a more forceful part with much less risk of deleterious consequences, even if there is disagreement. This is despite influence from the top being even more likely to exclude the contributions of the specialist departments (here the coefficient between the two is −0.80 compared to −0.45).

Most distinctively, success in business decisions has more of a link with resources. This accords with the findings by Bourgeois (1980) that performance was best when the means were agreed, despite differences in operationalization between his work and ours. Given the larger number of cases on which table IV is based compared to table III, there is here a noticeable positive relationship between realization and the availability of resources (r a.v = 0.40 and r a.y = 0.40). The more resources and information are available, the greater the chance that opportunities will be positively taken up. This is especially so if what is available is sufficient information on which to take a decision, since that clearly reduces unforeseen problems (when the measure of resources availability is dissembled into its composite variables, the availability of information correlates −0.70 with disturbance). If people know what they are doing, they are more able to make the most of the chances.

A cautious interpretation would be that there is nothing here to hinder top management successfully influencing decision making while ensuring that resources are available, including proper information, so that opportunities can be seized. Even if there is disagreement, compromises can be forced (r disagreement compromise = 0.73, but is negligible in the non-business organizations). Less cautiously stated, in business the influence of top management can drive decision making without the degree of sensitivity to the participation of others that seems necessary for success in non-business organizations. In short, there is more top-down, means-orientated successful decision making.

Further evidence for this is that it does not provoke the dissatisfaction that it might do in non-business organizations. It was mentioned earlier that in these a comparison of the most successful with the least successful decisions showed relative dissatisfaction with the distribution of influence in the least successful decisions. People wanted more influence lower down. This was not repeated to the same effect in the business-oriented decisions. There was comparative acquiescence in the hierarchical pattern of influence, even in the least successful decisions. It was not seen as hindering success, not even if it did arouse antagonism.

For example, when the management of one of the engineering firms decided to build a new depot near an old depot it was taken for granted that the personnel would transfer from the one to the other. It was assumed that poor performance and poor industrial relations would improve. But when the workforce discovered that their working day would be lengthened they rejected new methods of work, and the poor performance and poor industrial relations persisted. Yet management's non-participative style was not challenged. In manufacturing it was their prerogative.

Another decision among those regarded as unsuccessful was joint investment by an American parent corporation and its British subsidiary in a new product. This was a case of a higher management influencing a lower management. The latter, in the subsidiary, were sceptical about American forecasts of market potential and of costs. They saw both as unrealistically optimistic. The two managements did not see eye to eye over the validity of the data. None the less, the British management eventually went along with their parent corporation's plans. The product did not prove to be sufficiently competitive, and sales fell far short of the forecasts. This was a mistaken decision, paying too little attention to the quality of information that is crucial to business organization decisions, and swayed too far by the accepted influence of higher management.

A curiosity is the correlation in table IV between the duration of the process and successful propitiousness ($r = 0.41$) which suggests that, given time, more advantages will show up than were initially anticipated, a point that makes sense in itself yet fails to appear as an equivalent correlation for non-business organizations in table III. Why should it apply only to business firms? Is it that, however much time passes by, in universities and hospitals the interpersonal political hubbub prevents fresh advantages being seen?

Figure 2 again summarises this interpretation of the results. In business organizations, where despite the multiplicity of goals throughout the hierarchy, financial success is a cross-cutting common objective, successful decisions have comparatively more to do with the means for a decision and less with the social process itself. It is symptomatic that the minutes of meetings were found to record only the decision reached, whereas university and health service minutes also summarized the discussion that led to the decision. In business, timely, accurate and enough information seems primary, fostered by a diversity of interests which draw attention to a wide range of considerations. Higher management are not seen as getting in the way, or if they are, that is their prerogative. The hierarchy rules unchallenged.

LEVELS OF SUCCESS

The difference between the two kinds of organization is very much in the conditions that facilitate success, and not in the achievement of success. Their levels of achievement were much the same. There were no differences between them in their distributions of scores on the separate variables of successfulness, nor on the overall five-point rating of perceived success (on which, for example, the decisions in the non-business organizations had a mean of 3.3 and standard deviation of 1.4, compared to 3.4 and 1.4 for the firms, visibly no difference whatever, though as a check t-tests were run on the two groups of decisions on all variables). Hence, as reported by their own administrators and managers, the universities and health district were on average no less successful (and no more so) in their decision making than were private enterprise businesses. True, there was some indication that their administrators were more impatient with the time taken to reach decisions than were business managers, but this did not appear to adversely affect the results. The difference lay in the reasons for the results, not in their quality.

CONCLUSIONS

It is not news that non-business organizations and business organizations differ. It is not news that among the reasons are the contrasts in priority between goals, in the qualifications of personnel, and in control structure. What the findings presented here give is confirmation that the presumed effects of these contrasts do work through into managerial decision-making processes where they can be detected across a wide spectrum of cases covering many sorts of decisions.

Though caution has to be the watchword of organization theory, and nowhere more so than when interpreting these patterns of correlations. First, they are not strong in themselves. Secondly, they arise in groupings of organizations not numerous enough to yield any confidence bolstering degrees of significance.

Thirdly, the results are drawn from a limited range of organizations. Among the business organizations, commercially-oriented, there are no services such as financial advisers, insurance, or banking, no surface or air transport, no energy services such as electricity or gas. Though there are engineering, electronics, chemicals and confectionery companies, there is a wide range of manufacturing not covered. Even more limited are the non-business organizations, just hospitals and universities – no schools, local governments, or charities. Indeed, a list of what is not included would far exceed what is included. So brash generalizing must be avoided.

Further, the contrast that has been drawn is contaminated by ownership. The non-business universities and Health District are all publicly owned, and the business firms are all privately owned. At first sight, what we have argued is due to commerciality of purpose could as well be due to different ownership. Publicly owned organizations could just by reason of their ownership ignore commercial criteria. This is unlikely. Ownership by itself does not define the criteria of success. Aharoni and Lachman (1982) answered the question, 'Can the manager's mind be nationalized?', by convincingly showing that it cannot. In nationalized concerns in Israel, managers had the same commercial aims as did their counterparts under private ownership. It was not the ownership that fixed these aims but the environment, or sector, in which an organization operated. If it was in a business environment, its management applied business type criteria irrespective of ownership.

But this is case-based research. It is based on personal visits to and interviews with senior executives in organizations, and on a personal knowledge of recorded case histories. Indeed, though there are only eight organizations, the data from which the results are drawn cover 53 cases of decisions in these organizations, a substantial number of cases with data of this nature compared to what is commonplace in this field of research due to the difficulties of obtaining access and co-operation.

Persuasively, the results fit remarkably well what is to be expected in these two kinds of organizations.

So the conditions for success perceived in the making of decisions in the non-business organizations do seem likely to stem from their being what Mintzberg (1983) calls 'professional bureaucracies' of a non-commercial kind. Synthesizing research findings over the years, he defines their 'main design parameters' as 'vertical and horizontal decentralization' to highly trained personnel who receive all or most of that professionalized training outside the organization, probably prior to joining it. Academic faculty members, and medical doctors and nurses, are well-known examples. Their semi-autonomous hierarchies-within-hierarchies enable them also to lend their weight to others on occasion, for example, supporting student or patient protest. Successful decision making predictably would need an acceptable level of participation by them, and they set norms within the organization for other staff who might not otherwise be able to make themselves heard. In such organizations, successful decision making requires the acquiescence, if not assent, of these 'partisans', as Baldridge (1971) calls them in universities, taking the word from Gamson (1968), and they may defy influence from higher management. Layers of committees build up in these organizations, as was seen in the universities, Health Service Districts and municipality whose decision-making processes were studied by Hickson et al. (1986a), to absorb the potential conflict and smooth the path to a decision.

This accords with the finding by Nutt (1986, 1987) that in the hospitals, charities, professional societies and governmental agencies covered by his analyses, the tactics likely to successfully carry through the implementation of strategic plans were participative and persuasive in character. And that going about things by power-based edict does not work well. In these kinds of organizations people do not like being pushed around. However, he also found that the most successful tactic (though a rare one) was intervention, 'when a manager took charge and created an environment where plans that help to realize a strategy could be justified and understood' (Nutt, 1987, p. 12). At first sight, this does not mesh with the results presented here, which imply that in non-commercial organizations, and in particular in health and education services, top people should stand back rather than intervene. But Nutt's results concern implementation, whereas this paper is concerned with the processes of decision making leading up to authorized implementation, and so largely preceding it. Strictly, the two studies are not comparable. Yet if both are put together, they can be taken to imply that the most likely way in which top management can procure both success in making a decision and in implementing it, is never to force it through but occasionally to 'intervene' just enough to ensure a situation that facilitates what has to be done.

Further, no single criterion of managerial judgement expressable in a commonly recognized terminology, such as that of money, can be placed first and foremost among criteria. Education, research, health and similar imprecisely formulated aspirations yield a variety of indefinite goals. In the absence of defined and recognized priorities, agreement itself may be given greater weight as a criterion of success, including who participated in moving towards the agreement. As problems, solutions and participants drop haphazardly into the 'garbage-can' (Cohen et al., 1972), a metaphor said to apply most aptly to this kind of organization, so anything which produces some feel of orderly achievement is welcomed.

Whereas the logic of action of managements in the business sector is more obvious to all. People may have reservations about it, but they know it. It is the purportedly rational pursuit of success as judged by numerical criteria. Executives being interviewed frequently referred to numerical indicators such as profits or costs or productivity, especially with less successful decisions. In business-oriented 'machine bureaucracies', using Mintzberg's (1983) parlance again, money provides a common denominator. Managements operate under market rules, seeking resource maximization.

So what happens in the course of reaching a decision can be less important for success than in non-business organizations, and relatively less important than is the availability of resources, especially of information, to guide the decision. Rationally speaking, enough information should ensure a good decision, given proper hierarchical control. Hence, executives would stress that even though a decision turned out badly, it was taken at the time according to all the information that could be found or, at least, that it was in their capacity to find. In this sense, decision making in business organizations, more so than elsewhere, is an attempt to absorb uncertainty. The influence of higher management, which is not objected to in these organizations, can itself screen out alternative 'unspeakable' if not 'unthinkable' possibilities, arriving at the 'quasi-decisions' noticed by Hickson et al. (1986a) where there are foregone conclusions.

The institutional contrast heightened by this paper is, of course, ultimately 'all in the mind'. That is, in the minds of managers and administrators whose perceptions were part of the prevailing managerial culture. The two differing sets of conditions for success are those which these men perceived and remembered. These were the features of decision making that came to them, evoked by questions and conversation, as they looked back. In retrospect, these features were meaningful to them. Decision making can be understood through the conceptions that decision makers have of both the making and the implementing of decisions (Hickson and Miller, 1992). 'Cognitive politics' inscribes upon organization members common definitions of reality (Ramos, 1981), and the 'management of meanings' (Pettigrew, 1985) creates mutual parameters for action. Here two differing social realities had been constructed over the years. Scott (1987) and Zucker (1987) have emphasized that these realities vary between the organized institutions of a society, and the findings here affirm their point as shown in what counts towards successful decision making.

APPENDIX

Definitions of Variables (Operationalisations in italics)

Variables of successfulness

1. Closure

The degree to which the problem(s) which evoked the decision was (were) solved by the making of the decision.

The mean of total scores by respondents on three point ratings from 'Not solved' (scored 1) to 'wholly solved' (scored 3) of each of a number of problems (named by the respondent) which gave rise to the decision.

2. Realization

The degree to which the opportunity(ies) which evoked the decision was (were) taken.

The mean of total scores by respondents on three point ratings from 'not taken' (scored 1) to 'wholly taken' (scored 3) of a number of opportunities (named by the respondent) which gave rise to the decision.

3. Propitiousness
The extent to which unforeseen advantages were exposed by the decision process.
The total number of opportunities and advantages which interviewees reported unexpectedly appeared with the making of the decision.

4. Disturbance
The extent to which unforeseen problems were exposed by the decision process.
The total number of problems and difficulties which interviewees reported unexpectedly appeared with the making of the decision.

5. Perceived success
The degree to which a decision is perceived as being successful or unsuccessful.
The mean of total scores by respondents on five-point ratings from unsuccessful (scored 1 to very successful (scored 5).

Variable conditions for success

1. Resources availability
The amount of resources/information which are available for the making and implementation of the decision.
A factor score from a linear combination of constituting variables (Quantity of resources, Timeliness of resources, Quantity of information, Timeliness of Information, Accuracy and Generation of Information) according to their respective loadings on the factor. Reliability: standardized item alpha: 0.78.

1a. Quantity of resources
The extent to which resources were available when making the decision.
The mean of total scores by respondents on five point estimates of the availability of money, time, materials, labour, union co-operation, technology, customers/users, facilitating policies by government and competitors, and special know-how, from 'Not at all' (scored 1.00) to 'Very much' (scored 5).

1b. Timeliness of resources
The extent to which resources became available on time or late.
As 1a above, but from 'Well in time' (scored 1.00) to 'Very late' (scored 5.00).

1c. Quantity of information
The extent to which information was available when making the decision.
As 1a above, but omitting 'special know-how', and rating the amount of information on each from 'Not at all' (scored 1.00) to 'Very much' (scored 5.00).

1d. Timeliness of information
The extent to which information became available in time or later.
As 1c above, but from 'Well in time' (scored 1) to 'Very late' (scored 5).

1e. Accuracy of information
The extent to which information was felt to be correct.
As 1c above, but from 'Very inaccurate' to 'Very accurate'.

1f. Generation of information
How far the search for information was effective.
As 1c above, but rating the effectiveness of attempts to gather information on each from 'Not at all' (scored 1) to 'Very much' (scored 5).

2. Resources criticality

The extent to which resources/information were critical to the decision making.

A factor score from a linear combination of the scores of the constituting variables (Resources importance, Information importance) according to their respective loadings on the factor. Reliability: standardized item alpha: 0.66.

2a. Resources importance

The extent to which resources were important for the decision-making.

As 1a above, but rating the importance of each from 'Not at all' (scored 1) to 'Very much' (scored 5).

2b. Information importance

The extent to which special information was important for making the decision.

As 1c above, but rating the importance of each from 'Not at all' (scored 1) to 'Very much' (scored 5).

3. Diversity of interests

The range of interests in the decision process.

The number of interest units internal and external to the organization (see text for examples), which exercised influence in the decision process.

4. Specialists involvement

The number and level of functional specializations involved.

A combination of specialist involvement and its hierarchical level (see text for examples) being the number of specialized functions involved in the decision making, divided by the number of interests at higher management level.

5. Top management's influence

The relative influence exercised by interests at higher levels.

The total of respondent's five-point ratings of the influence of parent organization and top management (see text for examples) from 'Little' (scored 1) to 'A very great deal' (scored 5), divided by the equivalent for middle and upper middle management levels.

6. Disagreement

The extent to which there were expressed differences.

The sum of respondent's five-point ratings of disagreement from 'Not at all' (scored 0) to 'Very much' (scored 4), divided by the notional maximum disagreement (number of hierarchical levels multiplied by maximum possible disagreement score).

7. Compromise

The extent to which conflict was settled by mutual concessions.

The sum of respondent's ratings of compromise from 'Not at all' (scored 0) to 'Very much' (scored 4), divided by the notional maximum compromise (number of hierarchical levels multiplied by maximum possible compromise score).

8. Duration

The actual period of time between the recognition of the decision trigger and the authorization of implementation.

The sum of the standardized scores on the constituting variables (promptness and length). Reliability: standardized item alpha: 0.60.

8a. Promptness
How immediate was the response to the decision stimulus.
The time in months between the recognition of the need for a decision and initial decision activities.

8b. Length
The period of identifiable decision making activity.
The number of months between the first decision activities and the authorization to implement.

9. Tardiness
Hou far coping with the decision was perceived as slow.
The sum of the standardized scores on the constituting variables (delay in recognition and delay in the process). Reliability, standardized item alpha: 0.83.

9a. Delay in recognizing the decision stimulus
The extent to which commencement of specific decision action was later than it ideally might have been.
The number of months by which the commencement of decision activities was perceived to be needlessly late.

9b. Delay in the decision-making process
How far the decision-making process was seen as protracted.
The number of months by which a decision could have been quicker.

REFERENCES

AHARONI, Y. and LACHMAN, R. (1982). 'Can the manager's mind be nationalized?'. *Organization Studies*, **3**, 1, 33–46.

AXELSSON, R. and ROSENBERG, L. (1979). 'Decision-making and organizational turbulence'. *Acta Sociologica*, **22**, 1, 45–62.

BALDRIDGE, J. V. (1971). *Power and Conflict in the University*. New York: John Wiley.

BOURGEOIS, L. J. III (1980). 'Performance and consensus'. *Strategic Management Journal*, **1**, 3, 227–48.

BRAYBROOKE, D. and LINDBLOM, C. (1963). *A Strategy of Decision*. New York: Free Press.

COHEN, M. D., MARCH, J. G. and OLSEN, J. P. (1972). 'A garbage can model of organizational choice'. *Administrative Science Quarterly*, **17**, 1–25.

CROZIER, M. (1964). *The Bureaucratic Phenomenon*. Chicago, Ill.: University of Chicago Press.

CROZIER, M. and FRIEDBERG, E. (1980). *Actors and Systems*. Chicago, Ill.: Chicago University Press.

GAMSON, W. (1968). *Power and Discontent*. Homewood, Ill.: Dorsey.

HARRISON, STEVE (1982). 'Consensus decision making in the National Health Service'. *Journal of Management Studies*, **19**, 4, 377–94.

HICKSON, D. J. (1987). 'Decision-making at the top of organizations'. *Annual Review of Sociology*, **13**, 165–92.

HICKSON, D. J. and MILLER, S. (1992). 'Concepts of decisions: making and implementing strategic decisions in organizations'. In Heller, F. (Ed.), *Decision Making and Leadership*. Cambridge: Cambridge University Press.

HICKSON, D. J., BUTLER, R. J., CRAY, D., MALLORY, G. R. and WILSON, D. C. (1986a). *Top Decisions: Strategic Decision-Making in Organizations*. Oxford: Blackwell; San Francisco: Jossey Bass.

HICKSON, D. J., BUTLER, R. J., CRAY, D., MALLORY, G. R. and WILSON, D. C. (1986b). 'Governmental influence upon decision making in organizations in the private and public sectors in Britain'. In Wolff, R. (Ed.), *Organizing Industrial Development*. Berlin: De Gruyter, 107–16.

KENNY, G. K., BUTLER, R. J., HICKSON, D. J., CRAY, D., MALLORY, G. R. and WILSON, D. C. (1987). 'Strategic decision making: influence patterns in public and private sector organizations'. *Human Relations*, **40**, 9, 613–32.

LUKES, S. (1974). *Power: A Radical View*. London: Macmillan.

MARCH, J. G. and OLSEN, J. P. (1976). *Ambiguity and Choice in Organizations*. Oslo: Universitatsforlaget.

MINTZBERG, H. (1983). *Structure in Fives: Designing Effective Organizations*. Englewood Cliffs, NJ: Prentice-Hall.

MINTZBERG, H., RAISINGHANI, D. and THEORET, A. (1976). 'The structure of "unstructured" decision processes'. *Administrative Science Quarterly*, **21**, 246–75.

NUTT, P. C. (1984). 'Types of organizational decision processes'. *Administrative Science Quarterly*, **29**, 3, 414–50.

NUTT, P. C. (1986). 'The tactics of implementation'. *Academy of Management Journal*, **29**, 2, 230–61.

NUTT, P. C. (1987). 'Identifying and appraising how managers install strategy'. *Strategic Management Journal*, **8**, 1, 1–14.

PETTIGREW, A. (1973). *The Politics of Organizational Decision Making*. London: Tavistock.

PETTIGREW, A. (1985). *The Awakening Giant: Continuity and Change at I.C.I.* Oxford: Blackwell.

RAINEY, H. G., BACKOFF, R. W. and LEVINE, C. H. (1976). 'Comparing public and private organizations'. *Public Administration Review*, **36**, 233–44.

RAMOS, A. G. (1981). *The New Science of Organizations: A Reconceptualization of the New Wealth of Nations*. Toronto: University of Toronto Press.

SCOTT, W. R. (1987). 'The adolescence of institutional theory'. *Administrative Science Quarterly*, **32**, 493–511.

THOMPSON, J. D. (1967). *Organizations in Action*. New York: McGraw-Hill.

ZUCKER, L. G. (1987). 'Institutional theories of organization'. *American Review of Sociology*, **13**, 443–64.

[19]

Implementing Strategic Decisions: Four Key Success Factors

Susan Miller*

Susan Miller
Business School,
Durham
University,
U.K.

Abstract

This paper reports an empirical study aimed at elucidating reasons for success or failure in the implementation of strategic decisions. Eleven decisions in six organizations were examined using a case-study approach. Findings highlight four factors that appear to be critical for the successful management of implementation: backing, clear aims and planning, and a conducive climate — as long as chance events do not get in the way. Perhaps surprisingly, other factors, such as having relevant experience, giving implementation priority, having abundant resources, an appropriate structure and implementing flexibly, appear to matter rather less.

Descriptors: strategic decision-making, implementation, decision success, strategy, performance.

Decision-making Research

There is now a substantial body of research on the making of strategic decisions in organizations. From the early work of Simon (1947, 1960) and March and Simon (1958) to writers such as Braybrooke and Lindblom (1963); Pettigrew (1973); Mintzberg et al. (1976); Heller et al. (1983); Nutt (1984, 1993); Hickson et al. (1986); Eisenhardt (1989a) and Kriger and Barnes (1992), the emphasis has been on describing and explaining how decisions are arrived at. Though, to some extent, decision making and implementation are interwoven — some aspects of implementation may start before decision processes have been finalized and some sub-decisions may be taken thereafter — they can be distinguished for analytical purposes. Hickson et al. (1986), for example, used the point at which the decision was officially sanctioned (by the Board or CEO) to provide an empirically identifiable 'cut-off' point for their very extensive study of decision making which looked at the process through 'gestation' to 'authorization'.

The majority of these studies do not go beyond this 'authorization stage', though there are exceptions (e.g. Dean and Sharfman 1996; Rodrigues and Hickson 1995; Nutt 1986, 1987, 1989). It is therefore not possible to find in them anything concerning the 'success' of decisions once implemented (however 'success' is defined, a point returned to late), and this

Organization
Studies
1997, 18/4:
577–602

0170-8406/97
0018-0020 $3.00

has remained a relatively under-researched area (Dean and Sharfman 1996; Harrison 1992; Skivington and Daft 1991; Nutt 1987; Beyer and Trice 1978, 1982). Since strategic decisions concern 'substantial and all-pervading' issues (Hickson et al. 1986) and are of significance because of the 'actions taken, the resources committed, or the procedures set' (Mintzberg et al. 1976) this area warrants further attention.

Beyond the decision-making literature itself, work in the broad area of strategic change is tangentially pertinent to this. The significance of cultural and contextual issues has been particularly highlighted (e.g. Whipp et al. 1987, 1989; Johnson 1987). So has the institutional context in shaping the structures of organizing and mechanisms of control (Powell and DiMaggio 1991), including the kind of decisions that are taken and the legitimacy of how they are put into effect.

The concept of organizational archetypes — sets of systems and structures that reflect a dominant interpretative schema — (Greenwood and Hinings 1993; Hinings and Greenwood 1988) takes this further and has been developed alongside the study of organizational change. An archetype is the embodiment of past and current values, beliefs and organizational practices. These may serve to sanction some decisions rather than others and shape the process of implementation. However, as Greenwood and Hinings (1993: 1052) point out, this perspective centres on large-scale change, whereas micro-level change may be quite different. Certainly, changes at the level of the archetype, and institutional change in general, are likely to be gradual and incremental, rather than 'frame-breaking' (Nadler and Tushman 1989). In consequence these may be more difficult to analyze at finer levels of detail. Studies of individual decisions may be one way of gaining an insight into a narrower, but more focused aspect of the change process.

The successfulness of strategic change is most often assessed at the corporate level, but since corporate performance is a result of a range of complex and interrelated elements, this may reveal little about the impact of individual decisions. Firm performance 'is a function of a diverse array of factors which may mask the effect of decision processes' (Dean and Sharfman 1996: 371). This encourages research at the level of the strategic decision if outcomes are to be meaningfully evaluated.

Dean and Sharfman's (1996) work is one of the few studies of strategic decision-making to venture this empirically. In examining three areas: rationality, politicality and the effect of the environment, they found that rational processes were associated with effective outcomes, political processes were not, and that environmental instability moderated the effects of decision effectiveness (p. 389). However, even they did not extend this to see whether success also depends on the steps to implement decisions as well as to formulate them. They suggest that further work is needed to examine the relationship between implementation and success.

The study reported here is an attempt to do this by examining eleven case studies to explore how managers manage the implementation process. The research is exploratory in nature. Given that work on decision making does not focus on this area and the literature on strategic change does not provide a clear framework for the evaluation of strategic decisions, there is a need for fundamental concept-building research. The case studies were used to conceptualize the complex and multi-faceted notion of success and identify factors which appeared to influence it.

Comparable Cases, Contrasting Outcomes

A particularly graphic instance of what needs elucidating and explaining is provided by two cases which happen to be almost identical in all important respects: the same decision, implemented at about the same time, in two organizations situated a matter of a few miles apart, and operating in the same industry. They provide an intriguing comparison, illustrating how the same decision can bring either success or failure, and begin to suggest some factors which may be important in the management of successful implementation.

In the early 1980s a decision to radically alter fundamental operational and administrative systems was taken simultaneously, yet independently, in each of two British companies. Both companies operate in the mail-order industry and are active in the same markets. Each enjoyed a high level of success in the 1960s and early 1970s, but in the mid 1970s both were faced with identical problems: shrinking markets, increased competition and economic recession. In particular, both firms were suffering under the weight of burdensome and inefficient administrative systems, poor debt recovery and high labour costs.

Faced with these problems, each firm decided on the same technological solution — to reframe the entire business around major new computerized processes, including ordering, invoicing and stock control. In mail order, computers are not a mere management aid but the core technology.

Authorization to go ahead was given about the same time in each company. But here the similarities end. One firm, Great Northern[1], implemented the changes smoothly and after 6 months had an effectively working set of systems. The other, Easyshop, took 8 years, after which time it was still facing unresolved problems.

This paper will try to give reasons for this and other contrasts in performance.

Sample and Methods

Including these two cases, eleven decisions were covered in six organizations. Both organizations and decisions were chosen to give as broad a spread of activities as is possible in a small sample, to maximize the variety of rich and detailed data. The organizations covered public and private ownership, as well as manufacturing and service industries. The kinds of decisions studied ranged from the merger of two divisions of a chemical manufacturer, to the building of a water treatment works. A full list of organizations and cases is given in Appendix 1. As in other studies (Cray et al. 1988) the stipulation for inclusion was that each case had to be strategic in the view of the organization members.

Strategic decisions are often viewed as the province of top management (the CEO and senior directors); hence much research is carried out by interviewing this group only, or a single senior executive (Nutt 1989). Yet even if the making of decisions takes place predominantly at senior levels (and this view of decision making can be challenged), implementation will almost certainly require the involvement of others lower down (Schilit 1987; Kingsley and Reed 1991). Indeed, Beyer and Trice argue that separating adoption from implementation is desirable because different people are usually involved in each (1982: 596), so the case-study approach was used to obtain information from a wider range of informants. In all, 113 informants were interviewed, sometimes more than once, in semi-structured interviews which lasted from one to three hours. Of these informants, about a third were involved in making the decision, just over a third were involved in implementing it, and just under a third were affected by the decision although they were not directly involved in implementation. These categorizations are necessarily loose as they are not always mutually exclusive. Where significant individuals had left the organization through relocation or retirement, they too were followed up and interviewed. This variety of sources allowed a range of perspectives to be collated, compared and cross-referenced, providing a detailed account of the decision and especially its aftermath: the events, the activities, the problems, the outcomes. Illustrative examples of areas covered and questions asked during interviews are given in Appendix 2. Company documents and reports were also scrutinized. Data collection continued for over a year enabling some longitudinal information to be collected concerning the continuing repercussions of each decision.

Detailed 'implementation biographies' (Kimberly 1984) were compiled, chronicling the historical and contextual circumstances of each decision and implementation, the participants involved and the events that took place. As in Nutt's study (1987), these were then verified with informants to check for accuracy. As Cray et al. observed, 'all data on decision making relies on memory' and the longer recall necessary for these kinds of interviews means that 'the story becomes less cluttered and relatively simpler, not that it changes' (1988:23). The path of decisions, especially if they are of some moment, can be recalled. They leave identifiable traces, an imprint both in memory and reality: the computer systems are in place, the new building still stands, the departmental reorganization has taken place. Hence, as Alexander (1986) found, managers are able in retrospect to assess their long-run outcomes.

Temporal stability for information given by respondents in studies of decision making has also been demonstrated by Huber (1985). However, the use of multiple informants in this study did provide a check of the various accounts, overcoming many of the concerns in replying on sole respondents (Huber and Power 1985). In addition, the verification exercise showed a high degree of corroboration, with only a very few minor changes being made by informants to the biographies.

Data analysis proceeded in a step-wise fashion, each step being an attempt to synthesize and condense data into factors which best defined the concept of success, and factors which appeared to have most import for it. As Yin (1981) has suggested, case studies do not necessarily start with a conceptual framework. Indeed, Eisenhardt has argued that '. . . most importantly, theory-building research is begun as close as possible to the ideal of no theory under consideration and no hypotheses to test' (1989b:536). However, most research begins with some preconceptions, if only because fieldwork is costly and time-consuming for both researcher and researched alike. Hence eight pilot studies in other organizations were used to broaden understanding and suggest areas for preliminary exploration.

The first step in elucidating factors to describe and explain success involved carrying out a content frequency analysis to sift out features of each implementation process. All data pertaining to each decision were considered to try and distinguish the factors which appeared to affect the level of success. Decisions were then compared one with another in an effort to improve understanding of the range of factors which seemed to have import for success, and the frequency that they were mentioned. In this way, their significance was highlighted and their conceptualization refined. This process was repeated to operationalize the notion of 'success' in a way which captured the complexity of that term. This sorting and grouping of data allowed concepts to emerge as in 'grounded theory' (Glaser and Strauss 1967).

An example may help to illustrate this process. The preliminary scan of data relating to the installation of Vale University's heating and energy conservation system (Case 9) threw up a large number of aspects which different informants mentioned as having some bearing upon the outcomes. Further examination showed that one aspect was mentioned by nearly all informants. This was to do with the importance of clearly specifying implementation tasks and activities in advance. Analysis of other cases began to confirm the significance of this factor. It was mentioned again by informants at Great Northern when discussing computerization of the company's systems (Case 4). At Vale 'specificity' (the label finally given to this factor) was achieved by setting up a working party and producing written reports; at Great Northern the plan was largely unwritten, but the four or five individuals reponsible for implementation had discussed and planned comprehensively what had to be done. So although specificity appeared to be achieved in a number of ways, the important point is to what extent there was an opportunity to think things through beforehand in sufficient depth to be able to detail the tasks which implementation must encompass. Sometimes specificity was noticeable by its absence, as in the two cases at Wharf Chemicals. Here informants suggested that failing to be precise about what should be done both to set up the company and to merge two divisions played a part in their disappointing levels of success. Thus repeated examination of this factor within and across cases both highlighted its significance and gradually refined its conceptualization.

In this way, a number of concepts emerged to denote the factors which appeared to affect success. As discussed later, four of these were to prove especially influential. Three ways of defining success were also distinguished. Each resulted from the careful distillation of a wealth and variety of information. Illustrative excerpts from interview material and the final derived independent variables are given in Appendix 3. All variables are discussed below, and defined in Tables 1 and 2.

All data require interpretation, though the analysis of qualitative data has prompted particular concerns about its reliability and validity (e.g. see Miles 1979). For these reasons a second researcher carried out an independent content frequency analysis of one of the cases to check both the method of analysis and resulting concepts. An encouraging degree of consistency was found; over two thirds of the concepts were agreed immediately and the rest after some discussion, following which the other cases were re-analyzed. As with all work of this kind, the process was iterative. Full analysis took several months during which time the data were constantly re-examined, codified and reformulated.

As Eisenhardt suggests, the analysis of case-study data is the most difficult and the least codified part of the research (1989b:539). Both data collection and analysis closely followed the precepts on theory-building outlined in her paper, with the addition of reliability tests as described.

Defining Successful Implementation

Some authors take a straightforward approach to the definition of success, arguing that if a decision is adopted it may be said to be successful (Bourgeois and Brodwin 1984; Piercy 1989). Nutt (1989), building on Beyer and Trice (1982) also follows this line. However, this is too simple. Adoption does not necessarily lead to successful outcomes. For this reason, others have equated success with the achievement of certain results, which often take the form of financial or market indicators. Excellent companies (Peters and Waterman 1982) are those that are successful according to these kinds of criteria. The problems associated with such measures of success have been well documented (for a balanced critique see Guest 1992).

The three features of success distinguished in this study were *completion*, *achievement* and *acceptability* (Table 1). These emerged from the process of analysis previously described, in which some decisions were found to be more on time, some behindhand; some lived up to intentions more than others; some were more satisfactory to those concerned.

Table 1 Dependent Variables (*successfulness of implementation*)

Completion	The degree to which everything intended to be done, is done, within the expected time period.
Achievement	The degree to which what was done performs as intended.
Acceptability	The degree to which the method of implementation and outcomes are satisfactory to those involved in, or affected by, implementation.

Completion refers to how far the decision was implemented within an expected time period. Decisions are sometimes implemented in part and often take longer than decision makers expect (Alexander 1986). For the purposes of this research, a decision was considered to be completed to a high degree if the majority of the more significant implementation tasks was carried out within the time period anticipated.

Even fully implemented decisions may not live up to expectations, however. *Achievement* is a performance measure, referring to how far the objectives of those who made the decision were met. This compares with Dean and Sharfman's (1996) notion of decision effectiveness, which they defined as 'the extent to which (decisions) result in desired outcomes' (p. 368).

Even so, a decision may be implemented in full, may achieve all that is required and still be carried out in such a way, or have outcomes that are so widely unpopular, that it cannot be acclaimed an unmitigated success. *Acceptability*, sometimes cited as a criterion for evaluating strategic options (Piercy 1989), is used here as a third element in evaluating success.

In some sense, the first two measures can be viewed as somewhat more impersonal evaluations of performance derived from relatively objective information, while acceptability is a more personal evaluation of what occurred. However, since the data for all three are from the accounts given by informants, a sharp hard/soft distinction between them could not be sustained.

Of the two mail-order cases already recounted, Great Northern's computerization was highly successful along each of the three success dimensions; it completed on time, achieved everything expected, and all were satisfied with both what was done and how it was done. In fact, this case was one of the two most successful in the sample. On the other hand, Easyshop was the least successful in that it was late, underachieved even when mostly completed, and the changes were unacceptable to everyone in the organization.

Differential Contributions to Success

In all, ten factors potentially important for the successful management of implementation were deduced from the case data. They are *backing*, *assessability*, *specificity*, *cultural receptivity*, *propitiousness*, *familiarity*, *priority*, *resource availability*, *structural facilitation* and *flexibility*. Operationalized definitions are given in Table 2. Of these, it is the first four that appear to play the primary role in the explanation of success. *Backing*, *assessability*, *specificity* and *cultural receptivity* appear to have the greatest import for success, especially if the fifth,*propitiousness*, is favourable. There are therefore four crucial organizational factors and one that is beyond control. Together, these are named the 'realizers', since they help to realize the highest degree of success during implementation. The other five variables are given the name 'enablers', since they appear to support success without being fully capable of realizing it.

The significance of the realizer variables was highlighted during further analysis which began with a comparison across the cases. The methodological challenge was how to compare as many as eleven cases to see what pattern of factors, if any, was associated with the dependent, suc-

Table 2 Independent Variables (*factors affecting implementation success*)

	Realizers
Backing	The degree to which influence patterns favour implementation.
Assessability	The degree to which the success of implementation can be evaluated with precision.
Specificity	The degree to which precise details of implementation tasks and activities were decided beforehand.
Cultural receptivity	The degree to which organizational culture is conducive to the process of implementation.
Propitiousness	The degree to which any unforeseen external circumstances favour implementation.
	Enablers
Familiarity	The degree to which those involved have experience relevant to implementation.
Priority	The degree to which implementation is given precedence in the organization.
Resource availability	The degree to which resources for implementation (such as manpower, finance and time) are available.
Structural facilitation	The degree to which organizational structure is conducive to the process of implementation.
Flexibility	The degree to which the implementation process can be adapted to accommodate changing circumstances.

cess, variables. The approach chosen here was to rank cases on each variable using a method of 'paired comparison', adapted from Green and Tull (1978). This was used to arrive at an ordering of cases into higher, medium, or lower categorizations.

To give an example, with *backing* it was found that after comparing each case wth all the others, Great Northern's computer installation was one of two cases (the other being Vale University's heating system) that enjoyed the strongest and most universal support. In Great Northern, support came from the Managing Director and his senior team as well as the operatives who would have to install and use the new computer systems. No-one appeared to waiver, even though implementation was by 'edict' (Nutt 1989) with little prior consultation. However, during Easyshop's computer decision there was outright hostility from the Data Processing Director and his staff who, having already installed some automated systems in a piecemeal fashion, refused, for a long time, to invest more time in this new initiative. In fact, this case had the least support of all. Great Northern and Vale are therefore categorized as having higher backing, and Easyshop lower backing. The remaining cases were similarly compared with all the others, and ranked accordingly.

In the same way, cases were ranked on the success variables, comparing one case with another in terms of greater or less completion, achievement and acceptability. To check the ordering, all rankings were carried out independently by three other researchers.

The cases were then ranked on overall success, as in column 1, Table 3, by means of aggregating the rankings on the three success variables. Since there was no means of differentiating the weighing of one success variable against the other, the three were added, the combination giving a broader and firmer appreciation of success than taking any one alone. The mechanics involved awarding three 'points' for a higher rating, two for a medium rating and one for a lower rating, and adding these together. In this way, Great Northern's computer installation and Vale University's heating case were both rated higher on each success variable, so gaining a maximum nine points and placing them in joint first place in Table 3.

Thereafter, rankings on the ten variables were entered in the same ordering. Table 3 shows the final placings. Then it could be seen that though all ten had arisen from the case data which showed them as being influential, they did not all show the same kind of association with success when compared across all eleven cases.

Five, those now listed first in Table 3, showed a straight 'positive correlation' with success. That is, cases ranked high (H) on them ranked high on success (most obviously Great Northern's computer case and Vale University's heating case) and those ranking low were low on success (most obviously Easyshop's computer and both Wharf Chemicals' cases).

The other five did not show an obvious correlation with success. The

Table 3 Ranking of Cases According to Level of Success, Showing Placings on Realizer and Enabler Variables

Cases	Rank on success	Realizer Variables					Enabler Variables				
		Back	Asses.	Spec.	C.R.	Prop.	Fam.	Prior.	Res.A.	S.F.	Flex.
Great Northern — *computer*	1st	H	H	H	H	H	H	H	L	H	L
Vale University — *heating*	1st	H	H	H	H	H	M	L	H	M	H
Great Northern — *warehouse*	3rd	M	M	L	H	M	M	M	M	M	H
Central Water — *CADD*	4th	M	M	M	H	M	M	L	H	H	M
Central Water — *water works*	5th	L	M	M	M	L	M	M	L	L	M
S & D Chemicals — *transport*	5th	M	M	M	M	M	H	L	H	H	M
Vale University — *building*	5th	M	L	M	H	M	M	H	M	M	H
S & D Chemicals — *computer*	8th	M	M	M	M	M	L	M	M	M	M
Wharf Chemicals — *merger*	8th	M	L	L	L	M	M	L	M	L	M
Wharf Chemicals — *formation*	10th	L	L	L	L	M	L	M	M	L	M
Easyshop —*computer*	11th	L	M	M	L	L	L	M	M	L	M

Key: H=Higher M=Medium L=Lower
Realizer variables: backing, assessability, specificity, cultural receptivity, propitiousness
Enabler variables: familiarity, priority, resource availability, structural facilitation, flexibility

highly successful Great Northern computer was low (L) on two of the variables, and Vale University's successful heating case was low on one and only medium (M) on two. Among the less successful cases at the bottom of the table, there were many medium rankings, and among the cases middling on success there were many high rankings, so it was not necessary to have a high positioning on all of them in order to succeed. Lower positionings would do. Similarly, high positionings did not ensure high success.

It appears that the first five seem capable of fully realizing success, the second five of something less than that, only enabling it.

How these variables work in practice is now explained. For ease of exposition, Great Northern and Easyshop are again used as primary exemplars for illustrative purposes.

Four Critical Influences on Success

The way in which *backing*, one of the four key organizational factors, contributes to highly successful outcomes, has been mentioned already. While other work has shown that support is needed to push decisions along (Hickson et al. 1986; Pettigrew 1973); this research shows that *backing* is also needed to see them through. In particular, continuing support is required from those who authorize what goes on as well as support from those required to implement the changes. Although there is one clear example of a change 'champion' in the study (a middle manager at Central Water who was convinced of the advantages of computer-aided design but had to work hard before his ideas were taken up by senior management), these colourful individuals are less frequently encountered than the literature would perhaps suggest. What is more striking is the continuity of support provided by key decision-makers, whose sustained involvement and interest keep the decision on track during implementation. In all eleven cases, at least one influential decision-maker was also involved in implementation. In addition to these, commitment is now needed from those responsible for putting the decision into effect, as Great Northern's computer decision shows. The lack of *backing* was a clear hindrance in Easyshop. It is clear, therefore, that support is needed from those who have to implement the changes or who are powerful enough to get in the way, but this should not be confused with a requirement for a participative approach to implementing. The case of Great Northern suggests that a more consultative approach is not essential if people can themselves see the need for what is being done. 'Owning' the strategy (Giles 1991) is not always necessary.

In Great Northern, the objectives which were to be achieved and the tasks to be undertaken were spelt out with a high degree of precision. This *assessability* and *specificity* made the ultimate targets identifiable and ongoing tasks clear. In terms of *assessability*, managers knew what the new systems had to do; they were working towards a pre-existing, pre-conceptualized vision of what a fully developed and integrated system should offer. With the end point capable of being clearly defined, implementation activity was given focus and direction. Knowing where the end of the journey lies helps orientation along the way. Detailed planning of stages along the route — *specificity* — helps implementors know what has to be done to achieve progress. In Great Northern this took the form of frequent meetings, close 'hands-on' interaction between senior managers and other employees and regular de-briefings, which was particularly important as the vision of what the final systems would look like was really only understood by senior people.

All this was very different at Easyshop where it was much less obvious how success would be gauged or what individuals had to do to achieve it. Here, few had much idea of what was required or were prepared to set out the steps needed to make it happen. Good communication, or briefing, is known to be important (Bishop 1981), but clarity of vision must come first. What has to be communicated must first be analyzed in some detail. The importance of *specificity* in the implementation of new technology has been noted elsewhere (e.g. Leonard-Barton and Kraus 1993) but, though the example given here relates to computerization, this research suggests it is of more general significance.

The last of the organizational factors identified as helping to realize success is *cultural receptivity*. The Managing Director and many senior staff in Great Northern were new to the organization, having been brought in from a rival firm. As is often the case with such change, a new management team can revitalize an organization. Here they succeeded in re-framing some taken-for-granted company norms and ways of operating, fostering an acceptance of change and risk. Since the prevailing wisdom has it that change is often resisted (Bardach 1977; Mumford and Pettigrew 1975), and is retarded by individuals' 'myoptic blockages' (Lorange 1985) the introduction of a new group of powerful change agents can be an effective 'new broom', sweeping away entrenched ways of thinking. Informants were very aware of this transformation and contrasted the present situation with the previous conservative management under whom, it was felt, such a radical decision would never have been implemented. Easyshop again provides a stark contrast. Here, the view was widely held that senior managers were not catalysts for change. They had agreed to the decision but were not active in promoting it nor in providing a climate in which it could flourish. However, the pace picked up considerably at a late stage when a new chief executive was recruited to this company too.

Great Northern's experience could be regarded as a 'cultural transformation'. A top management team can be in a position to sanction particular values and norms that may bring about changes in attitudes and behaviour. The idea of *cultural receptivity*, introduced here, is not meant to infer that some generally facilitative corporate-wide culture is necessary, as has been sometimes suggested (Peters and Waterman

1982; Peters 1987), and culture is an amorphous notion. The finding here relates to a receptive context that is decision-specific. In this way, as Whipp et al. note, culture may well be a critical component of a more intricate equation (1989: 565) having some effect on performance, even if only in the short-term (Gordon and DiTomaso 1992).

Having support, being clear about what has to be done, spelling out how to do it, and operating in a facilitative context all contribute towards outcomes that are likely to realize expectations. It is these four factors that appear to be most clearly associated with successful implementation. They indicate that some level of analysis and planning in implementation is associated with successful outcomes. This accords with, and extends, Dean and Sharfman's (1996) findings that procedural rationality in decision-making is conducive to success. As it is in decision making, so it is in implementation.

There is an important qualifier, however. This work shows that not everything can be planned for. Managerial prescriptions need to allow for the unpredictable and unforeseen occurrences that are inherent both in decision-making (Alexander 1986; Whipp et al. 1987) and implementation. Chance events can get in the way. In this study, Easyshop's path was impeded by an unexpected take-over bid from a rival firm where sophisticated systems were already in place. Unforeseen and unwanted, it diverted attention and diluted momentum. The unforeseen is not always unfavourable, though. In another case — Vale University's heating installation — an offer by the local gas utility to provide cheap fuel allowed the organization to install a dual-fuel system which greatly increased performance, so it is the *propitiousness* of unforeseen events that has to be allowed for in explanations of success, as Rodrigues and Hickson (1995) confirm. Managers, however good they are, cannot control everything.

Enabling Factors

But what of the other five factors: familiarity, priority, resource availability, structural facilitation and flexibility? Intriguingly they appear to have much less import for success than might have been expected. They support the 'realizers', but of themselves do not appear to lead to successful outcomes. This finding is explored after they are briefly described below.

Strategic decisions are noted for their complexity in that they require the co-ordination of a multitude of interrelated tasks. Indeed, Hickson et al. (1986), with their distinctive interpretation of the term, found complexity to be a key feature in explaining the process of making decisions. However, when it comes to implementation, it is not just the complexity of what has to be done, but the *familiarity* of those doing it which is crucial. Great Northern's management team already had some experience of installing automated systems in their previous company and their prior experience smoothed the way. This does not mean that implementation was in any way simple or routine, but that it was more comprehensible. Easyshop, in contrast, was overwhelmed by their lack of *familiarity* with what had to be done.

Easyshop also failed to make this decision a *priority*, whereas Great Northern made it their foremost consideration; implementation of this decision was propelled forward and no other considerations were allowed to impede progress. In Easyshop the decision was not given this kind of prominence.

Resource availability, in terms of personnel, finance and time, is thought to be a crucial part of installing strategy (Alexander 1986), yet a surprising finding from this research is that no case suffered from a substantial deficit in resources. From this evidence it would seem that, for the most part, strategic decisions, once made, do tend to be resourced — not always lavishly, but enough in most cases. Indeed decisions which are best resourced are not necessarily the most successful. Great Northern's computer installation was the case where all resources were least abundant, being short of finance, people and working to a tight deadline, whereas Easyshop was in a somewhat better position, at least with regard to time and money.

The final two factors are to do with the organization's structure and the flexibility of the implementation process. With regard to *structural facilitation*, Easyshop's structural arrangements were clearly unhelpful. To by-pass the unsupportive Data Processing Director, responsibility for implementation was given to another Director. However, the data-processing department was still able to stall progress by withholding information and hardware so that the writing and testing of software was made more difficult.

Other cases demonstrate that structural reconfigurations can ease implementation. Central Water's computer-aided design and drafting (CADD) system was helped by the formation of a number of project teams brought together to oversee implementation. Different functional sections, managers, and users monitored progress, helped with problems and generally supported the process. Lorange (1985), Daft (1986), Owen (1993) and Skivington and Daft (1991) are among the writers who have drawn attention to the potentially beneficial effect of appropriate organizational design.

Finally, a degree of *flexibility* may be appropriate and the clearest example of this is in Great Northern's other case: the building of a new warehouse. Here, managers carried out frequent and wide-ranging reviews to ensure that the tasks which had been specified were being done satisfactorily and were still likely to produce the desired results. Particular elements of the decision, for example the internal layout of the building and choice of materials handling equipment, were deliberately taken at a very late stage so final requirements could be fine-tuned and advantage taken of technological advancements in products and materials. The emphasis throughout was on retaining flexibility to ensure appropriate responses in a dynamic context.

However, the surprising finding is that, contrary to expectations and much of the literature, these five factors do not distinguish between success and failure in the way that the 'realizers' do. Though cited by managers and theorists, they do not seem to provide the leverage to push implementation towards success.

The Importance of the Realizers: The Key Success Factors

So the four key variables of *backing*, *assessability*, *specificity*, and *cultural receptivity*, together with some good fortune, *propitiousness*, are those which appear to be associated with the highest level of success. The two most successful cases, Great Northern's computer installation and Vale University's heating system are placed uniformly highly on all five in Table 3, but none of the least successful implementations is highly placed on these variables, all being generally lower or at best medium in relative terms.

This means that to complete implementation, achieve everything which is intended, and do all of this in a way which is acceptable to organization members — this is, to attain comprehensive success — there needs to be support (especially from influential persons, and those implementing the decision), clarity about what the objectives are and how to reach them, a favourable climate within the organization and a little bit of luck — or at least no bad luck.

Great Northern's case has already been examined. At Vale there was full support from both decision makers and those implementing the heating/energy management system. It was believed that it would reduce costs significantly, as well as being more efficient, so the criteria for success were obvious to all and implementation was planned in detail. A National Energy Initiative provided a facilitative external context, while the university took great pains to prepare the ground internally by extensively publicising the new scheme. As already mentioned, the offer of cheap gas was an unexpected propitious occurrence.

In contrast, low down on the ordering, Wharf Chemicals' merger of two divisions was best with problems. Although senior managers were in favour, those directly affected were suspicious and refused wholehearted support. What the merger was to achieve was never made explicit, so what had to be done was unclear. The two divisions operated in completely different ways: one was well known to the rest of the industry for taking short cuts in safety and having a record of harmful emissions, the other was proud of its health and safety standards. A sharper cultural contrast could hardly be found, with each division having different values and ways of working. Unlike Vale, no propitious factors could help to overcome this daunting combination.

Overall what seems to be required is clear aims and means, with backing in the right climate, and no bad luck. These factors work together to help realize the highest level of success, but it is the pattern of them acting in concert which appears to be important. This interpretation is confirmed by the fact that, although the third and fourth cases in Table 3 (Great Northern's warehouse and Central Water's CADD system) are placed highly on cultural receptivity, this alone is far from enough to give a fully successful implementation. Their strength lies in their working together, which in turn strengthens their impact on success.

In contrast, the other five variables do not have seem to have the same import for success. Though they may be useful, they do not carry implementation far enough. It is for this reason that they have been termed 'enablers', a label borrowed from Daft and Becker (1978) who use it to refer to organizational characteristics which facilitate decisions to adopt innovations. Here the term refers to factors which provide minimum conditions for success but cannot of themselves, without 'realizers', take it to the full. They merely enable, they do not realize.

It can be seen, therefore, that although being familiar with what has to be implemented does help, as does making it a priority, providing at least sufficient resources, having a facilitative structure in place and implementing the change in a flexible way, these alone are not enough. Great Northern's computerization did not need to be flexible; Vale University's heating installation was low priority, but was successful, nevertheless.

So whilst three favourable 'enabler' factors (familiarity, priority and structural facilitation) supported Great Northern's very successful computerization, the three equally favourable 'enablers' (familiarity, resource availability and structural facilitation) at S & D Chemicals (lower in Table 3) were not sufficient to make up for a set of only moderately favourable 'realizers' and so their transport decision was less successful than it might have been. The building of the campus and university at Vale suffered in the same way — its relatively good 'enablers' could not take it far, when it had only a middling set of 'realizers'.

Looking at this the other way around, lower positionings on enabler variables do not *prevent* highly successful outcomes. The two top cases of Great Northern and Vale have already demonstrated this.

Organizational and Process Characteristics

Although this research has indicated some critical features in the management of implementation, are there, within what are available in this study, any characteristics of the organization or decision, as distinct from implementation, that have a bearing on final success?

It has already been shown that the same decision (computerization) can be implemented with quite different outcomes, so it is likely that the topic of what is being implemented is not a crucial determinant of success. In other words, a computer installation is no more and no less likely to do well than is a merger, and neither will, of itself, do better than new buildings, for instance. This would mirror the lack of significance of topics as such during decision-making that was shown by Hickson et al. 1986. But what of organization? Table 4 shows the cases, again in order of success, this time indicating whether they are in the public or private domain, and in service or manufacturing sectors. It also gives the duration of both decision and implementation in order to provide further dimensions for comparison.

On first appearance there is some evidence to suggest the effect of organizational factors. Both Great Northern's implementations were highly successful, both cases in Central Water and S & D Chemicals enjoyed moderate success, Vale had one highly successful and one moderately successful case and both of Wharf's were largely failures. However, this does not appear to be due to the effects of ownership. Of the two most successful cases, one organization is privately owned (Great Northern) and one public (Vale University). It is true that the four least successful cases are all in private organizations, but the inclusion of only two public-sector organizations in total is too few to allow more than speculation. Similarly, the sample contains only two manufacturers, so the effect of sector cannot be reliably tested. Nonetheless, it is interesting that neither manufacturer does particularly well, attaining only moderate success at best. Though some studies of decision making have found some differences between public and private sectors (Kingsley and Reed 1991; Coursey and Bozeman 1990), it would seem that the effect of organization is residual here (Hickson et al. 1986). What appears to be more important is the way in which implementation is managed by management, rather than the ownership of the firm or the sector in which it operates.

Lastly, how long is taken by the processes of deciding and implementing themselves? Table 4 depicts the duration of decision-making (the decision 'point' is when the decision was authorized) and the duration of implementation (when the decision was 'completed', that is, when most things intended to be done, were done). The mean time to arrive at a decision in this study was just over 11 months. Interestingly, the other major study of strategic decisions, the Bradford Studies, (Hickson et al. 1986), found that the mean of their sample of 150 decisions was 12.4 months showing that, on this dimension at least, there is mutual corroboration (though in only 11 cases the mean is heavily affected by just two lengthy decisions, Central Water's water works and S & D's computerization). This current work shows that implementing a decision takes much longer than making it in the first place. Only two cases, Central Water's water works and S & D's transport decision, took longer to decide than to implement. In Central Water this can be explained by the long planning-application process and feasibility studies needed for public works of this kind; in the chemical company the choice of a contract haulage company to deliver chemical consignments meant there was little to do during implementation other than to hand over the customer delivery details and pass on existing distribution systems to the outside contractor. On average, however, implementation takes about 39 months, though it can vary from under a year to anything up to the eight years of the struggling Easyshop computerization. In total, managers contemplating strategic decisions should expect to take about four years to get the decision through and then get it implemented. It is not something to embark upon lightly — or maybe a factor to consider when planning for retirement!

Table 4
Duration of Decision Making and Implementation by Ownership and Sector

Cases	Rank on success	Ownership	Mfg/ service	Duration (months) Decision	Implement-ation	Total
Great Northern (*computer*)	1st	private	service	1	6	7
Vale University (*heating*)	1st	public	service	6	34	40
Great Northern (*warehouse*)	3rd	private	service	8	41	49
Central Water (*CADD*)	4th	public	service	2	25	27
Central Water (*water works*)	5th	public	service	48	28	76
S & D Chemicals (*transport*)	5th	private	mfg	8	2	10
Vale University (*building*)	5th	public	service	10	36	46
S & D Chemicals (*computer*)	8th	private	mfg	24	84	108
Wharf Chemicals (*merger*)	8th	private	mfg	6	36	42
Wharf Chemicals (*formation*)	10th	private	mfg	3	36	39
Easyshop (*computer*)	11th	private	service	6	96	102
				mean: 11.1	mean: 38.6	mean: 49.6

Interesting though this is, there is nothing firm to associate length of either deciding or implementing with success. It can take about the same time to decide and implement a poor decision as a successful one. For instance, there is no pattern of the more successful cases towards the top of Table 4 being faster than those at the bottom in arriving at a decision. There is only the possibility that faster decisions can be either best or worst in outcomes, insofar as the most lengthy cases are in the middle. Speed may win the day, or haste may lose it, but there are far too few cases from which to draw firm conclusions. Other potential links between decision-making characteristics, implementation processes and success need to be explored in future work.

Conclusions

The main finding from this research is the distinguishing of key factors, the 'realizers', which influence implementation success. They represent the clarity of vision and purpose, and the positive context which are needed for a successful outcome. Whereas the 'enablers' provide the facilitating conditions of know-how, impetus, adequate resources, appropriate structures and flexibility, they do not embody the central driving force which pushes implementation further forward.

The identification of 'realizers' and 'enablers' suggests a theory of differential contributions to success that takes us beyond a mere list of undifferentiated factors. It helps to clarify the role of individual elements and transcends the implicit equal weighting which is usually given.

A provisional explanatory theory can be ventured as to why the 'realizers' should work together in this way. The common element which seems to link them is a sense of commonality and clarity of purpose. There is agreement about what has to be done and there is support for it.

Put another way, backing for a clarity implementable goal in a culturally receptive organization arises from a clear and shared aim. The 'realizers' act in concert to produce the best chance of success, especially when there is a little bit of luck, propitiousness, or at least no back luck along the way.

This will differ from decision to decision. The contrasts between cases in the same organization in this study show that a management cannot take it for granted that because the 'realizers' mesh together favourably for one implementation they will do so again for the next. This will not be a long-lasting and unchanging feature of an organization which impacts on all decisions in the same way, for what is being done and who supports it will change, so it will be a feature of some implementations more than of others.

In contrast, the 'enabler' variables are more heterogeneous and so do not work together in such a synergistic way. Although it can be argued that making implementation a priority may lead to the allocation of resources, and it is conceivable that being familiar with what has to be done can help devise a suitable structure. Beyond this, there is no apparent connection across all five 'enabler' variables to the extent that there is between the 'realizers'. This comparative heterogeneity means that their combined effect is not as powerful and, unlike the 'realizers', the resulting impact is not enhanced by the 'sum of the parts'.

In coming to this conclusion, this study is able to shed light on previous work, lending support to some views and not others. The political side of decision making has been emphasized by many authors (e.g. Eisenhardt and Bourgeois 1988; Pettigrew 1973; Baier et al. 1986; Hickson et al. 1986) and now *backing* is shown to be a prominent 'realizer'. It is demonstrated that political behaviour may be apparent at all stages of the decision, not only while it is being decided but beyond that, when it is being implemented.

The prominence of *assessability* and *specificity* among the 'realizers' confirms the role of planning, the mainstay of so much orthodoxy. It does help — in the 'realizer' sense of being clear about the targets which have to be hit and being precise about what has to be done to hit them. This may well imply that what is required for successful outcomes is increasingly rational managers, something which has been decried since Simon's (1947) 'administrative man' model circumscribed the rational economic ideal. Yet that criticism can go too far. An element of planning, clarity and precision gives management a better chance.

Cultural receptivity also affirms the importance of context (Whipp et al. 1989). A favourable climate is helpful, though this is decision-specific and may not be facilitative for other decisions in the same organization.

It has been shown, though, that it is not only internal organizational factors which must be taken into account. As Alexander (1986) found, and Nutt intimated (1989), external factors also play their part, for good or ill. Management often need favourable external circumstances, some *propitiousness*, on their side.

By identifying and defining four key success factors, the 'realizers', this exploratory research can contribute to a growing recognition of what is most likely — and not so likely — to take a decision through implementation to a successful outcome. Further work is now needed to test these findings on a more representative basis.

Appendices

1. Organizations and Cases

Central Water (public utility, studied prior to subsequent privatization)	1. Building a Water Treatment Works 2. Installation of a CADD (computer-aided design and drafting) system
Easyshop Mail Order (private company)	3. Installation of a new computer system
Great Northern Mail Order (private company)	4. Installation of a new computer system 5. Building a £40m+ new warehouse

S & D Chemicals (private company)	6. Development of a new transport and distribution system 7. Installation of a new computer system
Vale University (public organization)	8. Building the university and campus 9. Installation of a heating and energy management system
Wharf Chemicals (private company)	10. Formation of the company 11. Merger of two divisions

2. Indicative Check-List of Areas Covered During Interviews

Making the Decision

1. Please give details of how the decision was reached — sequence of events, who was involved, their favourability and influence.
2. What was the decision meant to achieve?
3. How was the success of the decision to be evaluated? Where there any targets to be met?

Implementing the Decision

1. Please give details of how the decision was implemented — sequence of events, who was involved, their favourability and influence.
2. How precisely was it laid down how the decision was to be put into effect?
   Very clearly specified 5
   Fairly clearly specified 4
   Specified only in part 3
   Vaguely specified 2
   Completely unspecified 1
   If specified, how?
3. How long was implementation expected to take? How long did it actually take? Was there a deadline?
4. How far was the decision implemented?
   Completely implemented 5
   Mostly implemented 4
   Partially implemented 3
   Mostly unimplemented 2
   Not implemented 1
   What aspects were not implemented, and why?
5. Did any impediments get in the way?
   How seriously did they affect the process?
   Extremely seriously 5
   Very seriously 4
   Rather seriously 3
   Quite seriously 2
   Not very seriously 1

6. Did anything help in any way? In what way? How favourably?

Extremely favourable	5
Very favourable	4
Rather favourable	3
Quite favourable	2
Moderately favourable	1

7. What kind of resources were needed to implement? List in order of importance and rate the availability of each:

Fully available	5
Mostly available	4
Available in part	3
Mostly lacking	2
Completely lacking	1

8. How far was the decision implemented as intended?

Wholly	5
Mostly	4
Largely	3
Partially	2
Not at all	1

9. How far did implementation succeed in achieving what was intended?

Completely successful	5
Mostly successful	4
Largely successful	3
Mostly unsuccessful	2
Completely unsuccessful	1

What was successful and what was not? Why?

10. Have there been any unintended consequences of the decision? What were these and why did they occur?

11. What changes, if any would you like to have seen in either the process or outcomes?

How far were you generally satisfied with what was done and the way things were done?

Wholly	5
Mostly	4
Largely	3
Partially	2
Not at all	1

3. Illustrative Excerpts from Interviews, and Derived Variables

Excerpts	Variables
The move was strongly supported by some employees who saw it as enhancing their careers, but some were sceptical. *(CADD Administrator, Central Water, talking about the installation of a CADD system)*	Backing
Implementation had to be gauged in terms of how far it led to cost-savings, but also its impact on customers.	Assessability

(Head of Logistics, S & D Chemicals, talking about the development of a new transport and distribution system)	
We very clearly defined what needed to be done at every stage ... *(Computer Director, Great Northern, talking about the installation of a new computer system)*	Specificity
In terms of this decision, the top people lacked risked-taking attitudes. *(Sales Systems Manager, Easyshop, talking about the installation of a new computer system)*	Cultural receptivity
An unforeseen take-over bid seriously delayed implementation for a couple of years. *(Finance and Customer Administration Director, Easyshop, talking about the installation of a new computer system)*	Propitiousness
We had already installed a new (computer) system at (previous company) so though we couldn't completely translate the whole system we had a chance to do it better and improve things with hindsight. *(Data Base Marketing Director, Great Northern, talking about the installation of a new computer system)*	Familiarity
The Vice-Chancellor was emphatic that the buildings had to be ready for the first students — he was very concerned about the students having nowhere to stay. *(Architect, talking about the building of Vale University)*	Priority
We were part-funded by a European Regional Development grant (so finances were sufficient), but the main building contractor was short of manpower. *(Project Manager, Central Water, talking about the building of a Water Treatment Works)*	Resource availability
One division was almost unstructured while the other was run in a very structured way, lots of layers of management, very formal, very rigid — almost the opposite, yet they had to work together. *(Operations Director, Wharf Chemicals, talking about the merger of two divisions)*	Structural facilitation
The building was still being changed as it was being built ... nothing is concluded until the work package goes on site, then things can still be changed at the last minute — this gives us more flexibility. *(Director, Great Northern, talking about the building of a new warehouse)*	Flexibility

Note

* The author wishes to thank Professor David J. Hickson for his guidance and unstinting encouragement, and three anonymous reviewers for their helpful comments.

1. All cases are real but company names are pseudonyms.

References

Alexander, Larry D.
1986 'Successfully implementing strategic decisions' in *Planning and managing change*. B. Mayon-White (ed.), 249–261. London: Harper and Row.

Baier, Vicki E., James G. March and Harald Saetren
1986 'Implementation and ambiguity'. *Scandinavian Journal of Management Studies* (May): 197–212.

Bardach, Eugene
1977 *The implementation game — what happens after a bill becomes law*. Cambridge, MA: Massachusetts Institute of Technology Press.

Beyer, Janice M., and Harrison M. Trice
1978 *Implementing changes: alcoholism policies in work organizations*. New York: Free Press.

Beyer, Janice M., and Harrison M. Trice
1982 'The utilization process: a conceptual framework and synthesis of empirical findings'. *Administrative Science Quarterly* 27, December, 591–622.

Bishop, Jeff
1981 'Briefing for implementation, the missing link?' in *Policy and action*. S. Barrett and C. Fudge, 163–181. London: Methuen.

Bourgeois, L.J., and David R. Brodwin
1984 'Strategic implementation: five approaches to an elusive phenomenon'. *Strategic Management Journal* 5: 241–264.

Braybrooke, David, and Charles Lindblom
1963 *A strategy of decision*. New York: Free Press.

Coursey, David, and Barry Boseman
1990 'Decision making in public and private organizations: a test of alternative concepts of "publicness" '. *Public Administration Review* (Sept/Oct): 525–535.

Cray, David, Geoffrey R. Mallory, Richard J. Butler, David J. Hickson, and David C. Wilson
1988 'Sporadic, fluid and constricted processes: three types of strategic decision-making in organizations'. *Journal of Management Studies* 26/1: 13–40.

Daft, Richard, L.
1986 *Organization theory and design*. St. Paul: West Publishing.

Daft, Richard, L., and Selwyn W. Becker
1978 *Innovation in organizations*. New York: Elsevier.

Dean, James W. Jr., and Mark P. Sharfman
1996 'Does decision process matter? A study of strategic decision-making effectiveness'. *Academy of Management Journal* 39/2: 368–396.

Eisenhardt, Kathleen M.
1989a 'Making fast strategic decisions in high-velocity environments'. *Academy of Management Journal* 32: 543–576.

Eisenhardt, Kathleen M.
1989b 'Building theories from case study research'. *Academy of Management Review* 14/4: 532–550.

Eisenhardt, Kathleen M., and L. J. Bourgeois
1988 'Politics of strategic decision making in high-velocity environments: towards a mid-range theory'. *Academy of Management Journal* 31/4: 737–770.

Giles, William D.
1991 'Making strategy work'. *Long Range Planning* 24/5: 75–91.

Glaser, Barney G., and Anselm L. Strauss
1967 *The discovery of grounded theory: strategies for qualitative research*. New York: Aldine.

Gordon, George G., and Nancy Ditomaso
1992 'Predicting corporate performance from organizational culture'. *Journal of Management Studies* 29/6: 783–798.

Green, Paul E., and Donald S. Tull
1978 *Research for marketing decisions*. London: Prentice-Hall.

Greenwood, Royston, and C. Robert Hinings
1993 'Understanding strategic change: the contribution of archetypes'. *Academy of Management Journal* 36/5: 1052–1081.

Guest, David E.
1992 'Right enough to be dangerously wrong: an analysis of the "*In search of excellence phenomenon*" ' in *Human resource strategies*. G. Salaman (ed.), 5–19. London: Sage.

Harrison, E. Frank
1992 'Some factors involved in determining strategic decision success'. *Journal of General Management* 17/3: 72–87.

Heller, Frank, A., J. D. Pieter Drenth, Paul Koopman, and Veljko Rus
1983 'A contingency model of participative decision making: an analysis of 56 decisions in three Dutch organizations'. *Journal of Occupational Psychology* 56/1: 1–18.

Hickson, David J., Richard J. Butler, David Cray, Geoffrey R. Mallory, and David C. Wilson
1986 *Top decisions: strategic decision making in organizations*. San Francisco: Jossey-Bass; Oxford: Basil Blackwell.

Hinings, C. Robert, and Royston Greenwood
1988 *The dynamics of strategic change*. Oxford: Basil Blackwell.

Huber, George P.
1985 'Temporal stability and response-order biases in participant descriptions of organizational decisions'. *Academy of Management Journal* 28/4: 943–950.

Huber, George P., and Danel J. Power
1985 'Research notes and communications, retrospective reports of strategic-level managers: guidelines for increasing their accuracy'. *Strategic Management Journal* 6: 171–180.

Johnson, Gerry
1987 *Strategic change and the management process*. Oxford: Basil Blackwell.

Kimberly, John R.
1984 'The study of organization: toward a biographical perspective' in *Handbook of organizational behaviour*. J. Lorsch (ed.), 223–237. Englewood Cliffs, N.J.: Prentice-Hall.

Kingsley, Gordon A., and Pamela Norton Reed
1991 'Decision process models and organizational context: level and sector make a difference'. *Public productivity and management review* 14/4: 397–413.

Kriger, Mark P., and Louis B. Barnes
1992 'Organizational decision-making as hierarchical levels of drama'. *Journal of Management Studies* 29/4: 439–457.

Leonard-Barton, Dorothy, and William A. Kraus
1993 'Implementing new tecnnology' in *Managing change*. C. Mabey, and B. Mayon-White (eds.), 125–131. London: Paul Chapman.

Lorange, Peter
1985 'Strengthening organizational capacity to execute strategic change' in *Organizational strategy and change*. Johannes M. Pennings et al. (eds.), 449–467. San Francisco: Jossey-Bass.

March, James G., and Herbert A. Simon
1958 *Organizations*. New York: Wiley.

Miles, Matthew B.
1979 'Qualitative data as an attractive nuisance: the problem of analysis'. *Administrative Science Quarterly* 24 (December): 590–601.

Mintzberg, Henry, Duru Raisingham and André Theoret
1976 'The structure of 'unstructured' decision processes'. *Administrative Science Quarterly* 21: 246–275.

Mumford, Enid, and Andrew Pettigrew
1975 *Implementing strategic decisions*. London: Longman.

Nadler, D.A., and M. Tushman
1989 'Organizational frame bending: principles for managing reorientation'. *Academy of Management Executive* 1: 194–204.

Nutt, Paul C.
1984 'Types of organizational decision processes'. *Administrative Science Quarterly* 29/3: 414–450.

Nutt, Paul C.
1986 'Tactics of implementation'. *Academy of Management Journal* 29/2: 230–261.

Nutt, Paul C.
1987 'Identifying and appraising how managers install strategy'. *Strategic Management Journal* 8:1–14.

Nutt, Paul C.
1989 'Selecting tactics to implement strategic plans'. *Strategic Management Journal* 10: 145–161.

Nutt, Paul C.
1993 'Formulation processes and tactics used in organizational decision making'. *Organizational Science* 4/2: 226–251.

Owen, Arthur A.
1993 'How to implement strategy' in *Managing change*. C. Mabey, and B. Mayon-White (eds.), 143–150. London: Paul Chapman.

Peters, Tom J.
1987 *Thriving on chaos*. London: Macmillan.

Peters, Tom J., and Robert H. Waterman
1982 *In search of excellence*. London: Harper and Row.

Pettigrew, Andrew
1973 *The politics of organizational decision-making*. London: Tavistock.

Piercy, Nigel
1989 'Diagnosing and solving implementation problems in strategic planning'. *Journal of General Management* 15/1: 19–38.

Powell, Walter W., and Paul J. DiMaggio
1991 *The new institutionalism in organizational analysis*. Chicago, IL: University of Chicago Press.

Rodrigues, Suzana Braga, and David J. Hickson
1995 'Success in decision making: different organizations, differing reasons for success'. *Journal of Management Studies* 32/5: 655–678.

Schilit, Warren Keith
1987 'An examination of the influence of middle-level managers in formulating and implementing strategic decisions'. *Journal of Management Studies* 24: 271–293.

Simon, Herbert A.
1947 *Administrative behaviour*. New York: Free Press.

Simon, Herbert A.
1960 *The new science of management decision*. New York: Harper and Row.

Skivington, James E., and Richard L. Daft
1991 'A study of organizational "framework" and "process" modalities for the implementation of business-level strategies'. *Journal of Management Studies* 28/1: 45–68.

Whipp, Richard, Robert Rosenfeld, and Andrew Pettigrew
1988 'Understanding strategic change processes: some preliminary British findings' in *The management of strategic change*. A. Pettigrew (ed.), 14–55. Oxford: Basil Blackwell.

Whipp, Richard, Robert Rosenfeld, and Andrew Pettigrew
1989 'Culture and competitiveness: evidence from two mature UK industries'. *Journal of Management Studies* 16/6: 561–585.

Yin, Robert K.
1981 'The case study crisis: some answers'. *Administrative Science Quarterly* 26 (March): 58–65.

[20]

How Organizations Can Overbalance

Decision Overreach as a Reason for Failure

DAVID C. WILSON
Aston University Business School, Birmingham, England
DAVID J. HICKSON
Bradford University Management Centre, England
SUSAN MILLER
Durham University Business School, England

A special case of the big bad decision is identified. It is called decision overreach. Two separate elements constitute overreach, namely, disproportionality and irreversibility. Four conditions seem to dispose managers to take decisions that are disproportionate and irreversible. These are small size of firm, relatively short duration of decision process, a lack of foresight, and overfamiliarity with products and markets. The data are drawn from U.K. manufacturing organizations.

The senior management team of a small brewery in England was contemplating expansion. This family-owned firm had experienced steady growth of sales for its beers throughout the past 10 years. Most of the directors favored expanding the company, and an unanticipated opportunity to purchase a relatively huge additional brewing plant seemed too good to miss. A vigorous future seemed to stretch ahead. Problems then began to arise, especially cash flow problems, which overwhelmed management. The decision that had purported to drive the company forward could be seen to have done exactly the opposite. It brought a takeover, which meant the end of the firm as an independent entity.

This is one of 55 cases of strategic decision making (Miller, Hickson, & Wilson, 1993) that are currently being studied in an attempt to explain more fully the success or failure of decisions. It was the particular characteristics of this brewery decision that drew attention to it beyond the generality of cases. The decision not only went too far but also went beyond reversal. This article discusses the likely constituents and causes of what is called decision overreach.

AMERICAN BEHAVIORAL SCIENTIST, Vol. 39 No. 8, August 1996 995-1010

AN ABSENCE OF OVERREACH

There are tangential references in the literature to overreach, but we could find no studies that address the concept directly. Only a few may be thought to have touched upon it, if their ideas are stretched to serve that supposition. Greenwood and Hinings (1993), for example, argue that broad "archetypes," such as patterns of beliefs among managers or strategic recipes, can be taken so far as to lead to decision failure, and Dutton and Duncan (1989) focus on the faults of strategic planning. Nutt (1986) emphasizes the role of key executives in holding the process within reach, and Huff and Reger (1987) point to information and decision support systems as keeping things under control. Miller (1990) analyzes how implementation can take a decision forward out of the "failure zone," but not how it gets into that zone.

Nor have others who have searched through and synthesized published research come up with any concept of this kind. Hickson (1987) reviews what had been written on managerial decision-making processes, the subject of decision, and the decision itself. He includes incrementalism, edging forward little by little, but no mention is made of the contrasting big move, let alone of any concept of a decision that goes too far. Listing those few studies that have ventured to project from process to performance, Rajagopalan, Rasheed, and Datta (1993) show that varying combinations of consensus, drive from the top, and decision speed are held to have affected economic and other performance criteria, yet again do not mention any concept remotely like overreach. Laroche (1995) takes a more interpretive stance, preferring to regard the idea of a decision as a representation by managers of what they think they are doing, a way "to organize the flow of action" as "participants make their way in the organizational mess." However, nothing emerges from this perspective either, nothing about how decisions that are "socially represented" might be taken too far in this socially constructed reality. The scale and the scope of managerial imagination are not mentioned at all.

Overreach is not to be confused with technical disasters such as the sinking of the *Titanic*, Three Mile Island, Bhopal, and Chernobyl (e.g., Perrow, 1984; Smith, 1995; Turner, 1978). It is a managerial overreach, not an operational calamity, that is the concern of this article.

CASES OF OVERREACH

As already stated, attention was drawn to decision overreach by the case of the brewery, conspicuous among the 55 decisions being studied in 14 public and private sector organizations, large and small. These decisions were a representative one third of the 150 cases covered by the "Bradford Studies" (Cray, Mallory, Butler, Hickson, & Wilson, 1988; Hickson, Butler, Cray, Mallory, & Wilson, 1986). That original research had traced and compared processes up to the point of decision, that is, to when implementation was authorized. Data had been collected during the later 1970s and early 1980s. The subset of 55 were revisited during 1990 to 1993 to obtain data on what happened subsequently, during implementation and afterward. The 55 case histories cover periods ranging from 15 to 20 years.

Preparatory to the second period of data collection, telephone inquiries had revealed that there were still senior executives in each organization, or otherwise locatable, who recalled meeting members of the research team during the original investigation, who had been closely involved personally in what had happened since then, and who were willing to talk about it.

The interviews with them were semistructured, commencing with a general history of how the decision had been implemented, the sequence of subsequent events, and a listing of who and which departments or other interests from the managerial echelons had been involved. This also included external interests, such as suppliers, customers, and competitors. Interviews continued with open questions about the success of the decision and reasons for success (or lack of it). A number of rating scales were completed, the results of which are not pertinent to this article. Typically, interviews lasted from 1 to 2 hours, and some were longer. The essentials of what was said were noted on semistructured interview guides rather than using a tape recorder, for earlier experience had shown that informants were frequently reluctant to record occasionally sensitive material verbatim. Where available, archival data such as internal reports and documents were also examined.

Discovering what came to be called overreach was a case of classic serendipity. There was no such idea in mind when the research began. Cases had been analyzed and reanalyzed, discussed and rediscussed, many times. Gradually, they had been grouped in terms of their successfulness, or lack of it, in implementation and the subsequent outcomes. There were many failures or, at least, performances that were disappointing to the managements responsible. There were various kinds of production problems, market changes, failures to sell, and lack of profitability. Yet the decision by the brewery was based on none of these. The market generally was good, and sales were rising. The problem was simply the purchase of a huge additional plant. Again and again discussion returned to the case history until it was recognized for what it was and thereafter seen in a fresh light.

Then reexamination of the other 54 cases in this light, deliberately seeking any more instances of overreach, found one other decision in an engineering factory with similar features, though not so pronounced as in the brewery. The brewery decision remains the exemplar, the extreme, or what can be termed an "ideal type."

The two firms in which the overreach decisions were made are given the fictitious names of Thomson, the brewery, and Jacobite, the engineering factory. In addition to the managers interviewed during 1978 and 1977 in the firms, respectively, about the original making of the decisions (Hickson et al., 1986), those now interviewed during 1990 and 1992 were, in Thomson, two of the small number of directors—being the former managing director (or president), who was visited at his home, and the former financial controller, who was seen at the firm to which he had moved. In Jacobite, they were the financial controller, the commercial manager, the quality control manager, and the former chairman and managing director (president) who, too, was visited at home. Some were seen once, others more than once. All had been included among the original informants. The two case histories are as follows.

THOMSON

Thomson was formed early in the nineteenth century as a small family-owned brewery. When first visited, it still employed only 35 people and was producing only a small quantity of beer. However, demand for quality beer was increasing rapidly and so the firm's owners and managers were considering what could be done to expand production. During these deliberations, an opportunity arose to purchase a closed down brewery some distance away. This would increase capacity to almost 8 times current production, and there was some doubt whether or not this relatively colossal increase was manageable and necessary. Doubts were short lived, however. Only one nonexecutive director stood his ground in opposition, and resigned. The cost of acquiring this eightfold capacity was substantially less than the cost of even just doubling production on the existing site. Further, it could be acquired straight away, avoiding prolonged construction. The only problem was raising the money. The banks were unhappy because Thomson already had a substantial overdraft, and they felt that Thomson had not really fully worked through the financial implications. There was no sufficiently detailed business plan or profitability projections. Eventually one bank was persuaded to finance the acquisition.

Problems began to arise, however, within months of production starting. The volume of beer could be brewed and got out, but the scale of what had been taken on proved too great to manage. In a plant of this size, more technical problems arose than had been anticipated. The boiler and the lifting gear were unreliable. The effluent treatment plant became inadequate for this volume under stricter government regulation. But more than anything, the inflow of revenue at this scale of operation was slower and with smaller margins than Thomson's management, used to a much smaller and tighter operation, had envisaged. They did not have enough capital to finance themselves through the resultant cash-flow crisis. In brief, over several years, this led to their succumbing to successive takeovers and their brands to being absorbed into the capacity of a larger competitor. They had overbalanced in reaching for such an immense relative increase in production volume, when they might have sustained a lesser increase.

Ten years after the decision to buy the additional brewery, Thomson was reduced to a nominal shell of a firm with only a little symbolic specialist brewing in their original tiny premises. They were back to where they started, but minus their independence.

JACOBITE

Jacobite had long held a premier position supplying components mainly to a small number of well-known industrial buyers that assembled Jacobite's precision engineering items into household name products. Their decision was a relatively massive investment in new buildings, a new plant.

Pressed by rising demand, top management had debated ways of adding to existing space and embarked on a series of costing exercises. These involved consultation with external organizations such as banks, major customers, and equipment suppliers, as well as with the internal functions of production, planning, engineering, sales, and finance. Discussions were led by Jacobite's vigorous chairman who was closely involved personally. It was decided to build extensive new factory premises on a contiguous site. This was a big decision in two ways. First, it assumed an increase in sales volume of up to 50% and, second, it was expensive, incurring substantial debts for the company to pay for it. All senior managers in Jacobite were in favor of the decision. Confidence in the future was high.

However, sales volumes peaked at no more than a 20% increase, while several years of economic recession forced drastic cost cutting. Jacobite was threatened with closure as capital ran out. The large site and premises, with the production equipment that had been installed, were unsustainable. Financial collapse was only narrowly averted, under new ownership, by halving the premises and radically changing ways of working.

The bulk of the older buildings were sold, and all the manufacturing equipment was moved into the newer buildings. Just-in-time production and cell-form manufacturing on more modern equipment replaced previous large batch and mass production methods. Soon, 200 employees were turning out what 700 had done before. From one point of view, this was a turnaround success story. From another, the company had come close to collapse because it had gone too far in expanding production floor space beyond what was needed. The original premises with relatively small improvements could have been big enough for the new equipment and production methods.

There was in Jacobite, unlike Thomson, an element of market miscalculation, but as in Thomson the scale of their move was relatively too big.

CONSTITUENTS OF DECISION OVERREACH

What do these two cases have in common? First, the move that was made was relatively huge, disproportionate, more so for Thomson than for Jacobite. Second, it was irreversible, wholly so for Thomson who could not recoup and was reduced to a mere front organization, not quite so irrevocably for Jacobite. Disproportionality and irreversibility appear to be the two characteristics that distinguish overreach.

Disproportionality denotes the scale of the move decided upon, relative to the size and scope of the organization. It could be regarded as inherent in any doubling or more than doubling of ongoing activity or capacity. It corresponds to Ross and Staw's (1993, p. 723) description of "the sheer size of the venture relative to the total size of the firm." The means of assessing disproportionality may vary from sector to sector and from organization to organization, but both cases reported here were described as being for high stakes. At Thomson, the owner-managers were venturing their entire company from the start. The stakes could not have been higher. They took on no less than 8 times their firm's previous capacity—wholly disproportionate. Jacobite did not go anything like so far. Although they more or less doubled their manufacturing capacity, they did survive the subsequent crisis. Had they reached further, they would have probably gone under.

Irreversibility is the second constituent of overreach. It is the critical one for failure. Conceivably, a decision that was only disproportionate might succeed if all went well. Conceivably, too, such a decision might not become catastrophic even if all should not go well, *provided* it was possible to draw back, to retract. But when in both the cases reported here all did not go well, management was in an irreversible situation. At Thomson this was wholly so, for their new plant's previous ties with sales outlets had been severed, and without these it was unsaleable. In England, each main brewery controlled inns and public houses and so ensured basic direct sales, as distinct from those through the wider retail trade. So Thomson was stuck with its acquisition. Jacobite's decision was not so absolutely irreversible. By halving premises (a reverse sidestep, so to speak), reducing the workforce from 750 to 200 employees, and rethinking and reequipping their production operations, they were able to get by.

OVERREACH AS A SPECIAL CASE

Our database contains four other decisions by manufacturers that turned out very badly but did not have the features of overreach. In the first case—a huge multinational, one of the leaders in an oligopolistic world market—a decision was taken to back the development of a new material in which their established principal product would be used, alongside their other continuing main outputs. After the investment of tens of millions of pounds over many years, and an apparently initially successful marketing, it eventually became clear that technical limitations to the new material would restrict its use to far less than had been assumed. So the rights to it were sold off to other firms for limited purposes.

A manufacturer of industrial chemicals decided to add to its product range a new chemical of a kind it had not handled before. The market looked promising. However, development and manufacturing costs were higher than expected, and it took longer than expected to reach a financially worthwhile volume of production. Before this was attained, if it ever could have been, cost cutting and a change in market strategy closed down this emerging product. Another poor decision by the management of the same company was to purchase land adjacent to their main industrial site on the presumption that it would be needed to expand their plant. Although plans for expansion were drawn up, the land was found to be difficult to build upon, and it proved cheaper to buy an existing extra plant elsewhere, and rent the land for farming.

Fourth, a manufacturer of model kits decided to add to its largely plastic-based kits a range made in a specific type of wood. Additional premises were rented on a government subsidized employment-creating scheme. But the wood, which had to be imported, proved to be diseased, and, simultaneously, demand for wooden kits began to tail off. The costs of the extra premises could not be sustained. Fortunately, they had been rented, not bought, and although the terms of the state subsidy required each tenant to find a substitute tenant if they withdrew, a substitute was found.

All these four cases were run-of-the-mill failures. They failed, or at least underperformed, because of technical and/or market reasons. Relative to the business concerned, they were significant and serious yet still well within the means of the firms. They were not disproportionate, nor were they irreversible. What was done could be disposed of or closed down, and without undue strain or undue risk.

Many bad decisions have also been mentioned in the literature. For example, Hage (1980) cites Ford's failed Edsel car, IBM's mistaken computer choices, and Du Pont's Corfam shoe as instances of American high-risk decisions that did not come off. Valentin (1994) describes the failure of a rapid expansion of retail outlets by Boise Cascade Corporation, also in the United States, within an increasingly "unwieldy conglomerate."

Overreach is something distinct from this more usual genre of failure. It is a special case of failure. It is probably not a common reason for failure, and it is not a necessary element in failure. It is one in which the disproportionality and irreversibility stand out and magnify the risk. Many decisions go wrong because of technical difficulties or market shortfalls such as beset Thomson and Jacobite, and others do so because of the kind of overwhelming financial squeeze that was the principal cause of calamity for both firms, but it was the disproportionality and irreversibility of what they did that laid them open, unduly so, to these perils.

They could not be accused of poor management generally. Both managements had a creditable record. Their other decisions that were studied went well. Thomson had, while still small, computerized and begun laboratory-based quality control in a way that was advanced for a small brewery. Jacobite set up a new marketing department and introduced new material into its components, and it too had computerized. Neither firm appeared to be in the condition of continual poor performance, vividly depicted by Meyer and Zucker (1989) as "permanent failure." Their managements were not breaking out of that condition, which we hypothesize can be a successful breakout but can equally be an "outright failure." The decisions in Thomson and Jacobite were not of that kind. Theirs were moves from a successful position to take advantage of buoyant demand. It was more likely that past success disposed their managements to the "immoderation" of risky, proactive innovation, as against the caution that can also follow success, according to Miller (1994). Even so, overreach is not just another name for bad management.

Nor is overreach equivalent to escalation. Escalation of commitment means going on and on, usually in a multichoice escalation, as Lipshitz (1995) has defined it, or perhaps a single-option escalation along a path without turnings, as he contends occurred in American decisions on Operation Desert Storm in the Gulf War with Iraq in 1990. Something of the sort happened also in the 1980s with the burgeoning aspirations and costs of the Expo 86 exhibition intended to boost the standing and economy of British Columbia in Canada (Ross & Staw, 1986). This is the "pouring good money after bad" fiasco, getting ever deeper into the "big muddy" (Staw, 1976). It is persisting with a course of action that seems to be going wrong in the hope that more effort and resources will put it right. Whereas overreach is not escalation, but one big move.

Nor is it a big move into the unknown. The managements of Thomson and Jacobite knew very well what they were about. Between them, they each had decades of experience in their industries, and what they did was nothing new. They were doing exactly what the famous counsel given by Peters and Waterman (1982) would have had them do, "stick to the knitting" they knew so well. It was the disproportionality of what they did that took them out of their depth, and its irreversibility that prevented Thomson from being able to retract the decision.

In short, an overreach decision has a relative scale and irretrievability that marks it out from the commonplace extension of core business. That more usual extension is likely to bolster survival, according to Mitchell and Singh (1995), whereas overreach jeopardizes survival.

CONTRIBUTORY FACTORS

Were there any circumstances that may have disposed the managements of Thomson, and to a lesser extent Jacobite, to decide on a step too far? Were there factors that disposed them and not other firms to overreach? For, as said earlier, their businesses were not in difficulties. They were not precipitated into rash moves by crises. Ruling that out, therefore, what else could have contributed?

First, both companies were on the small side. Then, these decisions were taken quickly, and with a lack of foresight. Finally, did overfamiliarity carry with it an intrinsic overconfidence? These four probable contributory factors are now considered, namely:

Management size
Decision process duration
Lack of foresight
Overfamiliarity.

We do not suppose this list is exhaustive. It is what attracts attention in the two cases of overreach examined here.

MANAGEMENT SIZE

Thomson had 35 employees, and Jacobite came down to 200; though when the decision was made, they had close to 750. But each firm was small enough for each top management echelon to be small, half a dozen men at most, dominated at Thomsons by two cousins from the owning family, especially the elder, and at Jacobite by the strong, driving figure of the chairman and managing director who had led the way for decades. Did mutual supportiveness and pressure in small groups with years of stable membership engender blinkered "groupthink," as Janis (1972) called it? At Jacobite there were no doubts about the decision that was taken. At Thomson, a third cousin who expressed doubts was overridden and left the scene.

Eisenhardt and Bourgeois (1988) found evidence in microcomputer firms that power sharing by CEOs and a consequent minimum of interpersonal competitive politics were associated with good performance. However, it might be that in the overreach cases, the men at the very top dominated the small managerial cadres too much, though it is difficult to be conclusive about this.

In any case, the managements of small organizations are less able to accumulate resources that are not immediately used in the conduct of everyday business. They have little "organizational slack" (March & Simon, 1958, p. 126). Large organizations can build up slack and so go further before their managers begin to go too far. This accords with Singh's (1986) study of organizational performance (using data from 173 U.S. and Canadian managers). He found that the key variables contributing to good performance were slack and decentralization. So small firms are less buffered by reserves, as the managements of Thomson and Jacobite found to their cost.

DECISION PROCESS DURATION

The 150 decisions studied by Hickson et al. (1986) were arrived at, on average, in 12.4 months, and so, almost exactly, were those reported by Mallory (1987) and by Hickson and Oliveira (in press). Against this strongly supported mean for British managements, the two overreach decisions are very quick. From earliest recalled mention of the possibility of the decision (that is, to implementation being agreed and authorized), each took 3 months, only a quarter as long. Speed may also be haste. Thomson's managing director at the time said, in retrospect:

> Really, we seized an opportunity rather than made a planned decision . . . we felt we could hardly turn it [the purchase of the brewery] down. We were planning to spend £150,000 expanding our own brewery and the acquisition only cost £115,000.

Eisenhardt (1989) shows startlingly fast decisions in her eight microcomputer businesses, in times ranging from 1½ to 12 months. The contrast with the range from a month up to 48 months, 4 years, reported by Hickson et al. (1986) is striking. All eight cases reach a decision in less than the Hickson et al. mean time. For Eisenhardt (1989), speed is good in a "high-velocity environment." However, that is what limits generalization of her finding. Speed is not necessarily good everywhere. Thomson and Jacobite were in vigorous but not dynamically "high tech" industries. Beyond that, they were in a different society. The faster American approach to management as compared to the British is consistently asserted (see Hickson & Pugh, 1995, for summary portraits of both).

Hence it is more likely that speed in the overreach decisions allowed vital information to be overlooked, or to be insufficiently considered. Although in Eisenhardt's (1989) particular industry, "fast decision makers use more, not less, information," that was almost certainly not so in Thomson and Jacobite.

LACK OF FORESIGHT

Moving fast, perhaps in haste, also leaves little time for *prévoyance*, as the French doyen of management writers Fayol (1949) put it; in other words, less time to plan and foresee.

As noted, Thomson's decision was opportunist rather than planned. They never foresaw their difficulty in managing the transition from a very small capacity to a larger volume, especially how much working capital would be needed and that getting it would lose them control over the business. Jacobite were more careful, with their chairman involved in every detail even to personally designing the pattern of the tiling in the new canteen. However, this care and detail was in the planning of the form of the new premises and the laying out within them of the existing production technology. It did not extend to foreseeing coming radical changes in technology or to widely scanning the market, because they relied on broad assurances by their main industrial buyers of continuing and larger orders, without themselves checking further.

SMALL MANAGEMENT SIZE, SHORT DECISION DURATION, AND LACK OF FORESIGHT ACTING TOGETHER?

Here, the likely interaction of size, duration, and prévoyance becomes evident. If the organization is small, there is less slack in every sense to enable prévoyance. There are less funds to pay for research or advice; fewer individuals to prepare financial, capacity, or sales forecasts; and fewer or none with the specialist training required for these tasks. It is also likely that there is no one at the top of the organization sufficiently removed from daily operational problems to enable strategic-level assessments to be made free of day-to-day distractions, and groupthink may trap those involved. If, then, the decision is made in a short time, and especially if in haste, a thorough scan of what lies ahead and an attempt to think as carefully as possible about whatever may be plannable are even less likely. Therefore, small size, short duration, and scanty planning are likely to act together in creating the circumstances in which management is most prone to decision overreach.

The contrast can be seen in the other poor decisions in manufacturers among our own cases, where lack of success was not due to overreach. The two new product launches were in much larger companies, took much longer to make (between 3 and 4 years), and were comprehensively planned. Although the decision in one of the same companies to purchase adjacent land was made more quickly, the land had always been there, physically visible every day, and this simple contingency purchase did not require any detailed data or planning. All three failed, of course, nevertheless. The point is that there were no factors conducive to failure through overreach.

The fourth decision, venturing into wooden model kits made in additional premises, did, however, show predisposing features. It was in a relatively small business of 300 employees. It was made very quickly, in no more than a month or so. It was opportunistic, prompted by the sales director chancing on cheap assignments of wood more than by weighing up the merits of the venture. Perhaps the management were lucky. Had it not been that the first deliveries of wood were diseased, would they have gone on too far? Had it not been that the state offered subsidized buildings for rent, would they have bought premises rather than renting and found it more difficult to draw back? Was this an overreach might-have-been?

OVERFAMILIARITY

The final contributory factor we have suggested as disposing a management to decision overreach is overfamiliarity. This is more speculative. We have no explicit evidence for it. It appears a self-evident concomitant of the other three factors.

The decisions in Thomson and Jacobite were an extension or expansion of the existing core businesses that managers knew well. None of these decisions moved outside the accustomed "knitting" (Peters & Waterman, 1982). Unlike the Boise Cascade Corporation that changed the pattern in the knitting by shifting its building materials division from principally wholesale supplies into consumer do-it-yourself retailing (Valentin, 1994), Thomson and Jacobite went on doing as they had always done. In straight product terms, their decisions did not entail learning anything new. Their managements knew all about brewing and engineering. They were not newcomers to the business and had many years of successful decision making behind them. All had been in the industry and the firm for a long time, most of them for life.

Could it have been that, as a result, they were less alert to the novel, nonproduct elements in what they decided? Probably, they were overconfident. Probably, too, this led to what has been termed "risky shift" decision making (Stoner, 1968), a shared state of mind that shifts attention from the degree of risk entailed, and so is more open to failure. So those in control of Thomson and Jacobite underrated or did not sufficiently reckon with the risks inherent in what they meant to do. They risked too much because they knew too well. They were overfamiliar with their business.

Doing more of the same has been proposed by many authors, such as Quinn (1980), as a recipe for achieving progressive and relatively less risky change. The reasoning is that the more familiar managers are with their products and markets, the less the uncertainty associated with strategic change. If this is in general a good thing, then there can be too much of it. Sticking to what is familiar can carry with it the bounding of awareness. Managers and organizations can become locked into particular frames of reference. These bind awareness, effectively preventing managers from seeing what might go wrong until it is too late. They can also lead, perhaps, to what Grinyer and McKiernan (1994) term the "hubris" effect. This is where successful managements, as those of Thomson and Jacobite were, develop pride in their ways of doing business and assume that these will always work in the future. Such misplaced confidence may be a result of managers being too familiar and not questioning their actions until after substantial commitments have been made. They do not see that their "sensemaking" may be gradually ceasing to make sense (Weick, 1995).

CONCLUSIONS

The two cases of failure described in this article are at the decision level of analysis. They are examples of failure by managers in exercising "strategic choice" (Child, 1972). Although there are only two such cases in our sample, we cannot avoid the conclusion that analyzing failure at the decisional level can help understanding of organizational failure. In each case, the outcome of the particular decision imperiled the whole organization. Perhaps overreach decision processes are the most likely to threaten the survival of the whole organization. The other cases of decision failure in our sample never threatened overall survival of the firm, despite being severe setbacks in their own right. They failed because of one or more of the predisposing factors cited by Zucker (1991), which include little or no investment in new technology, inadequate investment in research and development, and failing to achieve sufficient market penetration through advertising or brand strength. The two overreach patterns of failure are different, in that these "usual" factors for failure are not present in either case.

Figure 1 diagrams the model of overreach deduced from our cases. It postulates that both disproportionality and irreversibility are necessary, neither being sufficient on its own. It implies that there will be multiple factors contributing, in other words, a multivariate explanation, and stipulates the four factors identified in this article without being able—from just two cases—to estimate their proportionate contributions.

Both the cases analyzed come from manufacturing organizations. Are manufacturers more prone to overbalance in this way? We have no cases of overreach

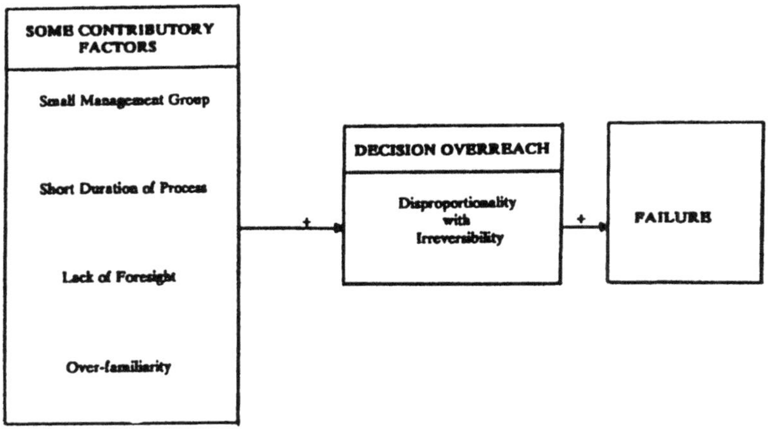

Figure 1: A Model of Overreach

from 31 decisions in service organizations, but 2 come from 24 decisions in manufacturers. In the absence of a broader study of manufacturers, we cannot be sure of any predilections. However, given that comparatively more decisions in manufacturers require substantial capital investment in tangible assets such as buildings and plans (e.g., Hickson et al., 1986; Pettigrew & Whipp, 1991), these may be more open than most decisions to being irrevocably overblown.

It is tempting to speculate about the influence of leadership upon the contributory factors. The popular press and much management literature (e.g., Bryman, 1992; Shackleton, 1995) make much of the leader as a cause for failure (and success) of an organization. According to this view, failure is an attribute of the individual rather than a decisional or organizational feature. Wise leaders bring success and poor leaders make foolish and ill-informed judgments, increasing the likelihood of failure. There is some limited evidence of this from our two cases. In Jacobite, the strong driving influence of the chairman and managing director was a key component of the strategic choice made. In the brewery (Thomson), leadership was shared between two powerful cousins from the owning family. In both cases, these leaders held sway over only small top management groups. There was little countervailing power to redirect the choices made. They were unlikely to bring in outsiders to dilute the overfamiliarity with the industry. As Strebel (1995) argues, if organizations are going to avoid failure they need entrepreneurial champions to maintain innovation and creativity. We would add that organizations may be at risk from "blinkered champions" whose parameters are too focused or short term.

Lindblom (1959) and Quinn (1978) both advocated incremental steps for reducing uncertainty in decision processes. Such small steps also build in the ability to retract the decision should it begin to go off course. It has never been possible to define how big or how small an incremental step is. However, it is possible in the overreach cases to see what it is not. The eightfold and twofold increases decided upon in Thomson and Jacobite were not on the scale of increments on what had been done before. They were on a far larger proportionate scale. They correspond rather to Ross and Staw's (1993) description of one-way big steps, which, once the organization has got moving, are almost impossible to stop.

Seeing failure at the decision level of analysis allows us to see more than the polar extremes of market selectivity (survival of the fittest firms) on the one hand, and the individual characteristics of effective leaders on the other. Of course, we need more cases of overreach to generalize, but in the two presented here, the prevailing patterns for avoiding this kind of failure are not to act too hastily, to plan carefully so that all aspects can be considered, and not to rely on too much personal knowledge derived from previous experience. This seems to be especially so for smaller organizations.

These findings might even be taken to imply that restless entrepreneurs and strong charismatic leaders may make for a colorful scenario, but they are likely to risk overbalancing the organization. Is uncertainty reduction in organizations best achieved after all by cooler, impersonal means?

REFERENCES

Bryman, A. (1992). *Charisma and leadership in organizations*. London: Sage.

Child, J. (1972). Organizational structure, environment and performance: The role of strategic choice. *Sociology, 6*, 1-22.

Cray, D., Mallory, G. R., Butler, R. J., Hickson, D. J., & Wilson, D. C. (1988). Sporadic, fluid and constricted processes: Three types of strategic decision-making in organizations. *Journal of Management Studies, 25*(1), 13-39.

Dutton, J. E., & Duncan, R. B. (1989). The influence of the strategic planning process on strategic change. *Strategic Management Journal, 8*(2), 103-116.

Eisenhardt, K. (1989). Making fast strategic decisions in high-velocity environments. *Academy of Management Journal, 32*(3), 543-576.

Eisenhardt, K., & Bourgeois, L. J., III. (1988). Politics of strategic decision making in high-velocity environments: Toward a midrange theory. *Academy of Management Journal, 31*(4), 737-770.

Fayol, H. (1949). *General and industrial management* (C. Storrs, Trans.). London: Pitman.

Greenwood, R., & Hinings, C. R. (1993). Understanding strategic change: The contribution of archetypes. *Academy of Management Journal, 36*(5), 1052-1081.

Grinyer, P., & McKiernan, P. (1994, September). *Sharpbenders revisited*. Paper presented at the British Academy of Management Conference, Lancaster University, England.

Hage, J. (1980). *Theories of organizations: Form, process and transformation*. New York: Wiley.

Hickson, D. J. (1987). Decision-making at the top of organizations. *Annual Review of Sociology, 13*, 165-192.

Hickson, D. J., Butler, R. J., Cray, D., Mallory, G. R., & Wilson, D. C. (1986). *Top decisions: Strategic decision-making in organizations*. Oxford: Blackwell, San Francisco: Jossey-Bass.

Hickson, D. J., & Oliveira, C. A. (in press). *Sensitivity to societal culture in managerial decision-making*.

Hickson, D. J., & Pugh, D. S. (1995). *Management worldwide: The impact of societal culture on organizations around the globe*. London: Penguin.

Huff, A. S., & Reger, R. K. (1987). A review of strategic process research. *Journal of Management, 13*(2), 211-236.

Janis, I. L. (1972). *Victims of groupthink: A psychological study of foreign policy decisions and fiascos*. Boston: Houghton Mifflin.

Laroche, H. (1995). From decision to action in organizations: Decision-making as a social representation. *Organization Science, 6*(1), 62-75.

Lindblom, C. E. (1959). The science of muddling through. *Public Administration Review, 19*(2), 79-88.

Lipschitz, R. (1995). The road to Desert Storm. *Organization Studies, 16*(2), 243-263.

Mallory, G. R. (1987). *The speed of strategic decisions*. Unpublished doctoral thesis, University of Bradford Management Centre, England.

March, J. G., & Simon, H. A. (1958). *Organizations*. New York: Wiley.

Meyer, M. W., & Zucker, L. G. (1989). *Permanently failing organizations*. Newbury Park, CA: Sage.

Miller, D. (1994). What happens after success: The perils of excellence. *Journal of Management Studies, 31*(3), 325-358.

Miller, S., Hickson, D. J., & Wilson, D. C. (1993, July). *Expansive gestures: Fancies and follies in strategic decision-making*. Paper presented to the 11th European Group for Organization Studies Colloquium, Paris.

Miller, S. J. (1990). *Successfully implementing strategic decisions*. Unpublished doctoral thesis, University of Bradford Management Centre, England.

Mitchell, W., & Singh, K. (1995). Spillback effects of expansion when product-types and firm-types differ. *Journal of Management, 21*(1), 81-100.

Nutt, P. (1986). Tactics of implementation. *Academy of Management Journal, 29*(2), 230-261.

Perrow, C. (1984). *Normal accidents: Living with high-risk technologies*. New York: Basic Books.

Peters, T., & Waterman, R., Jr. (1982). *In search of excellence: Lessons from America's top run companies*. New York: Harper and Row.

Pettigrew, A., & Whipp, R. (1991). *Managing change for competitive success*. Oxford: Blackwell

Quinn, J. B. (1978, Fall). Strategic change: Logical incrementalism. *Sloan Management Review*, pp. 7-21.

Quinn, J. B. (1980). *Strategies for change: Logical incrementalism*. Homewood, IL: Irwin.

Rajagopalan, N., Rasheed, A.M.A., & Datta, D. K. (1993). Strategic decision processes: Critical review and future directions. *Journal of Management, 19*(2), 349-384.

Ross, J., & Staw, B. (1986). Expo 86: An escalation prototype. *Administrative Science Quarterly, 31*(2), 274-297.

Ross, J., & Staw, B. (1993). Organizational escalation and exit: Lessons from the Shoreham nuclear power plant. *Academy of Management Journal, 36*(4), 701-732.

Shackleton, V. (1995). *Business leadership*. London: Routledge.

Singh, J. (1986). Performance, slack and risk taking in organizational decision making. *Academy of Management Journal, 29*(3), 562-585.

Smith, D. (1995). The dark side of excellence: Managing strategic failures. In J. Thompson (Ed.), *The CIMA handbook of strategic management*. London: Butterworth-Heinemann.

Staw, B. (1976). Knee-deep in the big muddy: A study of escalating commitment to a chosen course of action. *Organizational Behavior and Human Performance, 16*(1), 27-44.

Stoner, J. (1968). Risky and cautious shifts in group decisions: The influence of widely held values. *Journal of Experimental Social Psychology, 4*, 442-459.

Strebel, P. (1995). Creating industry breakpoints: Changing the rules of the game. *Long Range Planning, 28*(2), 11-20.

Turner, B. (1978). *Man-made disasters*. London: Wynham.

Valentin, E. K. (1994). Anatomy of a fatal business strategy. *Journal of Management Studies, 31*(3), 359-382.

Weick, K. (1995). *Sensemaking in organizations*. Thousand Oaks, CA: Sage.

Zucker, L. G. (1991). The role of institutionalization in cultural persistence. In W. W. Powell and P. J. DiMaggio (Eds.), *The new insitutionalism in organizational analysis* (pp. 83-107). Chicago: Chicago University Press.

Part VI
Doing the Research

[21]

RUMINATIONS ON MUNIFICENCE AND SCARCITY IN RESEARCH

David J. Hickson

These ruminations could as well have been called 'tales of two teams'. For they are a personal chewing over of memories of two research teams, end-on in my own life but otherwise unrelated, the first in conditions of munificence and the second in conditions of scarcity. In the first, there was both as much money and, for the central participants, as much time in each twenty-four-hour day as could be made use of; in the second, both were hard to come by and never enough. The first team, which studied power, was in Alberta, Canada; the second, which studied decision making, was in Bradford, England

It has to be said, even though it should be obvious, that these tales are told here in the manner in which they linger in a particular person's memory, my own. Ruminations are solitary. Other members of the same teams would tell the same basic stories, but would do so from the points of view of their own careers and feelings. My point of view is that of the originator of each team who set the balls rolling on two very different pitches, and was the only member who belonged to both.

Further, whilst these tales are one man's truth, they are not even for me the whole truth. They emphasize money and time, but there is more than this to research and there was more than this to the contrast between Alberta and Bradford. It has often been contended by members of both teams that what was attempted at Bradford was of a greater scale and complexity, so that differences in the nature of what was being done, as well as in the resources to do it, must go into the understanding of what took place. Doubtless that is so, but it is something that must await the telling somewhere else at some other time.

AN ALBERTA TALE
Munificent money

On second thoughts, perhaps it was not I but Charles Lee, a Texan enjoying the wide spaces of Western Canada around the boom city of Edmonton, who rolled the ball on to the pitch in Alberta. As Chairman of the Organizational Behavior section of the Faculty of Business Administration and Commerce, University of Alberta, he wrote to me in 1967 enquiring whether I would be interested in moving there to build up research. I was startled to find this letter out-of-the-blue on my desk in the room we all shared in the Research Unit at the University of Aston (Derek Pugh looks back on those days in Birmingham in chapter 8).

We did not intend the Aston team to break up, but we had more than once mused over the seven-year-bust-up tendency in other research groups. If they survived that long then around about that point they seemed to finally disintegrate, if not in name then in any real concerted work. We were on that point but getting along well. Maybe instead of being broken up by some uncontrollable influence we could engineer a controlled separation and then re-group? So my reply to the surprise letter did not say no. It outlined what might be needed for a couple of years to set up a research team. In the correspondence that followed all the possible needs in posts and money were matched by what was likely to be available. The Province of Alberta was – and still is – riding high on its mineral resources, especially oil, and Canada as a whole was doing well. To such munificence I could not say no. It was a chance to launch fresh research. It set off two years' concentrated effort, 1968 to 1970. Well, twenty-two months' working time, given the travelling to and fro and holidays.

I approached Bob Hinings, then at the University of Birmingham a few miles from Aston, but still working with us, to join the Albertan adventure (adventure it was, since at that time neither of us had ever been to North America, nor flown so far). Years afterwards the attractions of Alberta claimed him once more and he returned there permanently. A couple of months after Bob and I arrived in Canada, Hans Pennings joined us from the Netherlands. Charles Lee was already there, of course, and so was the fifth team member, Rodney Schneck, our only Albertan, immensely tolerant of this foreign body in his homeland. But then Albertans are used to people of many origins.

Later on there was Charley McMillan from the far end of Canada, whose talents were spotted by Rod Schneck, but he is the main character of a different story that will be alluded to here only in passing.

Held in common

We were high up in the umpteen-storey Tory Building, a disconcerting label to English eyes, but which had been the name of an Albertan celebrity and benefactor. In academic terms each research group should begin its research anew as far as that is humanly possible, but we did carry over some principles of team construction from the Aston experience. First and foremost, interpersonal competition should be minimized and cooperation maximized by holding in common what the team accomplished. This was achieved by agreeing that the names of all members should be on every publication, and be omitted only at the request of an individual who for some unforeseeable reason wished to come off. That would apply irrespective of whether individual contributions to the collective effort were more conceptual or more empirical or more in the final writing. All are vital to the end result. The writing cannot take place unless something has been done to write about, and what is done remains just a personal pastime if it is not communicated to others.

This did leave open for negotiation the question of whose should be the first names in the order in any lists of authors, but nevertheless it removed manoeuvring over who did what with an eye to ensuring future places on publications.

The blunders that can still be made could not be more vividly instanced than by what Bob Hinings and I later did. When the literature on power in organizations (the team's theoretical focus) had been reviewed it occurred to us that there might be a publisher for an edited selection, a reader on power. To our minds this was an incidental by-product of the research, and of little consequence. We saw journal papers as the real prize. Because we did not want to divert attention from this goal we did not involve the others in the notion of a book, but in an odd half hour or so had a list of possible contents typed out and mailed to publishers.

When what we had done so naively became known, it nearly shattered the team. To our colleagues who, unlike us, were aware of the money that could be made from book sales in North America, a book and not journal papers seemed at first sight the greater prize. Worse, here was I, the very enunciator of the held-in-common principle, ignoring it in order to line my pockets on the side. For hours we talked it out, but who knows whether complete trust was ever wholly regained. Perhaps it was fitting that no such book ever came into being.

A second team-building principle was a room in common. We did not ask for separate capacious offices, though they were there for the asking, but for a room large enough for desks for three or four, with a linked secretary's room. Common purpose and mutual stimulation do not come only from prearranged discussions or meetings for seminars. They come also from casual chats, passing comments that set someone else's mind going, mugs of coffee and tea drunk sitting on a desk edge, getting a sandwich together. These happen day by day in the normal course of things, above all fostered by constant contact working in and out of the same four walls.

Munificent time

The team did have to work against the difficulty that the original tenured Alberta faculty members had inevitable commitments and obligations due to their already established positions in the department. They could not abruptly drop these. Nor could they uproot themselves from their accustomed personal rooms and move into the research team room. They did everything they could by also having 'research desks' in the team room, which certainly helped, but we could not wholly overcome the difficulty. Those who moved in from outside, unencumbered by prior relationships, could fling themselves totally into the common effort. Those who were already there could not do so to quite the same degree.

For the newcomers, time was munificent. Not endless, since a two-year contract had been agreed, but as much each day as mind and body could give. We taught just one course each for a short academic year, and beyond that there were no research students to be supervised, no administrative jobs, no committee memberships, nothing to distract from or detract from the common aim. A comparatively undisturbed mental and emotional concentration was possible.

Bob Hinings's presence fulfilled a third team-building principle, that a minimum base for a viable team is two research-minded, full-time, fully committed members right from the beginning. They can hold on to the aims even if others are subjected to competing pressures, and in the last resort they can ensure continuity even if all goes awry.

The research task

Apart from a relative munificence of money and time, the team had another factor in its favour. It knew where it was going. It was going to explain power in organizations. It did not know what was meant by power, whose power was to be explained, nor what the explanation might be, but everyone could get down to work quickly on these questions without a long preparatory casting around to define the central aim. That aim had to be set in the initiating transatlantic correspondence during which a firm statement of the general objective was required so that funds could be applied for. It was premature insofar as research aims should be formulated by everyone, all together, and anyone who cannot participate in this is liable to be proportionately that less committed. However, this was offset by the team having a sense of direction right from the start.

In setting the general aim I had brought out a thought that had been at the back of my mind for years. In 1963, the Routledge edition had appeared of Blau and Scott's *Formal Organizations*, which seemed then to us at Aston the first thoroughgoing textbook in our field, an affirmation that a new subject, organization theory or the sociology of organizations, or what-you-will, was emerging. On page 175 a footnote had announced a forthcoming book by a Frenchman, not then much known beyond France, Crozier. The text said that 'Crozier suggests that bureaucratic formalization eliminates many areas of uncertainty. Power accrues to those who can control the remaining areas of uncertainty.' Although I did not really understand what this might mean, it had intrigued me, and when subsequently *The Bureaucratic Phenomenon* (1964) became available, I had seized on it. So for Alberta I proposed that we follow Crozier's lead. Hence the mixed European and North American team in Alberta owed its aims to Michel Crozier in Paris and to a footnote by Peter Blau and Dick Scott in Chicago.

Bob Hinings and I wanted to spell out theory more explicitly than had been done at Aston. So the five of us set out to search our minds, and those of everyone who had published anything relevant, for reasons why in organizations some had more power than others. Lawrence and Lorsch had just published encouraging results on 'subsystems' (Lawrence and Lorsch, 1967), and this view of organizations as interdepartmental systems fitted neatly with Crozier's idea, which had arisen from the tactics of the maintenance departments in French tobacco factories.

We worked out the rudiments of what was eventually published as a 'strategic contingencies theory', and went forth to test it in breweries, and in packaging factories, small organizations with virtually identical departments, a sampling that also owed a lot to Crozier. Because he had a set of small, simple, identical factories, a pattern of power repeated again and again had been plain to see, and we followed this example. We did not choose alcohol just because his study had been tobacco! We did so because of the peculiarities at that time of the Albertan liquor market. There were tight governmental controls. Alcohol was sold only from government liquor stores, windowless and advertless buildings in which a form filled in at the counter produced the required bottles from featureless shelves out of reach of the customer. Advertisements anywhere of any kind were carefully restricted. Though they were allowed on buses, for example, if they did appear and showed a glass then the glass must not touch the lips. The number of salesmen each brewery could employ was laid down. Only three companies were allowed to have breweries in the province, and imports over the provincial border were strictly limited.

So here were easily comprehended small organizations, with a simple product and technology, in the same highly defined market conditions. If there was any uncertainty, and if the theory worked, then it and the power should both be easily recognizable. Indeed, they were recognizable, subject to the conditions the theory states. In particular, there was the mystique of the brewer blending the hops so as to produce a standard beer despite uncertain crop variations.

Later, some small breweries in the United States and packaging manufacturers in British Columbia were added. Personally, I would have preferred chocolate factories! As it was, the others in the team got all the free beer samples that were going, and all I got were endless bought-in lunches of fast food spare ribs during interviews in one brewery, tasty at first but wearing week after week!

The project design demonstrates the advantages of a deliberately selected sample under controlled conditions when there is a clear theory. It became a textbook example of a hypothesis-testing design. And it worked. We did know what we were doing as much as anyone can in the research world. We had taken our initial theoretical inspiration from Crozier, but we did not look to any particular source for methods of data collection and data analysis. We tried to develop these for our particular research problem and sample. It is a mistake to believe in a method and repeat it whatever the problem. Methods should be devised to suit the task in hand. Naturally, accumulated experience is brought to bear with its preconceptions and predilections, and we worked within the structural functionalist approach, but we sought fresh ways of empirically getting at uncertainty and at the other major concepts, centrality and substitutability. We tried to get everything two ways, by open-ended interview and by questionnaire, so that variables were represented by two separate cross-checking sets of data.

Achievement

This was a team that realized its full potential. Of course, there was more to be done and more that we would have liked to do. Maybe other individuals might have done more, and they would certainly have done different. But this group of individuals did all that it could in twenty-two months. It achieved a drawing together of its ideas into a single explanation, it evolved this in interaction with empirical experience, and it published papers that have been cited by others.

Munificent money and time provided conditions in which the work could be driven forward with single-minded determination. Munificence created confidence and allowed concentration. Since the individuals who made up the team were confident of the two years they had wanted, and had got, they could concentrate on what they were doing and give to it all they respectively had.

The strain of the effort was still very great. There were the stresses in the team, due to the different degrees of concentration possible and to mistakes like the never-to-be power reader. There was also a little of the 'second generation' effect which Derek Pugh has described in chapter 8. Things are never quite the same for anyone who was not there in the first days and weeks when so much was still open, unthought of, unshaped. Coming later means coming into a situation already partly shaped. The 'second generation' then tends to leave earlier as the far end draws near. This was the fate of Hans Pennings who, having been unable to be present on day one, was first to move on as the conclusion of the project approached. Derek Pugh reports that those at Aston who were in this position did not continue to work in organizational research, but clearly this does not indicate some immutable law since Hans has continued to do so with distinction.

When the two years expired, Charles Lee and Rod Schneck stayed on to sustain Alberta in this academic field, but the team dispersed and the Research Unit as such came to an end. It was not continued in the same form. Its visible symbols, the common room, the secretary's office, and the filing cabinets, faded away. Research is so much the creation of individuals, within the situation and the thinking of their day. It does not march on regardless. It is not bureaucratizable.

Personal links persisted, of course. These included a relationship with Charley McMillan, mentioned earlier, who had joined the group to carry through a second project, a structural type comparison of American, Canadian and British factories. It led to him afterwards moving to Bradford to tackle a similar British, Japanese and Swedish comparison. In turn this brought a contact with Runo Axelsson in Sweden who had a decisive influence on what else then transpired at Bradford.

A BRADFORD TALE

Those at Bradford were not lucky enough to live in the comparatively secure confidence that sustained those at Alberta. The environment was not the same. Scarcity – relative scarcity – ruled. It called for a supreme determination to keep on whatever the adversities.

I went to Bradford from Alberta in 1970, with a brief to help build up the research side. Bradford Management Centre was still in its formative phase, and research activity was only just getting going. After a while Charley McMillan followed to undertake the cross-national comparison. Alongside this funds were fortuitously won from the Department of Health and Social Security for research staff to study local health centres. Again a Dutch link was forged when Ad Teulings applied for a temporary vacancy and came to Bradford for eighteen months. He and I had long discussions about possible research on power, and these and the arrival of Stewart Clegg amongst the first doctoral candidates kept my interest in power alive. Indeed, it was lively for Stewart and I had many stimulating and fruitful exchanges about what power did and did not mean.

Scarce money

With hindsight, the omens did not show the favour they had showed at Alberta. There were hindrances and delays from the start. On the same principle as before, that prolonged team research should be based on a minimum of two fully committed members, I wanted to recruit an experienced research-minded colleague. Moves to do so were twice frustrated, first when the departure of the Management Centre's founding Director created a temporary uncertainty, then by inapposite university appointments procedures.

At last things were on course when Richard Butler was attracted home from the United States in 1973 to make the stipulated pair. Neither he nor I knew the nature of what was ahead – a protracted research programme which required endurance from everyone involved, including the two of us who began it. As the Foreword to the ultimate book thirteen years later says, it was 'an uphill struggle to carry through large-scale, long-term research on small-scale, short-term grants' (Hickson *et al.*, 1986, p. xi). The principle of having two members with secure jobs who could hold on when all around were losing theirs, and to whom the others less fortunate could hold on, was fully borne out, though rather it had not been so tested.

The general economic and political omens also contrasted with those in oil-rich Alberta. The British economy was feeling the effects of the oil price increases by the OPEC producers. Suspicious political glances were being cast at the SSRC, the Social Science Research Council, and it had to be circumspect in what it did. Research pay-offs had to be foreseeable, and be not too long coming. It was a climate of opinion best evidenced by the subsequent change of title from SSRC to ESRC, the Economic and Social Research Council.

Nevertheless, we succeeded in obtaining a grant from the SSRC for a Research Fellow, for two years. We were pleased. In absolute terms this could be considered a good start. Yet it was half what we believed to be necessary for the magnitude of the work our intentions entailed. We had hoped for the security of an assured run of years. Our ideal was five years. So in relative terms the signal it gave was not so much of success as of an instant scarcity climate, an insecurity, which was to persist throughout.

As little as one year can be enough for a small-scale project re-using known concepts, whereas we were trying to think ourselves into an area where concepts were fuzzy and methods virtually non-existent. We found that it called for undistracted concentration, and the confidence to spend time on thoroughly clarifying concepts. Two years became inadequate, as we had feared. Although it sounds ample, and it can be sufficient for research which already has an explicit starting point and does not need further money beyond that, as the Alberta experience showed, the timetable it imposed on us was cramped. For the first month or two a new group has to shake down together. Then, if further funds are desired, work must commence inside six months on drafting a proposal, assuming submission of the proposal at the mid-point of the two years so that there is a chance of revising it if requested to do so and still obtaining money in time. And also assuming that unbroken employment is to be afforded to those contract researchers who have given themselves to the initial thinking and planning and to whom the research belongs as much as or more than to anyone else. Thus before anything much can be done on which to base a further proposal for money, that proposal has to be written. The group is distracted from the work on which it needs to concentrate by trying to dream up a persuasive proposal for a future before it has created a present.

All the time that a decision on new money is awaited the insecurity grows. Thought becomes pressured. The minds of contract members are in some measure diverted on to job vacancies elsewhere, and how long they can risk hanging on.

At Bradford, a self-reinforcing series of short-term research grants awarded to Richard Butler and me began. There were grants or grant extensions of two years, eighteen months, fifteen months, twelve months and four months, and finally a Personal Research Grant to myself for five months. At various points Graham Astley, David Cray, Geoffrey Mallory and David Wilson fell off at the end of one grant or another, the latter two even working for nothing in gaps between grants.

Conceptualizing and methodological consideration had again and again to be crumpled into shorter horizons than they demanded. There was never time to hammer things out as far as they possibly could be. Proposals for further money were always having to be concocted before we felt ready to do so. Therefore, each successive research proposal, whilst all right as far as it went, lacked that fuller assurance which ultimately comes from having worked ideas through and through as far as they can be taken. So, in their turn, our academic peers who toiled away for the SSRC and read these proposals never felt we deserved backing at any greater length. The sequence of proposals and grants reiterated itself round and round.

In all, we received SSRC grants on and off across nine years, including the gaps. To our peers with the SSRC it must have seemed like a series of generous acts of faith, constantly demonstrating goodwill despite a repeated lack of results. In all it ultimately did amount to a funding that was substantial in proportion to the total they allocated. But to us it was incessant insecurity and frustration, and a latent awareness that it was suppressing the potential that we thought was there to be had. The same amount of money awarded in longer grants might have got better value for money. We once reckoned that over the entire period Richard and I spent one quarter of our available time and attention not on research but on applying for money.

Scarce time

The core members of the team did not have the same freedom from other obligations as their equivalents had at Alberta. I had gone to Bradford to a Chair, as these positions are quaintly called. I found that this carried other furniture with it as well. Committees and policy discussions were always cropping up, not excessively as Chairs go, but nonetheless dislodging thoughts from their research focus.

Furthermore, as part of the creation of a research image, and as part of our contribution to the Management Centre, Richard and I took on the supervising of doctoral candidates. This was congenial enough, often stimulating, but whilst one is talking about or thinking about someone else's research you cannot have your mind on your own. For the same reasons we became Vice-Chairman and Chairman respectively of the doctoral programme, a most apt and complementary activity, but nonetheless another activity. Also for the same reasons, as well as for my own personal interest in it, I followed the doctoral chairmanship by accepting the editorship of *Organization Studies*, again a most pertinent occupation but a preoccupation nevertheless.

Desirable though all such commitments are if a research-orientated milieu is to be maintained, they fraction time and attention. We could never give our all to the main project to the extent that our Research Assistant and Research Fellow on contracts could, and this was a strain within the group.

The strain had been signified early on, before this project itself began, when I had attempted to join research staff in a common research room. All our desks were there, mine too. My allocated Professor's room opposite, measured out in the decreed number of square feet to encompass a Chair, was declared commonly available for anyone to retreat to for solitary work.

Tolerated for a while, my presence became intolerable. The interruptions to whatever was being done in the research room from calls and callers to me became too frequent. I had to move out to the Professor's room opposite. My time for research was too scarce. I was different. Though we successfully bore onwards from Alberta the principle of everyone's names being on common publications unless any individuals wanted theirs off, we could not sustain the common room.

The meaning of the word 'professor' is very different in Europe from its meaning in North America, of course. I knew this, but coming from Canada where we were all professors in title, I still had to learn its status divisiveness in Britain the hard way. In this, Britain and most of Europe lags behind.

There also were clear gaps between tenured members of the team and the others in age and experience, as well as in status. These criteria all cut through the group at the same point, whereas in Alberta they had criss-crossed around the group. So a second earlier attempt to overturn the realities had also failed. We had once decided to have a research group Chairperson, and had chosen Arthur McCullough, one of the forerunners to the project. It was a non-job. Requests and decisions had come to me anyway.

It is difficult for a Professor with a capital 'P' to get it right. If a Professor plays too large a part in research group affairs the potential of other members may be squashed out, should undue attention be paid to what he or she says. Play too small a part and the group misses what it could gain from contributed experience.

The research task

I had come from 'intraorganizational power' at Alberta, and Richard had come from work in interpersonal influence at Chicago, so we saw the new project heading somewhere into power and influence. This time there was not a specific antecedent such as Crozier had been for the Albertan team, but a general fashion to be followed. In 1973/74 the world of organization studies was just discovering *inter*organizational relationships anew. So why not study organizational power?

However, Runo Axelsson arrived from Sweden as the first Research Fellow. He applied for our advertised vacancy and was successful. David Wilson came as a Research Student. Runo was fresh from a jointly authored dual doctorate thesis, an academic novelty in itself, on decision making in colleges in Sweden. To him it was obvious that power or influence, whatever it is, is exercised when decisions are made.

Although Runo could not stay the full course and returned home because of the insecurity of his appointment and personal circumstances, he was crucial to all that transpired. As the point he made sank in, we turned away from the interorganizational literature and towards decision making as our subject for research. In any case, we realized that decision making must be heavily affected by interorganizational influences, as we later were able to show.

We found that whilst a composite picture of what decision making might be like could be sketched from the brilliant writings of the progenitors, no one had so far sorted out any different kinds of decision making. So scarcity notwithstanding, we set out to find ways of conceptualizing decision making processes among organizational elites, and to find explanations for any similarities or differences that we might come across.

Graham Astley, British but returning from the United States, succeeded Runo, and he saw clearly the distinction in the literature between the technical or task aspect of a decision and its political aspect. Our attempts to explain decision-making processes were thereafter shaped by this distinction.

We began fieldwork with six intensive case studies, progressing to a second phase using interviews with multiple informants for each case. We were well into this phase when once more we failed to obtain longer-term funding. We again had to review our plans. We had to so conduct the fieldwork that if this were the last money of all, when it ran out we would have enough time to make sense of what we had and would not be left with incomplete, unusable data. We were embarked on a large sample, which subsequently reached 150 cases of decision making from thirty organizations, in order to cover enough variation to be able to differentiate and explain. The crunch choice was whether to reduce either the number of cases, or the number of interviews per case. We chose to reduce the interviewees, which is why there was a third phase of cases that are the accounts of single principal informants and of those others whom they contacted for information. Long afterwards corroborations of one feature by another in the data, and by what was comparable in other published research, showed this to have been a valid choice, but nonetheless it was a regrettable necessity.

Since scarcity also forged repeated crisis choices between thinking some more or dashing out for more data while there was still time, some of us crying forwards and others crying that forwards would be retrograde, the concepts were not wholly defined nor the theory weaving them into an explanation wholly spelled out until the very end. The clarity of concepts attained comparatively quickly in Alberta, which accelerated work there, was not attained until later in Bradford. The defining of concepts and theory requires concentration in a less pressured situation, and not until someone did have a chance for that were the last kinks ironed out. It was I who had that chance. I was fortunate enough to obtain a year's Fellowship in 1982/83 at the Netherlands Institute for Advanced study in the Humanities and Social Sciences. Our debt to the Dutch for it is immeasurable. At NIAS I found that our theory had confused statements of phenomena, such as decision problems and decision processes, with the variable qualities of those phenomena. When this was sorted out the steps in the argument which had seemed all right, but not yet quite right, became clear and it could form the theme for the book which followed.

Sometimes some among us wondered whether studying processes was not more difficult than studying structures. Look at all that had been done on organization structure in the 1960s. It seemed easier to get a grip on structure. As we were finding it so hard to conceptualize processes and to grasp them empirically, surely they must be more elusive? This could be right, but to me it is not. Research always looks easy in retrospect, when the results are on neatly printed pages, to those who did not have to think of it in the first place. To study process is indeed to describe movement, but since all creation is in ceaseless flux I have never been really sure where process ends and how structure can differ from it in the final analysis.

Turning points

The lowest point was when we applied for a five-year Programme Grant from the SSRC and failed to get it. We got more months, not more years. Looking back on this eventuality, it can clearly be seen to have ensued from the lack of a secure period to think through what we planned to do sufficiently well, apart from any personal failings of mine or anyone else which there may have been.

Always juggling thinking time against fieldwork time against research-grant-proposal-composing time, we were at a stage when we had done most on the six initial intensive case studies. These therefore came over confidently and well to the SSRC visiting party, especially given David Wilson's capabilities in expounding what he had been largely responsible for since, within our allocation of tasks, it was he who had concentrated on them. The rest of the work, which was incomplete, and our future intentions, which were aspirations, must have seemed wishy-washy by comparison. It is easier to be convincing about what you have already done and so know well than about what you are doing or are about to do, even though it is the latter that are supposed to be under scrutiny.

Graham Astley's contract came to an end and he moved on, disappointed and despondent as we all were, another 'second generation' member unable to stay right through. His thoughtful contribution to organization theory has continued from the United States, like that of Hans Pennings of the Alberta group.

Geoff Mallory and David Wilson somehow managed to stay, with Richard and I, until the turnaround came. It arrived on another short grant in the person of David Cray from Wisconsin. His arrival brought new energy, and galvanized the team into further efforts when all might have appeared spent. The project surged ahead, a surge that eventually carried it to a successful conclusion.

However, the interminable insecurity again took its toll when David Cray, as the end of the grant that paid him approached, had to follow Graham Astley across the Atlantic, though not to the United States but to Canada. Richard and David Wilson switched by agreement to the study of strategies in voluntary organizations. But the fresh momentum that had been gained was enough. It carried Geoff Mallory and David Cray through final and indispensable data analyses on computers on opposite sides of the Atlantic, and me through final siftings of the evidence and book writing in Holland and at home in Yorkshire, alongside Geoff who as the surviving sheet anchor man at Bradford defied all the difficulties of successive 'generations'.

Achievement

Much was achieved, all the greater in the circumstances. An exceptionally wide empirical study was accomplished. Strategic decision-making processes, social processes, were holistically typified by characteristics they revealed over time so that differences among them can be recognized. The duration of processes, the consequentiality of what is being decided, and the influence of interests, were described. Which kind of process is most likely to happen was explained by the complexity and politicality of the matter under decision. Whether that process is due more to the matter under decision or to the organization in which it happens was examined. Journal papers, book chapters, and a book were published.

But for me the achievement might have been better still. Of course, such thoughts are about might-have-beens, and there always will be might-have-beens. There can never be a research project where more might not have been achieved in one respect or another had the fates been different. With puny research instruments, our human selves, all research is necessarily bad research, and the question is merely how bad it is. Yet in this instance there were more than a dozen years between preparatory discussions and the publication in 1986 of the book which gives the bulk of the results. Perhaps we could have worked more speedily and effectively. It is hard to say. But stop-go financing sapped confidence, distracted attention, and held productivity below what it could otherwise have been.

TALES' END

Both tales show clearly the benefits of researcher mobility from project to project and from nation to nation. The Alberta and the Bradford projects both gained from the variety of individuals they drew together. In Alberta we were from three scattered preceding locations and from four nations, Britain, Canada, the Netherlands and the United States. In Bradford we were in all from nine preceding locations and again from four nations, three the same as in Alberta, Britain, the Netherlands and the United States, and one different, Sweden.

Obviously these locations and nations were all within an international research culture in which the individuals drawn together had an acceptable degree of homogeneity in values and methodological assumptions. Equally obviously to the individuals themselves, they were far from identical. They brought differing preferences and, most important, they brought different bunches of concepts from their previous experience. The interactions between these preferences and these concepts determined what research problem was lighted upon, how it was perceived, and how it was approached methodologically. Both teams added perfectly to the evidence that effective research requires heterogeneity on a basic homogeneity. It requires argument but not dispute, variety but not confusion, novelty but not strangeness. Probably most of the ideas that go into it, perhaps all of them, are expressions of age old thoughts in a contemporary form, but each new mix has in it the possibility of a fresh and more currently relevant compound.

Both Alberta and Bradford also show how likely it is that there will be a constant internal strain in a team between those who can give the research virtually all their time and attention and those who cannot. In the more usual situation such as at Bradford, those who can are likely to be those who are on short-term contracts, the most insecure, and they rightly feel that everything they have is at stake, whereas those who cannot give so much time and attention risk either treading heavily when they do not know enough of what they are treading on, or feeling awkwardly diffident because they know less than they are expected to. A solution in the case of externally funded research might be to pay some or all of the salaries of tenured staff so that they can be released from their teaching and administrative obligations. This is puzzlingly rare when it ought to be commonplace.

The big difference between the two teams, as it seemed to me and with increasing hindsight continues to seem, was in their relative munificence and scarcity. Both tales tell of achievement. A great deal was accomplished. The question I have ruminated upon was whether at Bradford yet more could have been accomplished, given a better situation in which to do it. Of course, the munificent Alberta team did not float lightly along without a care in the world. There were only two years. Individual member had many worries over what they were doing and should do with their lives. Yet, relative to what was attempted, there was security and confidence enough for concentrated mono-purpose effort. The Bradford team made the same personal effort but, relative to what they attempted, did not have that degree of security and confidence.

This does not imply that researchers should have all the money in the world for an indefinite period. They need neither opulence nor infinity. In funded research there is always the challenge of getting something done by a given date. There is always the compulsion to guess at the incalculable so as to fit it into a finite number of years. On balance, and only on balance, this may have more advantages than disadvantages. But it is challenge enough, together with the overriding academic challenge, without it being taken to a degree where the disadvantages of the insecurity overwhelm any stimulus from the challenge. Notably, researchers with longer-term aspirations need enough time to fully think out what they are to do, before they are diverted into composing further proposals for funds, or into precipitate fieldwork because they dare not delay it any longer. The outstanding problem is how to assess who most needs and deserves that munificence.

APPENDIX: SOME SELECTED ALBERTA AND BRADFORD TEAM PUBLICATIONS TO DATE

Alberta

Hickson, D.J., Hinings, C.R., Lee, C.A., Schneck, R.E. and Pennings, J.M. (1971), 'A strategic contingencies theory of intraorganizational power', *Administrative Science Quarterly*, 16, pp. 216–29.

Hinings, C.R., Hickson, D.J., Pennings, J.M. and Schneck, R.E. (1974), 'Structural conditions of intraorganizational power', *Administrative Science Quarterly*, 19, pp. 22–44.

Bradford

Astley, W.G., Axelsson, R., Butler, R.J., Hickson, D.J. and Wilson, D.C. (1982), 'Complexity and cleavage: dual explanations of strategic decision making', *Journal of Management Studies*, 19, pp. 357–75.

Hickson, D.J., Butler, R.J., Cray, D., Mallory, G.R. and Wilson, D.C. (1985), 'Comparing one hundred and fifty decision processes', in J.M. Pennings (ed.), *Organizational Strategy and Change*, San Francisco, Jossey-Bass.

Hickson, D.J., Butler, R.J., Cray, D., Mallory, G.R. and Wilson, D.C. (1986), *Top Decisions: Strategic Decision Making in Organizations*, Oxford, Blackwell, and San Francisco, Jossey-Bass.

Hickson, D.J. (1987), 'Decisions at the top of organizations', *Annual Review of Sociology* (to appear in 1987 issue).

Mallory, G.R., Butler, R.J., Cray, D., Hickson, D.J. and Wilson, D.C. (1983), 'Implanted decision making: American owned firms in Britain', *Journal of Management Studies*, 20, pp. 191–211.

Wilson, D.C. (1982), 'Electricity and resistance: a case study of innovation and politics', *Organization Studies*, 3, pp. 119–40.

Wilson, D.C., Butler, R.J., Cray, D., Hickson, D.J. and Mallory, G.R. (1982), 'The limits of trade union power in organizational decision making', *British Journal of Industrial Relations*, XX, pp. 322–41.

Bibliography

Blau, P.M. and Scott, W.R. (1963), *Formal Organizations*, London, Routledge & Kegan Paul.

Crozier, M. (1964), *The Bureacratic Phenomenon*, London, Tavistock.

Lawrence, P.R. and Lorsch, J.W. (1967), 'Differentiation and Integration in Complex Organizations', *Administrative Science Quarterly*, 12, pp.1-47.

Name Index

For Product Safety Concerns and Information please contact our EU
representative GPSR@taylorandfrancis.com
Taylor & Francis Verlag GmbH, Kaufingerstraße 24, 80331 München, Germany

www.ingramcontent.com/pod-product-compliance
Ingram Content Group UK Ltd.
Pitfield, Milton Keynes, MK11 3LW, UK
UKHW050052200926
475702UK00019B/2794

* 9 7 8 0 3 6 7 2 4 9 3 7 3 *